MODERN TRANSPORT GEOGRAPHY

MODERN TRANSPORT GEOGRAPHY

Second, revised edition

Edited by

Brian Hoyle

Reader in Geography, University of Southampton

and

Richard Knowles

Reader in Geography, University of Salford

on behalf of the
Transport Geography Research Group
of the
Royal Geographical Society with the Institute of British Geographers

John Wiley & Sons
Chichester · New York · Weinheim · Brisbane · Singapore · Toronto

Other Wiley Editorial Offices

John Wiley & Sons, Inc., 605 Third Avenue,
New York, NY 10158-0012, USA

WILEY-VCH Verlag GmbH, Pappelallee 3,
D-69469 Weinheim, Germany

Jacaranda Wiley Ltd, 33 Park Road, Milton,
Queensland 4064, Australia

John Wiley & Sons (Asia) Pte Ltd, 2 Clementi Loop #02-01,
Jin Xing Distripark, Singapore 129809

John Wiley & Sons (Canada) Ltd, 22 Worcester Road,
Rexdale, Ontario M9W 1L1, Canada

Library of Congress Cataloging-in-Publication Data
Modern transport geography / edited by Brian Hoyle & Richard Knowles
on behalf of the Transport Geography Research Group of the Royal
Geographical Society with the Institute of British Geographers. —
2nd, rev. ed.
p.   cm.
Includes bibliographical references and index.
ISBN 0-471-97777-2
1. Transportation.   2. Economic geography.   I. Hoyle, B.S.
II. Knowles, R. D. (Richard D.)   III. Royal Geographical Society
(Great Britain). Transport Geography Research Group.   IV. Institute
of British Geographers.
HE147.5.M63   1998   98-27242
388—dc21   CIP

British Library Cataloguing in Publication Data

A catalogue record for this book is available from the British Library

ISBN 0-471-97777-2

Typeset in 10/12pt Times by Dorwyn Ltd, Rowlands Castle, Hants
Printed and bound in Great Britain by Antony Rowe Ltd
This book is printed on acid-free paper responsibly manufactured from sustainable forestry, in which at least two trees are planted for each one used for paper production.

CONTENTS

PREFACE AND ACKNOWLEDGEMENTS

The world of transport geography, and of transport in general, has moved on substantially since the first edition of this book was published in 1992. Transport remains a subject of universal interest and importance, and transport geography is a major component within an interdisciplinary framework. The investigation, analysis and understanding of transport issues are of concern to a wide variety of students, researchers and planners as well as to people directly involved in the operation of transport systems and services. No single discipline or author can realistically be expected authoritatively to cover the subject as a whole, such is the variety and complexity of problems involved.

From its inception in the early 1970s the Transport Geography Study Group of the Institute of British Geographers developed a close and active interest in the spatial dimensions of transport. Members published extensively within the field of transport geography and in 1982 established the Group's own monograph series. Since 1990, members have also produced a number of research-based books with external publishers. However, perhaps the most significant developments have been the creation of two new, diverse and substantial publications. The first edition of this book, published in 1992 as an outcome of a long-held ambition on the part of TGSG members, drew on collective expertise to present a wide-ranging and successful contribution to the study of modern transport geography of value to students in a variety of interrelated disciplines. A highly significant and parallel expression of these aims was the launch by the Group of the quarterly international *Journal of Transport Geography* in 1993, now widely recognized as a major research vehicle in this field.

More recently, and following the reintegration of the Institute of British Geographers within the Royal Geographical Society in 1996, the renamed Transport Geography Research Group has actively sought to strengthen its links with the Transportation Geography Specialty Group of the Association of American Geographers through research collaboration, joint conference sessions and publication. The second edition of this book, thoroughly revised, expanded and updated, contains several new chapters and contributions authored by colleagues from the United States and Canada, and their advice on the reorientation of this book for a wider international (and notably American) market has been of great value to us as editors.

Our policy throughout has been to encourage contributors to draw upon their own experience in the context of a particular problem or specific area of reference within this complex field. We have attempted to cover the major components of the subject, at a level appropriate to undergraduates following courses in geography and other cognate subjects, in an open-ended manner indicating where more detailed information may be found and where further research is needed.

We record our gratitude to our fellow contributors on both sides of the Atlantic for their cooperation in the preparation of this new edition. We recall with pleasure the role of Dr Iain Stevenson, formerly of Belhaven Press and more recently of John Wiley & Sons, who first encouraged us to write this work and later laid the foundations for this restructured revised edition. For its production we are indebted to Tristan Palmer and his colleagues at John Wiley & Sons, and to their international team of reviewers, for their support and encouragement.

Some of the maps and diagrams were prepared or amended by Bob Smith in the Cartographic Unit of the University of Southampton, under the general direction of Tim Aspden, and some were drawn by Gustav Dobrzynski in the Department of Geography, University of Salford. Others were submitted by authors in a finished condition, thus accounting for some variation in cartographic style. We also record our appreciation of the computational expertise of Dr Jim Milne, the photographic skills of Andrew Vowles and the secretarial support of Jackie Bailey and Marie Langford at Southampton, and of Moira Armitt and Lesley Harris at Salford.

Brian Hoyle
University of Southampton

Richard Knowles
University of Salford

May 1998

1

TRANSPORT GEOGRAPHY: AN INTRODUCTION

Brian Hoyle and Richard Knowles

Transport is part of the daily rhythm of life. Mobility is a fundamental human activity and need, but is restricted by the friction of distance. As a complex industry in terms of land use, employment and functions, transport is a major factor interlinked with the environment and with the spatial distribution and development of all other forms of economic and social activity. Geographical theories, methods and perspectives contribute significantly towards an understanding of transport problems and their eventual solution.

INTRODUCTION

Transport is a central dimension of the national and global production systems that are reshaping the world, and is therefore a topic of universal interest and importance. Most people wish to travel from one place to another, regularly or occasionally. Goods collected, extracted or manufactured, almost without exception, are distributed from place to place prior to consumption. If people need or wish to use services, which are generally provided at a limited number of places, they must travel in order to do so. Transport industries exist to provide for the movement of people and goods, and for the provision and distribution of services; and transport thereby fulfils one of the most important functions and is one of the most pervasive activities in any society or economy. "There is no escape from transport . . ." (Munby, 1968, 7). In advanced countries, modern transport systems involving road, rail and air networks are generally well-developed; global economic integration relies upon efficient maritime transport; and the development of the less-developed parts of the world is substantially dependent upon transport. "Even in the most remote and least developed of inhabited regions, transport in some form is a fundamental part of the daily rhythm of life" (Hoyle, 1973, 9).

The general importance of transport is not in doubt, but its very ordinariness leads to its general acceptance and to a widespread assumption that transport is not a particularly interesting subject of study, except when things go wrong. Transport is a focus of media attention when disasters occur, when strikes paralyse services, or when exciting innovations capture public interest or become the subject of controversy. Transport services cannot operate perfectly all the time, and to a greater or lesser degree the travelling public always has a ready-made target for complaints, justified or otherwise. Yet most rational people would agree that the vast majority of transport services operate at a reasonable level of efficiency for most of the time: were this not so, economic and social systems would grind to a halt.

Modern Transport Geography: second, revised edition. Edited by Brian Hoyle and Richard Knowles.
© 1998 John Wiley & Sons Ltd.

All transport systems, however, are capable of improvement: more extensive, faster and above all more efficient services are constantly in demand but there are increasing calls for transport to become less environmentally harmful and more sustainable (Black, 1996; Whitelegg, 1993). The level of efficiency and customer satisfaction achieved by any transport service is fundamentally a political issue, for it rests largely on the level and pattern of public-sector resource allocation to transport as opposed to other economic sectors and on the conditions under which private-sector investment in transport is permitted or encouraged. It follows that "almost every transport decision is a public issue" (Munby, 1968, 7); and that transport is "an enormously varied, exciting and controversial area of study" (Whitelegg, 1981, 4).

The study of transport is not the sole prerogative of any one academic discipline, and transport is too important to be left entirely in the hands of its practitioners. Transport, by its very nature, lends itself to multidisciplinary study and to interaction between those who operate or use transport systems and those who control or seek to analyse them. Economic theory plays a leading role in transport study, and the contributions of political scientists, sociologists, historians and lawyers must be acknowledged. The work of transport engineers is also critical to the design and development of transport facilities and systems. Geographers, too, have much to contribute to the study of transport, and transport geography is increasingly widely recognized as a useful and important component in the broad field of transport analysis. "Transport geography . . . emphasises the vital interactions between transport and other essentially spatial processes such as industrial location and urbanisation" (Tolley and Turton, 1995, 4).

WHY TRANSPORT GEOGRAPHY?

Why is transport *geography* important? There are two main reasons. Firstly, transport industries, facilities, infrastructures and networks occupy substantial areas of geographical space, constitute complex spatial systems and provide substantial numbers of widely spread jobs. Secondly, geography is concerned with interrelationships between phenomena in a spatial setting and with the explanation of spatial patterns; and transport is frequently one of the most potent explanatory factors. Transport is a measure of the interactions between areas; it also enables a division of labour to occur. Spatial differentiation, wider market areas and economies of scale in production are partly a product of transport availability and use; and the demand for transport, in turn, is partly a product of these factors (Gauthier, 1970; Hay, 1973; Button and Gillingwater, 1983). "Location remains all-important as technological innovations in transport and telecommunications continue to collapse space differentially" (Knowles, 1993, 5). Nodal "situations" change and the spatial qualities of centrality and intermediacy enhance the importance and traffic levels of strategically located hubs within transport systems (Fleming and Hayuth, 1994).

Transport geography is thus concerned with the explanation, from a spatial perspective, of the socio-economic, industrial and settlement frameworks within which transport networks develop and transport systems operate. The subject therefore centres upon dynamic interrelationships within transport itself and in transport-related contexts. A substantial and growing literature and an increasing interdisciplinary involvement on the part of transport geographers have led to an enhanced awareness of the importance of the spatial dimension in transport studies, and of the contributions transport geographers are making, individually and collectively, to the further understanding and eventual solution of contemporary transport problems. The holistic approach of geographers is particularly valuable in land-use and transport planning, in the design of transport systems and in addressing environmental problems. This book offers a wealth of examples of issues addressed by transport geographers and illustrates in detail some of the specific transport problems – environmental, urban and rural, for example – as well as many policy-orientated debates in the context of which a geographical perspective is not only illuminating but essential if realistic solutions are to be found.

Many contemporary issues have been highlighted at a series of conferences organized by the Transport Geography Research Group[1] of the Royal Geographical Society with the Institute of British Geographers. For example, in the early 1980s, transport geographers and planners examined a wide range of transport and recreation issues at a meeting in 1982 (Halsall, 1982). As the Conservative Government's policies of privatization, deregulation and competition were beginning to change the framework in which British transport operates, a range of public issues in transport were discussed by transport geographers (Turton, 1983). Transport geographers joined with planners, Transport 2000 and British Rail to identify problems of and prospects for rail-based rapid transit in Britain's increasingly congested and decentralized conurbations (Williams, 1985). Implications of the then imminent deregulation of local bus services were examined in depth at a symposium of transport geographers and economists (Knowles, 1985).

The Channel Tunnel and its estimated impacts on short Channel crossings and ferry terminals were evaluated by transport geographers, economists and planners together with representatives of Eurotunnel, British Rail, ferry companies and Dover Harbour Board (Tolley and Turton, 1987); and more recently an interdisciplinary seminar examined a wide range of geographical implications of the Channel Tunnel (Gibb, 1994). The effects of technological innovation in transport on spatial change were examined in relation to high-speed railways, minibuses, unconventional modes, small ports, retailing and telecommunications (Tolley, 1988). Green modes of transport and traffic-calming measures were analysed on a European scale at a symposium of transport geographers, planners and transport pressure groups (Tolley, 1990). A joint British–Italian seminar of geographers, economists and mathematicians evaluated aspects of transport policy and urban development (Knowles, 1989). The revitalization of derelict dockland and waterfronts

was examined on an international scale at a symposium of transport geographers, planners and political scientists (Hoyle, 1990). The effects of factors such as transport costs, investment and the Single European Market were assessed in relation to industrial location, property markets, physical distribution and supply systems (Moyes, 1991). Causes, consequences and ways of alleviating traffic congestion were the focus of an interdisciplinary seminar (Whitelegg, 1992). Aspects of the changing regional economics and inadequate transport systems of post-Communist states in Central and Eastern Europe were examined by a multidisciplinary group of researchers from across Europe (Hall, 1993). Equity, welfare, personal mobility, behavioural and environmental issues were the focus of a conference on transport and welfare (Smith, 1994). A second British–Italian seminar considered aspects of city-port development and regional change (Hoyle, 1996).

Further issues and ideas have been addressed in research papers published in the quarterly, international *Journal of Transport Geography* established in 1993 by Butterworth-Heinemann (now Elsevier Science) in association with the British Transport Geography Research Group[1]. The journal has provided a focus for research findings and has stimulated research and debate within transport geography's 10 research agendas, namely: policy practice and analysis; the impact of infrastructure provision; the declining friction of distance; the mobility gap and differential accessibility; demand modelling; transport, environment and energy; travel, recreation and tourism; challenges in theory and methodology; information for transport planning and operation; and effects of climatic hazards on transport operation (Knowles, 1993, 1994).

MOBILITY

The study of transport rests essentially on two cardinal principles. The first is that *mobility is a fundamental human activity and need.* "When the history of the late 20th century is written, there seems little doubt that mobility . . . will be one of its touch-stones'' (Johnston *et al.*, 1995, 13). Enhanced mobility is an attribute of an increasing globalization of the world space economy. In all societies, environments and economies the movement of goods and people – as well as capital and ideas – is a necessary element in functional and developmental terms. The word "transport" describes this activity, whether in terms of a relatively straightforward transfer of people or goods from one location to another, over a short distance, or in terms of the infinitely more complex systems involving many different directions, modes and locations on an international scale. The transport industries constitute, basically, a response to these activities and needs; transport facilities are normally provided in response to, rather than in anticipation of, demand; as in all demand-led industries, there can rarely if ever be a perfect match between the transport facilities and services required or desired by a population or economy and the available infrastructure at a particular time.

It follows that, although transport in one form or another is part of the daily rhythm of human life, in all societies and economies, most places and people suffer from restrictions on mobility. Such restrictions may be temporary or long-lasting – even, in personal terms, permanent; they may be very seriously disruptive or only marginally inconvenient. Most commonly these restrictions arise from economic factors, especially the cost of transport: most individuals and families cannot afford to make all the journeys they would ideally wish to undertake. In developed countries the mobility gap is widening, especially in rural areas, between the growing majority with regular access to a private car and the minority who are entirely dependent on declining public transport for access to shops, medical services, families and friends (Moseley, 1979). However, a continuous increase in personal mobility is unsustainable and fiscal measures are already in use in some countries to dampen demand for transport (Black, 1996; Whitelegg, 1993). Unconventional transport modes and community transport systems provide responses to transport demand in a variety of circumstances (Nutley, 1990). Industries and businesses naturally

attempt to reduce transport costs by limiting movements and few governments can afford to provide modern transport facilities and services to satisfy existing demand, let alone to cater for anticipated future requirements. Of course, demand for transport is in a sense a function of available facilities and services: people always want more than they can have. Similarly, the services and facilities provided are clearly a function of demand, for unless demand exists or is anticipated there is no point in providing them.

Restricted mobility is inevitably a brake on development, in every sense. In modern Western cities, particularly, people are increasingly used to seeing, expecting and perhaps using transport facilities for mobility-deprived individuals and groups: those confined to wheelchairs, for example, or who have difficulty in using public transport and need specially adapted vehicles and access points to buildings and public spaces. Political factors, too, directly restrict the movement of individuals – refugees, hostages, guest workers, would-be immigrants – and in some countries it is still difficult or not permitted for most people to travel beyond national boundaries. Indirectly, political decisions underpin resource allocation to the transport sector, so that governments can restrict or enhance mobility by withholding or advancing investment in transport facilities and services. More generally, however, it is usually the broad level of economic development, together with the technological level of transport provision, that creates a restrictive environment in transport terms.

Factors affecting the relative restriction of mobility are clearly interrelated, but we should also consider *the friction or restrictive impact of distance* itself. Everyone is aware that some places are more expensive than others to live and work in, or to trade from; and a major factor contributing to these spatial variations is the cost of transporting people to work and goods to market. Inland countries in West Africa, such as Mali and Niger, suffer economically because of the cost of transporting trade goods to or from coastal ports in neighbouring countries. The downward economic gradient that runs northwards from the coasts of Ghana, Côte d'Ivoire or Nigeria reflects ever-rising transport costs, as well as deteriorating environmental conditions, as distance from the sea increases (Hilling, 1996; Simon, 1996).

In Australia, where the phrase "the tyranny of distance" has gained a certain currency, "the distance of one part of the Australian coast from another, or the distance of the dry interior from the coast, was and is a problem as obstinate as Australia's isolation from Europe" (Blainey, 1966, viii). The peripheral distribution of population, urbanization and economic development is an expression of the high cost of transport between coastal ports and distant hinterlands as well as of the attractions of the coastal zones as compared with the frequently less favourable environments of interior areas. The Norwegian maxim "the forests divide, the mountain plateaux unite" reflects the fact that before mechanical transport became available, forests constituted a greater barrier to movement (Steen, 1942, translated in Knowles, 1976). The mountains also linked economically complementary areas thereby generating a demand for movement, unlike the valleys, which linked areas with similar economies. Distance – and its chief enemy, efficient transport – are potent factors in any explanation of the geography of economic and social activity.

MULTIDISCIPLINARITY

The second cardinal principle on which the study of transport rests is that *transport studies are essentially multidisciplinary*. Well-developed components within transport studies include: *transport engineering*, concerned with the design and development of transport infrastructures and facilities; *transport economics*, dealing with the analysis of transport demand and the costs of meeting that demand in relation to other forms of economic activity; and *transport history*, concerned with the evolution of transport facilities, partly in terms of their intrinsic interest, in relation to past societies and economies, and partly as an explanation of the origins of modern transport systems. Politics and law are other major fields of study, as well as activity, in which

transport issues loom large; for in all societies and economies, in various ways, transport is necessarily subject to some forms of political control and legal regulation, yet is itself a factor in the modification of political and legal systems (Banister and Hall, 1981). The study of transport networks, inherently a spatial phenomenon, is of concern not only to geographers but also to transport engineers, town planners and policy-makers, among others (Bell and Iida, 1997).

Transport studies are therefore *multidisciplinary* in character, and are sometimes *interdisciplinary* as well. Fields of enquiry and activity such as transport economics and transport law are necessarily discrete, up to a point, reserving to themselves a specific body of information and a specific range of methods or techniques derived from the wider experience of their particular disciplines. Yet the evolution of transport law, for example, is conditioned by transport economics; the history of transport is an expression of transport technology, and transport technology, in turn, is intimately connected with transport engineering, which is dependent upon transport economics.

In all these ways, no specific academic discipline, no subject-defined body of theory or methodology, can ever be totally self-contained; each must work with others, to a greater or lesser degree, drawing as required on a common fund of knowledge, in the pursuit of objectivity and truth. As in some other fields of study where interdependence is potentially a key to success, transport analysis requires that the scope and nature of any enquiry must be defined by the problem set, not by any preconceived notions of what is or is not relevant to a particular discipline.

THE ROLE OF TRANSPORT GEOGRAPHY

Transport geography lies at the heart of this interlocking web of relationships; for, as an integrative science, geography draws some of its materials from related subjects and focuses upon the analysis of interrelationships, especially those expressed in spatial dimensions. It is obvious that so vast, exciting and varied a field as the study of transport geography encompasses a great variety of approaches. "The skills which geographers have to offer are by definition useful ones and need no sterile efforts at carving out some indefensible space of disciplinary exclusivity" (Whitelegg, 1981, 4).

Transport geography, like the study of transport as a whole, rests on two essential ideas. The first is that *transport is itself a major complex industry in terms of land use, employment and functions*. Transport infrastructures and facilities occupy large areas of land and water space, and transport services provide substantial employment. In both these dimensions, transport is highly significant geographically. The second idea is that *transport facilities and services, taken as a whole or in terms of their component parts, are a major factor affecting the environment and the spatial distribution and development of all other forms of economic and social activity*. In this sense, transport is a major influence on virtually all other phenomena capable of analysis in terms of spatial variations and structures (Taaffe *et al.*, 1996).

In this context, it is possible to approach the study of transport geography from several different directions. Perhaps the most common method is the *modal* approach, which looks separately at road, rail, air and maritime transport systems and problems. This method is exemplified by Bird's (1963, 1971) studies of seaports and Sealy's (1966) and Graham's (1995) work on air transport. Such an approach is of course necessary for some purposes, especially the examination of specific issues, but it largely disregards the basic underlying intermodal interdependence of transport systems serving an area, however limited or substantial their degree of integration might appear to be. Another common approach to transport geography is through the study of factors – environment, economy, etc. – affecting the demand for, and the development of, transport networks (White and Senior, 1983). While this is a necessary element in an appreciation of the potentialities and limitations of transport systems, emphasis upon specific factors must avoid losing sight of the interdependent web of relationships of which they form a part. In this book traditional approaches based on

modes and factors are largely rejected in favour of integrated analysis based on issues, problems, principles and examples. This approach, transcending factors and modes *per se*, shows how geographical dimensions can contribute significantly towards an understanding of transport problems and towards their eventual solution. A complementary approach to transport geography by Tolley and Turton (1995) emphasizes spatial aspects of transport systems, transport problems and the evaluation of consequential social, environmental and policy issues.

EXPLANATION AND ASSESSMENT

It is, however, useful at the outset to suggest a broad, conceptual factor-based framework within which most if not all of the diverse elements of modern transport geography can be said to find a place. Figure 1.1 describes such a framework. The present-day transport system of any country or area cannot normally be explained by one factor alone. Explanations can be found, however, in a series of interrelated factors. Some of the more important factors are indicated in Figure 1.1, which shows how transport demand is influenced by economic and demographic circumstances, by patterns of land use and by trading conditions; how transport provision is constrained by political structures, inherited transport networks, environmental factors, available technology and finance; what affects transport usage and modal split; how the effects of transport are assessed at different scales and in different dimensions; and what influence transport has on land use, volume of activity, economic development and the environment (Blunden and Black, 1984; Barke, 1986; Fullerton, 1975).

The conceptualization of transport as an interactive system involving widespread demand for facilities and networks, the provision of varied and often interdependent and intermodal infrastructures in response to that demand, and ultimately the continuous assessment of that provision in technological, socio-political, economic and environmental terms,

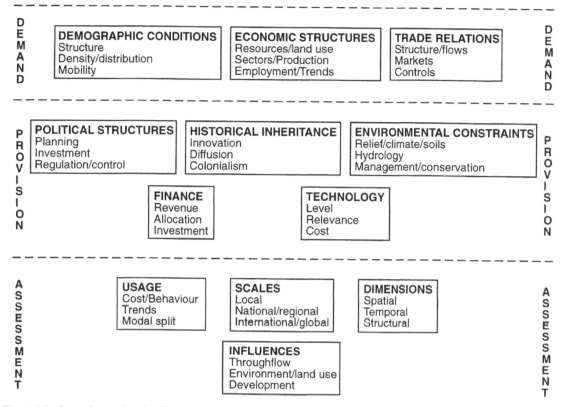

Figure 1.1 Some factors involved in transport demand, provision and assessment

is a useful overall perspective emphasising the interdependence and dynamics of transport systems at many different scales. Such factors are not only useful as sources of explanation and understanding of transport systems and patterns, past and present; they are also prominent areas of influence and concern in terms of assessment, traffic forecasting and planning for the future.

Changes in transport demand usually originate with changes in the pattern of resource exploitation and are often stimulated by changes in population structure, density, distribution or mobility as well as by people's desire to improve living standards. Resource exploitation involves the extraction, processing and marketing of resources, requires an increasingly specialized division of labour to generate higher living standards and although stimulated

by trading opportunities is limited by trade constraints.

The form of the transport network provided and the nature of the transport system that operates upon it is a product of competing constraints. Historical factors are essential to a proper understanding of modern transport systems, for all existing transport networks have been inherited from the recent or more distant past and from decision-making processes now modified or superseded. In Britain or France, this principle applies equally to Roman road networks and to recently constructed motorways. Although it is true that, as L.P. Hartley put it, "the past is a foreign country – they do things differently there" (Hartley, 1953, l), the importance of inherited transport systems and of superseded decision-making processes is that they provide part of the framework within which present-day decisions are taken and future developments planned. Historical legacies provide, in other words, one set of constraints that condition, positively or negatively, the ways and methods in which future transport systems can be designed and implemented.

The physical environment influences the development of transport infrastructures – roads, railways, seaports and airports – both directly and through the comparative costs of construction. The morphology of any specific component of a transport network – a railway station, an air terminal, a motorway, a container terminal – is set within a specific environmental context and its development raises particular environmental questions, problems and perhaps controversies.

All the factors discussed above are underpinned in many respects by technological factors. The technological characteristics of individual transport modes – pipelines, railways, canals, roads – impose limitations with regard to usage and maintenance costs, for example. Similarly, vehicles offer potentialities and impose limitations by reason of their individual or collective technological characteristics: bicycles, cars, ships, trains, aeroplanes, trucks and hovercraft all have appropriate physical, social and economic environments within which they operate and outwith which they either cannot operate or are unsuitable. Advanced technology is expensive, and transport costs are therefore frequently a reflection of technological inputs. Together, technology and cost factors are closely related to environmental issues, for the adaptation of a transport system to physical conditions or to environmental concerns is dependent upon technological capacity and available financial resources. In many port cities, for example, the relocation of port facilities and the consequent opportunities for inner-city renewal are basically derived from the evolution of global maritime transport technology (Hoyle *et al.*, 1988) while the restructuring of urban transport systems is virtually a continuous process in the context of urban economic evolution and rapidly changing technology (Hanson, 1995; Hudson, 1996; Malone, 1996).

There is a sense in which political factors transcend the logic of other factors discussed above and their interrelationships. Political decisions involving transport investment, like those in other spheres, hinge upon issues both broader and more specific than those outlined here. There is often a conflict between the demand for transport and the political will to provide it, or between the political objective of a transport innovation and its economic purpose or value. For example, the trans-Siberian railway, completed to consolidate Russian rule over Siberia, and the widespread introduction of railways in Africa during the early European colonial period, underscore the significance of political motivations for transport innovation. The political entity of Canada was created by the British North America Act (1867), which required the building of the Intercolonial Railway to link the four colonies of Ontario, Québec, Nova Scotia and New Brunswick so as to enable the new country to function as a political and economic unit (Leggett, 1973). The Canadian Pacific Railway was a similar but much larger-scale legal requirement. British Columbia entered the Canadian Confederation in 1871 under an agreement that guaranteed the construction of a railway connecting the Pacific coast with Ontario within 10 years. The controversies surrounding the Channel Tunnel and its connecting railways in Britain and France provide a contemporary example (Tolley and Turton, 1987; Gibb, 1994).

Political considerations are significant in another sense in relation to transport. Governments are a major source of capital for investment in transport infrastructure, although private investment is also very important in some countries. In addition, governments are involved in the regulation and deregulation of the supply of transport services, in the control of intermodal competition (to varying degrees), in safety control, in the coordination of investment allocation between modes and areas, and in decisions concerning pay and working conditions. In all these ways, governments are often in a position to decide what happens in transport terms, but decisions can only be taken in the context of consideration, evaluation, acceptance or rejection of all the relevant factors involved (Cloke and Bell, 1990).

Economic factors involve a different set of perspectives. Traditionally, economic approaches to transport have involved the assessment and analysis of traffic flows – the collection, dissection and discussion of movements along a line, through a node or within a network, in relation to demand and costs. The objective of such approaches underlines the essential economic perspective, based on demand–cost relationships and on the comparative claims of other forms of investment or activity for available finance. These perspectives have led transport economists and planners to develop sophisticated quantitative transportation models to attempt to forecast future traffic trends and to identify interrelationships between different transport modes, usually expressed as the *modal split*. Implications have been assessed for investment and planning.

Transport can be defined not only as an economic facility but also as a social enabler, so therefore it is impossible to disregard social factors in transport analysis and planning. Social activities and characteristics constitute a basis for transport planning, and they may be developed or modified by available transport facilities. The analysis of journey-to-work patterns provides an important spatial link between economic and social factors, as does the wider question of accessibility to modern transport services, especially in rural areas. Recreational travel and shopping patterns are two other areas where social characteristics form an important part of transport analysis. In rural and urban areas, each socially distinctive locality generates its own type and pattern of demand for transport, and responds in its own way to the services and facilities that are available.

Transport and land use therefore influence each other. The development of streetcar, underground railway and suburban railway systems, for example, enabled a separation to occur of workplace from place of residence (Hood, 1995; Kellett, 1969; Ward, 1964). The later developments of motor buses, lorries and above all of mass-produced cheap private motor cars enabled a much greater suburbanization and deconcentration of urban and economic activity

to occur. As a consequence it is now increasingly expensive to provide a decentralized urban area with adequate public transport services. City centres have become less accessible due to road congestion and parking difficulties, whilst bypasses and ring roads have enhanced the accessibility of the suburban fringe. However, where land-use and transport planning have been coordinated and the decentralization of urban activity has been tightly channelled over several decades (as for example in Greater Copenhagen, Greater Oslo and Greater Stockholm), the city retains its accessibility (Fullerton and Knowles, 1991).

Transport investment can positively influence economic development, and often does so. Improving the speed, capacity and reliability of transport or reducing its price provides opportunities for widening market areas and increasing market share. This will only occur if finance, productive capacity, entrepreneurial skill and trading conditions permit. The frictional effect of distance has steadily reduced over time. This has helped, together with lower tariff and technical trade barriers, to produce a worldwide area for the supply of many raw materials and a world market for many finished products. Lower-cost transport can however lead to economic decline where inefficient high-cost industries or areas of production were previously sheltered from lower-cost competitors by the cost barrier of distance.

The influence and effects of transport on the environment are widely regarded as a critical issue in terms of air pollution, noise pollution, the overcrowding of urban places and the deterioration of rural areas. Modern efficient transport can substantially improve the quality of life in many areas and ways, but any improvement inevitably brings costs of various kinds. Environmental impact assessment is therefore a critical element in transport planning.

In considering the relative importance of these and other factors affecting transport in a particular country or area, geographers not only use general models but also emphasize the diversity of place and the specific combination of factors that helps to explain an individual transport problem or situation. In some cases, one particular factor may be overwhelmingly important. In most cases, however, we can only understand how a transport system operates, how it has grown and developed, and how it is related to socio-economic progress, if we examine all the relevant factors involved and the relationships between them. This principle applies equally to countries and areas at any particular level of development, from the most advanced to the least developed.

CONCLUSIONS

Geography is concerned with environmental and human interrelationships in a spatial context, and transport geography is the study of transport systems and their spatial impacts. Just as population distribution is a delicate parameter of the interaction of a very wide range of environmental and human factors affecting people and their activities, so also transport is an epitome of physical and socio-economic interrelationships between individuals and groups in society, an ultimate yet dynamic expression of the demands and constraints that condition human mobility. In this wide-ranging context transport geography plays an important role. It rests on the principles of universal mobility and multi-disciplinarity; and is concerned with transport as an industry, a source of employment and a user of land and water space. Above all, however, transport geography investigates the effects of transport demand and availability on almost all other aspects of human society. Whether through modal, factor-based, demand-led or problem-based approaches, there is truly no escape from transport, and the study of transport geography helps us to understand why this is so. To a greater or lesser extent, the tyranny of distance affects us all.

Transport geography is not merely an explanatory tool, however, albeit a powerful one. As this book amply demonstrates, links between transport, technology, the environment and the global economy reveal an enormous spectrum of issues and processes. The world of logistics and transport management requires a good understanding of the essence of transport geography. The study of logistics focuses upon the complex national and international movements of components and services. These movements create a dynamic system dependent on technology and transport infrastructures on the one hand, and on economic and socio-political conditions on the other. Geographical patterns of transport routes, flows and nodes reflect and affect this system. In global terms, the modern world transport system and the logistical principles on which it is based are more widely dispersed across the globe than they once were, but at the national and local scales the critical nodes and flows are more concentrated and the key routes under greater pressure. These outcomes reflect not only traditional factors, such as those linking technology and distance, but also current trends such as privatization and corporate operation. As private market forces strengthen, and policy concerns emerging from environmental matters sharpen, the changing character of world transport systems continually presents new challenges for investigation, analysis and action.

NOTE

1. Formerly the Transport Geography Study Group of the Institute of British Geographers. In 1996 the Institute merged with the Royal Geographical Society and most Study Groups were renamed Research Groups.

REFERENCES

Banister, D. and Hall, P. (eds) (1981), *Transport and public policy planning* (London: Mansell).

Barke, M. (1986), *Transport and trade* (Edinburgh: Oliver and Boyd).

Bell, M.G.H. and Iida, Y. (1997), *Transportation network analysis* (Chichester: Wiley).

Bird, J.H. (1963), *The major seaports of the United Kingdom* (London: Hutchinson).

Bird, J.H. (1971), *Seaports and seaport terminals* (London: Hutchinson).

Black, W.R. (1996), "Sustainable transportation: a US perspective", *Journal of Transport Geography* 4 (3), 151–59.

Blainey, G. (1966), *The tyranny of distance: how distance shaped Australia's history* (Melbourne: Sun Books).

Blunden, W.R. and Black, J.A. (1984), *The land-use/ transport system*, 2nd edn (Oxford: Pergamon).

Button, K.J. and Gillingwater, D. (eds) (1983), *Transport, location and spatial policy* (Aldershot: Gower).

Cloke, P. and Bell, P. (eds) (1990), *Transport deregulation: market forces in the modern world* (London: Fulton).

Fleming, D.K. and Hayuth, Y. (1994), "Spatial characteristics of transportation hubs: centrality and intermediacy", *Journal of Transport Geography* 2 (1), 3–18.

Fullerton, B. (1975), *The development of British transport networks* (Oxford University Press).

Fullerton, B. and Knowles, R.D. (1991), *Scandinavia* (London: Paul Chapman).

Gauthier, H.L. (1970), "Geography, transportation and regional development", *Economic Geography* 46, 612–19.

Gibb, R. (1994), *The Channel tunnel: a geographical perspective* (Chichester: Wiley).

Graham, B. (1995), *Geography and air transport* (Chichester: Wiley).

Hall, D.R. (ed.) (1993), *Transport and economic development in the new Central and Eastern Europe* (London: Belhaven).

Halsall, D. (ed.) (1982), *Transport for recreation* (Transport Geography Study Group, Institute of British Geographers).

Hanson, S. (ed.) (1995), *The geography of urban transportation*, 2nd edn (New York: Guilford).

Hartley, L.P. (1953), *The go-between* (London: Hamish Hamilton).

Hay, A. (1973), *Transport for the space economy* (London: Macmillan).

Hilling, D. (1996), *Transport and developing countries* (London: Routledge).

Hood, C. (1995), *722 miles: the building of the subways and how they transformed New York* (Baltimore: Johns Hopkins University Press).

Hoyle, B.S. (ed.) (1973), *Transport and development* (London: Macmillan).

Hoyle, B.S. (ed.) (1990), *Port cities in context: the impact of waterfront regeneration* (Transport Geography Study Group, Institute of British Geographers).

Hoyle, B.S. (ed.) (1996), *Cityports, coastal zones and regional change: international perspectives on planning and management* (Chichester: Wiley).

Hoyle, B.S., Pinder, D.A. and Husain, M.S. (eds) (1988), *Revitalizing the waterfront: international dimensions of dockland redevelopment* (London: Belhaven).

Hudson, B.J. (1996), *Cities on the shore: the urban littoral frontier* (London: Cassell/Pinter).

Johnston, R.J., Taylor, P.J. and Watts, M.J. (1995), *Geographies of global change: remapping the world in the late twentieth century* (Oxford: Blackwell).

Kellett, J.R. (1969), *The impact of railways on Victorian cities* (London: Routledge and Kegan Paul).

Knowles, R.D. (1976), *An analysis of transport networks in selected marginal areas with special reference to Norway*, unpublished PhD thesis, University of Newcastle-upon-Tyne.

Knowles, R.D. (ed.) (1985), *Implications of the 1985 Transport Bill* (Transport Geography Study Group, Institute of British Geographers).

Knowles, R.D. (ed.) (1989), *Transport policy and urban development: methodology and evaluation* (Transport Geography Study Group, Institute of British Geographers).

Knowles, R.D. (1993), "Research agendas in transport geography for the 1990s", *Journal of Transport Geography* 1 (1), 3–11.

Knowles, R.D. (1994), "New horizons in transport geography", *Journal of Transport Geography* 2 (2), 83–6.

Leggett, R.F. (1973), *Railways of Canada* (Vancouver: Douglas and McIntyre).

Malone, P. (1996), *City, capital and water* (London: Routledge).

Moseley, M.J. (1979), *Accessibility: the rural challenge* (London: Methuen).

Moyes, A. (ed.) (1991), *Companies, regions and transport change* (Transport Geography Study Group, Institute of British Geographers).

Munby, D.L. (ed.) (1968), *Transport: selected readings* (Harmondsworth: Penguin).

Nutley, S. (1990), *Unconventional and community transport in the UK* (New York: Gordon and Breach).

Sealy, K.R. (1966), *The geography of air transport* (London: Hutchinson).

Simon, D. (1996), *Transport and development in the Third World* (London: Routledge).

Smith, J. (ed.) (1994), *Transport and welfare* (Transport Geography Study Group, Institute of British Geographers).

Steen, S. (1942), *Ferd og fest· reiseliv i norsk sagatid og middelalder* (Oslo: Aschehoug).

Taaffe, E.J., Gauthier, H.L. and O'Kelly, M. (1996), *Geography of transportation*, 2nd edn (Englewood Cliffs, NJ: Prentice Hall).

Tolley, R.S. (ed.) (1988), *Transport technology and spatial change* (Transport Geography Study Group, Institute of British Geographers).

Tolley, R.S. (ed.) (1990), *The greening of urban transport* (London: Belhaven).

Tolley, R.S. and Turton, B.J. (eds) (1987), *Short sea crossings and the Channel Tunnel* (Transport Geography Study Group, Institute of British Geographers).

Tolley, R.S. and Turton, B.J. (1995), *Transport systems, policy and planning: a geographical approach* (Harlow: Longman).

Turton, B.J. (ed.) (1983), *Public issues in transport* (Transport Geography Study Group, Institute of British Geographers).

Ward, D. (1964), "A comparative historical geography of streetcar suburbs in Boston, Massachusetts and Leeds, England: 1850–1920", *Annals of the Association of American Geographers* 54, 477–89.

White, H.P. and Senior, M.L. (1983), *Transport geography* (Harlow: Longman).

Whitelegg, J. (ed.) (1981), *The spirit and purpose of transport geography* (Transport Geography Study Group, Institute of British Geographers).

Whitelegg, J. (ed.) (1992), *Traffic congestion: is there a way out?* (Hawes: Leading Edge Press).

Whitelegg, J. (1993), *Transport for a sustainable future: the case for Europe* (London: Belhaven).

Williams, A.F. (ed.) (1985), *Rapid transit systems in the UK: problems and prospects* (Transport Geography Study Group, Institute of British Geographers).

2

TRANSPORT AND DEVELOPMENT: CONCEPTUAL FRAMEWORKS

Brian Hoyle and José Smith

Transport provides a key to the understanding and operations of many other systems at many different scales, and is an epitome of the complex relationships that exist between the physical environment, patterns of social and political activity, and levels of economic development. Viewpoints on relationships between transport and development continue to evolve. This chapter focuses on transport as a social facility and as an economic enabler at various levels within the transport spectrum. Through an analysis of selected models of global relevance, through discussion of a variety of scales, modes and contexts, and with reference to examples, it interprets the concept of transport as a permissive factor rather than as a direct stimulus to economic development or spatial change.

INTRODUCTION

Transport is an epitome of the complex relationships that exist between the physical environment, patterns of social and political activity, and levels of economic development. In advanced and developing countries, investment in transport is a matter for political negotiation, economic calculation and environmental consideration (Adams, 1981). Modern economies require, and assume, relatively sophisticated transport systems; yet changes are frequently contentious. A majority of the world's peoples, however, inhabit areas underprovided with even rudimentary forms of transport, and the need to facilitate economic development by providing improved transport services is often overwhelming (Hoyle, 1994; Owen, 1987).

Transport systems provide a key to the understanding and operation of many other systems at many different scales. At one extreme, intercontinental transport provides essential communication between the advanced and the developing worlds. At the other extreme, local transport to rural markets in many parts of the Third World is a vital component in changing dynamic socio-economic structures (Barke and O'Hare, 1984; Mabogunje, 1989; Todaro, 1989). Viewpoints on relationships between transport and development, at various levels in the development spectrum, continue to evolve (Gauthier, 1968; Hilling, 1996; Hoyle, 1973, 1988; Leinbach *et al.*, 1989; Simon, 1996; Ullman, 1956; Wilson, 1973). Theoretical approaches to transport network development provide useful perspectives, and historical evidence is often relevant, but present-day problems require a multifaceted approach.

This chapter examines the role of surface transport in the process of spatial change, in a variety of

Modern Transport Geography: second, revised edition. Edited by Brian Hoyle and Richard Knowles.
© 1998 John Wiley & Sons Ltd.

contexts, at various levels of development, and in terms of a selected range of modes and intermodal systems. The pivotal role of air transport in the ongoing globalization of economic activity – for example, in the emergence of world cities and in the regional economic fortunes of particular metropolitan areas – is dealt with in Chapter 14. Here the focus is on transport as an economic enabler and as a social facility, at various levels within the global development spectrum, and the interpretation rests on the concept of transport as a permissive factor rather than as a direct stimulus to economic development or spatial change.

While the main purpose of the chapter is to provide an introduction to a range of ideas and theories, and to underline the role of transport and communication as space-adjusting technologies affected by and affecting the globalization process, reference is made to a range of examples. On this basis, a number of relevant cases are examined in greater detail in Chapter 3.

THEORETICAL FRAMEWORKS

Five Essential Ideas

Relationships between transport and development are underpinned, in one sense, by five essential ideas, whatever theoretical frameworks are introduced, or whatever specific modes of transport or level of development under discussion might be.

Historical perspectives

The first is *the continuing relevance of historical dimensions*, in two senses. Firstly, theoretical ideas and concepts about the transport–development relationship have a long pedigree, and current thinking on this subject is informed by an appreciation of the evolution of ideas in the past. Secondly, all existing transport networks have been inherited from the recent or more distant past, and not infrequently were designed to serve purposes rather different from those they are now expected to fulfil. Transport his-

tory, like transport engineering or transport economics, is essentially complementary to transport geography (Vance, 1986). Critics of the inadequacies of transport systems should bear in mind the costly process of adaptation to present-day and foreseeable requirements.

Nodes, networks and systems

A second essential idea centres on *the critical role of transport nodes* in the context of the regional, national and international transport systems which they serve. Transport is fundamentally a question of nodes, links, networks and systems. Links between places, by a single mode or a variety of modes, and over shorter or longer distances, encourage the emergence of significant nodes where links converge or where modes change. A pattern of links and nodes produces a network, a physical arrangement of transport facilities; and the design, development and management of that network requires a multifaceted transport system, which is ultimately both a response to demand and an expression of technological capability and economic resources. Early work by Kansky (1963) and by Haggett and Chorley (1969) elaborated the essential foundations of these perspectives.

Cities, as nodes within multimodal transport systems, fulfil a critical role on an inter-urban basis, as well as experiencing the problematic complexities of intra-urban mobility. Similarly, by linking waterborne and land transport systems, seaports are well placed to act either as generative foci of development diffusion or, alternatively, as parasitic nodes drawing off resources from hinterlands and restricting economic growth.

Modes, choices, intermodalism and flexibility

A third basic idea concerns the links between different conventional transport modes – roads, railways, air and sea routes, canals and pipelines. Three dimensions are significant. Firstly, the *relative significance of different transport modes* is a dynamic aspect of the transport provision in any country or area, and today often focuses particularly on road/ rail competition and the declining importance of railways. Historically, railways provided the pioneer transport arteries in many world areas, but over time roads have proved more flexible and more competitive as well as providing more convenient door-to-door transport. Although rail track mileage is increasing worldwide, specialized networks such as urban rapid-transit systems are increasingly popular, and rail modernization schemes are frequently seen as a good investment, railways have nevertheless generally lost their arterial role.

Secondly, it is important to consider *the degree of intermodal choice* available to an individual, group or society. The selection of a specific transport mode for a particular purpose depends upon a range of factors including the range of modes available, their relative cost, safety factors and convenience. In some areas, however, relatively few modes are available and therefore choices are severely restricted. Very broadly, a relative lack of intermodal choice characterizes less-developed countries and areas, while people in more advanced parts of the world usually have a much wider choice available. The restrictive impact of limited transport availability is a major factor affecting the development process in poor countries, while conversely the availability of a wide range of modes facilitates socio-economic progress in more prosperous regions.

Thirdly, modern transport systems depend increasingly on the concept of intermodalism, the movement of goods from origin to destination in sealed containers by means of two or more transport modes (e.g. rail/road, road/rail/sea, rail/sea/rail). Introduced by the so-called container revolution of the 1960s, the concept of intermodalism and the use of multimodal transport methods together facilitated the rapid spread of containerized transport methods throughout much of the global transport system (Hayuth, 1987), and by the 1990s had effectively revolutionized transport logistics. Although the ultimate goal of a seamless international transport web is far from present-day reality, intermodalism has induced a rethinking of relationships between coastal ports and their traditional hinterlands and

forelands, as inland container-handling centres (sometimes termed "dry ports") have assumed increasing importance.

Deregulation and privatization

In the past two decades there has been a major worldwide move away from transport services that are heavily regulated by government, by controlling service patterns and charges, and operated by nationalized or municipally owned companies, towards deregulated or liberalized transport services operated by privately owned companies. This policy reflects neo-liberal "New Right" views that the State should confine its role to the adoption of minimal regulations designed to ensure fair competition and the safe operation of transport services (Green, 1987).

Deregulation, which has affected all modes of transport, has been underpinned by the *theory of contestable markets*, which contends that competition, through the free entry of new (private) operators into a transport market, is the key mechanism for improving efficiency and for providing cheaper and more innovative transport services (Baumol *et al.*, 1982; see also Chapter 4). In practice most transport markets have not been contestable and deregulation has often resulted in near-monopoly control by a single transport company. Potential abuses of monopoly power such as excessive prices and poor-quality services can be controlled by a form of re-regulation through a government-appointed regulator. In Britain's passenger rail industry regulators control fares and provide service quality incentives to transport operators through a reward/ penalty régime (Gibb *et al.*, 1996; Knowles, 1998).

Other motives for transport deregulation and privatization are reducing the cost of transport subsidies and raising enormous capital receipts from selling publicly owned companies such as British Airways, Canadian National Railways, Britain's National Bus Company and a host of other large and small companies in all modes of transport in a wide range of developed, former Communist and less-developed countries.

Franchising of services by competitive tendering for a fixed-period contract has sometimes proven to be a more successful method of introducing market forces into the provision of transport services. The franchising of Greater London's local bus services, for example, is regarded by most people as more successful than full deregulation in the rest of Great Britain (Kennedy, 1995).

Privatization continues unabated as most privately run transport companies have proved to be lower-cost and more market-orientated than their publicly owned predecessors and so there have been few calls for re-nationalization. Full deregulation, however, is a more controversial policy and there are strong arguments favouring partial liberalization or re-regulation especially where monopoly power could be detrimental to transport users.

Holistic approaches

It is important to emphasize, fifthly, that *transport systems are dynamic wholes*, and that their evolution and operation should ultimately be perceived and analysed in this context. In order to understand how any system operates today, what its problems are and how it might be improved, it is usually helpful to know how it has originated, grown and developed. Transport history, like history in general, is not bunk; it is part of human inheritance, and helps us to appreciate the potentialities and the limitations of the transport systems we have today or are planning for the future (Kessides, 1993; Nijkamp and Reichman, 1986). Transport policy, however, is often fragmented, especially in competitive market economies, and integrated transport systems are often regarded as unattainable in a world where individual transport modes, and elements within them (such as specific railway or road haulage companies or ports), operate in a competitive environment in which the demand for transport is ultimately unpredictable. In most cases, of course, individual transport modes were developed separately, both spatially and over time, and this partly explains why transport policy is often fragmented and why intermodal approaches

are traditionally difficult. In an era of intermodalism and increased attention to integrated transport policies, however, there are signs that these problems may be alleviated.

Factors Involved in Transport and Development

Many factors are involved in the complex relationships between transport and development, and the present-day transport system of a country or area cannot normally be explained by one factor alone. Explanations can usually be found, however, in a series of interrelated factors. Some of the more important factors are indicated in Figure 2.1, which shows how transport systems of various types are influenced by environmental characteristics and constraints; by historical trends and conditions; by economic, political and demographic circumstances; by technological changes; and by trading conditions.

Figure 2.1 emphasizes that these factors affect transport in different ways, influencing each other as well as affecting transport systems directly and indirectly. Transport systems themselves, together with the physical environment within which they are set, also influence all these different areas of human activity. Each factor may operate in a positive, negative or neutral way; each may affect transport on different scales, from the local to the global; and two basic dimensions – time and space – are involved. Examples of some of these factors at different scales of activity are given in Table 2.1.

In considering the relative importance of factors affecting transport in a particular country or area, geographers not only use general models but also emphasize the diversity of place, and the specific combination of factors, which help to explain an individual transport problem or situation. In some cases, one particular factor may be overwhelmingly important. In most cases, however, we can only understand how a transport system operates, how it has grown and developed, and how it is related to socio-economic progress, if we examine all the relevant factors involved and the relationships between them.

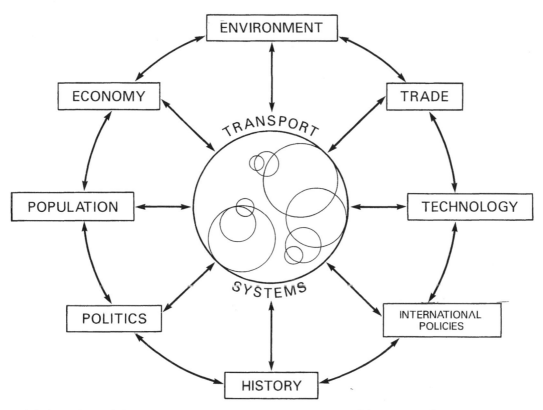

Figure 2.1 Some factors influencing the development of transport systems and the transport/development interface

This principle applies equally to advanced and less-developed countries.

MODELS OF GLOBAL RELEVANCE

Attempts to generalize on transport and development relationships at a global scale have resulted in a number of spatial models. Whilst there is considerable debate on the interpretation of such studies, a degree of consistency is apparent in the underlying factors. Most agree that the present pattern owes much to the emergence of a world mercantile system and the ensuing colonial period, which laid the foundations not only of the global links but also of the urban hierarchies that form the transport nodes.

The Vance Model

Based on his work on the eastern seaboard of America, Vance (1970) developed a five-stage "mercantile" model to illustrate the development of transport links and the growth of the urban hierarchy in North America (Figure 2.2). Although primarily concerned with trade, his model is important in that it stresses the impact of exogenous forces on the evolution of transport networks and their associated spatial patterns. In the initial stage, an accumulation of wealth in Europe prompted overseas expansion of an exploratory nature. Stage 2 sees the beginnings of the transatlantic trade routes based on the one-way trade in staple products such as fish, furs and timber. From 1620 permanent settlement occurs in North America: this results in Atlantic trade in both directions as settlers begin to produce commodities for export and

Table 2.1   Some examples of factors involved in the development of transport systems

Scale	Environmental	Historical	Technological	Political	Economic
Local	Soils/drainage Geomorphology	Settlement Culture	Roads	Enterprise Administration	Employment Core zones
Regional	Altitude Crop environments	Colonies	Railways	Trade	Road/rail competition
Continental	Distance	Colonialism	Sea routes	Independence	Markets
Global	Oceans	Isolation	Energy Air transport Telecommunications	Neo-colonialism	Interdependence Prices Demand level

consume manufactured products from a rapidly in-dustrializing Europe (stage 3). Internal transport links are limited but all are externally orientated, a process that results in linear patterns both along the coast and stretching into the interior.

The fourth stage of the model is characterized by the development of internal trade and an internal manufacturing industry. Despite the lessening of mercantile ties with Britain after 1783, the spatial impact of the first three stages remains strong. The initial points of attachment with Europe assume an independent status and, in turn, form the nodes from which the interior is settled. Competition between the various coastal settlements resulted in a number of east–west penetration routes, first by water, then by rail. The growth of internal nodes is also the res-ult of their long external links to the coast and, ul-timately, Europe. The final stage of the model is reached when internal trade dominates North America and is matched by a mature transport and urban system in Europe. Although North America was eventually to lead the world in transport de-velopments, the historical evolution is still apparent in both its transport network and its urban system.

The Rimmer Model

An alternative and complementary perspective is provided by Rimmer (1977) who outlined the de-velopment of a hybrid transport system in less-developed countries, derived from the colonization process by which metropolitan powers used revolu-tionary modes of transport to penetrate indigenous systems and to gain both political control and cultural and economic dominance. The resultant re-structuring of resource use, patterns of circulation, organization and outlook transformed the indige-nous system, and instituted an interdependent rela-tionship in which the colonizing power to a substantial extent controlled a two-way exchange of goods and services. This process eventually yielded a hybrid transport system in developing countries con-taining both indigenous and imported elements, often inadequately integrated.

Using terminology derived from Brookfield (1972, 1975), Rimmer identified four phases in the evolving interrelationships between metropolitan and Third World countries in transport terms (Figure 2.3):

1. A *pre-contact phase* involved no links between a Third World country and a distant power in the advanced world. Within the Third World country, a limited network of tracks, together with navig-able waterways, supported a relatively restricted socio-economic and political system.
2. An *early colonial phase*, secondly, involved the establishment of direct contacts by sea between advanced and developing countries but did not produce radical changes in Third World societies, Europeans being largely content to dominate sea transport routes and to establish foothold settle-ments such as trading posts and garrisons.
3. A third phase of *high colonialism* involved more fundamental changes including the introduction

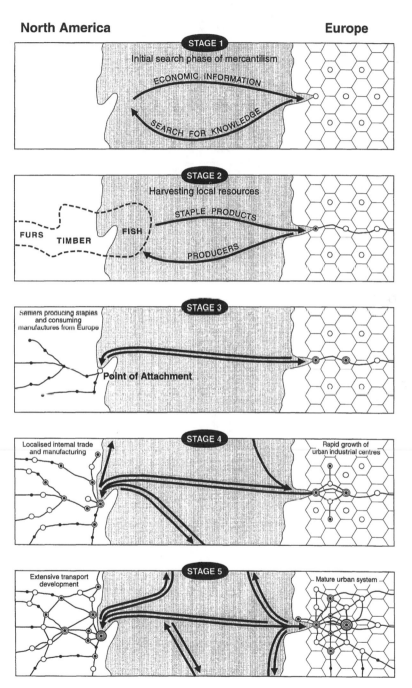

Figure 2.2 The Vance model

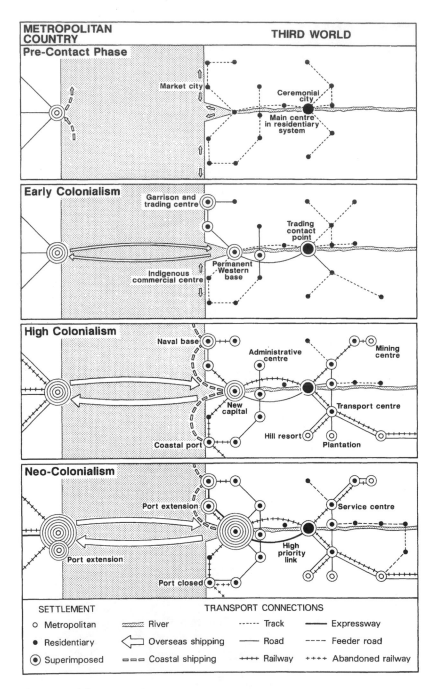

Figure 2.3   The Rimmer model

of roads and railways, port facilities and inland transport nodes, and the diversification of economic activity (including industrialization and commercial agriculture) and settlement patterns (including rapid urbanization).

4. A fourth *neo-colonial* phase involves a substantial further diversification of the economic development surface of the Third World country and continuing (if modified) trade links with the former metropolitan power. The modernization of the transport system in the Third World country involves, at this stage, elements of rationalization, adaptation and selective investment in response to changing demands. There is, however, no radical adjustment to the systems inherited from earlier phases.

The Taaffe, Morrill and Gould Model

The interrelationships between transport and development within a developing area of the world have been drawn together in a very well-known model (Figure 2.4a) first published by three American authors – Taaffe, Morrill and Gould (Taaffe *et al.*, 1963). The ideas it contains were originally derived from research in Ghana and Nigeria. Figure 2.4b shows an adaptation to East Africa. A series of six diagrams suggests how, in a hypothetical developing country, a transport network may gradually evolve from a pre-colonial situation of underdevelopment, through a period of external political intervention to the period of political independence.

The model represents the parallel evolution of political, economic and transport systems in a developing country. It is based on the usually valid assumption that, in such countries, transport networks are rooted, both physically and historically, in seaports, although the external, maritime element in the processes represented is largely ignored. The first of the six small diagrams in Figures 2.4a and 2.4b suggest how a scatter of small, unconnected coastal trading ports represents the initial points of political contact and economic exploitation, and forms a basis for the introduction of inland transport modes. Arterial railways and roads are introduced, and in time extended,

and feeder lines are added. Inland transport routes pass through or focus upon places of established political significance or economic opportunity, so the changing transport network in part controls, and is in part controlled by, the changing political and economic geography of the port hinterlands. As the sequence of diagrams indicates, some places grow and prosper, others decline, and the connectivity of the network is gradually increased. Eventually, in the final diagram of the series, the model suggests a fully integrated transport network closely attuned to a mature economy, a diversified development surface and a mature political system.

This model, like all models, is an oversimplification of reality. It provides a useful point of view but is open to discussion and reinterpretation. In terms of the relationship between transport and development, a number of questions may be asked. How, for example, does a developing country make the transition from one stage of the model to the next? What is the nature of the development process involved? How far do the processes implied in the model represent the real needs of developing countries rather than the aspirations of external, colonial powers? How relevant is the model to an understanding of pre-colonial roots of modern transport systems, or to present-day demands and objectives? Does the model bear any relation to the processes by which transport systems in advanced countries have evolved? All such questions admit a variety of answers, but whatever the nuances of interpretation, the intimate interrelationships between transport and development provide an essential underpinning.

Just as the Vance model was derived from Euro-American relations, the Rimmer model is essentially associated with South-East Asian experience, and the Taaffe, Morrill and Gould model was conceived in West Africa. All three models are useful, as external and very generalized viewpoints, in helping us to understand some of the processes of transport change. The model by Taaffe *et al.* "essentially identifies phases in the evolution of spatial organization", does not "deal effectively with issues of modal interlinkage and spatial integration and [says] little

(a)

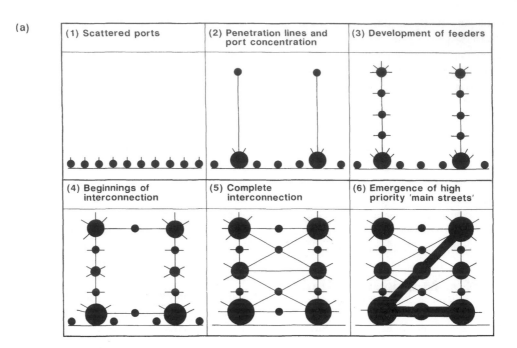

(b)

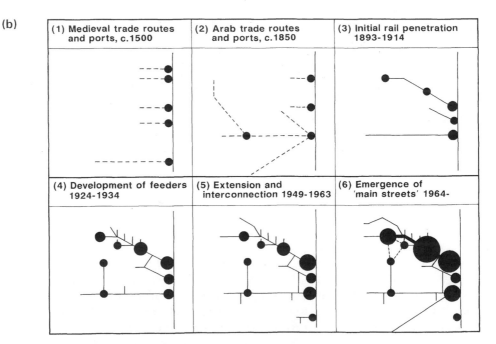

Figure 2.4   The Taaffe, Morrill and Gould model
(a) The original version (Taaffe *et al.*, 1963) and (b) an adaptation to East Africa (Hoyle, 1973)

about important questions of control and therefore power" (Hilling, 1996, 27; see also Taaffe *et al.*, 1996). Applied to the East African transport complex, the model works well (Hoyle, 1983) and has recently provided a basis for a new analysis of inter-port competition (Hoyle and Charlier, 1995). Rimmer's model, however, attempts "to incorporate transport into a wider political, administrative and even social context" (Hilling, 1996, 27). But because both models are broadly confined to the period of European colonialism and its immediate aftermath, they do not tell us much about how such transport systems may be expected to change during a more extended period of political independence. In this regard, the experience of the USA, Canada and Australia is relevant, and suggests a fifth *mature independence* phase characterized by continuing transport links along established lines (both within the former dependent territory and with the former colonizing power) together with substantial diversification and reorientation of external links and continuing intensification of internal networks. The final stage of the Vance model reflects these features.

The enduring relevance of these historical models of transport development is that they confirm that patterns are replicated across the globe and contribute towards our understanding of modern global systems. Applied to the USA, the Taaffe, Morrill and Gould model differentiates four phases of transport development: scattered East Coast ports, trans-Appalachian railway penetration, dominance of interconnected railroads, and intermodal competition (air, car, truck and sometimes rail) along "main streets". The Vance model illustrates how mercantilism created transport systems that supported advanced urban systems at the core and localized development in the periphery. Such models lay the foundations for later concepts which explain the growth in global interdependence and inequality that have come to dominate urban and economic development in the latter part of the twentieth century (Clark, 1996). As the physical transport systems on which globalization has been based are increasingly supplemented by telecommunications (Brunn and Leinbach, 1991), retaining a historical

perspective on transport expansion continues to play an important role in understanding the current globalization process.

MODELS OF NODAL DEVELOPMENT

Within this context, the associations between transport nodes and various forms of human settlement and economic activity are numerous and important. The relationships between public infrastructures, including transport, and regional economic development has generated a substantial literature (Duffy-Deno and Eberts, 1991; Munnel, 1992); and the specific problems of urban transport nodes and systems have been widely addressed (Abane, 1993; McGee, 1971; Tolley, 1990). Two basic issues are considered here: relationships between transport and the *form* of urban development; and the critical importance of cityports and airports as nodes where modes of transportation change.

Transport and Urban Form in Industrial Societies

Economic forces, especially capitalism as a dominant mode of production, were the fundamental determinants of urban growth in industrialized societies. However, within each growth phase, innovations in the transport system are viewed by many as the single most important determinant of urban morphology. Hartshorn (1992), based on the work of Adams (1970), has illustrated the significance of the historical evolution of transport for urban structures in North America. Knox (1987) has identified similar patterns in British cities. Although there are important differential impacts of successive transport technologies in cities in different regions and at varying times (Baerwald, 1984), there is considerable consistency in overall spatial patterns.

Prior to the advent of mechanized transport, the city depended on rudimentary water transport, horse-drawn vehicles and walking. The consequence was that for centuries the city exhibited a very compact form, typified by stage A in the Hartshorn model (Figure 2.5). Today, many older cities retain this imprint from the past, often, as in Europe, within a walled city centre, where everything is within walking distance. Not until the advent of trolley and rail technologies in the late nineteenth century could urban residents in major cities live beyond walking distance from their place of work.

In stage B, the fixed-rail and electric streetcar era of the late nineteenth century, mass transport became available to everyone at an affordable price. As cities grew in size, fuelled by industrialization, transport innovation allowed populations to decentralize away from the city core. Large-scale suburbs began to emerge especially along the transport routes catering for the working- and middle-class markets. As Figure 2.5 indicates, a star-shaped urban area began to replace the circular outline of the walking city. In parallel, commuter rail services and inter-urban links allowed further decentralization to beads of settlements along major transport routes.

In stage C of the model, road transport begins to make its impact. Between 1890 and 1930 cars were

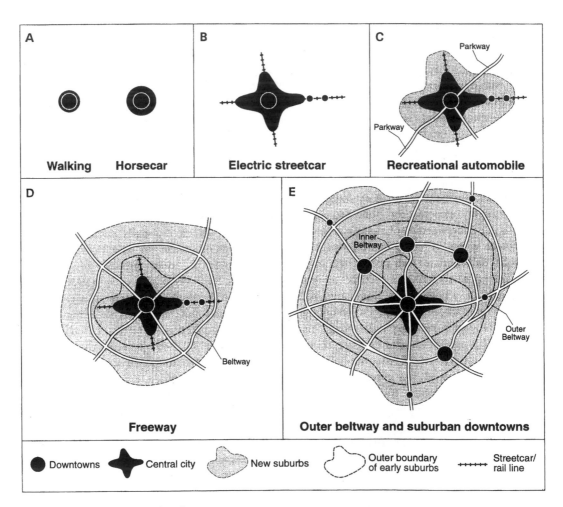

Figure 2.5 Transportation and urban form (after Hartshorn)

used mainly for recreation and had little impact on city structure although they allowed wealthy families to move further from the city centre. In contrast, the flexibility offered by buses allowed them to challenge streetcars from the 1920s onwards, and by the 1950s the transition to buses for public mass transit was almost complete. However, buses never dominated the urban transport scene to the same extent as streetcars, especially in the USA. As competition between buses and cars intensified, bus services found themselves unable to compete in the low-density suburbs with their networks of local roads. Buses became increasingly confined to the high-density central city areas and major arterial highways (stage D). In larger, older cities dominated by rail, overcrowding on the commuter rail lines prompted the search for alternative modes of travel to work. The car, which offered a greatly improved alternative to either bus, streetcar or rail, was not confined to rail corridors or major arterial roads and began to open up interstitial areas for suburban development. The decentralized form of development first created by mass transit was the perfect environment for the car, which rapidly came to dominate urban travel.

In the final stage E of the model in the USA, the post-1945 freeway building programme allowed the development of metropolitan areas with highway networks that permitted virtually random access between any two points. This led to further decentralization not just of residential land use but of retail, office and industrial growth. Many of these activities concentrated in the outer beltways where they formed a strong contrast to the declining inner-city areas. Ultimately such restructuring led to the fragmentation of urban spatial patterns, typified in North America by the growth of "edge cities" (Garreau, 1991). Although planning regulations limited the scale of decentralization in British cities, the same trends were apparent. Urban transport had become cheaper, faster and more ubiquitous, greatly enhancing the intensity of movement. In the process, as later chapters in this book illustrate, urban transport has created entirely new spatial patterns.

Seaport Development: the Anyport Model

In transport studies, much attention is given to urban problems, but seaports are often ignored in favour of roads, railways and other land-based modes; yet the pivotal position of seaports, like that of airports, within intermodal transport systems is indispensable (Bird, 1980, 1983). The term *cityport* is sometimes used to emphasize the interdependence of urban and transport forms and functions in locations where port facilities provided the original *raison d'être* of urban settlement (Hoyle and Pinder, 1981).

A port, as a node in a multimodal transport system, fulfils critical functions and the relative efficiency with which it does so can become a positive, neutral or negative factor in development. Ports reflect changing economic, political and technological circumstances over time and on different scales (Hoyle and Hilling, 1984). Ports and port cities have played a major role in development throughout the modern world, often as gateway settlements from the standpoint of a colonizing power or as windows on a wider world for the societies and economies of coastal and interior zones (Blaut, 1993). Imperial port cities – from ancient times to the nineteenth century – were critical nodes in the establishment of both transport networks and urban systems, helping to develop dependent territories within a globalizing economy. These key elements normally provided foundation stones of continuing importance in the context of present-day urban and transport systems.

The growth of ports is basically affected by four factors: the *land situation* and the *water situation*, and the *land site* and the *water site*. The water site (i.e. the physical conditions of the harbour) often provides the initial stimulus to development, but unless conditions in the other three categories are favourable, the settlement is unlikely to prosper. The level of port development, measured in terms of cargo-handling capacity or the volume and value of commodity flow, is chiefly a reflection of the land situation – the extent and pattern of economic development in the hinterland. The land site provides a direct control over urban growth, and the water situation affects relationships with major shipping routes. The prosperity of a port ultimately depends, however, upon the efficiency with which it is able to respond to demand and the degree to which it is able to enhance its competitive position.

The concept of a hypothetical *Anyport* was introduced by Bird (1963) in the context of British seaports, as a pattern and standard against which to compare the actual development of individual members of a port complex. Each historical stage in the development of Anyport involves a change in layout, and thus the way in which the present pattern of port facilities has evolved may clearly be seen. The six eras of the original model (Table 2.2a) reflect the emergence of a modern seaport node from primitive origins through the development of marginal quays, docks, deep-water berths and specialized quayage. Individual ports have not always followed this sequence precisely or at the same rate. The model outlines a general sequence, but also allows attention to be drawn to unusual or unique features in individual cases.

The *Anyport* model has been successfully used in a modified form to describe the evolution of the port system on the Indian Ocean coasts of the East African countries of Kenya and Tanzania (Hoyle, 1983). Table 2.2b outlines the growth of ports in this system from an ancient dhow traffic era through successive and sometimes overlapping eras involving lighterage, deep-water and specialized quays to the development of modern container terminals. In both the British and the East African cases, the model reveals the significance of maritime factors as primary influences in port development, as well as interdependent socio-economic and political factors affecting the level and pattern of port growth in specific locations.

The growth and development of ports clearly involve the interplay of many variables. Some factors operate at a local scale, such as those associated with port sites; others, such as the distribution of rainfall, population or feeder road systems, indicate regional conditions within a hinterland; while continental and global systems, often technological, political or

Table 2.2   The *Anyport* model

(a) Summary of the general theme of the development of a major British port

	Era	Terminated by
I	Primitive	Overflowing of the port function from the primitive nucleus of the port, or a change in location of the dominant port function
II	Marginal quay extension	Change from a simple continuous line of quays
III	Marginal quay elaboration	Opening of a dock or the expansion of the harbour
IV	Dock elaboration	Opening of a dock with simple lineal quayage
V	Simple lineal quayage	Provision of oil berths in deep water
VI	Specialized quayage	Occupation of all waterside sites between the port nucleus and the open sea

Source: Bird (1963, 34).

(b) Summary of the general theme of the development of a major East African port

	Era	Terminated by
I	Dhow traffic	Construction of the first port facilities on the modern harbour site
II	Primitive	Construction of the first lighterage quays
III	Marginal quay extension	Opening of the first deep-water berths
IV	Simple lineal quayage	Provision of oil berths in deep water
V	Specialized quayage	Development of a container terminal
VI	Containerization	Occupation of all deep-water sites within the confines of the harbour

Source: Hoyle (1983, 83).

economic in nature, involve wider circumstances and changes. Ports do not grow in isolation, but in response to changing opportunities and demands involving different times, areas, scales and intensities. They provide one set of dynamic, competitive instruments through which a country's external relations are conducted (Hayuth, 1985; Hilling, 1969; Hoyle and Charlier, 1995). All ports, whether studied individually or collectively, demonstrate the critical role of the port function in national and regional economic development, and the need to maintain and enhance each port's competitive position when looking towards the land and maritime transport systems of the twenty-first century.

The Airport as Multimodal High-Speed Hub

Major airports, primarily in Europe but also elsewhere, are increasingly evolving as multimodal "mainports". These are predicated upon the complementarity between air and high-speed train (HST) as the two transport modes most capable of shrinking the friction of distance. The key model, France's *train à grande vitesse* (TGV), is less a very rapid but essentially conventional train system as a new mode of transport offering a competitive product with patterns of access very similar to those of air transport (Gutiérrez *et al.*, 1996). The TGV, moreover, cannot be viewed in isolation, but rather as a transport mode that obtains added value when it interfaces with other high-speed systems (Thompson, 1995). Although early TGV development concentrated on city centre–city centre linkages, the most recent network additions include the bypass route around Paris, which links the existing TGV-Nord, Sud-Est and Atlantique lines (and eventually the TGV-Est to Strasbourg and beyond) and serves Europe's third busiest airport – Charles de Gaulle at Roissy. Additionally, Massy TGV in southern Paris is linked to the city's other airport at Orly – which ranks fourth in Europe – while a new TGV station has also been built at Lyon's Satolas airport. This functional interdependence, or complementarity, of air services with high-speed rail means that Paris CDG and Lyon Satolas have be-

come the first of a new wave of European multimodal airport hubs.

Although many airports in Europe and elsewhere are served by conventional rail links, the high-speed intermodal airport interchange is very different. The concept is central to the European Commission's plans to develop an integrated Trans-European Transport Network (TETN). A multimodal airport hub represents a rationalization of the economic, social and environmental benefits to be achieved by consolidating traffic flows, a terminal where passenger loads can be broken up by the most efficient mode (Varlet, 1992). Although France has by far the best-developed HST network of any of the EU countries, the system is being expanded throughout the Community (see Figure 13.1). Further multimodal high-speed airport hubs, including Brussels, Amsterdam, Dusseldorf, Munich, Frankfurt, Cologne–Bonn and Milan Malpensa, will be incorporated within this network, which will not be completed until after 2010.

Clearly, this particularly European approach has marked implications for the concept of the airport as a mainport. Two in particular can be emphasized here. Firstly, the development of the high-speed hub with its modal shift potential offers one means of tackling the major ground traffic congestion problems that bedevil large airports worldwide. Airport planners are constantly seeking means of shifting airport users from private cars to public transport, of which the HST is the most developed and perhaps most attractive form. Secondly, the multimodal high-speed airport hub is the only transport mode that can cater simultaneously for the point-to-point and transfer traffic markets catered for by any large airport. For point-to-point traffic, it has been shown that HSTs can compete effectively with air transport on inter-city journeys of less than three hours (approximately 500 km). Therefore, HSTs may well replace a considerable volume of air travel on shorter inter-city routes, particularly if the hub airport is served directly by this mode. Moreover, the development of multimodal airport interchanges will also allow HST substitution of at least some domestic and hub-feed airline services, a role of particular significance for transfer passengers. Intercontinental passengers, for example, can transfer directly to the terrestrial high-speed system, rather than having to take another connecting flight to reach their final destination or use conventional linkages to high-speed rail termini in city centres.

Ultimately, a successful integration of road, conventional rail, high-speed rail and air transport modes at airports could produce a succession of sophisticated mainports across Europe at which intra-urban, regional, national, international and global traffic flows are all seamlessly integrated (Graham, 1995) (Figure 2.6). The two poles of the complex are provided by (i) the airport–HST–autoroute–conventional national/regional rail interchange, with its regional, national, international and global focus, and (ii) the city-centre railway terminus, orientated primarily towards intra-urban, regional and national traffic, together with limited international services. The conventional airport–central station rail link remains a fundamental element in the model, linking the multimodal airport interchange to the city-centre termini. In sum, the model arguably offers a more rational approach to the problem of scarce airport capacity than does the construction of new runways. It is, however, one that is limited to densely urbanized regions that can sustain high-speed rail networks.

NETWORKS AND THEIR SPATIAL IMPACTS

Transport geographers are particularly concerned with the relationships that can be observed between nodes, networks and systems, and with the questions that arise when attempts are made to elucidate the impacts of transport network development on the environments and societies involved. Associations between rail network provision, or road network development, and wider aspects of economies and societies in advanced and less-developed countries are considered here, with reference to appropriate examples. More detailed case studies dependent upon these principles are presented in Chapter 3.

Railways and Development

Of all the transport modes, railways have exerted the greatest influence on the establishment of spatial patterns at a regional scale. Not only were they an integral part of the Industrial Revolution, but their development also coincided with the growth of European empires in Africa, Asia and Latin America. Consequently, they have played a crucial role in the development process in both advanced and less-developed societies. The experience of Africa, Europe and Japan is examined here.

Railways and development in Africa

Railways provide an important means of modern transport throughout Africa and their distribution and operation have been closely related to both political and economic developments (Figure 2.7). Their initial impact was profound, since they offered the first real alternative to head porterage, which was slow and labour-intensive (Hilling, 1996). In contrast to the traditional system, railways increased efficiency and reduced the cost of transport and

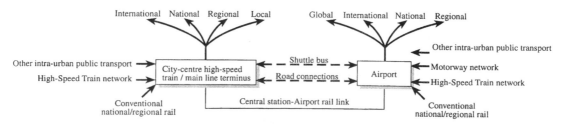

Figure 2.6   A model of a multimodal, high-speed airport mainport

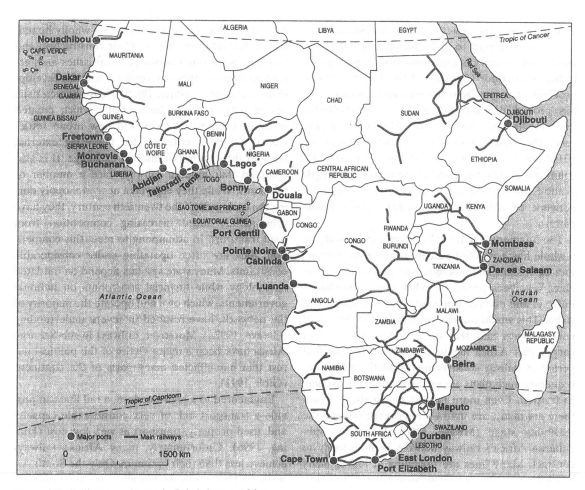

Figure 2.7 Railways and ports in Sub-Saharan Africa

were particularly suited to the movement of bulk goods. They facilitated the opening up of a modern commercial economy and initiated many of the development patterns that are still apparent today.

The majority of African railways were built during the late nineteenth and early twentieth century as essential elements of European colonial policy. Initially, built from coastal ports to interior nodes, they allowed European powers to demonstrate effective political control required to justify a claim to territory under the terms of the Berlin Conference of 1884–85. They also stimulated economic development through the development of cash crops and by facilitating mineral exploitation on a large scale. As

such, they were able to fulfil their principal objectives of exporting raw materials and importing capital goods, a role that they have retained to the present day.

The pattern of railway provision resulting from these colonial developments resulted in marked spatial inequality. Several landlocked African countries, including Chad, Central African Republic, Niger, Rwanda and Burundi, have no direct access to rail transport within their own boundaries. Most other tropical African countries have one or two major lines, usually linking major ports to interior economic cores. In some cases, such as the Tanzania–Zambia line, which is paralleled by a modern road and an oil pipeline system, an international railway from a coastal port to a distant interior zone in a landlocked country is one element in a multimodal transport corridor (Gleave, 1992b). Elsewhere, the problem of access from the interior to ocean ports has proved difficult and controversial (Griffiths, 1993; Hoyle and Charlier, 1995). South Africa possesses the most comprehensive railway network: its 20 005 km track, much of which is electrified, accounts for nearly one-third of the total track length in sub-Saharan Africa. It is the only African railway network to exhibit a grid rather than a linear pattern.

The fragmented nature of African rail networks as a whole has generated numerous proposals for further extensions and linkages. At a continental scale, plans have been proposed to link the existing linear railways and end the isolation of several landlocked states. This would require an estimated 15 000 km of new railways and the integration of the various gauges that Africa has inherited from the colonial period of railway construction (Siddall, 1969). Consequently, such plans are extremely unlikely to come to fruition. Even more modest proposals, of which there are many, are unlikely to progress beyond the feasibility stage (Mwase, 1996). In reality, sub-Saharan Africa's railway network is more likely to contract. Many lines are operating at low capacity and have good roads running in parallel. In this context, the World Bank and the International Monetary Fund have targeted a number of lines for closure with the aim of reducing public spending as part of Structural Adjustment Programmes. Consequently, any new developments will require strong economic justification, whilst network contraction (as in Sierra Leone) is likely to continue.

It is now widely accepted that, while railways may be a necessary condition for development, their existence is not a guarantee that it will follow. The assumption that new or extended railways actively promote development was questioned in the 1960s (O'Connor, 1965), and a distinction drawn in this context between the *initial* provision of modern transport facilities and the *elaboration* of established transport systems (Hoyle, 1970). Moreover, the ad-

vent of railways has not always been wholly beneficial or neutral in its effects. Their construction and financing were often highly political issues and, according to some opinions, resulted in underdevelopment and poverty (Pirie, 1982). Their characteristic spatial pattern of a "line-of-rail", which created zones of economic activity and new urban settlements, has been criticized for favouring external trade at the expense of internal exchange. It is also accepted that modern railways face a number of problems. While they enjoyed a near-monopoly during the early part of the twentieth century, they have subsequently faced increasing competition from road transport. In attempting to meet this competition, they are often operating under considerable constraints. Many state systems depend on outdated technology while financial constraints on national governments, which own and operate the majority of the network, have resulted in severe underfunding (Gleave, 1992a). Moreover, railways in sub-Saharan Africa have been a major victim of the political unrest that has afflicted many parts of the continent (Gibb, 1991).

Engineered to a high standard, a rail line can provide a transport link of very considerable capacity and, used properly, transport at very low cost (Hilling, 1996). Unfortunately, many African railways achieve less than their optimum. Only the South African system ranks technically and operationally among the most modern in the world. Elsewhere, the debt crisis and the subsequent Structural Adjustment Programmes have compounded the problems inherited from the colonial period. Investment in track has been affected by reductions in government expenditure while restrictions on imports have resulted in a shortage of spare parts and new rolling stock. To a limited extent, the impact of such programmes has been offset by international lending for railway rehabilitation. However, since railways are capital-intensive, they are most viable where they are intensively used. Unfortunately, Africa with its low population densities and limited economic expansion does not always offer ideal conditions for rail development. The role of rail networks in African development in the twenty-first century is likely to be less important than that which they currently fulfil.

High-speed rail networks in Europe and Japan

The earliest phases of railway building in advanced societies were associated with industrial expansion and emerging urban systems. Unlike Africa, rail networks emerged which were highly interconnected and incorporated most, if not all, of the urban hierarchy. The subsequent contraction of these railway networks from the 1960s onwards has been even more marked than in developing countries. However, in contrast to Africa, railway technology in industrial societies has continued to evolve, with consequent repercussions for spatial patterns. In particular, the development of high-speed trains and their associated networks is having an impact on both urban systems and regional development in Europe, the Far East and North America.

The spatial consequences that have arisen from this sequence of initial expansion, contraction and new technology are apparent in Japan (see Figure 8.3). Concentrating on urban accessibility, Murayama (1994) shows that the traditional urban system, linked by coastal shipping and a primitive road system, was completely reorganized by the emergence of the railways, which created new connections and greatly increased the speed of existing links. Between 1910 and 1960 concentrated investment in rail construction in Japan resulted in reduced travel times: for example, the journey time from Tokyo to Osaka fell from 11 hours in 1926 to 6 hours 30 minutes in 1961. The increase in inter-city accessibility encouraged the unity of the Japanese urban system, which incorporated all major cities. However, increasing competition from road transport meant that this network was unsustainable. The extent of the network peaked in the 1970s and hundreds of miles of track had been closed by 1985.

The introduction of a high-speed transit system, using the *Shinkansen* or bullet train, has both revitalized the Japanese railway system and destroyed the existing spatial structure (Murayama, 1994) (Figure 8.3). The Shinkansen has been introduced on three routes (Tokyo–Fukuoka, Tokyo–Morioka and Tokyo–Niigata), creating an east–west spinal system. Travel times between Tokyo and Osaka have been reduced by over half to 2 hours 52 minutes. Elsewhere savings are even greater, especially on journeys between Tokyo and such cities as Hiroshima, Fukuoka and Sendai. Cities on the Shinkansen lines have gained the greatest locational advantage while non-Shinkansen cities in remote regions became even more peripheral. Although the full implications of these changes are yet to be researched, strong evidence already exists for the convergence of Shinkansen cities and the divergence of other cities.

Gutiérrez et al. (1996) have suggested that similar changes in relative location are also expected of the European high-speed network, currently being developed (see Figure 13.1). The Commission of European Communities has placed great emphasis on this network, which is viewed as essential to the achievement of a Single Market and to the problem of regional development. The Commission argues that a truly free European market will be dependent on an open and flexible network in which transport and infrastructure provide efficient connections between all regions. Moreover, the high-speed network will improve the accessibility of levels of the regions of Europe, bringing them closer to each other. It is argued that the high-speed train, by reducing travelling times, reduces distances and that it is a powerful tool in regional planning (Thompson, 1994). Consequently, the European network will have a restructuring effect on community space and will play an important role in regional integration (Commission of European Communities, 1990).

As yet the network is in the early stages of development and consists of a number of unconnected lines in France, Germany, Italy and Spain. However, by 2010 the Outline Plan of the European high-speed network consists of 9000 km of new lines, 15 000 km of upgraded lines and 1200 km of new links (see Figure 13.1). As in Japan, the network offers considerable savings in travel time: journeys of 1000 to 1200 km could be accomplished in 4 to

5 hours while longer journeys of 1500 to 2500 km could be covered overnight in 8 to 12 hours (Community of European Railways, 1989). As Spiekerman and Wegener (1994) have argued, Europe is a shrinking continent. However, the contraction of space brought about by the high-speed train is far from continuous. Undoubtedly, peripheral regions will be brought closer to the centre, but only those regions which are on the network or well connected to it will benefit. As in Africa, the network will create islands of greater accessibility which will in fact favour the major conurbations and the corridors between them. Regions outside this new organization of space will decline unless they are well connected to the high-speed network (Plassard, 1991, 1992). This situation has considerable implications for the future development of national rail networks, especially in peripheral countries such as Britain, Greece, Portugal and Spain. As Dundon-Smith and Gibb (1994) have argued, the network offers the opportunity to link peripheral regions to Europe, but failure to develop national networks in conjunction with the high-speed network could also result in greater isolation.

Accessibility and Diffusion: Road Network Development

Although railways made a major contribution to the industrialization process, modern motor transport, with its flexibility and adaptability, now dominates the transport systems of most countries. More than any other mode, road transport has improved the mobility and accessibility of the majority of the world's population (Hilling, 1996). Despite its universality, it is also responsible for some of the greatest contrasts in development that have emerged during the twentieth century. In the developed world, the rapid expansion of motor transport after 1950 exposed the deficiencies of a conventional road network. In response, the industrialized nations invested in new limited-access highways specifically designed to carry large volumes of high-speed traffic. Motorway networks were constructed throughout Europe and Anglo-America for the purpose of link-

ing major cities and providing improved access within larger conurbations (Starkie, 1982). In contrast, the deficiency in road access in developing countries has been an underlying factor in underdevelopment (Owen, 1987). Many developing countries have struggled to find the resources to provide even basic levels of access, especially in their rural areas.

Road transport in less-developed countries

As in the developed world, road transport is now the dominant and universal mode of transport in less-developed countries. Both national governments and international agencies have invested heavily in the transport sector and road building has taken the major share. Early road developments focused on resource-rich areas, many of which had been initially opened up by the railways. In this respect, road building often duplicated the spatial patterns established by the railways and connected interior areas to the major ports. More recently, road networks have been expanded as national leaders have attempted to open up previously isolated and unexploited regions, to encourage economic development and to promote national integration (Airey, 1985; Filani, 1993). During the 1970s emphasis shifted away from the major trunk roads towards the expansion of secondary and feeder roads, especially in the rural areas (Barwell et al., 1985; Mwase, 1989). By 1977, 93 per cent of the total length of roads in projects funded by the World Bank were rural roads.

The spatial impact of such policies has been very varied. New trunk routes are few and their impact, whilst often substantial, is limited to specific areas such as the Amazon basin in Brazil (Hilling, 1996). However, continual advances in road-building technology have resulted in road improvement, often leading to realignment. The road-building programme that followed Nigeria's oil boom from 1974 to the early 1980s has been particularly well documented. Salau and Baba (1984) showed how the realignment of the Zaria to Kano road in northern Nigeria resulted in reorganized marketing opportunities and a substantial shift in population to the new route. However, as Porter (1995) has illustrated, such developments can have detrimental effects, especially on local feeder roads and off-road communities. The differential impacts of feeder roads, whilst location-specific, have also been highlighted. In general, their impact has been greatest where a marketable surplus exists, as in Kenya where a programme to provide 14 000 km of access roads was linked to the increased production of staple commodities such as coffee, tea and sugar. However, such roads have had little impact on other rural transport needs including the fetching of water and fuelwood.

Recent research has questioned the continuing sustainability of road programmes in the developing countries since many, especially the poorer African and Asian countries, are finding it increasingly difficult to maintain their existing road network. Economic Structural Adjustment Programmes imposed by the International Monetary Fund have had serious implications for road transport. Road maintenance in particular has been underfunded: by the late 1980s it was estimated that 90 per cent of Nigeria's unpaved roads were in poor condition. Shortage of foreign exchange and currency devaluation have limited the imports of new vehicles and essential spare parts. In Ghana 70 per cent of the vehicle fleet was found to be inoperative by 1983 owing to a lack of imported spares.

Clearly, the existing model of road transport provision requires modification. International agencies are increasing research into new initiatives in road maintenance which are labour- rather than capital-intensive. With low levels of vehicle ownership in both urban and rural areas, greater emphasis is being placed on encouraging the growth of indigenous vehicle manufacture and intermediate forms of transport such as bicycles and animal-powered transport. It is now widely accepted that there is no direct causal relationship between transport provision and development and that new roads are permissive rather than automatic triggers of development. However, in ensuring that road transport continues its universal role, greater emphasis will have to be placed on maintaining the existing network and providing wider access to motorized transport.

Road transport in developed countries

Although road transport had come to dominate the transport systems of industrial societies by the 1960s, network evolution has continued and long-distance, high-capacity, limited-access road networks now form a major feature of such transport systems. The Interstate Highway System in the USA and European motorway networks indicate the scale of capital investment that has occurred since the 1960s. Understanding the development implications of the road network improvements has been of major interest to transport geographers.

Early studies of the Interstate Highway System (IHS) concentrated on viewing the network as a graph consisting of a collection of nodes and linkages, and assessed accessibility through connectivity measures (Garrison, 1960; Garrison and Marble, 1974). Since these initial measures were rather general, the results in terms of the relationship between the network and locational shift were inconclusive. In view of the capital expenditure required for motorway building and the network's importance to strategic transport planning, interest in assessing the long-term role has generated a search for alternative approaches.

The IHS has emerged from public and private efforts over several decades and has vastly extended the transport system of the USA. Construction of initial linkages began in the 1960s, and the system now consists of 58 highway segments and over 40 000 miles. An important and recurring question, for which a definitive answer remains elusive, is the real impact of the IHS on environments, societies and economies. At the national level, clearly, the system has had a major impact on personal mobility and indeed has perhaps heightened dependence on the automobile. Another influence, however, has been felt through the process of "eminent domain", which has uprooted thousands of residents living in the paths of new proposed highway segments. Reduced travel times and increased accessibility have resulted in less-costly movements of goods and, in the first decade of the system's existence, highway ton-miles of freight increased by more than 60 per cent. The negative impact has fallen upon the railways where freight share declined from 50 to 25 per cent between 1950 and 1990, although rising again more recently. Although the environmental impact of the IHS is not very well documented, the construction industry has produced some well-known case studies of environmental impact mitigation. One example is that of Glenwood Canyon, Colorado, where construction was delayed for more than 20 years while a less harmful route than that originally proposed was designed for a segment near the Utah border. This segment ultimately cost more than $490 million and has two 4000 foot tunnels and 40 bridges (Briggs, 1980; Hamilton, 1988).

The literature surrounding the IHS includes a series of very interesting studies which reveal impacts on neighbourhoods and central business districts (CBDs) (Newman and Kenworthy, 1989) in metropolitan areas such as Los Angeles (Lowry, 1988), San Francisco and Washington, DC, as well as the growth of suburban nucleations. In a regional development context, the IHS has had an uneven impact. One major question is whether public-sector infrastructure is a key determinant of productivity. A recent study has examined the degree to which state highways provide productivity benefits beyond each state's borders (Holtz-Eakin and Schwartz, 1995). Although state highways, and the IHS, are designed with interstate linkages in mind, no evidence was found of significant productivity spillovers. On the other hand the IHS has had an important influence upon commuting patterns to employment (Fisher and Mitchelson, 1981; Mitchelson and Fisher, 1987), on economic activity surrounding many interchanges (Moon, 1994) and is strongly related to the industrial "filtering down" process into non-metropolitan areas (Cromley and Leinbach, 1981).

One especially interesting case study in this context involves economic restructuring and development in the I-75 corridor, which extends from Sault Ste. Marie, Ontario, to a point in south Florida near Miami (Figure 2.8). The 1600-mile link transects Michigan, Ohio, Kentucky, Tennessee, Georgia and Florida. As much as 15 per cent of capital spending on manufacturing in the USA occurs within this corridor. Of special significance is the fact that 25 per cent of Japanese investments are located here. The industrial clustering, which includes Mazda, Honda, Toyota and Komatsu as well as Ford, General Motors, GTE, Lockheed, Honeywell, Citicorp and other major US firms, is explained by branch plant development, increased reliance on suppliers, just-in-time manufacturing, heavy subsidies from individual states, abundant blue-collar, non-unionized labour and high land availability at minimum cost. Within the realm of automobile manufacturers and suppliers, the I-75 and I-65 are known as the "kanban" highways or the equivalent of "just-in-time" highways (Rubenstein, 1992). In fact of the 20 motor vehicle assembly plants started between 1980 and 1991, 16 were built within 100 miles of the corridors. Fragmentation of the US motor vehicle market has occurred as manufacturers produce a diversity of goods for consumer use. New assembly plants appear and supplier networks evolve. The IHS, given large-scale population redistribution, as well as labour problems and costs, has served this fragmented market and has essentially redefined the process of automobile assembly and distribution in the USA.

Linneker and Spence (1991) and Spence and Linneker (1994) have used market potential measures of accessibility to evaluate changes induced by the motorway network in Britain (Figure 2.9). By the 1990s the national strategic road network, which had been incrementally built over the previous 35 years, consisted of 3000 km of motorway and 12 500 km of trunk roads (Smith, 1992). Prior to the building of this network, London had the highest level of accessibility and peripheral areas of Scotland the lowest. Linneker and Spence were able to illustrate that all regions of Britain had experienced motorway-induced accessibility increases with greater increases in the first phase of construction (1971–76) than in the second (1976–89), with largest increases in the North West, Wales and the South West regions, and

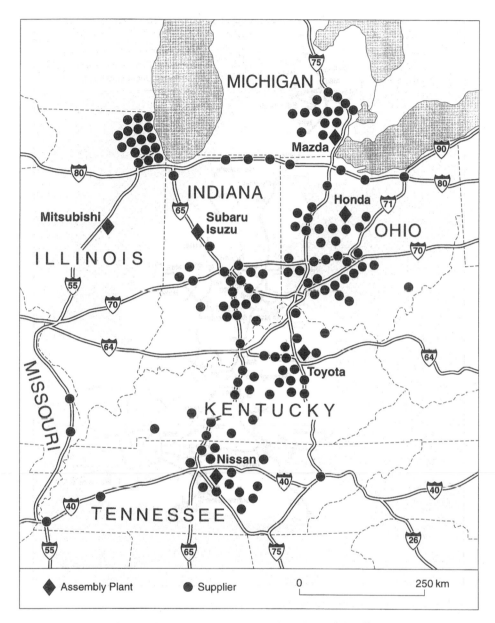

Figure 2.8   Japanese motor vehicle production in the I-65 and I-75 corridors of the USA
Sources: Moon (1994), after Rubenstein (1990)

more moderate increases in London and East Anglia. However, these changes were insufficient to offset the much greater changes in the national space economy brought about by population movement and large employment losses in the major conurbations. They conclude that motorways play a part in the evolving space economy but suggest that it is an enabling and facilitating one against a background of stronger, more structurally driven, economic forces for change (Spence and Linneker, 1994).

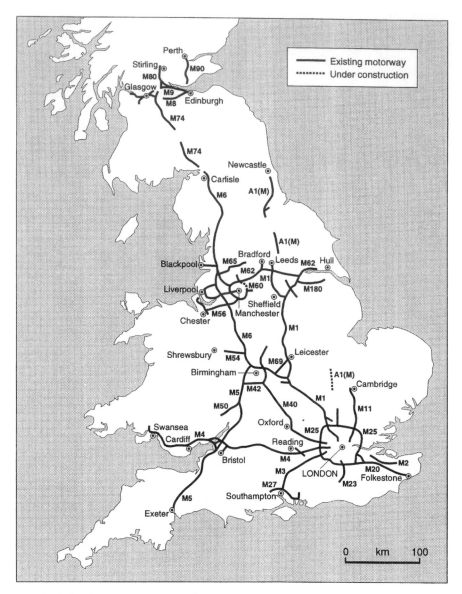

Figure 2.9   The United Kingdom motorway network

Although it is accepted that motorways influence accessibility, at present, the relationship with economic development is less clear (Damesick *et al.*, 1986). In addition, road building and the continued growth of road transport are beginning to create other concerns, especially in densely populated parts of Europe. There is a growing consensus that road capacity cannot be continually increased to match the forecast growth in demand. Congestion has reached unacceptable levels in many industrial societies and road construction can exacerbate the problem by generating new traffic flows. Above all, greater environmental awareness is creating a climate for policy changes towards further road building. Concerns over global warming are beginning to influence transport policies in the developed nations: for example, Britain has severely curtailed plans to expand and upgrade the motorway network during the 1990s. This trend could become more dominant in the twenty-first century.

CONCLUSIONS

This chapter has considered a range of ideas and examples chosen to illustrate the relationships between transport and development at scales ranging from sub-national to global. All such theories and case studies demonstrate the permissive nature of transport in the development process and the multi-faceted contexts in which transport systems operate in both advanced and developing societies. All confirm the importance of the historical dimension in understanding the spatial form of present-day networks and the processes that have created them. Above all, case studies reflect the evolutionary nature of the relationship between transport and development (Leinbach, 1995).

The dynamic nature of transport systems has played, and will continue to fulfil, an important role in the process of spatial change. Throughout the greater part of human history, transport has been a slow and laborious business. The nineteenth and twentieth centuries have been characterized by rapid technological advances, which have revolutionized the transfer of people, goods and information. Today, the technological transfer of information is virtually instantaneous, air transport has effectively reduced the world to a global village, and efficient multimodal networks have streamlined goods movement. Such changes both reflect and encourage socio-economic evolution, but must be assimilated and adapted in order to promote overall regional development. In most advanced societies, this has been best achieved by balancing the growth of strong external links with continuing intensification of internal networks.

Transport evolution in the less-developed countries has been in some ways more problematic. Most modern networks owe their origins to the European colonial period with its emphasis on external links rather than internal network development. Early models of the transport/development relationship accepted this external orientation as the norm, but more recent studies have questioned the validity of such views and called for a more "development-specific" approach to transport provision (Dimitriou, 1995). This has resulted in a more policy-orientated approach towards the further development of transport systems and towards development processes in the Third World. There are also signs that the relatively new links provided by telecommunications will offer some solutions to the limitations in the transport systems inherited from earlier phases of development.

A focus on the role of transport as a facilitator of social, economic and political change reveals and underpins two contrasting spatial patterns. Throughout the twentieth century transport modes have shown an increasing ability to overcome physical barriers and to reduce the friction of distance. As a consequence, the world is becoming a smaller place linked by intercontinental and global networks, a trend that will continue in the twenty-first century. On the other hand, global inequalities in development have never been greater. While advanced nations have developed relatively sophisticated transport systems, a majority of the world's peoples are underprovided with even rudimentary forms of transport. Although transport provision by itself can do little to reduce inequalities, appropriate transport strategies as part of multifaceted development programmes have a major role to play in overcoming the problems of regional and global polarization.

ACKNOWLEDGEMENTS

The authors of this chapter are indebted to Professor Brian Graham for information on airport hubs, to Dr Richard Knowles for material on deregulation and privatization, and to Professor Thomas Leinbach for details of the Interstate Highway System in the USA.

REFERENCES

Abane, A. (1993), "Modal choice for the journey to work among formal sector employees in Accra, Ghana", *Journal of Transport Geography* 1 (4), 219–24.

Adams, J. (1981), *Transport planning: vision and practice* (London: Routledge and Kegan Paul).

Adams, J.S. (1970), Residential structure of midwestern cities', *Annals of the Association of American Geographers* 60, 37–62.

Airey, A. (1985), "The role of feeder roads in promoting rural change in eastern Sierra Leone", *Tijdschrift voor Economische en Sociale Geografie* 76, 192–201.

Baerwald, T. (1984), "The geographic structure of modern North American metropolises", paper presented to the 25th International Geographical Congress, Paris.

Barke, M. and O'Hare, G. (1984), *The Third World* (Edinburgh: Oliver and Boyd).

Barwell, I., Edmonds, G., Howe, J. and De Veen, J. (1985), *Rural transport in developing countries* (London: Intermediate Technology Publications).

Baumol, W.J., Panzar, J.C. and Willig, R.W. (1982), *Contestable markets and the theory of industrial structure* (New York: Harcourt, Brace and Jovanovich).

Bird, J.H. (1963), *The major seaports of the United Kingdom* (London: Hutchinson).

Bird, J.H. (1980), "Seaports as a subset of gateways for regions", *Progress in Human Geography* 4, 360–70.

Bird, J.H. (1983), "Gateways: slow recognition but irreversible rise", *Tijdschrift voor Economische en Sociale Geografie* 74, 196–202.

Blaut, J.M. (1993), *The colonizer's model of the world: geographical diffusionism and Eurocentric history* (New York: Guilford).

Briggs, R. (1980), *The impact of the Interstate Highway System on nonmetropolitan growth* (Washington, DC: US Department of Transportation).

Brookfield, H.C. (1972), *Colonialism, development and independence: the case of the Melanesian Islands in the South Pacific* (Cambridge University Press).

Brookfield, H.C. (1975), *Interdependent development: perspectives on development* (London: Methuen).

Brunn, S.D. and Leinbach, T.R. (1991), *Collapsing space and time* (London: HarperCollins).

Clark, D. (1996), *Urban world/global city* (London: Routledge).

Commission of European Communities (1990), *Towards trans-European networks*, COM (90) 585 (Brussels: EEC).

Community of European Railways (1989), *Proposals for a European high-speed network* (Brussels: EEC).

Cromley, R.G. and Leinbach, T.R. (1981), "The pattern and process of the filter down process in nonmetropolitan Kentucky", *Economic Geography* 57, 208–24.

Damesick, P.J., Lichfield, N. and Simmons, M. (1986), "The M25 – a new geography of development?," *Geographical Journal* 152, 155–75.

Dimitriou, H.T. (1995), *A developmental approach to urban transport planning* (Aldershot: Avebury).

Duffy-Deno, K.T. and Eberts, R.W. (1991), "Public infrastructure and regional economic development", *Journal of Urban Economics* 30, 329–43.

Dundon-Smith, D.M. and Gibb, R.A. (1994), "The Channel Tunnel and regional economic development", *Journal of Transport Geography* 2, 178–89.

Filani, M.O. (1993), "Transport and rural development in Nigeria", *Journal of Transport Geography* 1 (4), 248–54.

Fisher, J. and Mitchelson, R. (1981), "Extended and internal commuting in the transformation of the intermetropolitan periphery", *Economic Geography* 57, 189–207.

Garreau, I. (1991), *Edge city: life on the new frontier* (New York: Doubleday).

Garrison, W.L. (1960), "Connectivity of the Interstate Highway System", *Papers, Regional Science Association* 6, 121–37.

Garrison, W.L. and Marble, D.F. (1974), "Graph theoretic concepts", in Eliot-Hurst, M.E. (ed.), *Transportation geography* (New York: McGraw-Hill), 58–80.

Gauthier, H. (1968), "Transportation and the growth of the Sao Paulo economy", *Journal of Regional Science*, 8, 77–94.

Gibb, R. (1991), "Imposing dependence: South Africa's manipulation of regional railways", *Transport Reviews* 11, 19–39.

Gibb, R., Lowndes, T. and Charlton, C. (1996), "The privatization of British Rail", *Applied Geography* 16 (1), 35–51.

Gleave, M.B. (ed.) (1992a), *Tropical African development* (Harlow: Longman).

Gleave, M.B. (1992b), "The Dar es Salaam transport corridor: an appraisal", *African Affairs* 91, 249–67.

Graham, B. (1995), *Geography and air transport* (Chichester: Wiley).

Green, D. (1987), *The New Right: the counter revolution in political, economic and social thought* (London: Wheatsheaf).

Griffiths, I.L. (1993), "The quest for independent access to the sea in southern Africa", *Geographical Journal* 155, 378–91.

Gutiérrez, J., González, R. and Gómez, G. (1996), "The European high-speed train network: predicted effects on accessibility patterns", *Journal of Transport Geography* 4, 227–38.

Haggett, P. and Chorley, R. (1969), *Network analysis in geography* (London: Arnold).

Hamilton, R. (1988), "Identification and ranking of environmental impacts associated with the US interstate highway system", *Transportation Research Record* 1166, 1–8.

Hartshorn, T.A. (1992), *Interpreting the city: an urban geography*, 2nd edn (Chichester: Wiley).

Hayuth, Y. (1985), "Containerization, inter-port competition and port selection", *Maritime Policy and Management* 12, 293–303.

Hayuth, Y. (1987), *Intermodality* (London: Lloyd's of London Press).

Hilling, D. (1969), "The evolution of the major ports of West Africa", *Geographical Journal* 135, 365–78.

Hilling, D. (1996), *Transport and developing countries* (London: Routledge).

Holtz-Eakin, D. and Schwartz, A. (1995), "Spatial productivity spillovers from public infrastructure: evidence from state highways", *International Tax and Public Finance* 2 (3), 459–68.

Hoyle, B.S. (1970), "Transport and economic growth in developing countries: the case of East Africa", in Osborne, R.H., Barnes, F.A. and Doornkamp, J.C. (eds.), *Geographical essays in honour of K.C. Edwards* (Nottingham: University of Nottingham), 187–96.

Hoyle, B.S. (ed.) (1973), *Transport and development* (London: Macmillan).

Hoyle, B.S. (1983), *Seaports and development: the experience of Kenya and Tanzania* (New York: Gordon and Breach).

Hoyle, B.S. (1988), *Transport and development in tropical Africa* (London: John Murray).

Hoyle, B.S. (1994), "The tyranny of distance: transport and the development process", in Courtenay, P.P. (ed.), *Geography and development* (Melbourne: Longman Cheshire), 117–43.

Hoyle, B.S. and Charlier, J.J. (1995), "Inter-port competition in developing countries: an East African case study", *Journal of Transport Geography* 3 (2), 87–103.

Hoyle, B.S. and Hilling, D. (1984) (eds), *Seaports systems and spatial change: technology, industry and development strategies* (Chichester, Wiley).

Hoyle, B.S. and Pinder, D.A. (1981) (eds), *Cityport industrialization and regional development* (Oxford: Pergamon).

Kansky, K.T. (1963), *Structure of transport networks: relationships between network geometry and regional characteristics* Research Paper 84, (Chicago: University of Chicago, Department of Geography).

Kennedy, D. (1995), "London bus tendering: an overview", *Transport Reviews* 15, 253–64.

Kessides, C. (1993), *The contribution of infrastructure to economic development: a review of experience and policy implications* (Washington, DC: World Bank).

Knowles, R.D. (1998), "Passenger rail privatization in Great Britain and its implications, especially for urban areas", *Journal of Transport Geography* 6 (1), 117–33.

Knox, P. (1987), *Urban social geography* (Harlow: Longman).

Leinbach, T.R. (1995), "Transportation and Third World development: review, issues and prescription", *Transportation Research* 29A (5), 337–44.

Leinbach, T.R., Chia, L.S., Kissling, C.C., Robinson, R. and Spencer, A.H. (1989), *South-east Asian transport: issues in development* (Singapore: Oxford University Press).

Linneker, B.J. and Spence, N. (1991), "Accessibility measures compared in an analysis of the impact of the M25 London Orbital Motorway on Britain", *Environment and Planning A*, 24, 1137–54.

Lowry, I. (1988), "Planning for urban sprawl", in *A look ahead: year 2020* (Washington, DC: Transport Research Board, National Research Council), 275–312.

Mabogunje, A.L. (1989), *The development process: a spatial perspective*, (London: Unwin Hyman).

McGee, T.G. (1971), *The urbanisation process in the Third World: explorations in search of a theory* (London: Bell).

Mitchelson, R. and Fisher, J. (1987), "Long-distance commuting and income change in the towns of upstate New York", *Economic Geography* 63, 48–65.

Moon, H. (1994), *The Interstate Highway System* (Washington, DC: Association of American Geographers).

Munnel, A. (1992), "Infrastructure investment and economic growth", *Journal of Economic Perspectives* 6 (4), 189–98.

Murayama, Y. (1994), "The impact of railways on accessibility in the Japanese urban system", *Journal of Transport Geography* 2 (2), 87–100.

Mwase, N.R.L. (1989), "Transport and rural development in Africa", *Transport Reviews* 9 (3), 217–34.

Mwase, N.R.L. (1996), "Developing an environmentally friendly transport system in Tanzania", *Transport Reviews* 16, 145–56.

Newman, P.W. and Kenworthy, J.R. (1989), *Cities and automobile dependence* (Aldershot: Gower).

Nijkamp, P. and Reichman, S. (1986), *Transportation planning in a changing world* (Aldershot: Gower).

O'Connor, A.M. (1965), "New railway construction and the pattern of economic development in Uganda", *Transactions of the Institute of British Geographers* 36, 21–30.

Owen, W. (1987), *Transportation and world development* (London: Hutchinson).

Pirie, G.H. (1982), "The de-civilizing rails: railways and underdevelopment in Southern Africa", *Tijdschrift voor Economische en Sociale Geografie* 73 (4), 221–8.

Plassard, F. (1991), "Le train à grande vitesse et le réseau des villes", *Transports* 345, 14–22.

Plassard, F. (1992), "L'impact territorial des transports à grande vitesse", in Derycke, P.-H. (ed.), *Espace et dynamiques territoriales* (Paris: Economica), 243–61.

Porter, G. (1995), "The impact of road construction on women's trade in rural Nigeria", *Journal of Transport Geography* 3 (1), 3–14.

Rimmer, P.J. (1977), "A conceptual framework for examining urban and regional transport needs in south-east Asia", *Pacific Viewpoint* 18, 133–47.

Rubenstein, J.M. (1990), "Japanese motor vehicle producers in the US: where and why", *Focus* 40, 7–11.

Rubenstein, J.M. (1992), "America's *just-in-time* highways: I-65 and I-75", in Janelle, D.G. (ed.), *Snapshots of America* (New York: Guilford), 432–35.

Salau, A.T. and Baba, J.M. (1984), "The spatial impact of the relocation of a section of the Zaria–Kano road: a study of change and development in rural Zaria", *Applied Geography* 4 (4), 283–92.

Siddall, W.R. (1969), "Railroad gauges and spatial interaction", *Geographical Review* 59 (1), 29–57.

Simon, D. (1996), *Transport and development in the Third World* (London: Routledge).

Smith, J.A. (1992), "Roads in the 1990s: expansion or restraint?", *Geography* 77 (1), 73–6.

Spence, N. and Linneker, B. (1994), "Evolution of the motorway network and changing levels of accessibility in Great Britain", *Journal of Transport Geography* 2, 247–64.

Spiekermann, K. and Wegener, M. (1994), "The shrinking continent: new time–space maps for Europe", *Environment and Planning* B, 21, 653–73.

Starkie, D. (1982), *The motorway age* (Oxford: Pergamon).

Taaffe, E.J., Morrill, R.L. and Gould, P.R. (1963), "Transport expansion in underdeveloped countries: a comparative analysis", *Geographical Review* 53, 503–29.

Taaffe, E.J., Gauthier, H.L. and O'Kelly, M. (1996), *Geography of transportation*, 2nd edn (Englewood Cliffs, NJ: Prentice Hall).

Thompson, I.B. (1994), "The French TGV system: progress and projects", *Geography* 79, 164–8.

Thompson, I.B. (1995), "High-speed transport hubs and Eurocity status: the case of Lyon", *Journal of Transport Geography* 3, 29–38.

Todaro, M.P. (1989), *Economic development in the Third World*, 4th edn (Harlow: Longman).

Tolley, R.D. (1990), *The greening of urban transport: planning for walking and cycling in western cities* (London: Belhaven).

Ullman, E.L. (1956), "The role of transportation and the bases for interaction", in Thomas, W.L. (ed.), *Man's role in changing the face of the Earth* (Chicago: University of Chicago Press).

Vance, J.E. (1970), *The merchant's world: the geography of wholesaling* (Englewood Cliffs, NJ: Prentice Hall).

Vance, J.E. (1986), *Capturing the horizon: the historical geography of transportation* (London: Harper and Row).

Varlet, J. (1992), *Interconnection of transportation networks in Europe*, Studies and Reports, 24, 92/1 (Paris: ITA).

Wilson, G.W. (1973), "Towards a theory of transport and development", in Hoyle, B.S. (ed.), *Transport and development* (London: Macmillan), 208–30.

3

THE ROLE OF TRANSPORT IN THE DEVELOPMENT PROCESS: CASE STUDIES FROM QUÉBEC, INDONESIA, ZIMBABWE AND CHINA

Brian Hoyle, Thomas Leinbach, José Smith and Andrew Spencer

On the basis of the discussion in Chapter 2 of some theoretical aspects of the relationships between transport and the development process, and the introduction of a wide range of examples, this chapter outlines in more detail the evidence from four contrasted case studies chosen from North America, Africa and Asia. By this method the chapter interprets, in a variety of contexts, the concept of transport as a permissive factor rather than as a direct stimulus to economic development or spatial change. A conclusion attempts to draw lessons from the individual case studies that may be of wider general relevance.

INTRODUCTION

This chapter examines the role of transport in the process of spatial change, in a variety of contexts, at various levels of development and in terms of a range of modes and intermodal systems. The essential focus is on transport as an economic enabler and as a social facility, at various levels within the development spectrum, in the more distant as well as the recent past, and with an eye to the present and to the foreseeable future. The interpretation rests on the idea, discussed in Chapter 2, that transport is normally a permissive factor in socio-economic terms rather than a direct stimulus to economic development or spatial change.

Four case studies – from Québec, Indonesia, Zimbabwe and China – allow varying interpretations of the balance between factors affecting the transport–development relationship. The broad sweep of Québec's history, in a North American context and in the context of Euro-American relations, illustrates the power of transport to mould and condition societies and economies as their political frameworks evolve. While China differs from Canada in almost every respect, the evolution of China's transport systems and services, and their relationships with economic development, nevertheless reflect Sino-European relations as well as China's characteristically introspective policies. Zimbabwe and Indonesia illustrate in other ways the impacts of colonialism as an initial provider of modern transport facilities, but equally demonstrate the problems faced by developing countries today where there is a widening gulf between transport demand and the resources available to meet that demand, and where increasing rather than reducing diversity in levels of

Modern Transport Geography: second, revised edition. Edited by Brian Hoyle and Richard Knowles.
© 1998 John Wiley & Sons Ltd.

transport provision acts as a brake on economic progress and national-scale integration.

Each case study reflects a complex web of relationships involving transport and a wide range of other physical and human factors, sometimes over specific periods of development and change, sometimes at particular points in time. At a detailed level, most of these relationships are specific to the areas or countries analysed and to particular development phases, but collectively they demonstrate some of the broad underpinnings of transport geography in a developmental context. While one purpose of presenting four contrasted examples is to demonstrate both the universality and the variety of the transport–development relationship, viewed globally, another is to encourage readers to investigate different but comparable case studies where similar or contrasted factors may have played an important role.

QUÉBEC: INTEGRATION, ISOLATION OR INDEPENDENCE?

The Canadian province of Québec provides a first case study and offers not only an illustration of relationships between transport and development in a variety of contexts, past and present, but also an exemplification of the general principles outlined in the models proposed by Vance (1970) and by Taaffe *et al.* (1963) (Chapter 2). Québec is Canada's largest province in area (1.7 million km²), but contains only about 6.5 million people, most of whom live in the St Lawrence lowlands, along the transport axis linking Montreal and Québec City (Yeates, 1975) (Figure 3.1). Transport is undoubtedly a fundamental factor that has affected the development and character of Québec's economy and society over time and continues to do so today (Allison and Bradshaw, 1990).

The Québec environment is not a particularly promising one for settlement and development, especially in climatic terms, in comparison with other North American areas into which European migrants moved over hundreds of years. Yet in this case the combination of the beaver, the offshore fisheries, the agricultural potential, the timber and above all the magnificent transport artery provided by the river made the St Lawrence lowlands a zone of attraction from an early date, and human use of this environment and in particular its arterial routeway has had significant politico-economic repercussions throughout much of North America (Lasserre, 1980).

Heartland and Hinterland: Québec as a Focus of In-Migration

Québec is the historic heartland of Canada, the location of the first substantial European settlements in North America, the historic context of the confrontation between Britain and France in this part of their colonial empires, and the geographical focus of French culture in present-day North America. In terms of the heartland and hinterland concept, Québec is historically the Canadian politico-economic core (Waddell, 1987). Modern Canada, however, has seen the migration of this core southwestwards towards the neighbouring province of Ontario and its capital Toronto, Canada's largest city, as well as to Ottawa, the federal capital. Today, although Québec remains a highly distinctive entity geographically, politically and socio-economically, this province has for some years appeared to be poised on the brink of secession from the Canadian federation. If Québec secedes, the geopolitical disintegration of the rest of modern Canada may follow.

In many ways, the geography of transport provides an essential key to an understanding of the Québec problem. From a historical perspective European intervention in North American affairs, based on transatlantic sea transport, took place in the context of earlier, overland migrations of so-called Indian peoples from another direction. Before the coming of the Europeans across the North Atlantic, much of Québec was inhabited by groups of "native" peoples. Following the retreat of the last Ice Age over 10 000 years ago, migrants from Asia had crossed via Alaska into Canada and gradually

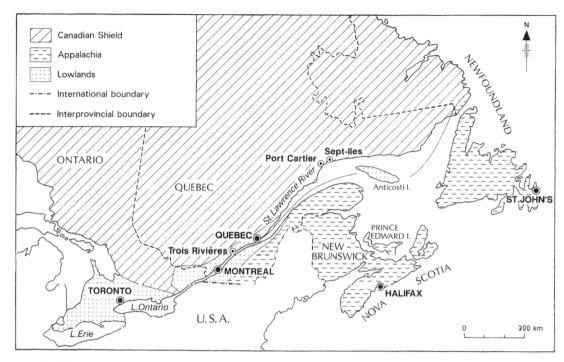

Figure 3.1 The St Lawrence artery

moved south and east, on foot or by canoe. For these Indians, the St Lawrence lowlands were an attractive but terminal zone in their long-continued migrations from the far northwest. For the Europeans coming westwards across the North Atlantic, in contrast, the St Lawrence artery provided ready-made access, a gateway into new North American territories ripe for exploitation.

New France

The beginnings of European settlement and economic exploitation in Québec, initially dependent upon sea transport, date back many centuries. European explorers came across the Atlantic in search of new resources and new ocean-transport routes to the Orient and its riches, and at first had no idea of the extent of the Americas or of the Pacific Ocean's existence. Thus, North America was labelled "Nova India" on some sixteenth-century maps, and its inhabitants termed "Indians". Quite early in this

process of exploration, the St Lawrence became known as a convenient navigational entry route into new lands of economic opportunity, and trading posts were set up along the river. Between 1570 and 1650 many French fur traders came to the shores of Québec, bartering with the Indians who brought furs down to the St Lawrence from the north and west, overland and by canoe. European traders were sometimes actively discouraged from penetrating inland, but at first there was no real need for them to do so.

New France, as areas coming under French influence in North America were known, centred on Québec City, founded in 1608 as a gateway in settlement and transport terms. The fur traders who set up their extensive supply and trading networks were known as *coureurs de bois* – literally, the runners of the woods – and moving around on foot, sometimes over considerable distances, was an important if elementary form of transport at the time. When New France was declared a crown colony in the 1660s this encouraged immigration and settlement, the development of transport facilities and the diversification of the economy. Explorers travelled west to the Rockies and south to Louisiana. At its greatest extent New France covered a vast area, at least in theory; but it was in practice no more than a trading empire, dependent upon slow, primitive forms of transport, especially rivers.

French pioneer settlers in seventeenth-century Québec lived off the land and off trade as far as possible; but they remained dependent on maritime transport for the expanding fur trade with Europe, for imported textiles and clothing, as well as for wines and brandy to help them survive the rigours of winter. The farm unit and the family were the keynotes of this peasant society, and river transport was the essential network tying the settler communities together. The later seventeenth and early eighteenth centuries were punctuated by Anglo-French wars in northeastern North America as settlements, transport routes and territories were fought over.

Eventually, Britain gained the upper hand: Québec City, the strategic gateway, was captured by the English in 1759 (an encounter in which the river played a crucial part); and all of New France was formally ceded to Britain in 1763. In spite of the advantages of the St Lawrence transport artery, therefore, the French endeavour in North America was relatively unsuccessful, partly because the English colonies along the eastern seaboard of the continent were far more accessible and more attractive to settlers. Ultimately, links between an emergent USA and the core zone of an emergent Canada in Ontario contributed to the marginalization of Québec as an anomaly in a predominantly anglophone continent.

British Rule

At first, the change from French to British rule did not fundamentally alter the Québec economic and transport systems, but as the nineteenth century progressed a society undergoing rapid transformation began to generate new forms of economic activity and new transport demands. The creation of an English Upper Canada (Ontario) and a French Lower Canada (Québec) in 1791 reflected Anglo-French rivalry and also reactions to the early politico-geographical evolution of the USA. The American Civil War (1861–5) convinced Canadians of their need to achieve political independence from Britain and to remain separate from the emerging USA; and, to these ends, produced a political climate favouring union between the various British colonies in Canada. The British North America Act of 1867 created the Canadian Confederation, signalling the end of the British colonial régime and the birth of modern Canada. These political changes at the Canadian national scale were in part a reflection of transport factors, notably the building of a trans-Canada railway, and within Québec as in other provinces they gave rise to new demands for urban and rural transport facilities and services.

Economic Expansion and Transport Development in an Independent Canada

The expansion of transport networks, especially railways, played a prominent part in the process of economic development in Canada. As the geopolitical and economic map of North America evolved, Québec's geographical location ensured an important role for the province in transport terms. The first great period of railway construction began in the 1850s, and by 1885 the Canadian Pacific Railway linked the Atlantic and Pacific coasts. The great port city of Montreal became a focal point within this system. By the 1870s industrialization, urbanization and the influx of French urban employees meant that Montreal had become eastern Canada's major economic and transportation centre, where entrepreneurs were investing heavily in industries, railways and banks.

The early twentieth century brought accelerated economic development in Québec, and Montreal became increasingly a nodal service centre for the development of the Canadian west – exporting wheat from the prairies through its growing port and sending its own industrial products along the railways to the pioneer fringe. During World War I the trans-continental Canadian Pacific Railway was repli-cated by the consolidation of other privately owned railways to form two further transcontinental lines, the Canadian Northern and the Grand Trunk Pa-cific, which were taken over by the Federal Gov-ernment during World War I to avoid closure and which together formed the Canadian National Railway in 1923. In Québec, new industries based on hydro-electric power exploitation began to appear – aluminium, chemicals – as well as a mod-ernized forestry and paper industry. This industrial progress, partly based on US investment, led to increased transport demands met by port develop-ment, road construction and rail-network improve-ments. While transport improvements helped to bind the emergent Canadian nation together in po-litical as well as economic terms, by the 1930s they also facilitated the beginnings of the migration of economic power southwestwards through the Ca-nadian heartland away from Montreal and towards Toronto.

Recent decades have seen a scientifically based modernization drive, as Québec has tried to keep its place in the forefront of twentieth-century North American development, although increasing econ-omic prosperity has been paralleled by increased dis-satisfaction with Québec's place within a federal Canada. Rapid post-World War II economic growth – in mining, manufacturing and service industries – involved rapid urbanization, improved transport and the further marginalization of the farming com-munity. Today, the Québec economy depends sub-stantially upon natural resource exploitation, including vast hydro-electric power resources, iron ore deposits, abundant timber and numerous other minerals including asbestos, copper, mica and lead. Growing industries include pulp and paper, chemi-cals, aircraft and food processing.

The Québec Port System

Ports and port cities have played, and continue to play, a particularly important part in the economic life of Québec. The development of the province, as in a sense the development of Canada as a whole, is rooted in maritime exploration and trade, and in the foundation of coastal settlements which provided an initial basis for movement into the interior. Today, several of Canada's major cities – including Montreal and Québec City – continue to function as seaports, although their urban economies are now greatly diversified.

The Province of Québec possesses a great variety of ports, paralleled by a complex management sys-tem involving federal, provincial and local govern-ment. Four of Canada's top 10 ports, measured by total cargo throughput, are located in Québec (Table 3.1). Two of these, Montreal and Québec City, are major multifunctional general cargo ports; the other two, Port Cartier and Sept-Iles, located on the north shore of the St Lawrence estuary, serve primarily as exporting ports for iron ores and other minerals extracted from the northern interior of Québec province. The province is also served by a variety of smaller ports such as Trois-Rivières that fulfil important local and regional functions. Table 3.1 lists all Canadian ports handling over 10 million tonnes in 1995 and shows that in this re-spect no individual Québec port approaches the leading Canadian port, Vancouver, which main-tains its traditional west coast dominance (For-ward, 1982) and has a largely different foreland. It is interesting to note, however, that Thunder Bay (Ontario), the interior terminal on Lake Superior of the route plied by ocean-going vessels using the St Lawrence Seaway, handles a total throughput approaching those of the four Québécois ports on the list. While the Seaway has accentuated a tend-ency for shipping to bypass Québec ports in favour of destinations further west, the need for tranship-ment (for example, in the grain trades), due to the Seaway's limited maximum ship size, has enhanced throughput levels at Montreal. In terms of inter-port competition, however, Québécois ports are disadvantaged in locational terms in comparison with US east coast ports such as Baltimore, Boston and New York.

Québec today is nevertheless an important com-ponent in the Canadian overseas trading economy,

Table 3.1 Leading Canadian ports by total throughput, 1990–95
In order of 1995 performance (million tonnes)

Port	1990	1991	1992	1993	1994	1995
1 Vancouver (BC)	64.5	68.4	61.3	58.9	64.6	69.5
2 Port Cartier (Qué)	20.6	22.9	21.3	19.3	21.7	24.9
3 Sept-Iles (Qué)	21.3	21.4	19.2	21.0	22.6	18.7
4 Saint John (NB)	14.4	17.2	15.6	19.3	20.9	18.7
5 Montreal (Qué)	21.1	16.2	16.6	15.8	19.6	18.6
6 Québec (Qué)	17.1	18.2	15.7	13.2	16.0	17.4
7 Halifax (NS)	16.8	14.2	13.8	14.2	14.4	13.2
8 Hamilton (Ont)	11.9	10.7	12.6	12.4	12.5	11.9
9 Port Hawkesbury (NS)	7.9	6.2	4.1	6.4	6.9	11.9
10 Thunder Bay (Ont)	13.9	16.9	12.7	11.3	13.7	11.5
11 Prince Rupert (BC)	12.5	13.0	12.6	11.3	13.5	11.4
All Canadian Ports	353.1	350.8	327.7	324.1	351.7	360.6

The table shows all ports handling more than 10 million tonnes in 1995, the year in which Port Hawkesbury entered the top 10 group for the first time.
Source: Statistics Canada, *Shipping in Canada* (Ottawa, annually).

exporting vast quantities of grains, ores and forest products to a wide range of destinations, as well as relying on international container trades for a wide variety of imported and exported goods. It follows that the efficiency of Québec's ports is a matter of critical provincial and national importance in developmental terms. Any port system is by definition dynamic, and the changing character of port activities, together with the broad sweep of late twentieth-century urban economic and social change, have radically altered the historic relationships between ports and cities, and between ports and hinterlands in recent decades. This has affected the character of individual Québec port cities, modified the provincial port system, and produced some striking examples of the now widespread phenomenon of waterfront revitalization. While continuing to serve as maritime terminals, older zones within port cities such as Québec and Montreal have acquired new functions and characteristics in their new role as tourist-historic cities. In this sense the sites of some of the earliest European settlements and transport foci in North America, doorsteps from which development spread far and wide, have themselves experienced further substantial changes as their functions are once more transformed.

INDONESIA: NEEDS, RESPONSES AND INTERMODAL BALANCE

A quite different but especially interesting case study of relationships between transport and development can be found in Indonesia (Figure 3.2). With an archipelago setting of huge geographical dimensions, a significant resource base, and a large population, the country has faced a major challenge in coping with transport demand, with the rapidly increasing need for enhanced transport capacity and with the need to provide transport facilities on an efficient and equitable basis (Leinbach and Chia, 1989). Nowhere is there a more conspicuous example of the real dilemma of satisfying regional and structural needs from limited resources. Yet Indonesia's emergence as one of the more dynamic economies in the South-East Asian region is testament to the fact that transport has responded to critical needs. This case study, which exemplifies some aspects of the Rimmer (1977) model (Chapter 2), discusses very briefly the historical background and then the economic bases associated with the development of transport in Indonesia. Most important are the critical needs involved in revitalizing an

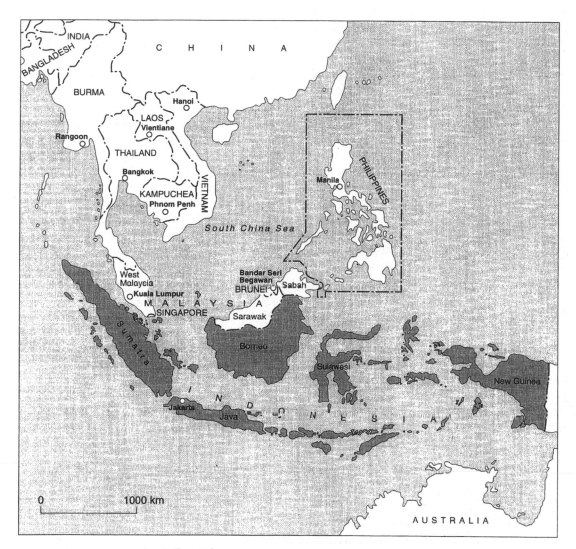

Figure 3.2   Indonesia in its South-East Asian context

archaic system, and the ways in which the government has responded. Changing priorities, problems and policies are addressed.

As with colonial intervention elsewhere in South-East Asia, water transport played a key role in early economic development for both intra- and inter-island movement. The significance of inter-island shipping has been emphasized in a recent study (Rutz and Coull, 1996). The development of land transport in Indonesia reflected the Dutch need to establish administrative control and simultaneously to encourage the growth of a spatially discrete agricultural economy. The first development attempts were carried out by the United East India Company, a Dutch trading firm, through a mastery of trade in spices, especially nutmeg, cloves and pepper. So-called "factories" or processing operations were established throughout Sumatra, Java, Sulawesi (then the Celebes) and the Moluccas during the seventeenth century (Van Goor, 1996). These isolated coastal operations had few internal transport connections. After the Dutch monopoly of shipping in the archipelago was broken by the Treaty of Paris in 1784, British and other vessels were free to trade in the area. Shortly after this, a new Dutch Governor-General emphasized a refashioning of the administrative system in order to exert better control and stimulate commerce. One aspect of this was the construction of interior roads. Another major development impact was the Dutch-introduced system of forced cultivation, known as the Culture System. Instead of paying taxes and rent in money, Javanese peasants were obliged to devote land and labour to the cultivation of export crops such as indigo, sugar and especially coffee. Earnings from these were not used in Java but rather transferred to the Dutch treasury and were used in part to finance construction of the Dutch railways. However, when these transfers ceased in 1878, more revenues from the East Indies were used for local development and especially for transport and irrigation.

Given the fragmented nature of the country, a decision was made at an early stage to concentrate the limited resources available for transport investment, both road and rail, in Java. While a railway was developed in Sumatra to support commercial agriculture, the fragmented lines there and the

absence of railways in the other Outer Islands (Sulawesi, Borneo, Moluccas) reflect a decision in the 1930s to concentrate on the development of a basic road system as the major form of land transport in these islands.

The earliest Dutch transport development effort focused upon Batavia with linkages to the other major administrative centres of Java, as well as the agriculturally productive areas of that island. Later, Sumatran agriculture was an important stimulus for road and railway building. The first major link in the Javanese system was the Great Post Road built by the Dutch between 1808 and 1811 in preparation for a possible British invasion. The road ran from the Sunda Strait to Jakarta (then Batavia) and along the north coast via the agricultural heart of central Java to east Java (Figure 3.3). This main link in the highway system provided essentially the route for the first state railway. Later, a shorter route via Cirebon, Semarang and the lower Solo Valley was used for both the main highway and railway lines. Coupled with this early growth, the gradual development of ports, first on Java and later elsewhere in the archipelago, also provided an important stimulus for the further development of the road network. Gradually, as the administrative and commercial impress of the Dutch diffused outwards, a maritime

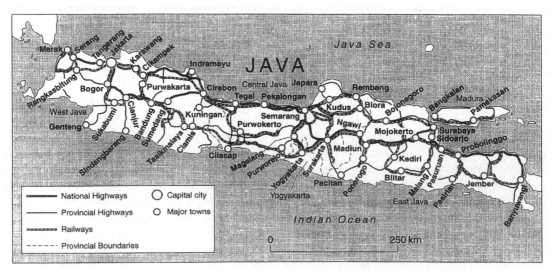

Figure 3.3   Highways, railways and ports in Java

emphasis became evident and is conspicuous today in patterns of interaction.

The early spatial focus of Dutch efforts produced a strong centre–periphery contrast in the pattern of development in Indonesia. Over 60 per cent of the current population of over 200 million is concentrated in Java and Bali where well-developed market economies exist. Concentrations also exist in select areas of Sumatra, Sulawesi, Kalimantan and other Outer Islands. Rubber, oil palm and other commercial crops dominate the lightly settled areas of portions of the Outer Islands. Agriculture and timber were the major revenue sources prior to the 1970s when oil became a key resource. Oil prices and the world market for this commodity have been closely tied to development investment. Transport expansion and upgrading benefited greatly from the strong oil revenues of the 1970s and 1980s.

However, recognizing the drawbacks of reliance on a single source of revenue, the government has now moved towards a policy of economic diversification in a range of bulk commodities and has expanded the production of plantation crops, such as oil palm, and emphasized the development of new basic industries such as fertilizer and cement. The allocation to transport in Five Year Development Plan budgets through the mid-1980s was dominated by an emphasis on roads. During the 1970s roughly 93 per cent of all goods and 99 per cent of all passengers were accounted for by the road system, but from 1979 to 1984 the modal allocation recognized the need for improvements in civil aviation and sea transport. This continuing trend reflects the improved quality and maturation of the road network as well as the need to extend assistance to other critical modes, given the fragmented nature of the spatial economy and population base.

Transport investment in Indonesia has increasingly been utilized since the mid-1970s as a policy instrument in development. Beginning with a series of highway rehabilitation projects funded by the United Nations Development Programme (UNDP) and the World Bank, progress in the diffusion of reliable access in the Outer Islands has been steady. Such higher-order linkages are forged to strengthen basic connectivity in the highway system but at the same time often serve as major developmental or penetration linkages, which are intended to stimulate growth in areas where poor transport has been a binding constraint on regional development. The notion of "bottlenecks" and "constraint points" in the transport system throughout Indonesia remains an important factor in policy decisions on new investment.

The Trans-Sumatra Highway is a prime example of such a linkage. The concept of a spinal highway developed in the 1970s from the notion that it would be a catalytic force and stimulate development along its length. The highway, which stretches from Banda Aceh in the northwest to Tanjungkarang opposite Java, is actually a synthesis of road segments built at various times, mostly during the Dutch period, and is now (mostly) a two-laned surfaced road (Figure 3.4). Funds for the project were initially provided by the World Bank as part of rehabilitation efforts in Sumatra. Later the objective was to close gaps in the highway mainly in support of nearby transmigration and plantation areas. While the catalytic impact on development has been somewhat overstated, there is little doubt that the development of a continuous through-road has integrated the major cities of Sumatra and lowered transport costs while improving trade within the island and the major market areas of Java. Plans for similar trans-insular highways exist for Sulawesi and Kalimantan but have not been fully implemented.

There is widespread agreement that a rationalization and more efficient use of the existing road network is possible and, moreover, desirable in lieu of new construction. Despite this acknowledgement, however, there are numerous instances throughout the archipelago where rapid growth and capacity constraints have created bottlenecks to economic development. One strategy in these situations has been to construct toll roads. These are viewed as a tax on the relatively affluent segment of the population and have been utilized in both inter-urban and intra-urban situations. In Java, the Jagorawi Highway linking Jakarta with Bogor was the earliest such facility (Photograph 3.1). With an emphasis on

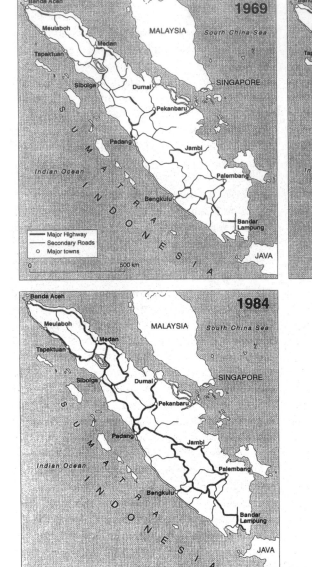

Figure 3.4   The development of the Trans-Sumatran Highway

liberalization, the concept of the toll road operated by private enterprise has grown considerably and currently many such projects are planned for Java. The toll road system is partially financed through the sale of bonds on the local market and operations and maintenance are financed through revenues (Table 3.2).

Rural Development

In the context of the development objectives for the Outer Islands, in particular eastern Indonesia, rural road improvements and the enhancement of port facilities have become high priorities. In the early

Photograph 3.1   The Jagorawi Highway, Indonesia, between Bogor and Jakarta (T. Leinbach)

1980s it was estimated that 30 per cent of Indonesian villages outside Java did not have vehicle access to main highways. A concentrated effort to improve rural roads came relatively late as a result of the critical need to rehabilitate basic highways especially after the Japanese occupation. However, this need has been a part of formal development plans since the mid-1980s as the country's rural development strategy has gained momentum.

Funds to implement and finance road improvements at the district level come from central government and foreign sources. The programme known as *Inpres Jalan* has been used internally to allocate funds provided by international assistance agencies to especially needy districts. In this connection the government also developed a programme called *Padat Karya Gaya Baru* that aims to provide supplemental cash incomes for unemployed labour through the construction of roads through labour-intensive methods (Photograph 3.2). Popular

through the early 1980s, the programme resulted in the growth of cash crops, improved marketing, attraction of regular transport services, expanded personal mobility and the more frequent use of social services such as family planning. Although employment was temporary, it provided a critical income injection for many poor families. At the same time negative impacts under this programme included the destruction of existing modes of production, which in turn created unemployment. Moreover, too often the new or upgraded access provides the most benefit to outsiders, not local residents. Another critical factor in the ongoing success of these small road projects has been the need to establish responsibility for maintenance.

Transport Sector Issues

The objectives of the transport sector are clearly tied to strategic development issues such as the

Table 3.2 Indonesia: toll road construction plans, early 1990s

Road Section	Length (km)	Investment (m rupiah)
1 Cawang–Tanjung Priok	17.6	371 000
2 Cibitung–Cikampek	47.5	78 000
3 Tangerang–Merak (1st stage) Tangerang–Ciujung (2nd stage)	34.2	260000
Ciujung–Merak	43.2	441 220
4 Surabaya–Gresik	20.0	183 000
5 Jakarta Outer Ring	39.8	1 252 843
6 Cikampek–Padalarang	59.0	834 352
7 Jakarta–Serpong	11.9	94 128
8 Medan–Binjai	21.9	138 655
9 Ujung Pandang	3.1	19 534
10 Jakarta Harbour Road	12.0	585 000
11 Cikampek–Cirebon	133.0	1 271
12 Semarang Arteri	8.0	97 465
13 Semarang Bawen	22.0	65 930
14 Surabaya–Mojokerto	38.0	400 000
15 Semarang–Batang	29.0	120 000
16 Gempol–Malang	55.0	87 600
17 Gempol–Pasuruan	27.0	81 000
18 Yogyakarta–Surakarta	60.0	123 700
19 Bogor–Bandung	120.0	703 253
20 Cirebon–Tegal	69.0	
21 Tegal–Batang	69.0	

Source: Ministry of Public Works.

promotion of non-oil exports, increasing food production, and supporting transmigration, industrial centres and tourism. In an effort to achieve these objectives, within the constraints of limited budgets, a number of issues have emerged (Leinbach, 1986, 1989). These include: the adequacy of public-sector investment and appropriate modal balance; inadequate transport sector management and intermodal coordination; government subsidies within the transport system; deregulation of the transport industry; the lack of road maintenance; utilization of rail capacity; and improved efficiency in the maritime and ports sector.

Debate and discussion on these issues are ongoing and no clear policy directions or strategies have emerged. Table 3.3 shows the general emphasis on roads and, in recent five-year plans, increased emphasis on railways, ports and airports, sometimes (as in Repelita IV) at the expense of roads allocations. Among the many issues under debate, several deserve special emphasis. These are the future of the railway in Indonesia, the restructuring and improved efficiency of ports, and the status and implications of government subsidies within the transport system, including the pioneer transport services programme.

The Indonesian Railway Dilemma

The Indonesian State Railway system provides a total track length of 6800 km, 30 per cent of which comprises three separate lines in North, South and West Sumatra (Figure 3.5) while the remaining 70 per cent serves Java (Figure 3.3). Despite an effort to carry out a railway rehabilitation and modernization programme, inadequate maintenance and the lack of re-investment in equipment have plagued operations and discouraged traffic. The railways have gradually deteriorated. Although the share of passenger and freight traffic improved between the mid-1970s and the mid-1990s, the system's financial performance declined. Revenues increased, but expenditure more than doubled and the deficit expanded four-fold. One explanation for this is the existence of cross-subsidies. Several essential commodities, but especially petroleum products, the largest single traffic item, were carried at rates much below the average tariff. Remedial measures have now been effected so that tariffs have increased. Yet the basic problem of inadequate demand persists.

The long-term role of the railway in the Indonesian transport system must lie in its effective bidding

Photograph 3.2   Indonesia: a labour-intensive road project under the PKGB programme (T. Leinbach)

Table 3.3   Indonesia: allocations for transport, 1969–94
(percentages)

	Repelita I 1969–74	Repelita II 1974–79	Repelita III 1979–84	Repelita IV 1984–89	Repelita V 1989–94
Transport percentage of development budget	17	16	14	12	18
Intermodal distribution of allocation					
Roads	75	78	67	46	63
Railways, road transport	6	7	8	18	12
Ports and shipping	10	10	13	22	11
Airports and aircraft	9	5	12	14	14
	100	100	100	100	100

Sources: For 1969–89, Indonesia, Directorate of City and Regional Planning; for 1989–94, *The Five-Year Plan IV (1984–89) and V (1989–94)*.

for the haulage of bulk commodities especially in Java but also in Sumatra. The government must also improve and restructure its tariff schedules for the railway so that it may operate more flexibly in order to compete with road transport. The long-standing problem of competition between these modes, especially over short distances in Java, is still relevant in Indonesia as elsewhere. At the same time

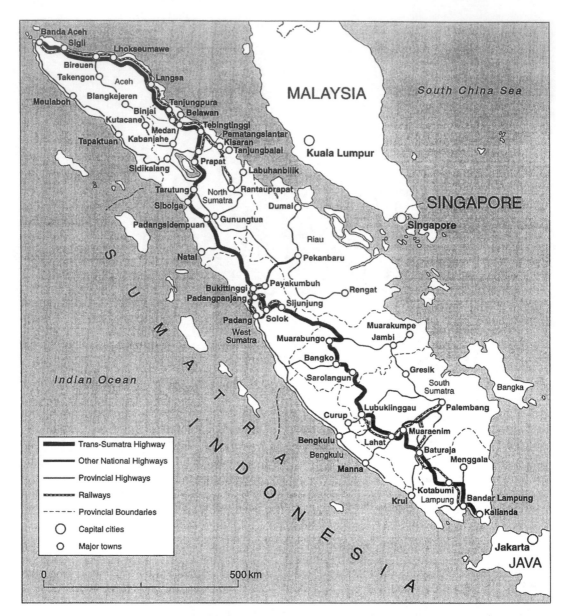

Figure 3.5 Toll roads, railways and ports in Sumatra

long-run variable costs must be covered and non-bulk services must be upgraded to entice users. Freight consolidation between major nodes in Java could result in additional substantial traffic. Impact analyses suggest that the railway could be an economical carrier of intermediate and long-haul passenger services. Given a Java-centred industrialization policy, traffic forecasts reveal healthy growth in freight and passenger traffic of 4 per cent and 7 per cent respectively. Major keys to future improvements might lie in the closure, as elsewhere in the world, of short inefficient branch lines and new strategies that seek additional traffic generation and operational efficiency.

The Indonesian Port System and Inter-Island Shipping

It is essential that a fragmented, island-based country such as Indonesia has an efficient port system especially now that a strong export policy is being pursued. While early efforts to improve ports largely failed, in the mid-1980s a recommendation for a trunk–feeder system was made. This system is intended to allow the transfer of cargo more efficiently from high-order to low-order ports. Operationally this has resulted in a "gateway" scheme whereby four ports (Tanjung Priok in Jakarta, Tanjung Perak in Surabaya, Ujung Pandang in Sulawesi, and Belawan serving Medan) were selected to serve as major export outlets for the country. These major ports are served by a series of collector (second-order), trunk (third-order) and feeder ports. This reorganization, while comprehensive and logical, required massive investment and heightened the demands on management. The results of this reordering strategy have been far from satisfactory. Port modernization, however, has proceeded in Tanjung Priok, Tanjung Perak and Belawan (Airriess, 1991).

The impact of port deficiencies is greater upon deep-sea shipping, however, than upon inter-island shipping. Being much smaller, inter-island ships are more easily able to obtain berths and make fewer demands upon mechanical cargo handling. Moreover, since they do not carry import cargo they are not impacted by warehouse congestion constraints. The impact of port quality is also clearly associated with firm efficiency and proper management skills. More efficient firms have used a variety of initiatives to circumvent the perceived deficiencies of smaller ports. For example, scheduling berth usage and using manpower around the clock are two techniques that have proved useful. In the smaller ports of the Outer Islands as well as in the larger ports of Java, *lokal* (local/feeder) and *prahu* (indigenous craft) operations are not constrained by the state of physical facilities. Despite the lack of modern infrastructure these ports function at a high level of productivity because there is much less bureaucracy and customs procedures are much more informal. Although cargo is manhandled, rates are high, damage low and pilferage much lower than elsewhere.

At the same time a strong environment of control developed, and a variety of restrictive regulatory measures were imposed. These measures reserved Indonesian cargo for Indonesian vessels, controlled the entry of foreign flag ships, and allowed transhipment container cargoes to and from Singapore to be reserved exclusively for Indonesian and Singaporean vessels. More important were customs regulations and long delays in ports which tended to constrain export expansion. This protected and strongly regulated system was shaken by a Presidential decree, INPRES No. 4 1985, intended to smooth the flow of goods, which essentially provided for streamlining and greater efficiency in customs and port procedures. A major improvement occurred as export goods were exempted from customs inspection and a Swiss firm was appointed to inspect cargoes. However, in contrast to this positive development, shippers were allowed access to foreign flag vessels, which in turn exposed inter-island shipping to international competition. Displacement of capacity, even in areas such as eastern Indonesia, resulted and the effect was to create financial uncertainty for Indonesian shipowners already plagued by overcapacity and depressed rates. Partial deregulation has essentially forced a survival attitude in the shipping industry. Despite some loosening of control the continuation of regulation reinforced the high cost of inter-island shipping, which in turn presents an obstacle to a growing domestic market. Premature replacement of ships and overinvestment in port facilities because of a "technology preoccupation" rather than a management focus were other negative side-effects. Such continued constraints on shipping will ultimately force more cargo towards a trucking industry unhampered by regulation (Dick, 1987). A completely deregulated inter-island shipping industry must be an important stimulus for regional development. This economic reform is now in the process of implementation.

Despite the tremendous growth of air transport, it is clear that inter-island freight and passenger shipping will continue to be critically important to development. Revenue evidence from low-income passengers (many higher-income users have switched to air) and the continuing influence of government policy in transmigration (voluntary resettlement of poor families to the Outer Islands) and regional development, especially the emphasis on eastern Indonesia, supports this statement. The current pattern of routes and frequency of services reflects a high intensity of connections from Aceh to Timor and especially from Java to the ports of Kalimantan and Sulawesi. Clearly the greatest demand for inter-island passenger connection is on the routes between Java and the nearby regional metropolises but, in fact, ships also serve the provincial capitals of eastern Indonesia as well as Jayapura, the capital of Irian Jaya (Rutz and Coull, 1996). Since 1985 regional centres in the more remote provinces have gradually become linked to the inter-island shipping network by the use of smaller vessels, which are accommodated in the shallower channels of these ports. Despite these improvements there continues to be unsatisfied demand for passenger shipping, for there are parts of the archipelago for which connections with Java are too slow and in other areas service is non-existent or too infrequent. When the required upgrading will be achieved will depend upon government priorities for investment, traffic demand and profitability as well as the future impact of deregulation (Rutz and Coull, 1996).

Transport Subsidies

With the objectives of income redistribution and national stability the Indonesian government has subsidized elements of the transport system (Leinbach, 1989). The subsidies have included those to transport fuels, controls on transport charges for select commodities, financing of the operating deficits of State-owned transport enterprises, and the less-than-full recovery of the costs of infrastructure provision from users. An example is the airport system, which in the recent past has operated in deficit and required a 42 per cent subsidy to cost including depreciation. Similarly numerous major and minor ports, and the railway system, as noted above, do not operate profitably and must be subsidized. The issue of fuel subsidies has been an important part of the overall controversy. Pertamina, the national oil company, has been provided with both "cost" (where production costs are in excess of revenues) and "economic" (the difference between fixed local market prices and prices at which the product could be sold in the global market) subsidies. While the fuel subsidy has been decreased by increasing the price of fuel, in the mid-1990s Indonesians paid considerably less for fuel than their South-East Asian neighbours. An interesting, but complex, question is the impact that these subsidies have had on the location and growth of economic activity in the Indonesian space economy.

Pioneer Services

As a final illustration of the dilemmas of providing access in a fragmented area, Indonesia's pioneer transport programmes are of interest. These services also link to our previous discussion of subsidies. Pioneer services, which exist for both sea and air transport, are essentially attempts to provide low-cost and efficient services to remote and inaccessible areas of the archipelago. These networks are intended to serve those areas where there is no other form of access, where commercial capacity is insufficient, or where low volumes of traffic have produced very high tariffs. The services operate through a complex system of subsidies, which are paid to semi-commercial (generally State-owned) companies to operate routes through schedules specified by the government. Subsidies take the form of capital costs for aircraft/vessels as well as operating costs. Both the air and sea programmes focus on eastern Indonesia and other remote parts of the nation. Clearly the purpose of these services is not only to offer basic transport for critical needs but also to stimulate regional development. The evidence of impact, as analysed to date, is quite mixed. The effects of sea pioneer services seem to indicate that the impact on regional development is positive but marginal. For example, constraints on development in the Nusa Tenggara area of eastern Indonesia are not primarily of a transport nature but rather are associated with deficiencies in human and production capital (Leinbach, 1995).

ZIMBABWE: TRANSPORT EVOLUTION UNDER SOCIALISM

Over the past 100 years the relationship between transport and development in Zimbabwe (Figure 3.6) has reflected the experience of many African countries. On achieving independence in 1980 Zimbabwe inherited a transport system adapted to the needs and aspirations of the colonial powers and which typified the colonial stages of the spatial models proposed by Taaffe *et al.* (1963) and Rimmer (1977) (see Chapter 2). Post-independence policies have sought to maintain this network and its external linkages, which are vital to the nation's economy (Griffiths, 1990; Smith, 1988).

However, development policies under the socialist government have given higher priority to the needs of the African population (Drakakis-Smith, 1987). The development plans of the 1980s placed great emphasis on State involvement in both rural and urban transport. The improvement of mobility and accessibility in rural areas has been a key feature in national development planning. In urban areas the focus has been on providing mass transport for the rapidly growing numbers of urban dwellers who do not have access to private transport. Although State involvement has continued throughout the 1990s, policies are being adjusted to take account of the World Bank's Structural Adjustment Programmes with their emphasis on economic liberation.

The Colonial Transport Network

The emergence of Zimbabwe's modern transport system dates back to the 1890s when Cecil Rhodes' British South Africa Company extended the South African railway network through Bechuanaland (now Botswana) to Bulawayo in 1897 and crossed the Zambezi at Victoria Falls in 1902. A second major penetration route was established from the east, linking the Mozambique port of Beira with Umtali (now Mutare) in 1898 and Salisbury (now Harare) in 1899. The two routes were connected in 1902 along the ridge of the high veld by the Bulawayo to Salisbury line (Kay, 1970). These early railway routes exerted considerable influence over subsequent network development and settlement patterns. The policy of settling Africans into reserves and selling land rights to European immigrants began in the 1890s and the patterns of land ownership were well established by the time of the 1930 Land Apportionment Act. European settlement, attracted by minerals or agricultural potential in climatically favourable areas, dominated the high veld and eastern highlands and the emerging urban hierarchy. Africans were confined either to reserves in the less-productive middle and low veld areas, or to townships on the periphery of European towns.

Such contrasts became more marked once road building began in Rhodesia during the 1930s. Main roads paralleled the railways linking major centres of European commercial development and were maintained in good condition, especially during the years of the Central African Federation (1953–63) and, for security reasons, during the period of Southern Rhodesia's illegal Unilateral Declaration of Independence (1965–80). Moreover, throughout the European commercial farming areas, rural councils invested local taxes in a substantial feeder road network. In contrast, lack of resources severely limited expenditure on the road network in the Tribal Trust Lands, which were heavily dependent on subsistence agriculture. The liberation struggle that preceded independence in 1980 prohibited even limited maintenance and many African rural areas were left without a basic transport infrastructure. Africans in the urban areas were similarly affected since they were confined mainly to the high-density housing developments served by a network of narrow, ill-kept lanes (Kay, 1970). Road building was strongly

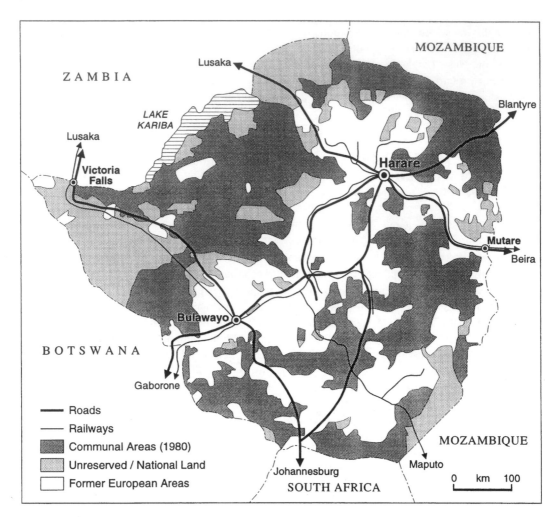

Figure 3.6   Zimbabwe: transport network

influenced by security issues and public transport, in the form of stage bus services, was controlled by European operators and existed mainly to link the townships with centres of employment.

Rural Transport and Agricultural Development

During the 1980s Zimbabwe focused much of its national development effort on the reconstruction of the Communal Areas (the former Tribal Trust Lands) (Figure 3.6). In 1980 57 per cent of the country's population lived in these areas, which were characterized by dependence on agriculture, land degradation and outward migration. Most were located in ecologically marginal zones and drought was a major problem. Upgrading the rural road network was regarded as a major prerequisite for improving the social and economic conditions in such areas. Between 1984 and 1992 the government invested in a Rural Roads Programme designed to facilitate the marketing of surplus agricultural produce, to offer equitable access for all households to basic facilities and service centres, and to provide all-weather roads suitable for bus transport. In total 16 600 km of primary rural roads were provided, of which 82 per cent were improved existing roads and the remainder totally new.

Since the Communal Areas lack nucleated settlements, household access to primary roads was a key element in the design of the feeder road network. "Scotch carts" pulled by animals (Figure 3.7) are the traditional form of transport in the Communal Areas and the network was designed so that ideally each household was within 10 km of a primary road (this distance represents a day's return journey using a scotch cart). Primary roads had all-weather surfaces suitable for bus transport and linked with rural service centres and the national road network. They were supplemented by a secondary road system (not all-weather) which aimed to reduce the homestead-to-road distance to 5 km. In hilly terrain, where scotch carts are impracticable and loads are carried by human porterage, only primary roads were provided but these aimed to limit the homestead-to-road distance to 3 km.

The provision of primary roads has encouraged the expansion of the long-distance rural bus network. Since Communal Areas are characterized by a lack of urban development, most services link these areas with major urban centres located in the former European commercial areas, especially Harare and Bulawayo. By 1985 nearly 200 firms operated throughout Zimbabwe: each tended to serve a specific locality, all were privately owned and most were family concerns. However, post-independence expansion has not been without its problems. The industry is highly dependent on imported equipment

and has faced rapidly rising costs and shortages of spare parts consequent upon the growth of Zimbabwe's foreign debt during the 1980s; fare increases have been limited by the government and have not kept pace with costs. Moreover, the network exhibited marked inequalities: marginal areas had low levels of service provision while some major routes, for example those linking Communal Areas of the northeast with Harare, offered up to 10 services a day.

Freight transport has faced similar problems. The railway-owned Road Motor Services (RMS), which was established during the colonial period, was the only operator offering a nationwide scheduled and contract freight service. However, although it operated in some Communal Areas, its scheduled routes were confined mainly to the main road network which runs predominantly through the large-scale commercial farming areas (Turton, 1991). Consequently, communal farmers depended on small-scale hauliers for freight transport. Like the bus industry, freight operators have faced escalating costs, limited foreign exchange and a shortage of spare parts. In 1992 the initiation of the World Bank's Economic Structural Adjustment Programme eased the financial situation and allowed the import of some spare parts for essential repair and maintenance. However, the investment was insufficient and farmers faced acute vehicle shortages during the harvesting season and with the transport of perishable crops. In response to these problems, a number of initiatives have been developed aimed at improving vehicle availability (Dawson and Barwell, 1993). Recognizing that many small-scale farmers are unable to purchase vehicles, State marketing boards collect crops from the Communal Areas. The District Development Fund, the organization responsible for the road-building programme, own trucks which they hire out to communities for the transport of their harvest to the nearest crop marketing point. The latter have also been increased in number: for example, grain buying points were expanded from five in 1980 to over 40 in 1990. This expansion has made markets more immediately accessible to the communal farmers.

Figure 3.7   A Scotch cart

Policy-makers have also realized that motorized transport is inappropriate for some rural activities and the importance of the traditional form of transport, the scotch cart (Figure 3.7), has also been emphasized. Such carts are manufactured on both large and small scales throughout Zimbabwe. In wealthier crop-producing regions, their supply is plentiful and purchase by farmers has been assisted through loans provided by the Agricultural Finance Corporation. In the poorer south, where demand is more sporadic, most carts are produced by local artisans. Technical assistance to these small manufacturers has been provided in the form of wheel-making equipment. Again farmers have been provided with loan facilities to purchase these simple but efficient vehicles (Dawson and Barwell, 1993). Such is the lack of transport in the Communal Areas that many farmers are able to recoup their capital outlay by hiring their cart to neighbours.

The rural roads programme, and improved vehicle availability, have together had a considerable impact on the expansion of agricultural output from the Communal Areas. Combined with schemes to promote smallholder cultivation, such as guaranteed prices, agricultural extension and credit, outputs of both staple and export crops have been increased (Rukuni and Eicher, 1994). In the State marketing sector, the most dramatic increases have occurred in the production of maize, Zimbabwe's staple food crop. Whereas communal farmers accounted for only 7.5 per cent of maize deliveries to the State-run Grain Marketing Board in 1980, their contribution had increased to 63 per cent by 1989 and has remained at this level throughout the 1990s. Cotton has also been developed as a cash crop for both home consumption and export: deliveries to the Cotton Marketing Board by communal farmers increased three-fold during the 1980s. Whilst it may be argued that transport developments alone cannot account for the expansion of maize and cotton, there is strong evidence to suggest that, as one of a range of measures, transport has had a positive effect in improving agriculture within the State sector.

Developments in the transport system have also enabled many communal farmers to participate in the private marketing sector and the urban economy, a point well illustrated by the results from a survey undertaken in the late 1980s (Smith, 1989). Horticultural crops are widely grown for home consumption on small plots of irrigated land throughout the Communal Areas. Although marketing opportunities are limited within the Communal Areas it is estimated that 65 per cent of farmers in northern Zimbabwe sell horticultural crops, mainly in Harare (Figure 3.8). Since less than 5 per cent of farmers have their own transport, most used non-motorized transport, especially Scotch carts, to reach the main road network (Table 3.4). Long-distance bus services were the most important mode for farmers transporting themselves and their produce to the city markets (Table 3.5). Substantial distances were a feature of the journey patterns: only 24 per cent travelled less than 50 km while 22 per cent of all journeys were over 100 km. Journeys were both time-consuming and costly: 66 per cent of growers surveyed stated that journey costs represented at least 20 per cent of the sales and most growers experienced trips in which they did not recoup their transport costs. However, such trips provided many families with an important source of regular income. In addition, most farmers used the opportunity whilst in Harare to undertake other activities such as purchasing household goods and agricultural inputs, thus benefiting from their links with the urban areas.

Table 3.4   Farm to main road journeys in Zimbabwe

Distance (km)	Percentage of Growers	Mode	Percentage of Growers
1.0 or less	32	Porterage	13
1.1–3.0	33	Wheelbarrow	10
3.1–5.0	14	Scotch cart	58
5.1–10.0	7	Private car	2
10.1 and over	2	Lorry	16
Not given	12	Other	1
Total (N = 182)	100		100

Source: Smith (1989).

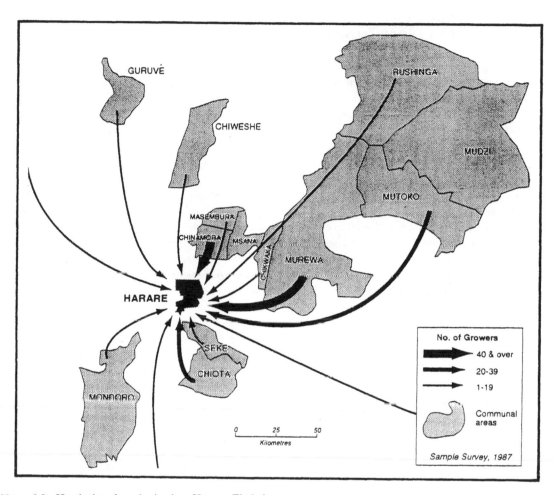

Figure 3.8   Horticultural marketing into Harare, Zimbabwe

Table 3.5   Journeys into Harare

Distance (km)	Percentage of Growers	Transport Mode	Percentage of Growers
1–25	3	Grower and produce by bus	70
26–50	21	Grower by bus/produce by lorry	6
51–75	24	Grower by bus and lorry/produce by lorry	5
76–100	30	Grower and produce by lorry	16
101–125	10	Grower and produce by private car	3
126–150	6		
151 and over	6	Total (N = 182)	100
Total (N = 182)	100		

Source: Smith (1989).

Urban Transport: the Development of Mass Transit

Transport policies for the urban areas of Zimbabwe have had less impact on the structure of networks and more on the public transport participants. The capital, Harare, typifies the urban structure of Zimbabwe's towns with its extensive urban area and apartheid social system which has remained until the present day. Greater Harare covers approximately 600 km^2 and in 1980 had a population of one million of whom 250 000 lived in Chitungwiza, its dormitory township. With an annual growth rate of 8.1 per cent, it is predicted that Greater Harare will have a population of two million by the year 2000. The city's transport problems stem from its urban structure. The central business district (CBD) is the main place of work and attracts over 50 per cent of commuter traffic, inducing long journeys to work between the high-density housing areas (the former townships) which account for over 60 per cent of the population. In 1980 conventional public transport accounted for 80 per cent of all travel requirements, walking 10 per cent and the remaining journeys were made by private car (Lefevre, 1991). Conventional public transport was provided mainly by a municipal bus company, which operated a monopoly service connecting residential and employment zones. Bus services were supplemented by both regular and illegal taxi services, which accounted for an increasing proportion of journeys to work.

In 1980 central government removed the power of local authorities and became the sole regulator of public transport. In 1981 the State refused to subsidize public transport operators and, as an emergency measure in 1982, legalized the informal sector operators. Unfortunately, the combination of these policies created considerable problems for both public transport operators and passengers. Although bus patronage increased in the early years of independence, fixed revenues and escalating costs resulted in decapitalization with a consequent deterioration of the bus fleet and quality of service. In parallel, the legalization without constraint of informal sector taxis allowed substantial growth and by 1989 taxis accounted for an estimated 38 per cent of journeys.

Whilst in theory these measures were intended to provide low-priced transport for the urban poor who often had long journeys to work, in reality they created an unreliable service with high accident rates.

Since 1988 the government has opted for a policy of partial deregulation coupled with direct State participation in the stage bus service in which it has become a majority shareholder. The subsequent improvement in the stage bus service, together with the introduction of commuter minibuses operating on a hail-and-ride basis, has led to an overall improvement in the bus service (Maunder *et al.*, 1994). Fleet expansion of 8.7 per cent per annum after 1988 has resulted in additional carrying capacity, which is now above the rate of population growth. Between 1988 and 1992, average passenger waiting times were reduced from 36 minutes to 22.8 minutes and new routes have been opened into low-income areas previously not served with public transport. As a result of these policies, overall bus patronage has increased, minibuses provide much-needed peak time capacity on busy routes and there has been a decline in the use of unregistered transport. Moreover, levels of passenger satisfaction have improved despite the fare increases which, since 1991, have been allowed to rise in line with costs.

CHINA: INDEPENDENCE WITH AUTARKY?

China stands out from the other case study regions discussed in this chapter in at least two respects. Firstly, it was never actually colonized although at certain crucial periods external powers could easily dictate terms to it. Secondly, its size, natural resources and history of technological and organizational achievement have given it a potential for autarkic development unmatched by any other non-European civilization except India. The history of China's transport and national development since the early nineteenth century reflects the interplay of these opposing factors.

Although China had for centuries had a complex economy, it displayed strongly autarkic tendencies.

While its porcelain, silk and tea were highly prized luxury items in the West, the domestic economy was so large that foreign trade mattered little to it; there seemed "no use for ingenious articles, nor . . . your country's manufactures", as the emperor Qianlong famously expressed it to a British trade mission in 1793. There were also fears of espionage and piracy. Even domestic trade was limited; grain, metals and salt were among the chief commodities moved to supply the major cities in the east of the country. The transport system was patchy. Apart from the major rivers such as the Yangtze or Chang Jiang and a dense network of canals in the south and east (the Grand Canal, stretching 1782 km from Hangzhou to Beijing, was the most important), carriers had to rely on narrow and poorly surfaced roads, built more for couriers and pack animals than for wheeled vehicles. In the 1870s it was estimated that moving freight by road was between 20 and 40 times more expensive than by water, while water was commonly faster as well: salt shipments covered up to 28 km per day by junk compared with 15 km by oxcart and 25 km by pack mule (Chiang, 1983). Coastal shipping was caught up in the general discouragement of seaborne trade.

Infrastructural problems were compounded by official policies. Salt was a government monopoly and its movement was closely controlled, while duties (*likin*) were levied on other internal freight movements. One 500 km route from a salt distribution centre was interrupted by no fewer than 10 checkpoints (Chiang, 1983) and a 320 km road journey from Shanghai passed through seven *likin* collecting points, which together could extract some 35 per cent of a good's price (Liang, 1982, 137). Controls on foreign trade were numerous and, to Western eyes, irksome, although the long and indented coastline afforded many opportunities for evasion to the more resourceful and less scrupulous traders (Chiu, 1973).

Transport difficulties had not prevented the Chinese from assembling both the resources and the finance to set up embryonic industrial economies producing such commodities as iron, timber and textiles. They relied for markets on a dense local population and on water transport where it was available. Their failure to develop into mechanized industrial regions on the European or North American pattern has been attributed to exhaustion of the local raw materials and the overabundance of cheap labour, which formed a disincentive to mechanization. "In these conditions, the sprouts of capitalism received little nourishment and inevitably made no growth" (Leeming, 1993, 53).

The Imperialist Period

For a government disposed to autarky the encounter with European and US mercantile traders was a culture clash of the first order. Matters came to a head with the Opium War (1839–42) which ended with China being forced to cede Hong Kong Island (and later the Kowloon peninsula) to Britain, to permit trade through five ports (Guangzhou, Xiamen, Fuzhou, Ningbo and Shanghai) and to allow foreigners to live there and carry on their businesses immune from Chinese law. Subsequent wars and treaties with various countries raised the number of treaty ports to 107; most were coastal, 10 more lined the Yangtze and several were on inland routes crossing from Indo-China, Burma or Russia (Williams, 1920). Although only a few were successful, notably Shanghai, China's economy became increasingly oriented around these port cities.

Mercantile penetration called for railways leading inland and here, again, the foreign powers had the ascendancy. Although Chinese capital funded the first successful line in 1881, this was purely a mineral railway serving coal-mines near Tianjin. Extensions to turn it into a genuine trunk line, linking Beijing with Mukden (now Shenyang), were beyond the promoters' resources and it came under the control of British financial interests. In 1896 the Russians secured a concession for a line across Manchuria to serve, first, their own port at Vladivostok and then a second – and ice-free – one at Port Arthur (now Lüshun), which they had seized in 1898. Both this latter line and its port came under Japanese control in 1905. Germany occupied the port of Qingdao in 1898 and began a line along the Shandong peninsula to exploit coal-mines near Jinan. The French began to extend a line northwards from their possessions in

Indo-China. Various foreign interests supported a line from Beijing to Hankou, while the British opened one from Hong Kong to Guangzhou. By now China's central government was in decline and Figure 3.9 graphically illustrates how the foreign powers were attempting to carve out spheres of influence. It was popular opposition to this heavy foreign investment – in what were seen as the arteries of China's future prosperity – which helped to trigger the downfall of the imperial government in November 1911 (Spence, 1990).

The Inter-War Years

Although official thinking in the new Republic followed the ideas of its architect, Dr Sun Yat-Sen, in urging the development of ports and new railway lines (Edmonds, 1987), lack of capital and political instability between 1911 and 1938 meant that expansion was painfully slow. Three major trunk lines were completed but only in Manchuria did a relatively dense network emerge. The major factor here was Japan's continued drive for political domination and industrial exploitation (Chou, 1971).

Despite the lack of progress the impact of the new railways on agriculture, at least, was appreciable. By lowering the costs of moving both inputs and produce, they helped to raise yields: a 1 per cent fall in transport costs raising outputs of grain crops by around 0.3 per cent. Wheat yields could be 17.1 per cent higher, and rice yields 7.8 per cent higher, in rail-served counties compared with counties in the same area without rail connections (Liang, 1982, 69 and 85). Access to large urban markets helped to assure farmers of higher and more stable prices. This in turn led to greater commercialization with increased cultivation of cash crops, growing agricultural surpluses and greater capital formation. Data collected between 1927 and 1934 show that in areas close to the Beijing–Hankou railway 85 per cent of the cotton grown, and 42–55 per cent of wheat, was marketed compared with 37 per cent and 26 per cent elsewhere (*ibid.*, 115). The opening of the Beijing–Shenyang line in 1907 led to a 100-fold increase in fruit prices and an expansion in the acreage planted, often at the expense of grain crops (*ibid.*, 99–102). Land values were higher in rail-served counties, agricultural credits were more widely taken up and research stations were generally located at railway centres from which agricultural innovations diffused, mainly along the railways themselves (*ibid.*, 93 and 115–8).

There were also adverse impacts. Growing commercialization enabled farmers to buy manufactured goods from factories in the cities in preference to locally produced products. In addition, the limited penetration of the rail network and the failure to improve road transport meant that the impacts of commercialization were spatially rather limited. Areas away from the railways could lose out in competition, though Liang (1982) saw this as a consequence of too little, rather than too much, investment in transport. Administrative inefficiencies also set limits on what was achievable. The fragmented network, set up by numerous companies funded from widely varying sources, made through-traffic from one line to another difficult, and while the *likin* had officially been abolished in 1931 it stubbornly persisted in the inter-war climate of corruption and warlordism. For Liang it was this factor, above all else, which limited the railways' ability to promote economic development (*ibid.*, 139). In the matter of industrialization, polarization was even more marked; a study in 1947 revealed that of the 20 most important cities 54 per cent of industrial employment was in Shanghai while the next most industrialized city, Tianjin, had only 8 per cent. In 1952 over 70 per cent of China's industrial employment was concentrated in the coastal provinces (Lippit, 1966).

Liberation and Reconstruction

China emerged from World War II and the Communist takeover of 1949 with its transport system in ruins. Reconstruction had largely been achieved by 1951 (Ginsberg, 1951), since when its development has been bound up with the shifting directions of economic and planning policies. It is common to identify three main phases.

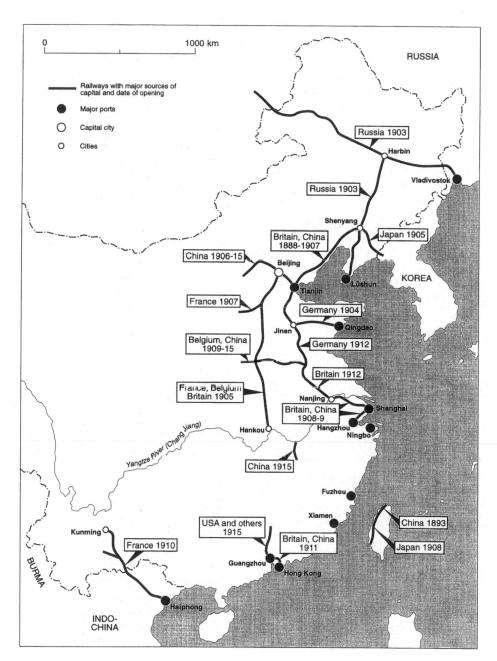

Figure 3.9 China: major ports and railways up to 1915
Sources: Chou (1971) and Darby (1945)

The first Five Year Plan: 1953–57

With the "classic" stimulus to development, overseas trade, almost extinguished, China was, once again, thrown back on autarkic development. Strongly influenced by Soviet ideas on planning, the emphasis was on resource-based industrial complexes in the interior such as the iron- and steelworks at Baotou, linked to areas of demand by rail (Lippit, 1966). In accordance with these aims the bulk of rail expansion was westward and southwestward. Port development, in contrast, virtually stagnated (Chiu and Chu, 1984).

The eclipse of central planning: 1958–78

By the late 1950s Soviet influence was on the decline and Mao Zedong's anti-centralist theories were generally dominant. The national autarky characterized by the first Plan was now increasingly echoed at provincial and local levels also. Paradoxically the effect of this was to hamper attempts to redistribute investment, which continued to flow predominantly to the east of the country (Table 3.6). Only between 1966 and 1970, the early Cultural Revolution years, was there any major shift in the trend as Mao's "Third Front" policy attempted to relocate industrial plants and research institutes to interior provinces so as to be out of reach of attack by foreign powers. In general, the result of all these policies was a proliferation of small and inefficient plants with more than 1200 iron- and steelworks spread across the country by 1979 (Leeming, 1985). During this period some major rail lines were completed but the emphasis

Table 3.6 China: percentage of capital construction investment by region

Region	1953–1957	1966–1970	1976–1980	1991–1992
East	36.9	26.9	42.1	49.5
Central	28.7	29.9	30.2	24.5
West	19.0	34.8	19.9	16.8
Unspecified	15.4	8.4	7.8	9.2

Data in this table exclude Hong Kong and Taiwan.
Source: Computed from Zhao (1996, Appendix 3).

shifted to local roads and other intra-provincial links (Lippit, 1966).

The "Open Door" policy: 1979–96

Although China's *détente* with the West from 1972 onwards was accompanied by a certain readiness to trade with overseas countries, the great reorientation had to await Deng Xiaoping's accession to power in 1976. The new policy might be characterized as a drive for economic growth centred on a modernization perspective on development. National autarky was effectively cast aside. As set out by Yang (1990) the policy comprised three major elements.

1. *Moves to attract foreign investment, technology and skills* by such means as tax privileges. To this end four Special Economic Zones were designated in 1979 in Zhuhai, Shenzhen, Shantou and Xiamen; these were followed by a series of other development areas, almost all of them on the coast.
2. *An embracing of the principle of comparative advantage,* under the assumption that regional specialization would increase productive efficiency. In the eastern region (Figure 3.10) it was intended that the new-found foreign investment would transform the industrial structure, displacing traditional heavy industries inland to the central region where their heavy demands on energy sources and raw materials could more easily be met. The western region, remoter still, would rely on its agricultural, forest and mineral resources.
3. *A belief that the interior regions would ultimately benefit from "trickle-down" effects.* Although some government support for these regions would remain it was hoped that they would benefit principally from partnerships with enterprises in the east. In practice many of these arrangements have involved the supply of raw materials and energy sources to feed the growing coastal industries.

Representative of these new policies has been the solution adopted to the coast's energy shortages.

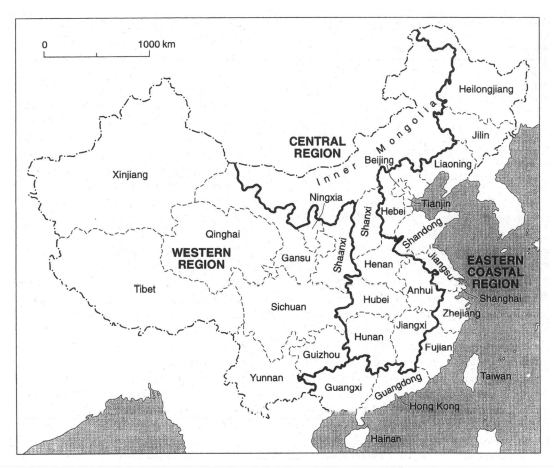

Figure 3.10 China: economic regions (administrative boundaries as at December 1996)

Economic growth in the eastern region and the lower Yangtze, particularly in Shanghai, Jiangsu and Guangdong, has increased their demand for energy; the central and western regions, in contrast, have an energy surplus (Table 3.7). Shanxi province, in particular, has some of the largest coal reserves to be found anywhere in the world and already supplies a quarter of China's annual requirements. The new policies in effect see its coal as a resource to be traded and increasingly heavy flows to the deficit regions have resulted (Figure 3.11). With the existing rail network already heavily taxed by growing freight traffic, China's planners have adopted a water-borne solution. New rail construction has concentrated on west–east links from Shanxi to the

coast: principally a double-track electrified line from Datong to the port of Qinhuangdao which, long neglected, has now been massively upgraded to admit ships of up to 50 000 dwt (deadweight tonnes). This has offered cost savings of up to 20 per cent over direct rail haulage to Shanghai although the capacity of the port installations has proved critical to the economics of the operation. A rail link has subsequently been created from southern Shanxi to a port at Rizhao in southern Shandong; improvements here have enabled this port to admit ships double the size of those using Qinhuangdao (Todd, 1996).

China's investment in its transport system since 1949 has been impressive. In the early Communist years

Table 3.7 China: regional energy self-supply balances, 1990
(million tonnes of coal equivalent)

Region	Production	Consumption	Balance
East	265.62	406.00	−140.38
Central	549.45	334.59	214.86
West	196.42	181.28	15.14
All China	1011.49	921.87	89.62

Data in this table exclude Hong Kong and Taiwan.
Source: Computed from Todd (1996, table 1).

there were 70 000 km of navigable waterways; currently there are 110 000 km of which 5800 km can accommodate vessels of over 1000 tonnes (Wei, 1987; *China Daily*, 1997a). Its 1942 rail network of 19 370 km reached 54 616 km in 1995 with over 800 km added during 1993–95 alone. The completion of the Beijing–Hong Kong and Nanning–Kunming lines, along with several others, has since added over 3500 km more and it is planned to have 70 000 km in operation by the end of the century. The network density of 5.71 km of line per thousand square kilometres of land area, though well below India's 19.06 km, compares well with 3.13 km in Brazil and 5.12 km in the Russian Federation, two other countries similarly faced with opening up a large and undeveloped interior; in fact, eliminating the largely rail-less regions of Qinghai, Tibet and Xinjiang raises the density to a respectable 8.65 km. It is interesting to compare these figures with what Sun Yat-Sen envisioned, back in 1922, as a "basic" system of 160 000 km, which would have given a density approaching India's (Lippitt, 1966; *Railway Gazette International*, 1996, 1998; Qian, 1997). What the early visionaries could not have foreseen has been a 15-fold increase in the highway network from 80 000 km in 1949 to nearly 1.2 million km by 1996, reaching virtually all of China's townships and over four-fifths of its villages (Li, 1990; *China Daily*, 1997a). More tellingly, since its inception in 1989 an expressway system of 375 km had grown to 3422 km by the end of 1996 and a further doubling by the end of the century is planned. And whereas in 1947 China had 26 airports listed in the ABC Air Guide with a total

of 304 domestic departures weekly, by 1996 the Official Air Guide listed 108 airports and 8985 weekly domestic departures (in both cases with Hong Kong and Macau, but not Taiwan, included as domestic).

The renewed emphasis on trade has meant an overhaul of the long-neglected seaports. Apart from the bulk handling facilities just mentioned there has been major expansion of container ports, notably at Dalian, Tianjin, Qingdao and Shanghai. All the same, Hong Kong remains China's biggest port. Its 1994 throughput of over 11 million TEUs (twenty-foot equivalent units) contrasts with a *total* throughput for the other mainland ports of 3.8 million (Lambert, 1997). More than 15 mainland ports have feeder container services connecting with liner services operating out of Hong Kong. Its harbour, infrastructure, facilities and services are incomparable and, despite some shortcomings, its overland links to the interior are superior to those from most other ports (Lin, 1995). Although China's leaders expressed reservations about continued port investment at Hong Kong, particularly in the run-up to its reversion to Chinese sovereignty, the completion in 1996 of a new railway linking it to Beijing powerfully symbolizes the exorcizing of the imperialist legacy as well as alleviating some bottlenecks.

China has experienced an alternation of autarkic and externally oriented modes of development, not always as a product of its own choosing. It is common, though not entirely accurate, to characterize the autarkic periods as times of stagnation but relative equality, the externally oriented ones as exhibiting strong but polarized growth. The imperialist period saw development focused on a system of treaty ports and inward-penetrating railway lines imposed on China by the foreign powers. China's experience in this context was comparable with, but different from, those of other world regions such as Africa or Latin America. Latterly the Special Economic Zones and open cities, admittedly under Chinese sovereignty but still predominantly coastal, have become the new foci for growth. As Table 3.6 shows, for most of the post-war period the largest share of government investment has gone to the eastern region; this dominance continues and 84 per

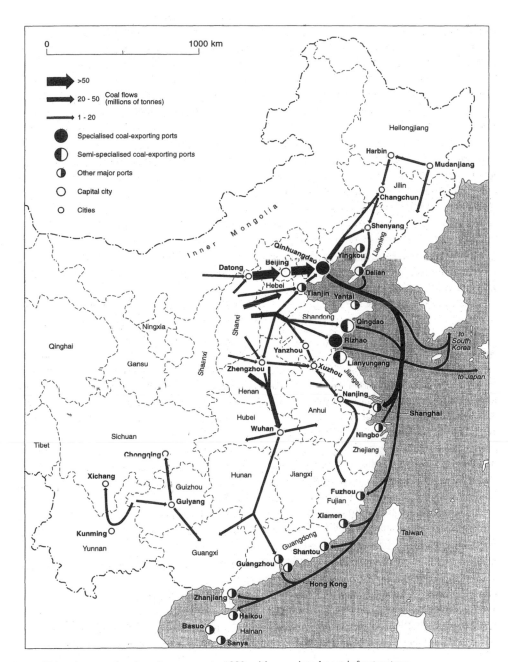

Figure 3.11 China: inter-regional coal movements, 1990, with associated port infrastructure
Source: Todd (1996)

cent of foreign investment between 1989 and 1992 was also directed here (Zhao, 1996). Up to 1985, 92 per cent of foreign joint ventures were located in coastal provinces and few had diffused inland (Leung, 1990). Provinces' per capita incomes can be shown to be positively correlated with the level of their foreign trade and economic linkages between coastal enterprises and those in inland provinces remain sparse (Fan, 1992). Reflecting these trends, the transport system is heavily biased towards the eastern part of the country. In 1996 the eastern coastal region accounted for 71 per cent of China's weekly domestic air departures despite having just 46 per cent of its airports. Major rail construction has continued in the east despite important expansions in the centre and west. And China's policy for expressways explicitly recognizes that the demand for road transport will be highest where there is an externally oriented, commodity-based economy: in short, the more developed regions (Li, 1990).

CONCLUSIONS

This chapter has considered specific case studies chosen to illustrate the relationships between transport and development at various scales. Each demonstrates the significance of the physical environment, the effects of changing political and economic circumstances, and the role of policy evolution. Essentially, the material presented here re-emphasizes the permissive nature of transport in the development process and the multifaceted contexts in which transport systems operate in both advanced and developing societies. The cases discussed all confirm the importance of the historical dimension in understanding the spatial form and economic functioning of present-day networks and the processes that have created them. Above all, the case studies reflect some of the complex ways in which the changing relationships between transport and development reflect the wider structures of economies and societies.

The four contrasted countries discussed in this chapter – Canada, China, Indonesia and Zimbabwe

– are likely to experience substantial changes in the twenty-first century both in terms of internal economic restructuring and political change and in terms of their relative positions in the world development spectrum. China is likely to assume an increasingly dominant place on the world stage in demographic and political terms, and perhaps in economic terms too. Indonesia and Zimbabwe are both likely to consolidate and enhance their status as progressive, newly industrializing countries with strong agricultural traditions. A major question mark stands against the Canadian confederation, which would be unlikely to survive the secession of one or more of its component provinces.

Whether Québec remains part of a federal Canada or follows a more independent pathway, the transport systems derived from the past and now serving the modern economy will continue to evolve in the service of one of the modern world's most diverse cultural regions (Trent *et al.*, 1996). Québec Province, like Canada as a whole, has progressed from a colonial to an industrial/post-industrial economy and transport has played a significant part in this evolutionary process. Yet the magnificent St Lawrence transport artery has not been magnificent enough to ensure continued centrality within the Canadian space economy. Ultimately, Québec plays a marginal role in modern Canada: the harsh environment, transport logistics, economic history, political realities and language policies all contribute towards a significant degree of marginalization – different from British Columbia, and not so marked as in the Atlantic Provinces – but nevertheless a factor underpinning pressures for secession. Disadvantaged by geography and history, Québec's place in twenty-first-century North America seems uncertain, and the geography of transport, at least in part, underpins and explains that uncertainty (Lamonde, 1996). In a continental context, the overall effects of the 1992 North American Free Trade Agreement on Canadian transport (Slack, 1993) may enhance the province's commitment to a distinctive future.

Indonesia provides a good example of a transport system that suffers from a lack of regionally balanced and modally coordinated planning, a failure to come to grips with maintenance throughout the system, imperfect regulatory policies and practices, and inadequate services by certain modes. Highly centralized planning is also problematic where too often decisions made in Jakarta are not informed by local circumstances and evidence. On the positive side the most recent five-year plan, Repelita VI (1994–99), maintains that the road-building programme will be the first to be devolved entirely to the regions, thus loosening the hitherto strong financial centralization. Another bright spot is the progress of deregulation of domestic sea transport which is beginning to provide the types and qualities of services needed by shippers at lower costs. Especially interesting is the regional development impact of this process of deregulation. In order for the railway to exist profitably without subsidization, full-cost recovery for medium- and long-distance passenger services as well as renewed efforts to capture freight traffic must be implemented. Perhaps the major policy issue that is currently being addressed is the policy conflict provided by national goals for a more equitable distribution of growth and simultaneously the creation of a more efficient transport system.

The provision of transport facilities, as a response to demand or in an attempt to facilitate socio-economic change, is invariably uneven, in both more-advanced and less-developed countries. Inequalities in transport provision, in geographical and structural terms, are however a marked feature of developing countries, as illustrated by Zimbabwe where post-independence policies under a socialist government have gone some way towards ameliorating the mobility and accessibility problems of the African population. Development plans during the 1980s placed great emphasis on the rural areas and improving conditions for 800 000 smallholders and their families in the Communal Areas. The provision of feeder roads and the development of rural bus and freight services facilitated the development of agricultural marketing in areas formerly dominated by subsistence agriculture. Maintaining this momentum has been more difficult in the 1990s as road maintenance and vehicle fleets have suffered from escalating costs and shortage of foreign exchange.

Similar problems have beset the urban areas with their dependence on public transport. Whilst vehicle ownership levels have risen since independence, they are still less than 50 per 1000 population and, for the foreseeable future, urban populations will depend on public transport, especially for the journey to work. A policy of deregulation combined with an increase in State ownership has improved public transport, especially in Harare. However, greater State involvement is unlikely, given the introduction of the World Bank's Structural Adjustment Programme with its emphasis on privatization and economic liberation.

In common with most other countries, whether advanced or less-developed, China's planners have acknowledged what they regard as the shortcomings of past transport policy. Apart from the general failure to expand capacity, they feel that they have emphasized railways unduly at the expense of other modes (Liu *et al.*, 1987). In similar vein the World Bank (1985, 83–5) has urged greater investment in roads in order to benefit local agriculture, passenger travel and the movement of high-value freight. Some foreign investors have attempted to distribute their products by road rather than rail, arguing that rail's lower costs are outweighed by delays and the risk of damage in transit (Anon., 1996). It will be hard for the government to resist further pressures for road building and environmental objections are unlikely to carry much weight. The ninth Five Year Plan (1996–2000) is ambiguous, presenting road expansion as a "priority" yet continuing to regard railway building as the principal means to expand transport capacity (*China Daily*, 1997b). Meanwhile autarkic tendencies remain, particularly at provincial and local level, where leaders are understandably seeking to attract development to their own areas (Auty, 1992). Ports are being expanded, locally funded road and rail links to them are being built, and provincial authorities have set up airlines and invested heavily in airports. Any perceived central government bias in development priorities is bound to arouse sensitivities in places which feel that they are losing out, and there is some evidence that under the 1996–2000 Plan attempts will be made to halt the widening disparity between the coast and the interior, for instance through increased road building in central and western China. How successful this will be remains to be seen.

Some interesting comparisons and contrasts emerge between the various examples discussed in this chapter. The impact of foreign technology on the development of port and rail systems in China has been outlined, and in developing countries such as Indonesia and Zimbabwe most modern transport networks owe their origins to the European colonial period with its emphasis on external links rather than internal network development. In all such cases, adaptation to modern postcolonial needs has been in many ways problematic. Models of the transport/development relationship (discussed in Chapter 2) based upon colonial experience were inclined to accept an external orientation as a normal feature of the global transport system, but postcolonial studies have understandably called for a more "developmental-specific" approach to transport provision, questioning the validity of earlier views and arguing for closer attention to the demand–provision–assessment relationships (outlined in Chapter 1) in the context of today's development priorities and needs. Indonesia and Zimbabwe are among many former colonial territories which show that postcolonialism has produced a more pragmatic, policy-orientated and development-centred approach towards the further development of transport systems.

The communications revolution induced by advances in tellecommunications is also beginning to affect Third World transport systems and this will not only accelerate the process of shrinking the globe in transport terms but will also provide some alternative solutions to the limitations of the transport systems inherited from earlier phases of development. In this context, the accelerating speed of change in transport technology is a critical factor. It is important to remember that transport has normally been a slow and laborious business throughout the greater part of human history, and for many people (especially in the less-developed countries) it remains so today. The nineteenth and twentieth centuries, however, have been characterized by rapid technological advances which have revolutionized the transfer of people, goods and information throughout the world, although the spatial effects of these advances have been far from uniform and many places and socio-economic groups still remain relatively untouched by these advances. Thus the dynamic nature of transport systems has played, and will continue to fulfil, an important role in the process of spatial change and in the differentiation of societies, economies and people. The technological transfer of information is today virtually instantaneous, air transport has effectively reduced the world to a global village, and efficient multimodal networks have streamlined goods movement. As the case studies developed in this chapter have shown, changes in transport demand and provision both reflect and encourage socio-economic and political evolution, but such changes must be carefully assessed in the context of the promotion of overall regional development. This has usually been best achieved in advanced societies by balancing the growth of strong external links with continuing intensification of internal networks. Developing countries are attempting, with varying degrees of success, to achieve a similar balance between internal networks and external linkages in order to enhance wherever possible the growing competitiveness of their economies.

The theoretical and empirical material presented in Chapters 2 and 3 has illustrated an interesting dichotomy in terms of global spatial relationships and in terms of modern transport geography, by focusing on the role of transport as a facilitator of social, economic and political change. The world development surface is forever very uneven, and it is apparent that as the rich get richer and the poor remain poor, global inequalities in development have never been greater. Advanced countries have developed sophisticated, technologically advanced transport systems, yet in less-developed countries there is still heavy reliance upon basic forms of transport such as head-loading, walking and cycling, and the use of animal-drawn vehicles. The increasing use of motorized transport brings, of course, its own benefits and problems. The provision of more modern transport facilities, in response to increasing demand, can by itself do relatively little to reduce inequalites, and sometimes on a local or regional scale can actually increase them. The incorporation of *appropriate* transport stragegies as part of multifaceted development programmes, however, must ultimately play a major role in overcoming problems of regional and global inequalities in development levels that are widespread today.

The global telecommunications revolution has accelerated a trend that had already become apparent throughout the nineteenth and twentieth centuries during which various transport modes have shown an increasing ability to overcome physical barriers and to reduce the friction of distance. As a consequence, the world has become a much smaller place linked by intercontinental and global networks, and this trend will not only continue into the twenty-first century but will also come to affect a far higher proportion of the world's peoples. To some extent, transport technology may ultimately have the effect of reducing some of the inequalities of the global development surface, although it is unlikely ever to obliterate them entirely.

REFERENCES

Airriess, C.A. (1991), "Global economy and port morphology in Belawan, Indonesia", *Geographical Review* 81 (2), 183 96.

Allison, R. and Bradshaw, M. (1990), *The concept of French Canada in a geographical context*, Canadian Studies Geography Project for sixth forms and colleges (Plymouth: College of St Mark and St John).

Anon. (1996), "No truck with trains", *Far Eastern Economic Review* 159 (3), 46.

Auty, R.M. (1992), "Industrial policy reform in China: structural and regional imbalances", *Transactions, Institute of British Geographers (New Series)* 17, 481–94.

Chiang, T.C. (1983), "The salt trade in Ch'ing China", *Modern Asian Studies* 17, 197–219.

China Daily (1997a), "More roads, waterways, ports to be developed through 2000", 8 September.

China Daily (1997b), "Government to double investment in transportation projects", 13 October.

Chiu, T.N. (1973), *The port of Hong Kong: a survey of its development* (Hong Kong University Press).

Chiu, T.N. and Chu, D.K.Y. (1984), "Port development in the People's Republic of China: readjustment under programmes of accelerated growth", in Hoyle, B.S. and Hilling, D. (eds), *Seaport systems and spatial change* (Chichester: Wiley), 199–215.

Chou, S.H. (1971), "Railway development and economic growth in Manchuria", *China Quarterly* 45, 57–84.

Darby, H.C. (ed.) (1945), *China proper*, vol. 3 (Edinburgh: HMSO).

Dawson, J. and Barwell, I. (1993), *Roads are not enough* (London: Intermediate Technology Publications).

Dick, H. (1987), *The Indonesian interisland shipping industry: an analysis of competition and regulation* (Singapore: Institute of Southeast Asian Studies).

Drakakis-Smith, D. (1987), "Zimbabwe: the slow struggle towards socialism", *Geography* 72 (4), 348–52.

Edmonds, R.L. (1987), "The legacy of Sun Yat-Sen's railway plans", *China Quarterly* 111, 421–43.

Fan, C.C. (1992), "Foreign trade and regional development in China", *Geographical Analysis* 24, 240–56.

Forward, C.N. (1982), "The development of Canada's five leading national ports", *Urban History Review* 10 (3), 25–45.

Ginsberg, N.S. (1951), "China's railroad network", *Geographical Review* 41, 470–4.

Griffiths, I. (1990), "The quest for independent access to the sea in southern Africa", *Geographical Journal* 155 (3), 378–91.

Kay, G. (1970), *Rhodesia: a human geography* (University of London Press).

Lambert, M. (1997), *Containerization International Yearbook 1997* (London: EMAP).

Lamonde, Y. (1996), *Ni avec eux ni sans eux: le Québec et les Etats-Unis* (Québec: Nuit Blanche).

Lasserre, J.-C. (1980), *Le Saint-Laurent: grande porte de l'Amérique* (Montreal: Hurtubise).

Leeming, F. (1985), "Chinese industry – management systems and regional structures", *Transactions, Institute of British Geographers (New Series)* 10, 413–26.

Leeming, F. (1993), *The changing geography of China* (Oxford: Blackwell).

Lefevre, C. (1991), "Management of Harare urban public transport: relations between informal transport and conventional transport since independence", in Heraty, M. (ed.), *Urban transport in developing countries* (London: PTRC Education and Research Services).

Leinbach, T.R. (1986), "Transport development in Indonesia: progress, problems and policies under the New Order", in MacAndrews, C. (ed.), *Central government and local development in Indonesia* (Singapore: Oxford University Press), 190–220.

Leinbach, T.R. (1989), "Transport policies in conflict: deregulation, subsidies, and regional development in Indonesia", *Transportation Research* 23A (6), 467–75.

Leinbach, T.R. (1995), "Transportation and Third World development: review, issues and prescription", *Transportation Research* 29A (5), 337–44.

Leinbach, T.R. and Chia Lin Sien (1989), *Southeast Asian transport issues in development* (Singapore: Oxford University Press).

Leung, C.K. (1990), "Locational characteristics of foreign-equity joint venture investment in China, 1979–1985", *Professional Geographer* 42, 403–21.

Li, P. (1990), "Reform brings vigour to road construction", *Beijing Review*, 26 November, 20–25.

Liang, E.P. (1982), *China: railways and agricultural development 1875–1935*, Research Paper 203 (Chicago: University of Chicago, Department of Geography).

Lin, K.P.K. (1995), "The development of port facilities in Hong Kong and southern China", *Proceedings, Chartered Institute of Transport* 4 (3), 13–26.

Lippit, V.D. (1966), "Development of transportation in Communist China", *China Quarterly* 27, 101–19.

Liu, G.G., Liang, W.S., Tian, J.H. and Shen, L.R. (1987), *China's economy in 2000* (Beijing: New World Press).

Maunder, D.A.C., Mbara, T.C. and Khezwana, M. (1994), "The effect of institutional change on stage bus performance in Harare, Zimbabwe", *Transport Reviews* 14 (2), 151–65.

Qian, L.X. (1997), "Jing-Jiu trunk line boosts north–south capacity", *Railway Gazette International* 153, 455–8.

Railway Gazette International (1996, 1998), Rail Business Report (supplement issues).

Rimmer, P.J. (1977), "A conceptual framework for examining urban and regional transport needs in south-east Asia", *Pacific Viewpoint* 18, 133–47.

Rukuni, M. and Eicher, C.K. (1994), *Zimbabwe's agricultural revolution* (Harare: University of Zimbabwe Publications).

Rutz, W.O.A. and Coull, J.R. (1996), "Inter-island passenger shipping in Indonesia: development of the system, present characteristics and future requirements", *Journal of Transport Geography* 4 (4), 275–86.

Slack, B. (1993), "The impacts of deregulation and the US–Canada free trade agreement on Canadian transportation modes", *Journal of Transport Geography* 1 (3), 150–5.

Smith, J.A. (1988), "The Beira Corridor Project", *Geography* 73 (3), 258–61.

Smith, J.A. (1989), "Transport and marketing of horticultural crops by communal farmers in Harare", *Geographical Journal of Zimbabwe* 20, 1–15.

Spence, J.D. (1990), *The search for modern China* (London: Hutchinson).

Taaffe, E.J., Morrill, R.L. and Gould, P.R. (1963), "Transport expansion in underdeveloped countries: a comparative analysis", *Geographical Review* 53, 503–29.

Todd, D. (1996), "North–south energy resource transfers in China and the port intermediary", *Tijdschrift voor Economische en Sociale Geografie* 87, 195–208.

Trent, J.E., Young, R. and Lachapelle, G. (eds) (1996), *Québec-Canada: nouveaux sentiers vers l'avenir* (Ottawa: University of Ottawa Press).

Turton, B.J. (1991), "The role of the RMS in the rural road transport sector in Zimbabwe", *Geographical Journal of Zimbabwe* 22, 46–61.

Vance, J.E. (1970), *The merchant's world: the geography of wholesaling* (Englewood Cliffs, NJ: Prentice Hall).

Van Goor, J. (1996), "Dutch factories in Asia, 1600–1800: bridgeheads of political, economic and cultural interaction", in Everaert, J. and Parmentier, J. (eds), *Shipping, factories and colonization* (Brussels: Académie Royale des Sciences d'Outre-Mer), 71–92.

Waddell, E. (1987), "Cultural hearth, continental diaspora: the place of Québec in North America", in McCann, L.D. (ed.), *Heartland and hinterland: a geography of Canada* (Scarborough, Ontario: Prentice Hall Canada), 149–72.

Wei, Q.Y. (1987), "The development of water transport in China", *Transport Reviews* 7, 1–15.

Williams, E.T. (1920), "The open ports of China", *Geographical Review* 9, 306–34.

World Bank (1985), *China: long-term development courses and options* (Baltimore: Johns Hopkins University Press).

Yang, D.L. (1990), "Patterns of China's regional development strategy", *China Quarterly* 122, 230–57.

Yeates, M. (1975), *Main street: Windsor to Québec City* (Toronto: Macmillan).

Zhao, S.X.B. (1996), "Spatial disparities and economic development in China, 1953–92: a comparative study", *Development and Change* 27, 131–63.

4

TRANSPORT DEREGULATION AND PRIVATIZATION

Richard Knowles and Derek Hall

In this chapter reasons are identified to explain the increasing regulation of public freight and passenger transport services and the trend towards public ownership up to the 1970s and for worldwide moves subsequently to deregulate and privatize transport. Case studies examine road transport deregulation in Third World contexts, deregulation of United States domestic air services, privatization of British Airways and international air transport deregulation, bus deregulation and privatization in Britain, and rail privatization.

INTRODUCTION

Regulation and Public Ownership

The tradition of transport regulation is well established throughout the world (Button, 1991). Most governments have intervened in the transport market for many years to protect customers and employees by introducing quality and safety controls, by controlling the quantity of services to ensure a comprehensive transport network, by controlling the price of services, by regulating the entry of new transport operators and sometimes by public ownership of transport companies. These controls were built up from the nineteenth century through to the 1970s to stop the market creating significant social and financial differences between areas and groups (Leyshon, 1992).

In this protected system, operators were expected to provide some services for social rather than for commercial reasons. An early British example was the requirement of the 1844 Railway Act that any new railway should provide "parliamentary" trains, at fares not exceeding 1 (old) penny per mile, so as to spread the benefits of cheap mechanized travel to all sections of the population (Jenkins, 1995). Britain's 1930 Road Traffic Act introduced a system of road service licences and fares controls to regulate the often chaotic and unsafe free market for bus services experienced in the 1920s. Bus operators were protected from unregulated competition but were expected to cross-subsidize unprofitable rural services from profits made elsewhere (Knowles, 1989). Button and Gillingwater (1986) identified the 1930s as a particularly active period of regulation, much of it reversed since the 1970s.

Public ownership of transport occurred initially when there were strategic or social requirements for new routes, especially in thinly populated areas, which the private sector was unable to finance. In the Scottish Highlands, for example, the British Government paid for the Crinan and Caledonian Canals to be built during the Napoleonic wars to enable warships to transfer more quickly between the Irish and North Seas, whilst for social reasons at the end of the nineteenth century it paid for railway lines to be completed from Stromeferry to Kyle of Lochalsh and from Banavie to Mallaig. In comparison in Norway most railway development was State-financed and -operated from the 1860s.

During the twentieth century, social democratic and communist governments, in for example France and the UK and China and the Soviet Union respectively, nationalized various modes of transport for ideological reasons. In most countries air transport was publicly owned from an early stage owing to high capital and operating costs and the political requirement for rapid access within large countries and to far-away colonies (Graham, 1995).

Public ownership of urban passenger transport companies occurred in most countries either by municipal development of transit systems (usually electric streetcars or buses but sometimes including underground railways, suburban railways, electric trolleybuses or light railways) or by municipal purchase of privately owned transit companies. Even in the USA, public-sector investment in transit systems started more than 100 years ago, and by 1940 a substantial minority of transit systems were in State or local government ownership or control (Neff, 1998).

Deregulation and Privatization

Deregulation, or liberalization, measures started in an *ad hoc* way in response to the requirements of individual modes of transport. For example inter-state road freight transport was deregulated in Australia in 1954 (Scrafton, 1997). Swedish Railways were divided into commercial and social networks as early as 1963, while Swedish road haulage was deregulated by 1968 (Fullerton, 1990). British road haulage was deregulated in 1968 as were US domestic air services in 1978. In the late 1970s the theory of contestable markets suggested that the free entry, or even just the threat of entry, of new operators into the transport market was the key mechanism to ensure efficiency, price moderation and welfare maximization (Bailey and Baumol, 1984; Baumol, 1982;

Baumol *et al.*, 1982; Hibbs, 1985). Regulation was held to be responsible for increasing prices by limiting competition. State and municipal ownership and operation of transport services was widely viewed as inefficient, bureaucratic and unresponsive to the market. Neo-liberal "New Right" advocates of transport deregulation and privatization agreed that the State should confine its role to the adoption of minimal regulations that ensured fair competition and safe operation of transport services (Green, 1987).

Contestability theory was used to underpin the ideological moves to deregulate and privatize transport, which started in the USA and Great Britain at the end of the 1970s. This process then spread rapidly throughout the world and included many less-developed countries often at the instigation of the World Bank and the International Monetary Fund (Bell and Cloke, 1990). In the USA, the 1978 Airline Deregulation Act, the 1980 Staggers Rail Act, the 1980 Motor Carrier Act and the 1982 Bus Regulatory Reform Act liberalized inter-state transport with consequential effects on intra-state regulation (Button, 1991). In Great Britain the 1980 Transport Act abolished fare controls on all bus services and deregulated express bus services, while the 1985 Transport Act deregulated local bus services outside Greater London by abolishing road service licences (Knowles, 1989). Other measures reduced and capped the level of public transport subsidies. A widespread privatization programme from 1982 onwards sold off publicly owned British transport companies including the National Freight Corporation, British Transport Docks Board, Seaspeed Hovercraft, British Transport Hotels, Sealink Ferries, British Airways, British Airports Authority, National Bus Company, Scottish Bus Group and many municipally owned bus companies (Knowles, 1989).

Since the mid-1980s contestability theory has been challenged increasingly as the outcome of deregulation and privatization has often been oligopolistic control of particular transport markets instead of competition (Button, 1991; Dempsey and Goetz, 1992; Kahn, 1988; White, 1997). Optimal regulatory systems are now seen by many as those systems such as franchising and compulsory competitive tendering which stimulate competition in bidding for service contracts but control services, quality and fares by preventing the misuse of monopolistic or oligopolistic power. This type of competition reduces operating costs and public subsidy without destroying the integrated network of public transport services (Kennedy, 1995; Knowles, 1985; Mackie *et al.*, 1995). London Regional Transport, for example, put out to competitive tender nearly a quarter of its bus route network from 1986 to 1989, reducing costs by 15 per cent whilst increasing bus service reliability (Gayle and Goodrich, 1990).

In 1989 and 1990 the sudden collapse of the Communist political system and centrally planned economies throughout Eastern Europe, in favour of multi-party democracy and market economies, heralded a new phase in transport deregulation and privatization (Hall, 1993a,b). It quickly became clear that the highly centralized Soviet Unified Transport System (Mellor, 1975) would be obsolete as in future sources of raw materials and finished products and modal split would be determined more by the market than by the State.

Deregulation continues to gather momentum in the rest of the world. For example domestic air services have been gradually liberalized in Australia, Canada, the EU, Japan, Korea and Taiwan (Graham, 1995, 1997; Small, 1993). Road freight deregulation has been completed in New Zealand and the Irish Republic and started in the USA. Interstate bus services have been deregulated in Australia followed by intra-state services in New South Wales. Here the Canberra to Sydney coach services have cut fares and increased frequencies but the previous monopoly operator still dominates the market and train services have been cut from four to one per day (Higginson, 1990). New Zealand deregulated all scheduled passenger services on 1 July 1991 including buses, taxis and rail services, whilst Denmark began competitive tendering of Copenhagen Capital Region bus services in 1990 to reduce soaring costs (Fullerton and Knowles, 1991; Higginson, 1990). In the European Union the introduction of the Single

European Market on 1 January 1993 accelerated a process that will result in the eventual harmonization and liberalization of national transport regulations. Further privatizations in developed countries include Air Canada, Air New Zealand, British Railways, Canadian National Railways, Icelandair, JAL, Japanese National Railways, KLM Dutch Airlines and Qantas, all designed to improve operating efficiency, reduce government debt and help balance budgets.

Welfare states such as Sweden and Norway have also been attracted by the ability of the free market to increase efficiency and adapt public transport services to match demand. Deregulation, however, threatens the viability of minimum transport services in marginal areas and restricts the accessibility of the car-less population to jobs and to retail and health services. Some regulation of transport is therefore necessary to protect the most vulnerable people. In 1988 Swedish coach services were deregulated and a National Railway Infrastructure Authority took over fixed rail infrastructure. This infrastructure is charged for on the basis of the marginal cost of use and on a fixed charge equivalent to road tax on each wagon (Fullerton, 1990). Swedish Railway services were redivided into four groups – a profitable business railway and subsidized county railways, Northern Inland railway and the iron ore railway from the inland iron mines to the Baltic and North Atlantic coasts. Norway deregulated its internal freight transport in 1986 to the benefit of road transport with subsidies decreasing by 5 per cent in one year and new operators increasing by 41 per cent (Higginson, 1990).

CASE STUDIES

Road Transport Deregulation in Less-Developed Countries

Since the early 1980s deregulation and privatization policies have been central to structural adjustment and economic recovery programmes in less-developed countries and a condition of further aid from developed countries and international agencies (Simon, 1996). In less-developed countries deregulation is often hampered by import restrictions, owing to a lack of foreign exchange, causing a shortage of vehicles and spare parts. In Sri Lanka, for example, all bus routes were deregulated in 1979 but the impact was blunted by the continuing subsidies to State-owned buses. Communist China has deregulated long-distance coach services and fares are allowed to vary by up to 15 per cent. Demand-responsive and flexible paratransit services are a common feature of many developing countries as an essential part of the informal economy, but often operate in at best illicit circumstances, providing "unsafe and unreliable services at unregulated fares" (Higginson, 1990, 61; Adeniji, 1983; Rimmer, 1986). Many governments now recognize the commercial and operational benefits of paratransit. Harassment of paratransit operations has often changed to regularization or even legalization. Kenya, for example, legalized and licensed its *matatu* (converted pickup trucks) in 1984 requiring annual inspection, insurance and drivers' licences (Simon, 1996). Often revealing more extreme manifestations than in Europe, the practice of deregulation and privatization in Africa (Banjo, 1994) and Korea (Kang, 1995), reversions to elements of State control (Maunder *et al.*, 1994) and the efficiency of public ownership (Bhattacharyya *et al.*, 1995) in developing countries have stimulated wide-ranging debates that UK policy went some way in nurturing. In Chile, after 11 years of deregulation, the authorities reintroduced some regulation in 1989 – including route franchising and emission controls – after bus fares had more than doubled in real terms and the external effects of traffic congestion, atmospheric pollution and road accidents had greatly increased (Koprich, 1994).

The franchising of Jamaican urban bus services involved the legalization of the mainly illegal minibuses that had creamed off much of the profitable traffic and had put the State-owned Jamaica Omnibus Service deep into debt and then in 1983 out of business (Anderson, 1990). This problem of illegal competition from minibuses and adapted vehicles is widespread in the less-developed world, causing similar problems, for example, in Chiang Mai (Thailand) and Lagos and Ibadan (Nigeria), with the Ibadan City Bus Service liquidated in 1976 (Adeniji, 1983; Rimmer, 1986; Thomson, 1978). In 1983 the Jamaican Government franchised the 65 bus routes in the Kingston Metropolitan Region into 10 packages which were then resold at a higher price to minibus owners, most of whom own one vehicle. Overcrowding occurs in the peak period and illegal competition survives in the peak and off-peak periods on routes abandoned by the franchise holder because of worries about personal safety. Timetabling has broken down because of competition. Short operation sometimes occurs with services turning back before the end of the route. Non-designated stops are frequent and tickets are rarely issued. In the peak period there is discrimination against school children and pensioners carried at concessionary fares. The objective of franchising is to remove government subsidy and provide conditions for genuine, permanent competition with an effective division of responsibility between private ownership and limited government control. This form of deregulation has produced negative effects on the quality of service, working conditions and increased road traffic accidents.

Deregulation of United States' Domestic Air Services

The US airline industry was regulated by the Civil Aeronautics Board (CAB) from 1938. The CAB's policy was to preserve the 16 "trunk airlines" that existed in 1938, but these were reduced to 11 by mergers (American, Braniff, Continental, Delta, Eastern, National, North West, Pan Am, TWA, United and Western). Routes were awarded to these airlines and fares specified by the CAB, which in return ensured safe airline operating practices (Pickrell, 1991). Its major service initiative was to allow a group of local service airlines to start subsidized feeder services during the 1950s to connect small communities with the cities served by the trunk airlines. Subsidy payments to local airlines increased rapidly as new aircraft replaced ex-military planes.

The CAB then began to award more profitable longer-distance routes to local service airlines to offset feeder service losses. Many acquired jet planes and evolved into regional airlines.

Strong economic growth increased domestic air passengers 10-fold from 1950 to 1970 but fares stabilized owing to the lower operating costs of modern aircraft. After 1970 fares rose with the cost of fuel and labour. Demand was suppressed as the mileage formula for fares overpriced profitable long-haul routes and underpriced the often loss-making short-haul routes. The oil crisis of 1973–4 increased pressure for deregulation. A Congressional Committee recommended relaxing the controls over fares and new airlines entering the market, which occurred from 1975. American Airlines started to discount tickets by up to 45 per cent in 1977, in response to charter carriers and low-fare airlines, leading to 60 per cent traffic increases on some routes and copycat fares by competitors. The 1978 Airline Deregulation Act phased out the CAB's route licensing powers over three years and its fares controls over five years. Commuter airlines were permitted to receive subsidies for routes to small communities. The CAB itself was abolished in 1984.

Alfred Kahn, the US Transportation Secretary who introduced deregulation, advocated (Kahn, 1988) that it would:

- make airlines more competitive;
- offer large reductions in average fares and distribute the benefits more equitably;
- provide new lower-fare and quality options;
- be more efficient;
- make airlines less likely to take part in cost-inflating competition;
- continue to serve pre-existing networks;
- not subject the airline industry to severe financial distress.

Since 1982 the domestic US airline market has been open to any national carrier. The most significant result of route deregulation has been the development of "hub-and-spoke" route networks. Services from smaller towns are fed into large city airports, or hubs, and the hubs are then linked by regular direct flights. Hubbing reduces costs, raises load factors and frequencies on hub-to-hub flights and the cheaper seat/mile costs of larger aircraft can lower fares on competitive routes. Hubbing can raise the entry costs for new operators as an airline needs to develop many spoke routes to achieve sufficient density of feeder traffic to achieve economies of scale. On-line connections by a single airline are a strong competitive advantage. A change of airline is now only required on 1 per cent of US domestic airline trips compared with 15 per cent in 1978 (Graham, 1995). The proportion of passengers boarding flights at major link airports rose for example from 19.9 per cent in 1977 to 31 per cent in 1984. This has paradoxically caused congestion and delays at some airports. The extra employment and increased accessibility that a hub airport brings to a city are seen as major economic advantages of hub status, outweighing the adverse environmental consequences of increased noise and air pollution and higher fares at the fortress hubs dominated by one airline.

Competition has reduced the real cost of air travel with 75 per cent of passengers travelling in markets with reduced fares. The top 20 domestic city pair markets experienced a 31 per cent average real cost reduction in one-way air fares from $128 in 1979 to $88 in 1994 (Bureau of Transportation Statistics, 1996). However, the important Los Angeles–San Francisco, Boston–New York and New York–Washington DC city pairs respectively showed real increases of 35, 23 and 15 per cent. Average fares have fallen most on long-haul routes and discount tickets. By 1987, 90 per cent of passengers used discount fares compared with only 15 per cent in 1976 before deregulation. Almost 40 per cent of domestic passengers now travel in markets where low-cost carriers compete (Bureau of Transportation Statistics, 1996). Reed (1995) maintains that fares are now less closely related to product costs than ever before. Airline costs have been cut by higher productivity and lower pay whilst the leisure market has accepted lower frequencies and higher load factors, which yield lower fares. The Federal Aviation

Administration claim that safety standards have continued to increase despite the sacking of most air traffic controllers who were on strike in 1981, and accident rates have remained low.

Following deregulation, eight former local service airlines (Frontier, Hughes Airwest, North Central, Ozark, Piedmont, Southern, Texas International and USAir) grew rapidly and began to compete with the smaller trunk airlines. In the early 1980s they were joined by five intra-state airlines (Alaska and four new carriers Air Cal, Air Florida, PSA and Southwest) and three new commuter airlines (Air Wisconsin, Empire and Horizon). After 1984 however the number of regional or national competitors was reduced by financial failures, mergers or takeovers to 10 airlines by 1988 and only five (Alaska, America West, Midway, Southwest and USAir) by 1994.

By the end of 1991 only six of the 11 pre-deregulation trunk airlines survived. Braniff, Eastern and Pan Am (which had taken over National in 1981) were bankrupt and had ceased operating, whilst Western had been taken over by Delta. The main US international airlines Pan Am and TWA had sold off assets including international route licences to London Heathrow to United and American respectively to offset losses but only in TWA's case did this ensure survival (*The Guardian*, 1991a,b). Heavy losses by the surviving trunk airlines in 1990–93 led to withdrawal from some hubs and more point-to-point competition with the increasingly successful low-fare/high-frequency "no frills" airlines such as Southwest (Graham, 1995).

The market share of the eight largest airlines, which fell from 81 per cent in 1978 to 70 per cent in 1985, rose to 90 per cent by 1988. By the mid-1990s, 16 of the 19 major US hub airports were dominated by one airline which usually handled over 70 per cent of passenger boardings. The other three major hubs, Chicago O'Hare, Dallas/Fort Worth and Phoenix, were each similarly dominated by two airlines. This demonstrates the monopolistic nature of the airline market after deregulation. Competition cannot be effective so long as the entry of new airlines is so costly. Other sources of monopoly power are the ownership of computerized reservation sys-

tems, which bias displays of seats and fares available to customers, joint marketing agreements with commuter and regional airlines including code-sharing by connecting flights, frequent-flier programmes and travel agent commission overrides.

Pickrell (1991) showed that 137 out of 183 US airports increased their number of flights between 1979 and 1988, often by more than 50 per cent. However, 46 airports showed a decline due to deregulation mainly of 10 to 50 per cent. Seat capacity per plane fell at all except the largest city airports as airlines switched to smaller, often turbo propeller, aircraft for spoke routes.

The Privatization of British Airways and International Air Transport Deregulation

British Airways (BA) was privatized in 1987 to make it more efficient and to remove the need for government financial support. BA's poor productivity levels, in comparison with other international airlines, were improved by cutting staffing levels, modernizing its aircraft fleet and improving its terminal facilities (Ashworth and Forsyth, 1984).

The international airline industry remains heavily regulated. Routes are licensed usually on a bilateral basis by pairs of countries who each usually designate their national airline. The frequency of flights is limited and fares are high and government-approved (Sealy, 1966). In recent years route licensing has been relaxed in some markets, for example between UK and West Germany in 1984, UK and Belgium in 1985 and UK and Canada in 1987, liberalized within the EC in 1988, 1990 and 1992 and totally abolished within the European Union since April 1997 when full cabotage was established giving any EU airline the right to carry traffic between any two airports. However, as most EU airlines are still State-owned the full effects of deregulation await privatization (Meersman and van de Voorde, 1996). A 1991 UK–USA agreement allowed a second British airline to fly from London Heathrow to North America, allowed British airlines to fly via Europe to the USA and beyond, and permitted better marketing deals with US domestic airlines (*The Guardian*, 1991b). In return United's $290 million deal to buy Pan Am's Heathrow routes and American's $445 million deal to buy TWA's Heathrow routes were allowed to try to stave off bankruptcy, and enabled United and American to use Heathrow as a hub to serve Europe. This replaced the 1977 agreement which allowed cities in the USA to be served direct from the UK by two airlines from each country except for New York, Los Angeles, Boston and Miami, which were limited to one airline each from each country.

BA has benefited from regulation as it receives most of the bilateral route licences and its oligopoly powers enables it to charge high airfares and make supernormal profits. However, domestic deregulation in the USA, Canada, Australia and the UK generated pressure for international deregulation especially within the European Union. Liberalization within Europe, for example, resulted in London to Frankfurt flights increasing from 68 to 97 per week between the summers of 1983 and 1987 (Monopolies and Mergers Commission, 1987). The growth of mega-airlines and the internationalization of the industry allowed the BA/British Caledonian merger and BA's takeover of Dan Air to be approved despite its near monopoly power in Britain. Other agreements helping to transform BA into a global airline include a BA/USAir code-sharing alliance in 1993 yielding connecting flights in the USA and minority shareholdings in Qantas, Deutsche BA, TAT, Air Russia and USAir. The latter was sold when BA proposed an alliance with American Airlines in 1996 and USAir scrapped its code-sharing agreement.

Since privatization, BA has increased its profits on airline operation from £183m in 1986/87 to £728m in 1995/96 falling to £673m in 1996/97. Whilst European turnover is increasing, its profits have fallen to zero owing to deregulation and competition. BA's Americas services account for over half of all its profits, and 13 per cent on turnover, probably due to tight regulation limiting competition. BA's Far East and Australasia routes yield a 12 per cent profit, and African, Middle East and Indian subcontinent routes a 14 per cent profit, all in tightly regulated markets (British Airways, 1997).

BA faces a much more competitive future with more international deregulation, competition from high-speed trains using the Channel Tunnel on short European routes from London to Paris and Brussels, erosion of its dominant share of frequencies from London Heathrow, privatization of other large State-owned airlines, an increase in global and regional code-sharing and the growth of a few major airlines to rival the United States' big three, American, Delta and United. Debbage (1994) argues that the most efficient air transport systems to emerge from the transition from State-owned carriers and restrictive bilateral agreements to multinational strategic alliance route networks and multilateral air service agreements will achieve a competitive advantage in the global economy. BA and the three US mega-carriers are currently the best placed.

Bus Deregulation and Privatization in Britain

UK public-transport policy has long experienced political partisanship. In the 1980s the government set about pursuing the deregulation and privatization of public-transport services, with road-passenger transport foremost in that process. As a consequence, not only have routes and services been deregulated, but the fundamental structure of Britain's bus and coach operating industry has been dramatically altered at a time when the structure of the vehicle manufacturing industry was also undergoing substantial readjustment.

The UK bus operating industry

The UK's first licensed urban motor bus service began operation in 1898. Six years later, with growing numbers of motorized vehicles, a registration system was introduced. But it was not until the 1930 Road Traffic Act that the notion of regulation through route licensing was established, to eradicate what was seen as a dangerous vying for passengers by increasing numbers of competing buses on the streets of London and other major cities.

From then on, until 1986, the local bus operating industry remained highly regulated. Route licensing through the office of Traffic Commissioners – a field agency of central government – regulated and regularized public bus services. New potential bus operators needed to conform to certain standards of organization, and applications for a route licence could be opposed – and often were, successfully – by incumbent bus and railway operators.

The 1948 Transport Act nationalized companies within the large Thomas Tilling group and the Scottish Motor Traction Company (SMT). Four groups of bus companies emerged: (i) those in full public ownership under the auspices of the British Transport Commission (from 1962 the Transport Holding Company) (London Transport was also established as a directly run central government operation); (ii) those of the British Electric Traction group, in which the government had a minority holding; (iii) municipal companies, run by local county boroughs and municipal boroughs; and (iv) completely independent private companies. Of the four groups, the first two were made up of relatively large organizations, which dominated much of the country's bus operation, particularly inter-urban and urban–rural services. Municipal companies operated within the confines of their administrative boundaries, sometimes under the terms of joint schemes with a BTC or BET company, sometimes crossing boundaries in joint schemes with adjacent municipal operators.

Independent operators were mostly small, although with some notable exceptions such as Barton, Gosport and Fareham (Provincial), OK, South Yorkshire and West Riding. Independents were – and still are – particularly important in rural and remote areas, holding detailed local knowledge and patronage where the larger companies were unable to derive economies of operating scale.

UK bus passenger numbers reached their peak in the early 1950s, after which time increasing car ownership and new patterns of spatial mobility saw bus ridership decrease substantially, with services being commensurately reduced in rural and suburban areas and at off-peak times. Partly reacting to this situation, the Labour Government's 1968 Transport Act established the National Bus Company (NBC) as a corporate State enterprise encompassing all former BTC and BET companies, as well as some others, and amalgamating units perceived to be too small to derive economies of scale. North of the border, the Scottish Transport Group was established on a similar basis. The Act also set up comprehensive passenger transport authorities in urban conurbations in advance of local government reform in the mid-1970s. Passenger Transport Authorities and Executives (PTAs and PTEs) were publicly controlled and owned to provide locally determined integrated public-transport systems. Government subsidies were introduced for certain types of services and vehicles; attempts to standardize bus design into just a few models through the provision of bus grants possessed parallels in the structural concentration taking place within the bus manufacturing industry itself.

By the 1970s, over 95 per cent of local bus services were being operated by either NBC or municipally owned companies. Meanwhile, UK bus patronage continued to decline: from just over 8000 million journeys in 1975 to just over 6000 million in 1985, a fall of almost a quarter (Fairhurst and Edwards, 1996). Passenger receipts, at 1986 prices, fell from £2600 million to £2300 million over the same period, a decline of 12 per cent. Numbers of staff employed in the bus and coach operating industry fell from 224 400 in 1975 to 174 300 in 1985, a reduction of some 22 per cent (Department of Transport, 1987, 106–7, 111). The decline in bus passenger traffic and revenue required an operating subsidy to maintain a comprehensive local service. Nationally, subsidies rose by 1300 per cent between 1972 and 1982, from £10 million to £520 million. Fares rose 35 per cent in real terms, while services declined by 12 per cent (Knowles, 1989, 82).

The UK bus manufacturing industry

As in the car industry, structural rationalization through mergers and take-overs saw bus and coach manufacturing increasingly concentrated into fewer hands. The industry had traditionally entailed two essential elements – chassis and body manufacture – the two groups of activities usually being undertaken by separate companies. Famous chassis manufacturers such as AEC, Bristol, Daimler and Guy, and body builders Eastern Coach Works (ECW), Park Royal and C.H. Roe, were absorbed into a larger and seemingly more cumbersome and inefficient Leyland Group, such that customer choice noticeably dwindled as both UK chassis and bodies, encouraged by 50 per cent government grants on new buses, became more standardized and concentrated in the hands of one major manufacturing group.

While in the short term this may have been appropriate for a dwindling home market, it did little for export opportunities, and the Leyland Group, with assured sales to home companies based on standard bus types, began to lose overseas markets. Meanwhile, foreign manufacturers began penetrating the British market. In 1988, after the government had written off debts of £55 million, Leyland Bus was bought out by a management consortium. Within months, following the enforced redundancies of 750 workers, the company was resold to Volvo Bus of Sweden: this appeared to sound the death knell for the wholly UK-owned bus manufacturing industry.

Structural reorganization of operating units

Although several mergers and absorptions amongst NBC subsidiaries had taken place in the early 1980s in advance of privatization and deregulation, moves towards decentralization and company individuality began with larger operating units being (re-)subdivided. The most comprehensive approach to this task was taken in Scotland. In June 1985 the seven nationalized Scottish Bus Group companies were broken down into 11 smaller units. All but one of the existing companies' operating area boundaries were redrawn, partly providing a closer geographical relationship with Scottish administrative regions.

The Transport Act, 1985

The Conservative Government argued that the existing regulatory system had three inherent shortcomings: (i) preventing competition, which would keep costs, subsidies and fares down; (ii)

inhibiting innovation such as the use of minibuses and midibuses; and (iii) suppressing passenger demand by overcharging profitable traffic in order to be able to cross-subsidize unprofitable routes. Early responses to this situation were enshrined in the Transport Act, 1980, which abolished fare controls on all bus services and deregulated express bus provision (Photograph 4.1). Local "stage-carriage" services remained subject to the provisions of the 1930 legislation on route licensing, but the entry of new operators was eased by shifting the onus of proof in licence application and objection from the applicant to the objector, in a particular attempt to encourage the better provision of rural bus services (Knowles, 1989, 82–3). The perceived success of the 1980 legislation encouraged the government to press further ahead with the implementation of "free market" measures in the public-transport arena. The *Buses* White Paper (Department of Transport, 1984), and the subsequent Transport Act, 1985, were the outcome. Their overriding aims were to: (i) deregulate – introduce far greater competition into – UK bus services (initially to exclude Greater London); (ii) considerably reduce public subsidy to the bus operating industry; and (iii) shift the bulk of bus operation from the public to the private sector, in line with other privatization policies being pursued by the government.

The introduction of route competition

The Transport Act, 1980 deregulated long-distance express bus operations and stimulated some competition, higher-quality service and cheaper fares on such trunk routes as between London and Newcastle. Overall, traffic increased by 60 per cent from 1980 to 1982, although direct coach services on secondary routes between smaller, less popular centres were cut back. The Act also allowed for the setting up of trial areas for bus service deregulation and the Hereford trial area was deemed by government to be a success (Evans, 1988). The demonstration effect of this legislation was critical for the subsequent 1985 Act, which abolished road service licensing. Provided that operators had a valid PSV Operator's

Photograph 4.1   London commuter bus services
The 1980 Transport Act stimulated a number of commuter service operators and revived an interest in double-deck coaches. Maidstone and District adopted the brand name *Invictaway* for its commuter services to London from the Medway towns. Here, one of its Leyland Olympian coaches is leaving the 1930s architecture of London's Victoria Coach Station for Sheerness (D.R. Hall)

("O") licence, they could now introduce, change or withdraw a service simply by registering details with the appropriate Traffic Commissioner's Office, notifying the relevant local authority (which had the role of coordinating and publicizing public transport in its area), and waiting for a 42-day period to elapse. The government argued that greater competition would provide more choice for the travelling public: more buses, greater frequencies and lower fares. While this may have been the case on trunk routes in urban areas, where lucrative pickings were to be had, in Scotland, in the first year and a half of deregulation, passenger journeys dropped by 6.5 per cent, twice the average decline since 1977, and only one completely new operator survived (Photograph 4.2).

The 1980 Act explicitly demolished area coordination and integration schemes, some of which dated back to the 1940s. All metropolitan areas with PTEs had developed such schemes, perhaps the most notable of which was that in Tyne and Wear, which integrated bus, metro, rail and ferry services. This was now abandoned: the bus companies had to compete with each other, and with Tyne and Wear PTE's bus operations, which were now run by an "arm's length" company. They were all also in competition with the PTE's own light rail Metro system, which had been expressly designed to be integrated with other forms of public transport.

While arguing that fares appeared to have been largely unaffected by deregulation, an early

Photograph 4.2   A Guide Friday service, Edinburgh, Scotland
One almost eccentric consequence of bus deregulation in the UK has been the rise, alongside the growth of urban and heritage tourism, of the Guide Friday bus company, which specializes in open-top bus circular services. Here, exceptionally, a Guide Friday uses an elderly closed-top second-hand bus on the Edinburgh city centre to airport route in competition with the existing Lothian Region service (D.R. Hall)

government-sponsored report (Balcombe *et al.*, 1988) pointed to the significantly increased fares and inconvenience brought about by the loss of through-ticketing and pre-paid tickets, as a result of the abandonment of coordinated schemes.

Reducing public subsidy

Within the Act, two types of service were recognized: commercial and tendered. Bus companies were now to operate services as a business and not as a public service, registering as "commercial" routes considered to be economically viable. The legislation forbade the cross-subsidy of routes, as had often happened in the past. The appropriate local

authority or PTE was charged with assessing the transport needs not met by registered commercial networks. With a restricted amount of central government subsidy and its own limited resources, the authority was empowered to put out to competitive tender routes that it considered essential for social or other reasons such as school bus provision (White and Tough, 1995; Mercer and Tielin, 1996). However, given the ever-changing nature of the registered commercial services, particularly in areas of strong competition, local authorities and PTEs have faced an extremely difficult task in keeping ahead of new developments and in assessing future need for tendering purposes: one of the most significant long-term public concerns about the consequences of deregulation has been the uncertainty that continually changing patterns of services and operators brings. Within the metropolitan areas, for example, in 1988 Greater Manchester experienced over 1900 new and changed registrations, affecting 90 per cent of all services, some changing three or four times during the year.

Even after deregulation, however, the concept of a free-market service industry is more apparent than real. By the very nature of their statutory role, local authorities subsidize services through the formal tendering procedures, and more indirectly subsidize the operating companies by providing publicity and information on all transport services, both tendered and commercial. Bus companies also continue to receive central government subsidy through the fuel tax rebate system.

Looking at the financial results of the first year of deregulation, a government-sponsored report (Balcombe et al., 1988) pointed to substantial savings made in direct bus service subsidies, but also argued that these were partially offset by increases in administrative and publicity costs to local authorities, and by the costs of establishing the new "arm's length" companies. A report undertaken for the Association of Metropolitan Authorities (Tyson, 1988) found a reduction in subsidy levels of about 10 per cent for the metropolitan areas, but also recognized that part, at least, of this saving had been obtained by deflating wages rather than by any real increase in efficiency. Uncertainty amongst passengers had led to significant lost patronage – between 7.5 and 12.5 per cent for most PTE areas, but a hefty 32.5 per cent in Merseyside. These losses partly reflected the substantial fare increases experienced due to previous low-fare policies and the loss of such facilities as through-ticketing. After two years of deregulation, fares in metropolitan areas had risen 27.5 per cent above inflation (Tyson, 1989). In non-metropolitan areas, a government-sponsored study (Rickard et al., 1988) also suggested that early cost savings might not be sustainable for local authorities, and that operators had cut costs largely by wage level cuts and redundancies. Department of Transport calculations neglected to take into ac-

count fuel duty rebate, greatly increased administrative costs, and the unquantifiable loss of amenity to large numbers of non-car-owners.

After 10 years of deregulation, privatization, subsidy withdrawal, tendering formulae and abolition of the route licensing system, clear trends have emerged (Mackie et al., 1995; White, 1995). Operating costs have fallen more steeply than earlier opponents of deregulation expected, largely due to increased labour productivity through reductions in engineering and management staff as well as through mechanisms to deflate drivers' wages. Both fare costs in real terms and service levels have risen. Patronage has declined faster since deregulation, with the result that cost per passenger journey has been little changed, but average loads have dropped. Apart from the use of minibuses, little impact has been felt from other forms of innovation. Public expenditure has fallen substantially, but the operating industry has only remained marginally profitable, stimulating a number of the larger companies to seek diversification, not least in terms of horizontal and vertical integration.

The case of London

The 1984 London Regional Transport Act removed control of London Transport from the elected Greater London Council and vested it in central government in order to reduce subsidy levels. Within the overall coordinating ambit of London Regional Transport (LRT: later to take on the old name of London Transport), London Buses Limited (LBL) and London Underground Limited (LUL) were established for the day-to-day running of their respective modes and given company status in April 1985. In preparation for the likelihood of deregulation, LBL was restructured into 11 (later 12) operating units during 1988.

Although the LRT operating area was excluded from the provisions of the 1985 Transport Act for full deregulation, under the 1984 Act LRT was empowered to put out groups of routes to competitive tender with the stated aim of providing LBL with the discipline of competition. This process began in

1985 and the first service to be lost by LBL to a competitor commenced operation with its new private operator in July of that year (Kennedy, 1995).

After the timetable for full deregulation in Greater London had apparently been put back several times, in March 1991 a consultation paper was published (Department of Transport, 1991) indicating the government's intention to introduce legislation in the 1991/2 Parliament to fully deregulate bus services in London and to privatize the now 12 operating units of LBL. Acknowledging the already severe traffic congestion problems of the capital, the Department of Transport would be accompanying deregulation with a review of bus lanes and other bus priority measures.

Having been mooted for 1995, deregulation was again deferred. However, the further franchising of routes and comprehensive privatization of London's bus operating companies during 1994–5 appeared to satisfy government intent. Indeed, following relatively favourable comments concerning the efficiency, cost reduction and patronage support of the London franchising system compared to full deregulation elsewhere in the country (e.g. Mackie *et al.*, 1995), there were signs that the Conservative Government were beginning to rethink their policy approach to bus service provision.

Privatization of the Bus Operating Industry

The 1985 Act provided for the sale of the National Bus Company (NBC) in whole or in part to the private sector within three years. Its constituent companies were subsequently divided into three groups of non-adjacent operating areas, in order that sales of adjacent companies should not be sold to the same purchaser and thereby establish a geographical monopoly. On the other hand, to ensure that no NBC company was too big to dissuade competitors from taking advantage of deregulation, in February 1986 the government insisted that the four largest NBC companies be broken down into smaller units before deregulation day. The main short-term aims were therefore to produce medium-sized companies

without monopolistic advantage but with commercial appeal.

The NBC had been the world's largest bus and coach operator, at its height employing 80 000 staff and running 20 000 vehicles. By the time of privatization these numbers had been reduced to 48 000 and 14 000 respectively. By mid-1988 all NBC subsidiaries and assets had been sold, well within the three-year period stipulated by the 1985 Act. Of the 62 NBC subsidiary companies disposed of, 18 were sold to a single bidder for less than their asset value, with, in some cases, discounts of more than 65 per cent (Department of Transport, 1990).

The 1985 Act also required local authorities and PTEs to transfer their bus operations to separate public-transport companies and the government soon made it clear that this was just one step towards full privatization of municipal and PTE bus operations, a process that was almost complete by 1997.

Increasingly, inter-company take overs helped to establish a limited number of large private groupings such that, after 10 years, perhaps the most notable trend to have emerged from privatization has been the rise of new and older corporate names such as FirstGroup (formerly FirstBus), Arriva (formerly Cowie) and Stagecoach, expanding through takeover, merger and not a little predatory operational activity in some cases. Further, having replaced public near-monopolies by private near-monopolies, but just short of the extent that would cause the Monopolies and Mergers Commission to intervene, the industry has seen the stronger bus companies moving into rail privatization and pursuing new forms of horizontal integration.

The company most emblematic of deregulation and privatization is Stagecoach, which started from small beginnings in Perth in response to coach service deregulation in 1980. Britain's largest bus company by the early to mid-1990s, by 1997 Stagecoach had dropped to number three in terms of size of fleet behind FirstBus and the Cowie Group (now renamed Arriva). But by then UK bus operations only accounted for a quarter of the Stagecoach group's business. During 1996, acquisitions of Swebus, which made it the biggest operator in Scandinavia, and securing the franchises for UK's South West Trains and Island Line (Isle of Wight) and the train leasing company Porterbrook Leasing, more than doubled the size of the Stagecoach group, producing an annualized turnover of £1.4 billion (Anon., 1997). Other overseas bus operations involve activities in New Zealand, Malawi, Kenya, Portugal, Norway, Denmark and Finland. In total 18 British passenger rail company franchises passed to groups with strong bus operating interests.

Minibuses: the user-friendly symbols of deregulation?

Until the mid-1980s, the operation of minibuses as public-transport vehicles had been restricted to relatively small numbers, small group private-hire work or remote rural services. The UK legal definition of a "minibus" still refers to a vehicle of between nine and 16 seats, but usually public minibuses can carry between 16 and 25 seated passengers. Use of the term "midibus" is often applied to vehicles of the 25 to 35 seating capacity range, which confusingly includes shortened versions of standard single-deck vehicles, and stretched versions of minibuses.

From a local experiment in Exeter in 1984, the operation of minibuses by large bus companies grew rapidly, encouraged by the *Buses* White Paper (Department of Transport, 1984). The changing nature of the labour market also encouraged minibus introduction, as wages in the industry were being depressed through the elimination of national agreements, and with three million people nationally unemployed, bus companies outside South-East England were well placed to offer lower salary levels to minibus drivers. The Transport Act 1980 reinforced this process by lowering the minimum age for public service vehicle (PSV) drivers from 21 to 18. Indeed, it could be argued that an important underlying aim of large-scale minibus deployment was to depress wage rates. Minibus working agreements in some cases hastened the demise of national pay and conditions of service negotiating frameworks, while in others they followed in the wake of such disintegration. Given the economies of small bus oper-

ation, large fleets of minibuses could only have been deployed on an economically viable basis with driver wage levels significantly lower than they had been in the 1970s.

NBC subsidiaries led this rapid development (Turner and White, 1987), with over 500 minibuses purchased by major companies in 1985, compared to 83 in 1984 and just 22 in 1983. Such purchases, coupled with the ending of bus grants in 1984, together with a growing uncertainty of what lay beyond the 1985 Act, saw the beginnings of a slump in new full-size bus purchases: for the 1983–5 period, NBC company PSV deliveries as a whole decreased by 37.8 per cent.

Immediately prior to deregulation, in October 1986, some 1800 minibuses were being operated by former or current NBC subsidiaries. By the end of 1986, after the initial impact of deregulation, some 3000 minibuses were in regular service, and by the end of 1987, the figure for those in operation with major companies was approaching 6000. By contrast, approximately 55 000 full-size buses remained in operation (White and Turner, 1987). The reasons for this growth in such a relatively short period reflected the need for companies to establish and maintain a "competitive edge" in preparation for the new "market" conditions of deregulation. Minibuses were seen to be able to fulfil several criteria (Hall, 1988):

1. To increase the frequency of service.
2. To improve service penetration of outlying residential areas along roads that were unsuitable for larger buses.
3. To permit passengers to board and alight anywhere safe along the route through the taxi-like "hail-and-ride" system. This practice also obviated the need to provide bus stops, thereby enhancing the potential flexibility of service provision.
4. To provide a faster service through the use of smaller vehicles with good acceleration and fewer passengers to pick up and set down.
5. To provide a friendlier service. Smaller vehicles were often marketed in such a way as to

encourage personal identification, with regular, familiar and specially trained drivers employed to reinforce a "customer-friendly" on-board atmosphere.

However, if the government aimed to encourage the small private operator or completely new small bus businesses, their objective was confounded by the highly protective actions of the pre-existing major companies in wishing to maintain, and even enhance, their market share. NBC bulk purchases of at least 1500 minibuses – buying out the complete remaining UK production runs in 1986 – did not represent entrepreneurial enterprise so much as panic buying to keep out the potential deregulated competition. Further, novel, eye-catching liveries and fleet names were adopted, and new forms of "product marketing" came to the fore.

For more than a decade, minibuses have been a familiar sight on many urban streets. If they are the only major tangible innovation to have arisen out of deregulation, their low cost, often crude structure and operational flexibility symbolized the early stages of the process (Photograph 4.3). The development of larger, more sophisticated vehicles, often barely distinguishable from "full-size" buses, has represented one element of a maturing post-deregulation bus operating environment. But with a renaissance of confidence in the industry, the 1990s has witnessed a return of substantial large orders for

Photograph 4.3 Minibus operation in residential areas
An Aline Mercedes minibus in suburban Gateshead reveals two elements of deregulation: (a) the Tyne and Wear PTE sticker over the nearside windscreen to indicate that the vehicle is operating a subsidized "secured" service, and (b) the hand-written route numbers and lack of route information blinds, suggesting that the operating company was ill-prepared on the first day of its taking over the route from Go-Ahead Northern (D.R. Hall)

new buses, and thus far, one of the major success stories of the decade has been the substantial re-entry into the bus manufacturing market of Dennis Vehicles with its particularly popular single-deck, full-size vehicles.

Deregulation of the taxi industry

In England, entry deregulation in the taxi trade was introduced in January 1986 when the discretion previously granted to local authorities to limit the number of "hackney carriages" in their area was abolished. Three subsequent nationwide studies of taxi licensing policy suggest that it has attained only limited success (Toner, 1996). Vehicle numbers have not increased at a noticeably greater rate in districts that have deregulated, and there is little evidence to suggest that increased competition in deregulated districts has resulted in lower fares. In restricted markets, a substantial and increasing licence premium is enjoyed by licence holders. In deregulated districts, generally lower standards of quality enforcement have been observed along with severe shortages of rank capacity. This suggests that further liberalization, without concomitant requirements to ensure fares and quality requirements are set appropriately, is unlikely to yield significant benefits to consumers. Studies in Canada (Cairns and Listonheyes, 1996) and Sweden (Garling et al., 1995) tend to confirm such views.

Overall effects

An impartial observer might argue that the credit/debit balance sheet for the British road public-transport deregulation and privatization process was roughly balanced out. Urban trunk routes witnessed more buses, greater frequencies, and in some cases cheaper fares as the result of competition, but often at the expense of congestion and increased traffic hazards. More especially, just as in the previous US deregulation of air transport or the UK deregulation of coach services, the trade-off saw reduced services in less-populated and less- or non-profitable areas. In the case of bus services this has meant poorer rural and off-peak and Sunday urban services.

In the late 1990s – with increasing widespread concern over the negative externalities of road traffic pollution, congestion, exploitation of finite fossil fuels, accidents and health hazards – a major longer-term criticism has been the loss of the ability to use local bus services as an instrument of urban planning policy (Mackie et al., 1995; Tyson, 1995; Simpson, 1996). Some local authorities – often in public–private sector partnerships – have grasped the opportunity to assist the development of "supertram" light rail schemes, partly at least so as to be in a position to exert a more direct influence over shifting modal splits, environmental impacts, the spatial distribution of urban road transport and major retailing, recreational and other land uses associated with it (Owens, 1995; Knowles, 1996; Hall, 1998).

Rail Privatization

Privatization of heavily subsidized State-owned railways presents a formidable challenge to the private sector to increase revenue quickly and reduce costs.

Japan

Japan was the first major industrialized country to privatize a heavily subsidized State-owned railway (Winston and Kuranami, 1996). Japanese National Railways (JNR) was privatized in 1987 having previously received an average annual subsidy of $4.9 billion. JNR was divided geographically into six potentially profitable passenger companies and a single break-even Japanese Freight Railway, whilst the loss-making JNR Settlement Corporation deals with inherited long-term JNR debt and remains unprofitable. Annual government subsidy has now been reduced to $1.2 billion. The three passenger companies on the main island of Honshu each contain high-speed *Shinkansen* services and are very profitable whilst the companies serving the three smaller islands of Hokkaido, Kyushu and Shikoku are just profitable (Figure 4.1, Table 4.1). This turnaround from heavy public-sector subsidy to private-sector profitability has been achieved by cost cutting through labour shedding and three-fold productivity

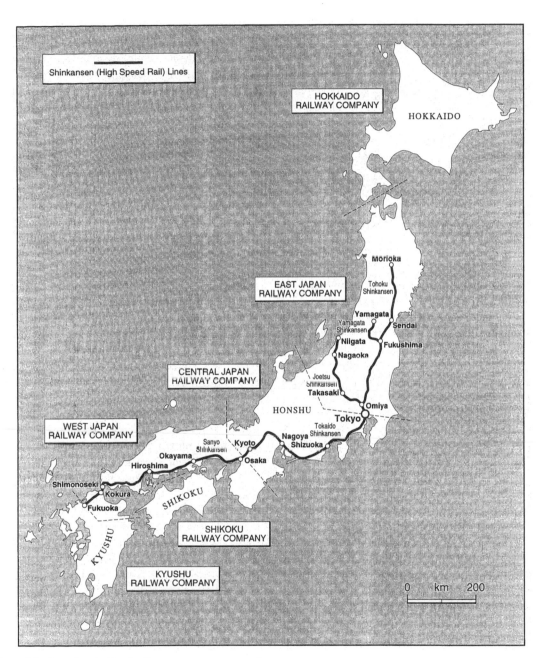

Figure 4.1 Japan's privatized railway passenger companies

Table 4.1   Japanese railway company profitability, 1996
(billion yen)

Railway Company	Revenue*	Pre-tax Profit/Loss	Percentage
East Japan	1956.3	103.0	5.3
Central Japan	1108.9	64.7	5.8
West Japan	940.4	52.0	5.5
Kyushu	176.8	1.8	1.0
Shikoku	50.2	0.2	0.4
Japan Freight	205.7	0.2	0.1
Hokkaido	105.2	−3.7	−3.5
Total	4543.5	218.2	4.8

*Projected.
Source of data: *Nikkei Weekly*, 15 April 1996, in Winston and Kuranami (1996).

increases between 1981 and 1991 and by increasing revenue through real estate developments on railway-owned land and better marketing of services. The increased emphasis by the privatized railway companies on successful non-railway enterprises, such as real estate development, offers a lot of potential for rail privatization in other Asian countries where urban real estate markets are more similar to Japan's than those of European and North American countries (Winston and Kuranami, 1996).

Great Britain

British Rail, State-owned since 1948, was privatized in two phases. Firstly, in the 1980s the non-railway businesses such as British Transport Docks Board, British Transport Hotels and Sealink Ferries were sold as were some non-core rail businesses such as station catering and rolling stock construction and repair (Farrington, 1985; Gibb *et al.*, 1996). Private-sector investment in freight terminals, wagons and locomotives was also encouraged. Secondly, under the provisions of the Railways Act 1993, the core passenger and freight rail businesses were privatized between 1994 and 1997. The privatized rail industry is highly regulated under the control of a Rail Regulator and a Director of Passenger Rail Franchising.

Railtrack, a separate infrastructure company, was created in 1994 by taking over British Rail's track, signalling, stations, land and depots, and was privatized in 1996. Its income comes from charging train operators for access to the network, by leasing stations and depots and by developing railway land. Railtrack is also required to invest in improved infrastructure. The Rail Regulator grants licences to operate railway assets, regulates access to track, stations and depots, and enforces domestic competition laws.

The seven rail freight transport businesses were privatized in 1995 and 1996. US-owned Wisconsin Central bought five of them: the three domestic bulk commodity companies Loadhaul, Mainline and Transrail (renamed English, Welsh and Scottish Railways); International Freight, which handles European intermodal and automotive freight mainly via the Channel Tunnel; and Post Office mail. Freightliner, which handles domestic intermodal freight mainly carrying containers between inland terminals and major ports, and Red Star Express parcels were both sold to management buy-outs.

Three Rolling Stock Companies (ROSCOs), which were created by transferring British Rail's railcars, carriages and passenger locomotives, were privatized in 1996. Their income comes from leasing rolling stock to passenger operators. Twenty-five Train Operating Companies (TOCs) were created to operate passenger services in designated and largely discrete areas, most stations and depots. The 25 TOCs were franchised by the Office of Passenger Rail Franchising (OPRAF) to the private sector by competitive tender to minimize OPRAF subsidies or maximize premium payments to OPRAF. The franchises, which came into operation between February 1996 and March 1997, are for periods of between five and 15 years, but are mostly for about seven years. Passenger Service Requirements specified a minimum service level for each franchise at or close to previous British Rail levels. Most franchises also require investments in station and rolling stock and specified service enhancements. Most ticket prices are regulated at or below the Retail Price Index and incentive or penalty payments are intended to secure punctuality and reliability.

This complex, highly regulated and bureaucratic structure more than doubled the pre-privatization Government rail subsidy of £1.07 billion in 1993/94 to £2.19 billion in 1996/97 due mainly to high Railtrack access charges and ROSCO leasing charges (Bradshaw, 1996; Knowles, 1998) (Photograph 4.4). Sliding-scale franchise payments will reduce the total subsidy paid to £1.84 billion in 1997/98, the first full year of private rail operation, to £1.09 billion in 2001/02 and £0.54 billion in the final year of all 25 franchises, by which time eight TOCs will be making annual premium payments to OPRAF. To achieve these ambitious targets, the franchise operators need to secure substantial increases in revenue by better marketing and reduce costs particularly by increasing productivity. From the outset the bus industry has dominated the privatized passenger rail market by controlling 18 TOCs, and holding minority shares in a further two TOCs (Table 4.2). Two companies,

National Express Group and Prism Rail, control over one-third of the rail franchises. Where the same bus company also dominates the local bus market, this could provide customer benefits through integration of bus and rail timetables and fares or disbenefits through reduced bus services or increased bus fares.

CONCLUSIONS

Since the late 1970s a wave of transport deregulation and privatization has swept across the world predicated on the theory that transport markets are contestable and that competition would generate consumer benefit and lower public subsidies. Deregulation and privatization have been encouraged by "New Right" politicians and have become prerequisites for international financial institutions offering aid and restructuring packages to indebted

Photograph 4.4 Manchester Piccadilly Station
The complex structure of Britain's privatized railways is illustrated at Manchester Piccadilly railway station, one of only 14 large stations operated as well as owned by Railtrack – all other stations are owned by Railtrack but operated by a Train Operating Company. From Manchester Piccadilly trains are operated by six TOCs – North Western Trains, Inter City West Coast, Virgin Cross Country (all illustrated here), Regional Railways North East, Central Trains and ScotRail (R.D. Knowles)

Table 4.2   Control of British passenger rail franchises

Franchises	Franchise Revenue*		Franchises		Train Operating Companies
	£ million	(%)	Number	(%)	
Bus industry	**2873.0**	**67.0**	**18**	**72**	
National Express Group plc	837.8	19.5	5	20	Central Trains; Gatwick Express; Midland Main Line; North London Railways; ScotRail
Connex Rail Ltd	601.0	14.0	2	8	South Central; South Eastern
Prism Rail plc	397.7	9.3	4	16	Cardiff Railway Company; LTS Rail; South Wales & West; West Anglia Great Northern
MTL Trust Holdings Ltd	391.9	9.1	2	8	Merseyrail Electrics; RR North East
Stagecoach Holdings plc	337.4	7.9	2	8	Island Line; South West Trains
Go-Ahead Group plc†	158.2	3.7	2	8	Thameslink; Thames Trains
FirstBus plc	149.0	3.5	1	4	Great Eastern (and 24.5% of Great Western Trains and North Western Trains)
Others	**861.1**	**20.1**	**4**	**16**	
Virgin Rail Group Ltd	516.7	12.1	2	8	CrossCountry Trains; West Coast Trains
Sea Containers Ltd	270.5	6.3	1	4	Great North Eastern Railway
GB Railways Group plc	73.9	1.7	1	4	Anglia Railways
Management buy-outs (MBOs)	**551.4**	**12.9**	**3**	**12**	
Great Western Holdings	512.9	12.0	2	8	Great Western Trains; North Western Trains
M40 Trains Ltd	38.5	0.9	1	4	Chiltern Railways

*Fares revenue 1995/96 plus year 1 subsidy or less year 1 premium payment.
†GOVIA (Via GTI 35%) and Victory Railway Holdings Ltd (MBO 35%).
Source: Knowles (1998).

governments, especially in the less-developed world. However, in most cases transport markets have proven to be not fully contestable with oligopoly control by the private sector replacing previous public-sector monopolies. Although consumers have usually benefited from lower prices on US domestic air services and British express buses, the use of Regulators has been necessary to ensure consumer benefit in the privatized British rail industry. Franchising transport services through competitive tendering for fixed-period contracts has proven to be more successful than open competition. Private operation of transport has proven to be usually more efficient and innovative but the main beneficiary has been the taxpayer as the amount of government subsidy for transport services has fallen sharply and in some cases has been eliminated.

REFERENCES

Adeniji, K. (1983), "Nigerian municipal bus operations", *Transportation Quarterly* 37 (1), 135–43.

Anderson, P. (1990), "Jamaica's urban bus system: deregulation or public responsibility", in Gayle, D.J. and Goodrich, J. N. (eds), *Privatization and deregulation in global perspective,* (London: Pinter), ch. 15.

Anon. (1997), "Stagecoach aims for £2 billion turnover", *Buses* 49 (503), 9.

Ashworth, M. and Forsyth, P. (1984), *Civil aviation policy and the privatization of British Airways* (London: Institute of Fiscal Studies).

Bailey, E.E. and Baumol, W. J. (1984), "Deregulation and the theory of contestable markets", *Yale Journal on Regulation* 1 (2), 111–38.

Balcombe, R.J., Hopkin, J.M. and Perrett, K.E. (1988), *Bus deregulation in Great Britain: a review of the first year,* TRRL Report RR161 (Crowthorne, UK: Transport and Road Research Laboratory).

Banjo, G.A. (1994), "Deregulation of urban public transport services", *Third World Planning Review* 16 (4), 411–28.

Baumol, W.J. (1982), "Contestable markets: an uprising in the theory of industrial structure", *American Economic Review* 72, 1–15.

Baumol, W.J., Panzar, J.C. and Willig, R.W. (1982), *Contestable markets and the theory of industrial structure* (New York: Harcourt, Brace and Jovanovich).

Bell, P. and Cloke, P. (eds) (1990), *Deregulation and transport: market forces in the modern world* (London: Fulton).

Bhattacharyya, A., Kumbhakar, S.C. and Bhattacharyya, A. (1995), "Ownership structure and cost efficiency: a study of publicly owned passenger-bus transportation companies in India", *Journal of Productivity Analysis* 6 (1), 47–61.

Bradshaw, B. (1996), "The real costs of rail privatization", *Public Transport Information* 8 (4), 8–9.

British Airways (1997), *Reports and accounts 1996–97* (London: British Airways).

Bureau of Transportation Statistics (1996), *Transportation statistics annual report 1996* (Washington, DC: US Department of Transportation).

Button, K.J. (ed.) (1991), *Airline deregulation: international experiences* (London: Fulton).

Button, K.J. and Gillingwater, D. (1986), *Future transport policy* (London: Routledge).

Cairns, R.D. and Listonheyes, C. (1996), "Competition and regulation in the taxi industry", *Journal of Public Economics* 59 (1), 1–15.

Debbage, K.G. (1994), "The international airline industry: globalization, regulation and strategic alliances", *Journal of Transport Geography* 2 (3), 190–203.

Dempsey, P.S. and Goetz, A.R. (1992), *Airline deregulation and laissez-faire mythology* (Westport, CT: Quorum Books).

Department of Transport (1984), *Buses* (London: HMSO).

Department of Transport (1987), *Transport statistics Great Britain 1976–1986* (London: HMSO).

Department of Transport (1990), *Sale of the National Bus Company. Report by the Controller and Auditor General* (London: HMSO).

Department of Transport (1991), *A bus strategy for London*, Consultation Paper S15/21 (London: HMSO).

Evans, A. (1988), "Hereford: a case-study of bus deregulation", *Journal of Transport Economics and Policy* 22 (3), 283–306.

Fairhurst, M. and Edwards, D. (1996), "Bus travel trends in the UK", *Transport Reviews* 16 (2), 157–67.

Farrington, J.H. (1985), "Transport geography and policy: deregulation and privatisation", *Transactions of the Institute of British Geographers NS* 101, 109–19.

Fullerton, B. (1990), "Deregulation in a European context – the case of Sweden", in Bell, P. and Cloke, P. (eds), *Deregulation and transport: market forces in the modern world* (London: Fulton), 125–40.

Fullerton, B. and Knowles, R.D. (1991), *Scandinavia* (London: Paul Chapman).

Garling, T., Laitila, T., Marell, A. and Westin, K. (1995), "A note on the short-term effects of deregulation of the Swedish taxi-cab industry", *Journal of Transport Economics and Policy* 19 (2), 209–14.

Gayle, D.J. and Goodrich, J.N. (eds) (1990), *Privatisation and deregulation in global perspective* (London: Pinter).

Gibb, R., Lowndes, T. and Charlton, C. (1996), "The privatization of British Rail", *Applied Geography* 16 (1), 35–51.

Graham, B. (1995), *Geography and air transport* (Chichester: Wiley).

Graham, B. (1997), "Air transport liberalization in the European Union: an assessment", *Regional Studies* 31 (8), 807–12.

Green, D. (1987), *The New Right – the counter revolution in political, economic and social thought* (London: Wheatsheaf).

The Guardian (1991a), "When freedom turns out to be licence", 11 February (London).

The Guardian (1991b), "Anglo–US deal widens air horizons", 12 March (London).

Hall, D.R. (1988), "The changing nature of minibus technology and deployment in UK public transport strategies with particular reference to the Tyne and Wear area", in Tolley, R.S. (ed.) *Transport technology and spatial change* (Stoke-on-Trent: Transport Geography Study Group, Institute of British Geographers), 31–78.

Hall, D.R. (1993a), "Impacts of economic and political transition on the transport geography of Central and Eastern Europe", *Journal of Transport Geography* 1 (1), 20–35.

Hall, D. R. (ed.) (1993b), *Transport and economic development in the new Central and Eastern Europe* (London: Belhaven).

Hall, D.R. (1998), "Urban transport environmental pressures and policy options", in Pinder, D.A. (ed.), *The new Europe* (Chichester: Wiley), 435–54.

Hibbs, J. (1985), "Bus licensing – arbitration or franchise", in Knowles, R.D. (ed.), *Implications of the 1985 Transport Bill* (Salford: Transport Geography Study Group, Institute of British Geographers), 35–44.

Higginson, M. (1990), "Introduction to international transport deregulation", in Bell, P. and Cloke, P. (eds), *Deregulation and transport: market forces in the modern world* (London: Fulton), 53–64.

Jenkins, R. (1995), *Gladstone* (London: Macmillan).

Kahn, A.E. (1988), "Surprises of airline deregulation", *American Economic Review; Papers and Proceedings* 78, 316–22.

Kang, Y.I. (1995), "The development of urban bus regulatory policy in Korea reviewed", *Transport Reviews* 15 (4), 357–70.

Kennedy, D. (1995), "London bus tendering – an overview", *Transport Reviews* 15 (3), 253–64.

Knowles, R.D. (ed.) (1985) *Implications of the 1985 Transport Bill* (Salford: Transport Geography Study Group, Institute of British Geographers).

Knowles, R.D. (1989), "Urban public transport in Thatcher's Britain", in Knowles, R.D. (ed.), *Transport policy and urban development: methodology and evaluation* (Salford: Transport Geography Study Group, Institute of British Geographers), 79–104.

Knowles, R.D. (1996), "Transport impacts of Greater Manchester's Metrolink light rail system", *Journal of Transport Geography* 4 (1), 1–14.

Knowles, R.D. (1998), "Passenger rail privatization in Great Britain and its implications, especially for urban areas", *Journal of Transport Geography* 6(2), 117–33.

Koprich, D.F. (1994), "The modernization of Santiago's public transport, 1990–1992", *Transport Reviews* 14 (2), 167–85.

Leyshon, A. (1992), "The transformation of regulatory order – regulating the global economy and environment", *Geoforum* 23 (3), 249–67.

Mackie, P., Preston, J.M. and Nash, C.A. (1995), "Bus deregulation: ten years on", *Transport Reviews* 15, 229–51.

Maunder, D.A.C., Mbara, T.C. and Khezwana, M. (1994), "The effect of institutional changes on stage bus performance in Harare, Zimbabwe", *Transport Reviews* 14 (2), 151–65.

Meersman, H. and van de Voorde, E. (1996), "The privatization of air transport in Europe", *Built Environment* 22 (3), 177–91.

Mellor, R.E.H. (1975), "The Soviet concept of a unified transport system and the contemporary role of the railways", in Symons, L. and White, C. (eds), *Russian transport: an historical and geographical survey* (London: Bell), 75–105.

Mercer, A. and Tielin, D. (1996), "Competitive tendering strategies in the bus industry", *Journal of the Operational Research Society* 47 (12), 1452–60.

Monopolies and Mergers Commission (1987), *BA plc and BCal plc – a report on the proposed merger* (London: Monopolies and Mergers Commission).

Neff, J. (1998), "Government investment in transit before 1940", unpublished paper presented at the Association of American Geographers Annual Meeting, Boston, MA (Washington, DC: American Public Transit Association).

Owens, S. (1995), "Transport land-use planning and climate change: what prospects for new policies in the UK?", *Journal of Transport Geography* 3 (2), 143–5.

Pickrell, D. (1991), "The regulation and deregulation of US airlines", in Button, K.J. (ed.) *Airline deregulation: international experiences* (London: Fulton), 5–47.

Reed, P. (1995), "Flying into trouble", *New Economy* 2 (1), 9–13.

Rickard, J.M., *et al.* (1988), *Deregulation of local bus services: interim results from non-metropolitan study areas* (Crowthorne, UK: Transport and Road Research Laboratory).

Rimmer, P.J. (1986), *Rikisha to rapid transit: urban public transport systems and policy in Southeast Asia* (Sydney: Pergamon).

Scrafton, D. (1997), "Transport deregulation in Australia and the changing role of the private sector", paper presented at the Transport Geography Research Group symposium, Exeter.

Sealy, K. (1966), *Geography of air transport* (London: Hutchinson).

Simon, D. (1996), *Transport and development in the third world* (London: Routledge).

Simpson, B.J. (1996), "Deregulation and privatization – the British local bus industry following the Transport Act 1995", *Transport Reviews* 16 (3), 213–23.

Small, N.O. (1993), "A victim of geography, not policy? Canada's airline industry since deregulation", *Journal of Transport Geography* 1 (3), 182–94.

Thomson, J.M. (1978), *Great cities and their traffic* (Harmondsworth: Peregrine).

Toner, J.P. (1996), "English experience of deregulation of the taxi industry", *Transport Reviews* 16 (1), 79–94.

Turner, R. and White, P. (1987), *NBC's urban minibuses: a review and financial appraisal* (Crowthorne, UK: Transport and Road Research Laboratory).

Tyson, W.J. (1988), *The first year of bus deregulation* (London: Association of Metropolitan Authorities).

Tyson, W.J. (1989), *A review of the second year of bus deregulation* (London: Association of Metropolitan Authorities).

Tyson, W.J. (1995), "Bus deregulation – the planning dilemma", *Transport Reviews* 15 (4), 307–13.

White, P.R. (1995), "Deregulation of local bus services in Great Britain – an introductory review", *Transport Reviews* 15 (2), 185–209.

White, P.R. (1997), "What conclusions can be drawn about bus deregulation in Britain?", *Transport Reviews* 17 (1), 1–16.

White, P.R. and Tough, S. (1995), "Alternative tendering systems and deregulation in Britain", *Journal of Transport Economics and Policy* 29 (3), 275.

White, P.R. and Turner, R. (1987), "Minibuses: the way ahead?", paper presented to Planning and Transport Research and Computation (PTRC) International Association Conference.

Winston, B. and Kuranami, C. (1996), "Effects of rail privatization in Japan", in Salveson, P. (ed.), *World railway equipment and technology update 1996/7* (London: Kensington Publications), 230–33.

5

Transport and the Environment

Colin Hunter, John Farrington and William Walton

This chapter considers the relationship between transport and the environment, focusing on major environmental impacts associated with transport development and on policies aimed at dealing with these impacts. Concern about the environmental consequences of transport development and operation is not new, and the historical context is significant. Transport has taken a central position in the environmental debate, and relationships between transport and sustainability are outlined. Five specific types of impacts of transport on the environment and their mitigation are analysed. Policies designed to address the most critical problem of air pollution from transport emissions in the UK and the USA are examined. Measures to improve air quality in urban areas are the most favoured method of moving towards sustainable transport activity.

INTRODUCTION

The Historical Context

Concern over the environmental consequences of transport development is long-standing. For example, many canal and railway proposals in Britain faced opposition from landowners, artists and urban authorities throughout the eighteenth and nineteenth centuries on environmental grounds, including visual intrusion, land-take and land severance (Carpenter, 1994). When the objection was successful, the canal or railway company would have to make a concession, such as a route alteration. If a canal or railway caused severance to a landed property by dividing it, an occupation bridge could be built. If the general amenity of a landscape was threatened by the sight and sound of the barges on a canal or by the passage of steam locomotives, then screening by cutting, tunnelling or even re-routing might be the only way of placating the opposition. A railway company might be obliged to construct an extensive Italianate station building or a mock-Gothic tunnel portal to meet a landowner's demands. More far-reaching consequences resulted from the successful opposition in 1882 by Canon Rawnsley to the building of a railway along the shores of Derwentwater in the Lake District. Rawnsley's experience led him to become one of three founder members of the National Trust (Battrick, 1982).

The canals and railways of Britain gave rise to considerable environmental impacts, both directly in their construction and operation, and indirectly through the industrial and other land uses they encouraged. Kellett (1979) gives details of the impacts of railways in the five largest cities in Victorian England and Scotland. The main direct impacts on the urban environment were in land-take, severance and housing demolition. The land-take of railways in

Modern Transport Geography: second, revised edition. Edited by Brian Hoyle and Richard Knowles.
© 1998 John Wiley & Sons Ltd.

central areas of cities in 1900 varied between 5.3 per cent in Birmingham and 9.0 per cent in Liverpool. Similar proportions were apparent in US cities, with a high of 12.8 per cent in a major transit point like Kansas City (Kellett, 1979, 290). Large blocks of land were also required for railway use in the areas outside the central districts of cities. Connection between these facilities required many lines, often elevated on embankments, which frequently created a barrier effect between housing areas. Demolition of inner-area housing arose from the construction of large urban railway terminals and their approaches. Approximately 20 000 people were displaced by demolition for railway purposes in central Glasgow, and at least 120 000 people in London between 1840 and 1900 (Kellett, 1979, 327). These were mainly in slum areas where tenants had no chance to prevent demolition.

Growing Awareness of a Growing Problem

It is clear that transport's environmental impacts, and concern about them, is not new, but our level of awareness is now much greater than it was. The environmental implications of transport development have become very widely recognized, with a plethora of local, national and international governmental and non-governmental organizations contributing to the debate by producing their own policy prescriptions and agendas for action. In part, this heightened concern reflects the growing importance of transport to the functioning of modern societies and, more generally, a greater awareness of a range of environmental issues, such as pollution, the loss of natural habitats and the possibility of global environmental change. Another factor in this concern is the growth in transport activity in general, and in road transport in particular. The number of vehicles in Britain increased from 2 million in 1950 to 9 million in 1963 and in 1996 to 26.3 million. Forecasts suggest that the 1996 total of 22.2 million cars could double in number by 2025, reaching levels already seen in the USA, where there is close to one car per person on average. It is thought that this is getting close to a saturation level, but there is also a trend for cars to be used to travel greater distances, and for a greater proportion of trips, so that overall traffic can still grow. The distance travelled by car in Britain increased 10-fold between 1952 and 1993 (Royal Commission on Environmental Pollution, 1994).

Many observers feel that this growth, which has given millions of people unprecedented mobility, cannot be sustained and threatens vital aspects of the environment and of human life itself. Increasingly, the debate surrounding transport development and environmental quality is arousing strong passions (House of Lords, 1996), and transport has taken a central position in the environmental debate generally, as exemplified by Banister (1998) and Banister and Button (1993). Transport produces approximately one-third of the greenhouse gases in the UK. For comparison, the use of energy in buildings contributes about half, of which two-thirds is from housing (Building Research Establishment, 1991).

In considering the relationship between transport and the environment we are immediately confronted with a potential paradox: on the one hand, modern industrial societies (and those seeking this description) pursue economic growth through the open exchange of people, raw materials, energy, goods and services in an increasingly global marketplace, yet, on the other, the transport systems required to allow such exchanges may be exerting pressures on the environment that degrade the functional integrity and quality of natural ecosystems to the extent that the prospect of maintaining or achieving a high quality of life in many human societies is threatened. In short, we cannot apparently live without transport development, but neither may we be able to cope with its side-effects over the long term. This view, although simplistic, is nonetheless reflected in important policy statements. The European Union's Fifth Environmental Action Programme, for example, states that transport is "vital to the distribution of goods and services, and to trade and to regional development" (Commission of the European Communities, 1992, 6), but argues that current trends towards increasing transport demand are likely to result in "greater inefficiency, congestion, pollution, wastage of time and value, danger to life and general economic loss" (*ibid.*, 33).

In trying to reconcile the apparent contradiction between transport development and environmental protection, a possible way forward in terms of guiding principles may be found in the broader concept of "sustainable development". Following the publication of the Brundtland Commission's report *Our common future* (World Commission on Environment and Development, 1987), sustainable development has become a very widely used phrase, which captures the need to achieve the continued socio-economic development of human societies in ways that adequately protect the natural resources which ultimately provide opportunities for development both now and for future generations. In other words, sustainable development is "a process of change in which the exploitation of resources, the direction of investments, the orientation of technological development, and institutional change are all in harmony and enhance both current and future potential to meet human needs and aspirations" (*ibid.*, 46).

A complex debate on the precise conditions and requirements of sustainable development has emerged, and still continues, following the Brundtland report. While an account of this debate is outside the scope of this chapter (but is dealt with more fully in Chapter 15), what can be said is that, despite profound disagreement on how the term can and should be interpreted (see, for example, Turner *et al.*, 1994), sustainable development as a headline concept retains an appeal in terms of its succinct description of a need for some kind of change in the way societies exploit natural resources. The importance of sustainable development was reaffirmed with its adoption as the basis for global development at the 1992 Earth Summit in Rio de Janeiro. This summit culminated in the Declaration on Environment and Development, and was accompanied by a global plan of action agreed by 179 nations, which is commonly referred to as Agenda 21. Although none of the 40 chapters of Agenda 21 deals specifically with transport, Longhurst *et al.* (1996) point out that the principles set out in many of the chapters, such as those concerned with protecting the atmosphere and land management, carry direct implications for the transport sector.

In the light of the above discussion, it is possible to formulate a perception of "sustainable transport" as the contribution of transport development to the sustainable development of human societies more broadly. This approach has been adopted by the UK government, for example, in its strategy for sustainable development (Department of the Environment, 1994). Chapter 26 of this strategy considers transport. The strategy recognizes the dependence of commerce and industry on an effective transport system, and the role of transport in shaping contemporary social and recreational lifestyles. The following aspects are provided as critical components of a sustainable transport framework (*ibid.*, 169):

1. To strike the right balance between the ability of transport to serve economic development and the ability to protect the environment and sustain future quality of life.
2. To provide for the economic and social needs for access with less need for travel.
3. To take measures that reduce the environmental impact of transport and influence the rate of traffic growth.
4. To ensure that users pay the full social and environmental costs of their transport decisions, so improving the overall efficiency of those decisions for the economy as a whole and bringing environmental benefits.

This chapter examines some of the major environmental impacts of transport infrastructure development, and ends with an examination of policy approaches and techniques designed to better manage transport impacts. The implications of applying sustainability to transport are discussed more fully in Chapter 15.

TRANSPORT MODES AND UNDERSTANDING ENVIRONMENTAL IMPACT

The impact of transport development depends in large part on the nature of the transport proposal, i.e. its mode and purpose. The major types of transport system are shown in Table 5.1. Potentially, infrastructure development associated with any of these transport systems could result in a very large number of changes to the environment both locally and at a larger scale. These changes could encompass alterations to natural and built components of the physical environment, or impacts on the social and economic activities of the local and wider human population. This chapter focuses on negative (adverse) changes to the natural environment, including related impacts on human health, although the issue of energy consumption is not considered, being the subject of detailed analysis elsewhere in this book.

In keeping with any other type of development project, a transport infrastructure development may give rise to environmental impacts in one of three ways:

- due to its physical presence (e.g. land-take, visual intrusion);
- due to its use of resources (e.g. fossil fuels, building materials);
- due to its generation of waste (e.g. emission of air pollutants).

In the environmental assessment of development proposals it is also the convention to consider potential impacts during the construction, operational and decommissioning (abandonment) phases of the project. Again, the impacts of specific transport projects can usefully be appraised using this temporal classification, although the abandonment phase is not usually considered as part of the environmental assessment of transport infrastructure proposals. In terms of the precise nature of individual environmental impacts, then these may be seen to be:

- positive (beneficial) or negative (adverse);
- short-term or long-term;
- reversible or irreversible;
- direct, indirect or induced;
- linear, nodal or areal;
- local, regional, national or global.

Factors that will determine the nature, magnitude and perceived significance of environmental impacts are not just related to the type of transport system and its associated vehicles. The geographical context or characteristics of the area affected will also be critical, as will characteristics of the transport operation such as the volume of traffic, traffic speed, the loads to be carried and their loading factors (i.e. how full vehicles will be). Given the often subtle differences in these factors between projects that might appear similar, the task of accurately predicting the nature and degree of environmental changes brought about by transport infrastructure developments is frequently extremely daunting. However, it is possible to categorize the major potential impacts of new infrastructure developments based upon a growing body of work conducted to assess the impacts of existing transport activities.

Table 5.1 Types of transport system

Mode	Purpose
Aircraft	Passenger/freight
Boat	
inland	Passenger/freight
marine	Passenger/freight
Road	Passenger/freight
Rail	Passenger/freight
Pipeline	Freight

MAJOR ENVIRONMENTAL IMPACTS OF TRANSPORT INFRASTRUCTURE DEVELOPMENT

Reviews such as those provided by the Department of the Environment (1994), the House of Lords (1996), Mwase (1996), Varma *et al.* (1992a,b) and Vougias (1992) allow the rapid synthesis of major, negative impacts of transport development on the natural environment. Such a synthesis is given in

Table 5.2. It is probably true to say that, of these impacts, it is air pollution that has received the greatest attention in recent years, particularly in relation to human health effects. However, all the potential impacts listed in Table 5.2 may be highly significant, certainly in a local context. Therefore, a brief description of each impact area is provided in the following paragraphs. It should become evident that impacts are often strongly interrelated, and not easily isolated from one another. For example, ecological degradation may occur as a direct consequence of land-take, or as a result of long-term exposure to a cocktail of transport-related air pollutants. In either case, the loss of biological diversity may have a knock-on impact on the aesthetic appeal of the local landscape.

Land Consumption and Landscape Damage

Obviously, the provision of land-based transport requires the direct utilization of land. Long strips of land are consumed, and large areas effectively divided into smaller ones (severance). Previous land uses, such as forestry, agriculture, housing and nature reserves, may be displaced, and zones adjacent to the new development rendered unsuitable for a wide range of activities. The latter aspect is true of pipelines carrying volatile materials (such as pressurized gas), for example, where a corridor of land along the route must be kept undeveloped for safety reasons, even if the pipeline itself causes no direct

Table 5.2 Major potential impacts of transport infrastructure development on the natural environment and human health

---

Nature of Impact

Land-take, severance and displacement
Landscape damage, loss of aesthetic quality
Disruption of hydrological processes and water
  pollution
Ecological degradation
Air pollution
Noise
Traffic accidents

---

consumption of land. Ironically, severance may seriously restrict the movement of people and animals between previously contiguous areas, with consequences for the quality of community life and the functional integrity of ecosystems.

Airports are such large blocks of land that they create severance in their particular location. Some severance effects, notably those of non-motorway type roads, are only partial, though increasing traffic density and speed increases the danger of pedestrian crossings on the same level. Traffic engineers have introduced more light-controlled crossings in recognition of this problem. The use of road tunnels or viaducts can reduce severance, especially in urban areas, though the latter introduce significant visual impact, and both solutions are costly. As remarked earlier, large-scale severance was first experienced in Britain by the Victorians, and an early example of proposed railway construction in Glasgow brought a comment which echoes much more recent concerns about the construction of motorways, airport runways and high-speed railways (*Citizen*, November 1845, quoted by Kellett, 1979, 235):

> Whatever comes in [the railway's] way will inevitably be crushed and trampled down. It cares as little for old associations as it does for old houses, and offer what opposition we will, every year that passes will see iron lines dashed with remorseless sweep, through the faded handwriting which bygone ages have left on the earth's surface.

Generally, roads are the most hungry in terms of land-take. In the UK, roads are estimated to occupy some 1.5 per cent of the land surface, with railways occupying substantially less, at around 0.2 per cent (Department of the Environment, 1994). It is possible to estimate the width of land lost to different modes of land transport as a function of passengers transported per hour. On this basis, roads may transport only some 225 passengers per metre width per hour (assuming 1.5 people per car), whereas rail may allow approximately 8700 passengers per metre width per hour to be transported (TEST, 1991). In short, roads generally require far more land area to transport the same volume of passengers (and freight) than do railways. Land consumption is not just a direct consequence of transport development; it may also occur indirectly as land is utilized for the extraction of the raw materials (principally aggregate) required for construction. An average of 76 000 tonnes of aggregate is required per kilometre of road lane, and approximately 90 million tonnes of aggregates are used in the UK every year in the construction and repair of roads (Royal Commission on Environmental Pollution, 1994).

Clearly, a major impact of transport-related land loss and land-use change may be a decline in the visual amenity or aesthetic attraction of the landscape. Visual impact may be essentially linear in nature for road, rail and inland waterway developments, or nodal in character as with the large terminal installations of sea- and airports. Information on the scale of transport-related landscape damage and loss of visual amenity is not widely available, partly due to the difficulties of assessing existing landscape quality. Obviously, however, the impact of adverse landscape change is likely to be much more significant in areas of high scenic value, such as national parks and mountain passes, or where a flat topography allows visual intrusion over a wide area. Unsympathetic transport development close to important historic sites and monuments may, in the eyes of many, threaten cultural heritage (Vougias, 1992).

In their linear characteristics transport systems are unique as a land use. While elements of a road or railway, such as a bridge or intersection, can be considered separately in terms of their visual impact, it is often more satisfactory to attempt an overall assessment of impact along the length of the line. However, while measurement of the direct visual effect of a new road or railway is straightforward, the assessment of its impact in a particular context is difficult. The physical dimensions of an embankment, cutting or viaduct can easily be measured and scaled against the surrounding environment. Difficulties arise with the judgement involved in assessing the significance of the visual impact. The perception by individuals and groups of any particular piece of transport infrastructure is likely to vary. These groups include developers, planners and transport operators, local residents, transport users and interest groups. Complete consensus is therefore most unlikely (Photograph 5.1).

The time dimension has a role to play in assessing visual impact. The railways and canals, opposed in the nineteenth and twentieth centuries because of their intrusion in the landscape, are now supported with equal passion by those concerned about the environment, either as valuable landscape components or as modes that are environmentally preferable to others, such as air and road transport.

It is clear that the passage of time can transform the perceived impact of transport systems, and this is most clearly seen in the case of visual impact. A large-scale canal aqueduct or railway viaduct is likely to be valued as a landscape element, while a similar structure for a new road or railway is much less likely to find favour. This is partly because such a new structure would be an additional landscape element, but also because we feel that many of the older engineering and architectural structures form part of our heritage and therefore have more merit than newer structures. An indication of this perspective is given by Pratt (1976) for canal architecture, and Biddle and Nock (1983) for railway architecture (Photograph 5.2).

Where the "time threshold of acceptance" of a structure should be drawn is not clear. Perhaps it has to be threatened with demolition before its visual value increases. Since this is rarely the case as yet with road or air transport, we do not see their merits as visual elements. Roads in particular are also rather ubiquitous and, apart from a few structures such as major bridges and viaducts, have no scarcity value, as well as being relatively recent.

The ability to picture precisely what a new transport system will look like in its environment is a useful tool in assessing impact and evaluating mitigation measures. Artists' or engineers' impressions have long been used for this purpose, supplemented more recently by superimposed photographs. The use of computer simulations has taken the process an important step further. It is now possible to produce a three-dimensional image of a landscape with specified structures located within it, and to examine their appearance from various viewing points. This

Photograph 5.1   The M3 extension at Twyford Down, Hampshire, England
This has been one of the most controversial road projects in recent years. The construction of this motorway section (designed to complete the M3/M27 links between London and the south coast, especially the port of Southampton) through downland has major visual, land-take and aesthetic impacts (R.D. Knowles)

helps in changing the design of transport structures to mitigate visual impact. Mitigation measures may include resiting the whole project, or perhaps cut-and-cover construction or tunnelling for new road or rail lines, as planned for the proposed high-speed rail line linking the Channel Tunnel with London, although such measures are costly. Less expensive mitigation measures include alignments following land contours, giving a route more in sympathy with its landscape, or shallow cutting, earth or fence barriers (also useful for noise reduction), retention of trees, reinstatement of habitats, screening by tree-planting, detailed design of structures, and colour selection for clad or painted structures, to harmonize with the landscape as far as possible.

However, visual impacts are bound to remain to some extent. Grade-separated road junctions with their concrete elevated sections and bridges, large road signs and traffic-control systems, overhead wires on electrified railways, extensive car parking at terminals or city centres, are all elements difficult to hide (Photograph 5.3).

Ecological Degradation

The degradation of terrestrial and aquatic eco-systems, as measured by indicators such as reduced habitat/species diversity, primary productivity or the areal extent of ecologically valuable plant and animal communities, provides one of the most emotive aspects of the tension between transport development and environmental quality. As this section is being written, the author is (half) listening to a radio report on the slow but steady removal of environmental protesters from trees and tunnels in and around the proposed site for a new runway at

Photograph 5.2   The Leeds and Liverpool Canal
Canals were often opposed because of intrusion in the landscape. Now we tend to value them as landscape components, recreational facilities and aquatic habitats, as in this section of the Leeds and Liverpool Canal near Wigan, Lancashire (J.H. Farrington)

Manchester airport in England. Central to the protesters' case is their perceived need to preserve a deciduous woodland habitat. For many "environmentalists", the complete and direct removal of such a (relatively small) wildlife habitat in the name of the enhanced (global) movement of people and goods is unacceptable. Such direct destruction is the most overt manifestation of the ecological impacts that may accompany transport development projects.

Severance is another direct consequence of land-based transport development. The physical division of natural or semi-natural ecosystems may inhibit the movement of animal and plant species across transport lines, and the associated reduction in size can threaten the viability and/or biodiversity of the smaller remnants. Likewise, the death of individual animals through collision with vehicles will be an all-too-familiar direct consequence of road transport for many readers. A recent report by Scottish

Natural Heritage (1994) included a study which put the annual road-kill loss of breeding amphibians in Scotland at 20–40 per cent, with an annual kill of barn owls of at least 3000 individuals.

However, as pointed out by Varma *et al.* (1992b), the indirect or secondary effects of transport development may also be responsible for many adverse impacts on wildlife, including those associated with air, water and noise pollution (described below). With reference to water pollution, for example, one could point to the ecological destruction associated with catastrophic, and internationally reported, oil leaks from stricken tankers, or the contamination of coastal ecosystems resulting from the more routine (albeit often illegal) flushing out of oil tanks by the same ships.

Little can be done to alleviate the direct destruction of habitats, though some relocation may be possible and, in the case of pipelines, reinstatement is normal. Careful route alignment can avoid

Photograph 5.3   A viaduct carries the Autostrada del Sole across rugged terrain in Italy
This can be classed as "visual intrusion" but will it take its place as a valued landscape element in time? (J.H. Farrington)

protected sites or areas of special interest. The separation of habitats may be partially overcome by the construction of underpasses for the movement of animal species. Quite recently, the positive ecological potential of some transport lines has been recognized. Canals provide aquatic habitats in inland locations. Railway and motorway cuttings and embankments provide thousands of miles of non-agricultural habitats.

Disruption of Hydrological Processes and Water Pollution

Much transport infrastructure development involves the covering of permeable soil surfaces with impermeable materials such as concrete and tarmac. This tends to reduce the infiltration of rainfall and increase the risk of standing water and flooding. Rainfall landing on road surfaces, for example, is often drained rapidly to the nearest watercourse in order to avoid the accumulation of standing water. However, this may simply heighten the risk of downstream flash flooding in the recipient stream or river during or shortly after large storms as the channel may be unable to cope with large volumes of water being discharged into it over short time periods.

Impermeable surfaces and the increased overland movement of rain water will also tend to allow the easy and rapid transport of deposited materials into adjacent watercourses, adding to the pollution load. Runoff from roads, for example, may contain a wide range of substances linked to vehicular use including: rubber, bitumen and other tyre derivatives; metals; petrochemicals and other hydrocarbons from exhaust fumes; petrol and oil; aggregate; tarmac derivatives and particles; de-icing salt and grit in winter; and spills from any type of transported load (Haslam, 1990). Many of these pollutants will be toxic to aquatic plant and animal communities, either individually or in combination. Indeed, ecological damage may occur even before a new stretch of road becomes operational, as a result of increased suspended sediment loads in receiving waters during construction brought about by the erosion of exposed soil surfaces. Reductions in the abundance of fish and large bottom-dwelling invertebrates during, and shortly after, road and road bridge construction near or over streams and rivers have been well documented (e.g. Ogbeibu and Victor, 1989). Such changes can be prolonged. Taylor and Roff (1986), for example, observed changes in the relative abundance of different species downstream of a road construction site in southern Ontario for up to six years.

The mitigation of such impacts is difficult. Existing drainage patterns can be modified and realigned, though this itself may affect local water tables and habitats, and cannot compensate for the presence of pollutants.

Noise and Vibration

Noise is the propagation of sound waves through the air and is produced by all forms of mechanized transport. The measurement of noise is relatively simple and it is usually expressed in decibels on the dB(A) scale: a scale weighted towards those sound frequencies of most relevance to human hearing. This easy measurement, however, does not necessarily make it a simple task to determine the levels at which sound or background noise may become problematic and intrusive for those exposed. In this respect, additional factors may be very important, such as distance from source, the mode of transport and the time of day.

Transport noise is obviously not a natural phenomenon and so it is reasonable to expect it to impact on wildlife populations in some way, perhaps through restricted movement in order to avoid noise. Although animals are known to suffer physiological and behavioural changes after exposure to loud noise, little is known about the tolerance levels of individual species. Much more research has been carried out on noise effects in humans, and it is clear that prolonged exposure to excessive noise (above around 75 dB(A), typical of a busy urban street) can directly impair hearing on a permanent basis, while the human pain threshold occurs at around 120 dB(A) (comparable to a jet aircraft taking off at about 160 metres). However, in the context of transport, it is subtler physiological and psychological changes and their impact on human health and well-being that are generally of greatest concern. Some forms of noise, particularly regular exposure to sudden, loud noises and noise that disturbs sleep, may cause long-term and even permanent physiological changes, including the constriction of blood vessels and high blood pressure, both associated with cardio-vascular and circulatory disorders. Psychologically, noise may fuel aggression, annoyance and personal grievance, and also impair learning and workplace performance.

In terms of the number of people disturbed, the primary source of transport noise is road traffic. It is likely that well over 100 million people in OECD countries are currently subjected, on a daily basis, to road traffic noise levels of over 65 dB(A), a level widely regarded as an upper acceptable limit (Organization for Economic Co-operation and Development, 1990). At a national scale, recent evidence from Norway suggests that some 260 000 people (out of a total population of 4.3 million) are subjected to noise levels above recommended standards (Stenstadvold, 1996). High levels of noise may also be found around airports and along railway lines (especially if high-speed lines or steeply graded uphill and used by diesel locomotives). Carpenter (1994) discusses railway noise in some detail. Although the impact of noise from jet aircraft can be decreased by reducing the thrust used at take-off when over built-up areas, in many cities (e.g. Mexico City, Lima, Bogota and Buenos Aires) the major airport is located in densely populated areas and this tactic is less successful.

Overall transport noise levels in the developed world have tended to stabilize in the last decade and are expected to fall slightly in the foreseeable future. This is due to mitigation measures, which are now briefly reviewed. Noise mitigation can be approached under four headings (after Nelson, 1987, 1.4), which are complementary rather than mutually exclusive. Maximum mitigation will be obtained only if all are incorporated in an overall approach.

1. *Reduction of noise at the source*. This includes vehicle design, traffic management, tunnelling and noise abatement procedures for aircraft (Figure 5.1).
2. *Measures to control noise along its transmission path*. These consist mainly of barriers such as fences and embankments, and the use of buildings as noise barriers. A two-storey building may reduce noise levels on the "lee" side by about 13 dB(A) (Nelson, 1987, 11.1.5).
3. *Measures to protect the observer from noise at the point of hearing*. Buildings can be designed to reduce noise impacts on their occupants, for example by locating smaller windows on the noisiest facade. Double or triple glazing and acoustic insulation can have significant benefits, but may require air conditioning to compensate for lack of ventilation.

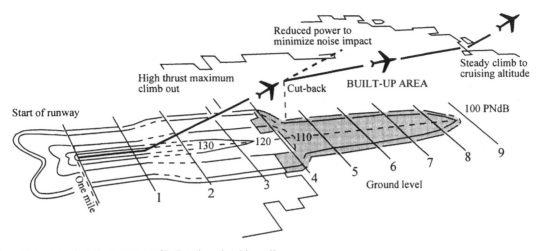

Figure 5.1   A typical departure profile for aircraft taking off
This has been designed to reduce noise impacts in the built-up area beneath the flight path. Such noise abatement procedures are voluntarily followed by many airlines and are standard practice at many airports
Source: after Nelson (1987), courtesy Butterworth

4. *Land-use planning and zoning.* This approach is the most effective in reducing noise levels at the larger scale, because it locates housing and workplace further away from noise sources (Stratford, 1974, 51). There is a long time lag in its application as a corrective measure, but it helps to ensure that new noise nuisances are not created. Planning consent around airports is normally determined by zoning based on current and predicted "noise footprints", or contour lines of noise levels.

The air transport industry has made significant progress in mitigating noise pollution, though as Graham (1995) points out, increases in aircraft movements may largely erode these improvements. Vibration from transport sources has two main components:

- low-frequency noise (mainly from exhausts), which can cause parts of buildings, such as windows, to vibrate; and
- ground vibration transmitted to buildings via their foundations.

The effects of vibration on buildings and on people are not yet fully assessed. It seems likely that rattling window frames and crockery can add to the personal stress induced by noise nuisance. Damage to buildings from traffic vibration is difficult to quantify, but is probably small in relation to other causes of damage such as drought or frost. On the other hand, specific locations such as historic buildings may suffer discernible damage. Subsurface pipes and cables can also be damaged.

The gradual increase in permitted lorry weights has emphasized the need to reduce vibration by attention to the smoothness of the road surface and to vehicle suspension design. Further research will enable a more precise estimate of vibration impacts in future, and of the compensation or charging levels that might need to be applied to the recipients and sources of vibration if reductions are to be made.

Air Pollution

Transport-related air pollution can be a severe problem, especially over congested urban streets where a cocktail of pollutants may produce conditions undoubtedly harmful to human health (see, for example, Haughton and Hunter, 1994). Frequently, such pollutants are transported considerable distances away from urban centres, extending the area within which ecological damage (in the form of plant stress or acidic deposition, for example) may also occur. Lack of space prevents anything other than the most cursory examination in the following paragraphs of some major air pollutants, their sources and effects.

Although transport-related construction activities may create significant dust problems, it is the operation of land-based vehicles that gives the greatest cause for concern; or more precisely, the human health effects of long-term exposure to pollutants largely derived from the combustion of fossil fuels used in motorized transport. Air pollution from transport arises from either primary pollutants (those emitted directly into the atmosphere from a vehicular source), or secondary pollutants formed in the atmosphere as a result of interactions between primary pollutants and normal atmospheric constituents. The major air pollutants are:

- oxides of sulphur, especially sulphur dioxide;
- oxides of carbon, especially carbon monoxide and carbon dioxide;
- oxides of nitrogen, especially nitric oxide and nitrogen dioxide;
- particulates, including smoke, dust, acidic droplets and salts;
- volatile organic compounds (VOCs), including hydrocarbons such as benzene;
- photochemical oxidants, including ozone and peroxyacetyl nitrates (PANs);
- metals, especially lead.

It is extremely difficult to attempt to calculate the contribution of transport to the total anthropogenic emission of these pollutants into the atmosphere, and the relative importance of different transport modes (although road vehicles as a whole generally contribute most in both developed and developing countries), but some estimates are available (see, for example, Commission of the European Communities, 1992; House of Lords, 1996; Royal Commission on Environmental Pollution, 1994; Varma *et al.*, 1992a,b; Vougias, 1992). For example, transport may be responsible for up to 37 per cent of anthropogenic carbon dioxide and 90 per cent of carbon monoxide emissions worldwide. Likewise, in most countries transport accounts for approximately half of all releases of oxides of nitrogen, perhaps one-third of VOC emissions, and 90 per cent of lead emissions. In heavily built-up areas, some 50 per cent of atmospheric particulates and hydrocarbons may originate from the transport sector. Precise emission rates of these pollutants vary with many factors, including engine technology and traffic speed. Prevailing weather conditions will also be important in determining the build-up, or otherwise, of air pollution.

Some of the potential human health effects associated with individual pollutants are given in Table 5.3. It is important to remember, however, that it may well be the combined influence of pollutants acting together which carries the most significance for human health. In a study on the health effects of general air pollution on 100 traffic policemen working in the city of Jaipur, India, Sinha (1993) found extremely high rates of occurrence of respiratory, digestive, ocular and skin problems and diseases, often within a few weeks of the policemen taking up their jobs. More specifically, the possible link between increasing asthmatic disease and rising air pollution from road traffic has received much attention in recent years. Niven (1995) reviews the possible link between asthma and a number of pollutants, including ozone, sulphur dioxide, oxides of nitrogen, small particulates and black smoke, and concludes that, whilst general air pollution is unlikely to cause asthma directly, there is strong evidence that it can aggravate the condition, given the presence of another "trigger" such as a range of allergens (e.g. pollen or dust mite protein). Small particulate matter may be particularly important as an aggravating factor (Table 5.3). This pollutant on its own may kill as many as 10 000 people annually in Britain and cost some £17 billion a year through death, sickness and lost working days (Hamer, 1996). Most of this matter is emitted by diesel engines.

Table 5.3   Some major potential health effects of individual air pollutants

Pollutant	Effect on Human Health
Carbon monoxide	Can exacerbate cardiovascular disease symptoms, particularly angina. Can also affect the central nervous system, impairing physical coordination, vision and judgement, creating nausea and headaches. Sustained exposure to high concentrations can result in death. Odourless and colourless
Sulphur dioxide	Can affect lung function
Nitrogen dioxide	Can be an irritant and exacerbate respiratory diseases
Particulates	Fine particulates may be toxic, or may carry toxic and carcinogenic organic and inorganic substances. May also penetrate deep into the respiratory system irritating lung tissue. Episodes of high atmospheric concentration often correlate highly with asthma attacks and deaths from respiratory illnesses
VOCs	Both benzene and benzidine may be carcinogenic. Carbon tetrachloride is a potential teratogen (a substance that produces abnormal changes in foetus development)
Ozone	Can be an eye and throat irritant, and cause coughs and headaches
Lead	Can impair the synthesis of haem, adversely affecting oxygen transport in the blood. Can also impair neurotransmitter functions, affecting behaviour and learning performance in children

Sources: Haughton and Hunter (1994), House of Lords (1996).

POLICY APPROACHES TO IMPACT REDUCTION

Policies at national and supranational levels have been evolving to try to meet the implications of these impacts, but have not yet fully come to terms with the continual growth in transport flows, particularly in road traffic. Problems in doing this include the political difficulty of introducing potentially unpopular measures such as restrictions or taxation on car use, and the unwillingness to increase the costs of the transport processes that are so important for economic activity.

It is now commonly accepted that the demand for travel as a whole should be influenced by policy. Many policy measures set out by the European Union and its member States so far have addressed specific negative externalities of the transport sector (Barrett, 1995), but some policy elements are now aimed at the suppression of demand itself. EU legislation so far has been related to vehicle noise and exhaust emissions, and policies now being debated are concerned with the development of biofuels to account for 5 per cent

of transport fuels by 2005, and the introduction of a carbon tax on oil to reflect assessments of the environmental costs of carbon dioxide emissions. This would result in an increase in petrol prices of 5 to 6 per cent, and diesel prices of 7 up to 9 per cent, too little to have more than a marginal effect on road vehicle kilometres and energy consumption (Barrett, 1995). Other policy measures under discussion include further reductions in emission limits, moves to reduce the sulphur content of fuels, and tougher speed limits (with safety, as well as environmental, aims).

However, although these measures address problems to some extent, the indications are that travel demand in the six largest EU countries will continue to grow by about 55 per cent by 2010, with energy consumption and carbon dioxide emissions increasing by about 40 per cent. Critics argue that policy needs to reflect the underpricing present, particularly in road transport, where the total external costs may exceed the total tax burden on the sector by two to three times. This suggests that demand will have to be suppressed by significant tax increases or by restrictions on movement, or both.

In Britain in the mid-1990s there were signs that the government, while not introducing policies that fundamentally challenged the predominant position of the private car, at least began to acknowledge the problems by introducing measures aimed at reducing reliance on the car. For example, planning authorities have been instructed to prevent the further growth of out-of-town shopping centres, and also to give priority to the redevelopment of "brown-field" and town-centre sites for housing in preference to those at or beyond the urban edge (Department of the Environment, 1996). Fuel prices have been increased by 5 per cent per year in real terms in order to achieve a reduction in demand, although the Royal Commission on Environmental Pollution (1994) wanted a greater increase, to achieve a more significant reduction in demand.

More far-reaching policies are in prospect from the Labour Government from 1997. It is likely that the previous government's commitment to increasing the costs of car use may be expanded to include such measures as urban road pricing, strict parking limits and differential taxation on larger cars, together with efforts to improve integration between the different modes and to increase the share of walking, cycling and public transport. The previous government's reductions in the road-building programme are set to continue or to be increased, and the proposals to give local authorities powers to achieve defined air quality standards, for example by restricting vehicle access to urban areas, will be implemented, while the idea of statutory traffic reduction, with appropriate measures, is also being discussed. Measures such as bus lanes, road pricing, parking charges, park-and-ride schemes and pedestrianization will continue to be applied in an effort to achieve significant modal shift away from the car. This will not be easy, and some of the measures may have adverse side-effects. For example, pricing and taxing car use impacts adversely on those who use cars and rely on them the most, including rural dwellers, particularly those on low incomes. Encouraging a move towards smaller cars may bring somewhat higher rates of fatalities in accidents, though this may be outweighed by health benefits

from lower emission levels (Farrington et al., 1997). However, the overall imperative of taking steps to deal with the continued growth in car use will require significant policy changes. There are clear signs that British governments are moving towards the reflection of the true value of the environment in the price of transport, rather than treating environmental components as "free goods" (Banister and Button, 1993).

In the USA, federal legislation in the form of the Clean Air Act was introduced in 1970 and amended in 1990 (Seagriff, 1995; Atash, 1996). This sets standards for ozone, carbon monoxide, nitrous oxide, sulphur dioxide, lead and particulates. Standards are applied on the basis of air basins, defined geographically. The California Clear Air Act, implemented in 1989 and amended in 1992, is generally more stringent than the federal legislation. It establishes a legal mandate to control vehicle trips and vehicle-kilometres travelled. Areas that do not meet the required air quality standards have to prepare an Air Quality Management Plan and every three years this has to be shown to be implemented effectively (Seagriff, 1995). Federal Intermodal Surface Transportation Efficiency Act (ISTEA) legislation directly ties air quality compliance to funding for transportation projects. Non-attainment areas regarding National Ambient Air Quality Standards (NAAQS) are subject to having transportation project funds withdrawn if future plans cannot be shown to bring the region into compliance.

The Southern California basin has the worst air quality in the USA but as a result of the reductions in vehicle emissions due to lead-free petrol, better engine management systems and catalytic converters, pollution levels in this area have generally fallen. Ozone levels have been reduced by almost half over the last 30 years. However, standards continue to be exceeded, notably by ozone, particulates and carbon monoxide. As Seagriff (1995, 151), notes: "The widespread availability of lead-free petrol and catalytic converters is therefore not enough", and other measures are needed. Land-use and travel patterns need to be changed, alternative forms of propulsion introduced, improvements in public transport made, and a greater role for walking and cycling developed. Progress is being made in these areas by integrating the roles of the various agencies involved, and this is one of the lessons to be learned from the Californian experience. Another is the difficulty of changing lifestyles and travel patterns towards a more sustainable profile that reduces car dependence, particularly when long-term changes such as land-use patterns are required. But the use of air quality standards as a method of driving transport, land-use and related fiscal policies, as adopted in the USA, appears to be the approach with the best chance of success.

POLICY EVALUATION: TOWARDS STRATEGIC ENVIRONMENTAL ASSESSMENT

A set of techniques of potential value in achieving the aim of a more sustainable set of transport and related policies are those of Environmental Assessment (EA) and Strategic Environmental Assessment (SEA). EA operates at the level of individual projects, such as a length of major road or railway, or an airport. The formal requirement for this process was introduced in European legislation in 1985, effective in the UK in 1987, though EAs of Department of Transport road schemes had been prepared since the 1970s. Increasingly the development of such projects is also assessed by another type of impact statement known as a Traffic Impact Analysis (TIA) (Institution of Highways and Transportation, 1994).

These assessments (EA and TIA) provide a systematic framework for the identification, estimation and evaluation of the predicted impacts of a specific project, and are generally accepted as a reasonable tool for this purpose, although they may well be contentious in their prediction of the magnitude of impacts and of their significance. Attaching monetary values to impacts is increasingly common but presents difficulties (Glasson *et al.*, 1994). Other problems include their failure to give full consideration to

the generation and testing of alternatives, and the fact that they are normally undertaken by the developer (see, for example, Wathern, 1988, 88). Their main limitation, however, lies in the case-by-case basis on which they examine projects, together with their confinement to new, major projects. The problem is that projects are the product of policies, programmes and plans (in increasing order of detail), and it is the formulation of policies themselves that needs to be subjected to testing in an environmentally based framework. For example, as discussed elsewhere in this book, it is policy at the national (British) level that has produced rail privatization, bus deregulation and the land-use and fiscal regimes that have such an important bearing on such things as travel generation and the choice of mode. Only by assessing the environmental consequences of policy and its constituent elements in a holistic way can systematic progress be made towards more sustainable transport policies with maximum environmental and social benefit.

SEA seeks to carry out such an assessment, by predicting and evaluating the environmental consequences of policies (Glasson *et al.*, 1994). Ideally it should be part of the policy formulation process so that alternatives can be evaluated before implementation, but it can be applied to existing policies. For example, Carpenter (1994), in his review of the impact of railways on the environment, argues for comprehensive social and environmental evaluation of transport modes in the context of different transport needs, presenting a strong case for the effectiveness of railways, particularly where routes already exist. This type of strategic approach in the UK will probably require legislation at the EU level. EU efforts to introduce a requirement for SEA have so far been rebutted, the UK Government in particular fearing that such a measure would hamper development unnecessarily without achieving significant benefits. However, SEA offers potential gains if it can help to produce more environmentally sustainable policies that do not have unacceptable social and economic consequences. Indeed, it is being argued more frequently that there is a shared social and economic benefit to be gained by recognizing the reality of the environmental costs that transport causes. All parties benefit from, say, policies that prevent our cities from being polluted and our streets from being clogged up, and not just those who traditionally advocate "green" policies. Put another way, not only do the pedestrian and cyclist stand to gain, but also the central city business and the motorist, since they are already experiencing significant economic, as well as environmental, costs due to traffic congestion. In this spirit, Goodwin has argued that transport may be able to make the "pivotal contribution" to environmental policy by charting a path step by step so that people are given "opportunities to benefit themselves, their communities and their economies by recognizing the reality of environmental costs and reducing their impact" (Banister and Button 1993, 268).

Photograph 5.4   Large-scale development of road systems Such development is not now regarded as a viable solution to congestion because it generates more traffic and cannot in itself prevent ultimate gridlock (Madden, 1991)

CONCLUSIONS

Transport as a whole causes significant impacts on the environment, and thus on people. The largest impact arises from road transport and from car use in particular. It is generally accepted that the present trends towards continued growth in car use are not sustainable, especially because of the consequential levels of atmospheric pollution where traffic is concentrated, such as urban centres and densely trafficked inter-urban routes. As roads become more congested the pollution consequences increase, so that congestion becomes an environmental problem as well as an economic and social one. It is also becoming more widely accepted that transport modes should pay for the environmental damage they cause. This would raise revenue, particularly from road users, which could be used to finance more favourable modes.

Selective investment in road improvements can achieve environmental, economic and safety benefits but large-scale development of the road system is not now regarded as a viable solution (Photograph 5.4). Instead, other measures are needed which will modify our dependence on cars, by providing better facilities for alternatives such as public transport,

walking and cycling, together with pricing measures to reduce the demand for car use (though these need to have regard for the situation of rural low-income dwellers who may have no practicable alternative to the car). Similarly, Graham (1995) recognizes the need for measures to reduce the demand for air travel as part of overall policy.

In urban areas, pedestrianization, the pricing of car parking and road space, and the planning of park-and-ride systems, have a role to play in adjusting the balance between the car and alternative modes. Some help is also possible from new technologies for providing alternative forms of propulsion. In the longer term, changing land-use patterns will reduce the need for travel. As Whitelegg (1993, 162) expressed it: "A phased reduction in dependence on motorised transport and a gradual shift in the organization of land uses and activities will deliver material rewards as well as dramatic increases in health, psychological well-being and employment."

Transport policies in Britain and the USA are beginning to get to grips with the problems but there is still a long way to go. Air quality management has been chosen in the USA as the mainspring of policy to achieve a better mix of transport modes, particularly in urban areas, and similar approaches are being adopted in Britain. Strategic Environmental Assessment can be a useful technique in tuning policies to meet environmentally sustainable objectives and could usefully be supplemented by social and economic assessment of transport policies so that the full spectrum of policy impacts is assessed. It seems clear that transport policies and other related policies such as energy and land use must in future set their agenda increasingly within an environmental framework so that we move closer to the goal of safeguarding our environment not only for ourselves but for future generations.

REFERENCES

Atash, F. (1996), "Reorienting metropolitan landuse and transportation policies in the USA", *Land Use Studies* 13 (1), 37–49.

Banister, D. (ed.) (1998), *Transport policy and the environment* (London: Spon).

Banister, D. and Button, K. (1993), *Transport, the environment and sustainable development* (London: Spon).

Barrett, G.M.J. (1995), "Transport emissions and travel behaviour: a critical review of recent European Union and UK policy initiatives", *Transportation* 22, 295–323.

Battrick, E. (1982), "The watchdog of the Lake District", *National Trust Magazine* 3, 13–15.

Biddle, G. and Nock, O.S. (eds) (1983), *The railway heritage of Britain* (London: Michael Joseph).

Building Research Establishment (1991), *BREEAM/New homes: an environmental assessment for new homes* (Watford: BRE).

Carpenter, T.G. (1994), *The environmental impact of railways* (Chichester: Wiley).

Commission of the European Communities (1992), *Towards sustainability: a European Commission programme of policy and action in relation to the environment and sustainable development* (Luxembourg: CEC).

Department of the Environment (1994), *Sustainable development: the UK strategy* (London: HMSO).

Department of the Environment (1996), *Household growth: where shall we live?* (London: HMSO).

Farrington, J.H., Needle, C. and Sleightholme-Albanis, G. (1997), "A contribution to the debate on fuel price increases: some possible safety implications", *Journal of Transport Geography* 5 (1), 73–7.

Glasson, J., Therivel, R. and Chadwick, A. (1994), *Introduction to environmental impact assessment* (London: UCL Press).

Graham, B. (1995), *Geography and air transport* (Chichester: Wiley).

Hamer, M. (1996), "Clean air strategy fails to tackle traffic", *New Scientist*, August, p. 6.

Haslam, S.M. (1990), *River pollution: an ecological perspective* (London: Belhaven).

Haughton, G. and Hunter, C. (1994), *Sustainable cities*, Regional Policy and Development Series No. 7 (London: Jessica Kingsley/Regional Studies Association).

House of Lords (1996), *Towards zero emissions for road transport*. Select Committee report on science and technology (London: HMSO).

Institution of Highways and Transportation (1994), *Traffic Impact Analysis: a good practice guide* (London: IHT).

Kellett, J.R. (1979), *Railways and Victorian cities* (London: Routledge).

Longhurst, J., Gibbs, D.C., Raper, D.W. and Conlan, D.E. (1996), "Towards sustainable airport development", *The Environmentalist* 16, 197–202.

Madden, C. (1991), *When humans roamed the Earth* (London: Earthscan Publications/Kogan Page).

Mwase, N. (1996), "Developing an environment-friendly transport system in Tanzania: some policy considerations", *Transport Reviews* 16 (2), 145–56.

Nelson, P.M. (ed.) (1987), *Transportation noise reference book* (London: Butterworth).

Niven, M.L. (1995), "A review of the medical evidence for a link between air pollution and asthma", *The Environmentalist* 15, 267–71.

Ogbeibu, A.E. and Victor, R. (1989), "The effects of road and bridge construction on the bank-root macrobenthic invertebrates of a southern Nigerian stream", *Environmental Pollution* 56, 85–100.

Organization for Economic Co-operation and Development (1990), *Environmental policies for cities in the 1990s* (Paris: OECD).

Pratt, F. (1976), *Canal architecture in Britain* (London: British Waterways Board).

Royal Commission on Environmental Pollution (1994), *Transport and the environment* (London: HMSO).

Scottish Natural Heritage (1994), *Transport policy guidance note 94/2* (Edinburgh: SNH).

Seagriff, E. (1995), "Southern California Air Quality Plans in the 1990s and the effects on transport policy", *Transport Reviews* 15 (2), 141–65.

Sinha, R.K. (1993), "Automobile pollution in India and its human impact", *The Environmentalist* 13 (2), 111–15.

Stenstadvold, M. (1996), "Institutional constraints to environmentally sound integrated land use and transport policies: experiences from the Norwegian integrated land use and transport planning scheme", *Journal of Environmental Planning and Management* 39 (4), 593–605.

Stratford, A. (1974), *Airports and the environment* (London: Macmillan).

Taylor, B.R. and Roff, J.C. (1986), 'Long term effects of highway construction on the ecology of a southern Ontario stream', *Environmental Pollution (Series A)* 40, 317–44.

TEST (1991), *Wrong side of the tracks? Impacts of road and rail transport on the environment: a basis for discussion* (London: Transport and Environment Studies).

Turner, R.K., Pearce, D. and Bateman, I. (1994), *Environmental economics: an elementary introduction* (London: Harvester Wheatsheaf).

Varma, A., Souba, J., Faiz, A. and Sinha, K.C. (1992a), "Environmental considerations of land transport in developing countries (part 1)", *Transport Reviews* 12 (2), 101–13.

Varma, A., Souba, J., Faiz, A. and Sinha, K.C. (1992b), "Environmental considerations of land transport in developing countries (part 2)", *Transport Reviews* 12 (3), 187–98.

Vougias, S. (1992), "Transport and environmental policies in the EC", *Transport Reviews* 12 (3), 219–36.

Wathern, P. (ed.) (1988), *Environmental Impact Assessment: theory and practice* (London: Unwin Hyman).

Whitelegg, J. (1993), *Transport for a sustainable future: the case for Europe* (London: Belhaven).

World Commission on Environment and Development (1987), *Our common future* (London: Oxford University Press).

6

Urban Travel Patterns

Genevieve Giuliano

This chapter examines urban passenger travel patterns and trends. Urban passenger travel in developed countries is characterised by increases in car use, declining use of public transit and other modes, the negative effects of cars on urban environments and changes in urban form and lifestyle resulting from the use of cars. Rising affluence, social and demographic changes, and shifts in economic structure are identified as primary explanatory factors for these trends. Rising car use and the associated changes in urban spatial patterns generate large social costs. The chapter also examines why policies designed to control car use, in order to reduce negative external effects, have failed to stop increases in car use.

INTRODUCTION

The most dramatic trend in urban travel during the twentieth century has been the rise in car ownership and use. The first major surge occurred in the 1920s in the USA with Henry Ford's Model T, the first car mass-produced and sold at a price affordable to working-class households. Although the USA has led the way, car ownership and use is rising throughout the world. Economic growth and rising per-capita incomes over the past three decades have increased car use in Europe. In the 1990s, the fastest growth rates of car ownership are observed in developing countries around the world.

The purpose of this chapter is to discuss and examine urban travel patterns. This is a broad subject: travel patterns vary greatly between countries, from the almost complete domination of the private car in the USA to the still extensive reliance on non-motorized modes in developing countries. Urban travel patterns include movement of goods as well as people, and here too there is great variation. Urban transport inevitably generates large social costs. Such a broad subject cannot be comprehensively dealt with in a single chapter, and attention is directed here towards urban *passenger* transport in the advanced economies of North America and Europe. In most metropolitan areas, passenger transport accounts for over 90 per cent of all vehicle travel and is therefore a key factor in determining infrastructure needs and overall travel demand.

Urban travel is mostly about cars – about growing car use, about the declining competitiveness of other modes of transportation (particularly public transit), about the negative effects of cars on urban environments, and about changes in urban form made possible by the car and by lifestyle changes that make the car an integral part of most people's daily activity patterns. Planners and policy-makers are increasingly concerned about car use. Traffic congestion and accidents, environmental pollution, loss of open space and natural habitat, and the decline of

Modern Transport Geography: second, revised edition. Edited by Brian Hoyle and Richard Knowles.
© 1998 John Wiley & Sons Ltd.

central cities are some of the major problems associated with the automobile. Many policies have been implemented in an effort to control car use in order to solve these problems, yet travel by car continues to increase. This chapter aims to provide some understanding as to why this is the case.

THE ROLE OF TRAVEL IN DAILY LIFE

As noted in Chapter 1, travel is a fundamental human activity. Travel is necessary to engage in spatially dispersed activities – work, shopping, visits to friends, etc. In economic terms, travel is an intermediate good, because demand for travel is derived from the demand for other spatially separated goods and services. Thus one travels in order to engage in work or to do shopping or see a film. Apart from sightseeing and some types of holiday, rarely do people travel simply for the sheer pleasure of the trip.

Like other goods and services, travel has a cost. When an individual makes a trip, he or she values the destination activity sufficiently to incur the trip cost. The cost of travel usually has two components, time and money. Time spent travelling is time not spent doing other things, hence those who value their time highly will be willing to spend more money in order to save time by using a faster mode. For example, business travellers may use air travel or high-speed trains to economize on time spent travelling from one engagement to another, while retirees and university students – for different reasons – are among those who are quite willing to use cheaper and slower buses and local trains. Research has shown that the value of time is positively correlated with wage rates or income levels (Small, 1992); hence as real income increases over time, the demand for faster modes of travel also increases.

ACCESSIBILITY

Accessibility refers to the ease of movement between places. As movement becomes less costly – in

terms of either money or time – between any two places, accessibility increases. The propensity for interaction between any two places increases as the cost of movement between them decreases, all else being equal. Accessibility also includes the concept of attractiveness: the opportunities or activities that are located in a given place. Thus accessibility is a function both of spatial structure and of the transportation system.

Some geographers distinguish between accessibility and mobility (e.g. Hanson, 1995). Accessibility is used to describe the spatial distribution of activity sites with respect to a given location, while mobility describes the ability to move between activity sites. The concept of mobility is often applied to individuals and thus describes the individual's ability to travel between activity sites. All else being equal, as land-use patterns become more dispersed, individuals require more resources (cars, money) to maintain mobility. For any given land-use distribution, an individual's mobility increases with the supply of transportation services available and the ability to use or purchase these services.

Accessibility is typically expressed as a gravity-type function:

$$A_i = \sum \frac{O_j}{d_{ij}^b} \qquad (6.1)$$

where A_i is the accessibility of zone i, O_j is the number of opportunities in zone j, and d_{ij} is some measure of the distance between them. The parameter b is called the impedance factor, and reflects the rate at which increasing distance reduces accessibility. Empirical research shows b to be in the range of 0.5 to 2 (Haynes and Fotheringham, 1984). Such measures are useful for making general comparisons of accessibility across metropolitan areas, or comparing the accessibility of different modes, such as private car and public transit.

Measures such as equation (6.1) of course do not capture many aspects of accessibility. For example, if we consider access to a specific set of opportunities, say shopping, then we also need information on the quality and variety of shops, their hours of operation, etc. In addition, accessibility measures based on zonal-level data are averages, and hence do not reflect the variation among individuals and their location within the zone.

ACTIVITY-BASED MODELS OF TRAVEL DEMAND

Travel demand can be examined at the level of individuals or households, or at the level of population segments, by location or population characteristic. Models of individuals or households are termed *disaggregate* models; models of population segments are termed *aggregate* models. In this section I restrict the discussion to disaggregate models.

Much of the disaggregate research is trip-based. That is, travellers are assumed to be rational utility maximizers making choices on specific trips (journey to work, to shop, etc.). However, if travel is a derived demand, it follows that travellers are making choices about activities, and the travel we observe is the outcome of these activity choices. Consequently, understanding travel behaviour requires under-

standing the underlying patterns of people's daily activities. Activity-based models seek to capture the complex process of choosing a set of daily activities and their location, timing and sequencing. These models draw from the work of Chapin (1974) on activity choices and Hägerstrand (1970) on choice availability.

Chapin (1974) conceptualizes activity patterns as an outcome of demand and supply, demand being the motivation to take an action, and supply being the opportunity to do so, as illustrated in Figure 6.1. Motivation or desire to act depends on the person's household role and individual characteristics. Opportunity depends on the availability of resources required to act, and on the perceived value of the act.

Hägerstrand's (1970) work focuses on the interplay of space and time; since activity locations are distributed in space and time, time resources are required in order both to access locations as well as to participate in the activity itself. Hagerstrand identified three categories of time and space constraints that affect activity opportunities:

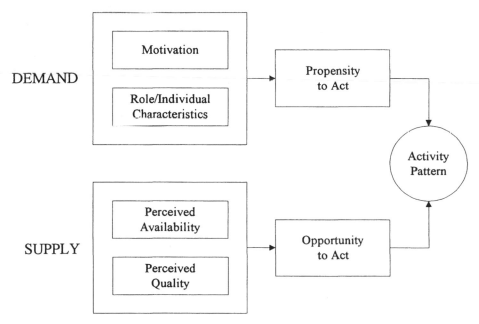

Figure 6.1 Chapin's model of activity patterns
Source: after Chapin (1974)

1. *Capability constraints* describe the limits of the physical system, the transportation technology available and the fact that one can only be in one place at a given time.
2. *Coupling constraints* describe the schedule dependences of activities, such as the hours of operation of stores, or an individual's work schedule.
3. *Authority constraints* describe the legal, social or political limitations placed on access, such as the age requirement for a driver's licence.

The set of opportunities available to a given individual are those which meet all three sets of constraints. For example, you can go to the Chinese restaurant for lunch only if (i) the restaurant is open (coupling constraint) and (ii) you can get there, eat and return to work within the duration of your permitted lunch break (authority constraint). If you need to use your car in order to get there and back quickly enough, but your car is in the workshop for repairs (capability constraint), you will not be able to have Chinese food for lunch.

Hagerstrand developed the *space–time prism* to illustrate the opportunities in time and space available to a given individual. Here is a simple example. Betty must be at work from 8 a.m. to 4 p.m. and her job is located 10 miles from home. Her household responsibilities require that she cannot leave home before 7 a.m. and must return home no later than 6 p.m. What is her opportunity space for non-work activities? In Figure 6.2a, I assume she takes public transport to and from work, and her travel time is one hour each way. The space–time graph shows her path, leaving home at 7 a.m., arriving at work at 8 a.m., etc. Before work, she has no time available. After work, she has two hours before she must be home. The rectangle in Figure 6.2a shows all the possibilities in time and space that are accessible to her during this period. The more time she spends travelling, the less time she has for other activities such as shopping for a new pair of shoes. If no shoe shops are located within the rectangle, she cannot shop for shoes. Similarly, if there are shoe shops, but they close at 5 p.m., her opportunities are vastly reduced.

Now suppose that Betty buys a car, and her travel time to work is reduced to 30 minutes each way. Figure 6.2b shows how her after-work time–space prism has increased as a result of greater travel speed. Note that the increased travel speed is reflected in the flatter slope of the lines in Figure 6.2b. Betty also has some time available before work. However, this time does not help her very much, since most shops and services are not open before 8 a.m. She therefore decides to ask her employer if she can shift her work schedule to 7:30 a.m. to 3:30 p.m. Figure 6.2c shows the resulting after-work time–space prism. This example shows how relaxing constraints leads to greater spatial access and therefore more activity opportunities.

Historically we observe a consistent trend towards relaxation of coupling and capability constraints. For example, shops and services have extended hours to evenings and weekends. In large US metropolitan areas, it is not unusual to find retail activities that are open 24 hours per day. Catalogue sales and other forms of home-based shopping are available around the clock to anyone with a telephone. Employers are engaging in more flexible work arrangements: flexible work schedules, telecommuting and part-time jobs reduce schedule constraints associated with employment. Private cars and high-speed roads have increased travel speed, making it possible to travel longer distances in less time. The space–time prism makes it easy to see why greater accessibility is highly valued and consequently enthusiastically pursued. The aggregate travel patterns we observe are the outcomes of choices made by many individuals, and these choices are based on the simple principle of arranging one's daily schedule so as to best utilize one's resources.

URBAN TRAVEL TRENDS

I turn now to some empirical observations of aggregate travel patterns. Throughout the developed world, people own more private vehicles, use them more frequently, drive more miles, and are more likely to drive alone than ever before. The world's

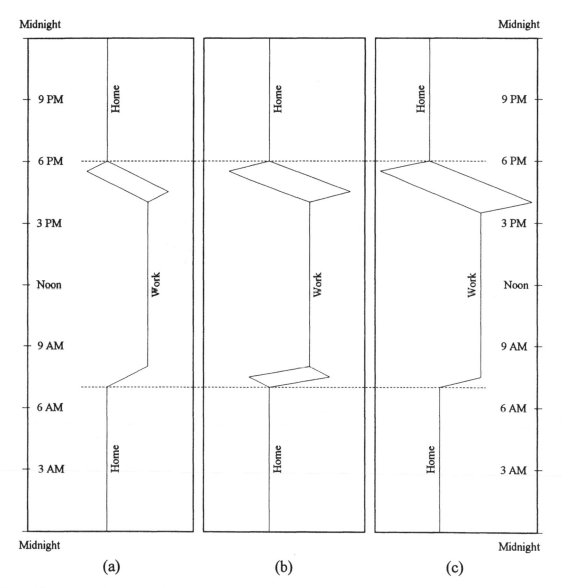

Figure 6.2 An example of space–time relationships in an urban transport context
Source: developed by the author from Hagerstrand (1970); a similar illustration is included in Hanson (1995)

motor vehicle fleet has grown immensely over the past two decades. The total number of cars and trucks increased from 246 million in 1970 to 617 million in 1993, with most of the growth occurring outside the USA, as illustrated in Figure 6.3. Average annual growth rates in the motor vehicle fleet over this period are 2.6 per cent for the USA, 4.4 per cent for other OECD countries, and 6.5 per cent for non-OECD countries.

Patterns of vehicle ownership are further illustrated in Table 6.1, which gives average annual growth rates for car registrations in selected countries, grouped by level of per-capita income and weighted by population. The low- and low/middle-

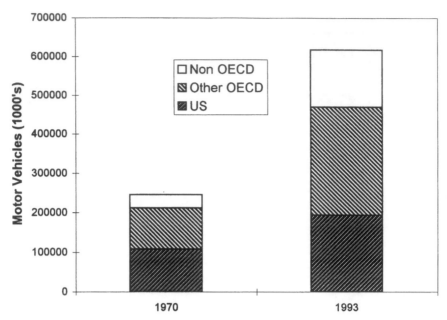

Figure 6.3   The World motor vehicle fleet, 1970–93
Source: US Department of Transportation, (1996), p. 208

Table 6.1   Growth in car ownership, by country per capita income category, 1970–92

Income category	Annual Growth Rate (%) 1970–92		Cars/population 1992
	Cars	Population	
Low-income economies (e.g. India, China, Nigeria)	9.4	2.3	0.0034
Lower/middle-income economies (e.g. Peru, Thailand, Turkey)	9.6	2.5	0.0350
Upper/middle-income economies (e.g. Mexico, South Korea, Brazil)	7.2	2.4	0.0860
High-income economies (e.g. USA, Japan, Germany	3.3	0.9	0.4760

Source: US Department of Transport (1996, 219).

income countries have the lowest car ownership rates, but the highest growth rates. These numbers suggest that, in the absence of severe policy intervention, the world car fleet will grow enormously in the coming decade as developing countries achieve higher levels of per-capita income. It bears noting that China has the lowest 1992 car ownership rate (car per population ratio of 0.00162), even though the vehicle fleet increased by more than a factor of 10 between 1970 and 1992. Another increase of this magnitude or greater is quite possible in the coming decade. At the opposite end of the spectrum, the

USA continues to have the highest car ownership rate (car per population ratio of 0.6) but it had the slowest growth rate (2.2 per cent) during this period, suggesting that car ownership in the USA may finally be reaching saturation.

Car ownership is significantly related to per-capita income. Figure 6.4 plots car ownership per 1000 population against the natural logarithm of 1992 GDP per capita in US dollars for several European countries (East and West), the USA, Canada and Japan. The graph suggests that, as economic well-being improves in lower-income countries, car ownership will increase. The graph also shows that the greatest dispersion of car ownership rates is found among the higher-income countries, with the USA at one extreme and Denmark and Japan at the other. Later in this chapter I will discuss some possible explanations for these differences.

More car ownership means more car use; annual vehicle-kilometres travelled have increased at about the same rate as car ownership. To illustrate, Table 6.2 gives annual average VKT (vehicle-kilometres travelled) growth rates for the USA, Japan and selected European Union (EU) countries. These data indicate that car ownership and use are increasing throughout the world, but they do not reflect the still large differences in the degree or intensity of car use across different countries. Comparing British national travel survey data of 1965 and 1985, May (1993) observed that total person-kilometres in motorized vehicles increased by 61 per cent, an average annual rate of 2.4 per cent. The increase was allocated as 4 per cent due to increased population, 22 per cent due to more trips, and 35 per cent due to longer trips. More and longer trips are made possible by the personal car; by 1989 private vehicles accounted for 79 per cent of UK person-kilometres

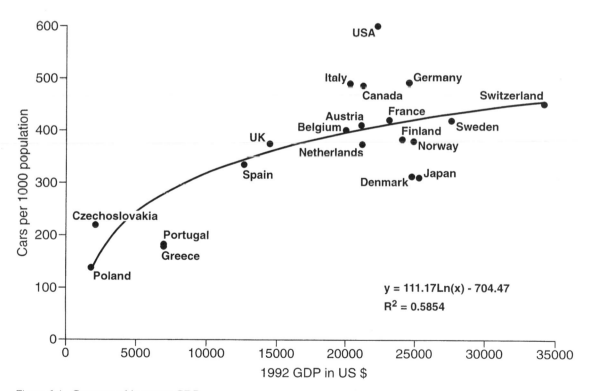

Figure 6.4 Car ownership versus GDP
Source of data: Pucher and Lefevre (1996)

Table 6.2   Growth in car use, by country, 1970–93

| Country | Average Annual Growth Rate (%) | |
	VKT	Cars
USA	2.7	2.2
France	3.2	3.0
W. Germany	3.0	3.6
Great Britain	3.8	3.2
Japan	6.5	6.9

Source: US Department of Transport (1996, 209).

(Jones, 1996). In the EU, the number of passenger-kilometres increased by 85 per cent from 1970 to 1990, with most of the increase attributable to private car use (European Commission, 1992).

Table 6.3 illustrates the great differences in the extent of car use across different countries. The USA continues to lead the world in both car ownership and use, with the highest rate of car ownership, the greatest distances travelled by car, and the largest share of all person-trips by car. Canada has a similar but less extreme pattern. The EU countries have car ownership rates comparable to Canada, but travel fewer kilometres by car and make more extensive use of public transit and the "soft modes", bicycle and walking. Although much of the public policy debate regarding transport focuses on car versus public transport use, it is noteworthy that differences in use of soft modes are quite striking, and that, with the exception of Canada, the soft modes account for a far greater share of all trips than public transport. It is possible that the low population density of much of Canada and the USA limits the potential for very short walks or bike trips.[1]

In addition to per-capita income, differences in car ownership and use across countries are attributed to population density, the density of cars relative to land area or road supply, and car ownership and fuel costs. High population density and limited land area may promote implementation of restraint policies on car use to reduce congestion and other negative effects associated with such travel in densely developed areas. Table 6.4 gives information on these factors for selected countries (limited data availability prevents using the same set of countries as in Table 6.3). Comparing the policies listed in the last two columns of the table, the countries with extreme values (Denmark, The Netherlands, USA), either high or low, have car ownership levels and use consistent with expectations. Road capacity appears to have no relationship; note that road capacity per motor vehicle in Denmark is even higher than that of the USA; road capacity in Germany and Italy is relatively low, while car ownership is relatively high. With the exception of the USA,

Table 6.3   Measures of car use, selected countries

| Country | Ownership, 1992 (cars/pop) | Use, 1992 (km) | Modal Share, 1990, All Person-Trips | | |
			Car	Public Transit	Bike and Walk
USA	0.600	9728	84	3	10
Canada	0.486	8746	74	14	11
Denmark	0.310	5790	42	14	41
France	0.420	5824	54	12	34
Germany	0.492	6228	52	11	37
Netherlands	0.374	5270	44	8	46
UK	0.375	6000	62	14	20
Italy	0.490	5438	25	21	54
Japan	0.313	3108	n/a	n/a	n/a

Source: Adapted from Pucher and Lefevre (1996).

car ownership and use also do not appear to be related to population density. Table 6.4 of course provides only limited information; countries also vary in terms of public transport and car-parking policy, factors that also affect mode choice. Moreover, gross national measures do not directly reflect levels of urbanization or metropolitan size, or the frequently wide variations that occur within individual countries.

Travel patterns within countries are highly varied, yet, with a few exceptions, the same general trend of increasing car use is evident. Comparable travel statistics are very scarce; consequently I present only a few examples. Table 6.5 gives information on mode shares for urban areas in various countries. Care must be taken in making such comparisons, because data are collected differently, and mode and trip definitions may differ across countries and across years. Data for all trips are not available for urban areas in the UK; hence only data for London and for the journey to work for Manchester are presented. Because London is such a large metropolitan area, it is not representative of the general level of car use in other UK urban areas. In all countries, the trend of increasing car use is obvious, but the rate of increase varies greatly. In the USA, where car use was already very high in 1969, increases have been quite small. In contrast, large increases have occurred in the urban areas of Norway and West Germany, as well as in Manchester.

Increased car use has come at the expense of both public transport and non-motorized travel, depending on the urban area. In Germany, the public-transport share has remained quite stable, while the non-motorized share has decreased. In the other countries, both public-transport and non-motorized shares decreased. Decreases in non-motorized trips suggest substitution of longer trips for short trips, as well as population shifts out of core city areas to less dense (and therefore less bike- or pedestrian-accessible) areas.

The exceedingly high rate of car ownership and use in the USA merits further elaboration. Rising car ownership is also illustrated by the decrease in the number of households with no vehicles and increase in households with more than one vehicle. US Census data show that about 21 per cent of all households had no vehicles in 1960; by 1990 the percentage dropped to 11 per cent. In contrast, the share of households with three or more vehicles increased from 2.5 per cent in 1960 to 17 per cent in 1990 (Rosetti and Eversole, 1993).

Observed increases in private vehicle travel in the USA over the past decade have been far in excess of population or employment growth. Between 1983 and 1990, private VKT increased by 37 per cent, while population increased by just 4 per cent. Growth in VKT reflects increases in the number of trips, longer trips, more trips by private vehicle, and more driving alone (Vincent *et al.*, 1994).[2] In

Table 6.4 Explanatory factors for differences in car use, selected countries

Country	Car Ownership, 1992 (cars/pop)	Population Density, 1990 (pop/km^2)	Road Supply, 1990 (road/mv)*	New Car Sales Tax, 1990 (%)	Gasoline, 1992 (US$/litre)
Denmark	0.301	121	60	105–180	1.02
France	0.420	104	47	25	1.07
Germany	0.492	257	26	14	1.04
Italy	0.490	194	18	n/a	1.37
Netherlands	0.374	370	32	18–27	1.20
UK	0.375	236	26	22.7†	0.98
USA	0.600	27	55	5–8	0.31

*Roadway kilometres per motor vehicle.
†Includes VAT of 15% as well as sales tax of 10% wholesale, equivalent to 7.7% retail.
Sources: Compiled from Pucher and Lefevre (1996), Korver *et al.* (1993), Pucher *et al.* (1993).

Table 6.5 Mode share trends, all person-trips, selected urban areas

London	1975–76	1985–86	1989–91
Car	41	44.3	47.8
Public transport	20	17.3	17.0
Bike	3	2.8	1.7
Walk	35	35.0	32.7

Manchester*	1971	1981	1991
Car	32	50	64
Public transport	39	24	16
Bike	2	2	2
Walk	21	19	16

Norwegian City Regions	1970	1985	1990
Car	32	60	68
Public transport	20	11	7
Walk and bike	48	29	25

West German Urban Areas	1972	1982	1992
Car	34	43	49
Public transport	17	17	16
Bike	8	10	12
Walk	41	30	23

USA Urban Areas	1969	1977	1990
Car	79.8	82.3	84.3
Public transport	4.9	3.4	2.8
Bike	0.7	0.7	0.7
Walk	11.5	10.7	9.1

*Journey to work only.
Sources: Pucher and Lefevre (1996), Hervik *et al.* (1993), Brog and Erl (1996).

contrast, public-transport use has continued to lose market share; it accounted for just 2 per cent of all person trips and 5.5 per cent of all journey-to-work trips in 1990 (Hu and Young, 1993).

A second trend over the past few decades is an increase in trip distances. The average journey-to-work distance in France increased from 9 km in 1974 to 11 km in 1986 (Jansen, 1993) and, according to Pucher and Lefevre (1996), to 14 km in 1990.[3] In the UK, average trip distance increased from 11.4 km in 1985 to 12.5 km in 1989 (Pucher and Lefevre, 1996). Between 1983 and 1990, average trip distance in the USA increased from 10.77 to 11.70 km; for the journey to work, the increase was from 13.33 to 16.32 km (Vincent *et al.*, 1994). These increases have not been accompanied by proportionate increases in travel time. In France, travel times have remained stable. The 22 per cent increase in US work-trip length was accompanied by a 6 per cent increase in travel time. Travel speeds have increased as a result of shifts to faster modes (private cars), as well as population and employment decentralization (Gordon *et al.*, 1991; Orfeuil and Salomon, 1993).

The purpose of trip-making has also changed; the work trip constitutes a declining share of all travel, in terms of both trips and travel distance. In The Netherlands urbanized areas, the work-trip share declined from 27.4 per cent in 1980 to 23.4 per cent in 1990; figures for the UK are 46 per cent in 1965 and 33 per cent in 1993 (Pucher and Lefevre, 1996). In terms of travel distance, the work-travel share of all person travel in the UK decreased from 22 per cent in 1975–76 to 19.3 per cent in 1985–86 (Banister and Banister, 1994). Trends have stabilized in the USA. The work-trip share was 23 per cent in 1983 and 22 per cent in 1990; comparable percentages for distance travelled are 26 in 1983 and 27 in 1990 (Hu and Young, 1993).

The declining share of work trips has taken place despite increased labour-force participation rates, especially for women. Thus absolute numbers of work trips are increasing, but travel for other purposes is increasing even faster. US data show that the greatest increase is in "other family/personal business" trips (i.e. not shopping). The ECMT attributes increased non-work travel to changing lifestyles: shorter working weeks, more holidays, smaller households, and increasing affluence (European Conference of Ministers of Transport, 1995). US research suggests that the increased labour-force participation of women – especially those with dependent children – does not change women's roles and responsibilities within the household, so work travel is simply added to already busy daily schedules, hence generating more non-work trips (Hanson and Pratt, 1995; Rosenbloom and Burns, 1993).

WHY THE RISE IN CAR USE AND DECLINE IN USE OF OTHER MODES?

Major explanatory factors for the rise in automobile ownership and use include increased affluence, changing demographics and household structure, labour-force participation and changing land-use patterns.

Rising Affluence

Figure 6.4 showed that national car ownership rates are related to per-capita income. Trip-making and travel are increasing functions of household income, and as travel increases, more trips are made by car. Figure 6.5 presents person-trips and kilometres travelled for US households, by household income category for 1990. Both trips and travel distance increase, but distance increases more than trips: average trip length increases from 10 km for the lowest-income segment to 17.4 km for the highest-income segment. Longer trips mean more trips by car. The increasing rate of car travel with income is illustrated in Table 6.6, which gives mode shares for the same household income categories. For car trips, I separate trips made as driver and trips made as passenger. The "trucks and other" category also refers to personal vehicles; unfortunately, the survey data do not distinguish driver and passenger trips within this category. It is quite evident that the lowest-income households make many more non-motorized trips than other households, and that these households have the smallest share of drive-alone trips. Even among the lowest-income households, most trips are made in private vehicles, and public transport is a distant third share. As household income increases, private vehicle trips (and particularly drive-alone trips) replace non-motorized trips. Note that the share of trips made as car passenger is quite consistent across income categories.

Higher income implies higher value of time, making travel time relatively more important in travel choice decisions. As the value of travel time increases, faster modes will be preferred, all else being equal. The personal car is by far the fastest and most

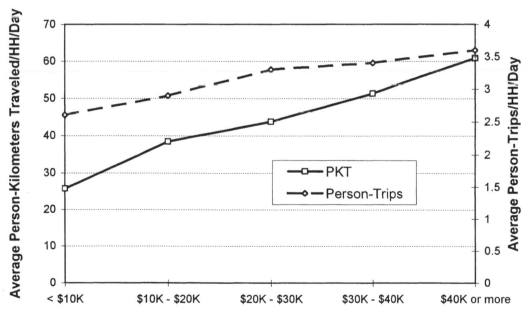

Figure 6.5   US person-trips and travel by household income, 1990
Source of data: Hu and Young (1993)

Table 6.6   US mode shares by household income category, all person-trips, 1990

Mode	Household Income (US $'000)				
	10 or less	10 –20	20 –30	30 –40	over 40
Car driver	41.6	52.6	53.9	54.3	58.1
Car passenger	21.0	20.7	21.1	20.8	21.9
Truck/other	7.4	11.3	12.5	13.5	10.9
Public transport	3.7	2.8	2.0	1.3	1.2
Walk/bike	22.4	9.2	7.9	6.9	5.2

Columns to not add to 100, because other modes (taxi, school bus, etc.) are not included.
Source: Hu and Young (1993, 4–58).

convenient mode of travel, except in the most heavily congested urban core areas. It is therefore not surprising that car use has increased most rapidly outside these core areas.

Household Structure

Household size has declined both in the USA and in Europe for several decades. Average number of persons per US household in 1990 was 2.63, down from 2.75 in 1980. Moreover, household composition is changing; the most rapid increase (29.2 per cent) was among non-family households, e.g. persons living alone or with other non-family persons (Pisarski, 1996). These changes reflect trends of the past few decades, including: rising divorce rates; ageing of the population, which results in more women living alone upon the death of a spouse; and young adults leaving home and forming independent households.

Similar patterns have been observed in European countries. Household size in the UK fell from 2.91 in 1971 to 2.48 in 1991; in Germany from 2.8 to 2.3; and in Italy from 3.6 to 2.8 for the same period (Masser *et al.*, 1992). Masser *et al.* provide the following explanatory factors: declining fertility rates, rising divorce rates, breaking up of the extended family system, ageing of the population, and growing economic independence of women and young people.

Declining household size means more travel for personal or household needs. Regular household activities (food shopping, laundry and cleaning, home maintenance, social visits, etc.) are shared among fewer household members. In addition, non-family households are less likely to share resources; therefore we would expect such members to behave more like individuals living alone, hence generating more household trips.

Labour-Force Participation

In both the USA and European countries, observed increases in the labour-force participation rate are mainly due to increased participation by women. For example, the UK female participation rate increased from 36 per cent in 1976 to 48 per cent in 1985; in Italy the increase was even greater: from 14 to 34 per cent (Masser *et al.*, 1992). Figure 6.6 shows that female participation rates vary greatly across countries, and that the female participation rate increased between 1984 and 1994 in every country listed. In the USA, female participation surged in the 1960s and 1970s, but the rate of increase slowed in the 1980s, as the female rate approached that of males.

Increased participation in the labour market by women has at least two significant effects on travel. Firstly, more working women means more households with multiple workers. In the USA, 70 per cent of all working households had two or more workers in 1990 (Pisarski, 1996). Housing location choice decisions are more complex for households with multiple workers; all else being equal, it is more difficult for such households to live close to work, given dispersed job locations. Although research shows that women generally travel shorter distances to work than men, it seems reasonable to attribute some of the observed increases in commuter travel distances to the rise in multiple-worker households.

Secondly, increased participation of women in the workforce has not been accompanied by any major changes in household responsibilities. As noted above, the task of paid work tends to be added to existing tasks. Working women are normally subject to greater time pressure, and consequently attribute high value to the efficiency of driving alone. The

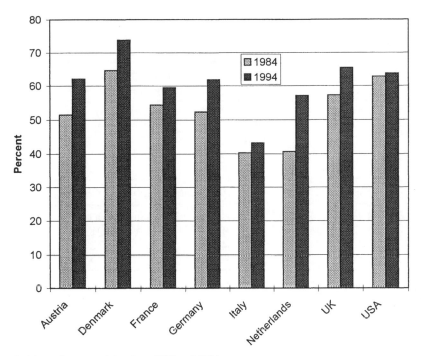

Figure 6.6 Female labour-force participation, 1984 and 1994
Source of data: US Department of Commerce, Bureau of the Census (1996), Table 1348, p. 842

value women place on driving alone is demonstrated in the USA by the higher likelihood of women driving alone than men when household income is controlled (Rosenbloom, 1995). Also, although US women in 1990 still drove fewer annual VKT than men, the rate of increase in VKT since 1983 has been higher for women (Pisarski, 1992).

Changing Land-Use Patterns

The major trend in urban spatial patterns for several decades has been decentralization. Suburbanization of population and employment has been evident in the USA throughout the twentieth century, despite the conventional wisdom that it is a phenomenon associated with the surge in car ownership and highway building that occurred after World War II. Large-scale population suburbanization was followed by large-scale employment decentralization

and by the emergence of major agglomerations outside the traditional downtown (Muller, 1995). More recently, decentralization has been accompanied by dispersion, with most growth occurring outside major urban centres. A similar process of population and employment decentralization is also evident within most metropolitan areas in Europe, although from a very different starting point and with a wider degree of variability of experience. Indeed, decentralization has been documented in major metropolitan areas throughout the developed world.

Table 6.7 gives population growth rates for US metropolitan areas with 1 million or more population, by decade, 1960 through 1990, using US Census data. In each decade, population growth was more rapid in suburban counties than in central counties. In 1960, central counties accounted for a majority of the metropolitan population, but by 1970 the majority shifted to suburban counties. The

Table 6.7 Population growth for US metropolitan areas with 1 million or more population, central and suburban counties

(a) Population growth rates (%)

Years	Total Area	Central County	Suburban Counties
1960–70	18.50	10.20	27.35
1970–80	7.78	2.82	12.35
1980–90	11.81	9.22	13.79

(b) Population shares (%)

Year	Central County	Suburban Counties
1960	51.60	48.40
1970	47.99	52.01
1980	43.28	56.72
1990	42.27	57.73

Source: Rosetti and Eversole (1993).

suburban county share continued to increase through 1990.

Population decentralization has been accompanied by employment decentralization. Empirical evidence of this trend is extensive. Gordon and Richardson (1996) calculated average annual employment growth rates for 54 US metropolitan areas for 1976–80 and 1980–86. Areas were segmented into the CBD (central business district), the remainder of the central city, and the remaining metropolitan area excluding the central city. Results are shown in Table 6.8. In all cases, growth rates are highest outside the central city. In other work, Gordon *et al.* (1996) used annual US employment data

Table 6.8 Employment growth within US metropolitan areas*

	1976–80	1980–86
CBD	0.0190	0.0128
Remainder of central city	0.0392	0.0276
Metropolitan area outside central city	0.0545	0.0381

*Average annual growth rate calculated from 1976, 1980 and 1986 data.
Source: Gordon and Richardson (1996, 1738).

by county, 1969 through 1994, and found that average annual employment growth rates in suburban counties exceed those of central counties in nearly all cases.

Similar trends are evident in European metropolitan areas. Table 6.9 gives population and employment changes for several metropolitan areas, for core city areas and their suburbs. In all but one case (Liverpool employment), population and employment grew faster (or declined more slowly) in the suburbs than in the core city. Note that the table includes metropolitan areas in several different countries, and that the most recent series ends in 1985. It is possible that more recent data would reveal an acceleration of these trends, given the effects of globalization and the shift to an information-based economy. On the other hand, it is possible that the greater regulatory controls over land use that exist in most European countries may lead to some attenuation of these trends.

Before these trends were clearly evident and documented in European and other developed countries, decentralization was perceived as a uniquely American US phenomenon. Explanatory factors commonly identified included the following:[4]

Table 6.9 Population and employment decentralization in selected european cities, average annual percentage change

City	Population			Employment		
	Years	Core City	Suburbs	Years	Core City	Suburbs
Antwerp	1970–81	−0.8	+1.2	1974–84	−0.7	+0.4
Copenhagen	1970–85	−1.5	+1.0	1970–83	−0.3	+3.2
Hamburg	1970–81	−0.8	+1.9	1961–83	−0.8	+1.9
Liverpool	1971–80	−1.6	−0.4	1978–84	−2.6	−3.1
Milan	1968–80	−0.6	+1.3	1971–81	−0.9	+1.9
Paris	1968–80	−1.1	+1.1	1975–82	−1.1	+0.9
Rotterdam	1970–80	−1.6	+2.2	1975–84	−1.1	+1.5

Source: Jansen (1993).

1. Federal tax and mortgage policies that made suburban residential development more economically attractive.
2. Tax and pricing policies favourable to car ownership and use.
3. The Federal Interstate Highway construction programme.
4. Changing industrial technology that favoured horizontal manufacturing structures and shifts to service-sector activities less reliant on central location.
5. Political fragmentation of local government that enabled escape from urban social and fiscal problems.
6. Ethnic and racial segmentation.
7. Historical preferences for single-family home ownership.
8. The tradition of private property rights.

In the light of similar trends throughout the developed world, explanatory factors for decentralization merit further consideration. It would appear that economic forces – rising per-capita incomes and economic restructuring – play a more important role than previously thought. Rising income increases demand for consumer goods, including housing. Preferences for single-family homes, for example, may not be so uniquely American after all. One small piece of supporting evidence comes from a 1985 survey conducted in West Germany. Respondents were asked, "How would you like to live?" Replies were 59 per cent for a detached house, 18 per cent for a "row" house, and the remainder for apartments and condominiums. At the time of the survey, just 40 per cent of the respondents actually lived in detached or row houses (Masser *et al.*, 1992, 115). As demand for single family housing increases, households seek more affordable locations in the suburbs in Germany, France, the UK, or the USA.

US patterns of shopping and retailing are also evident in many European metropolitan areas. The out-of-town shopping centre, conveniently accessible only by car and typically offering free parking, can be found along expressways in the suburbs of London, Milan, Munich, Paris and most other cities. More recently, "big box" retailing ("superstores") and discount malls have appeared. A recent British report states (Royal Commission on Environmental Pollution, 1995, 16):

There have been major changes in the way people shop. Between 1982 and 1992 more than half of new retail floorspace opened was at out-of-town sites, compared with only one seventh between 1960 and 1981. Between 1988 and 1992, the number of superstores . . . increased by more than half. . . . The last decade has seen the creation of a small number of massive out-of-town shopping centres, each containing hundreds of shops. . . . In all, 37% of retail sales in 1992 were in out-of-town locations, compared to only 5% in 1980.

The Royal Commission attributes these changes in UK shopping patterns to rising affluence; shopping has become a leisure activity, and people are less willing to patronize the closest shops or facilities. Rather, people are choosing "to travel further to obtain a quality or kind of service which they see as more desirable" (Royal Commission on Environmental Pollution, 1995, 17). The UK central government has issued planning guidelines to discourage further development of out-of-town shopping centres (Curtis, 1996); however, the effectiveness of such guidelines remains to be determined.

Changes in economic structure also promote decentralization.[5] The shift to a service-based economy implies greater firm mobility (service activities require less infrastructure investment than manufacturing, and therefore are more easily relocated). As the population decentralizes, service firms follow, seeking access to the labour-force. Improvements in information and communications technology (ICT) reduce the benefits of agglomeration, and hence firms place less value on central locations and seek lower-cost (suburban) locations. Declining agglomeration benefits also imply that congestion and other costs of agglomeration will not be as easily offset, and thus will promote additional decentralization.

Improvements in ICT are expected to continue and intensify. These improvements have made possible vertical disintegration of firms, spatial dispersion of firm activities, outsourcing of routine functions, and a variety of flexible production methods. The effect of these changes is to overcome the friction of distance – to take advantage of specialized resources and labour markets, wherever they may be located. A US analysis summarizes ICT effects as follows (US Congress Office of Technology Assessment, 1995, 61):

> In sum, technology is connecting economic activities, enabling them to be physically farther apart, reducing the competitive advantage of high-cost, congested urban locations, and allowing people and businesses more (but not total) freedom to choose where they will live and work.

COMMUTING PATTERNS

Decentralization of population and employment is reflected in commuting patterns. To summarize, traditional commuting to the city centre is no longer the dominant commuter flow. Commuting between suburban locations is now the major flow in the USA, and is also the fastest-growing commuter flow in European metropolitan areas. Table 6.10 gives commuter flow data for the USA, drawn again from US Census data. Since the Census only began asking for work location in 1980, comparisons are available only for 1980 and 1990. The data are compiled by county, a local political jurisdiction that can include one or more cities. Central counties therefore encompass the central city of the metropolitan areas as well as adjacent cities and county areas. "Central county" therefore overstates the central city portion in nearly every case. Nevertheless, the US Census is the most reliable data source for national data, so it is used here. Several observations are to be drawn from Table 6.10. Firstly, central counties were the location of the greatest share of job destinations in both years, but the share declines. Conversely, the share of job destinations in suburban and exurban locations increases. Secondly, the suburban resident worker share increases, as illustrated previously in Table 6.8. Thirdly, the largest flow is central county to central county in 1980, but is suburban county to suburban county in 1990. Using more disaggregate data, Pisarski (1996) allocates the increase in commuter flows between 1980 and 1990 as follows: 58 per cent suburb to suburb, 20 per cent suburb to central city, 12 per cent central city to suburb, and 10 per cent city to city. Thus suburb-to-suburb commuting continues to be the fastest-growing commuting flow segment.

With more suburban job destinations and fewer central city job destinations comes more use of the private car. Table 6.11 gives mode share for US journey-to-work trips by destination location category. I include the carpool category, because in the USA it is considered a separate mode, and its share is second only to driving alone. Even in the USA, public transport still carries a significant portion of work trips to central city destinations. In contrast, more people walk or bike to suburban jobs than take public transport, and the private vehicle accounts for 90 per cent of all trips.

Table 6.10 Commuter flows in US metropolitan areas, 1980 and 1990

(a) 1980: 31 metropolitan areas

| Place of Residence | Place of Work | | | |
	Central County	Suburban County	Outside Area	Subtotal
Central county	41.90	2.70	0.83	45.43
Suburban county	12.14	40.90	1.53	54.57
Subtotal	54.03	43.60	2.36	100.00

(b) 1990: 39 metropolitan areas

| Place of Residence | Place of Work | | | |
	Central County	Suburban County	Outside Area	Subtotal
Central county	38.05	3.57	0.83	42.44
Suburban county	11.68	43.52	2.34	57.55
Subtotal	49.73	47.09	3.17	100.00

Source: Computed from Rosetti and Eversole (1993).

Table 6.11 Journey-to-work mode choice, 1990, by job location, USA

| Job Location | Mode Share (%) | | | | |
	Drive Alone	Car Pool	Public Transport	Walk/Bike	Other*
Central city	68.2	13.4	11.0	4.7	2.9
Suburbs	77.5	12.9	2.0	3.5	3.3

*Includes work at home.
Source: Pisarski (1996, 84).

The same trend of dispersing commuter flows is evident in the EU. Once again, limited data make possible only a few examples. Firstly, Table 6.12 gives information similar to that of Table 6.11, but for the Greater London metropolitan area. No distinction is made between driving alone and carpools, so the private vehicle share in Table 6.12 is comparable to the total of the first two columns of Table 6.11. As would be expected, differences in mode shares across the four geographic areas are quite pronounced. Fully three-quarters of Central London workers travel by public transport, while that share falls to just 7 per cent in the outermost area. Private vehicle use shows the opposite pattern. Note also

that (i) even in the most remote parts of the London metropolitan area, there is a greater share of both public transport and walk/bike than in the US suburbs; (ii) the large share of walk/bike in the "Rest of South East" area suggests that many work trips are quite short, in contrast to the US; and (iii) most jobs are located in the suburban areas, where the private car is the dominant mode.

Secondly, Table 6.13 gives percentage change in commuter flows for the Paris region between 1975 and 1982. The greatest decline occurred in the central city to central city flow, while the greatest increase occurred in outer suburb to inner suburb commuting. Other large increases took place in

Table 6.12   Journey-to-work mode choice, 1995, by job location, Greater London

Job Location	Mode Share (%)*				Number of Workers
	Private Car†	Bus/Rail	Walk/Bike	Other‡	
Central London	17	75	5	2	972 000
Rest of Inner London	40	41	16	2	738 000
Outer London	67	18	13	1	1 315 000
Rest of South-East England	76	7	17	1	4 030 000

*Excludes work at home.
†Includes car, van, minibus.
‡Motorcycle.
Source: Department of Transport (1996).

Table 6.13   Percentage change in commuter flows, Paris region, 1975–82

Place of Residence	Place of Work		
	Paris	Inner Suburbs	Outer Suburbs
Paris	−14	−5	19
Inner suburbs	−8	−7	18
Outer suburbs	7	21	11

Source: Jansen (1993).

central city to outer suburbs, and inner suburbs to outer suburbs. These shifts imply significant dispersion of travel flows and longer-distance commuting, which in turn implies greater use of private vehicles.

The final example comes from Germany. Between 1970 and 1988, the share of workers living and working in the same city declined from 72 per cent to 61 per cent. The increase in commuting by car that occurred over this period is the result of both longer-distance commuting and generally increased demand for car travel. For example, among those living and working in the same city, the car share increased from 25 per cent to 42 per cent. Most of this increase was taken from the soft mode share, which decreased from 52 to 44 per cent. Among those working in a different city, the car share increased from 59 to 79 per cent, and this increase was taken primarily from public transport, which declined from 35 to 15 per cent (Jansen, 1993).

CONCLUSIONS

This chapter has described major aspects of urban travel patterns within the context of rising car ownership and use. I have shown that people are travelling more in terms of both trips and travel distance, and most of the increase is due to use of the car. The car provides people with unprecedented levels of mobility; as per-capita income rises, people use their resources and take advantage of this mobility to live, work, shop and conduct leisure pursuits where they most prefer. Rapid and convenient mobility also allows people to conduct busy, time-pressured daily activity schedules. Access to the private car, for example, makes it possible for mothers of young children both to work outside the home and to fulfil household and childcare responsibilities. Access to the private car also makes it possible to conduct business meetings in several locations over the course of a day. People who prefer to live in the countryside can keep their jobs in the city, if they are willing to drive the longer commuting distances involved. Given the benefits of "car mobility", we should not be surprised by the trends described in this chapter.

Rising car use has been supported by larger economic trends that have increased per-capita income and favoured employment as well as population decentralization. As the decentralization process advances and land-use patterns become more complementary to the car, other modes become less competitive. Consequently, rising car use has been accompanied by declines in both public transit use and the soft modes. Public transit cannot compete with the superior travel times of the private automobile for longer trips. The soft-mode share declines as trip distance increases; having a car available makes it possible to substitute a short walk trip with a longer car trip. At the same time, as suburbanization continues, an increasingly large proportion of the population will live in lower-density areas where walk and bike accessibility are poor.

The social, environmental and financial consequences of these trends are of course significant. Growing reliance on the private car may not be sustainable: a large proportion of the world's known energy resources are consumed by transport; air and water pollution are causing damage to human health and to the natural environment; and the economic vitality of central cities may be threatened. Developing alternative concepts of "sustainable cities", and specifying more clearly the social costs of transport, have consequently become major objectives of planning and policy research.

There are no easy solutions to the problem of restraining the private car, however. As we have seen, individuals reap large benefits from using their cars and, as private vehicle use continues to spread and alternatives to the car become less viable, democratic governments will find it increasingly difficult to implement automobile restraint policies. Nevertheless, the negative aspects of the private car must be addressed. It is hoped that this chapter has conveyed some understanding of the underlying forces at work, and therefore will help to enlighten and inform policy discussion.

NOTES

1. Population density in persons per square kilometre is: USA 27, Canada 3, France 104, Germany 257, UK 236, Italy 194, Japan 336 (Pucher and Lefevre, 1996).
2. There is some disagreement on the increase in travel distance. Lave (1996) claims that this increase, estimated from national travel survey data, is excessive. Using other data sources, Lave estimates a VMT (vehicle-miles travelled) annual growth rate of 1.4 to 1.5 per cent over the same period, compared to the 2.7 per cent increase implied by the above numbers (results in kilometres not available).
3. Pucher and Lefevre (1996) do not provide a source for this number.
4. For reviews see Jackson (1985) and Muller (1981).
5. There is an extensive literature on economic restructuring and regional development. See for example Graham and Marvin (1996), Hepworth (1989) and Scott (1988).

REFERENCES

Banister, D. and Banister, C. (1994), "Energy consumption in transport in Great Britain: macro-level estimates", *Transportation Research A* 29, 21–32.

Brog, W. and Erl, E. (1996), "Germany", in *Changing daily urban mobility: less or differently?* Report of the 102nd Round Table on Transport Economics (Paris: European Conference of Ministers of Transport).

Chapin, F. (1974), *Human activity patterns in the city: things people do in time and space* (New York: Wiley).

Curtis, C. (1996), "Can strategic planning contribute to a reduction in car-based travel?", *Transport Policy* 112 (3), 55–65.

Department of Transport (1996), *Transport statistics Great Britain 1996* (London: HMSO).

European Commission (1992), *Green Paper on the impact of transport on the environment: a community strategy for "sustainable mobility"* (Brussels: European Commission).

European Conference of Ministers of Transport (1995) *Urban travel and sustainable development* (Paris: Organization for Economic Co-operation and Development).

Gordon, P. and Richardson, H. (1996), "Employment decentralization in US metropolitan areas: is Los Angeles an outlier or the norm?", *Environment and Planning A* 28, 1727–43.

Gordon, P., Richardson, H. and Jun, M. (1991), "The commuting paradox: evidence from the top twenty", *Journal of the American Planning Association* 57 (4), 416–20.

Gordon, P., Richardson, H. and Yu, G. (1996), "Settlement patterns in the US: recent evidence and implications", paper presented at the TRED Conference, Cambridge, MA.

Graham, S. and Marvin, S. (1996), *Telecommunications and the city* (London: Routledge).

Hägerstrand. T. (1970), "What about people in regional science?", *Papers, Regional Science Association* 24, 7–21.

Hanson, S. (1995), "Getting there: urban transportation in context", in Hanson, S. (ed.), *The geography of urban transportation*, 2nd edn (New York: Guilford).

Hanson, S. and Pratt, G. (1995), *Gender, work and space* (New York: Routledge).

Haynes, K. and Fotheringham, A.S. (1984), *Gravity and spatial interaction models,* Scientific Geography Series, 2 (Beverly Hills, CA: Sage).

Hepworth, M. (1989), *The geography of the information economy* (London: Belhaven).

Hervik, A., Tretvik, T. and Ovstedal, L. (1993), "Norway: crossing fjords and mountains", in Salomon, I., Bovy, P. and Orfeuil, J.-P. (eds), *A billion trips a day: tradition and transition in European travel patterns* (Dordrecht: Kluwer Academic), 349–66.

Hu, P. and Young, J. (1993), *1990 NPTS databook, nationwide personal transportation survey,* Report FHWA-PL-94-010A (Washington, DC: Federal Highway Administration).

Jackson, K. (1985), *Crabgrass frontier* (New York: Oxford University Press).

Jansen, G. (1993), "Commuting: home sprawl, job sprawl and traffic jams", in Salomon, I., Bovy, P. and Orfeuil, J.-P. (eds), *A billion trips a day: tradition and transition in European travel patterns* (Dordrecht: Kluwer Academic).

Jones, P. (1996), "United Kingdom", in *Changing daily urban mobility: less or differently?* Report of the 102nd Round Table on Transport Economics (Paris: European Conference of Ministers of Transport), 101–28.

Korver, W., Klooster, J. and Jansen, G. (1993), "Car: increasing ownership and decreasing use?", in Salomon, I., Bovy, P. and Orfeuil, J.-P. (eds), *A billion trips a day: tradition and transition in European travel patterns* (Dordrecht: Kluwer Academic), 75–100.

Lave, C. (1996), "Are Americans really driving so much?", *Access* 8, 14–17.

Masser, I., Sviden, O. and Wegener, M. (1992), *The geography of Europe's futures* (London: Belhaven).

May, T. (1993), "Transport policy and management", in Banister, D. and Button, K. (eds), *Transport, the environment and sustainable development* (London: Spon).

Muller, P. (1981), *Contemporary suburban America* (Englewood Cliffs, NJ: Prentice Hall).

Muller, P. (1995), "Transportation and urban form: stages in the spatial evolution of the American metropolis", in Hanson, S. (ed.), *The geography of urban transportation*, 2nd Edition (New York: Guilford).

Orfeuil, J.-P. and Salomon, I. (1993), "Travel patterns of the Europeans in everyday life", in Salomon, I., Bovy, P. and Orfeuil, J.-P. (eds), *A billion trips a day: tradition and transition in European travel patterns* (Dordrecht: Kluwer Academic), 241–56.

Pisarski, A. (1992), *Travel behaviour issues in the 90s* (Washington, DC: Federal Highway Administration).

Pisarski, A. (1996), *Commuting in America II* (Lansdowne, VA: Eno Foundation).

Pucher, J. and Lefevre, C. (1996), *The urban transport crisis in Europe and North America* (Basingstoke: Macmillan).

Pucher, J., Ioannides, D. and Hirschman, I. (1993), "Passenger transport in the United States and Europe: a comparative analysis of public sector involvement," in Banister, D. and Berechman, J. (eds), *Transport in a unified Europe: policies and challenges* (Amsterdam: North-Holland), 369–416.

Rosenbloom, S. (1995), "Travel by women", in *NPTS demographic special reports* (Washington, DC: Office of Highway Information Management, Federal Highway Administration), chapter 2.

Rosenbloom, S. and Burns, E. (1993), "Why working women drive alone: implications for transportation demand management programs", *Transportation Research Record* 1459, 39–45.

Rosetti, M. and Eversole B. (1993), *Journey to work trends in the United States and its major metropolitan areas, 1960–1990* (Washington, DC: Federal Highway Administration).

Royal Commission on Environmental Pollution (1995), *Transport and the environment, eighteenth report* (Oxford: Oxford University Press).

Scott, A. (1988), *Metropolis: from division of labour to urban form* (Berkeley, CA: University of California Press).

Small, K.A. (1992), *Urban transportation economics* (Chur, Switzerland: Harwood Academic).

US Congress, Office of Technology Assessment (1995), *The technological reshaping of America,* Report OTA-ETI-643 (Washington, DC: US Government Printing Office).

US Department of Commerce, Bureau of the Census (1996), *Statistical Abstract of the United States, 1996* (Washington, DC: Bureau of the Census).

US Department of Transportation, Bureau of Transportation Statistics (1996), *Transportation statistics annual report 1996* (Washington, DC: Bureau of Transportation Statistics).

Vincent, M., Keyes, M. and Reed, M. (1994), *NPTS urban travel patterns: 1990 nationwide personal transportation survey,* Report FHWA-PL-94-018 (Washington, DC: Federal Highway Administration).

7

URBAN TRANSPORT PROBLEMS AND SOLUTIONS

Brian Turton and Richard Knowles

In towns and cities of the developed world the principal transport difficulties are caused by the dominance of the private car, leading to severe congestion on urban roads, together with a steady decline in the patronage of public transport. In Third World cities public-transport facilities are grossly inadequate and inner areas are congested with a mixture of motorized, animal-drawn and pedestrian traffic. Solutions to transport problems include new road construction, traffic-management schemes, rail-based rapid-transit systems, transport coordination programmes, congestion pricing and non-transport solutions that reduce demand.

INTRODUCTION

In towns and cities of the developed world the principal transport problems are caused by usage of the private car, which creates severe congestion on often inadequate road systems and has led to a sharp decline in the patronage of public transport. Car ownership levels are very low in cities of the developing world and public-transport services are also grossly inadequate, with inner areas congested with motorized vehicles, animal-drawn vehicles and pedestrians. Current solutions to these problems include improved infrastructure, traffic management, new initiatives in public transport, transport coordination programmes and, in the longer term, more effective urban land-use planning in order to reduce levels of traffic generation.

Almost all of the world's urban areas experience difficulties in planning for the wide variety of personal and commodity journeys described in Chapter 6. Major cities in particular provide an arena in which the principal modes exist in a competitive environment, creating what is often an inefficient system of movements. Devising and implementing solutions to ensure a more efficient use of the urban-transport infrastructure has been a principal concern of policy-makers, planners and transport operators. Many of the issues involved, such as transport policy, administrative control and environmental conflict, are discussed elsewhere in this book, and this chapter concentrates upon the leading difficulties and the currently available remedies. These two are interrelated in the urban transport-planning process, involving the identification and classification of travel patterns, the forecasting of future movements in the context of urban developments and modes of transport available, and finally the implementation of the most appropriate plan to cater for traffic in the most acceptable manner (Dimitriou, 1990a). In this chapter attention is focused upon the spatial aspects of this transport-planning process. The nature and scale of transport problems vary with the size and

Modern Transport Geography: second, revised edition. Edited by Brian Hoyle and Richard Knowles.
© 1998 John Wiley & Sons Ltd.

shape of the urban area, the balance between use of private and public transport, and the level of road and public-transport infrastructure that exists. One major contributory factor is the tendency for an increasing separation of home and the most common destinations, resulting in a higher level of personal trip-making and lengthier journeys. These in turn impose greater demands upon road and public-transport systems that are already nearing or exceeding their capacity (Hanson, 1995a,b). Traffic congestion is thus one of the most common problems encountered to some extent in almost all urban areas. To this must be added pollution and other related environmental issues, and the complex problem of equity in terms of personal accessibility for the different groups within urban society.

PROBLEMS

Congestion

Traffic congestion occurs when urban transport networks are no longer capable of accommodating the volume of movements that use them. The location of congested areas is determined by the physical transport framework and by the patterns of urban land use and their associated trip-generating activities. Levels of traffic overloading vary in time, with a very well-marked peak during the daily journey-to-work periods. Although most congestion can be attributed to overloading, there are other aspects of this basic problem that also require solutions. In the industrialized countries increasing volumes of private car, public transport and commercial vehicle traffic have exposed the inadequacies of urban roads, especially in older city centres where street patterns have survived largely unaltered from the nineteenth century and earlier. The intricate nature of these centres makes motorized movements difficult and long-term car parking almost impossible. In developing countries the problem is particularly acute: Indian and South-East Asian cities often have cores composed of a mesh of narrow streets often accessible only to non-motorized traffic. The rapid growth in private

car ownership and use in Western cities in the period since 1950 has rarely been accompanied by a corresponding upgrading of the road network, and these increases will probably continue into the twenty-first century, further exacerbating the problem. In less-developed countries car ownership in urban areas is at a much lower level (Table 7.1) but there is evidence of an increased rate in recent decades, especially in South America and South-East Asia (Rimmer, 1986). Satisfactory definitions of the saturation level of car ownership vary but if a ratio of 50 cars to 100 persons is taken then in several US cities the figure is now over 80 per 100, whereas in South-East Asian cities the level rarely exceeds 10 per 100. One factor contributing to congestion in developing world cities is the uncontrolled intermixing of motorized and animal- or human-drawn vehicles. The proliferation of pedal and motor cycles causes particular difficulties (Simon, 1996).

Public-Transport Decline

Congestion on urban buses and trains is a major problem but is only one of a group of interrelated factors initiating a cycle of decline that results in deteriorating services and reduced revenue. Buses and tramcars contribute to the overall problem of excessive vehicle flows and there is frequently overcrowding and unacceptable conditions for passengers within vehicles. Urban railway systems also experience congestion when, even at maximum frequency and capacity, trains are incapable of meeting demands, and overcrowding becomes a permanent and unpopular feature of travel during the morning and late afternoon peaks.

One common difficulty directly attributable to the growth of car usage is the decline in public-transport patronage. The resultant reduced revenues often inevitably lead to lower frequencies and higher fares, which in turn further discourage the use of services, producing a cyclic effect which, unless arrested, can result in the virtual elimination of public transport in smaller towns and a substantial rationalization in larger cities. There are also marked reductions in the use of public transport outside the peak periods, and the concentration of traffic into the latter creates

Table 7.1   Basic transport data for selected Third World cities

City	Population, 1985 ('000)	Cars per 1000 Population, 1980	Cars: Annual Growth Rate, 1970–80 (%)	Buses per 1000 Population, 1980
Bangkok	6100	71	7.9	1.22
Bogota	4500	42	7.8	2.13
Bombay	10 100	21	6.1	0.36
Buenos Aires	10 900	53	10.0	1.20
Cairo	7700	32	17.0	1.10
Calcutta	11 000	10	5.6	0.33
Hong Kong	5100	39	7.4	1.83
Jakarta	7900	33	9.8	0.72
Karachi	6700	35	8.4	2.32
Manila	7000	45	8.0	5.30
Mexico City	17 300	105	–	1.23
Rio de Janeiro	10 400	104	12.1	1.20
Sao Paulo	15 900	151	7.8	1.28
Seoul	10 300	15	11.7	1.55

Source: Dimitriou (1990b).

serious problems for operators when attempting to provide the most efficient services in terms of staff and vehicle deployment. Demands during the peak cannot be satisfactorily accommodated, and at other times patronage is often insufficient to justify the provision of services.

Car Parking

The provision of adequate car parking space within or on the margins of central business districts (CBDs) for city workers and shoppers is a problem that has serious implications for land-use planning. A proliferation of costly and visually intrusive multistorey car-parks can only provide a partial solution and supplementary on-street parking often compounds road congestion. The extension of pedestrian precincts and retail malls in city centres is intended to provide more acceptable environments for shoppers and other users of city centres. However, such traffic-free zones in turn produce problems as they create new patterns of access to commercial centres for car-borne travellers and users of public transport, while the latter often lose their former advantage of being conveyed directly to the central shopping area (Roberts, 1981).

Changing Land-Use Patterns

The increasing trends towards siting retailing complexes, leisure centres and business parks on the peripheries of major urban areas have also created new transport problems. Bus routes, which traditionally focus upon city centres, rarely offer convenient access to these new marginally located complexes and larger retailers often introduce their own bus services to attract customers from neighbouring housing areas. Car-borne shoppers using these new centres on the urban fringe often create traffic problems as they drive through suburban areas, and similar cross-city trips are made by leisure centre patrons and workers in business and science parks (Hall, 1989). The development of these peripheral centres was initially seen as desirable as they reduce the volumes of traffic destined for city centres, but planners are becoming concerned at the decline of central business districts and are now restricting new fringe expansions.

City Problems in Developing Countries

The difficulties faced by urban populations in the developing countries are often far greater than those encountered in the Western world, and Dimitriou has assembled a comprehensive list of the principal problems involved. They include rapid traffic growth, poorly maintained transport infrastructure, inefficient operations, a mix of old and new transport technology, ineffective traffic management and enforcement, inadequate public-transport services, transport problems of the poorest groups, high accident rates and weak institutional support for transport facilities (Dimitriou, 1992).

Many of these problems are shared with industrialized countries, but in the developing world the opportunities for implementing solutions are fewer. Although rising car ownership is a feature of urban expansion, most journeys are still made either on foot, by bus or, to a more limited extent, by rail. The extension of low-income immigrant settlements on city fringes exerts increasing pressure on already inadequate bus services. This problem of expanding demand would be more serious if it were not for the fact that low disposable incomes prevent many workers from making regular use of public transport (Roth, 1984). For example, in Indian cities the costs of using public transport, expressed in terms of GDP per capita, can be four times those in the UK, and in Delhi up to 36 per cent of disposable income can be spent on bus travel (White, 1990). Those who can afford to use buses endure long, slow, uncomfortable trips on poorly maintained vehicles and heavily congested roads, and wherever practicable urban migrants try to live as closely as possible to their workplaces. Purchase of new buses and the maintenance to a satisfactory standard of existing vehicles is frequently hampered by a shortage of foreign currency. It is not unusual for between 60 per cent and 80 per cent of a fleet to be out of service because of a lack of spare parts and skilled mechanics, yet a 70 per cent level of availability is generally seen as the minimum acceptable to ensure satisfactory services (Dimitriou, 1990b). Because of these shortages of both new and existing buses, few companies in the developing countries are able to satisfy the demand for services in existing areas or in newly established immigrant settlements.

With continuing rapid population growth in the twenty-first century the users of public transport will encounter increasing difficulties, especially in the larger cities of Brazil, China, Indonesia, India and Nigeria. A comparison of bus availability levels illustrates the difficulties faced by many developing countries. Whereas in the UK there are 0.9 buses per 1000 population, the ratio in the developing countries is about 0.6 per 1000, falling to only 0.3 in some Indian cities. However, the relative smallness of the bus fleets is compensated for by a much more intensive usage of the vehicles, each bus travelling for 70 000 km per annum in some countries compared with only 45 000 km in British towns and cities (White, 1990).

These inadequacies in the formal public-transport sector have encouraged the expansion of paratransit modes which flourish, legally and otherwise, on routes alongside conventional vehicles and in those urban areas where larger buses cannot operate in the narrow streets. A substantial share of this informal traffic is now carried by minibuses, and although these, together with hand-drawn and motorized rickshaws and similar vehicles, do meet a demand for transport, they in turn create serious difficulties with their slow speeds and frequent stops to pick up and set down passengers. Because of the usually small scale of these paratransit undertakings, their owners often concentrate their activities along corridors where revenue is most likely to be maximized, and other areas where some form of public transport is needed tend to be ignored or poorly served.

The Transport-Deprived Groups

Urban communities contain several clearly defined groups who experience considerable difficulty in securing acceptable levels of mobility and of accessibility to essential daily or periodic facilities. The elderly, the sick and disabled, those on low incomes and those below the legal driving age are those most commonly disadvantaged in this respect. The numbers of persons who suffer transport deprivation, being described as the "transport-poor", are increasing: in the UK six million people, or about 12 per cent of the adult population, suffer from some form of disability, and by 2025 some 20 per cent will be aged over 65, with at least two million over 80 years old (Oxley and Benwell, 1985). In the USA a survey of Worcester, Massachusetts, indicated that the proportion of persons aged over 65 rose from 11.9 per cent to 13.4 per cent between 1960 and 1980 and that the proportion of families defined as being below the poverty line increased from 5.4 per cent to 7.5 per cent in the decade 1970–80 (Hanson, 1995b). Although many people in these categories are currently able to drive or to be driven, eventually their level of mobility is bound to decline and they become totally dependent upon relatives, friends or public transport. Some bus and rail undertakings do meet the needs of the disabled traveller with wheelchair ramps and low level access buses, but these modifications need to be more widely introduced.

Surveys of the elderly in urban areas indicate that this group make much less use of cars than the employed and that they experience more difficulties when travelling in buses, trains or on foot. Certain facilities used regularly, such as shops and post offices, are accessible on foot, but longer trips requiring bus travel present problems in terms of access to the bus, and timings are not always convenient. Unavoidable and essential trips, such as those to doctors, clinics and hospitals, can cause particular problems for those who cannot secure assistance from car-driving friends and relatives and who cannot afford taxis. Distances travelled overall by the elderly are shorter than the average, indicating that their radius of action and hence the range of facilities available to them is also limited.

These problems increase with advancing age as mobility is gradually diminished by events such as the death of the car-driving partner or physical infirmity (Hopkin *et al.*, 1978). Those too young to drive legally can also be identified as transport-deprived, although many social and leisure trips are made as a family unit. In many advanced urbanized countries trips to school and college are confined to acceptable distances by a planned distribution of institutions and catchments throughout the built-up area and by the use of free or subsidized buses. In the UK most children who live within 1–2 km of their school can either walk or cycle, but traffic accidents and other hazards are making this a less popular option.

Environmental Problems

The contribution made by the transport industry to environmental degradation is discussed elsewhere in this volume. It is sufficient at this point to state that within urban areas both the current problems associated with transport systems and the solutions devised to combat them can have severe environmental implications. Excessive traffic flows within built-up areas cause atmospheric pollution, high noise levels, vibration that can undermine older buildings and visual intrusion. Construction of new urban highways and some railways can in turn lead to community disruption and inflict upon adjacent residential areas the same level of excessive noise as that produced by traffic on those routes that they are intended to supplement.

Road Safety

Within the UK, the USA and other industrial nations the greater proportion of serious accidents occur in urban areas. Roads in built-up zones display an accident rate up to three times greater than in other road categories. Pedestrians and cyclists are especially vulnerable, and 95 per cent of pedestrian accidents in Britain are recorded in urban areas, with one-half of these occurring in town centres. For the young the pattern of accidents is often highly localized: 90 per cent of accidents to the under-fives are recorded within 0.5 km of home, usually on minor roads in residential areas. The vulnerability of the young to traffic accidents in the UK is closely related to the problem of the transport-deprived, in that children account for almost one-third of pedestrian trips and form 39 per cent of all pedestrian casualties (Whitelegg, 1987).

SOLUTIONS

The urban-transport planning process generates a wide variety of proposals designed to solve problems caused by passenger and freight movements. Comprehensive plans for transport-improvement programmes in major towns and cities usually span periods of up to 20 years, but there is frequently an urgent need for more immediate short-term proposals to provide temporary relief for localized difficulties such as traffic "bottlenecks". Although solutions may be categorized according to their principal objectives and methods of application, it must be recognized that urban-transport problems are usually interrelated, and so the plans adopted are similarly interlinked. The introduction of a scheme to alleviate congestion on one part of an urban road network may well create difficulties elsewhere. Also, as noted above, the building of motorway or rapid-transit systems can have detrimental effects upon the physical and social structure of existing communities through which they pass, a fact noted in the earlier period of transport planning (Buchanan, 1963; Schaeffer and Sclar, 1975). The costly schemes introduced in Western cities also contrast markedly with the limited extent to which developing countries have been able to combat their transport problems. Many of the latter were initially tackled using Western urban-transport planning techniques, but it soon became apparent that such approaches were inappropriate, and proposals more suited to developing countries are now devised.

Investment in Additional Road Capacity

One of the most commonly adopted methods of combating road congestion in small towns or in districts of larger centres is the construction of bypasses to divert through-traffic. In the UK these date from the 1930s, and the extension of the principle to the orbital or sub-orbital highway has produced routes such as the M25 motorway around London and the M42, which interconnects the M5, M6 and M40 motorways converging upon Birmingham. Orbital routes can themselves also soon become overloaded if the initial traffic forecasts have been inaccurate, especially in terms of generated traffic, i.e. additional traffic attracted to the new facility. Ten years

after the M25 was opened in 1986, long sections are being provided with additional traffic lanes in both directions.

Mid-twentieth-century planners saw the construction of additional road capacity in the form of new or improved highways as the acceptable solution to congestion within major towns and cities. Since the pioneer transportation studies of the 1950s and 1960s were carried out in the US metropolitan areas, where the needs of an auto-dominated society were seen to be paramount, the provision of additional road capacity was accepted for several decades as the most effective solution to congestion, and urban freeways were built in large cities such as Chicago, San Francisco and Los Angeles (Dunn, 1981). Western European transport planners incorporated many of their American counterparts' concepts into their own programmes and the urban motorway featured in many of the larger schemes (Muller, 1995). However, it soon became evident that the generated traffic on these new roads rapidly reduced the initial advantages. The construction of an urban motorway network with its access junctions requires large areas of land and the inevitable demolition of tracts of housing and commercial properties. By the 1970s planners and policy-makers came to accept that investment in new highways dedicated to the rapid movement of motor traffic was not necessarily the most effective solution to urban transport problems (Starkie, 1982).

Although many US cities contain complex freeway networks, urban authorities in Western Europe have tended to be more selective and cautious in their adoption of motorways, and in the UK urban road-building programmes have often been substantially modified from their original designs. What has been described as "heroic structural change" has been replaced by a concern to make the most efficient use of existing roads. In London, for example, comprehensive plans for a series of concentric inner-orbital highways aroused fierce opposition and were abandoned in favour of a scheme based upon more selective road improvements (Bayliss, 1977).

Traffic-Management Measures

Temporary and partial relief from road traffic congestion may be gained from the introduction of traffic-management schemes, involving the reorganization of traffic flows and directions without any major structural alterations to the existing street pattern. Among the most widely used devices are the extension of one-way systems, the phasing of traffic-light controls to take account of traffic variations, and restrictions on parking and vehicle loading on major roads. On multi-lane highways that carry heavy volumes of commuter traffic certain lanes can be allocated to incoming vehicles in the morning and to outgoing traffic in the afternoon, producing a tidal-flow effect. Recent experiments using information technology have been based upon intelligent vehicle highway systems (IVHS), with the computerized control of traffic lights and entrances to freeways, advice to drivers of alternative routes to avoid congestion, and information on weather and general road conditions. The IVHS can be linked up with advanced vehicle control systems, making use of in-car computers to eliminate driver error and control automatic braking and steering when accidents are imminent (Plane, 1995).

Traffic management has been extensively applied within urban residential areas, where excessive numbers of vehicles produce noise, vibration, pollution and, above all, accident risks, especially to the young. "Traffic calming" has been introduced to many European cities and aims at the creation of an environment in which cars are permitted but where the pedestrian has priority of movement. Carefully planned street-width variations, parking restrictions and speed-control devices such as ramps are combined to secure a safe and acceptable balance between car and pedestrian (Tolley, 1990).

Bus Priority and Allied Proposals

Many transportation planning proposals are aimed specifically at increasing the speed and schedule reliability of bus services, and many European cities have introduced bus-priority plans in an attempt to increase the attractions of public transport. Bus-only lanes, with or against the direction of traffic flow, are designated in heavily congested roads to achieve time savings, although such savings may later be dissipated when buses enter inner-city areas where priority lanes are absent. Buses may also be accorded priority turns at intersections and certain streets may be restricted to buses only, particularly in pedestrianized shopping zones.

An effective use of buses may be made by incorporating bus-only lanes within new highways, allowing both public and private traffic to benefit from the new route. In the USA this method is the main means of providing bus priority and dates from the early 1970s, when bus lanes were established on freeways approaching Washington, New York and San Francisco. In its first year the exclusive bus lane on the link between the New Jersey Turnpike and the Lincoln Tunnel carried a daily average of 34 000 passengers in 800 buses, but these totals are well below the potential maximum capacity of a busway, which can accommodate up to 20 000 persons per hour (White, 1995). The latter total is, however, far in excess of current demand; although many bus lanes are not fully utilized they do provide a highly efficient method, when compared to the car, of carrying passengers into and out of city centres.

Where entirely new towns are planned there is an opportunity to incorporate separate bus networks within the urban road system, enabling buses to operate free from congestion. In the UK, Runcorn New Town, built as an overspill centre for the Merseyside conurbation, was provided with a double-looped busway linking shopping centre, industrial estates and housing areas. About 90 per cent of the town's population was within five minutes' walk of the busway and operating costs were 33 per cent less than those of buses on the conventional roads. Although the system is not used to the extent originally envisaged, it successfully illustrates how public transport can be integrated with urban development. Bus-only roads can also be adapted to vehicle-guidance systems, whereby the bus is not steered but controlled by lateral wheels, with the resumption of conventional control when the public road network is re-entered. Such systems have been adopted in Adelaide and experiments have been made in many other cities (Adelaide Transit Authority, 1988). The bus can also be given further advantages in city centres where major retailing and transport complexes are being redeveloped. The construction of covered shopping malls and precincts can incorporate bus facilities for shoppers, and reconstruction of rail stations can also allow bus services to be integrated more closely with rail facilities. The "park-and-ride" system, now adopted by many European cities, enables the number of cars entering city centres to be reduced, particularly at weekend shopping peak periods. Large car-parks, either temporary or permanent according to need, on the urban fringe are connected by bus with city centres, with charges generally lower than central area parking costs. The advantages of the bus over the car as an efficient carrier are secured, and the costs of providing the fringe car-parks are much less than in inner-city zones. Rail commuters can also be catered for in a similar manner with the provision of large-capacity car-parks adjacent to suburban stations.

Unconventional Bus Services

Many towns and cities have attempted to attract passengers back to bus transport by increasing its flexibility and level of response to market demand. In suburban areas the dial-a-ride system has met with partial success, with prospective passengers booking seats by telephone within a defined area of operation. Such vehicles typically serve the housing areas around a district shopping centre and capacity is limited, so they are best suited to operations in conditions of low demand or in off-peak periods. Fares are higher than on conventional buses since the vehicle control and booking facilities require financing (Martin, 1978). Experiments have also been made with small-capacity buses that can be stopped and boarded in the same way as a taxi and which can negotiate the complex street patterns of housing estates more easily than larger buses. However, with the widespread introduction of scheduled minibus

services in the UK following deregulation in 1986, most of these unconventional initiatives have been withdrawn.

Vehicle Restraint Schemes

The various priority measures designed to increase the attraction and efficiency of bus services can be combined with plans to restrain the use of inner urban streets by private motorists. A filter system can be applied which restricts congested inner-city roads to fully occupied cars, promoting a more effective use of such vehicles than would otherwise occur. Restraints upon car use can also be achieved by fiscal means, with the levying of premium tolls or taxes upon drivers wishing to enter congested inner zones. This "congestion pricing" penalty can be applied electronically with roadside computers and "smartcards" in each vehicle. A US study in 1994 estimated that the nationwide adoption of this pricing policy would cut average commuting times by 20 per cent and save $5–10 billion in fuel and time (Plane, 1995).

These schemes have the potential to make substantial reductions in the flows of cars to and from city centres, but they are generally unpopular with the private car driver: where the plans are proposed by local rather than national planning authorities, the political future of the authority can be threatened as these measures can antagonize the motoring public.

Rail Rapid Transit

Investment in rail-based rapid-transit schemes has been used to encourage suburban development, to provide an alternative to congested urban roads, and more recently to help regenerate the declining economies of city centres, inner cities and derelict docklands (Church, 1990; Roberts, 1985; Williams, 1985). Trains, horse-trams and later electric trams (streetcars) were the most notable nineteenth-century mass-transit modes, and enabled the first complete separation of place of residence from workplace and led to the development of star-shaped cities (Adams,

1970; Kellett, 1969; Ward, 1964). Underground railways are mainly twentieth-century developments, although they started with London's Metropolitan Railway in 1863 and London's first deep-level electrified "tube" line in 1890. In some countries rapid suburbanization was further encouraged by low flat fares, which removed the cost friction of distance in urban areas: for example in the USA on Boston's electric trams from 1888 and on New York's underground metro from 1904 where the uniform fare was retained at 5 cents until 1947, and in Denmark on Copenhagen's electric trams from 1911 (Fullerton and Knowles, 1991; Moorhouse, 1988; Vance, 1991).

From the 1920s transport constraints on urban expansion were relaxed by the widespread introduction of motor buses that could go wherever the demand warranted it. Buses therefore followed residential development whereas streetcars had previously directed it (Adams, 1970). More significantly, mass car ownership encouraged suburbanization and urban dispersal to occur on a much larger scale and in a less concentrated form, and urban areas became increasingly multi-centred instead of the traditional focus on a single city centre (Vance, 1991). Motor vehicles competed for congested urban road space with trams that ran on the road, except for a few segregated suburban lines. Trams were regarded as an outdated mode of transport and the British response from the late 1930s onwards, encouraged by government advice from 1946, was to replace trams with buses in all towns and cities. This was typically completed by Manchester in 1949 and London in 1952, although trams survived in Sheffield until 1960 and in Glasgow until 1962 and were retained along the Blackpool seafront. In contrast, the German response was to modernize trams into *Stadtbahn* (Light Rail) systems and put them underground in congested city centres and inner cities to avoid conflict with road traffic. Cologne, Essen and Hannover provide good examples (Hall and Hass-Klau, 1985).

An alternative response was to develop and/or electrify suburban railway lines as in Copenhagen, Glasgow and London, or underground metros as in London, Munich and Stockholm. This was par-

ticularly successful where land-use zoning powers were used to concentrate high-density suburban development around railway stations. The three Scandinavian capitals provide notably successful postwar examples with Copenhagen's five suburban rail corridors developed from its famous 1947 Finger Plan, and Stockholm's numerous metro lines and Oslo's four metro lines developing similar suburban corridors (Fullerton and Knowles, 1991).

In the UK the most widespread response to urban congestion in the early 1960s was to try to provide more road space for the sharply increasing volume of cars by building or widening roads, and by traffic management. American transport consultants ignored rail-transit investment and advised city after city to build extensive urban-motorway networks (Starkie, 1982). Urban-motorway plans were soon abandoned or curtailed because of cost and an environmental backlash, and transport consultants started advocating mass rail transit schemes. Recommendations for suburban rail electrification and re-opening the Argyle Line in Glasgow in 1968, a Link and Loop suburban rail connection underneath central Liverpool in 1969 and the Tyneside (light rail) Metro in 1971 were all accepted and built within 10 years, partly financed with government grants (Fullerton and Openshaw, 1985; Halsall, 1985; Robinson, 1985; Westwell, 1983). In London the Victoria and Jubilee underground (metro) lines were opened in 1968 and 1979 respectively, the first such lines since the 1920s. However, Manchester's Picc–Vic suburban rail underground link was rejected on cost grounds in 1975 (Knowles, 1985).

Metros need a large volume of potential users to justify the expense of tunnelling and the long period of disruption to city streets during construction. Metros are, therefore, rarely built in cities of under 500 000 people, and are more typical of million-plus cities and conurbations. The former Soviet Union actually had a policy of building a metro when a city had grown to a million people (Jackson, 1989). Metros are usually fully segregated from other rail traffic with stations 0.5 to 1 km apart in city centres, and about 2 km apart in the suburbs. They can carry up to 30 000 people per hour in one direction and extend up to 24 km from the city centre (Table 7.2). Metro systems are widespread with 90 operational worldwide, 33 of them in Europe and a further 10 under construction and 18 planned (Bushell, 1995; Knowles and Fairweather, 1991) (Table 7.3). The World Bank advises Third World countries not to invest in metros in their burgeoning capitals unless cheaper and more flexible road-based public-transport systems cannot cope.

Suburban rail provides frequent local passenger services on main-line surface railways up to about 40 km from the city centre as in Dublin, London, Manchester, New York, Tokyo and hundreds of other cities in dozens of countries in all six conti-

nents (Bushell, 1995; Knowles and Fairweather, 1991). Suburban rail is sometimes separated from long-distance rail routes and can be extended under city centres through short sections of tunnel, as in Copenhagen, Glasgow, Liverpool, Munich and Paris. Suburban trains are longer, with stations more widely spaced, gradients shallower and speeds higher than for metro systems (Table 7.2).

The revival of metro investment in Europe and North America gave way, in the 1980s, to light-rail investment. Electrified light-rail systems offer many of the advantages of metros and suburban rail, but at much lower cost as the routes are less heavily engin-eered and the lighter carriages can travel up steeper

Table 7.2 Typical characteristics of urban rail systems

		Streetcars	Light Rail	Suburban Rail	Metro
A	**Urban size**				
	Population	200 000–500 000	100 000–1 million	Over 500 000	Over 1 million
	CBD employment	Over 20 000	Over 20 000	Over 40 000	Over 80 000
B	**Route characteristics**				
	Route length from CBD	Under 10 km	Under 20 km	Under 40 km	Under 24 km
	Track	On street	Over 40% segregated	Segregated	Segregated
	CBD access	Surface	Surface or underground	Surface to CBD edge	Underground
	Station spacing in suburbs	350 m	1 km	1–3 km	2 km
	Station spacing in CBD	250 m	300 m	–	500 m–1 km
	Maximum gradients	10%	8%	3%	3–4%
	Minimum radius	15 m–25 m	25 m	200 m	300 m
	Engineering	Minimal	Light	Medium	Heavy
C	**Rolling stock**				
	Carriage weight	16 tonnes	Under 20 tonnes	46 tonnes	33 tonnes
	Number of carriages	1 or 2	2 or 4	Up to 12	Up to 8
	Carriage capacity	50 seats 75 standing	40 seats 60 standing	60 seats 120 standing	50 seats 150 standing
	Carriage access	Step	Step or platform	Platform	Platform
D	**Performance**				
	Power current	DC 500–750 V	DC 600–750 V	DC 600 V–1.5 kV or AC 25 kV	DC 750 V
	Power supply	Overhead	Overhead	Overhead or third rail	Third rail
	Average speed	10–20 kph	30–40 kph	45–60 kph	30–40 kph
	Maximum speed	50–70 kph	80 kph	120 kph	80 kph
	Typical peak headway	2 minutes	4 minutes	3 minutes	2–5 minutes
	Maximum hourly passengers	15 000	20 000	60 000	30 000

Source: Knowles and Fairweather (1991).

Table 7.3 Metro systems in operation, 1996

Country	Number of Systems	Cities
Africa	**1**	
Egypt	1	Cairo
Asia	**20**	
China	3	Beijing, Shanghai, Tianjin
Hong Kong	1	Hong Kong
India	1	Calcutta
Iran	1	Teheran
Japan	9	Fukuoka, Kobe, Kyoto, Nagoya, Osaka, Sapporo, Sendai, Tokyo, Yokohama
North Korea	1	Pyongyang
Singapore	1	Singapore
South Korea	2	Pusan, Seoul
Taiwan	1	Taipei
Europe	**33**	
Austria	1	Vienna
Belgium	1	Brussels
Bulgaria	1	Sofia
Czech Republic	1	Prague
Finland	1	Helsinki
France	5	Lille, Lyon, Marseille, Paris, Toulouse
Germany	6	Berlin, Cologne, Frankfurt am Main, Hamburg, Munich, Nuremburg
Greece	1	Athens
Hungary	1	Budapest
Italy	3	Milan, Naples, Rome
Netherlands	2	Amsterdam, Rotterdam
Norway	1	Oslo
Poland	1	Warsaw
Portugal	1	Lisbon
Romania	1	Bucharest
Spain	3	Barcelona, Bilbao, Madrid
Sweden	1	Stockholm
United Kingdom	2	Glasgow, London
Latin America	**9**	
Argentina	1	Buenos Aires
Brazil	3	Brasilia, Rio de Janeiro, Sao Paulo
Chile	1	Santiago
Colombia	1	Medellin
Mexico	1	Mexico City
Peru	1	Lima
Venezuela	1	Caracas
North America	**13**	
Canada	2	Montreal, Toronto
United States	11	Atlanta, Baltimore, Boston, Chicago, Cleveland, Los Angeles, Miami, New York/Newark, Philadelphia, San Francisco/Oakland, Washington DC
Former Soviet Union	**14**	
Armenia	1	Yerevan
Azerbaijan	1	Baku
Belarus	1	Minsk
Georgia	1	Tbilisi
Russia	7	Gorky, Kuybyshev, Moscow, Nizhni Novgorod, Novosibirsk, St Petersburg, Samara
Ukraine	2	Kharkov, Kiev
Uzbekistan	1	Tashkent

Sources: Bushell (1995), Knowles and Fairweather (1991).

gradients and around tighter curves. Light rail requires at least 40 per cent of its track to be segregated from road traffic to avoid road-traffic congestion, and this differentiates it from trams or streetcars (Table 7.2). A further distinction needs to be made between light-rail systems such as London Docklands Light Railway, which are fully segregated and can be automatically driven, and those such as the Manchester Metrolink, which are partly segregated. Light-rail systems typically operate up to 20 km from city centres and carry up to 20 000 passengers per hour. They are usually found in urban centres with between 100 000 and 1 million people, such as Charleroi in Belgium (200 000) and Hiroshima in Japan (900 000). When they occur in larger urban areas such as Vienna (1.5 million) they normally complement a metro system (Knowles and Fairweather, 1991).

Light-rail systems are operational in 117 cities, mainly in Europe and North America, but also in the Third World (Table 7.4). Light-rail systems are being built, planned or considered in hundreds of cities worldwide to relieve and avoid urban road congestion or help regenerate run-down areas. A successful example is Manchester Metrolink, which opened in 1992 without operating subsidy, exceeded its patronage forecast and attracted 2.6 million former car trips at the same time as car traffic volumes fell on parallel radial roads (Knowles, 1996). Regeneration routes include London Docklands Light Railway and the Don Valley Route Two of the Sheffield Supertram. Light-rail systems, especially in Germany, are sometimes upgraded from streetcars, as in Stuttgart, while others such as London Docklands run on mainly new alignments. A final group, including Manchester Metrolink, Los Angeles, Tyne and Wear and Vancouver Sky Train, utilize old railway routes. An increasing number of newer light-rail systems, such as Manchester Metrolink, Sheffield Supertram and Zürich, cross the city centre on surface routes on wholly or partially segregated streets, where they are driven ''on sight'' with priority at traffic lights. This is much cheaper than tunnelling and is also more accessible and safer for passengers.

Streetcars are still found in about 250 towns and cities worldwide but they are mainly in the former Soviet Union and other former Communist countries, where road congestion is less significant as private car ownership has been severely restricted (Table 7.2). It is expected that most of the streetcar systems will either be upgraded into light rail or abandoned as urban road congestion increases.

Transport Coordination

Successful transport planning relies substantially upon the integration of the various modes of transport available to meet demand, and the coordination of their operations. Major metropolitan councils have established transport authorities with overall powers in order to achieve an efficient urban transport system and the USA pioneered such authorities in the 1940s. The city of Chicago was one of the first in the world to acquire control over the majority of its rail and bus undertakings.

In the UK the 1968 Transport Act enabled the formation of Passenger Transport Authorities (PTAs) and Passenger Transport Executives (PTEs) in major conurbations, charged with providing integrated and efficient public passenger-transport systems within their respective areas. The PTAs are responsible for policy and funding decisions while the PTEs plan the operation of transport services provided by bus and rail undertakings. In many cities the PTEs inherited bus systems from the local authorities and became responsible for their operation. Following the reorganization of UK local government areas in 1974, the PTAs and PTEs assumed responsibility for all public-transport policy and planning in the major conurbations, which were now under unified control of the Metropolitan County Councils. The extent to which these transport authorities achieved their objectives is closely influenced by the socio-economic nature of their areas and the types of road and rail networks subject to their control.

In the USA the Mass Transit Authorities, which corresponded roughly to the UK PTAs and PTEs, had legal powers to acquire bus and rail companies within their areas if such action was thought to benefit the public: New York, Philadelphia and several

Table 7.4 Light-rail systems in operation, 1996

Country	Number of Systems	Cities
Africa	**3**	
Egypt	2	Alexandria, Helwan
Tunisia	1	Tunis
Asia	**10**	
China	1	Dalian
Hong Kong	1	Hong Kong
Japan	3	Hiroshima, Kyoto, Tokyo
Philippines	1	Manila
Turkey	4	Ankara, Istanbul, Izmir, Konya
Australia	**2**	Melbourne, Sydney
Europe	**72**	
Austria	1	Vienna
Belgium	3	Antwerp, Brussels, Charleroi
Bosnia	1	Sarajevo
Czech Republic	2	Brno, Prague
France	8	Grenoble, Lille, Marseille, Nantes, Paris, Rouen, St Etienne, Strasbourg
Finland	1	Helsinki
Germany	21	Bilefeld, Bochum-Herne*, Bonn, Braunschweig, Bremen, Chemnitz, Cologne, Dortmund*, Duisburg*, Düsseldorf*, Essen–Mulheim*, Frankfurt am Main, Freiburg, Gelsenkirchen*, Hannover, Karlsruhe, Krefeld*, Leipzig, Mannheim–Ludwigshafen, Stuttgart, Wurzburg
Hungary	1	Budapest
Italy	3	Genoa, Rome, Turin
Netherlands	4	Amsterdam, Rotterdam, The Hague, Utrecht
Norway	1	Oslo
Poland	5	Czestochowa, Krakov, Poznan, Szczecin, Warsaw
Romania	6	Brasov, Cluj, Constanta, Craiova, Poleisti, Resita
Slovakia	1	Bratislava
Spain	1	Valencia
Sweden	2	Gothenburg, Stockholm
Switzerland	6	Basle, Berne, Geneva, Lausanne, Neuchatel, Zürich
United Kingdom	5	Blackpool, London Docklands, Manchester, Sheffield, Tyne and Wear
North America	**22**	
Canada	4	Calgary, Edmonton, Toronto, Vancouver
United States	18	Baltimore, Boston, Buffalo, Cleveland, Denver, Detroit, Fort Worth, Los Angeles, Newark, New Orleans, Philadelphia, Pittsburgh, Portland, Sacramento, San Diego, San Francisco, San José, St Louis
Latin America	**5**	
Argentina	1	Buenos Aires
Brazil	1	Rio de Janeiro
Mexico	3	Guadalajara, Mexico City, Monterrey
Former Soviet Union	**3**	
Russia	2	Naberezhyne-Chelny, Volgograd
Ukraine	1	Krivoy Rog

*Stadtbahn Rhein–Ruhr.
Sources: Bushell (1995), Knowles and Fairweather (1991).

other large cities exercised this right. In contrast the British PTAs could not buy up railways but entered into contracts with British Rail (BR) to improve services. Infrastructure and rolling-stock investments were made by the PTAs but the services were run by BR. Although the coordination of all public-transport facilities within conurbations was not always achieved the transport authorities can be credited with improvements such as through-ticketing facilities on all modes, joint road–rail fare structures, and better dissemination of travel information to the public. They were also responsible for new infrastructure such as the Tyne and Wear Metro, the central Liverpool underground rail loop and the completion of the Strathclyde suburban electric rail system. With transport deregulation the powers of these authorities are now much more limited, particularly in respect of transport integration.

"Non-Transport" Solutions

A wide range of policies, strategies and plans have been introduced in an attempt to solve transport problems in the world's cities. However transport planners recognize that conventional patterns of social and economic activities, with their emphasis upon standardized working hours, dictate corresponding demand patterns for transport which cannot always be met in the most efficient or effective manner. As a result many urban transport planners now actively support proposals for changes in these established activity patterns as a means of securing greater levels of success in their transport-planning programmes.

One of the most obvious targets is to reduce the volume of commuter travel by encouraging the spread of job start and finish times over longer periods during each day (Plane, 1995). This move towards what may be described as a shift system would be unpopular with much of the urban workforce and difficult to promote, but the extension of each journey-to-work period over four to five hours rather than the current two could lead to a substantial reduction in the congestion caused by commuting and to a more efficient use of public-transport

resources. Already the widespread adoption of "flexitime" in the service sector has helped to flatten the commuter-travel peaks in many cities in the late twentieth century.

Another "non-transport" approach to solving the congestion problem is the recent growth of home-based economic activity using telecommunications, personal computing facilities and information technology. Many jobs in the financial and commercial sector traditionally carried out in city-centre offices can now be accomplished as effectively at home, using computer linkages with head offices. Significant increases in the numbers of employees who could work at home would again help to reduce the demand for transport during the peak hours. An extension of the trading hours of city-centre retailers during the week would also encourage more workers to shop later and delay their homeward journey.

Solutions for the "Transport-Deprived"

Various remedies have been implemented to cater for the special needs of the "transport-deprived" in urban areas. For the mobility-impaired who require some form of public transport to make trips beyond the range of electric wheelchairs, the taxi is the most acceptable mode but costs are high in comparison with other possible alternatives. Buses may be frequent and provide transport to most of the required destinations but physical access problems can be difficult although many buses and light-transit vehicles now have lower floors and entrances. Where the disabled are members of clubs, minibuses adapted for carrying wheelchairs are often provided for trips into city centres and other locations. These facilities are generally more acceptable than any provided by public transport. Rail journeys can present even greater difficulties but increasing numbers of urban stations are now provided with ramp or elevator access to platforms and much of the rolling stock has space for wheelchairs. In Manchester the Metrolink light-rail system is fully accessible to the disabled, but at an extra cost of £10 million for the first phase of the project.

CASE STUDIES

This chapter concludes with a series of case studies of individual cities to illustrate planning strategies for solving the more outstanding transport problems. Examples are drawn from North America, Europe, the Far East and the developing countries to demonstrate the complexity of the interaction between transport demand and the response from private- and public-sector undertakings.

Glasgow – Urban Deprivation and Transport Innovation

The Clydeside conurbation, with Glasgow as its core, contains almost half of the population of Scotland in a region characterized by some of the highest unemployment rates in the UK, low levels of car

ownership and extensive areas of recent urban renewal. The Passenger Transport Authority and Passenger Transport Executive created in 1972 became responsible for a complex system of public transport comprising a city-owned bus network, other bus services provided by over 40 state or private companies, an underground railway and an extensive system of local railways that is the largest outside London. The responsibilities and functions of the PTA and PTE were then taken over by the Strathclyde Regional Council in 1975, following local government reorganization.

Transport planning in Clydeside has had to take into account several social and economic trends. The inner-city population fell by almost one-third between 1961 and 1981, with large numbers being relocated on new peripheral housing estates (Law *et al.*, 1984). Demolition of many older residential and

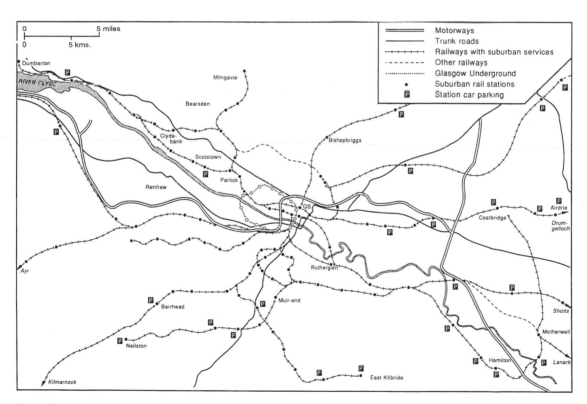

Figure 7.1 Principal roads and railways in the Strathclyde conurbation

industrial areas bordering the Clyde had released landfor new roads and the proportion of car-borne commuters was rising steadily. Travel by bus and rail declined by one-third in the 1970s, and although the level of government subsidy increased, operating costs also rose, creating a situation that could only be remedied by service reductions, higher fares or revenue support from local ratepayers.

Many infrastructural improvements were undertaken in an effort to arrest the declining patronage of public transport. Electrification of the suburban railways north and south of the Clyde was begun in the 1960s and the two sections were united in 1979 with the reopening of the Argyle line passing under Glasgow Central Station (Figure 7.1). The underground railway loop, opened in 1897 to serve the city centre and lower Clydeside west to Govan, was refurbished in 1980, with new bus or surface rail exchanges at each of its 15 stations and park-and-ride facilities at several. The coordination of bus and rail, and of the bus services run by different undertakings, was a keystone of the PTE's planning and what was seen as undesirable competition was fought vigorously in order to secure maximum integration of services. The PTE financially supported the newly electrified Glasgow–Ayr railway, which carried a substantial commuter traffic, and successfully opposed the introduction of bus services parallel to the line. However, competition was sanctioned by the 1980 Transport Act and Ayr to Glasgow bus services have captured some of the rail traffic (Westwell, 1983). Although the injection of State capital enabled suburban railway modernization to be completed by 1980, patronage has continued to decline and 90 per cent of all Clydeside passengers now travel by bus. Since deregulation in 1986 the attraction of the bus, especially in the outlying housing estates, has been enhanced with the use of small-capacity vehicles which can offer a more flexible service than the older larger buses. However, the vigorous competition between the numerous bus companies for passengers in the inner city has added to the congestion created by the car and the level of coordination of services achieved by the PTE has been severely reduced.

The most recent proposals for a light-rail transport system, more suburban rail stations and further bus priority measures are all designed to increase the share of travelling within the public-transport sector (Strathclyde PTE, 1990).

The South-East Asian City – Private Car Restraint and Rapid Mass Transit

Recent plans for transport improvements in South-East Asian cities indicate a changing attitude towards the non-motorized vehicles, such as rickshaws, which still play a very significant part in carrying passengers in many urban areas. Although such vehicles are often the only type of transport affordable by the urban poor there are proposals by transport planners substantially to reduce their role in the total urban transport system on the grounds of congestion and their outdated image (Simon, 1996).

Singapore and Kuala Lumpur provide two examples of cities that have grown rapidly since the 1960s as commercial and administrative centres, creating a range of formidable transport problems. In both cities the improvement of public transport is seen as the most effective remedy, but Singapore has made much more progress in this direction than the Malaysian capital. Singapore, with a population of three million, is surrounded by a ring of satellite towns along corridors radiating out from the city centre (Figure 7.2). In order to meet the travel demands of an island with a high population density, transport planning has been focused upon public transport in the form of a mass rapid-rail-transit network coupled with schemes for car restraint. Plans for the 67-km rail system were initiated in 1982 and the two routes were opened in stages between 1987 and 1992. The Public Transport Council established in 1987 regulates fares and services on this system and also on buses and taxis, and the two major bus companies provide feeder services to the stations on the mass-transit system. The latter is expected eventually to carry one-third of all public-transport trips

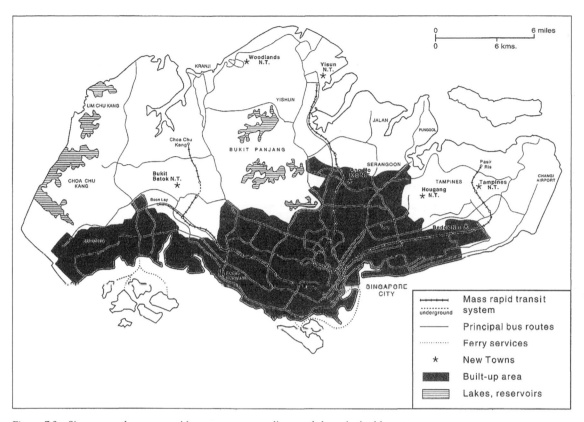

Figure 7.2   Singapore: the mass rapid-transport system lines and the principal bus routes

but the system at present concentrates upon fast ser-vices between the satellite towns and the city centre, and other housing areas are not so well provided for (Simon, 1996).

It is estimated that most of Singapore's population are within five minutes' walk of one of the 250 bus routes in operation and 80 per cent of services have frequencies of 10 minutes or less. Despite these facil-ities car traffic has continued to increase and since 1975 an Area Licensing Scheme has been in force to control peak-hour road traffic. Supplementary licences are required for all except fully occupied cars for access to the city centre during the morning peak period. The success of this scheme may be judged by the fact that incoming car traffic has de-creased by 20 per cent since 1975, despite an esti-mated 30 per cent rise in the number of city workers. The objective now is to make all Singapore public-

transport under-takings financially self-supporting and the mass-transit railway in particular must main-tain its passenger levels and minimize operating costs (Rimmer, 1986; Gray, 1988).

Proposals for transport improvements in Kuala Lumpur date from 1972 and were incorporated into the 1984 Master Plan for the city. The principal aims are the completion of inner urban ring roads, an expansion of the bus fleet, building of a rapid-transit network and introduction of area traffic control (Rahim, 1988). The latter would give priority on highways to buses, minibuses and fully loaded taxis and cars, and a limited form of area licensing has also been considered. It has been estimated that the reduction of road congestion would require a 40 per cent shift from private to public transport, but the securing of this objective is highly unlikely and the emphasis upon car usage remains (Figure 7.3).

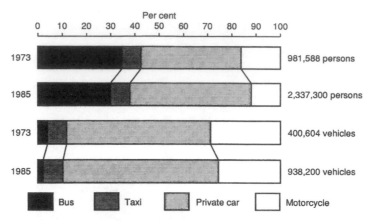

Figure 7.3 Kuala Lumpur: changes in the use of transport modes and in the number of vehicles, 1973 and 1985
Source: Rahim (1988)

The African City – Remedies for the Current Inadequacies of Public Transport

Although car ownership is steadily rising in many African cities, walking can still account for up to 40 per cent of all trips (Table 7.5) and the majority of urban travellers continue to rely upon the bus for motorized journeys. The major problem facing transport planners is thus to improve the efficiency of conventional bus services and to make the most effective use of the variety of paratransit operations (Table 7.6). Many cities in Nigeria and other West African states have either no or only poorly organized conventional bus services and the majority

of people travel in minibuses or shared taxis (Adenji, 1983). The population of Benin City in Nigeria is currently served by about 600 minibuses operated by many small undertakings with no effective route-licensing system. Most of the services radiate out from the city centre and connect with intercity taxi routes on the urban fringe. This minibus fleet accounts for about 38 per cent of all trips and shared taxis take a further 40 per cent of the market, especially for journey-to-work and social travel (Wiredu, 1989). In larger metropolitan centres such as Lagos, however, private car traffic has increased to a critical level, which has prompted the introduction of experimental vehicle-

Table 7.5 The importance of walking in selected Indian and African cities

	Population (million)	Proportion of All Trips by Walking	Average Walking Distance (km)
Jaipur	1.0 (1981)	39	1.2
Vadodara	0.7 (1981)	40	1.2
Patna	0.9 (1981)	36	1.3
Delhi	6.1 (1981)	40	1.1
Dar es Salaam	1.5 (1987)	25	1.7
Jos	0.4 (1986)	23	1.2
Douala	1.1 (1987)	28	1.2
Yaoundé	0.8 (1987)	30	1.7
Harare	1.3 (1987)	42	1.6

Source: Maunder and Fouracre (1989).

Table 7.6 Typical paratransit operations

(a) Paratransit in selected cities

City	Type	Fleet Size	Share of Motorized Trips (%)
Delhi	Autorickshaws: converted scooters	28 000	20
	Pedal rickshaws	5000	–
Istanbul	*Dolmus*: shared 5- and 7-seat taxis	16 000 }	50
	Minibuses	4000 }	
Jos	Shared taxis	1900 }	60
	Donfo minibuses	250 }	
Manila	*Jeepnies*: shared taxis (based on military Jeeps)	28 000	54
Nairobi	*Matatu*: mainly minibuses and converted pickups	2000	50
Surabaya	*Bemos*: 10-seater minibuses	3200	30
	Becaks: tricycle pedicabs	38 000	–

Source: Armstrong-Wright (1993).

(b) Transport modal split, Harare, 1989–94 (%)

Year	ZUPCO* stage bus	Emerg-ency taxi	Com-muter omnibus	Meter taxi	Motor car or cycle	Cycle	Walk	Other	Total
1988	18	7	–	0.5	30	1.5	42	1	100
1991	24	10	–	1	16	1	45	3	100
1992	31	9	–	1	17	5	36	1	100
1993	23	18	1	1	16	3	38	–	100
1994 (Jan)	25	18	4	1	14	3	35	–	100
1994 (Sept)	20	9	16	0.5	14	5.5	34	1	100

*ZUPCO = Zimbabwe United Passenger Company.
Source: Maunder and Mbara (1995).

restraint schemes similar to those in Singapore (Ogunsanya, 1984).

Harare, the capital of Zimbabwe with a 1995 population of 1.2 million, has the bulk of its African workforce resident in high-density suburbs on the city periphery, and almost entirely dependent upon public transport for access to the industrial zones and the commercial centre. A widespread network of conventional bus services is supplemented by a fleet of shared "emergency taxis" which operate on fixed routes from the centre to suburban termini. The lack of sufficient buses creates severe operating difficulties, resulting in regular overcrowding and lengthy waits for vehicles. The rapid growth of the satellite town of Chitungwiza (1995 population estimated at 275 000) has created particularly severe problems as workers rely upon buses for the 20 km journey into Harare (Atkinson Williamson Partnership, 1984; Rakodi, 1995). Proposals to improve public transport have included a scheme for mass rapid transit, combining the use of existing railway routes into Harare with two new lines linking the centre with the airport, the Southerton industrial estate and Chitungwiza. It is unlikely that this scheme will be implemented and the most significant recent development has been the use of small-capacity buses known as "commuter omnibuses". These vehicles were introduced in 1993 as part of a transport deregulatory process and have the effect of reducing pressure on conventional buses and providing paratransit for the first time in other housing areas. By 1994 these commuter omnibuses were carrying about 16 per cent of all passengers, having displaced the emergency taxis as the second-ranking form of motorized public transport after the conventional buses, which still account for 20 per cent of public travel (Maunder and Mbara, 1995).

The Californian City – a Reappraisal of Public Transport in Auto-Dominated Societies

The conurbations of San Francisco and Los Angeles typify the development of an intra-urban travel pattern which has been dominated by the car since the mid-twentieth century. Both cities possess highly complex freeway networks designed to meet the ever-growing demand for additional road capacity (Figure 7.4). In San Francisco the central business district, located on the peninsula between the Pacific coast and the Bay, and the suburbs along the bay shores to the north and south of the core are connected by bayside freeways and three toll bridges. By the mid-1960s congestion on the road approaches to central San Francisco had become so acute that the existing suburban railways were reconstructed as the Bay Area Rapid Transit (BART), with suburban station car-parks and, wherever possible, feeder bus services. Weekday traffic on the system in 1993 was 253 000, only slightly less than the total projected for the opening year of 1972, but the BART has improved urban mobility and accounts for about 50 per cent of all commuter trips into the centre. The system has also encouraged new commercial developments in central areas (Giuliano, 1995). Congestion on the Bay road crossings has prompted experiments in a premium toll charge in peak periods on the San Francisco–Oakland Bay bridge, using electronic collecting techniques (Hanson, 1995b).

The Los Angeles metropolitan region is polycentric in form and the central business district contains less than 10 per cent of all jobs in the county. The need for rapid interconnection between the constituent settlements of the region was initially met by a network of freeways carrying some of the highest urban traffic volumes in the world. A mass-transit system has also been built but its contribution to commuter transport is much lower than that made by the BART in San Francisco, although both systems are recognized as making an important contribution to the reduction of congestion on urban freeways.

The investment in public transport in these two cities exemplifies one of the two significant changes made in US transport policy since the 1960s, namely, the reappraisal of a continual programme of increasing urban road capacity and the acceptance of mass-transit systems as a feasible option for passenger transport (Orski, 1982; Fielding, 1983). Although the latter have succeeded in capturing a proportion of the car market, the enormous investments involved have been questioned. Since 1980 the emphasis has been placed upon securing a more efficient use of existing urban public transport and road systems at lower costs.

CONCLUSIONS

Transport planners have had to grapple with an increasing array of problems in the late twentieth century. Although a wide range of solutions have been devised and applied with various levels of success, an acceptable resolution of many of the basic difficulties has yet to be achieved. The reconstruction of existing roads and the building of additional expressways has alleviated congestion in many urban areas, but it has created additional difficulties with the inevitable generation of further volumes of traffic attracted to the extra road space. The eventual realization that the demands for road space from the continually increasing volumes of private cars could never be adequately met, except at an enormous cost to the urban environment, stimulated transport

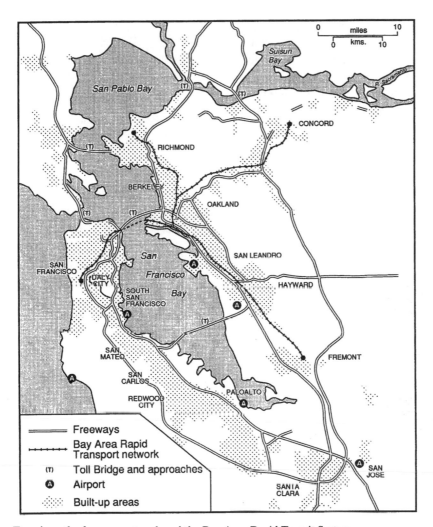

Figure 7.4   San Francisco: the freeway network and the Bay Area Rapid Transit System

planners to reappraise the potential of the public sector. Here, it was hoped, carefully allocated new investment could revitalize rail and bus networks, increase their attractiveness to the car driver, and thus raise their share of the total urban travel market.

This process of public-sector modernization still features prominently in many contemporary transport plans in the cities of leading industrial countries, although the proportion of the total passenger market which new mass-transit and similar costly schemes acquire is rarely at the forecast level. Compromise proposals, involving physical and fiscal restraint of private motoring, coupled with improved public-transport efficiency, and, where appropriate, providing extra capacity with light-rail systems, are now increasingly being incorporated within transport-planning programmes.

Cities in the developing countries, with few exceptions, have yet to experience the problems posed by excessive volumes of cars, and here the principal concern is to ensure that public transport, represented almost entirely by buses, can be improved so as to offer a sufficient level of mobility to urban dwellers who still depend upon the bus for all their regular basic trips. Whereas bus services in the Western world have, until recent moves towards deregulation, been subject to rigid licensing procedures, the situation in the developing nations is much more informal, with conventional buses sharing the available market with paratransit services. An inability to secure adequate financial resources generally prevents the larger cities in the developing world from installing the elaborate mass-transit systems now common in Europe and North America. This solution is in fact only suited to these larger cities and most analysts believe that a lower level of technology based upon established bus transport would, in most cases, be the more effective way of solving the imbalance in developing countries between public-transport demand and supply.

REFERENCES

Adams, J.S. (1970), "Residential structure of Midwestern cities", *Annals of the Association of American Geographers* 60, 37–62.

Adelaide Transit Authority (1988), *Report on guided busways* (Adelaide).

Adenji, K. (1983), "Nigerian municipal bus operations", *Transportation Quarterly* 37 (1), 22–23.

Armstrong-Wright, A. (1993), *Public transport in Third World cities, TRL state of the art review 10* (London: HMSO).

Atkinson Williamson Partnership (1984), *Study of the Zimbabwe road passenger transport industry: final report*, vol.1 (Harare: Ministry of Transport).

Bayliss, D. (1977), "Urban transportation research priorities", *Transportation* 6 (3), 4–17.

Buchanan, C.D. (1963), *Traffic in towns* (Harmondsworth: Penguin).

Bushell, C. (ed.) (1995), *Jane's urban transport systems*, 14th edn (Coulsdon, Surrey: Jane's Information Group).

Church, A. (1990), "Waterfront regeneration and transport problems in London Docklands", in Hoyle, B.S. (ed.), *Port cities in context: the impact of waterfront regeneration* (Transport Geography Study Group), 5–37.

Dimitriou, H.T. (1990a), "The urban transport planning process", in Dimitriou, H.T. (ed.) *Transport planning for Third World cities* (London: Routledge), 144–83.

Dimitriou, H.T. (1990b), "Transport problems of Third World cities", in Dimitriou, H.T. (ed.), *Transport planning for Third World cities* (London: Routledge), 50–84.

Dimitriou, H.T. (1992), *Urban transport planning: a developmental approach* (London: Routledge).

Dunn, J.A. (1981), *Miles to go: European and American transportation policies* (Cambridge, MA: Lexington).

Fielding, G.J. (1983), "Changing objectives for American transit", Parts I and II, *Transport Reviews* 3, 287–99.

Fullerton, B. and Knowles, R.D. (1991), *Scandinavia* (London: Paul Chapman).

Fullerton, B. and Openshaw, S. (1985), "The Tyneside Metro in full operation", in Williams, A.F. (ed.), *Rapid transit systems in the UK: problems and prospects* (Transport Geography Study Group), 27–45.

Giuliano, G. (1995), "Land-use impacts of transportation investments: highway and transit", in Hanson, S. (ed.), *The geography of urban transportation*, 2nd edn (New York: Guilford), 305–41.

Gray, M.G. (1988), "Planning and public transport issues in Singapore", *International Union of Public Transport, Conference report* (Singapore).

Hall, D.R. (1989), "The Metrocentre and transport policy", in Knowles, R.D. (ed.), *Transport policy and urban development* (Transport Geography Study Group, 105–29.

Hall, P. and Hass-Klau, C. (1985), *Can rail save the city? Rail rapid transit and pedestrianization in British and German cities* (Aldershot: Gower).

Halsall, D. (1985), "Rapid transit in Merseyside: problems and policies", in Williams, A.F. (ed.), *Rapid transit systems in the UK: problems and prospects* (Transport Geography Study Group), 76–91.

Hanson, S. (ed.) (1995a), *The geography of urban transportation*, 2nd edn, (New York: Guilford).

Hanson, S. (1995b), "Getting there: urban transportation in context", in Hanson, S. (ed.), *The geography of urban transportation*, 2nd edn (New York: Guilford), 3–25.

Hopkin, J.M., Robson, P. and Town, S.W. (1978), *Transport for the elderly* (Crowthorne: Transport and Road Research Laboratory), SR 419.

Jackson, C. (1989), "Metro plans span the world", *Developing Metros 1989, Railway Gazette International Supplement*.

Kellett, J.R. (1969), *The impact of railways on Victorian cities* (London: Routledge and Kegan Paul).

Knowles, R.D. (1985), "Rapid transit in Greater Manchester", in Williams, A.F. (ed.), *Rapid transit systems in the UK: problems and prospects* (Transport Geography Study Group), 46–75.

Knowles, R.D. (1996), "Transport impacts of Greater Manchester's Metrolink light rail system", *Journal of Transport Geography* 4 (1), 1–14.

Knowles, R.D. and Fairweather, L. (1991), *The impact of rapid transit*, Metrolink Impact Study Working Paper 2 (Department of Geography, University of Salford).

Law, C.M., Grundy, T. and Senior, M.L. (1984), *The Greater Glasgow area* (Salford: University of Salford).

Martin, P.H. (1978), *Comparative assessment of unconventional bus systems* (Crowthorne: Transport and Road Research Laboratory).

Maunder, D.C. and Fouracre, P.R. (1989), "Nonmotorised travel in Third World cities", paper presented to the Transport Geography Study Group, Institute of British Geographers Annual Conference, Coventry.

Maunder, D.C. and Mbara, T.C. (1995), *Initial effects of introducing commuter bus services in Harare, Zimbabwe* (Crowthorne: Transport and Road Research Laboratory), TRL 123.

Moorhouse, G. (1988), *Imperial City: the rise and rise of New York* (London: Hodder and Stoughton).

Muller, P.O. (1995), "Transportation and urban form: stages in the evolution of the American metropolis", in Hanson, S. (ed.), *The geography of urban transportation*, 2nd edn (New York: Guilford), 26–52.

Ogunsanya, A.A. (1984), "Improving urban traffic flow by traffic restraint: the case of Lagos", *Transportation* 12 (2), 40–45.

Orski, C.K. (1982), "The changing environment of urban transportation", *Journal of the American Planning Association* 48, 309–14.

Oxley, P.R. and Benwell, M. (1985), *An experimental study of the use of buses by elderly and disabled people* (Crowthorne: Transport and Road Research Laboratory), RR 33.

Plane, D.A. (1995), "Urban transportation: policy alternatives", in Hanson, S. (ed.), *The geography of urban transportation*, 2nd edn (New York: Guilford), 435–69.

Rahim, M.N. (1988), *Public transport planning in Malaysia* (University of Keele, Department of Geography, Occasional Paper 14).

Rakodi, C. (1995), *Harare* (Chichester: Wiley).

Rimmer, P. (1986), *Rikisha to rapid transit: urban public transport and policy in South-East Asia* (Oxford: Pergamon).

Roberts, J. (1981), *Pedestrian precincts in Britain* (London: TEST).

Roberts, J. (1985), "Lightrail: what relevance for London's Docklands?" in Williams, A.F. (ed.), *Rapid transit systems in the UK: problems and prospects* (Transport Geography Study Group), 98–137.

Robinson, S.E. (1985), "Tyne and Wear Metro: development of an integrated public transport system", in Williams, A.F. (ed.), *Rapid transit systems in the UK:*

problems and prospects (Transport Geography Study Group), 4–26.

Roth, G. (1984), "Improving the mobility of the urban poor", in Richards, P.J. and Thomson, A.M. (eds), *Basic needs of the urban poor* (London: Croom Helm), 215–42.

Schaeffer, K. and Sclar, E. (1975), *Access for all: transportation and urban growth* (Harmondsworth: Penguin).

Simon, D. (1996), *Transport and development in the Third World* (London: Routledge).

Starkie, D. (1982), *The motorway age: road and road traffic policies in post-war Britain* (Oxford: Pergamon).

Strathclyde P.T.E. (1990), *Strathclyde transport development study: public transport for the 21st century* (Glasgow).

Tolley, R.S. (1990), *Calming traffic in residential areas* (Tregaron, Dyfed: Coachex).

Vance, J.E. (1991), "Human mobility and the shaping of cities", in Hart, J.F. (ed.), *Our changing cities* (Baltimore: Johns Hopkins University Press), 67–85.

Ward, D. (1964), "A comparative historical geography of streetcar suburbs in Boston, Massachusetts, and Leeds, England, 1850–1920", *Annals of the Association of American Geographers* 54, 477–89.

Westwell, A.R. (1983), "Public issues of transport in the west of Scotland", in Turton, B.J. (ed.), *Public issues in transport* (Transport Geography Study Group), 5–30.

White, P.R. (1990), "Inadequacies of urban public transport systems", in Dimitriou, H.T. (ed.), *Transport planning for Third World cities* (London: Routledge), 85–116.

White, P.R. (1995), *Public transport*, 3rd edn (London: UCL Press).

Whitelegg, J. (1987), "The geography of road accidents", *Transactions of the Institute of British Geographers* 12 (2), 161–76.

Williams, A.F. (ed.) (1985), *Rapid transit systems in the UK: problems and prospects* (Transport Geography Study Group).

Wiredu, Y.K. (1989), "Minibuses in an African city", *Paratransit* 4, 22–3.

8

INTER-URBAN TRANSPORT

Brian Turton and William R. Black

Much of what we call spatial interaction in the geography literature is travel or transport between major cities or production areas. Here we examine the bases for such interaction using theoretical ideas from the era of the 1950s and before. The notions of complementarity, intervening opportunity and transferability are fundamental for understanding in an elementary way why travel and transport take place. These ideas are derived from the work of Edward L. Ullman and it is said that his source was the work of Bertil Ohlin, an economist concerned with trade theory. We also examine some of the inter-regional trade literature in an attempt to understand more clearly the reasons why transport takes place. Some of the theoretical ideas have been operationalized by the use of an elementary mathematical model called the gravity model. We will examine this model and explain how it works in its basic form. This will be followed by an examination of transport modes, patterns and networks of several European, African and Asian countries. A case study of the US transport system concludes the chapter.

INTRODUCTION

One of the classic papers in geography was written by the transport geographer Edward L. Ullman (1956). He was very much influenced by the writings of Bertil Ohlin (1933). Both of these scholars were concerned with explaining why interaction takes place. Ullman as a geographer approached the question from a fundamentally geographic perspective of uneven distribution of markets and raw materials. It is certainly true that in the absence of geographical variation there would be no need for transport. If all areas were the same in terms of economic activities and resources there would be no need to interact or trade with any other areas. So it is essentially the variation of resources that gives rise to interaction, but this is not the whole idea.

Ullman stated that transport would take place between different areas if "complementarity" existed between the areas. He defined complementarity as the presence of a surplus of supply in one area and unsatisfied or excess demand in the other area. Both have to be present, not just one. One country may have a significant surplus of some type of grain at the end of a harvest season. Another country may be completely without the grain, but interaction may not take place because the second country relies solely on some other foodstuff, for example rice, and as a result it has no demand for the grain. If both countries consume large amounts of the grain normally and one area has a drought leaving it with a shortage after harvest (unsatisfied demand) while the other produces far more of the grain than it can consume (excess supply), then

Modern Transport Geography: second, revised edition. Edited by Brian Hoyle and Richard Knowles.
© 1998 John Wiley & Sons Ltd.

complementarity exists and the areas should trade the grain in question.

Ullman (1956) recognized that there were two factors that interfere with such trade. The first of these was what he called "intervening opportunities". An intervening opportunity can be thought of in the above grain example as simply a nearer possible trade partner that also has an excess supply of the grain in question. All three countries have a state of complementarity existing between them, but trade should, other things being equal, take place between the two nearest partners that have a state of complementarity present. However, even in the presence of complementarity and no intervening opportunities, we do not always have trade taking place. The reason is that the transport costs of getting the product to the area of excess demand from the area of surplus supply are just too great. Ullman labelled this factor "transferability". It may be that the product becomes too expensive when its transport cost is added to the factory price.

Although not really discussed by Ullman, it would appear there is a fourth factor that may also be critical in some cases, and we can simply call this "political factors". Political factors are the reason that the USA secures sugar from Hawaii, rather than Cuba. In part, the fact that Hawaii is a state of the USA may give them a trade advantage with the rest of the United States, but it is the embargo against trade with Cuba that supports the Hawaiian trade. This factor also explains why Israel does not trade with neighbouring Arab countries, and vice versa. In addition, there are trade blocs that have existed for many years between countries and these blocs favour internal trade between the members. The Warsaw Bloc countries of Eastern Europe once constituted such a bloc, but other examples exist, such as the member states of the British Commonwealth, or the recent European Union or the North American Free Trade Agreement (NAFTA). In these cases there is a preference given to membership in the organization and this will overrule the intervening opportunities or in some cases the transferability requirement.

If we examine all the major types of human interaction over distances that occur today, the above factors explain just about all of these. We travel to stores to buy goods, we travel to doctors or dentists for treatments, we travel to visit relatives, we travel to work, because we demand certain goods or services or types of interaction that cannot be satisfied where we are. Even the movement activity of migrating to find a job has the unemployed (from areas of excess demand for jobs) moving to areas of high employment (surplus positions): the presence of complementarity. In some cases positions will not be filled if the migrant can find a closer job, or if the cost of getting to the job is too great.

Ohlin's (1933) ideas were not very different from Ullman's ideas. He preceded Ullman by a number of years, and spoke in terms of "factor endowment", which can be taken to mean the geographical distribution of resources. He viewed this as critical for the development of specialization which was also necessary in order to have economies of scale that would allow enough of a production cost decrease to lead to trade. The ideas expressed here have been the subject of models of spatial interaction. Let us examine these briefly since they make the nature of spatial interaction clearer.

Assume we have a closed system of five cities A–E, and we are interested in the interaction that takes place between one of these (A) and the other four (B–E). In general, economic activity varies with city size; as cities become larger they produce and consume more. If our cities B–E have populations of 100 000, 200 000, 300 000 and 400 000, we would assume (other things being equal) that our city A would have 10, 20, 30 and 40 per cent of its interurban interaction with these same four cities B–E. We could represent the interaction of our city A with any particular one of the other four cities B–E by the equation

interaction =

$$\frac{\text{population of particular city}}{\text{population of all four cities}}$$

More abstractly, the potential interaction of a city i with one of the other j cities is

$$I_{ij} = \frac{P_j}{\Sigma P_j}$$

However, other things are not equal and one obvious factor that influences the level of interaction is the cost of transport or movement, which may be represented by simply the distance from our city to each of the other four cities in our system.

We might therefore decrease the influence of each city by dividing its population by how far it is away from our city of interest. Symbolically,

$$I_{ij} = \frac{P_j}{d_{ij}}$$

Summing these terms and dividing the sum back into each component tells us the proportion of total interaction that should be attributable to any one of the four places. This would be represented as

$$I_{ij} = \frac{P_j/d_{ij}}{\sum\limits_{i=1}^{4} (P_j/d_{ij})}$$

Of course we do not know exactly how distance affects interaction. It may very well differ geographically, by goods transported, by purpose of travel, or as a function of travel time. Empirical work has suggested that the distance value should be squared for inter-city interactions in this formulation.

Returning to our earlier ideas the population values above represent some aspect of complementarity and transferability, and intervening opportunities are incorporated in the distance variable. In the case of shipping economic products, many manufacturing firms charge a price for the product that is equal to the plant price plus an average transport cost. This has the effect of removing the role of distance. Nearer customers pay more than they should while more distant customers pay less than they should. From a societal point of view this is good since it allows everyone to purchase the product at a reasonable price, even if they live in a remote place.

Some retailers charge a price for their product that includes a plant price plus the actual transport cost and a profit for their efforts. New motor vehicles are often priced in this manner. Most physical interaction over geographic space has a cost that is in some way related to distance. As a result interaction with more distant places, other things being equal, is less than it is with nearer places.

These are the theoretical ideas that have been passed down over the decades and constitute our basic understanding of spatial interaction today. Many of the ideas were brought into transport geography by Americans, such as Ullman, and this is an important point. In many cases these conceptual ideas and models work best in North America. This is due to two factors. Firstly, the distances over which interaction takes place on that continent are much greater than they are elsewhere, as for example in Europe. Secondly, there are far fewer countries – and boundaries and tariffs – to contend with in North America. More and smaller countries tend to lead to commodity flow patterns that favour buying from within the boundaries of your own country. The European Union should eliminate some of these barriers to interaction and one would expect the models to perform better in a Europe of the future.

In the sections that follow we will examine the characteristics of inter-urban transport modes (railways, roads, domestic airways, pipelines and inland waterways), the traffic distribution between modes for personal and commodity movements, and the networks of several different countries in Europe, Asia and Africa. The nature of the inter-urban flows that take place in any country is very much influenced by the modes and networks available. The final section of the chapter examines the USA as a case study. The development of the current networks, and the movement of goods and people over these networks, are examined.

CHARACTERISTICS OF INTER-URBAN MODES

Railways

Railways played a dominant role in linking the growing manufacturing centres of the Western industrialized nations during the nineteenth and first half of the twentieth centuries and also in developing European colonial territories. The advantages of the railway for long-distance carriage of freight and passengers gave it a near-monopoly of inter-urban traffic in many advanced countries until it was first seriously challenged by road motor transport in the 1920s. In most nations the railway is now a minority partner in long-distance transport and survives by concentrating upon the types of freight and passenger traffic to which it is best suited and, in many countries, through the support of state subsidies to meet revenue shortfalls.

Railways usually own their track and ancillary equipment and have exclusive control over traffic operations. This degree of overall management enables rail transport to be organized without encountering the congestion problems experienced by road traffic, but the costs of maintenance and repair of track and supporting infrastructure as well as motive power and rolling stock fall exclusively upon the railway undertaking. These fixed costs form a large proportion of total expenses. The rates for freight and passenger traffic reflect this, with the costs of transport over any distance being based upon both traffic handling costs at terminals and the variable costs of train operation. In some countries, notably Australia, differences between gauge in individual states have hampered through-traffic. Within the European Union the Spanish railway network has a 1.67 m gauge and transfers are necessary at the border with France, although some through passenger trains are operated. The former Soviet Union constructed an extension of its 1.52 m gauge network into Poland in order to link up with the Upper Silesian coalfield–industrial area. With increasing competition from road freight transport in both industrialized and developing countries railways now concentrate upon long-distance haulage of low-value bulk commodities such as coal, ores and heavy chemicals, with the rates to the consumer generally falling with increasing distance. Freight rates can also be reduced by the introduction of high-capacity wagons (called hopper cars in the USA) dedicated to a specific commodity, enabling trainloads of over 10 000 tonnes to be operated.

In industrial countries levels of passenger traffic on inter-urban services generally fell from mid-century until the 1980s, when they often stabilized. Increasing shares of the long-distance market have been lost by rail to the private car and, to a lesser extent, to domestic air and coach transport. Over distances of 300 to 400 km, however, rail can often offer the fastest journey times between city centres, and the progressive electrification of many rail systems has resulted in the recapture of much traffic lost to competing modes (Table 8.1). In the UK, for example, the franchisees of the former InterCity undertaking operate over 700 trains daily and account for about 12 per cent of the long-distance journeys made each year (Prideaux, 1988). The speed advantage possessed by rail over road transport is now being further exploited with more powerful electric traction and the building of entirely new railways permitting average speeds of over 190 kph. In Japan the *Shinkansen*, introduced in 1964, is the world's pioneer high-speed train and in France the *Train à Grande Vitesse* (TGV) has been operating since 1982. When the Paris–Lyon service was first introduced, with speeds of up to 270 kph on an entirely new track, it diverted one million passengers from the road and two million from domestic airlines.

Despite these advances, however, the railway will probably continue to occupy a subordinate role in inter-urban transport patterns in Western industrial nations. In China and Russia, however, where car ownership levels are low, the railway systems still carry the bulk of inter-urban traffic although the quality of service is very poor by Western European standards. Railways have the particular advantage over other inter-urban modes of offering the greatest capacity for traffic in terms of the volume of passengers or freight that can be carried over a given

Table 8.1 National railway networks and electrification
(all countries with over 10 000 km route in 1995)

Country	Rail kilometres in operation ('000)	Percentage of Network Electrified
USA	176.0	<1.0
Russia	87.6	44.1
Canada	66.1	<1.0
India	62.5	18.0
China	54.0	15.6
Germany	41.4	39.1
Australia	35.1	8.9
Argentina	33.8	<1.0
France	31.8	42.4
Brazil	27.2	4.1
Poland	24.3	47.9
Japan	23.4	64.7
Ukraine	22.6	36.9
Mexico	20.4	<1.0
South Africa	19.9	29.1
United Kingdom	16.5	19.8
Italy	16.1	62.9
Spain	14.0	52.8
Romania	11.3	32.9
Turkey	10.4	10.5

Sources: Jane's World Railways, 1996; Department of Transport (1996).

Table 8.2 Distribution of passenger traffic by surface modes in selected countries, 1994

	Percentage of Total Passenger-Kilometres		
	Private Road Transport	Public Road Transport	Rail (Excluding Metros)
USA	95.7	3.8	0.5
Germany	84.5	8.1	7.4
Italy	82.7	10.7	6.6
France	86.6	5.6	7.8
United Kingdom	89.0	6.7	4.3
Spain	79.1	14.7	6.2
Netherlands	84.0	8.0	8.0
Japan	53.5	9.5	37.0

Source: Department of Transport (1996).

distance in a given time period. Although this advantage can rarely be exploited to the full on contemporary inter-urban routes the railway does retain this ability to adjust to fluctuating market levels. In terms of energy consumption the railway is also more efficient than other modes in the carriage of both passengers and freight, and the extension of electrification can bring environmental benefits to inter-urban corridors that road transport cannot match (Table 8.2).

Roads

Inter-urban road services, unlike rail, are provided and operated by a variety of public and private undertakings. Routes are provided and maintained by the state, or by private companies in the case of some toll routes, and freight haulage and public passenger facilities are run by enterprises in both the public and private sectors. The European turnpike roads of the eighteenth and nineteenth centuries were the first attempts to improve inter-urban facilities but were soon superseded by canals and later by railways. It was only with the perfection of the petrol-fuelled vehicle in the early twentieth century that the road again became effective as a long-distance link, and subsequently developed to achieve the commanding position it now occupies within the inter-urban sector of most advanced countries. Whereas railway pricing structures are based upon the integral operation of the entire system, road rates are composed primarily of vehicle movement costs, with terminal and depot expenses representing only a small proportion of the total. Road services can thus offer strongly competitive rates in the market for freight and passenger movements over distances of up to 300–400 km, journey lengths that account for a high percentage of all inter-urban trips in many countries.

Commercial goods vehicles form a high proportion of total trunk-road traffic and users benefit from a flexibility of operation between origin and destination that the railways cannot match. The majority of inter-urban road passenger traffic in advanced countries consists of private cars; long-distance transport by coach and bus now accounts for only a small proportion of all personal trips (Table 8.2).

Roads designed specifically for motor traffic date from the early 1920s, when the first Italian autostrade were opened. The extensive freeways or motorways that now carry large volumes of inter-urban traffic are all constructed with intersections at two or more levels, allowing an uninterrupted route for through-traffic. Although the effectiveness of these roads in meeting the demands for medium- and long-distance travel is frequently questioned, especially by advocates of the railway, most advanced nations have continued to build motorways as the most acceptable alternative to heavily congested conventional road networks (Table 8.3).

Domestic Airways

Inter-urban air transport services have expanded since the 1960s to offer a substantial challenge to the railway for distances over 400–500 km. In very large territorial units, such as the USA, Canada and Australia, they are now the dominant means of travel although ticket prices are higher than those of rail. Where the pattern of towns is not only dispersed,

but separated by tracts of undeveloped or sparsely inhabited land with difficult terrain, surface links between towns may not exist and air services provide the only feasible links. The growth of internal air transport has also been fostered by the expansion of international services, as one airport will often be used for both types of flight. Such airports offer passengers with a foreign origin or destination a more convenient means of travelling than do road or rail, where an additional connecting journey between city land transport terminal and airport is necessary.

Although inter-urban airlines can offer the advantage of much higher average speeds than land-based modes, this benefit can only be realized on routes where the overall journey time between city centres, including the trips to and from airports of departure and arrival, is less than that by an alternative mode. Rail frequently has the time advantage over distances up to about 400 km but, as connections between city centres and airports are constantly being improved, inter-urban flights will become more competitive over these shorter distances. Many airports in the USA, such as Chicago O'Hare, Atlanta Hartsfield and Dallas Fort Worth, handle over 40 million domestic passengers each

Table 8.3 Motorways and principal roads in selected countries, 1994

	Length of Motorway Network ('000 km)*	Principal Road Network (Including Motorways) ('000 km)†	Motorways as Percentage of Principal Road Network
USA	90.0	657.2	13.7
Germany	11.1	40.1	22.6
France	8.0	37.8	21.1
Spain	7.5	25.9	28.9
Italy	6.4	52.1	12.2
Japan	5.4	52.0	10.4
United Kingdom	3.3	15.7	21.0
Netherlands	2.2	4.2	52.3
Belgium	1.7	14.6	11.6
Austria	1.6	11.8	13.5
Switzerland	1.6	20.0	8.0

*Includes all motorways and freeways with multi-lane carriageways and with limited access from the conventional road network.
†Definitions of principal, trunk and first-class roads vary between countries but the category generally comprises the major inter-urban roads.
Source: Department of Transport (1996).

year. Airlines in the USA and Russia currently carry the largest shares of internal long-distance passenger traffic.

Pipelines

The pipeline is similar to the railway system in offering an exclusive mode of transportation for freight. It provides a convenient, safe and economic means for the movement of petroleum and its refined products in large volumes. Whereas rail, trunk-road and domestic airline networks normally reflect the distribution of urban populations, pipelines generally connect major coastal oil terminals and refineries to inland industrial centres and thus play only a limited part in the overall freight distribution system of a state. Since pipelines are only constructed where the flows of crude oil are sufficiently high to justify the large capital costs involved, the more complex networks are confined to Anglo-America, Europe and Russia. Where regular transfers of over 10 million tonnes a year are made, pipelines of up to one metre in diameter are built, offering maximum economy in transfer costs. Annual quantities of oil of less than this total are handled by smaller pipes and on some routes the rates charged by inland waterways or coastal tankers can be competitive.

Inland Waterways

The constraints imposed by terrain upon canal construction or the improvement of natural waterways result in this mode of inland transport being far less extensive or flexible than roads or railways. Inland waterways are capable, however, of offering very competitive rates for the carriage of bulky low-value freight such as coal, mineral ores and building materials in unit loads of up to 1500 tonnes where speed of transit is not a critical factor. High transhipment costs at interchange depots with road and rail transport do, however, restrict the use of barges to longer hauls, as these fixed expenses account for a high proportion of total operating costs. Inland waterways are of especial value where they possess a large estuarine port; the Rhine, with Rotterdam at its

mouth and its linking canals and rivers, is still an indispensable means of inter-urban freight transport in Western Europe. These waterways carry over 500 million tonnes annually between riverine industrial cities and towns in Belgium, the Netherlands, France and Germany (Rissoan, 1994).

TRAFFIC DISTRIBUTION BETWEEN MODES

The distribution of passenger and freight traffic between modes is determined by economic factors, principally the rates chargeable to the consumer, logistical considerations, perception of the quality of services on offer and by government transport policy and legislation (Hay, 1973; Fowkes *et al.*, 1987). It is difficult to present reliable comparative analyses for different countries as the bases for data collection vary, and national statistics rarely contain separate data on long-distance or inter-urban transport. The international data that are available illustrate the wide variations in the proportional use made of modes for freight and passenger traffic. In most countries road and rail are the principal competing modes but waterways still play an important part in freight carriage in Western and Central Europe, Russia and China (Table 8.4).

Fundamental shifts in national economies from industrial to post-industrial have several implications for the transport sector. Freight movements are now often in smaller unit loads, moving over longer distances, and there are demands from the consumer for enhanced levels of service and reliability. These have been met by improving the performance of existing modes, applying information technology to mode operations, increasing the efficiency of the infrastructure, adopting advanced logistics and ensuring that the commercial aspects of each mode are becoming more responsive to consumer demand (Giannopoulos and Gillespie, 1993). In particular the rationalization of the distribution network of large wholesale and retail companies has also affected inter-urban goods movements (McKinnon, 1989; Quarmby, 1989).

Table 8.4   Distribution of freight traffic by mode in selected countries, 1994

	Percentage of Total Tonne-Kilometres			
	Road	Rail	Inland Pipeline	Inland Waterway
USA	31	38	19	12
Germany	51	23	5	21
Japan	92	8	0	0
Italy	85	10	5	<1
France	60	25	11	4
Spain	92	5	3	0
United Kingdom	85	8	7	<1
Netherlands	38	5	8	49

Source: Department of Transport (1996).

Personal Travel

Analyses of modal choice for personal trip-making involve a complex range of factors and employ highly sophisticated methodologies, and in this chapter it is only possible to consider the basic issues. Mode selection for inter-urban travel is influenced by journey purpose, overall trip length, travel costs, timing of trip and the range of transport options available. The business and commercial trips that account for a large proportion of all inter-urban travel involve complex multipurpose movement patterns, and the car is invariably selected as the most convenient mode, an obvious choice given the extensive practice of providing employees with company cars. Journeys from a city origin can make use of high-speed rail or air services over distances in excess of 300 km, although even here the car can still be a viable option despite the large amount of the working day that has to be devoted to travelling. The advent of the mobile phone now enables business persons to utilize their journey for keeping in contact with their office bases, and the combination of phone and laptop computer now enables the train to be used as a "mobile office", a factor that may favour this mode rather than the car for the longer trips.

Social and recreational trips at the inter-urban scale rely heavily upon the car, as total costs for a family will be much lower than those for rail or coach if only the car movement expenses are taken into account in the selection process. Several railway companies in Europe are successfully expanding their share of the social and recreational market with the issue of concessionary tickets for families, students and the retired, although privatization and fragmentation of rail services, as in the UK, have raised doubts about the future of these innovations. Inter-urban express coaches usually cater for those without access to private transport and without the financial resources or desire to patronize the faster rail or air modes. Passenger choice of a public mode also now takes into account the quality of travel information and communications, and technical innovations such as high-speed rail and computerized on-line reservation systems (Capello and Gillespie, 1993).

Freight Haulage

Since data on inter-urban freight movements are not usually recorded separately from national data the following discussion is based upon statistics that usually include freight flows in urban areas as well as on trunk roads. Within the UK, for example, freight haulage is now dominated by road transport, which accounted for 86 per cent of all freight tonne-kilometres in 1996. Consignments of the principal bulk commodities, however, still make some use of rail, water and pipelines (Table 8.5) and, in the case of petroleum, road accounts for only 8 per cent of all movements. Over the period 1985–95 the tonnage of metals, building materials and oil carried by the UK railways has not changed markedly but only 6 per cent of all freight, measured in tonne-kilometres, is now hauled by this mode.

Information on inter-urban freight flows is rarely available for developing countries but road transport is generally continuing to expand its share of the market. In 1960, when Nigeria gained its independence, 77 per cent of all freight was carried by road, but by the mid-1980s, following an extensive road-improvement programme, this share had been increased to 94 per cent. In Zimbabwe, however, the railway still has a significant role in the haulage of coal, iron ore and agricultural products and it is estimated that only about 10 per cent of all medium- and long-distance freight travels by road (Turton, 1989). Of the principal industrialized countries, Russia, Poland and China rely most heavily upon rail transport. Inland waterways carry over 20 per cent of freight in China and Japan (principally coastal services) and play an important role in the USA, the Netherlands, Belgium and Germany. Elsewhere road networks are dominant and carry at least 60 per cent of all freight tonne-kilometres in the leading members of the European Union (Table 8.4).

With the expansion of cargo unitization, and especially the advent of container services in the late 1960s, a greater measure of coordination and integration between the principal freight modes has

been achieved. Unitized freight can now be transferred between road and rail at strategically located container terminals at coastal and inland sites, but such operations still represent only a small proportion of all inter-urban goods traffic.

CONTEMPORARY INTER-URBAN NETWORKS

Much of the research into inter-urban linkages has focused upon the geographical significance of the technical innovations designed to improve the effectiveness of existing networks, the investments in Central and Eastern European networks following the establishment of democratic governments, and the changes in organization of movement patterns, again with the aim of securing more efficient services. Technical developments include the introduction of high-speed rail services and these are discussed in the case study section of this chapter. Recent and projected changes in Eastern Europe are also reviewed later in the chapter. Within the freight sector changes have taken place in movement patterns, particularly to cope with the requirements of manufacturing companies that have adopted "post-Fordist" production techniques and the associated reorganization of inwards and outwards goods traffic. The established "Fordist" approach to industrial production required quantities of standardized components which were normally often assembled on a regular basis by long-distance

Table 8.5 Great Britain: movement of principal types of freight by mode, 1995

Freight	Percentage of Total Tonne-Kilometres			
	Road	Rail	Pipeline	Water*
Petroleum and by-products	9.2	2.9	19.6	68.3
Coal and other solid fuels	34.6	42.3	23.1	–
Ores and metal waste	46.9	53.1	–	–
Minerals, building materials	74.4	8.2	–	17.4
Machinery and other manufactured goods	89.9	6.3	–	3.8

*Including coastal shipping.
Source: Department of Transport (1996).

transport, and this type of flow was well served by motorway networks and containerization. The adoption of the "post-Fordist" processes has often brought about an increased specialization of production, and the requirements for long-distance haulage are now more likely to arise from the distribution stage, with the growth of storage depots at strategic locations to serve the market (Giannopoulos and Gillespie, 1993).

The changes in the organization of inter-urban movement patterns for passenger and freight traffic can best be illustrated by the increasing use of the "hub-and-spoke" system. This system has been adopted by goods distribution companies and, in the passenger sector, by airlines, in order to achieve efficiencies in variable costs and, for freight in particular, in handling costs (Phillips, 1987). The concept involves the location of a hub or exchange point, represented for example by a warehouse, at the centre of a goods transport network in order to maximize efficiency of distribution through the market area. The solution to the hub network design problem requires the use of locational analysis and spatial interaction theory.

The hub network comprises (i) service nodes, from which flows originate and terminate, (ii) the hub itself, defined as a service node which also allows the entry and exit of through-flows, and (iii) arcs, which connect nodes and hubs. Hub design is carried out in four stages: identifying the optimal locations for the hub, assigning non-hub origins and destinations to the hub, discovering what linkages exist between hubs, and finally establishing routes for flows through the network (O'Kelly and Miller, 1994). The relevance of this hub design and operation to inter-urban routes is that hub networks can aid the solution of the many-to-many point distribution problem, one well represented by a complex system of towns and connecting routes. If appropriate hub networks can be constructed in terms of goods distributions or passenger flows, then improvements in transport costs and quality of services can be achieved (Shaw, 1993). Other approaches to investigating inter-urban route patterns make use of the accessibility concept, and in particular how levels of access to certain centres can be increased by infrastructural improvements derived from upgrading existing linkages or adding new routes, such as motorways.

The gradual spatial extension of the European Union and the need for integration between member states have stimulated many studies of the transport infrastructure. An investigation into the passenger transport network within the EU carried out in the mid-1970s was based upon international linkages, but the level of interaction between member states is sufficiently high to justify using this study as an example of inter-urban travel patterns (Organization for Economic Co-operation and Development, 1977). The network was defined as linkages, by road, rail and air, between all national capitals and cities with populations of over 750 000, plus what were identified as major transport centres, regional capitals and regional development centres. This produced a total of 77 urban nodes interconnected by 49 447 km of road, 47 000 km of rail and 259 direct air services. Motorways and other high-speed highways, the result of generally recent investment, accounted for 39 per cent of the network and 64 per cent of the rail net had two or more tracks. Within the EU there were wide variations in the quality of national networks, with the highest proportion of motorways in Germany, Italy, Belgium and the Netherlands. On the air services network the dominant focal airport cities were London, Paris, Frankfurt, Rome, Milan, Amsterdam, Zurich and Madrid, and passenger movements through these nodes accounted for almost one-half of all air traffic.

A more recent analysis of accessibility within the EU measures the impact of the projected trans-European Road Network Outline Plan, promoted to coordinate member states' own plans for improvements to their infrastructures. The main objectives are the creation of major routes, adequate facilities for international traffic, elimination of congestion points, the integration of landlocked and peripheral regions, and better linkages on land–sea routes. The Plan identified a 54 000 km road network, of which 37 000 km were in use in

1992, with schemes to upgrade a further 12 000 km by 2002. In order to determine a measure of access to the network, corridors 80 km wide were superimposed upon each road link and in 1992 an estimated 70 per cent of EU territory was within this zone, with percentages of over 90 being recorded in Germany, Belgium and the Netherlands. If the projected improvements are completed by 2002, then the accessible zone within the EU should rise to 85 per cent. A composite accessibility indicator using individual network node accessibility values, travel time and the GDP of economic activity centres was then devised, the zone with the highest values being the triangle defined by the cities of Paris, Brussels and Aachen. It is not expected that this pattern of accessibility will change by 2002, but the greatest improvements in access to inter-urban routes should occur in the peripheral regions of the UK, the Iberian Peninsula and Greece (Gutiérrez and Urbano, 1996).

The quality of linkages between urban centres can be measured in time or in travel costs, and the wide variations in levels of toll charges on European motorways clearly affect vehicle flows, acting as an impedance to certain types of traffic. In the early 1990s one-third of the European motorway network was subject to tolls, with France, Spain and Italy together accounting for 88 per cent of all the sections with tolls (Table 8.6). Toll motorways are intended for high-speed inter-urban travel and, given the high costs of construction, private investment is seen as an acceptable means of providing such routes in countries where public road funding is not available. These privately built toll roads therefore represent a means of providing high-quality inter-urban links for those types of traffic able to bear the tolls, but for others these charges are a deterrent. The choice between a toll road and the alternative route will depend upon journey length, the quality of the toll-free roads and the amount of congestion encountered on them. In France most freight and business traffic uses the toll motorways but about one-third of private car drivers make use of the conventional inter-urban routes (Munro-Lafon and Musset, 1994).

Table 8.6 Motorway tolls in Europe, 1989

Country	Percentage of Motorways Subject to Toll	Toll Rates (UK pence per km)	
		Private Cars	Goods Vehicles
France	71.9	3.5	7.3
Greece	100.0	0.4	0.6
Italy	81.4	3.5	4.3
Spain	79.5	5.1	9.3

Source: Munro-Lafon and Musset (1994).

Germany

As a pioneer of the motorway concept Germany had, by 1939, built a nationwide network of autobahnen focusing upon Berlin, the Ruhr and the Baltic port of Hamburg. Following partition in 1949 the Federal and East German states were obliged to reorientate their inter-urban networks and the Federal Republic embarked upon a massive programme of road reconstruction and extension to meet the demands of its new territory and, later, those of its Economic Community neighbours. The new West German network required the strengthening of north–south connections between Bavaria, the industrial Rhine valley and Baltic ports. To achieve this aim the 2100 km of autobahnen inherited from the 1930s had been extended to 8800 km by 1989 and all major towns and cities are now located on the motorway system or the supplementary framework of federal trunk highways. During the 1980s emphasis was shifted to improving the latter routes rather than the motorways and funds initially intended for additional autobahnen were diverted to federal road building (Scott, 1985) (Figure 8.1). Following political unification of Germany in 1990 and the reinstatement of Berlin as the national capital, substantial changes in the road network have been initiated and the former East German motorways in particular are being upgraded to match their Western counterparts.

In common with other European states the Deutschesbundesbahn has initiated high-speed train services (ICE) between major cities, involving the

Figure 8.1   The development of the German autobahnen network to 1997
Source: Road maps published 1930–96

construction or upgrading of 2000 km of track by the year 2000. There has been a continuing increase in both local and long-distance rail traffic and the ICE trains now carry 65 000 passengers per day and account for 30 per cent of all inter-urban passenger traffic revenue. Speeds of up to 250 kph are possible on the Hannover–Wurzburg and Mannheim–Stuttgart lines although access to these routes is restricted to principal stations. These new services have greatly reduced journey times but are of benefit principally to a restricted range of business travellers (Whitelegg, 1988). Trains are still operated over 40 500 km of passenger lines in Germany but 7000 km of these have been identified as under-used and passenger services on 12 000 km are under review. The Deutchesbundesbahn is to be divided into four separate companies in 1999 but the undertaking will continue in State ownership (Anon., 1997).

Domestic air services are provided by Lufthansa, with Frankfurt, Munich and Berlin as the principal hubs. As in France and the United Kingdom improved rail services have attracted air traffic over shorter distances but air links between major cities in the former Federal and Democratic German Republics have been improved, with the upgrading of airports in the East.

The United Kingdom

In the United Kingdom the railways and many long-distance passenger and freight road services were acquired by the state in 1948, with government policy being directed towards coordination and subsidization of much of this system. Since 1980, however, public investment in the inter-urban passenger sector has been greatly reduced, and express coach transport was deregulated in that year to encourage competition and lower public travel costs. The inter-urban motorway system, totalling 3300 km in 1996, now carries about 20 per cent of all trunk-road traffic but, in contrast to networks in France, Germany and the Netherlands, the UK motorways do not provide a fully comprehensive set of linkages between all main urban centres (Starkie, 1982). For example, motorways in Scotland and North-East England are

still isolated from the national network whilst Manchester and Sheffield lack both a motorway and a dual-carriageway road link.

As a network is expanded accessibility levels between nodes will increase and in turn affect prospects for economic development. A recent analysis of these processes in the UK has been based upon 280 urban regions, using time and distance measures and vehicle operating costs on the motorway system. These are combined to calculate market potential values, which are highest in the London region and lowest in the periphery of Scotland. All regions of the UK have become more accessible as the motorway net has been extended, with the highest increases in North-West and South-West England and in Wales (Spence and Linneker, 1994).

Within the railway system the InterCity sector, where the average trip length is about 175 km, provides a high-quality service with an increase in patronage during a period in which it has been required to become self-supporting. However the privatization of the UK railways has created very many new operating companies, and it is possible that with this fragmentation the quality of inter-urban rail travel may be reduced unless through-ticketing is organized effectively. On the shorter inter-urban routes there is often intense competition between rail and road modes and within the road passenger sector. The London to Oxford corridor (85 km), for example, has a frequent rail service and two high-speed coach companies who together provide a 20-minute service interval, decreasing to 10 minutes at peak periods, as there is substantial commuter traffic along this route. On the longer inter-urban routes, for example between London and Glasgow, the high-speed electrified railway can compete with air transport, and within the latter sector there is vigorous competition between the various private companies (White and Doganis, 1990; White, 1995) (Figure 8.2).

Eastern Europe

Political changes in Eastern Europe and the creation of new states such as Bosnia, Slovenia and Slovakia have necessitated a reassessment of national

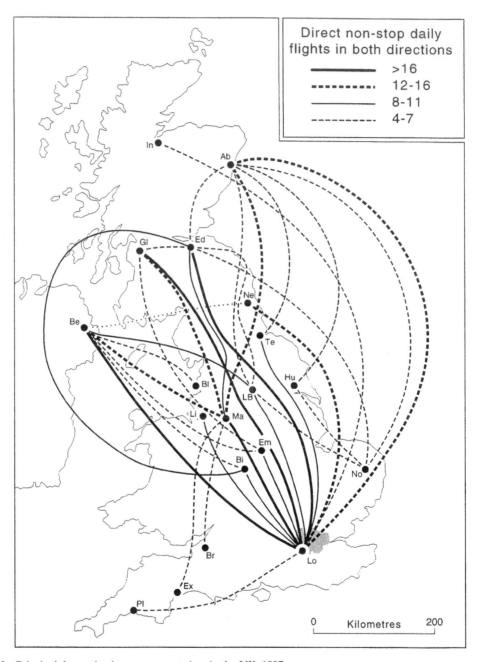

Figure 8.2 Principal domestic air passenger services in the UK, 1997
Flights to and from London make use of Heathrow, Gatwick and Stansted airports. Key to airports: Ab, Aberdeen; Be, Belfast; Bi, Birmingham; Bl, Blackpool; Br, Bristol; Ed, Edinburgh; Em, East Midlands; Ex, Exeter; Gl, Glasgow; Hu, Hull; In, Inverness; LB, Leeds–Bradford; Li, Liverpool; Lo, London; Ma, Manchester; Ne, Newcastle; No, Norwich; Pl, Plymouth; Te, Teesside
Sources: current airline timetables

transport infrastructures, particularly with regard to the integration of these networks with those of the European Union. It has been estimated that the union of East and West Germany will lead to an increase in traffic between the two formerly separate states of 24 per cent on the waterways, 30 per cent on the railways and 818 per cent on the roads in the period 1988–2010. If similar increases occur in Eastern European states the need for improvement of road and rail networks will become even more urgent. In Central and Eastern Europe 30 per cent of the road network is of trunk route status but 82 per cent of this requires major upgrading in order to carry the anticipated increases in long-distance traffic. The density of inter-urban road networks in Eastern Europe is similar to those in the West, but there is a need for better traffic management, improved surfaces, bypasses to towns and cities and a

reduction in accident rates, which are often five-fold those in Western Europe. Investment for these Eastern European states has to consider the intermodal split on inter-urban routes, the balance between long-overdue maintenance and new construction, the replacement and expansion of road and rail vehicle fleets and the need to allocate resources to both international corridors and domestic networks (Buchhofer, 1995; European Conference of Ministers of Transport, 1996; Hall, 1993).

Japan

During the 1950s and 1960s the severe strains placed upon the Japanese inland-transport system by the rapid growth of the economy were remedied by ambitious motorway- and rail-improvement programmes (Figure 8.3). The national narrow-gauge

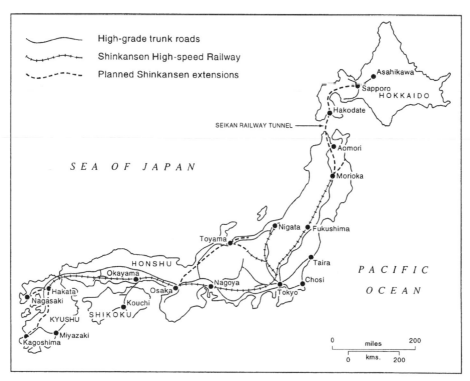

Figure 8.3   The Shinkansen railway and high-grade trunk-road networks in Japan
Sources: Saito (1989), *Jane's World Railways, 1996, International Railway Journal*, 37, 1997

rail network was steadily losing passenger traffic to both road and air transport. In 1964 the first 500 km high-speed standard-gauge Shinkansen route with electric traction was opened between Tokyo and Osaka to relieve existing lines and to counteract these growing challenges. This new line was extended in 1975 to Hakata on Kyushu and further routes linking Tokyo with Morioka and Niigata were built. These lines are restricted to passenger trains travelling at speeds of up to 220 kph but the initial expansion of traffic has not always been sustained, although traffic has risen on the original Tokaido and Sanyo routes. In mid-1997, 1800 km of Shinkansen railways were in service and a further 400 km are planned, with speeds to be increased to 260 kph. These Shinkansen services have dramatically enhanced levels of accessibility between major Japanese cities and increased the unity of the urban system (Murayama, 1994). Many of the new railways have also benefited from the construction of fixed links between the principal islands, with tunnels, notably the Seikan tunnel between Honshu and Hokkaido, and bridges replacing ferries (Knowles, 1996). Domestic air services however continue to carry a substantial proportion of all inter-urban traffic, especially between the major islands, and air transport has greatly reduced the intended significance of the Seikan tunnel as a rail link.

China

Chinese transport policy has been designed to fulfil several requirements of a centrally planned state first established in 1949 and inheriting a road and rail infrastructure that was severely damaged during World War II. Railway investment was initially concentrated upon the repair and improvement of existing inter-urban lines in the eastern coastal areas and on the extension of this core network westwards to peripheral provinces such as Inner Mongolia and Yunnan. The Chinese achievement in expanding their railway system since the Communist state was founded in 1949 is unparalleled anywhere else in the world. Of the 55 000 km now in use, 57 per cent has been built since 1949 and current plans aim for a

further 24 000 km to be completed by about the year 2000. All provincial capitals apart from Lhasa are now connected to Beijing by rail, compared with only half of these centres in 1949; in order to achieve this aim the annual rate of construction between 1949 and the early 1970s was 1000 km.

Before 1949 only one-fifth of the national network lay west of the main north–south Beijing–Guangzhou line but by the late 1980s this share had increased to almost 50 per cent. Almost 80 per cent of the system is still single-track but in the east many lines are now double-track, including the trunk routes linking the capital with Wuhan and Guangzhou and the Tientsin–Shanghai railway. The electrification programme focuses upon bulk freight-carrying lines, such as that between the Shanxi coalfield and the port of Qinhuangdou, which has an annual capacity of 100 million tonnes. The 2400 km Jing-Jiu line from Beijing to Shenzhen and Hong Kong was completed in late 1996 as China's largest single railway project and is designed to improve links with major east–west railways and to consolidate the newly acquired Hong Kong territories into mainland China. It meets the need for additional freight and passenger traffic capacity between the north and south and coal in particular will form the principal freight, with branches from the Jing-Jiu line into the Shanxi coalfield and to the coast being planned (Qian, 1997).

Both economic and strategic motives have been involved in this railway-building programme, and although the phenomenal construction rates achieved in the 1950–80 period are unlikely to be repeated many lines are to be upgraded and electrified. Although the Chinese government now accepts that the road system could carry a larger share of short-haul freight, thus relieving congestion on the railways, an expansion of road transport is greatly hampered by a lack of suitable vehicles and, in some areas, poor road conditions.

Although internal air transport in China can offer greatly reduced journey times, as compared to rail, between major cities, the existing services carry only a negligible share of all inter-urban passenger traffic and they are used mainly by government officials and business travellers.

The Less-Developed Countries

Proposals for transport improvements in less-developed countries have often been criticized for their shortcomings in the inter-urban sector: the relative merits of long-distance road and rail transport as effective contributors to the development process are particularly open to debate. Investment in inter-urban rail has to compete for limited resources that are also urgently required for the road, where modern high-capacity trucks offer lower freight rates on trunk roads, which are being steadily improved (Addus, 1989). The introduction in the 1990s of economic structural adjustment programmes in many African states has produced some privatization and deregula-

tion in the road-transport sector, which has lowered rates and led to even more aggressive competition with railway undertakings which are often still under rigid state control (Simon, 1996).

Within Zimbabwe plans for long-distance national transport are closely related to the regional transport policies of the Southern African Development Community (Figure 8.4). The First and Second National Development Plans saw the integration of inter-urban road and rail facilities as a principal aim. The state-owned railway still carries a substantial proportion of all long-distance freight, with rates that are often below operating costs as part of the government policy to encourage use of the railway for inter-urban goods transport (Zimbabwe, 1986,

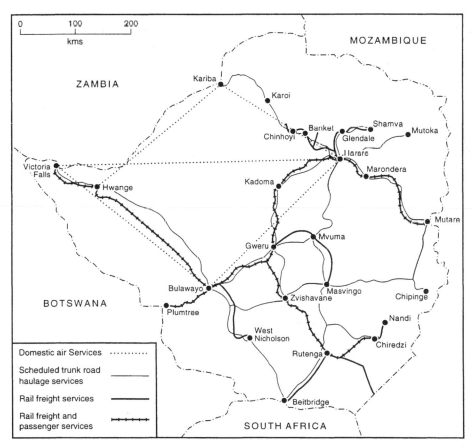

Figure 8.4   Principal road, rail and domestic air routes in Zimbabwe, 1997
Sources: NRZ rail timetables, Air Zimbabwe timetables, information from road haulage companies

1991). The market for inter-urban bus and rail travel is largely confined to the African population, which has a low level of car ownership, and most business and tourist journeys are by private car or by air. Domestic air services have until recently been the monopoly of the state-controlled Air Zimbabwe but competing airlines are now allowed to operate over some internal routes (Turton and Mutambirwa, 1996). Zimbabwe has also initiated the policy of involving the private sector in road construction and maintenance, with plans to convert the major Harare–Bulawayo and Harare–Mutare trunk roads into toll routes.

In many other developing countries roads act as the dominant inter-urban link and investment in railways inherited from colonial governments has rarely been seen as a priority. In Nigeria, for example, the first three national plans allocated up to 74 per cent of the transport budget to roads and the railway network now plays only a minor part in long-distance transport (Ezeife, 1984).

THE UNITED STATES: A CASE STUDY

The USA has the longest, high-quality highway network of any of the advanced nations in the world. Within this network the highest-quality tier is occupied by the Interstate Highway System, a 45 074 mile limited-access highway connecting the contiguous mainland states (Figure 8.5). Legislation authorizing the construction of these highways was enacted in 1956 and in less than two decades the bulk of the system was completed, although sections continue to be added from time to time as need merits their construction. The system was proposed in response to the excessive highway congestion that occurred in the post-World War II period. By the mid-1950s most of the nation's highways in urban areas were congested. This created significant problems for the movement of commodities by motor carriers and it was realized that something had to be done to facilitate the transport of goods. The proposed solution was a highway system named the

National System of Interstate and Defense Highways, which during the height of the Cold War virtually assured its passage as part of the Federal Aid Highway Act of 1956. The system as conceived would connect all of the nation's urban areas, which would be surrounded by beltways (often referred to as ring roads in Europe).

A few years later it became apparent that the system was dumping more traffic on the fringes of urban areas than the local streets could handle. Legislation was enacted that would take the Interstate Highways into the central part of the nation's major metropolitan areas in 1962 as a solution to the fringe congestion problem. While viewed as logical at the time, the urban extensions simply relocated the congestion to the central city. In addition the construction of highways within the metropolitan areas required the virtual destruction of large quantities of urban housing and neighbourhoods. This created a backlash against highway construction that continues in some areas to this day (Moon, 1994).

The Interstate Highway System and its urban extensions generated more impacts than were anticipated at the time of its construction. To some extent it was too good at a time when the railroads of the country were too bad. The freight railroads began to lose market share to the motor carriers, and the passenger railroads began to lose their traffic to automobiles. Bus services began to lose patrons as automobile commuting became the popular mode of urban travel. Federal legislation was necessary to preserve bus transit in urban areas and rail passenger services: the Urban Mass Transportation Assistance Act in 1964 and the Rail Passenger Service Act of 1970.

A series of legislative initiatives in the 1970s and 1980s virtually deregulated most transport services in the USA. It was thought that such actions were necessary in order for the various modes to compete and remain profitable. This deregulation eliminated controls in most cases over three areas that had been heavily regulated prior to this: freedom of entry, freedom of exit, and flexibility on pricing. Freedom of entry meant that if anyone could demonstrate a reasonable financial status, they could begin

Figure 8.5   The US interstate highway system, 1997

operating one of the transport modes. Many independent truckers formed their own small firms and numerous regional and short-line railroads started up. These took over the routes and lines abandoned by the freedom of exit provisions of the new legislation. Pricing freedom is less obvious to those outside the transport sector except in the area of rail passenger services. There have been several studies undertaken since enactment of the Airline Deregulation Act of 1978 to determine whether travellers have cheaper or more expensive fares now than they did before. The results are inconclusive, but it seems that fares have fallen on more popular routes (due mostly to competition) and risen on less popular routes.

Flexibility of routing has allowed many air carriers to offer services over what is called a hub-and-spoke system. Passengers on flights offered by such carriers pass through a hub en route to their final destination, and direct flights have become unusual except to major markets or to and from hubs. This may have kept air fares lower than they would have been otherwise. At the same time hubbing seems to have some diseconomies that no one is talking about. Passengers waste at least an hour on every hubbed flight as the planes land and taxi to the terminal, passengers disembark and reboard or board another flight, and the planes taxi and take off. For all passengers this is a waste of time; for business travellers it is a very expensive waste of time. It is interesting to note that some of the newer, no-frills airlines are beginning to offer direct flights between major cities as a way of establishing a market niche. They appear to be having some success.

For urban areas that have the hubs the additional flights generate more noise and air pollution than is common for other cities of their size. There seems to be no environmental assessment of hubbing prior to its establishment at an airport, and this is probably something that will be assessed with more care in the future. However, most cities are happy to become hubs owing to the additional employment this will bring to the urban area; therefore, regulation of hubbing will most likely come at the federal level if it is to be successful.

Personal Inter-Urban Travel Patterns

Personal travel in the USA is a product of the systems discussed above and the legislation that has created and modified them. It should not be surprising that most inter-urban travel (trips longer than 48 km) is made by automobile (Table 8.7). In reality there are not a lot of choices when it comes to inter-urban travel in the USA. If you live near the Amtrak (rail passenger) system you can use that system, but it is a "thin" network and it may not offer the access or the train frequency that you would like (Figure 8.6). Inter-urban bus operations have also come on hard times and are not nearly as important today as they were 10 years ago. Most non-motor-vehicle travellers choose to travel by airline because of its speed and accessibility to other parts of the country. The system of commercial airports is very dense, but only 694 of these have more than 1000 passenger enplanements per year (Figure 8.7).

Inter-Urban Goods Movement

Goods move between urban areas by every possible mode in the USA, but for most commodities the dominant modes are rail and motor carrier. If we look at the overall pattern of movement for ship-

Table 8.7 Modal split for personal trips longer than 48 km (sample survey)

Mode	Number of Trips	Percentage
Motor vehicles	10 583	94.9
Bus, streetcar	133	1.2
Rail/subway	164	1.5
Amtrak	19	0.2
Bike	3	0.0
Walk	1	0.0
School bus	46	0.4
Airplane	131	1.2
Other	66	0.4
Total	11 153	100.0

Source: Federal Highway Administration (1993).

ments of different length the pattern is as we would expect: motor carriers dominate at short distances and railroads at longer distances (Table 8.8). In general for all goods transported in the USA, motor carriers appear to be the dominant mode choice up to about 499 miles. At or about that point rail becomes the major mode choice. At very long

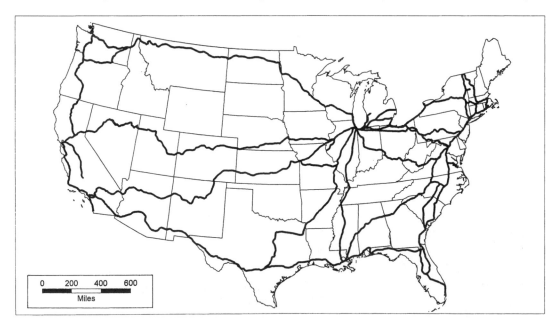

Figure 8.6   The Amtrak rail passenger system, 1996

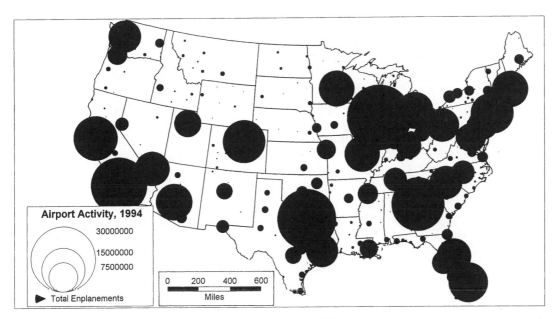

Figure 8.7 US airports with more than 1000 enplanements a year, 1994

distances motor carriers pick up some of the traffic again. In all cases in the table the traffic drops off with increasing distance, an example of distance decay.

It may be a little misleading to think that all traffic follows the pattern of Table 8.8. In reality there are many different products that go into the data of this table. Some of these products are bulk goods that move primarily by rail whenever it is feasible. Other goods of high value may be moved only by motor carriers. When we throw these data all together it

gives us the data of Table 8.8, but the percentages in the table may not apply to a single product.

Even the very elementary notion of assigning a mode to a particular shipment can be difficult. Table 8.9 illustrates the number of modal categories used by a recent commodity flow survey in the USA. In that case 17 different modes or modal combinations were used. Goods shipments must be viewed as primarily intermodal. Modes used in many cases are dependent on the value, weight or distance the commodity has to move. High-value goods move long

Table 8.8 Modal split of commodities between rail and motor carriers in the USA, 1993

Shipping Distance (miles)	Railroad ('000 tons)	Motor Carrier ('000 tons)	Total Tonnage ('000)	Rail (%)	Truck (%)
<99	415 304	4 496 287	4 911 591	8.5	91.5
100–249	258 616	662 455	921 071	28.1	71.9
250–499	316 681	330 581	647 262	48.9	51.1
500–749	250 532	159 879	410 411	61.0	39.0
750–999	148 593	87 069	235 662	63.1	36.9
1000–1499	119 863	59 270	179 133	66.9	33.1
1500–1999	26 756	31 432	58 188	46.0	54.0
>2000	7802	24 317	32 619	23.9	76.1

Source: Bureau of the Census (1996).

distances by air; heavy, low-value goods move by rail; and motor carriers perform the movements between these extremes. There are exceptions to this if water transport or pipelines are available and feasible for low-value goods transport. In many cases we can imagine door-to-door transport by a single mode, but in most goods transport there are multiple modes involved in the shipments. In some cases these intermodal shifts work well, but in other cases local conditions can obstruct the transfer between modes. This was part of the reason for the passage of the 1991 Intermodal Surface Transport Efficiency Act in the USA. It was an attempt to provide funds for improving intermodal flows of goods as well as people.

The basic rail network of the USA and the density of rail traffic (in millions of gross tons per mile) are shown in Figure 8.8. The "land bridge" moving traffic from Asia across the USA for shipment to Europe is evident in the traffic shown as are the major import and export ports of the East, West and Gulf coasts.

In comparison to rail and motor carriers the other modes are minor. Air freight accounts for less than 0.1 per cent of the value of goods shipped, while it represents an insignificant amount of the total tonnage. Pipelines move 1.5 per cent of the value and 5 per cent of the tonnage; this is primarily petroleum. Inland water moves 0.7 per cent of the commodities by value and 3.7 per cent by weight; this traffic is primarily coal and chemical products. Perhaps the fastest-growing mode, which is actually multimodal, is parcel shipments. Made up primarily of moves by

Table 8.9   Modal and intermodal shipment characteristics for the USA, 1993

Mode	Value		Tons		Ton-miles		Average miles
	Millions of Dollars	%	'000 Tons	%	Millions of Ton-miles	%	
All modes	5 846 334	100.0	9 688 493	100.0	2 420 915	100.0	424
Single modes							
Parcel, postal or courier	563 277	9.6	18 892	0.2	13 151	0.5	734
Private truck	1 755 837	30.0	3 543 513	36.6	235 897	9.7	52
For-hire truck	2 625 093	44.9	2 808 279	29.0	629 000	26.0	472
Air	5200	0.1	148	0.0	139	0.0	1180
Rail	247 394	4.2	1 544 148	15.9	942 561	38.9	766
Inland water	40 707	0.7	362 454	3.7	164 371	6.8	(S)
Great Lakes	1173	0.0	33 041	0.3	12 395	0.5	(S)
Deep-sea water	67	0.0	(S)	–	(S)	–	(S)
Pipeline	89 849	1.5	483 645	5.0	(S)	–	(S)
Multiple modes							
Private truck and for-hire truck	22 565	0.4	34 123	0.4	4639	0.2	197
Truck and air	133 887	2.3	2991	0.0	3870	0.2	1423
Truck and rail	83 082	1.4	40 624	0.4	37 675	1.6	1403
Truck and water	9392	0.2	67 995	0.7	40 610	1.7	1417
Truck and pipeline	349	0.0	(S)	–	(S)	–	(S)
Rail and water	3636	0.1	79 222	0.8	70 219	2.9	627
Inland water and Great Lakes	2448	0.0	13 501	0.0	(S)	–	(S)
Inland water and deep-sea	19 682	0.3	109 916	1.1	95 215	3.9	1903
Other modes							
Other and unknown modes	242 691	4.2	544 335	5.6	96 972	4.0	229

(S) indicates data not published due to sampling variability.
Source: Bureau of the Census (1996).

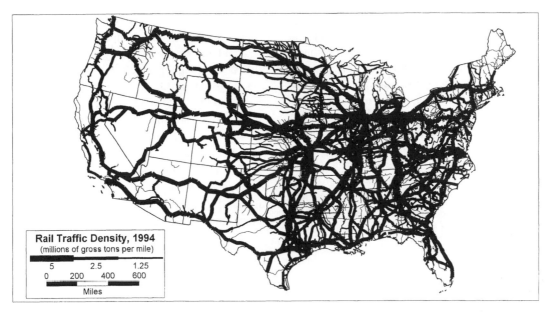

Figure 8.8   Rail traffic density in millions of gross tons per mile of track, 1994

air freight and motor carriers this sector moved 9.6 per cent of the value of all goods shipped in 1993, but only 0.2 per cent of the tonnage.

CONCLUSIONS

The theory and use of gravity models give us relative indicators of the strength of flows between places in the USA and to a lesser extent in countries such as the UK and France. If tariffs, political factors or international boundaries are involved these introduce factors that are incorporated in neither the theory nor the model and as a result their utility is somewhat limited in these situations. Nevertheless, the key variables identified by Ullman several decades ago, i.e. complementarity, intervening opportunities and transferability, are still relevant today in the analysis of major flows of goods and people.

The real world of travel is not made up of abstract flows but of passengers in automobiles, aircraft or rail cars, and of goods in containers, tractor trailers and lorries, wagons or box cars. When these flows are disaggregated into business trips or shipments of metal goods, Ullman's (1956) variables are still important but so are the modes and networks available. It is for this reason that we focus our discussion on these very real components of transport in the latter part of this chapter.

Innovations such as motorways and high-speed railways are able to change the relative pattern of accessibility for a system of cities and can result in some cities acquiring a new significance as focal points, but they cannot overcome geography if the investments in infrastructure are uniform. A well-equipped French port city with a good harbour will always be on the fringe of Europe's networks and within that context will always be among the least accessible of major urban places, but if it is designated as the key port for European container operations to and from North America its geography changes and it becomes central to the broader network of trade between these continents. Geography changes networks, and networks can change geography.

Mode availability is as important as it is detrimental. Environmental quality and congestion levels in Europe were probably better before the increases in automobile ownership of the last two decades. Americans are criticized for their over-reliance on the automobile, but they have fewer alternative modes available having allowed rail services practically to disappear and bus transit services to be barely worthy of the name. A mix of modes should be recognized by all national transport policymakers as desirable, not financially reckless.

There have been substantial changes in the past two decades on both sides of the Atlantic as governments have relinquished their levels of control over rail, road and air transport. These changes have taken the form of deregulation in North America and privatization and deregulation in Europe and South America. It should not be surprising that modal choices are fewer and network sizes are smaller today than they were 20 years ago. While the new networks may offer a higher quality of service it is difficult to see some of these as major accomplishments. It is easy to be impressed with the rail passenger service of the Northeast Corridor of the USA in 1998, but if one considers the rail passenger network of that country in 1948, the track in this corridor today is recognizable as a remnant of a network that was formerly much better. So it is not immediately clear at this point in time if the changes we have seen in terms of ownership and regulation are a success story or the prelude to yet smaller networks and fewer modal choices.

Many developing countries, and especially the independent states in Africa and South-East Asia, employed rigid centralized planning for investment in their transport sectors from the 1960s to the late 1980s. The lack of sufficient funding prevented many projects for improved inter-urban links from being realized and these states are now adopting economic structural adjustment programmes which have reduced state involvement in the management of road and rail undertakings and allowed other private companies to provide competition on these links.

In Europe and North America the two related aims of making increasing use of energy-efficient modes and minimizing the environmental impact of new transport routes will exert a major influence on inter-urban transport in the early twenty-first century. But the gains in energy efficiency and decreases in environmental impacts may be offset by the rapid motorization taking place in Asia and other developing regions. There is a possibility that some personal and business inter-urban travel will be replaced by electronic interaction made possible by increases in communications technology, but this is not certain. In the past, increases in communication have led to increases in transport, not less. Even if this does occur, the increases in leisure travel and increases in global trade will ensure that high-quality inter-urban connections need to be maintained.

REFERENCES

Addus, A.A. (1989), "Road transportation in Africa", *Transportation Quarterly* 43 (3), 421–33.

Anon. (1987), *International Railway Journal* 37 (4), 27–8.

Buchhofer, E. (1995), "Transport infrastructure in the Baltic States during the transformation to market economies", *Journal of Transport Geography* 3 (1), 69–75.

Bureau of the Census (1996), *1992 Census of transportation, communications and utilities, 1993 Commodity flow survey, United States* (Washington, DC: US Department of Commerce).

Capello, R. and Gillespie, A. (1993), "Transport, communications and spatial organisation", in Giannopoulos, G. and Gillespie, A. (eds), *Transport and communications innovation in Europe* (London: Belhaven).

Department of Transport (1996), *Transport statistics Great Britain, 1995–6* (London: HMSO).

European Conference of Ministers of Transport (1996), *Transport infrastructure and systems for a new Europe*, Report of the 1995 Round Table on Transport Economics (Paris: ECMT).

Ezeife, P.C. (1984), "The development of the Nigerian transport system", *Transport Reviews* 4 (4), 305–30.

Federal Highway Administration (1993), *Nationwide personal travel survey, 1990 NPTS databook*, vol. 1 (Washington, DC: US Department of Transportation).

Fowkes, A.S., Nash, C.A., Tweddle, G. and Whiteing, A.E. (1987), "Forecasting freight mode choice in Great Britain", *PTRC Proceedings, Seminar G* (University of Bath), 43–54.

Giannopoulos, G. and Gillespie, A. (eds) (1993), *Transport and communications innovation in Europe* (London: Belhaven).

Gutiérez, J. and Urbano, P. (1996), "Accessibility in the European Union: the impact of the trans-European road network", *Journal of Transport Geography* 4 (1), 15–25.

Hall, D. (1993), "Impacts of economic and political transition on the transport geography of central and eastern Europe", *Journal of Transport Geography* 1 (1), 20–35.

Hay, A. (1973), *Transport for the space economy* (London: Macmillan).

Knowles, R. (1996), "Fixed links and short sea crossings", in Hoyle, B.S. (ed.), *Cityports, coastal zones and regional change* (Chichester: Wiley), 213–33.

McKinnon, A. (1989), *Physical distribution systems* (London: Routledge).

Moon, H. (1994), *The Interstate Highway System* (Washington, DC: Association of American Geographers).

Munro-Lafon, J.P. and Musset, J.W. (1994), "European inter-urban toll roads", in Farrell, S. (ed.), *PTRC financing transport infrastructure* (London: PTRC), 57–63.

Murayama, Y. (1994), "The impact of railways on accessibility in the Japanese urban system", *Journal of Transport Geography* 2 (2), 87–100.

Ohlin, B. (1933), *Interregional and international trade* (Cambridge, Mass.: Harvard University Press).

O'Kelly, M.E. and Miller, H.J. (1994), "The hub network design problem", *Journal of Transport Geography* 2 (1), 31–40.

Organization for Economic Co-operation and Development (1977), *The future of European passenger transport* (Paris: OECD).

Phillips, L.T. (1987), "Air carrier activity at major hub airports", *Transportation Research A* 21 (3), 215–22.

Prideaux, J. (1988), "InterCity: profits of change", *Transport* 9 (1), 27–30.

Qian, L. (1997), "Jing-Jiu trunk line boosts north–south capacity", *Railway Gazette International* 153 (7), 455–8.

Quarmby, D.A. (1989), "Developments in the retail market and their effects on freight distribution", *Journal of Transport Economics and Policy* 23 (1), 75–88.

Rissoan, J.P. (1994), "River–sea navigation in Europe", *Journal of Transport Geography* 2 (2), 131–42.

Saito, C. (1989), "Transportation coordination debate and the Japanese National Railways problem in postwar Japan", *Transportation Research A* 23 (1), 13–18.

Scott, D. (1985), "The West German transport system", *Geography* 68(3), 266–71.

Shaw, S.-L. (1993), "Hub structures of major US passenger airlines", *Journal of Transport Geography* 1 (1), 47–58.

Simon, D. (1996), *Transport and development in the Third World* (London: Routledge).

Spence, N. and Linneker, B. (1994), "Evolution of the motorway network and changing levels of accessibility in Great Britain", *Journal of Transport Geography* 2 (4), 247–64.

Starkie, D.A. (1982), *The motorway age* (Oxford: Pergamon).

Turton, B.J. (1989), "Railways and the national economy of Zimbabwe", *Geographical Journal of Zimbabwe* 19, 47–57.

Turton, B.J. and Mutambirwa, C.C. (1996), "Air transport services and the expansion of international tourism in Zimbabwe", *Tourism Management* 17 (6), 453–62.

Ullman, E.L. (1956), "The role of transportation and the bases for interaction", in Thomas, W.L. (ed.), *Man's role in changing the face of the earth* (Chicago: University of Chicago Press), 862–80.

White, P. (1995), *Public transport* (London: UCL Press).

White, P. and Doganis, R. (1990), *Long-distance travel within Britain*, Rees Jeffreys Discussion Paper 17 (Oxford: Transport Studies Unit).

Whitelegg, J. (1988), "High-speed railways and new investment in Germany", in Tolley, R.S. (ed.), *Transport technology and spatial change* (Stoke-on-Trent: Institute of British Geographers, Transport Geography Study Group).

Zimbabwe, Ministry of Finance (1986), *First National Development Plan* (Harare: Central Statistical Office).

Zimbabwe, Republic of (1991), *Second National Development Plan* (Harare: Government Printer).

Learning Resources
Centre

9

RURAL AREAS: THE ACCESSIBILITY PROBLEM

Stephen Nutley

In the world's rural areas the low density of population causes economic problems for public transport leading to varying degrees of hardship and isolation for the people affected. The central issue is lack of accessibility to essential service locations. In economically advanced countries car ownership and mobility rates are high but deprived minorities remain. In the more densely populated countries, as in Europe, adequate public transport might survive, but in more sparsely settled countries such as the United States and Australia the automobile is assumed to be universal. In developing countries the lack of rural roads severely retards development prospects and vast populations are condemned to isolation and poverty.

INTRODUCTION

The problematic nature of transport in rural areas stems directly from the inherent characteristics of the rural environment itself. It is always difficult to define rural areas and to demarcate them clearly from "urban", especially in more densely populated countries. In advanced industrialized countries social and economic indicators show increasingly complex patterns across urban and rural zones (Cloke and Edwards, 1986), obscuring a distinctly separate "rural" transport sector. Nevertheless, the crucial factors are relatively low population density, a dispersed settlement pattern with low population totals at any point, a scattered pattern of small service outlets, a concentration of middle- and high-order facilities in widely separated urban nodes, and hence long and costly travel distances. Essentially, the "problem" is defined in terms of *public* transport, and therefore bears upon those people dependent upon this sector. It also refers to the *local* scale of passenger demand, i.e. the ease or difficulty of carrying out everyday journeys such as shopping, it does not refer to major traffic flows that happen to pass through rural areas between one city and another. It is predominantly concerned with passenger rather than freight movements, although in many parts of the world where remoter rural regions suffer economic underdevelopment goods carriage is also an important issue.

Hence the "demand surface" for transport is totally at variance with the optimum economic conditions for public transport or common carrier operation. In terms of infrastructure, a high aggregate length of road or railway track is required to cover the spatial extent of a rural region which is disproportionate to the population or traffic potential of that region. Similarly with respect to services, to maintain a geographical coverage of all settlements in a rural region, even at low frequencies, means providing an aggregate vehicle capacity that is excessively high relative to the likely patronage.

Modern Transport Geography: second, revised edition. Edited by Brian Hoyle and Richard Knowles.
© 1998 John Wiley & Sons Ltd.

Transport supply, at the level of the individual bus or train, is indivisible, and cannot be broken down into very small units to match the scale of demand. There is a fundamental mismatch between the type and scale of transport provision and the nature of demand.

This chapter reviews these issues as they are expressed through various economic, cultural, political and geographical situations. To simplify the enor-mous variation here, a suggested categorization is based upon the level of national economic develop-ment, population density and the nature of rural areas, and car ownership as an indicator of mobility (Figure 9.1). Hence the chapter is divided into three (unequal) sections. The developed countries of the world are characterized by high car ownership rates, but these are usefully divided into the high-density industrialized regions such as Western Europe, and

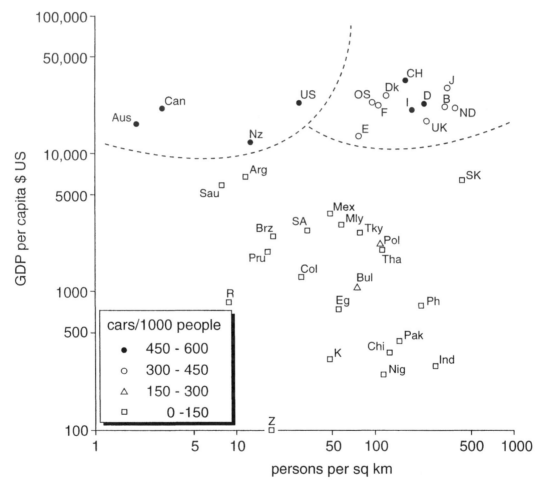

Figure 9.1 National income, population density and car ownership
Key to countries: Arg, Argentina; Aus, Australia; B, Belgium; Brz, Brazil; Bul, Bulgaria; Can, Canada; CH, Switzerland; Chi, China; Col, Colombia; D, Germany; DK, Denmark; E, Spain; Eg, Egypt; F, France; I, Italy; Ind, India; J, Japan; K, Kenya; Mex, Mexico; Mly, Malaysia; ND, Netherlands; Nig, Nigeria; NZ, New Zealand; OS, Austria; Pak, Pakistan; Ph, Philippines; Pol, Poland; Pru, Peru; R, Russia; SA, South Africa; Sau, Saudi Arabia; SK, South Korea; Tha, Thailand; Tky, Turkey; UK, United Kingdom; US, United States; Z, Zaire
Source of data: United Nations

the more spatially extensive affluent countries such as the United States and Australia. The less-developed world is extremely diverse, but generalizations are possible, and selective examples are used.

BASIC CONCEPTS

It is essential to appreciate that the purpose of transport is to provide *accessibility*, or the ability to make a journey for a specific purpose. Transport is not consumed for its own sake, but is merely a means to an end (a derived demand). Hence residents in location A seek *access* to location B in order to acquire goods or services or partake in activities that are not available at A. If A and B are beyond walking distance apart, then transport is needed to overcome the distance barrier that separates them. Commonly, A is a rural village and B a town or market centre. In rural areas a greater proportion of desired facilities (shops, doctors, work and leisure places, etc.) are likely to be at distant locations. Hence there is a *greater need for transport* in the countryside, in an environment where (except for car users) it is less likely to be available. In most Western countries this is exacerbated by the decline of local service outlets. It is normally assumed that access to a basic minimum range of facilities is economically and socially necessary for the pursuit of a normal way of life. The rural "problem" therefore is *lack of accessibility*.

An alternative approach is to focus on travel behaviour patterns. *Mobility* is simply the ability to move around, without any particular destination. *Potential mobility* is determined by various factors such as physical fitness and car ownership (both of which discriminate among population subgroups), as well as public transport availability. *Actual mobility* is measured in terms of traffic levels or trip rates (trips per person per week). Low trip rates by some social groups might, arguably, be interpreted as indicators of difficulty or hardship: rather than demonstrating a lack of "demand", they are more likely to reflect an absence of transport opportunities (Nutley and Thomas, 1995).

HIGH-DENSITY DEVELOPED COUNTRIES

"The Rural Transport Problem"

Within the literature of transport studies and geography, the problems of the rural environment have been analysed most vigorously in the context of high-density developed regions such as Western Europe, with the United Kingdom in particular generating a lot of research. This is because such countries have incomes high enough to support steadily rising car ownership but are not able to achieve near-universal levels likely to overcome rural isolation. Such countries also have a long history of good public transport services, sustained by relatively high rural population densities and moderate distances. Where bus and train services are forced into decline, there remain many people without the use of a private car who experience inconvenience and hardship. Thus the "rural transport problem" – a term first used by Thomas (1963) in a study of Devon, England – has remained strongly in the public consciousness in the districts affected.

Traditional public transport in rural areas has always been extremely vulnerable to competition from modes better suited to the dispersed pattern of demand. Other things being equal, by far the most appropriate mode for rural environments is the private motor car. It does not suffer from the fixed linear routes and timetables of the bus or train; it is personal and individualist, convenient and flexible; it can carry heavy loads. Moreover, it does not suffer the problems experienced by cars in urban areas; in the countryside there are no congestion or parking problems (except in some tourist areas in summer) and pollution is rarely an issue. Car ownership rates have always been higher in rural areas, ever since the first cars were acquired in the early 1900s by the landed gentry to run about their country estates. The main reason is *need*, not wealth. Precisely the same geographical, "rural" factors that make public transport so difficult make car ownership so necessary and attractive. Hence the enduring "rural transport problem" is suffered by those people who are unable to exploit the car's advantages and remain dependent upon public modes.

Rising car ownership inevitably triggered off the initial decline in bus services as the public-sector market contracted. Bus companies cannot compete with the long-term process towards greater car ownership and use, and their possible responses are limited. Reduction of network length or service levels, and fare increases, either reduce the market further or risk consumer resistance. This produces a permanently unstable situation, with each adjustment failing to halt a downward trend of services and passenger numbers. Feedback effects reinforce this process, in that perception of inadequate public transport encourages more people to acquire cars

and to use them more. Hence the frequently cited "vicious circle" of decline (Figure 9.2). Another available response in many cases is to seek external subsidy, but to maintain a stable service level then means a continuous increase in claims. Some countries and some governments are more sympathetic than others on this principle. Essentially the same process occurs on the railways, with decline taking the form of frequency reductions and infrastructure deterioration. Eventually, the "final solution" of closure is proposed and, once implemented, is irrevocable.

The United Kingdom

Rural transport issues have received a great deal of attention in the UK, and more work has been done

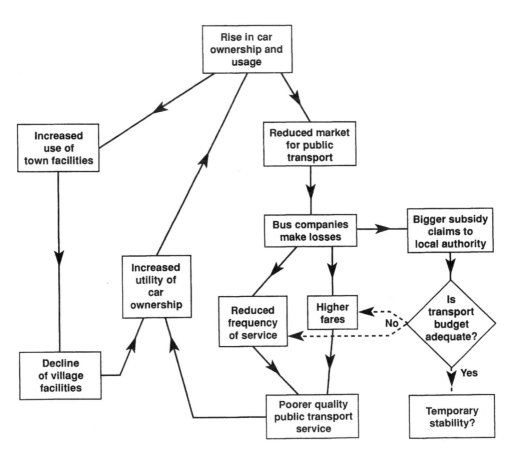

Figure 9.2 Rural transport "vicious circles"

here by geographers than in any other country. General works are Cloke (1985), Cresswell (1978), Halsall and Turton (1979), Moseley (1979), Tolley and Turton (1995, 231–62) and White (1995, 142–60). Much of this research has been done through detailed local case studies, e.g. Banister (1980), Cloke *et al.* (1994), Jordan and Nutley (1993), Kilvington and McKenzie (1985), Moseley *et al.* (1977), Moyes (1989), Nutley (1983), Nutley and Thomas (1992, 1995), Smith and Gant (1982) and Stanley and Farrington (1981).

Car ownership

Ownership of private cars in the UK began to increase dramatically in the 1950s, with the ending of post war restrictions and growth in the economy. For various reasons the costs of car purchase and use have risen by less than the overall cost of living, while public-transport fares have risen by more. Hence car acquisition has come within the means of successively lower income groups, and although a boon for rural people this has reinforced the public-transport vicious circle of decline. Car ownership rates vary spatially and socially. The map pattern (Figure 9.3) displays an intriguing blend of two influences.

1. *Rurality.* Predominantly rural counties and regions have significantly higher rates than cities, because of the dispersed location of facilities in the countryside, longer distances and the shortcomings of public transport. Many relatively poor rural families make great sacrifices to keep their car going.
2. *Income.* Among the rural counties/regions rates are markedly higher in the more prosperous south. Areas with relatively more cars are both rural and affluent, with the highest rates in urban fringe commuter zones such as London's stockbroker belt.

Apparently high car ownership rates by household may imply that the whole family has constant access to the vehicle. Commonly, the main wage earner takes the car to work, leaving the rest of the family deprived during the day, during which time they might require a shopping journey and a school journey. Even two-car households may have some demand for public transport. Realistically, in rural areas 20–35 per cent of households and 40–60 per cent of adult individuals are still without a car. Government has belatedly recognized that the market for rural public transport is not just a "declining minority", but there is an irreducible minimum population that will always need it. The young and the elderly may be unable to run a car because of age, infirmity and/or income; the disabled, those on low incomes or State benefits may be similarly deprived. Even wealthy retired people who have chosen to live in the countryside must accept that eventually they will have to give up their car and face an unfamiliar isolation. Social dimensions of car ownership and mobility are illustrated in Tables 9.1 and 9.2. These demonstrate the greater travel distances and greater car dependence in rural areas compared to urban, and the existence of some social groups with very low mobility rates. The carless are sometimes labelled "transport-poor", suffering "transport-induced deprivation", as their lack of mobility prohibits them from consuming other economic and social activities.

Bus issues

The use of buses in the UK, measured by passenger journeys, has more than halved from its peak in 1955. It is rarely possible to find transport statistics for rural areas only, but here the decline was probably steeper. The end of post-war depression, rising car ownership and rural depopulation all contributed to the cycle of decline. Historic route maps show a remarkable density of services in earlier years, an abundance that had encouraged dependence and high expectations of public services among the rural population, now acutely aware of its loss (Photograph 9.1). Despite this, spatial coverage remains quite good, with no more than 5 per cent of the population of any rural region having no services at all. While the basic network remains intact, *frequencies* are often very low. A basic network of

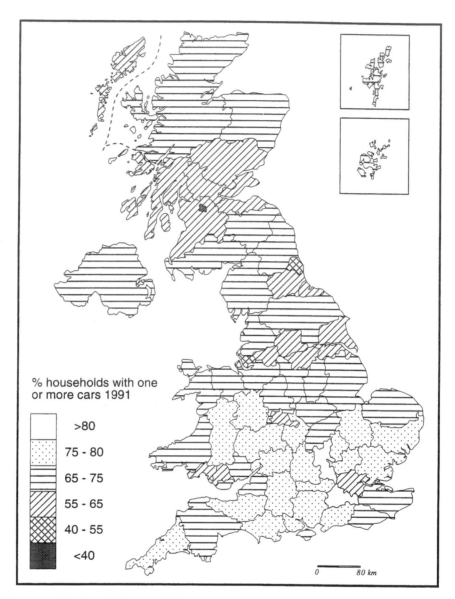

Figure 9.3   Car ownership, United Kingdom, 1991
Source of data: UK Census

once-daily services prevails in the Scottish High-lands; once-a-week services (usually market day) are not uncommon, e.g. in mid-Wales.

Beyond the more accessible lowland areas, Sun-day services have virtually disappeared. Early morn-ing and late evening workings have largely been cut out, and Saturdays (when the family car is usually available for shopping trips) may have thinner fre-quencies. Leisure trips by bus are extremely difficult. As rural commuters are overwhelmingly car owners, Monday–Friday peak timings are aimed primarily at school journeys, although the "school contract"

Table 9.1   Some social characteristics of travel in rural and urban UK

(a) Average journey length (km), 1985/6

	Urban	Rural
In households with cars		
main drivers	13.8	17.3
other drivers	12.2	13.9
non-drivers	9.9	12.8
In households without cars	8.3	10.1
Journey purpose 1985/6		
work	13.8	18.9
education	5.4	9.8
personal business	7.2	10.9
leisure	15.5	18.6
All journeys	11.7	15.4

(b) Distance travelled (km) per person per year, 1989/91

	Urban	Rural
Population group		
children	5859	10078
men age 16–59	15715	22150
women age 16–59	9899	15542
all adults age 60+	5998	8684
All persons	9832	14624

(c) Travel mode: distance (%) per person per year, 1989/91

	Urban	Rural
Walk	4.0	1.7
Car driver	46.9	53.5
Car passenger	30.6	33.3
Other private	3.5	3.9
Local bus	4.6	2.1
Rail	7.0	3.4
Other public	3.4	2.0
Average journey length (km)	12.5	17.6

Source: UK National Travel Surveys 1985/6 and 1989/91.

from the Local Education Authority will often support off-peak services (e.g. shopping) at marginal cost. A particular problem is making occasional but important journeys such as to hospitals. Compared with the national average, the rural bus market is dominated by education and shopping journey purposes (White, 1995, 142–60). Apart from school-children, the clientèle consists predominantly of women and pensioners.

Since about 1960, however, the most persistent and intractable issue has been the *finance* of bus services in this unrewarding environment. The traditional expedient was internal cross-subsidy, by which deficits on poorly patronized rural routes were

Table 9.2 Trip rates (excluding work and school) by social group, 1989, sample survey, County Antrim, Northern Ireland, UK

	Mean Trip Rate (trips per household per week)		
	Total including Walking	Motorized Trips Only	Percentage of Households With Car
All households	7.00	4.13	74.5
Non-car households	6.13	2.57	0.0
All households with cars	7.32	4.67	100.0
one car households	7.36	4.49	100.0
two+ car households	7.17	5.25	100.0
Households with			
one or more unemployed	6.93	4.04	62.9
one or more elderly	5.55	3.21	59.2
no employed persons	6.02	3.08	48.1
one person alone	4.76	1.66	23.1

Source: Nutley and Thomas (1995).

Photograph 9.1   Traditional rural public transport, Western Isles, Scotland
Although this photograph was taken in 1985, these buses look 20 years older. Contemporary standards are far higher, but this picture reflects a popular image of rural transport (S.D. Nutley)

compensated by profits from other sectors, such as town or inter-urban services, private hires and excursions, and school contracts. Over the course of time such profitable sectors have themselves been squeezed, putting further pressure on uneconomic routes unless external funding could be found. Payments by Local Education Authorities to bus operators for the carriage of schoolchildren have been vital – in many areas school buses have more routes and carry more people than public stage carriage services. Integration of public and schools traffic has been widely pursued as a means of making more efficient use of resources.

Despite this, external subsidy from public funds is normally regarded as indispensable to the survival of rural bus services. Belatedly introduced in 1968, "revenue support" (subsidy) has been administered by local authorities for "unremunerative" routes. Justification for this is the liberal "social service" argument: it is unreasonable to expect rural services to pay their way, yet local people depend on them for basic levels of mobility and access to facilities that are taken for granted in urban areas. An analogy is implied with health, education and the social services. The problem with subsidies is that once established they tend to get bigger. It must be emphasized, however, that despite the popular image of empty rural buses, their subsidy is lower per passenger than in the conurbations and the great majority of the national subsidy bill accrues to urban areas (White, 1995, 142–60). Successive governments have tried to keep subsidies under control by new procedures, such as by linking them to transport planning mechanisms, or by deregulation.

Commencing in 1986, the deregulation of the British bus industry was implemented primarily from ideological and financial motives, with little commitment to upholding service levels. Operators who register as "commercial" need no route licences but receive no subsidy; uneconomic routes regarded as important for the community are put out to tender by the local authority. Contrary to expectations, many rural routes were declared commercial, thus making it possible for the others to be supported financially. This plus other factors allowed the over-all cost of subsidies to be reduced considerably. Nationally, the supply of bus services has increased but patronage has fallen. In rural districts, studies have reported little change in service levels even if in some areas tendering together with privatization have caused new bus companies to appear (Astrop, 1993; Bell and Cloke, 1990; Moyes, 1995). The effect on passengers has not been properly analysed, but there is evidence of inconvenience and confusion (Cahm and Guiver, 1988).

Rail issues

Railways are more highly capitalized and less flexible than buses and are even more difficult to adapt to adverse circumstances. The current sparsity of rural lines in Britain is widely attributed to the "Beeching Report" of 1963 (Patmore, 1965). While the national railway network had remained at roughly its maximum extent throughout the period 1910–45, the passengers carried had declined steadily since 1920 and the system was plagued by financial crises both before and after nationalization in 1947. Historical overprovision and inefficiency were the main causes. The result was that by 1970 there was 30 per cent less route mileage and 57 per cent fewer stations than there had been in 1962. Inevitably rural regions suffered most, particularly Wales (Figure 9.4), East Anglia, the South West and parts of the Midlands, although northern Scotland was largely reprieved. Despite enormous criticism at the time, it must be conceded that most of the lines closed were hopeless cases and major surgery was essential to bring the national railway system up to date. Motivations, however, were overwhelmingly financial and political (Henshaw, 1994): no consideration was given to the social consequences on a line-by-line basis. The legacy is still apparent, not merely in terms of abandoned track and decaying structures, but also in the reduction of travel mode choice of rural people and the narrowly financial attitudes to further closure proposals (Photograph 9.2).

There have in fact been very few line closures since 1970 and successive Transport Ministers have

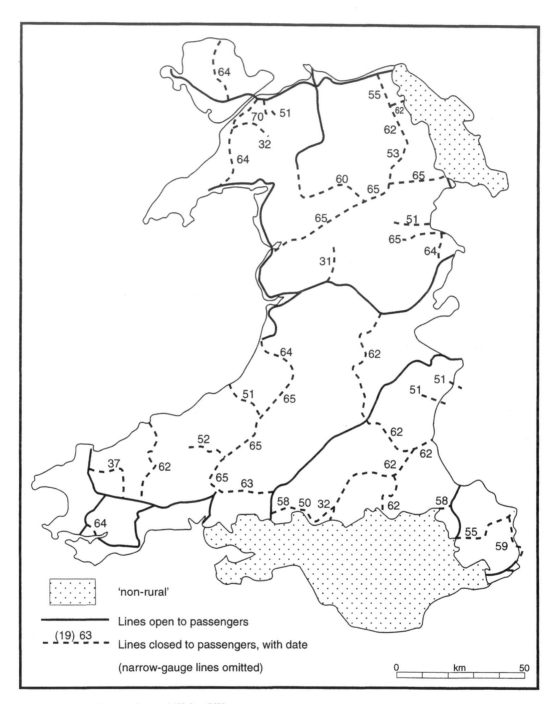

Figure 9.4 Railway closures in rural Wales, UK
(urban south and north-east excluded)

Photograph 9.2 The fate of many rural railway lines, Derbyshire, England
The station building is now a private house, and the trackbed a recreational footpath (S.D. Nutley)

declared their opposition to substantial cuts in the network, but this has not inspired confidence. A persistent theme in the post-Beeching era has been a political climate of uncertainty which ensures that rural lines appear to be constantly under threat. The economic options are discussed by Kilvington (1985) and the social and political implications by Whitelegg (1987). Very briefly, the arguments against rural line closures are as follows:

1. Displaced rail traffic adds to congestion on the roads.
2. Substitute bus services have proved to be inadequate.
3. Closure causes serious hardship to former users. They tend to make fewer journeys: some trips prove impossible, others are made less often or diverted to other destinations. The carless, the elderly and the low paid suffer most (Hillman and Whalley, 1980).

4. The main network suffers disproportionately when a branch line is closed, as connecting passengers are lost to the main lines.
5. The legal closure procedures are biased towards financial matters, and there is no requirement to do a social cost–benefit analysis, which would permit all relevant factors to be appraised (Whitelegg, 1984).
6. The financial savings from closure have been exaggerated.
7. State-run railway corporations under pressure from government may have to run down marginal lines to a little-used and neglected condition, so that closure seems "inevitable".
8. No attempts are made to invest in rural lines and actively promote them (e.g. for tourism).

Without unlimited subsidy the main strategy for rural lines has been to reduce costs. The "low-cost rural railway" is based on simplification and basic minimum standards, such as single-line track, "paytrains" with unstaffed stations and automatic signalling. Associated with this is the opportunity to replace obsolete stock and infrastructure with simpler lightweight train technologies (Ford, 1986). Some new stations have been opened, often with external funding. However, these limited attempts to sustain rural railways have been overtaken by the government's policy of privatizing the entire national network, commencing in 1993. The ability of rural lines to survive in a new commercial climate is again open to question.

New modes

Conventional public transport is severely hampered in rural areas by its rigid mode of operation, fixed routes and timetables and large vehicles, and hence greater success might be achieved by developing more flexible modal types. These are known in the UK as "unconventional modes" or, where voluntary labour is used, "community transport". Note that the internationally accepted term is *paratransit*, although in most other countries such operations occur mainly in urban areas. Unconventional features are: flexible routing and timing (perhaps demand-responsive); multipurpose operation, by combining different types of business on the same vehicle; management and/or operation by local volunteer labour, and the use of private vehicles; restricted eligibility to specific client groups and/or destinations; alternative sources of funding; and the use of new design and technology. Table 9.3 classifies 18 types, although this list is not definitive: operational details and examples are given in Nutley (1988, 1990).

Unconventional and community transport in the UK has been encouraged by government experiments, permissive legislation and small grant schemes. Another influence has been systems in other countries, such as postbuses in continental Europe, dial-a-rides in North America and shared taxis in parts of the Third World. From the 1980s public expenditure cuts have forced local authorities to seek "low-cost solutions", and perhaps to pass the burden on to the voluntary sector. Community transport is part of the "self-help" movement, build-

ing on a long tradition of charitable assistance with transport, primarily for the elderly, sick and disabled. Most "unconventional" operations serve specialized sectors of the market and have a local importance (Photograph 9.3). They are not a general solution to the rural problem, but it is possible that many commercial buses could adopt "unconventional" characteristics for the mutual benefit of bus companies and consumers.

Policy

In the UK there has never been any distinctive or coherent government policy exclusively for *rural* public transport. This sector merely has to operate within the prevailing *national* transport policy – which itself fluctuates sharply with every change of government. Macro-policy has alternated between nationalization and privatization, regulation and de-regulation, State intervention and *laissez-faire*, planning/coordination and free market/competition, yet it is by no means obvious which of these has been most successful. There was a reluctance to recognize firstly that a problem exists which would not be solved by rising car ownership. Secondly, attention should be directed not primarily at the economic problems of bus operators nor at the cost to the taxpayer, but at the lack of accessibility for rural people.

The Rest of Europe

Rural areas in the remainder of Western Europe have experienced social and economic trends broadly similar to those which have influenced transport in the UK. A number of countries, especially Germany and Italy, have even higher car ownership rates. While potential "problems" are equivalent, the widespread view is that most countries have achieved more stable bus and rail networks through their greater willingness to provide State subsidies for marginal services (Whitelegg, 1988). An exception is the Irish Republic, where continuing State control and rigid regulation have overseen the severe erosion of rural public transport (Barrett, 1982,

Table 9.3 "Unconventional" and "community" transport modes, in the context of the UK

Demand-responsive diversion	Stage carriage bus diverting from fixed route/schedule on demand-responsive basis, or operating flexible routes on similar basis
Multiple service bus	Stage carriage bus operating separate routes for different types of traffic at different times of day or on different days per week
Contract bus	Stage carriage bus "bought in" for specific service by agency without normal transport responsibilities, e.g. district, town or parish council
Subscription bus (cooperative bus)	Stage carriage bus contracted by local association and financed by subscriptions; no fares charged to members
Free shoppers' bus	Bus paid for by local traders/retailers to bring customers to shopping centre; no fares
School bus	Bus contracted or owned by Local Education Authority for transport of school pupils, also carrying fare-paying adult passengers
Postbus	Vehicle operated by Post Office for mail collection and delivery services, adapted to carry passengers
Community bus (CT)	Small vehicle owned and managed by committee of local volunteers, operating a variety of stage carriage or demand-responsive services, excursions and hires, with volunteer drivers
PSV dial-a-bus	Public Service Vehicle operated in demand-responsive mode according to telephone requests, using "hi-tech" control equipment
"Welfare" dial-a-bus (CT)	Vehicle run by community group in demand-responsive mode for people with special needs, such as the elderly and disabled; usually with adaptations such as wheelchair lifts
Social car (CT) (voluntary car)	Private car run by volunteer owner/driver to carry persons on essential trips impossible to make by other means; pool of cars coordinated by local committee
Hospital car (CT)	Private car run by volunteer owner/driver to carry outpatients to hospital; organized either by health authority to supplement ambulance service, or as social car exclusively for hospital trips
Lift-giving scheme (CT)	Informal arrangement by private car owners to give lifts, perhaps on a regular basis, to other persons; with local advertising but no central organization
Car pooling (CT)	Arrangement among car owners to use a single vehicle for regular trips (mainly the journey to work) on an alternate basis
Shared taxi/hire-car	Taxi or hire-car authorized to admit passengers sharing the vehicle, at separate fares
Passenger/freight service	Stage carriage bus modified to carry some freight, parcels, sundries; routes may be determined by regular freight delivery runs
Demountable vehicle	Vehicle with interchangeable bodies, detachable from single chassis/cab unit, e.g. bus body interchangeable with freight van
Railbus	Light rail vehicle (diesel multiple unit) consisting of bus body mounted on rail underframe

(CT) = "community transport" mode.
Source: Nutley (1990).

Photograph 9.3   An unconventional mode: a postbus in county Fermanagh, Northern Ireland
Buses operated by post offices are common in Western Europe, and postbuses in the UK are specifically designed for their dual-purpose role (S.D. Nutley)

1991, 72–129). Elsewhere, the basic "welfare" argument prevails. Regional development, demographic and agricultural factors strongly influence rural support policies. National railway systems are politically favoured and uneconomic lines are much less likely to be closed than in the UK. Rail/bus integration is frequently impressive, with public- and private-sector bus companies enjoined to cooperate and not compete with railways. Rural bus systems are commonly run by the railways or the post office and integrated with school transport. There is a general policy consensus about such matters in continental Europe, and transport is not the political football that it is in the UK.

Scandinavia provides an excellent example of the conflict between the ideals of service provision to low-density areas and modern economic realities (Fullerton, 1988). Across the region, a traditional concern for the maintenance of high standards of welfare and opportunity for all people regardless of where they live, together with strong environmental and regional lobbies, has directed minimum standards for transport and other services, subsidized where necessary by the state. Road-building, railways, buses, coastal shipping and ferries, and "third-level" air services have been State-funded with varying degrees of generosity. The low density of population and long distances make this a high-cost policy (Douglas, 1986; Knowles, 1979; Pedersen, 1981). Such policies are contradicted, however, by the equally valued principle of consumer choice, which makes governments reluctant to protect public transport from road competition; car ownership has grown to high levels.

Free competition obtains where traffic allows, as in road haulage, most coastal shipping and most air services, while intermodal competition exists on major routes and in less-remote areas. In north and

west Norway the trend is to circumvent highly subsidized ferries by new roads. A new approach is to
subdivide large transport systems to achieve market
segmentation and local accountability, such as Sweden's "social railway". Devolution of transport responsibilities to local authorities enables funding
allocations to be spent on the basis of overall community benefit. In remote areas this might mean any
combination of school buses, postbuses, taxis, dial-
a-rides, ferries and small-scale air services. Strict approval is needed for service closures.

Generous support to public transport in Western
Europe is under threat in the 1990s by forces of
economic restructuring and European integration.
France, for example, has been forced to accept that
it can no longer support its extensive rural railway
network, virtually unchanged since the 1960s, and
heavily subsidized by the state. The policy response
in 1995 was "regionalization", which would dismem-
ber the network and remove protection from uneconomic rural lines: drastic cuts are forecast (*The
Independent*, 1995; *The Times*, 1996). Apart from the
familiar themes of economy versus welfare, an overriding issue is the French government's need to reduce public expenditure in order to qualify for
European monetary union. Hence local people find
their living standards determined by ever more remote forces of change.

Countries of Eastern Europe and the former
USSR are radically different in their transport characteristics and in many ways are closer to the Third
World (see Figure 9.1). Horse-drawn vehicles and
steam trains may still be seen. The main legacy of
the long era of State Socialism is the dominance of
public transport (Hall, 1993; Jenkins, 1994). Car
ownership has always been very low and, unlike the
West, is higher in cities than in the countryside. It is
now increasing significantly in Eastern Europe, but
in rural parts of the former USSR it is still less than
10 per cent by household. Most local transport is still
provided by heavily subsidized State-run bus companies, using old vehicles with high maintenance
costs. In Eastern Europe buses provide a high level
of service in the countryside and are well used, but in
the former USSR they are sparse, unreliable and

strongly deterred by inadequate rural roads. There is
an extraordinary dependence on railways, which are
undercapitalized and overloaded. The most urgent
problem in the countryside is the lack of surfaced
roads, which is a severe impediment to the agricultural economy. In Russia, 25 per cent of farms
have no roads (Crouch, 1985); vehicles are commonly driven across fields, and people get lifts on
trucks and tractors. Added to the poor current
standards and vast distances, attempts to restructure
for a market economy have led to severe problems
in resource allocation. Most investment is going into
roads, but there is a problem of prioritizing development such that local access does not lose out to regional demands (Bougromenko *et al.*, 1996).

LOW-DENSITY DEVELOPED COUNTRIES

"Everyone Has a Car"

Where rural populations are sparse and distances
long, societies with suitable incomes and levels of
development have enthusiastically adopted the
automobile as the ideal solution to problems of
mobility and accessibility (Figure 9.1). Often encouraged and subsidized by governments, very high car
ownership and car-dependent lifestyles have fatally
undermined whatever public transport had previously existed. Remaining non-car populations are
likely to face severe difficulties.

The United States

With the world's highest car ownership rate, the
USA presents an opportunity to see if the automobile can "solve" problems of rural isolation. In
rural America cars are owned by about 95 per cent
of households (over 600 cars per 1000 people), with
relatively little geographical variation (Figure 9.5).
Particularly striking are the levels of multi-car
ownership, with two-thirds of rural households having two or more cars (Table 9.4); the car is regarded
as an individual possession rather than a household

asset. Hence it is unsurprising that in the USA car ownership is assumed to be universal, and there is no clear recognition or understanding that the rural environment might pose problems for some people in getting around. Long distances are cancelled out by the low cost of gasoline (e.g. roughly one-third of that in the UK). The small proportion without a car is dominated by disadvantaged minority groups. Geographers and other scholars in the USA have shown little interest in the rural transport situation, not perceiving it as a significant "problem" (Nutley, 1996).

The obsession with cars has caused a collapse of public transport with very few alternatives for local journeys. Less than 1 per cent of work journeys are by public modes (Table 9.4), reflecting lack of opportunity rather than choice. Historically, although most towns had a railroad, much of rural America passed from horse-drawn vehicles directly to the automobile age, with no intervening public-transport phase (unlike in Europe). Buses operate primarily long-distance inter-town routes, while outside the main cities nearly all railroads provide freight services only. Both modes have fallen between the private convenience of the automobile and the speed of the aircraft. The decline of bus transit in the USA is described in Briggs (1981),

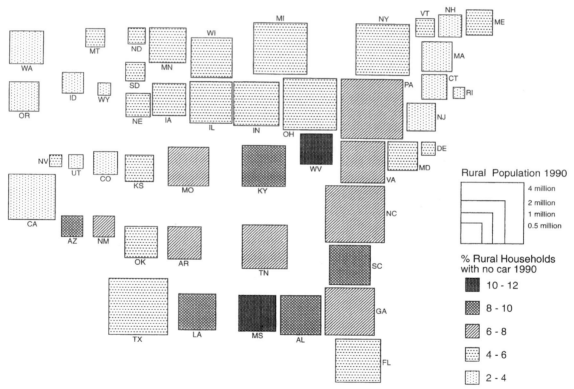

Figure 9.5 Car ownership, United States, 1990
The diagram is for rural areas and non-car households. Key to states: AL, Alabama; AR, Arkansas; AZ, Arizona; CA, California; CO, Colorado; CT, Connecticut; DE, Delaware; FL, Florida; GA, Georgia; IA, Iowa; ID, Idaho; IL, Illinois; IN, Indiana; KS, Kansas; KY, Kentucky; LA, Louisiana; MA, Massachusetts; MD, Maryland; ME, Maine; MI, Michigan; MN, Minnesota; MO, Missouri; MS, Mississippi; MT, Montana; NC, North Carolina; ND, North Dakota; NE, Nebraska; NH, New Hampshire; NJ, New Jersey; NM, New Mexico; NV, Nevada; NY, New York; OH, Ohio; OK, Oklahoma; OR, Oregon; PA, Pennsylvania; RI, Rhode Island; SC, South Carolina; SD. South Dakota; TN, Tennessee; TX, Texas; UT, Utah; VA, Virginia; VT, Vermont; WA, Washington; WI, Wisconsin; WV, West Virginia; WY, Wyoming
Source: Nutley (1996)

Table 9.4   Car ownership and travel to work – USA and UK

	USA (1990)	USA Rural	UK (1991)	UK Rural (estimates)*
Percentage of households with				
no car	11.5	5.9	33.4	20 to 32
one car only	33.8	26.8	43.5	40 to 50
2+ cars	54.7	67.3	23.1	20 to 35
(of which) 3+ cars	17.3	25.1	4.0	3 to 8
Persons/car	1.57	1.43	2.7	2.3 to 2.8
Cars/household	1.67	1.97	0.9	0.9 to 1.1
Percentage of no-car households				
over age 65	43.1	55.7		
below poverty level	41.0	52.7		
non-white	41.6	24.2		
Percentage of travel to work				
solo car driver	73.1	75.8	54.1†	45 to 60†
car sharing	13.4	14.7	8.0‡	7 to 12‡
public transport	5.3	0.6	15.8	2 to 8
walk	3.9	3.0	12.1	10 to 20
no journey	3.0	4.8	5.1	5 to 15

*Note that there is no official definition of "rural" in the UK, so figures are estimates.
†All drivers.
‡All passengers.
Source: Nutley (1996).

Burkhardt (1981) and Kihl (1985, 1988, 1990). A 1978 survey found that inter-city bus services did not exist in 89 per cent of places with populations under 2500, and in 57 per cent of places with 2500–10 000 population. Deregulation in 1982 has hastened the trend of decline, with roughly 10 per cent of communities losing service each year in the subsequent period. Note the contrast with Europe, where almost all settlements of similar size have a bus service of some kind and the main interest is the frequency, standard and accessibility provided.

It is true that the demand in the USA for public or alternative transport is relatively small and fragmented. Minorities lacking access to a private car and suffering problems of immobility seem to be confined to the poor, young, elderly and disabled, and non-white ethnic groups. Also there are persons in car-owning households who do not have use of a vehicle when required (Kidder, 1989). It is remarkable that US commentators share a belief that to

have "only" one car in the household is a problem condition! The US literature concentrates on the elderly and poor as the only significant problem groups. Unlike in other countries, the American older generations have lived all their lives with the automobile and many remain "reluctant drivers" for lack of an alternative (Kihl, 1993). Where there are alternatives for local transport in rural areas, these are likely to be paratransit modes such as taxis, jitneys[1], car-sharing schemes, demand-responsive or subscription buses (Saltzman, 1976), depending on the availability of state subsidies and volunteer drivers. Rucker (1984) found that over 60 per cent of transit vehicles in non-metropolitan areas belong to welfare-based "human service agencies".

Observers from outside the USA might find it extraordinary that "problems" are attributed to car owners also. Despite the fact that motoring in the USA is notoriously cheap by international standards, there are many complaints that the accumulated costs of motor transport in rural regions have a severe impact on personal finances and local economies (Gillis, 1989). The single-car household and the elderly driver are perceived as problems. Poverty is related to immobility, but in unexpected ways. In the USA, most of the rural poor feel obliged to get cars, but these are invariably old, in poor condition and very expensive to keep running. In a study of rural Georgia, Maggied (1982) explained that remote areas generate excessive car dependence and long-distance commuting; persons lacking a car or attempting to run a car on a low income have great problems of access to workplaces; such people are forced to take low-paid jobs nearby, withdraw from the labour market or leave the area; this perpetuates low personal incomes and relative immobility.

Transportation is very much a rural and regional development issue in the USA. The profitability of farms, businesses and ultimately whole communities is seen to be strongly related to the availability of suitable trucking, railroad and airline services, and to the freight rates charged (Gillis, 1989). Many rural roads and bridges are inadequate to cope with the increasing size of trucks, and some county roads are unsurfaced, but local communities often lack the resources for improvements. Deregulation of the trucking industry in 1980 was generally beneficial (Allen, 1990), but smaller and more isolated producers still have problems. Despite the dominance of trucking, the neglect and "abandonment" of freight railroad lines continues to cause great concern in small towns and rural businesses. Deregulation in 1976–80 has made line closures easier. Studies have tended to show that the feared negative impacts have been exaggerated, mainly due to the existence of road freight alternatives (Allen and Due, 1977; Due, 1990; McFarland, 1991). However, there has been a parallel trend for restructured rail companies to take over and continue to operate marginal lines (Rockey, 1987). Long distances also enhance the importance of air services, even to relatively small towns, although these traditionally survived on regulation and subsidy. While deregulation in 1978 was generally successful, concessions were made to soften the impact on smaller nodes, but

traffic reductions have still been experienced (Crum, 1990; Kihl, 1988).

A serious gap in the analysis of rural transportation in the USA is the general absence of local-scale case studies with evaluations of mobility and accessibility levels experienced by different social groups. Maggied's (1982) study of Georgia at county level goes part way, while Rucker's (1984) calculation of a transport "needs index" is also of interest. However, there is no clear information on how trip patterns adjust to long distances, or how the non-car population responds to its relative immobility. The widespread perception is that very high car ownership *does* solve problems of rural accessibility, implying also that those without cars are isolated politically as well as geographically.

Other Countries

The overall situation described for the USA can be expected to have much in common with affluent, low-density and spatially extensive countries such as Australia (Lonsdale and Holmes, 1981), Canada and New Zealand. Private car and truck availability and usage are overwhelming, and hence the condition of the rural road network attracts much attention. Otherwise, rural public-transport resources in Canada (Sullivan and Suen, 1981) compare easily with the US situation: bus and rail services are primarily long-distance inter-city; short-distance local services are highly variable in type and effectiveness; school buses, taxis and other paratransit are important. Air transport plays an exaggerated role for small places in the settlement hierarchy. Similar generalizations can be made for Australia. Where public transport is available to rural settlements, in Canada and Australia, as in the USA, these are normally dependent on intermediate stops along inter-city rail and bus lines, and consequently suffer the effects of policy changes dictated at national level. For example, the railway closures issue in both Canada (Stabler, 1986) and Australia (Parolin *et al.*, 1993) reveals similar features, in the rationalization of public or private facilities, in the emphasis on freight traffic, and in fears of damaging effects on local economies.

Canada and Australia share the problem of human populations living at very low densities throughout vast areas of "backcountry", putting a high premium on transport and communications to ensure their survival. The decline and continued viability of small remote settlements, loss of services and the problems of delivering essential State functions like health and education are pervasive issues, although contemporary macro-economic forces are more significant than the transport factor alone. Both Canada and Australia have extensive intermediate zones which are relatively remote but continuously settled, such that transport and service infrastructures are maintained with some difficulty. Here, population levels and economic prospects are determined by various quality-of-life factors controlled largely by distance, such as access to health, education and consumer services (Everitt and Gfellner, 1996; Joseph and Bantock, 1984; Stimson, 1981). Where vehicle ownership is very high and air transport is available, the "transport" factor is regarded in terms of the time and cost of travel to urban centres. In Canada, where there is a policy commitment to supporting transport to remote communities, the high costs are unavoidable but the effect on local development is not decisive (Bone and Green, 1986; Jones and Rosenberg, 1992). In outback Australia, extreme isolation has forced reliance on air transport and telecommunications to deliver health and education services (Brownlea and McDonald, 1981; Fitzpatrick, 1983). Reduced service availability might normally be compensated by more journeys to urban supply points, but the behavioural response to remoteness is to make less frequent trips to town as distance increases (Figure 9.6), with the most isolated homesteads exhibiting localized rural contact networks (Holmes and Brown, 1981).

LESS-DEVELOPED COUNTRIES

The rest of the world varies enormously with respect to culture, environment and levels of economic development. Despite this diversity, a common factor is that car ownership is so very much lower that it is often not a relevant issue (Figure 9.1), and hence "rural transport" has an entirely different meaning to that in the West. A major difference is that car ownership is higher in urban areas than rural, reflecting the privileges of political and commercial élites who live in cities. But in the poorest countries car ownership is below 30 per 1000 people, and in the countryside is negligible.

In the newly industrializing countries of the Middle East and South-East Asia roads and other transport infrastructure may be up to Western standards, although investment is concentrated in cities and inter-urban routes, but some rural areas are reasonably well served. Similarly in South Africa and some countries of Latin America, the economic core areas have good or adequate infrastructure. In outlying rural districts, and throughout the poorer countries, the basic problem is the lack of surfaced roads, non-availability of suitable motorized vehicles, consequent isolation and endemic poverty (Barwell et al., 1985; Hilling, 1996, 157–96; Howe and Richards, 1984; Owen, 1987; Tolley and Turton, 1995, 231–62).

Transport issues in the Third World are essentially tied up with the struggle for economic development at national level (see Chapter 3 of this volume). Governments have been preoccupied therefore with freight transport, railways, seaports, trunk roads, urban areas and resource-rich regions. Rural areas have received low priority, despite containing very large populations. Unlike in the West, the rural economy in developing countries is overwhelmingly an agricultural one; villages are occupational communities. The purpose of rural transport is primarily to service agricultural demands, either at a subsistence level within villages or at a commercial level through local markets or regional export. The needs of people for basic levels of mobility and access to services within their own localities might be recognized, but even simple infrastructural improvements are beyond the capacity of many national administrations.

To a large extent rural poverty in underdeveloped countries is attributable to the absence of decent roads over vast areas. In tropical Africa local routes

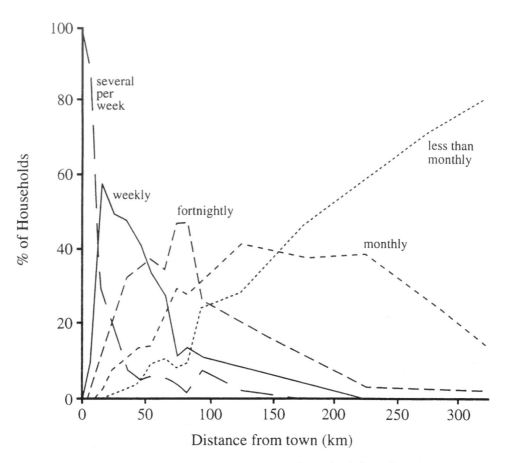

Figure 9.6   Distance and travel frequency to town in a remote area, Queensland, Australia
Note the distance scale!
Source: Holmes and Brown (1981)

are no more than tracks worn out by historical usage and suitable only for pedestrians and pack animals. Wider and reasonably graded tracks allow wheeled transport, usually some form of animal-drawn cart and perhaps bicycles. A gravel surface would permit some types of lightweight truck, if these are available. The greatest need is for all-weather surfaces, to permit operation of a wider range of motor vehicles, to reduce time and cost of journeys, and to lower the risk of environmental hazards. Typical road densities in African countries are under 10 km per 100 km², and only 5–20 per cent are sealed; many farms and villages are distant from a motorable road (Addus, 1989; Ogunsanya, 1987; Tolley and Turton, 1995, 231–62).

The absence of adequate roads and transport vehicles is exacerbated by long distances to the locations of basic commodities such as water, fuel and foodstuffs. Distances to fields can be long, and walking time reduces effective work in agriculture and precludes labour-intensive crops. Alternatively, land close to home may be overworked. Livestock requires a lot of movement by herders, nearly always on foot. It is still common in tropical Africa for everyday needs for goods to be supplied by head-loading, mainly by women. Pack animals are invaluable in difficult terrain. Significant improvement in load capacity can be obtained by animal-drawn carts if suitable routeways exist, but such upgrading also requires higher incomes at community level. Bicycles and freight-carrying adaptations may be used where surfaces are reasonable, especially in South-East Asia. Appropriate technology plus cultural preferences lead to a variety of ingeniously improvized conveyances (Barwell *et al.*, 1985; Hathway, 1985). For all such modes, whether measured by time, energy or human effort, costs are enormous and efficiency very low (Immers *et al.*, 1988; McCall, 1985; Mwase, 1989); some basic performance indicators are given in Table 9.5. Where motorized transport is possible and affordable, some form of open lorry normally carries all types of goods, and people. A variety of small lightweight motorized utility vehicles can be seen in South-East Asia and Latin America, often assembled locally. Bus services are inevitably confined to the better-quality all-weather roads and hence are beyond reach of most of the rural population. Buses are well used and often overcrowded, but the vehicles are usually old and unreliable (Photograph 9.4).

This lack of roads means that large populations are prohibited from entering the market economy and may be condemned to subsistence (Owen, 1987). Any kind of economic advancement requires access for delivery of fertilizers, seed, fuel, water supply equipment and building materials, and for export of even basic products. Provision of education and medical services may be difficult or impossible. Non-agricultural employment in other places cannot be reached. Development efforts are increasingly focusing on the phased upgrading of local rural roads, perhaps as part of an integrated programme including related projects such as school-building, irrigation works or power supply. Prioritization of roads to receive the very limited funding for improvement work must be linked to anticipated economic gains.

Western methodologies based on cost–benefit analysis or travel-time savings are very rarely suitable, and simple techniques are often more effective. For example, Dhir *et al.* (1987) describe a simple method of planning minimum road networks in rural India, using graph theory and traffic potential based on village populations. Road construction should make the best use of local resources, often using a high degree of manual labour. A systematic approach is proposed by Beenhakker *et al.* (1987). Policies, usually aimed at improving access within the constraints of local resources, are translated into strategies for implementation. Planning then has to deal with the interaction of various transport-related sectors, requiring the evaluation of accessibility levels, transport modes, infrastructure, maintenance and storage. Application in the field with locally available labour and material resources requires technical advice that is practicable and inexpensive, within the "appropriate technology" ethos, with special reference to climatic hazards.

Numerous studies have been done on the effects of road improvement upon local agriculture, incomes and access to services. Some find that transport cost reduction brings clear benefits in terms of "opening up" land resources, higher market prices and modernization of farm practices (Amadi, 1988; Filani, 1993). However, if the aim is the alleviation of poverty through income redistribution, it is argued that road development should benefit smallholders rather than big producers (Howe and Richards, 1984), and should be accompanied by other measures such as raising land productivity and providing vehicles. Other studies from Africa agree that feeder road provision is a necessary but not sufficient condition for sustained development. Indirect benefits of road improvement

Table 9.5 Local transport modes, rural Africa

Mode	Load Capacity (kg)	Average Speed (km/h)
Headloading	25–40	2–5
Wheelbarrow	60–120	2–5
Handcart	150–300	5
Bicycle	50–100	10–15
Bicycle-trailer/tricycle	100–300	10–15
Donkey	50–100	5
Mule	80–120	7
Camel	200–300	4
Donkey-cart	250–400	2–3
Ox-cart	600–750	3–5
Improved double ox-cart	1000–3000	5

Source: Hathway (1985), Hilling (1996), McCall (1985), Mwase (1989).

Photograph 9.4   Public transport in rural Africa: bus service near Arusha, Tanzania
The tarmac road indicates that this is an inter-urban route, but buses of this type are relatively rare and often absent in remote areas (S.D. Nutley)

are the growth of amenities, clinics, schools and better housing. Population groups with better access to transport have greater mobility and higher consumption of goods and services (Airey, 1985; Wanmali, 1991). While new roads might improve accessibility to hospitals, for example, usage is constrained by institutional, cultural and cost barriers (Airey, 1991; Okafor, 1990). A priority now must be to facilitate the supply of motor vehicles within the means of poor communities. There is a desperate shortage of simple, robust trucks, while for non-motorable roads the best policy might be to develop more efficient bullock carts or combined freight/passenger wagons.

ACCESSIBILITY

With such a diversity of environments and socio-economic circumstances, from the United States to tropical Africa, perhaps the only common theme is *accessibility* (or the cost of access). Useful generalizations may be futile, but at least it can be said that governments must recognize firstly that there is a problem in rural areas which handicaps people and local economies, and secondly that inadequate accessibility is the core issue. Traditional interpretations were *economic*. In Western countries until the 1970s discussion was largely confined to the financial problems of bus companies or railway branches, and decision-makers identified primarily with service providers. Accessibility requires a consumer view. In line with this, transport operations and planning should not be "demand-led" as at present, but "needs-based". Current attitudes see transport – whether private or public sector – as a commercial business with a duty to make a profit, not as a piece of social infrastructure to provide a service to the community.

Where a significant proportion of the population does not have regular use of a car and is dependent on public transport, it is common to find that the latter accounts for only a small share of total trips, and that non-car-owners have low trip rates (Tables 9.1 and 9.2). This is often seen by officialdom as evidence that there is little demand for bus or train services and hence that they are not worth supporting. The crucial error in this reasoning is to assume that low patronage of rural transport services is an accurate expression of demand or need for them. The reality is that service provision has declined to such low levels that these now act as a severe constraint on the trip opportunities available to consumers. Many travel needs are frustrated because of the absence of suitable transport services (*suppressed* or *latent* demand). Merely to equate low bus patronage with low demand is to argue the problem out of existence – the whole point is that total demand exceeds transport supply.

A serious gap now exists between the degree of accessibility needed by the local population and that which can be provided under the prevailing land-use/transport system. This is the crux of the problem. While understandable in general terms, measurement requires a definition of *need*, i.e. which local facilities the population needs access to, and under what conditions, e.g. how often? A certain proportion of needs will be satisfiable by the facilities and transport in any area, but the residue of *unfulfilled needs* can be taken as a measure of the scale of the "problem". In this context, needs are usually assessed by normative methods, where a set of desired facilities and minimum conditions are specified externally. This has the advantage of consistency and allows comparisons among areas and population groups.

Analysis must be undertaken at the local scale, the level at which problems are experienced in everyday life. It is essential also that the population is disaggregated into social groups such as the elderly, working people, housewives and schoolchildren, as each has different needs and personal circumstances. Travel behaviour in rural environments is a function of needs, under the influence of constraints. These constraints are (i) the social and economic characteristics of the population, such as income, car

ownership and the proportion of elderly people, (ii) the number, quality and relative location of desired facilities, and (iii) the frequency, timing and cost of public transport services (Stanley and Farrington, 1981).

Methodologies for integrating these variables to derive realistic accessibility measures for local case study areas are explained in Moseley *et al.* (1977), Moyes (1989) and Nutley (1983). Briefly, needs are defined by normative standards, with respect to destination facilities required by each social group and desirable frequency of usage. Opportunities available to population subgroups in specific demand locations (e.g. villages) then depend on the relative location of suitable facility outlets and the adequacy of connecting transport services. It is an exercise in time–space coordination, with transport schedules and facility opening hours needing to be compatible with people's "time budgets". Accessibility is the opportunities potentially achievable as a percentage of the hypothesized needs. Results can be expressed spatially by origin (demand) locations, by destination facilities, or socially, as represented in Figure 9.7.

Adaptations to the method can be used to produce a high-resolution coverage of a wider region, showing an intense degree of spatial variation (Figure 9.8). Such results can be qualified by the proportion of the population that does not have a car and is "public-transport-dependent" (Jordan and Nutley, 1993). Another adaptation might be to assess *historic change*. The method is easily extended, given adequate data, to compare present access levels with those of the past, in order to evaluate the effects of population changes and the decline of public transport and of other services. Studies in the UK suggest that the closure of local facilities has had a greater impact than cuts in public transport. A particularly important application is *policy appraisal*. By taking a "before and after" approach, access levels prior to and following the introduction of a specific policy measure (such as transport service changes) can easily be compared. It can be discovered which groups of people benefit the most and which the least. Accessibility gains might be regarded as the

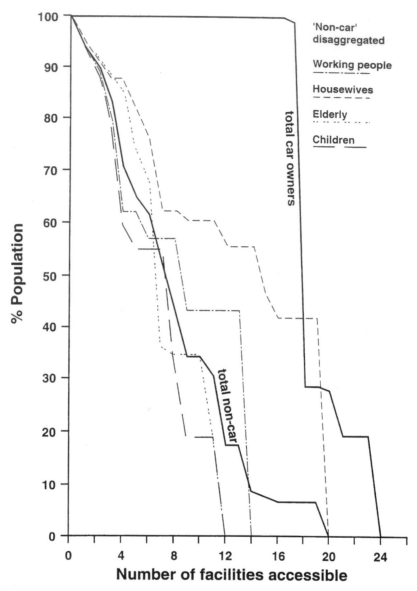

Figure 9.7   Local accessibility by social groups, part of Powys, Wales, UK
Source: Nutley (1985)

"benefits" of that policy, to be evaluated against the costs (Nutley, 1983). A similar approach might also be used to underpin the subsidization of public transport, such that financial support could be related to the extent of "needs" satisfied, or accessibility provided, by individual services.

The above methods are applicable where there is a significant non-car population and scheduled public transport is available. Traditional measures of accessibility are quite different. These are based on network analysis or graph theory, travel times to service centres or the number of facilities within

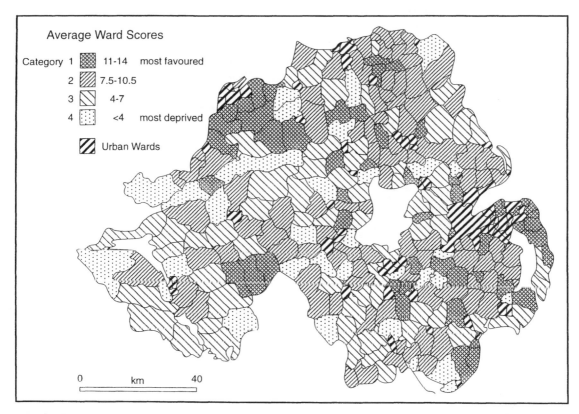

Figure 9.8 A composite index of public transport accessibility at the regional scale, Northern Ireland, UK
Source: Jordan and Nutley (1993)

successive time bands, potential surfaces or gravity model formulations. Implementation of these techniques may now be facilitated by the use of geographical information systems (Geertman and van Eck, 1995). Such approaches are aggregative and more suited to the regional scale; they may also be more appropriate where travel is dominated by cars and trucks and regular public transport is absent, as in much of North America (e.g. Joseph and Bantock, 1984) and Australia.

In rural parts of less-developed countries where, owing to poverty and poor roads, cars are non-existent and trucks and buses are very rare, it is debatable which is the most effective expression of accessibility. Official data sources may also be poor. Hence Okafor (1990) uses average distance to estimate accessibility to hospitals in Nigeria. In the same country, Ogunsanya (1987) uses road density, which

is possibly an acceptable surrogate for the difficulty of travel. Not only is the mapped pattern (Figure 9.9) a powerful testament to the difficulties of access for any purpose, but the severity is magnified by the large populations living in such areas.

In all environments it has to be remembered that *physical* accessibility might be modified, or further constrained, by other factors such as social and cultural values, institutional, legal and bureaucratic barriers, and of course costs, which are difficult to evaluate and virtually impossible to integrate satisfactorily with the methods described above.

Different Approaches

Where a problem is recognized to exist, and if it is understood in accessibility terms, then techniques

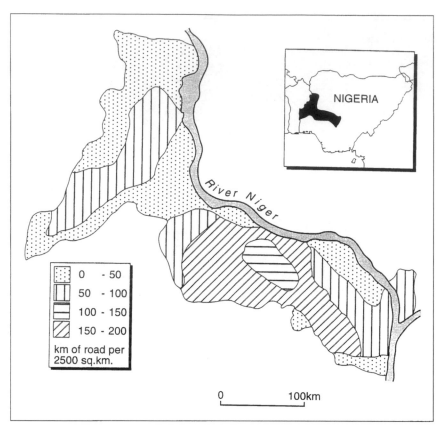

Figure 9.9   Accessibility to motorable roads, Kwara State, Nigeria
(The population density of this area is roughly 40 persons per square kilometre)
Source: Ogunsanya (1987)

are available to maximize the accessibility benefits to the population relative to costs and other resources (Nutley, 1984, 1985). As the issue is one of an integrated transport/land-use/settlement system, policy inputs might be applied to any one or more of these elements. Hence, there are alternatives to looking only at the "transport option" (Moseley, 1979).

1. The *mobile services option* involves the delivery of goods and services to the people by vans or specially adapted vehicles. Mobile shops and libraries are fairly common in the rural UK and other developed countries; other services such as banking (Photograph 9.5), some types of recreational, health and advisory facilities are also provided in this way (Moseley and Packman, 1983).

Peripatetic services are common in developing countries.

2. The *fragmented service option* is where small-scale facilities are dispersed among the rural hinterland, closer to their customers. This remains common in developing countries, but advanced economies have long since discarded this mode of provision.

3. The *key village option* requires the population to be concentrated into larger settlement units where basic facilities could be more efficiently sited. Largely a theoretical construct, it is by no means clear how this might be achieved.

For most countries, these three options are either expensive, impracticable, or contrary to political realities.

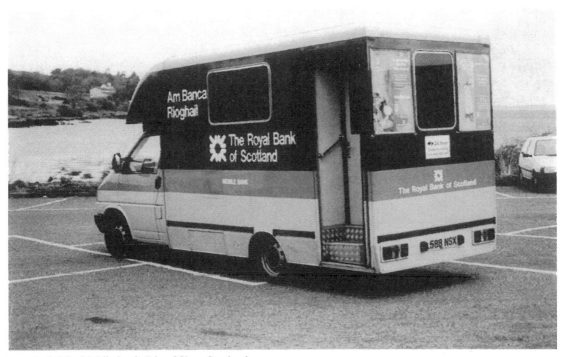

Photograph 9.5   Mobile bank, Isle of Skye, Scotland
An alternative means of maintaining accessibility is to bring services to the people. Mobile shops have a patchy distribution in developed countries, while more specialized services such as banks depend upon local circumstances (S.D. Nutley)

A further option is *telecommunications*, which have the potential to abolish distance in sparsely populated areas. The telephone is able to replace journeys for social, information and financial purposes, but usage is dominated by the better-off and mobile, and it may actually generate *more* trips (Clark and Unwin, 1981). Advanced computer-based technologies are now available, and prescriptive studies confirm that the benefits from such investment in rural regions are potentially great (Eskelinen, 1993; Hansen *et al.*, 1990). The main beneficiaries would be rural businesses, while community use, perhaps through "telecottages" (Qvortrup, 1989), encounters problems of finance, implementation and social acceptability. Telebanking, teleshopping and telecommuting are still very rare. It is probable that the disadvantaged, elderly and immobile would benefit the least. However, the development of satellite-based information systems for educational purposes in countries as diverse as Australia, India and Malaysia shows what can be achieved.

CONCLUSIONS

The real and perceived significance of transportation and accessibility problems in rural regions varies enormously around the world. In terms of the numbers of people affected, priority consideration should obviously be given to the less-developed countries where isolation and lack of surfaced roads prevent participation in the market economy and reinforce poverty (Hilling, 1996, 157–96; Owen, 1987; Tolley and Turton, 1995, 231–62). Infrastructure and communications should be integrated into development programmes that do not raise aspirations of high mobility. Deriving essentially from the dispersal of population and services, it is arguable that the problem is basically not a transport one but

Photograph 9.6   Localized rural traffic congestion, Dorset coast, England
Very high rural car ownership rates and a "car dependence" culture in Western countries lead to an increasing problem of localized *rural* traffic congestion, especially at popular recreation sites (S.D. Nutley)

a rural one. The integrated, rural-centred policies that this implies have not generally found favour in more affluent countries. Indeed, in Western Europe, political trends in the 1980s and 1990s towards non-intervention, deregulation and privatization have undermined possible mechanisms for systematic policy remedies, despite a high popular awareness of the problem. The USA shows that even saturation levels of car ownership do not eliminate the problem for everyone, but that disadvantaged minorities become marginalized and politically invisible (Nutley, 1996). While it is generally recognized that the rural transport problem in developed countries will not go away, governments are steadily disclaiming responsibility for it, perpetuating the division between the affluent and mobile (Photograph 9.6) and the isolated and underprivileged.

NOTE

1. A jitney is a cross between a small bus and a taxi, running more or less regular routes but without a fixed timetable, departing when full of passengers. Associated with Third World cities, such vehicles are known by a variety of names, e.g. *matatu* (Kenya).

REFERENCES

Addus, A. (1989), "Road transportation in Africa", *Transportation Quarterly* 43, 421–33.
Airey, A. (1985), "The role of feeder roads in promoting rural change in eastern Sierra Leone", *Tijdschrift voor Economische en Sociale Geografie* 76, 192–201.
Airey, A. (1991), "The influence of road construction on the health care behaviour of rural households in the Meru District of Kenya", *Transport Reviews* 11, 273–90.
Allen, B. (1990), "Small community trucking service", in Due, J., Allen, B., Kihl, M. and Crum, M. (eds), *Transportation service to small rural communities. Effects of deregulation* (Ames: Iowa State University Press), 46–72.

Allen, B. and Due, J. (1977), "Railway abandonments. Effects upon the communities served", *Growth and Change* 8 (2), 8–14.

Amadi, B. (1988), "The impact of rural road construction on agricultural development: an empirical study of Anambra State in Nigeria", *Agricultural Systems* 27, 1–9.

Astrop, A. (1993), *The trend in rural bus services since deregulation*, Project Report 21 (Crowthorne: Transport Research Laboratory).

Banister, D. (1980), "Transport mobility in inter-urban areas: a case study approach in South Oxfordshire", *Regional Studies* 14, 285–96.

Barrett, S. (1982), *Transport policy in Ireland* (Dublin: Irish Management Institute).

Barrett, S. (1991), *Transport policy in Ireland in the 1990s* (Dublin: Gill and Macmillan).

Barwell, I., Edmonds, G., Howe, J. and de Veen, J. (1985), *Rural transport in developing countries* (London: Intermediate Technology Publications).

Beenhakker, H., Carapetis, S., Crowther, L. and Hertel, S. (1987), *Rural transport services. A guide to their planning and implementation* (London: Intermediate Technology Publications).

Bell, P. and Cloke, P. (1990), "Bus deregulation in rural localities: an example from Wales", in Bell, P. and Cloke, P. (eds), *Deregulation and transport. Market forces in the modern world* (London: Fulton), 100–21.

Bone, R. and Green, M. (1986), "Accessibility and development of Métis communities in Northern Saskatchewan", *Canadian Geographer* 30, 66–71.

Bougromenko, V., Generalova, J., Gertsen, A., Krysanov, V., Martianova, N., Oplesnin, K., Rodionov, A. and Smoliakov, A. (1996), *The white book of motor roads of Amur Region* (Moscow: Geogracom).

Briggs, R. (1981), "Federal policy in the US and the transportation problems of low density areas", in Lonsdale, R. and Holmes, J. (eds), *Settlement systems in sparsely populated regions. The United States and Australia* (New York: Pergamon), 238–61.

Brownlea, A. and McDonald, G. (1981), "Health and education services in sparseland Australia", in Lonsdale, R. and Holmes, J. (eds), *Settlement systems in sparsely populated regions. The United States and Australia* (New York: Pergamon), 322–46.

Burkhardt, J. (1981), "Rise and fall of rural public transportation", *Transportation Research Record* 831, 2–5.

Cahm, C. and Guiver, J. (1988), *A passenger view of bus deregulation* (London: Buswatch, National Consumer Council).

Clark, D. and Unwin, K. (1981), "Telecommunications and travel: potential impact in rural areas", *Regional Studies* 15, 47–56.

Cloke, P. (ed.) (1985), *Rural accessibility and mobility* (Lampeter: Institute of British Geographers, Rural Geography Study Group).

Cloke, P. and Edwards, G. (1986), "Rurality in England and Wales 1981: replication of the 1971 index", *Regional Studies* 20, 289–306.

Cloke, P., Milbourne, P. and Thomas, C. (1994), *Lifestyles in rural England* (Salisbury: Rural Development Commission), 110–45.

Cresswell, R. (ed.) (1978), *Rural transport and country planning* (Glasgow: Hill).

Crouch, M. (1985), "Road transport and the Soviet economy", in Ambler, J., Shaw, D. and Symons, L. (eds), *Soviet and East European transport problems* (London: Croom Helm), 165–88.

Crum, M. (1990), "Small community air service", in Due, J., Allen, B., Kihl, M. and Crum, M. (eds), *Transportation service to small rural communities. Effects of deregulation* (Ames: Iowa State University Press), 112–79.

Dhir, M., Lal, N. and Mital, K. (1987), "The development of low-volume roads in India", *Transportation Research Record* 1106, 235–46.

Douglas, J. (1986), "Route to the Arctic", *Geographical Magazine* 58, 409–14.

Due, J. (1990), "Small community rail service", in Due, J., Allen, B., Kihl, M. and Crum, M. (eds), *Transportation service to small rural communities. Effects of deregulation* (Ames: Iowa State University Press), 8–45.

Eskelinen, H. (1993), "Rural areas in the high mobility communications society", in Giannopoulos, G. and Gillespie, A. (eds), *Transport and communications innovation in Europe* (London: Belhaven), 259–83.

Everitt, J. and Gfellner, B. (1996), "Elderly mobility in a rural area: the example of South West Manitoba", *Canadian Geographer* 40, 338–51.

Filani, M. (1993), "Transport and rural development in Nigeria", *Journal of Transport Geography* 1, 248–54.

Fitzpatrick, J. (1983), "The changing nature of outback isolation: an educator's perspective", *Australian Geographer* 15, 318–21.

Ford, R. (1986), "The DMU replacement story", *Modern Railways* 43, 315–20.

Fullerton, B. (1988), *Scandinavia adopts the new realism in transport policy*, Department of Geography Research Series 15 (Newcastle-upon-Tyne: University of Newcastle).

Geertman, S. and van Eck, J. (1995), "GIS and models of accessibility potential: an application in planning", *International Journal of Geographical Information Systems* 9, 67–80.

Gillis, W. (ed.) (1989), *Profitability and mobility in rural America* (University Park, PA: Pennsylvania State University Press).

Hall, D. (ed.) (1993), *Transport and economic development in the new Central and Eastern Europe* (London: Belhaven).

Halsall, D. and Turton, B. (eds) (1979), *Rural transport problems in Britain: papers and discussion* (Keele: Institute of British Geographers, Transport Geography Study Group).

Hansen, S., Cleevely, D., Wadsworth, S., Bailey, H. and Bakewell, O. (1990), "Telecommunications in rural Europe. Economic implications", *Telecommunications Policy* (June), 207–22.

Hathway, G. (1985), *Low-cost vehicles. Options for moving people and goods* (London: Intermediate Technology Publications).

Henshaw, D. (1994), *The great railway conspiracy* (Hawes: Leading Edge).

Hilling, D. (1996), *Transport and developing countries* (London: Routledge).

Hillman, M. and Whalley, A. (1980), *The social consequences of rail closures*, Report 587 (London: Policy Studies Institute).

Holmes, J. and Brown, J. (1981), "Travel behaviour of isolated rural populations in inland Queensland", in Lonsdale, R. and Holmes, J. (eds), *Settlement systems in sparsely populated regions. The United States and Australia* (New York: Pergamon), 215–37.

Howe, J. and Richards, P. (1984), *Rural roads and poverty alleviation* (London: Intermediate Technology Publications).

Immers, B., Malipaard, E. and Oldenhof, M. (1988), "Transport in rural areas of developing countries: empirical findings from Western Province, Zambia", *Transportation Research Record* 1167, 51–8.

The Independent (1995), "Trains halt as France takes axe to branch lines", 30 November (London).

Jenkins, I. (1994), "All change – new directions for the road transport industries of Russia, Ukraine, Kazakhstan and Belarus", *Transport Reviews* 14, 289–320.

Jones, J. and Rosenberg, M. (1992), "Regional development, remote communities and alternative transportation services", *Geografiska Annaler Series B*, 74, 199–209.

Jordan, C. and Nutley, S. (1993), "Rural accessibility and public transport in Northern Ireland", *Irish Geography* 26, 120–32.

Joseph, A. and Bantock, P. (1984), "Rural accessibility of General Practitioners: the case of Bruce and Grey Counties, Ontario, 1901–1981", *Canadian Geographer* 28, 226–39.

Kidder, A. (1989), "Passenger transportation problems in rural areas", in Gillis, W. (ed.), *Profitability and mobility in rural America* (University Park, PA: Pennsylvania State University Press), 131–45.

Kihl, M. (1985), "The impact of bus deregulation on small towns", *Transportation Research Record* 1012, 65–71.

Kihl, M. (1988), "The impacts of deregulation on passenger transportation in small towns", *Transportation Quarterly* 42, 243–68.

Kihl, M. (1990), "Small community bus service", in Due, J., Allen, B., Kihl, M. and Crum, M. (eds), *Transportation service to small rural communities. Effects of deregulation* (Ames: Iowa State University Press), 73–111.

Kihl, M. (1993), "The need for transportation alternatives for the rural elderly", in Bull, C. (ed.), *Aging in rural America* (Newbury Park: Sage), 84–98.

Kilvington, R. (1985), "Railways in rural areas", in Button, K. and Pitfield, D. (eds), *International railway economics* (Aldershot: Gower), 271–96.

Kilvington, R. and McKenzie, R. (1985), *A technique for assessing accessibility problems in rural areas*, Contractor Report 11 (Crowthorne: Transport and Road Research Laboratory).

Knowles, R. (1979), "Road Equivalent Tariffs: the Scandinavian experience and the Scottish prospects", in Halsall, D. and Turton, B. (eds), *Rural transport problems in Britain: papers and discussion* (Transport Geography Study Group), 113–26.

Lonsdale, R. and Holmes, J. (eds) (1981), *Settlement systems in sparsely populated regions. The United States and Australia* (New York: Pergamon).

McCall, M. (1985), "Accessibility and mobility in peasant agriculture in tropical Africa", in Cloke, P. (ed.), *Rural accessibility and mobility* (Lampeter: Institute of British Geographers, Rural Geography Study Group), 42–63.

McFarland, H. (1991), "Railroad abandonment policy in the 1990s", *Transportation Practitioners Journal* 58, 331–40.

Maggied, H. (1982), *Transportation for the poor. Research in rural mobility* (Boston: Kluwer Nijhoff).

Moseley, M. (1979), *Accessibility: the rural challenge* (London: Methuen).

Moseley, M. and Packman, J. (1983), *Mobile services in rural areas* (Norwich: University of East Anglia).

Moseley, M., Harman, R., Coles, O. and Spencer, M. (1977), *Rural transport and accessibility* (Norwich: University of East Anglia).

Moyes, A. (1989), *The need for public transport in mid-Wales: normative approaches and their implications*, Rural Surveys Research Unit Monograph 2 (Aberystwyth: University College of Wales).

Moyes, A. (1995), "Local bus services in Wales: changing supply patterns since deregulation", in Day, G. and Thomas, D. (eds), *Contemporary Wales*, vol. 8, *An annual review of economic and social research* (Cardiff: University of Wales Press), 183–211.

Mwase, N. (1989), "Role of transport in rural development in Africa", *Transport Reviews* 9, 235–53.

Nutley, S. (1983), *Transport policy appraisal and personal accessibility in rural Wales* (Norwich: Geo Books).

Nutley, S. (1984), "Planning for rural accessibility provision: welfare, economy and equity", *Environment and Planning A* 16, 357–76.

Nutley, S. (1985), "Planning options for the improvement of rural accessibility: use of the time–space approach", *Regional Studies* 19, 37–50.

Nutley, S. (1988), " 'Unconventional modes' of transport in rural Britain: progress to 1985", *Journal of Rural Studies* 4, 73–86.

Nutley, S. (1990), *Unconventional and community transport in the United Kingdom* (London: Gordon and Breach).

Nutley, S. (1996), "Rural transport problems and non-car populations in the USA. A UK perspective", *Journal of Transport Geography* 4, 93–106.

Nutley, S. and Thomas, C. (1992), "Mobility in rural Ulster: travel patterns, car ownership and local services", *Irish Geography* 25, 67–82.

Nutley, S. and Thomas, C. (1995), "Spatial mobility and social change: the mobile and the immobile", *Sociologia Ruralis* 35, 24–39.

Ogunsanya, A. (1987), "Rural accessibility problems and human resource development: case study from Nigeria", *Journal of Rural Studies* 3, 31–42.

Okafor, F. (1990), "The spatial dimensions of accessibility to general hospitals in rural Nigeria", *Socio-Economic Planning Science* 24, 295–306.

Owen, W. (1987), *Transportation and world development* (London: Hutchinson).

Parolin, B., Filan, S. and Ilias, A. (1993), "Impact assessment of rail branch line closure: the Tamworth–Manilla line, NSW", *Australian Geographical Studies* 31, 189–200.

Patmore, J.A. (1965), "The British railway network in the Beeching era", *Economic Geography* 41, 71–81.

Pedersen, P.O. (1981), "Planning the structure of public transport networks in low density areas", *Transport Reviews* 1, 25–43.

Qvortrup, L. (1989), "The Nordic telecottages. Community teleservice centres for rural regions", *Telecommunications Policy* (March), 59–68.

Rockey, C. (1987), "The formation of regional railroads in the United States", *Transportation Journal* 27 (2), 5–13.

Rucker, G. (1984), "Public transportation: another gap in rural America", *Transportation Quarterly* 38, 419–32.

Saltzman, A. (1976), "Role of paratransit in rural transportation", *Transportation Research Board Special Report* 164, 137–42.

Smith, J. and Gant, R. (1982), "The elderly's travel in the Cotswolds", in Warnes, A. (ed.), *Geographical perspectives on the elderly* (Chichester: Wiley), 323–36.

Stabler, J. (1986), "Branch line abandonment and Prairie towns – one more time", *Canadian Journal of Regional Science* 9, 207–19.

Stanley, P. and Farrington, J. (1981), "The need for rural public transport: a constraints-based case study", *Tijdschrift voor Economische en Sociale Geografie* 72, 62–80.

Stimson, R. (1981), "Problems of living in isolated communities: the Eyre Peninsula and Port Lincoln, South Australia", in Lonsdale, R. and Holmes, J. (eds), *Settlement systems in sparsely populated regions. The United States and Australia* (New York: Pergamon), 189–214.

Sullivan, B. and Suen, S. (1981), "Surface rural public transportation in Canada", *Transportation Research Record* 831, 63–69.

Thomas, D. (1963), *The rural transport problem* (London: Routledge).

The Times (1996), "End of line for French rail romance", 15 June (London).

Tolley, R. and Turton, B. (1995), *Transport systems, policy and planning. A geographical approach* (Harlow: Longman).

Wanmali, S. (1991), "Determinants of rural service use among households in Gazaland District, Zimbabwe", *Economic Geography* 67, 346–60.

White, P. (1995), *Public transport. Its planning, management and operation* (London: UCL Press).

Whitelegg, J. (1984), "Closure of the Settle–Carlisle railway line. The case for a social cost–benefit analysis", *Land Use Policy* 1, 283–98.

Whitelegg, J. (1987), "Rural railways and disinvestment in rural areas", *Regional Studies* 21, 55–63.

Whitelegg, J. (1988), *Transport policy in the EEC* (London: Routledge).

10

TRANSPORT FOR RECREATION AND TOURISM

Stephen Page

The development of recreational and tourist travel is, inter alia, *a direct result of transport infrastructure to facilitate this leisure time activity. Understanding the patterns and processes shaping such travel poses many challenges for transport geographers since it is based on a discretionary use of time where transport is used to further the pursuit of pleasure and enjoyment. However, such enjoyment can also pose many problems of congestion, environmental damage and various planning dilemmas. Transport can also form the focus of tourist activity as the example of recreational boating on the Norfolk Broads (UK) illustrates.*

INTRODUCTION

Relationships between transport, recreation and tourism have largely been researched by geographers who have used concepts developed by spatial scientists to understand the interactions and locational aspects of transport systems as they impact and depend upon recreation and tourism activities. Research involving transport and its relationship with tourism and recreation is not yet, however, particularly well developed within the field of transport geography. Reviews of progress in transport geography (e.g. Knowles, 1993) reveal a notable absence of substantive research efforts in this area. This is surprising given the growing number of geographers now teaching and researching tourism and recreation, with an increasing number located within University Business Schools (Hall and Page, 1999).

In some respects, transport tends to be viewed as a passive element by geographers in the recreation and tourism context rather than as an integral part of tourism and recreational activity. Comparatively little progress has been made by researchers in this area of study since the influential work undertaken in the 1970s and 1980s by geographers (e.g. Wall, 1971; Patmore, 1983). Useful syntheses (e.g. Halsall, 1992) provide bibliographies of past investigations, but few studies have been made by geographers in the 1980s and 1990s explicitly to develop an understanding of the way in which transport facilitates and in some cases conditions the type of recreational and tourism activity that occurs.

These general observations remain pertinent despite notable exceptions. Transport geographers have looked at the implications for tourism of new transport infrastructures such as the Channel Tunnel between England and France and the planned high-speed rail link through Kent (Goodenough and Page, 1994) and at the ways in which these innovations may affect patterns of recreational and tourism activity in the later 1990s and in the twenty-first century. A good deal of research by transport geographers in the 1990s published in the *Journal of Transport Geography* has been preoccupied with air travel (Chou, 1993; Shaw, 1993; Feiler and Goodovitch, 1994; O'Connor, 1995; Raguraman, 1997), until recently another somewhat neglected field (see Chapter 14), although little of this output is directly related to tourism and recreation. The continued neglect of transport in the analysis of recreation and tourism has also been compounded by the perception among some other geographers who have not conceded the importance of tourism and recreation as serious areas for research until the late 1980s and 1990s. Even today, it is often relegated to a minor research area despite the rapid growth in tourism and recreational courses in most countries.

Recent texts such as Tolley and Turton (1995) highlight the need to consider recreation and tourism in the context of transport geography but do not devote much space to the topic. Other studies that have sought to place transport for recreation and tourism on the research agenda include occasional publications by the Transport Geography Study Group of the Institute of British Geographers (Halsall, 1982; Tolley and Turton, 1987). In these studies and in more recent reviews (e.g. Halsall, 1992) the emphasis has often been on modal forms of recreational and tourist travel (e.g. land-based transport and the use of trails, water-borne transport and heritage transport for nostalgic travel) (Page, 1993, 1994a). This can now act as a basis for geographers to develop substantial contributions to the management, planning and development of transport for recreational and tourist travel (Page, 1994b).

Geography has an underlying paradigm concerned with space, location and place, and the predominant concern in a recreational and tourism context has traditionally been to analyse the spatial expression of human activity related to recreation and tourism. One of the themes that continues to dominate research on transport, recreation and tourism is the vital role which transport plays in linking the generating and receiving areas for recreational and tourist activities at a variety of spatial scales. Such scales range from the world scale for tourism (Pearce, 1995) through the national, regional and local scales. In this respect, transport is a fundamental factor enabling human activity to take place in a recreational and tourism context.

This chapter begins with a discussion of the relationship between transport, recreation and tourism, which explores some of the conceptual, semantic and practical issues associated with establishing the role of transport in this context. This is followed by a review of some of the principal approaches used by geographers to simplify the real-world interaction of transport, recreation and tourism in the form of spatial models. While the discussion is weighted towards tourism models, this is counterbalanced by a review of recreational models that have been more behaviourally derived. Later on there is a critical discussion of the role of the car in recreational and tourist travel, emphasizing its impact and its integral role in developed countries to facilitate recreation, domestic tourism and to a lesser degree international tourism between countries.

Examples from New Zealand, the United Kingdom and North America (the Great Lakes region which borders Canada and the United States) illustrate how spatial patterns of activity have been shaped by road-based travel. A case study of recreational boating on the Norfolk Broads (UK) illustrates some of the conflicts and management problems that such recreational transport may pose in contrast to the effect of the car, and highlights how transport can also be the focus of a recreational and tourist activity as opposed to a means of travelling to a recreational and tourism environment. In this context, the car can be the containing context for an activity in the same way as a cruise ship provides the context for tourist activity. Such case studies also raise a number of issues related to the sustainability of transport for recreational and tourism activity, and the example of cycling is explored as a truly sustainable mode of transport which can be developed to fill a niche in the special interest adventure tourism market. However, before discussing the ways in which transport geographers approach the analysis of recreation and tourism, it is appropriate to consider the relationship between transport, recreation and tourism in order to understand how these activities are constructed in social and economic terms and the difficulty of distinguishing between transport for recreational and for tourism purposes.

THE RELATIONSHIP BETWEEN TRANSPORT, RECREATION AND TOURISM

Within the growing literature on recreation and tourism, there is a debate which recognizes that recreational and tourism activities are a subset of leisure. This implies that leisure activities are discretionary because they occur in juxtaposition to work and other household functions. In other words, according to Patmore (1983), these activities occur in three contexts: (i) time not required for work or basic functions such as eating and sleeping; (ii) activities or recreation within leisure time; and (iii) an attitude of mind based upon a perception of pleasure and enjoyment (Patmore, 1983, 5–6, cited in Halsall, 1992, 155). Patmore recognizes that there may be blurring within and between these areas.

A further complication in seeking to understand the relationship between leisure, recreation and tourism is that, in the post-war period in developed countries, the amount of leisure time has increased as the hours of work have decreased. But for certain social groups such as women, and housewives in particular, leisure may actually mean work. So while leisure time has become a firmly ingrained element in the routine of many people, often defined as non-work time, the growth in daily, weekly and annual leisure time has not been distributed evenly in social and spatial terms. Williams (1995), for example, highlights the relationship in urban recreational patterns in British cities where residents in the most affluent neighbourhoods have relatively easy access to recreational and leisure resources. This is reflected not only in the spatial distribution of such resources but also through the increased levels of car ownership in such neighbourhoods compared to residents in poorer districts. Although certain researchers see recreation as dependent upon a range

of facilitating factors in social and economic contexts (i.e. the availability of time and financial resources to capitalize on leisure opportunities), the distinction between leisure and recreation activities has remained somewhat obscure and open to differing interpretations.

While conventional definitions of recreation tend to emphasize the outdoor context and non-home-based nature of such activities, when one attempts to distinguish between the use of transport for leisure and for recreation it becomes increasingly difficult. For example, on a rail journey through a National Park, a train may be carrying local passengers who are enjoying a passive use of their leisure time by sightseeing and it may also be carrying fell-walkers who are using the train as a mode of transport into the National Park to reach the starting point for their walk and their participation in outdoor recreation. The train may also be carrying non-residents journeying from point A to B. These may be domestic tourists, perhaps staying away from home for more than 24 hours, or international tourists on holiday. Herein lies the complexity of disentangling the complex relationship between leisure, recreation and tourism and the fact that tourists also undertake recreational activities at their destination area. How does one define tourism in this context?

Tourists may thus be defined in functional terms by their journeys and their stay at destinations for temporary leisure periods away from their normal place of residence, but the domestic and international contexts of such journeys create a complex array of spatial patterns. Few geographers have modelled and analysed these patterns at the domestic, intra-regional and international scales (Pearce, 1995). More socially constructed definitions of tourism (e.g. Urry, 1990) are useful in understanding the separate and regulated spheres of work and leisure time and in showing how individuals do not necessarily distinguish between leisure, recreation and tourism as has been observed by various researchers (e.g. Shaw and Williams, 1994). In spatial and social terms, differentiating between leisure, recreation and tourism remains a semantic and somewhat tautological issue since no clear boundary exists between each, the issue is perhaps not particularly critical here, and there is a significant interaction between each form of activity since, for example, "recreational environments . . . are important tourism destinations" (Smith and Godbey, 1991, 97). Halsall (1982, ii) identified the fundamental relationship between transport and leisure time as follows:

> Transport is an integral part of much recreational behaviour, both as an aid to access to recreational opportunities, and as a recreational activity in its own right . . . Progressive reductions in the relative costs of travel, and in the frictional effects of distance, have dramatically increased the demand for recreational trips. In particular, the growth of car ownership has extended both the distances travelled and the range of recreational foci.

Halsall (1982) focuses on domestic tourism, the volume of which – as Pearce (1995) acknowledges – is up to 10 times greater than international tourism at a global scale. Nevertheless, tourism has also been a major beneficiary of these changes in accessibility by encouraging people to travel further afield as package holidays and charter flights have widened access for international travel (see Chapter 14). The development of package tourism from the 1950s (Holloway and Robinson, 1995) expanded opportunities for people in developed countries to travel overseas on holiday because package holidays (also known as inclusive tours) were able to offer a lower unit price for the transport component of the holiday (and also for the accommodation) which had hitherto been prohibitively expensive. In the case of Britain, Figure 10.1 illustrates that between 1971 and 1995 British residents' propensity to take holidays of four nights or more increased by 43 per cent. In 1995 the number of holidays taken was 59 million. In terms of trends, propensity to take overseas package holidays in the 1970s, 1980s and up to the mid-1990s increased while domestic holiday-taking experienced a relative decline. However, these data conceal a trend within domestic holiday-taking in Britain towards shorter holidays (e.g. short breaks), which have shifted from conventional coastal resorts to inland urban and rural locations. In an urban context, Page (1995) documents the growth in urban

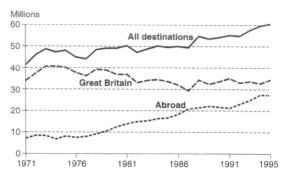

Figure 10.1 Holidays of four nights or more taken by Great Britain residents, by destination, 1971–95
Source: HMSO (1997, 213) using data from British Tourist Authority

tourism holiday-taking and the transportation and logistical problems it poses for small historic cities such as Canterbury, York and Chester and the consequent need for visitor and town centre management.

Other notable developments in tourist transport that have also seen a growth in tourist patronage are related to the cruising industry. Douglas and Douglas (1996) outline the growth of cruising in the Pacific and Table 10.1 illustrates the effect of cruise ship arrivals on individual Pacific islands, island groups and countries. Such arrivals have significant economic, social and cultural impacts on tourism (Hall and Page, 1996), and recent research has examined the profile of travellers on cruise ships (Morrison *et al.*, 1996), the economics of cruising (Bull, 1996) and the impact of cruise tourism on Australia (Dwyer and Forsyth, 1996). As Morrison *et al.* (1996, 16) argue, "the cruise ship industry has been one of the most exciting growth areas in North American tourism in the past 25 years. Its average rate of growth has been far greater than any other vacation category". Table 10.2 shows that the number of cruise ships serving the North American market in 1993 was 131 with a total capacity of 103 062 berths. By the year 2000, it is expected that there will be up to eight million passenger trips per annum on cruise ships in North America. The North American market accounts for 80 per cent of the world cruise market and reflects the high levels of disposable income

Table 10.1 Cruise ship passenger arrivals at selected pacific Island ports, 1988–93
Numbers and as a percentage (in brackets) of total tourist arrivals

Destination	Year										
	1988		1989		1990		1991		1992		1993	
Fiji	19 991	(9)	30 392	(11)	27 874	(9)	27 332	(10)	29 835	(10)	7 933	(3)
New Caledonia	42 762	(41)	33 169	(29)	42 158	(33)	35 330	(30)	49 802	(38)	38 742	(31)
Solomon Islands	4 547	(30)	2 981	(23)	2 616	(23)	2 649	(19)	4 886	(28)	2 656	(19)
Tonga	7 536	(25)	7 120	(23)	5 789	(20)	5 760	(19)	7 338	(22)	4 442	(13)
Vanuatu	50 932	(74)	41 311	(63)	41 867	(54)	37 023	(48)	59 346	(58)	43 059	(49)

Source: Adapted from Douglas and Douglas (1996) and World Tourism Organization *Compendium of Tourism Statistics*.

required to engage in this tourism activity focused on a form of tourist transport.

One of the important ways in which geographers have attempted to explain the relationship between transport, recreation and tourism is in terms of the development of models. Johnston (1991) examines the development of models in geography in the logical-positivist tradition. Although such models do not adequately accommodate the role of the individual traveller and their behavioural traits, they do provide an insight into the transport–recreation–tourism interface.

USING MODELS TO EXPLAIN THE RELATIONSHIP BETWEEN TRANSPORT, RECREATION AND TOURISM

Pearce (1979, 1995) provides the most extensive discussion of models in tourism research, but there is insufficient space here to review these models in detail and only the most fundamental models are discussed. According to Pearce (1995, 1) "the spatial interaction arising out of the tourist's movement from origin to destination has not been examined explicitly in much of the geographical literature on tourism" and recreation. In terms of transport geography, Tolley and Turton (1995) examine a variety of models that seek to explain spatial patterns of transportation. It is necessary, however, to understand the fundamental difference between recreational and tourist trips and other types of trips for work and everyday use. Human route-selection models based on the assumption of rational human decision-making posit that route selection is based on the least-cost principle. However, this does not incorporate the concept of travel for pleasure where the purpose of the trip does not necessarily rely upon selecting the shortest journey time or route from A to B. Research by Schaeffer and Sclar (1975) identifies a three-fold classification of trip purpose and frequency:

1. *extrinsic* trips, where the journey has a precise purpose such as to or from work;
2. *intrinsic* trips, where recreational or leisure activities are undertaken and which increases as the amount of leisure time increases;
3. *transport-generated trips* such as to fill the car up with petrol or to have it repaired.

Eliot-Hurst's (1974) research is also interesting in this context since it identified the concept of "movement space" where the type and length of trip were used to delimit the time–space dimensions of travel. For example, the majority of trips were made over short distances within the core areas of conurbations in advanced developed societies and these dominated the trip patterns. This was complemented by the second category, a "median area" in which were found less frequently performed trips such as recreational and tourist trips. The total spatial extent in which people interact and travel was defined as the

Table 10.2   Major cruise lines and cruise-line capacities, 1993

	Cruise Line	Passenger Capacity	Percentage Share of Total Capacity	Percentage Cumulative Share	Number of Ships	Average Ship Size (berths)
1	Royal Caribbean	14 228	13.8	13.8	9	1581
2	Carnival	12 514	12.1	25.9	8	1564
3	Princess	10 080	9.8	35.7	9	1120
4	Norwegian	8 408	8.2	43.9	6	1401
5	Holland America	7 515	7.3	51.2	6	1253
6	Celebrity	6 037	5.8	57.0	6	1006
7	Costa	5 948	5.8	62.8	7	850
8	Cunard	4 563	4.4	67.2	7	652
9	Epirotiki	3 840	3.7	70.9	8	480
10	Regency	3 747	3.6	74.5	5	749
11	Premier	3 038	3.0	77.5	3	1013
12	Royal	2 239	2.2	79.7	3	746
13	Dolphin	2 143	2.1	81.8	3	714
14	Cunard Crown	2 126	2.1	83.9	3	709
15	American Hawaii	1 489	1.4	85.3	2	745
16	Sun Line	1 098	1.1	86.4	3	366
17	Majesty	1 056	1.0	87.4	1	1056
18	Paquet French	1 016	1.0	88.4	2	508
19	Royal Viking	970	0.9	89.3	2	485
20	Crystal	960	0.9	90.3	1	960
21	American Family	874	0.8	91.1	1	874
22	Fiesta Marina	862	0.8	91.9	1	862
23	Renaissance	856	0.8	92.7	8	107
24	Orient Line	845	0.8	93.5	1	845
25	Club Med	772	0.8	94.3	2	386
26	Commodore	744	0.7	95.0	1	744
27	Seawind	624	0.6	95.6	1	624
28	Delta Queen Steamboat Co.	592	0.6	96.2	2	296
29	Dolphin Hellas	568	0.6	96.8	1	568
30	Cunard EuropAmerica River	456	0.4	97.2	3	152
31	Windstar Sail Cruises	444	0.4	97.6	3	148
32	World Explorer	440	0.4	98.0	1	440
33	Seabourn	424	0.4	98.4	2	212
34	Star Clipper	360	0.4	98.8	2	180
35	Diamond	354	0.3	99.1	1	354
36	Clipper	240	0.2	99.4	2	120
37	Seven Seas	172	0.2	99.6	1	172
38	American Canadian	160	0.2	99.8	2	80
39	Classical	140	0.1	99.9	1	140
40	Oceanic	120	0.1	100.0	1	120
	Totals	103 062	100.0	100.0	131	787

Source: Cruise Lines International Association (1994) cited in Morrison *et al.* (1996).

"extensive area". The key points emphasized by Schaeffer and Sclar (1975) and Hurst (1974) were that recreational and tourist trips were less common than commuter trips and the spatial extent and impact of such trips is less prescribed and not necessarily based on a logical choice when compared to the routine of daily trips to work.

It is this less predictable component which has continued to prove difficult to model in abstract and behavioural interpretations of travel flows of recreationalists and tourists. This is due to the flexibility that different forms of transport provide – the supply of resources – in terms of opportunities for activities. This is far more complex to analyse and understand than modelling by transport geographers of, for example, journey-to-work patterns. The literature and degree of sophistication with which geographers analyse recreational and tourist trips are far less developed than the research methodologies used to assess other forms of spatial interaction in transport geography (Tolley and Turton, 1995).

Probably the most fundamental relationship examined in geographical analyses of leisure activity involves the linkages between origin and destination areas. Pearce (1995) identifies four types of models used by geographers to examine tourism and recreational travel: "those emphasising the travel or linkage component, origin–destination models, structural models and evolutionary models" (Pearce, 1995, 1). Mariot (1969, cited in Matley, 1976) proposed three different routes that may link an origin area to a tourist centre (or a recreational site). As Figure 10.2 shows, the model identifies an access route, a return route and a recreational route. While the access and return routes are similar and work on the principle of selecting the most direct route, the recreational route highlights how the basic spatial principles developed in many of the models on minimizing trip distance do not readily apply to recreational and tourist travel (Tolley and Turton, 1995). The model by Mariot indicates that the traveller may enter the recreational route at any time for only part of the journey, making modelling even less predictable given the range of possible options and

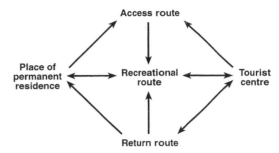

Figure 10.2   Mariot's model of tourist flows between two locations
Sources: Mariot (1969) and Matley (1976)

motivations to tour. The most important spatial principle inherent in Mariot's model is that of touring – the concept of visiting several places during one trip, rather than travelling directly from A to B.

For example, Figure 10.3 shows how the development of a scenic circuit in New Zealand's Northland region may result from using simple principles such as touring to encourage car-based drivers and those in camper vans to visit a much larger geographical area in order to explore and visit key attractions and resources which are off the main routeway. In the Northland case a scenic touring initiative has been used to promote visits by independent travellers, especially to the Kauri Coast region, based on good-quality signposting and closely following the coastal environment. To take advantage of these opportunities, tourists need to make a conscious detour from the direct route between the main tourist centres of Auckland and the Bay of Islands (Photographs 10.1 and 10.2). This case is based on a similar principle to that outlined by Lew (1991) in his discussion of scenic roads as a means of promoting rural tourism development in North America.

These principles are also embodied in Campbell's (1967) model of travel away from an urban area. As Figure 10.4 shows, Campbell identified a range of users according to the relative importance of the travel and stay components of their trips. As Pearce (1995, 1) argues:

For the recreationalist the recreational activity itself is the main element whilst for the vacationist the journey as such constitutes the main activity of the

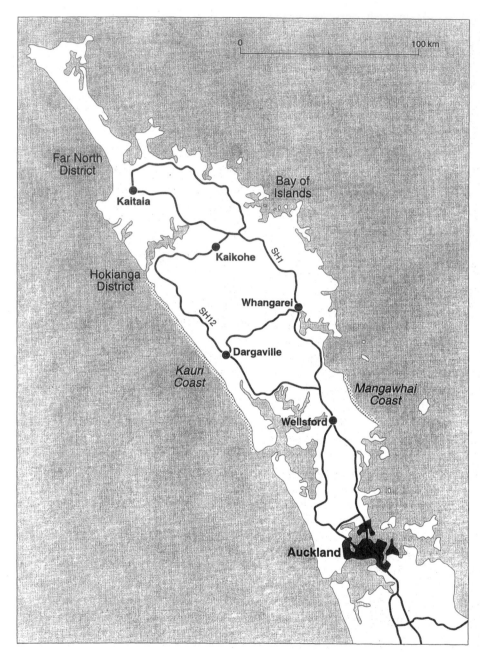

Figure 10.3   Scenic circuit tourism route in Northland, New Zealand

Photograph 10.1   Car ferry at Rawene, Hokianga District, Northland, New Zealand
Tourists and recreationalists mix with local residents in the peak season on this 12-car ferry operated by the Far North District Council (S.J. Page)

trip, with a number of stopovers being made on a round trip away from the city. An intermediate group, the recreational vacationist is shown to make trips from some regional base.

As a result, recreational travel is diffuse and scattered radially from the urban area whereas tourist travel (by vacationists) is mainly linear in form and recreational vacational travel is a mixture of both forms. Research by Rajotte (1975) found that this model could be applied in Québec. However, Pearce (1995) highlights the semantic problems of distinguishing between different types of travel, when in essence the main purpose is sightseeing and travelling.

In terms of domestic tourism, the prevailing research tends to rely on the concept of declining volumes of traffic from the generating centre. Greer and Wall (1979) highlighted the application of this principle of declining traffic volumes from the

source in urban areas as a function of time, money and demand. The result is a series of recreational uses with travel distance and blocks of land available as a series of zones: a day-trip zone, a weekend zone (which may be related to an area of second-home ownership) and a holiday or vacation zone. Figure 10.5 illustrates the location of these zones where transport is a major determinant (together with time and money) of the zonation of recreational uses. The diagram shows a series of zones of visitation where demand may rise inversely to distance from the urban area.

The potential recreational and vacation opportunities also increase geometrically from the city as land is available for use in greater quantities. Greer and Wall (1979) rejected the notion of a simple distance-decay function within each zone, a feature implicit in many transport models in geography. Pearce (1995) has also reviewed a number of other

Photograph 10.2   Fullers Ferry, Paihia, Bay of Islands, Northland, New Zealand
The ferry offers a sightseeing trip for tourists and recreationalists to look at marine activities in the Bay of Islands (S.J. Page)

models by geographers which highlight the role of cities as major generators of tourist and recreational travel and thereby examine demand to explain how tourist flows and the structure of tourist and recreational space evolve and develop. Oppermann (1992) also points to early work by geographers on dependence and diffusion theory (e.g. the work of Hagerstrand) in explaining spatial patterns of travel for tourism and recreation. The basic principle of reciprocity occurs in tourism since areas have receiving and generating functions and it is transport that facilitates the flow of travellers between places, yet there is a relative absence of the tourist and tourism industry in such models which are spatially abstract. Research on recreational travel models, however, is probably more highly developed from a spatial perspective than many of the fundamental models developed in tourism geography and more concerned with the user in relation to transportation and activities.

RECREATIONAL TRAVEL MODELS

Halsall (1992) analysed the range of recreational foci that had expanded in the post-war period as a function of the car, which had extended the range and distances people could travel. This develops a recreational geography focus largely articulated by Patmore (1983) where recreational travel is related to a range of factors. These factors include access, which provides the link between recreational choice and use of resources. Early research by Ullman (1954) examined spatial interaction between areas of supply and demand for recreation and the ability for areas to develop as intervening opportunities and to substitute one destination for another based on earlier models in population geography. As Elson (1979) observed, recreational trip-taking in the UK led to a range of research that focused on the

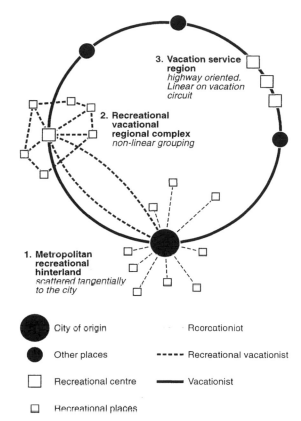

3. **Vacation service region**
highway oriented. Linear on vacation circuit

2. **Recreational vacational regional complex**
non-linear grouping

1. **Metropolitan recreational hinterland**
scattered tangentially to the city

- City of origin
- Other places
- Recreational centre
- Recreational places
- Recreationist
- - - - Recreational vacationist
- ──── Vacationist

Figure 10.4 Campbell's model of recreational and vacational travel
Source: Campbell (1967)

problems of increased traffic from urban areas destined for the countryside. Such trips pose significant stress on countryside resources and result in a range of management issues. Elson examined the responses to solve the spatial problems posed by urban recreationalists in the countryside. These included research on spatial interaction and four types of models were developed to try to explain why people chose and travelled to specific sites or resources:

- trip generation models (number of trips from the origin area, typically an urban centre);
- trip attraction (the likelihood of each competing or complementary destination to attract people);
- models of distribution (where the trips are destined);
- assignment models (which trips are chosen).

Pigram (1983, 31) highlighted the obvious relationship where "the strength of interaction declines as distance increases . . . this means that recreation sites at a greater distance, or for which the journey is perceived as involving more time, effort or cost, are patronised less". This contrasts somewhat with the tourism models reviewed by Greer and Wall (1979). Geographers have also examined the concept of time-budgets (i.e. how people allocate their leisure time) and a range of studies have identified both the seasonal and weekly use of time (Glyptis, 1981).

Patmore's (1983) classic study of recreation highlights the significance of geographical research and the need to set it against a context of opportunities and constraints for recreation. The constraints are mainly related to socio-economic factors such as age, income and household structure. Yet in terms of transport, mobility remains one of the fundamental constraints. For example, the car remains a potent force in shaping the ability of different groups to engage in recreation. Conversely, mobility constraints exist in terms of women's access to cars and the follow-on effects for children's recreation, and the ability of disabled persons to participate in recreational opportunities. Moseley (1979) analysed the significance of such mobility for deprived groups in the population. Elson (1979), however, questioned the geographers' focus on constraints to recreational travel, arguing for a decision-making approach measured through cognitive maps.

A focus on cognition and spatial choice highlights the dissatisfaction with spatial modelling to predict and analyse human behaviour, reflecting the importance of individual sets of stimuli promoting recreational travel. This incorporates the role of impulse and the role of psychological factors which Smith (1983) discussed in terms of motivation for travel, being the interaction of push and pull forces evident from the action space of individuals and groups. Pigram (1983) identified the central role of travel in the recreational decision-making process (Figure 10.6). This was symptomatic of the wider dissatisfaction in human geography in the 1970s with model-building as a route to explanation since many of the models were devoid of the complexities and problems associated with trying to predict patterns of human behaviour.

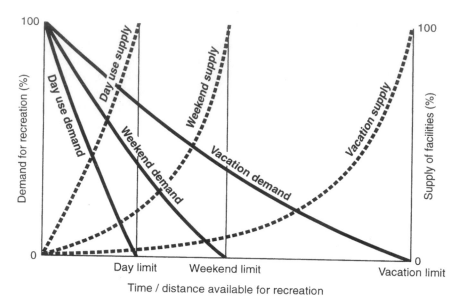

Figure 10.5   Greer and Wall's distribution of recreational resources model
Source: Greer and Wall (1979)

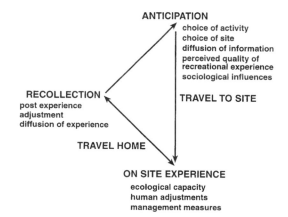

Figure 10.6   The Clawson five-phase model of the recreational experience
Source: Pigram (1983)

THE CAR AND RECREATIONAL TRAVEL

In the post-war period, the growth of car ownership has not only made the impact of recreational and tourist travel more flexible but has also induced overuse at accessible sites. This ease of access, fuelled by a growth in road-building and the upgrading of minor roads in many developed countries, has been a self-reinforcing process leading to over-use and a greater dominance in passive recreational activities.

Probably the most influential study of car usage among recreationalists was Wall's (1972) study of Kingston-upon-Hull in 1969. Wall identified the two principal types of study used to analyse recreational activity – namely site studies (of particular facilities or areas) and national studies such as the widely cited Pilot National Recreation Survey (British Travel Association and University of Keele 1967, 1969). Wall supplemented data from the national survey with a regional sample of 500 Hull car-owners in 1969. While the results are now very dated, this study highlighted the importance of seasonality and timing of pleasure trips by car and the dominance of the car as a mode of transport for urban dwellers. It also highlighted the role of the journey by car as a form of recreation in itself as well as the importance of the destination. These results emphasized the importance of the car as more than just a means of transport.

Wall's study also has a degree of similarity with others that followed such as Coppock and Duffield's (1975) survey of recreation and the countryside. This focused on patterns and processes of recreational activity in Scotland and mapped and described patterns of recreational travel, especially those of caravanners. At the same time, the study noted the tendency for many recreationalists not to venture far from their car at the destination, a point reiterated by Glyptis' (1981) innovative and seminal study of recreationalists using participant observation in Hull. Wall also found that the majority of pleasure trips were day trips less than 100 km away from Hull, being spatially concentrated in a limited number of resorts along the Yorkshire coast and the southerly part of the region. Other research (Burton, 1966; Wager, 1967) highlighted the versatility of the car and its use to venture into the North York Moors National Park. Burton and others explained the attraction of the car to recreationalists, allowing them to enjoy the countryside and observe its visual characteristics rather than have physical contact.

More recent research by Eaton and Holding (1996) identified the growing scale of such visits to the countryside by recreationalists in cars. In 1991, 103 million visits were made to National Parks in the UK (Countryside Commission, 1992), the most popular being the Lake District and Peak District Parks. In terms of car usage, car traffic was estimated to grow by 267 per cent by the year 2025 from the levels current in 1992 (Countryside Commission, 1992). In fact, the greatest pressures of rising car usage have been the decline in public-transport usage for recreational trips; many National Parks seem unlikely, however, to be able to cope with the levels of usage predicted for the year 2025 given their urban catchments and their relative accessibility by motorway and A-roads in the UK. Eaton and Holding (1996) review the absence of effective policies to meet the practical problems of congestion facing many sites in the countryside in Britain. Schemes such as the Sherpa Bus routes in the Snowdonia National Park have been introduced (Mulligan, 1979) but have not been incorporated into any wider policy objectives for transport. This combines with a failure to design

public transport to suit the needs and perceptions of users to achieve reductions and solutions to congestion in National Parks. Thus it is clear that the car poses a major problem not only for urban areas and for the continued use of cars by commuters and recreationalists but also in terms of the sheer growth in volume of cars in areas not designed for large numbers of car users. This problem is aggravated when spatially concentrated at "honeypot" locations which attract large numbers of cars and visitors within a confined area. National Parks in the UK have attempted to ameliorate this situation by introducing transport controls and visitor management initiatives. In some areas "rural policies encompass schemes to reduce car penetration to sensitive areas . . . to supplement inadequate capacity for cars which cannot be increased without great detriment" (Halsall, 1992, 171). In the Goyt and Derwent valleys of the Peak District a minibus park-and-ride scheme is in operation in summer and total car bans apply on Sundays and Bank Holidays. Similarly, there are plans in the USA to introduce a total ban on private cars in the Yosemite National Park.

The UK Tourism Society's response to the Government Task Force on Tourism and the Environment (English Tourist Board/Employment Department, 1991) highlighted the impact of the car by commenting that:

> No analysis of the relationship between tourism and the environment can ignore transportation. Tourism is inconceivable without it. Throughout Europe some 40 per cent of leisure time away from home is spent travelling, and the vast majority of this is by car . . . Approaching 30 per cent of the UK's energy requirements go on transportation . . . [and] . . . the impact of traffic congestion, noise and air pollution . . . [will] . . . diminish the quality of the experience for visitors.

Various management solutions exist, such as encouraging urban areas to develop "intervening opportunities" in the urban fringe through networks of Country Parks in the UK (see Harrison, 1991) which are capable of absorbing large numbers of visitors seeking a countryside experience. Such parks are able to fulfil the need for local recreational demand

and to reduce the need for recreationalists to seek out countryside sites, thereby reducing the impact of transport on other sites. However, car ownership in the UK developed rather later than in North America and for this reason it is pertinent to focus on one region in North America where it has had a major influence on recreational and tourist travel – the Great Lakes area.

Chubb's (1989) study of the Great Lakes region of North America highlighted the role of the car in cross-border travel. The region, which contains the world's largest complex of fresh water, also contains a diversity of recreational and tourism resources including lakes, forests, large park areas, cottages and resort complexes (Figure 10.7). Recreational cottages line many of the lakes as second-home development (Coppock, 1977) and other seasonal residences are distributed throughout the region which owners drive to for weekend and vacation use

from May to September. A range of resort areas also exists. The region experiences a high usage of recreational vehicles such as caravans and campervans.

Table 10.3 outlines a range of tourism flows which complement recreational travel within the region. For example, the majority of cottage owners who travel into Ontario are from the United States. The cross-border flows of car traffic produce a range of spatial forms which are related to the configuration of the Great Lakes and location of hotels, motels and camping grounds. As Chubb (1989, 300) illustrated, a number of straight-line and circuit routes exist which cross the international border between Canada and the USA. The straight-line routes include: the highway north from Minneapolis to Thunder Bay; Interstate 75 north through Michigan, along Lake Superior; and the Niagara Falls–Toronto–Georgian Bay route. The circuit routes which incorporate a touring component and cross

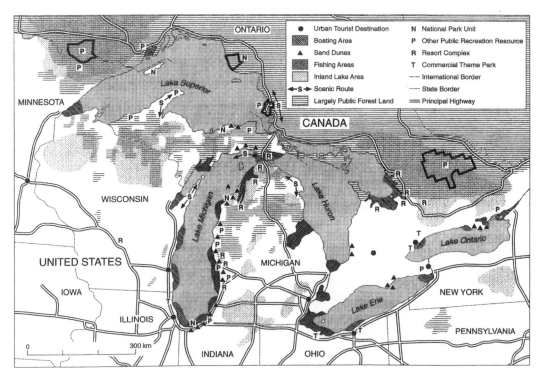

Figure 10.7   The Great Lakes region, North America
Source: adapted from Chubb (1989)

Table 10.3 Recreational and tourist flows in the Great Lakes region

Type of Activity	Destinations of Ontario Residents	Destinations of American Residents	Motivations: Primary	Motivations: Secondary
Short-term shopping/ Entertainment	Niagara Falls, NY Buffalo Detroit	Windsor Niagara Falls, Ontario Toronto	Novelty Proximity Prices	Exchange rate
Longer-term shopping/ Entertainment	Minneapolis Chicago Cleveland	Toronto	Goods and services available Novelty	Exchange rate Sales tax rebate
Visiting friends and relatives	Adjacent areas in USA, especially E Michigan	Adjacent areas in Ontario, especially SW portion	Early history Settlement patterns	Proximity
Power or sailboat cruising	Mackinac City Detroit area Cleveland	Toronto Owen Sound Parry Sound	Proximity Sheltered waters	Marina facilities Shore facilities
Travel to own cottage		Lake Erie and Huron shorelines Lake areas across S Ontario	Proximity Time of acquisition	Ethnic origin
Long-term fishing excursion	Saginaw Bay W Michigan Salmon areas	Georgian Bay Interior lakes in SE and N Ontario	Chance of success Fish species and size	Environmental facilities
Automobile touring	Various routes around one or more of the four Great Lakes		Well known natural and commercial attractions Proximity Length	Facilities

Source: Modified from Chubb (1989)

the border include: the Lake Ontario route (800 km) which is the shortest; the Lake Erie route (1000 km) which includes Niagara Falls; and the Lake Superior and Lake Huron routes, each of which is approximately 1600 km in length.

It is clear that while the car has an overwhelming influence on the choice of recreation and tourism, it is also used for passive recreation, especially day-trips. Likewise, in North America, distance is not so much of an inhibiting factor for recreational and tourist travel as the example of the Great Lakes implies. Distances are greater and the car is a fundamental catalyst in the region's development of a recreational and tourism infrastructure to serve the needs of visitors and recreationalists from within Ontario and from the USA. Yet while the car is labelled the main cause of over-use, congestion and environmental damage of recreational sites through transporting visitors, other modes of recreational transport pose a range of planning and management problems as the case of the Norfolk Broads (UK) will show. In this instance, it is not travel to the recreational and tourism environment that is of interest, but the use of a form of transport as the recreational and tourism activity in itself.

TRANSPORT–ENVIRONMENT CONFLICTS IN THE 1990s: MANAGING THE HIRE BOAT INDUSTRY ON THE NORFOLK BROADS (UK)

The Norfolk Broads comprise a wetland region in East Anglia (Figure 10.8), created in medieval times through a series of flooded peat diggings and focused on a number of rivers such as the Bure, Yare and Waveney and their tributaries in the eastern part of Norfolk and the northern part of Suffolk. Although the region, with 200 km of tidal rivers and 3640 ha of water space, is not large compared to the previous example of the Great Lakes region in North America, it is an area of natural beauty and an area for intensive recreational boating. The area was originally identified as a potential candidate for National Park status but was not included under the original designations. The 1981 Wildlife and Countryside Act highlighted the problem of reconciling agricultural and commercial practices with environmental conservation in this and other UK areas. In 1989, however, the area was accorded virtual National Park status when the Broads Authority was established by the 1988 Norfolk and Suffolk Broads Act. This granted the Broads Authority the same autonomy as a National Park in terms of finance, policy and administration and thus it receives a 75 per cent grant from central government (Glyptis, 1991).

Boating for pleasure on the Norfolk Broads dates back to the 1870s when the early wherries (local sailing vessels that carried cargo) began to carry passengers for pleasure. In the 1880s, John Loyne pioneered the hire boat industry and in 1908 the present-day company H. Blake and Co. was established to rent purpose-built vessels to visitors who travelled to the area by rail. Thus the provision of transport for recreational day use and for much longer holiday use led to the development of a particular form of recreation and tourism which was water-based and transport-dependent. The number of boats hired has fluctuated during the 1980s and 1990s but in 1995 boat companies owned 1481 motor cruisers and launches, which were hired to approximately 200 000 visitors. A number of environmental concerns have developed over the last 30 years related to their use, notably:

1. the erosion of river banks and the destruction of the protective reed fingers, which have implications for all river bank users and farmers;
2. the enrichment of the nutrient content of the water with nitrates and phosphates; this has contributed to the process known as *eutrophication*, which leads to excessive growth of a limited number of plant species and the extinction of the diverse range of flora and fauna.

These problems signify a recreational resource under pressure. The region comprises essentially a series of interconnected linear parks, and access has undoubtedly contributed to greater recreational pressures given the region's proximity to the urban centres in South East England, the Midlands and towns in East Anglia. There are two competing arguments for and against the continued growth and development of recreational boating in the Broads.

On the one hand, there is the physical environmental debate, which highlights the damage motor boats cause to the local ecosystems through their wash turbidity, as their propellers cause a suction effect on the river bed. This also impacts upon reed beds and causes abrasion on the river banks as well as polluting the water through petrol and oil emissions. However, boats alone are not the main cause of environmental damage as agricultural fertilizers and domestic sewerage are also major contributors to overenrichment and species extinction problems. Anglers may also be to blame for damage to river banks. Yet the problem with the hire boat industry is that it is spatially and temporally concentrated (see Table 10.4): heavy usage occurs at weekends in the northern parts of the river system (e.g. Thurne Mouth and the middle reaches of the river Bure at Horning and at Wroxham/Hoveton, and to a lesser degree the lower reaches of the river Ant). This places intense pressure upon attractions within that region, especially during the very short summer

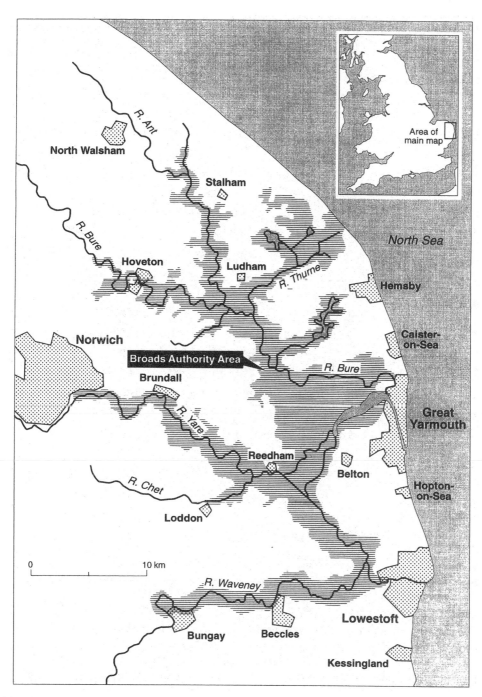

Figure 10.8   The Norfolk Broads, UK
Source: The Broads Authority, Norfolk

Table 10.4   Hire craft operators on the Norfolk Broads, UK

Location	Number of Operators	Motor Cruisers	Day Launches	Sailing Cruisers/Day Craft
River Waveney				
Burgh St Peter	1	0	2	0
Burgh Castle	1	0	1	0
St Olaves	2	9	2	0
Somerleyton	1	8	0	15
Beccles	4	42	17	0
Oulton Broad	5	23	16	0
Total	14	82	38	15
River Chet				
Loddon	5	46	3	0
River Yare				
Reedham	2	24	0	0
Brundall	12	190	2	0
Thorpe	5	113	7	0
Total	24	373	12	0
River Bure				
Acle	4	86	10	0
S. Walsham	1	9	2	0
Upton	1	0	0	16
Horning	7	128	32	19
Wroxham/Hoveton	14	209	124	13
Belaugh	2	74	0	0
Total	28	506	168	48
River Thurne				
Ludham	2	11	0	17
Potter Heigham	3	124	69	1
Martham	2	19	7	29
Hickling	1	9	6	2
Total	8	163	82	49
River Ant				
Ludham Bridge	1	0	7	1
Sutton	1	12	0	0
Stalham	4	357	6	2
Wayford	2	6	9	0
Total	8	375	22	3

Source: Broads Authority (1997) based on the Broad's Authority Register of Boats 1995.

season. A Broads Authority boat movement census in 1994 highlighted that on one peak Sunday in August there were 6296 craft movements recorded at 14 census points. In contrast, the upper reaches of many rivers are protected by their relative inaccessibility and, in a few cases, by low bridges.

In contrast to the environmental arguments for moderation and control there are powerful economic arguments for continuing to promote the development of recreational boating. The hire boat industry is estimated to contribute £25 million annually to the local economy and generates approximately £9000 for the economy for each boat rented

(Broads Authority, 1997). In 1991, a survey of boatyards by the Broads Authority found that in the 105 responding, boating employed 1622 people: 884 full-time, 148 part-time and 590 people on a seasonal basis. Furthermore, recreational and tourist spending indirectly contributes to 5000–5500 jobs in the hospitality sector, at local tourist attractions as well as in the local marine industry. Even though boating has been in recession within the area in the 1990s, boatyard diversification to develop facilities for the needs of visitors (e.g. the construction of accommodation) has also posed planning problems for the Broads Authority since such diversification changes the traditional image of the area.

Given these two competing arguments over recreational boating, it is pertinent to ask who is responsible for decision-making and planning for boating in this region? Much of the decision-making is fragmented across a number of public- and private-sector bodies responsible for influencing planning, each with particular powers, responsibilities and visions relating to boating. Some of these bodies are outlined below.

1 National government working through the Countryside Commission has debated the issue of the most appropriate administrative structure for the region, and this led to the Broads Authority being established. Yet other government departments (such as the Ministry for Agriculture, Fisheries and Food) have a very different view of the region's function from that of the Countryside Commission which is not recreational or conservationist in focus.

2. The Broads Authority can regulate planning proposals for the new boatyards and extensions to existing ones. It can also develop new waterside facilities such as public moorings in accordance with its overall management plan (Broads Authority, 1997).

3. The Great Yarmouth Port and Haven Commissioners are responsible for all navigation on the Broads and rivers. They license boats and have imposed speed restrictions, enforced by river inspectors, and they can also regulate river traffic charges.

4. The East Anglian Tourist Board and its parent body the English Tourist Board can promote the region to visitors together with local districts. Each body has a degree of choice over the image they choose to portray and the markets they target and can advocate alternative tourist activities in the region.

5. The hire boat companies and their marketing agencies have undertaken publicity campaigns to try to influence the behaviour of visitors and to encourage a greater consciousness of the natural environment. Boat companies could restrict the number of vessels hired at particular places and at certain times if they felt it was in their long-term interest to do so.

6. A variety of other bodies have responsibilities such as the regional water authority (Anglian Water) while the National Rivers Authority has powers over water quality and land drainage. There are also many pressure groups which have a strong lobby function such as the National Farmers Union, the Nature Conservancy Council and the local Broads Society. Although no one group has direct influence over the hire boat industry, they can exert pressure on decision-makers in the other bodies to influence planning outcomes.

This case study illustrates that it is not so much the volume of boats but rather the intensity of resource use in time and space as well as the behaviour of users which conflict with the natural environment. There is no all-embracing solution to the conflicts posed by these forms of transport, recreation and administration. Coexistence with the fragile ecosystem is therefore a major challenge for recreation management. Environmental deterioration is not a problem that can be solved quickly, but the Broads Authority has a management plan for the area which is viewed as a long-term vision for the Broads. It is a workable strategy and while a general decline in recreational boating holidays occurred in the late 1980s and early 1990s, it is anticipated that demand will rise again in the new millennium.

Since any form of management for the Broads needs to be accompanied by objectives that inform

Table 10.5   A range of broads Authority aims and policies for the management of recreational boating

Aim 13: Recreation
The Broads Authority will encourage quiet open-air, water-based recreation based on the area's distinctive beauty, culture, traditions, history and wildlife. The type, scale of activity should be compatible with the Authority's objectives for the natural and built environment and public enjoyment of the area.

Policy 69: Navigation Rights
The Broads Authority will assert and retain legitimate navigation rights throughout its area, taking account of its other statutory duties.

Policy 70: Extending the Waterspace
The Broads Authority will examine the opportunities for the extension of navigation waterspace, including the re-opening of old navigations, the creation of new water areas, and the provision of by-pass channels. The navigational and recreational benefits as well as the environmental impact of any such development will be evaluated in the context of the management, conservation and restoration aims of the Broads Authority and its statutory duties.

Policy 71: Boating in Sensitive Areas
The Broads Authority will oppose development in: the Upper Thurne, the Trinity Broads system, which is likely to lead to increased boating use.

Policy 72: Zoning for Wildlife
The Broads Authority will negotiate zoning in sensitive areas of Broads navigation where disturbance from craft is causing or likely to cause, significant conservation damage.

Policy 73: Zoning and the Navigation
The Broads Authority will keep restrictions to the minimum when, to ensure that wildlife and plant communities are not damaged or disturbed, it is considering the need for temporary, limited voluntary zoning in specified sensitive areas.

Policy 75: Promotion of Sailing
The Broads Authority will promote sailing opportunities in the Broads, maintaining a toll differential in favour of sailing craft.

Policy 77: Sailing for People with Disabilities
The Broads Authority will promote opportunities for sailing for people with disabilities in the Broads.

Policy 82: Motor Boating
The Broads Authority will discourage any further growth of motor boating.

Policy 83: Influencing Boat Numbers
The Broads Authority will investigate ways in which to influence boat numbers and their location.

Policy 84: Day Boats
The Broads Authority will encourage the introduction of day boats which have good wash characteristics, and those which are electrically powered. The Authority will continue to work with day boat operators and ensure that they provide adequate information to hirers.

Policy 131: Sustainable Tourism
The Broads Authority supports the concept of sustainable tourism, which improves the local economy, drawing on local skills and traditions, while ensuring the long-term conservation of the environment.

Policy 133: Hire Boat Industry
The Broads Authority will support and encourage the hire boat industry for the Broads provided its nature and scale of activities are appropriate.

Source: The Broads Authority (1997, 156–64).

overall strategy, sustainability is a prime concern for the region (Broads Authority, 1997). As Table 10.5 shows, the Broads Authority has developed a number of policies to address the issue of coexistence of the recreational boating industry with its underlying objective, which is to foster sustainable management and development. Each of these policies not only requires active coordination of the various agencies involved with the hire boat industry, but also an ongoing dialogue with all parties affected by the Broads management plan. By fostering an ongoing partnership between public- and private-sector groups, the management plan will remain a workable strategy for the future and will ensure that the boating industry is an integral but managed element of tourism and recreational activities available in the region. The case study also illustrates that there is growing concern over the management of the impacts of recreational boating and that sustainable policies and practices are developed in relation to recreational and tourism transport systems. The role of recreational and tourist cycling as a sustainable transport option is a worthwhile consideration in this context.

CYCLING AS A SUSTAINABLE FORM OF RECREATIONAL AND TOURIST TRANSPORT

Sustainability has become one of the vogue terms of the 1990s (see Chapter 15). However, in the context of recreational and tourist transport, this concern has not led to any widespread or dramatic changes in the operation and management of transport systems, but in many cases merely to some readjustments to accommodate green issues. Some researchers maintain that it is impossible to talk about sustainability in the context of recreation and tourism without a fundamental re-evaluation of the concept and necessity of pleasure travel. Wood and House (1991) argue that, while transport operators need to pursue good environmental practices, tourists also need to audit their trips very carefully. This audit is based on a number of questions:

- Why go on holiday? Consider your motivations and whether you need to travel.
- Choose the right type of holiday to meet your needs.
- Consider travelling out of season to less well-known destinations.
- Choose the right tour operator by asking environmentally related questions to ascertain what the company is doing to minimize environmental impacts.
- Is public transport, cycling or walking an option as opposed to hiring a car? This raises the issue of using sustainable and low-impact forms of transport at the destination, particularly the use of cycling.

According to Lumsdon (1996) the market for recreational cycling activities can range from day or part-day casual usage through to long-distance touring holidays. In fact cycling can present tourists and recreationalists with unique views of rural areas and is particularly appealing to free independent travellers. Beyond the seminal study by Tolley (1990) there is only a limited number of studies on cycle tourism (Beoiley, 1995; Lumsdon, 1996; Schieven, 1988, Sustrans, 1997). In northern England the C2C route, a 170 mile coast-to-coast cycle route, is estimated to have generated nearly 15 000 cycle tourists in its first year of operation (Sustrans, 1995). The development of a national UK cycle network, following a £42.5 million award from the Millennium Commission in 1996 to Sustrans, will arguably create the potential for up to 100 million journeys by bicycle, on foot or by wheelchair. This will require the development of 6500 miles of routes free of motorized traffic linking urban centres, using traffic-calmed roads and incorporating redundant railway lines, river and canal paths. Up to 40 per cent of the expected usage will be for leisure purposes and the ultimate aim is that the route network will be within a 10 minute cycle ride from about 20 million households.

In the UK, cycle tourism now generates approximately £535 million a year from leisure day-trips, domestic holidays and overseas trips (Beoiley, 1995). Cycling can also make a major contribution to environmental management where it forms a pollution-free form of recreation. For example, the Scottish Tourist Board (1991) recognized the early potential of cycling and developed a strategy to enhance cycle tourism and the Broads Authority initiated a "Broads Bike Hire" network in 1996 supplemented by the development of a series of short circular routes that avoid sensitive areas for wildlife and main roads. Each route in the Broads begins and ends at a cycle hire shop.

In the Netherlands, such schemes are even more highly developed as Tolley and Turton (1995) show, as in the case of Delft where cycles are segregated from motorized traffic to reduce the risk of conflict and accidents. This can enhance the use of cycles for recreational and other uses. The Dutch National Environmental Policy Plan has also improved cycle parking at stations to aid commuters and intermodal transfer to assist in promoting sustainable transport options.

In New Zealand, the central Otago region in the South Island has followed the lead of several other countries by converting former rail routes into linear cycle routes for recreational and tourist traffic. The Central Otago Rail Trail (Ritchie, 1997) is the only one of its kind in the South Island and complements the growing interest in long-distance cycling by tourists who tend to use secondary routes (equivalent to B-grade roads in the UK). While the majority of cycle tourists interviewed by Ritchie were experienced cyclists, they conformed to an international profile of cyclists tending to be aged 20–34 years of age, predominantly male and travelling with a partner or alone. While issues such as signposting, quality of roading and safety issues are rated highly, participating in tourist activities seemed of less importance.

Ritchie's (1997) study has important implications for the spatial distribution and planning of sustainable transport modes such as cycling. Countries seeking to promote this form of recreational and tourist travel need to develop a national strategy or cycle network. Such networks, as the experience in the Netherlands suggests, need to be safe and able to provide opportunities for rural tourism development by providing opportunities for cyclists to stop. The national cycling strategy in the UK is expected to generate a growth in cycling by the year 2000 through the stimulation of demand through the national cycling network (Sustrans, 1997). As a non-polluting and less-intrusive form of transport, cycling can expand the opportunities for recreationalists and it can fulfil a wide range of recreational and tourism motivations.

CONCLUSION

Halsall's (1992, 175) comments that "transport provision is a permissive factor in much tourist/recreation development, itself a product of increasing mobility, leisure time and affluence" remain a valid assessment of the relationship between transport, recreation and tourism. Yet geographers have largely failed to raise the issue of this relationship more prominently on the research agenda. There is growing evidence, however, that the sustainability debate and growth in special interest tourism (Weiler and Hall, 1992) are providing a renewed interest in this area of research, especially in the case of cycling. Much progress was made by geographers in analysing the transport, recreation and tourism interface in the 1960s and 1970s. With tourism and recreational research now a legitimate area for geographers to focus on, many opportunities exist to develop further many of the early studies based on new conceptual and empirical insights.

Such longitudinal studies are necessary to establish how cultural and environmental factors are shaping the use of transport for recreation and tourism. There is considerable scope for geographers to develop a renewed interest in transport as an integral element in facilitating and stimulating tourism and recreational activity and development, and thereby to illustrate the real significance of transport in the overall social construction of holidaymaking and day-trips by urban and rural populations in the developed and less-developed worlds. A spatial perspective is critical to understanding many of the fundamental issues underlying present-day planningproblems associated with tourism and recreation, as the example of the Norfolk Broads illustrates. Tourism and recreation continue to grow at a significant rate in most developed and many developing countries, and finding new and diverse opportunities for such activities may mean a greater concern for the more economic use of existing forms of transport for recreation and tourism and may also require, particularly, the development of more innovative schemes to manage the volume and spatial distribution of visitors in sensitive natural environments.

ACKNOWLEDGEMENT

This chapter is dedicated to the memory of Professor Sue Glyptis, formerly Professor of Recreation Management at Loughborough University, who died in 1997 and who made a major contribution to the study of recreational geography.

REFERENCES

Beoiley, S. (1995), "On yer bike – cycling and tourism", *INSIGHTS*, September, 17–31.

British Travel Association and the University of Keele (1967, 1969), *Pilot national recreation survey* (Keele: British Travel Association and the University of Keele).

Broads Authority (1997), *Broads plan* (Norwich: Broads Authority).

Bull, A. (1996), "The economics of cruising", *Journal of Tourism Studies* 7 (2), 28–35.

Burton, T. (1966), "A day in the country: a survey of leisure activity at Box Hill in Surrey", *Journal of the Royal Institute of Chartered Surveyors* 98, 378–80.

Campbell, C. (1967), *An approach to research in recreation geography*, Occasional Paper 7, Department of Geography, University of British Columbia, Vancouver.

Chou, Y. (1993), "Airline deregulation and nodal accessibility", *Journal of Transport Geography* 1 (1), 36–46.

Chubb, M. (1989), "Tourism patterns and determinants in the Great Lakes region: populations, resources, roads and perceptions", *GeoJournal* 19 (3), 291–96.

Coppock , J.T. (1977) (ed.), *Second homes: curse or blessing?* (Oxford: Pergamon).

Coppock, J.T. and Duffield, B. (1975), *Recreation in the countryside* (London: Macmillan).

Countryside Commission (1992), *Trends in transport and the countryside* (Cheltenham: Countryside Commission).

Douglas, N. and Douglas, N. (1996), "P & O's Pacific", *Journal of Tourism Studies* 7 (2), 2–14.

Dwyer, L. and Forsyth, P. (1996), "Economic impacts of cruise tourism in Australia", *Journal of Tourism Studies* 7 (2), 36–45.

Eaton, B. and Holding, D. (1996), "The evaluation of public transport alternatives to the car in British national parks", *Journal of Transport Geography* 4 (1), 55–65.

Eliot-Hurst, M. (1974) (ed.), *Transportation geography: comments and readings* (London: McGraw-Hill).

Elson, M. (1979), *State of the art review 12: countryside trip-making* (London: Sports Council/Social Science Research Council).

English Tourist Board/Employment Department (1991), *Tourism and the environment: maintaining the balance* (London: English Tourist Board).

Feiler, G. and Goodovitch, T. (1994), "Decline and growth, privatization and protectionism in the Middle East airline industry", *Journal of Transport Geography* 2 (1), 55–64.

Glyptis, S. (1981), "People at play in the countryside", *Geography* 66 (4), 277–85.

Glyptis, S. (1991), *Countryside recreation* (London: Longman).

Goodenough, R. and Page, S.J. (1994), "Evaluating the environmental impact of a major transport infrastructure project: the Channel Tunnel rail link", *Applied Geography* 14 (1), 26–50.

Greer, T. and Wall, G. (1979), "Recreational hinterlands: a theoretical and empirical analysis", in Wall, G. (ed.), *Recreational land use in southern Ontario*, Publication Series No. 14, Department of Geography, University of Waterloo.

Hall, C.M. and Page, S.J. (1996) (eds), *Tourism in the Pacific: issues and cases* (London: International Thomson Business Press).

Hall, C.M. and Page, S.J. (1998a), *Geography of tourism and recreation: environment, place and space* (Routledge: London).

Halsall, D. (1982) (ed.), *Transport for recreation* (Transport Geography Study Group).

Halsall, D. (1992), "Transport for tourism and recreation", in Hoyle, B.S. and Knowles, R.D. (eds), *Modern transport geography* (London: Belhaven), 155–77.

Harrison, C. (1991), *Countryside recreation in a changing society* (London: TML Partnership).

HMSO (1997), *Social trends* (London: HMSO).

Holloway, C. and Robinson, C. (1995), *Marketing for tourism* (London: Longman).

Johnston R.J. (1991), *Geography and geographers*, 4th edn (London: Edward Arnold).

Knowles, R.D. (1993), "Research agendas for transport geography in the 1990s", *Journal of Transport Geography* 1 (1), 3–11.

Lew, A. (1991), "Scenic roads and rural development in the U.S.", *Tourism Recreation Research* 16 (2), 23–30.

Lumsdon, L. (1996), "Future for cycle tourism in Britain", *INSIGHTS*, March, 27–32.

Matley, I. (1976), *The geography of international tourism*, Resource Paper No. 76–1, Association of American Geographers, Washington, DC.

Morrison, A., Young, C., O'Leary, T. and Nadkarni, N. (1996), "Comparative profiles of travellers on cruises and land-based resort vacations", *Journal of Tourism Studies* 7 (2), 15–28.

Moseley, M. (1979), *Accessibility: the rural challenge* (London: Methuen).

Mulligan, C. (1979), "The Snowdon Sherpa: public transport and national park management experiment", in Halsall, D. and Turton B.J. (eds), *Rural transport problems in Britain, papers and discussion* (Transport Geography Study Group), 45–55.

O'Connor, K. (1995), "Airport development in Southeast Asia", *Journal of Transport Geography* 3 (4), 269–79.

Oppermann, M. (1992), *Tourismus in Malaysia, Sozialwissenschafliche studien zu internationalen probemen* (Saarbrucken: Verlag Breitenbach).

Page, S.J. (1993), "European rail travel", *Travel and Tourism Analyst* 1, 5–30.

Page, S.J. (1994a), "European coach travel", *Travel and Tourism Analyst* 1, 4–18.

Page, S.J. (1994b), *Transport for tourism* (London: Routledge).

Page, S.J. (1995), *Urban tourism* (London: Routledge).

Patmore, J. (1983), *Recreation and resources* (Oxford: Blackwell).

Pearce, D. (1979), "Towards a geography of tourism", *Annals of Tourism Research* 6 (3), 245–72.

Pearce, D. (1995), *Tourism today: a geographical analysis* (London: Longman).

Pigram, J. (1983), *Outdoor recreation management* (London: Croom Helm).

Raguraman, K. (1997), "Airlines as instruments for nation building and national identity: case study of Malaysia and Singapore", *Journal of Transport Geography* 5 (4), 239–56.

Rajotte, F. (1975), "The different travel patterns and spatial framework of recreation and tourism", in *Tourism as a factor in national and regional development*, Occasional Paper 4, Department of Geography, Trent University, Peterborough.

Ritchie, B. (1997), "Cycle tourism in the South Island of New Zealand: infrastructure considerations for the twenty-first century", paper presented at the *Trails in the Third Millennium* Conference, Cromwell, New Zealand, December, 325–34.

Schaeffer, K. and Sclar, E. (1975), *Access for all: transportation and urban growth* (London: Penguin).

Schieven, A. (1988), *A study of cycle tourists on Prince Edward island*, unpublished Masters thesis, University of Waterloo, Canada.

Scottish Tourist Board (1991), *Tourism potential of cycling and cycle routes in Scotland* (Edinburgh: Scottish Tourist Board).

Shaw, G. and Williams, A. (1994), *Critical issues in tourism: geographical perspectives* (Oxford: Blackwell).

Shaw, S. (1993), "Hub structures of major US airlines", *Journal of Transport Geography* 1 (1), 47–58.

Smith, S.L.J. (1983), *Recreation geography* (London: Longman).

Smith, S.L.J. and Godbey, G. (1991), "Leisure, recreation and tourism", *Annals of Tourism Research* 18, 85–100.

Sustrans (1995), *The national cycle network: the bidding document to the Millennium Commission* (Bristol: Sustrans).

Sustrans (1997), *The tourism potential of national cycle routes* (London: Tourism Society).

Tolley, R. (1990) (ed.), *The greening of urban transport: planning for walking and cycling in western cities* (London: Belhaven).

Tolley, R. and Turton, B.J. (1987) (eds), *Short-sea crossings and the Channel Tunnel* (Transport Geography Study Group).

Tolley, R. and Turton, B.J. (1995), *Transport systems, policy and planning: a geographical approach* (London: Longman).

Ullman, E.L. (1954), "Geography as spatial interaction", reprinted in Eliot-Hurst, M.E. (ed.) (1974), *Transportation geography: comments and readings* (New York: McGraw-Hill), 27–40.

Urry, J. (1990), *The tourist gaze: leisure and travel in contemporary societies* (London: Sage).

Wager, J. (1967), "Outdoor recreation on common land", *Journal of the Town Planning Institute* 53, 398–403.

Wall, G. (1971), "Car-owners and holiday activities", in Lavery, P. (ed.), *Recreational geography* (Newton Abbot: David and Charles).

Wall, G. (1972), "Socioeconomic variations in pleasure trip patterns: the case of Hull car owners", *Transactions of the Institute of British Geographers* 57, 45–58.

Weiler, B. and Hall, C.M. (1992) (eds), *Special interest tourism* (London: Belhaven).

Williams, S. (1995), *Urban recreation* (London: Routledge).

Wood, K. and House, S. (1991), *The good tourist* (London: Mandarin).

11

SHIPS, PORTS AND BULK FREIGHT TRANSPORT

David Hilling and Michael Browne

Many commodities and products are transported in bulk and sea transport is the dominant mode. Importantly, the economics of bulk transport strongly influence decisions about industrial location, and ports are often a focal point for economic activity. In northern Europe a small number of ports have emerged as major transhipment hubs for a complicated mix of reasons. Among the most significant are: economies of scale in bulk sea transport, government policies and commercial practices.

INTRODUCTION

In maritime transport it has been normal to distinguish between two main types of cargo: bulk and break-bulk (Bird, 1971). The former comprises homogeneous materials without packaging (ores, coal, grain, raw sugar, cement, crude oil and oil products, etc.) usually for a single consignee and destination, while the latter, often known as general cargo, consists of an almost infinite variety of freight, usually in small consignments for numerous consignees and packaged in a variety of bags, bales, boxes, crates and drums of diverse shape and size.

The term "bulk" cargo is sometimes used (Stopford, 1988) for any commodity that may be carried in ship loads – bananas, refrigerated meat, cars – while the term "neo-bulk" is used for cargoes such as forest products when carried in large quantities in a standardized form. The question of shipment size is important in determining the method of movements: large consignments of grain will be carried in bulk but small quantities of rice or malting grain may be bagged. Similarly, small quantities of oil products (e.g. lubricants) may be carried in barrels but large volumes in bulk.

Recent developments in cargo-handling technology for both bulk and break-bulk cargo would suggest a refinement of the above classification. Thus, much of the break-bulk cargo is now carried in a unitized form with individual items grouped or "bulked" into larger, standardized units. This is done by *packaging* (crating, strapping together of plank timber), the use of *pallets* (wooden or metal platforms on which goods can be stacked and strapped), the use of *containers* (internationally standardized boxes) and the lorries, trailers and railway wagons in *roll-on/roll-off* operations. Containers are also used for the bulk rather than bagged movement of commodities such as coffee and cocoa beans; and tank containers are in use for a variety of liquid cargoes such as beer, wine and chemicals. Even lump coal for domestic use is now moved by container between Garston and Northern Ireland to reduce the fragmentation that is a consequence of bulk handling.

Modern Transport Geography: second, revised edition. Edited by Brian Hoyle and Richard Knowles.
© 1998 John Wiley & Sons Ltd.

Within the bulk category the physical characteristics of the cargoes are very different. Each has specific requirements with respect to stowage in the ship, methods of transfer between ship and shore, and the inland transport (Table 11.1). Bird (1971) suggested that the cargo type is reflected in the associated port activity. For the higher-unit-value break-bulk cargo (now mainly in unitized form) a port is usually the "gateway" through which the cargo passes to the hinterland, while for the bulk cargo it acts as a terminal – the cargo is stored and often processed before onward movement. This idea of port-related industries associated with the bulk cargoes is one to which we shall return.

While the unit and possibly the total value of bulk cargoes may not compare with those of general cargo, the sheer volumes involved give them a special significance in transport systems. For the railway systems of many countries the volume, regularity and generally simple movement patterns of the bulk traffic provide one of the few areas of profitable operation; most new railway line construction will have to be justified by the availability of such traffic. Recent examples are the Sishen–Saldanha line for iron ore in South Africa, the Cerrejon line for coal in Colombia and the Carejas line for iron ore in Brazil. The survival and improvement of inland-waterway transport in North America, Europe, the former Soviet Union and China is explained almost completely by the need to move bulk cargoes.

In 1994 (Organization for Economic Co-operation and Development, 1996) out of a total world seaborne trade of 4475 million metric tonnes, oil (crude and products) accounted for 1755 million (39 per cent) and the five principal dry bulk cargoes (iron ore, coal, grain, bauxite/alumina and phosphate rock) a further 1013 million tonnes (23 per cent). It may be argued that raw materials themselves now play only an insignificant part in influencing industrial location in general. Nevertheless, there are a

Table 11.1   Bulk cargoes – handling and movement

Commodity Type	Examples	Ship–Shore Transfer	Inland Movement
1 Liquid			
(a) Normal temperature and pressure	Crude oil, most oil products, wine, slurried coal, limestone	Pump/pipe	Pipeline
(b) Other temperature and pressure	Liquefied gases, heavy oils, latex, bitumen, vegetable oils	Pumps, temperature-controlled pipelines	Temperature-controlled pipelines
2 Dry bulk			
(a) Flowing	Grain, sugar, powders (alumina, cement)	Pneumatic/suction, conveyor, grabs	Pipes, conveyors, barge, rail wagon, lorry
(b) Irregular	Coal, iron ores, non-ferrous ores, phosphate rock	Grab, conveyor	Conveyor, barge, rail wagon, lorry
3 Neo-bulk	Forest products, steel products, baled scrap	Lift-on/lift-off, roll-on/roll-off	Barge, rail wagon, lorry
4 Wheeled units	Cars, lorries, rail wagons	Roll-on/roll-off	
5 Refrigerated/chilled cargo	Meat, fruit, dairy produce	Lift-on/lift-off, conveyor	Rail wagon, lorry

Source: Modified from Stopford (1988).

number of basic heavy industries – mineral and chemical refining most obviously – where the volume of bulk materials does have a profound impact on the location of processing industries and also on shipping markets (Evans, 1994), patterns of trade and port activity, and this provides the justification for the focus adopted in this chapter. If as is sometimes claimed the shipping industry provides a barometer for world economic conditions, then it is the bulk trades which are the dominant influence. In the context of maritime bulk trades, this chapter examines recent changes in transport technology and operations and assesses their impact on the geography of ports and associated industrial activity.

TRANSPORT AND INDUSTRIAL LOCATION

At a local level for small industries it may be that raw materials are available and can be processed at a location that also provides the market. As industries increase in scale and become more complex and organized on a global scale with diverse inputs and outputs in large volumes, this becomes impossible; transport is the prerequisite for spatial interaction. Models of industrial location have also become more complex and greater reality has been introduced by the incorporation of behavioural considerations (Greenhut, 1956; Pred, 1967) but it can still be argued that the "economics of procurement, and production distribution combined is the important – even deciding – location consideration" (Hamilton, 1962).

This is not too far removed from the basic thinking behind Weber's (1909) least-cost industrial location model. Weber has rightly been criticized for the unreality of many of his assumptions about freight rate systems and long-haul economics, labour supply and human behaviour, yet the model still has value in the basic distinctions it identifies between "sporadic", "ubiquitous", "gross" and "pure" raw materials. Thus, fuels and ores, the bulk materials of international trade, are localized (sporadic) while some materials (sands, clays, stone and water) although not ubiquitous are certainly found more

widely. It is also the case that some materials, which Weber termed gross, lose weight in processing while others (pure) do not. This was the basis for his "material index" (the weight of raw material inputs divided by the weight of the end-product) and his suggestion that where there is greater weight loss (high material index) the processing is likely to take place nearer the raw material source. He also recognized that this is a significant influence on location where the total weight of inputs is considerable.

For Weber, therefore, the least-cost location was strongly influenced by the relationship between the cost of assembling the raw materials and the cost of distributing the end-product – essentially the cost differences in the movement of bulk materials and manufactured products. Changes in the transport of bulk materials that are considered below have undoubtedly resulted in a modification of the cost differential.

Hoover (1948) provided a more elaborate analysis of the relationship between transport costs and industrial location. In particular he emphasized the difference between the cost to the transporter and the charge to the shipper (freight rates can and often have been manipulated for political or business reasons), the nature of rate structures (e.g. in relation to distance), and the importance of directional traffic (e.g. low rates on lightly loaded back-hauls – the "Cleveland" effect). He also emphasized the significance of the size of consignments, and the total volume of shipments and the relative transferability of the commodities concerned.

Goods of high value per unit of weight are able to bear higher transport costs than those of low value. Thus, where the transport cost makes up a high proportion of the delivered price of the good, distance will be reduced to a minimum (e.g. aggregates) and the cheapest possible form of transport will be utilized. Many bulk raw materials have low value in relation to weight and will be sensitive to transport costs.

In a situation where a production plant has one source of raw materials and one market (Figure 11.1a), Hoover suggests that generalized procurement and distribution cost curves are likely to produce an ideal location (i.e. least cost in terms of transport) which is at the source of the raw material or the market and not at some intermediate location. If, however, at some intermediate point tranship-ment between transport modes is necessary (Figure 11.1b) it is at this intermediate point that the trans-port costs are likely to be minimized. The act of transhipment itself greatly increases the cost of transport, which is why in recent years so much effort has been put into improving the efficiency and reducing the cost of transhipment for both bulk and break-bulk cargo. For the same reason much indus-try is located at ports (Bird, 1971; Takel, 1974)

especially in the case of heavy industries where the raw materials are in large volumes and transhipment costs therefore high in relation to the unit value of the commodity. Cleveland, America's Lake Erie metallurgical centre, developed as just such a tran-shipment point from lake to rail transport in the movement of iron ore from Lake Superior to Penn-sylvania. The iron and steel industry of Sparrow's Point, Maryland, provides another example.

TRANSPORT OF BULK CARGO

It can be argued that much port industry is a conse-quence of commodities moving in bulk and that for cargo to be moved in this way certain criteria have to be satisfied (Stopford, 1988). Firstly, the com-modity must have physical characteristics that al-low it to be handled and moved in bulk. Secondly, the demand for the commodity must be such that the cost of special ships and handling equipment is justified. The smallest practicable consignment size will effectively be that of the smallest bulk carrier available. There has been rapid expansion of the mini-bulker fleet in recent years (Tinsley, 1984; Heinimann and Cheetham, 1996) with vessels of 1200 to 3000 tonnes replacing the traditional short-sea vessels of 250 to 700 tonnes capacity (Photo-graph 11.1). A figure of 1000 tonnes has been sug-gested as a minimum threshold for bulk handling (Stopford, 1988).

Thirdly, the bulk-shipping operation must be adapted to the overall transport system. In the case of iron ore exports from Carejas in Brazil, the rail-way, port and even the ship (365 000 tonnes) were designed as integral parts of the whole. At the other end of the scale, relief grain has sometimes arrived at African ports with inadequate handling equip-ment, storage and onward transport facilities. Fourthly, the individual consignment size must be geared to the stocks that can be held at either end of the transport link. This will be related to the actual demand at the consuming end, to the storage space available at each end and to the frequency of shipment.

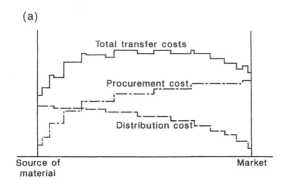

(a)

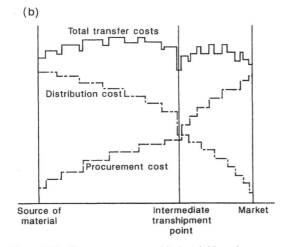

(b)

Figure 11.1 Transport costs and industrial location (a) with through-transport and (b) with transhipment
Source: after Hoover (1948)

Photograph 11.1   Crescent Shipping's *Stridence*
This vessel has a length of 85 m, beam of 11.5 m, draught of 3.45 m and a bridge which can be lowered hydraulically to give a maximum air draught of 4.5 m. These dimensions give a carrying capacity of 1800 tonnes but allow the penetration of inland waterways and access to smaller coastal ports which is necessary in short-sea transhipment trades (Cochrane Shipbuilders)

The availability of storage space is an important determinant of the efficiency and productivity of any port since there is an almost inevitable mismatch between the rate at which cargo arrives and departs by sea and the rate at which it enters and leaves the port on the landward side (Takel, 1974, 1981). Storage space acts as the essential surge-bin to balance the flows on the sea and land sides. This is important for general cargoes, but it becomes critical for large volumes of bulk cargo. Tankers of 250 000 to 350 000 tonnes are now common. Many dry-bulk carriers are in the 100 000 to 150 000 tonnes range and all can be discharged in several days (Gardiner, 1992).

The amount of space for storage is a function of the density of the commodity. A tonne of coal will require 1.4 m³, bauxite 0.7–0.8 m³, alumina 0.6 m³, crude oil 1.2 m³, latex 1.0 m³, vegetable oils 1.1 m³ and cement 0.9–1.5 m³. Storage space must allow for access and handling equipment such as stackers, cranes, conveyors and reclaimers, so that packaged timber will store at 4375 to 7500 tonnes per hectare and iron ore at just under 100 000 tonnes. Additional storage space will be needed where materials are sorted by grade or type (e.g. coals, ores and crude oils) and possibly to accommodate changes consequent upon conditions (e.g. wet and dry ores or coal).

A regular flow of bulk raw materials is essential for any industrial process. Storage is vital in reducing the effects of flow variations but storage replenishment for a given tonnage can be either by frequent small shipments or by less frequent large shipments.

This clearly involves the question of vessel size (Table 11.2) and choice is influenced by an interplay of three main factors: economies of scale; the consignment size in which the cargo is either available at source or acceptable at destination; and the physical constraints provided by the routes, ports and handling equipment (Stopford, 1988).

Shipping is less limited by size constraints than other modes and is able to capitalize on what has been called the "cube law". Simply put, this means that for a doubling of the ships' dimensions the carrying capacity is cubed. Also, the design and construction costs and operating costs (crew, fuel) do not increase in proportion with size. A 500 000 tonne tanker is able to operate with a crew no larger than that needed for a vessel one-twentieth the size, although there will be variations depending on

national flag regulations, level of automation and company organization (e.g. the amount of emphasis on shipboard maintenance).

The cost savings increase with vessel size and voyage distance and this is why there has been such dramatic growth in the size of bulk carriers and tankers in particular. Table 11.3 shows the size of vessels in service, but this conceals the extremes which in the case of oil tankers are in excess of 500 000 tonnes and for dry-bulk carriers around 350 000 tonnes (Photograph 11.2). Many bulk trades are effectively one-way traffic with return voyages in ballast. To reduce this empty running and to increase operational flexibility and revenue there has been increasing use of combination carriers (e.g. OBO – oil/bulk/ore; Conbulk – container/bulk). It is worth noting that in the 1990s many of the ULCCs,

Table 11.2   Factors influencing ship size

Cargo Type	Trade Characteristics	Vessel Size
General cargo		
(a) Conventional	Varied small consignments Numerous consignees Slow handling rates Various routes Numerous ports	Small
(b) Unitized	More uniform cargo Rapid handling Many ports	Small–medium
Dry bulk		
(a) Grain	Small–medium consignments Varied handling rates Many restrictive ports	Small–medium
(b) Ores/coal	Large consignments Long hauls Moderate–good handling rates Specialized terminals at few ports	Medium–large–very large
Liquid		
(a) Crude oil	Very large consignments Long hauls Few main routes Specialized terminals Few ports	Very large–ultra large
(b) Oil products	Smaller "parcels" Numerous consignees Many ports	Small–medium ("handy")

the largest tankers, have been laid up or scrapped (McLellan, 1997) (Photograph 11.2). However, while consignments of such size may be available from oil and ore producers and acceptable at the processing plant, this would not be the case in many bulk trades. Also, there is no financial advantage in using large vessels if the loading and unloading rate is slow and the vessel is kept unduly long in port. A

Table 11.3 Numbers and size of vessels in service, end-1996

Deadweight Tonnage (dwt)	Tankers	Dry-Bulk Carriers	Combination Carriers (OBO)*
<14 999	4 444	282	53
15 000–24 999	250	911	2
25 000–49 999 (Handy)	703	2 330	12
50 000–79 999 (Panamax)	290	922	63
80 000–99 999	388	44	27
100 000–199 999 (Cape)	355	425	79
>200 000	448 (ULCC/VLCC)†	43 (VLOC)†	13

*OBO: oil, bulk, ores.
†VLCC (Very Large Crude Carrier): >200 000 dwt,
 ULCC (Ultra Large Crude Carrier): >300 000 dwt,
 VLOC (Very Large Ore Carrier): >200 000 dwt.
Source: Lloyd's *World Fleet Statistics, 1996.*

Photograph 11.2   The World's largest dry-bulk carrier the *Berge Stahl* (365 000 tonnes)
With a length of 323 m, beam of 54.3 m and loaded draught of 20.5 m, this vessel is on long-term charter hauling iron ore from Ponta da Madeira, Brazil, to Rotterdam (Bergensen Dy Asa)

60 000 tonne and a 250 000 tonne tanker typically pump at rates of 6500 and 18 000 cubic metres per hour respectively (Stopford, 1997).

The ultimate constraint on vessel size must be the physical characteristics of the port (channel depths, turning circles, lock gate dimensions and berth lengths) and the routes along which the ships operate (McLellan, 1997). It is normal now to talk of Panamax (290 m × 31.7 m × 12.8 m) or the largest vessel that can transit the Panama Canal, a bulk carrier of about 55 000 to 65 000 tonnes, and Suezmax where the limit is a draught of 19.5 m which is a loaded tanker of about 150 000 tonnes or a 350 000 tonner in ballast. A tanker of 250 000 tonnes can transit the Malacca Strait on a voyage from the Gulf to Japan but any larger vessel would have to make a much longer voyage by way of the deeper Lombok Strait (Smith, 1973). The port of Rotterdam has had to increase channel depths continuously in order to accommodate ever larger bulk carriers, from 12.5 m in 1960 to 24.8 m in 1996.

The United States, an important exporter of bulk grain and coal, has shallow coastal waters and few bulk terminals with draughts in excess of 13.7 m and many of much less. In the grain trades normal shipments are of about 55 000 tonnes maximum and this may be adequate given the restricting capacity of most receiving ports. However, with vessels of just over 100 000 tonnes the largest that can be handled for coal at Hampton Roads, the United States is at a competitive disadvantage. Further, even where physical conditions might allow, mounting environmental opposition to dredging programmes is making it difficult to increase channel depths.

PORTS AS INDUSTRIAL AREAS

It has been argued (Hoyle and Pinder, 1981) that industrialization at seaports provides the most important sphere in which port functions and urban processes interact. However, this interaction can only be fully understood when seen against the wider relationships that include traffic generation by the hinterland, land-transport systems, foreland links and market factors.

At the outset a port is likely to develop industries relating to the ship itself – ship-building and repairs, sail-making, marine engineering – but as time goes on industries related to the processing of the cargoes are likely to emerge. This may be either the processing of hinterland materials for export or the processing of imports for the hinterland market. The significance of the port as a break-of-bulk point in the transport chain has already been noted. For a variety of economic, technical, administrative and logistical reasons, the act of transhipment provides a basis for the storage and possibly the processing of the commodities concerned. The port may well be as close to the source of the raw materials as an industry can be and any primary processing at the port will provide inputs for secondary processing. The port is ideally located to produce forward and backward linkages and for this reason some planners see ports as potential growth poles (e.g. San Pedro in Côte d'Ivoire and Tema in Ghana) although the spread effects are often slow to develop (Hoyle and Pinder, 1981).

There have been various attempts to classify port industries (Amphoux, 1949; Bird, 1971). A simple distinction can be drawn between: *industrial ports* in which industry has dedicated port installations; *general port industry* in which the industry does not have a dedicated terminal but is nevertheless dependent directly on the port as a break-of-bulk point; and *urban industries* which are attracted to the port because it is a centre of population and a market in its own right. In the first category are oil refineries, large metallurgical processing plants, chemical industries, cement works, paper mills and grain mills; while in the second group are rubber, tobacco and food processing and timber industries. There is clearly a continuum from those industries for which a dockside location is essential to those for which such a location is unnecessary.

The specific location of a particular processing plant in relation to the quayside will also be a function of the physical nature of the cargo and the technology that is required to discharge it from the ship and move it away from the quayside. As a general rule, the more difficult and costly the handling the nearer the processing plant will be (Takel, 1981). However, the handling costs for bulk products are strongly influenced by scale economies and the volumes involved will be a critical factor (Photograph 11.3).

Liquid bulk cargoes can be pumped and piped cheaply and easily over long distances if the volumes are large and this allows for geographical separation of the cargo terminal and the processing plant. Examples include the crude oil pipeline from Loch Long in western Scotland to the refinery at Grangemouth on the east coast and that from Rotterdam to the Ruhr. Movement cost by pipeline for small quantities is relatively expensive and the pro-

cessing of liquid latex, molasses and vegetable oils is often undertaken close to the quayside. Similarly, commodities such as grain or alumina where suction discharge methods are used are likely to be adjacent to the quayside, although at Tema, Ghana, alumina is moved over two kilometres on an enclosed conveyor belt from the port storage to the smelter.

MARITIME INDUSTRIAL DEVELOPMENT AREAS

Industrial development is therefore a normal characteristic of ports although to explain all cityport industrialization in terms of the maritime factor is clearly too simplistic (Verlaque, 1970; Winkelmans,

Photograph 11.3   Le Havre–Antifer, opened in 1976 is a terminal specifically built to accommodate Ultra-Large Cruse Carriers (ULCCs)
ULCCs carry in excess of 500 000 tonnes of oil with draughts of 25.5 m which excluded them from most other ports. Antifer is now underutilized and used mainly by Very Large Crude Carriers (VLCCs) of 250 000 to 350 000 tonnes which provide greater flexibility but higher unit cost of haul than ULCCs (Port of Le Havre)

1980). However, in the late 1960s the idea of a Maritime Industrial Development Area (MIDA) was introduced (ZIP – *Zone Industrielle Portuaire* – in French) for planned industrial development in coastal areas where the dominant influence was maritime. In particular this reflected a vast increase in the scale of processing in the oil, iron and steel industries, the need for much larger quantities of the raw materials and the requirement that the sea transport had to be by the largest possible vessels in order to maximize scale economies. The new MIDAs were therefore associated with revolutionary changes in maritime transport and the adoption of Very Large and Ultra Large Crude Carriers (VLCCs and ULCCs) and ever larger dry-bulk carriers to reduce maritime transport costs (Vigarié, 1981).

The essential requirements of any such MIDA will be deep water, large areas of land suitable for storage and industrial plant and a well-developed land transport system. In a study undertaken for the National Ports Council in Britain (Peston and Rees, 1970) the specific criteria adopted were 15.2 m water depth and 2000 ha of land. Four stages of MIDA development have been identified (Vigarié, 1981). The first generation of MIDAs were based on what Vigarié has termed the Rhine model. In Rotterdam, starting in 1958 with the Botlek scheme, there has been planned industrial and port development extending seawards through Europoort and Maasvlakte and embracing an area of 10 000 ha with heavy emphasis on oil refining and petrochemicals. A 1955–65 port development plan for Antwerp was associated with new oil refineries, a wide range of chemical and petrochemical industries (Bayer, Monsanto, Essochem, BASF) and vehicle assembly. In France the 1965–70 port plan resulted in large-scale port–industrial development of iron and steel, oil refining and petrochemicals at Dunkerque (Tuppen, 1981), of oil refining, chemicals, metal refining, wood processing and vehicle assembly at Le Havre (Gay, 1981), and iron and steel, oil and chemicals at Fos (Tuppen, 1975). In Japan, the need to reclaim land from the sea for large-scale industrial development combined with the need to import nearly all basic raw materials and fuels resulted in port development plans for 1965–9 and 1971–5 which created large MIDA areas (*kombinato*) such as Mizushima and Kashima (Rimmer, 1984).

There was a reaction to the large-scale industrial development involved in the MIDA on both social and environmental grounds and the recession of the later 1970s slowed their growth. The second-generation developments, as a consequence, have placed less emphasis on heavy industries and more on lighter secondary and tertiary activities including warehousing and distribution. In Rotterdam the development of a series of Distriparks typifies this trend and whereas some 84 per cent of land in early Japanese MIDA developments was devoted to industry the percentage has now dropped to as little as 24 (Vigarié, 1981). MIDA development is also found on a smaller scale in some Third World countries: Vigarié's third-generation MIDA. The varied industrial development at Tema, Ghana (Hilling, 1966) provides an example, as do the port-related phosphate industry at Gabès, Tunisia and plans for MIDA development in Thailand (Robinson, 1981).

If in the cases cited, port-related industrial development has been a result of design and planning, in Britain such areas may be seen as a product of historical process and default. On the Tees, Humber, Thames, Southampton Water and Severn there are elements of port-related industry but at no place has the development been planned in an integrated manner or on a very large scale. At Port Talbot and Redcar existing iron- and steel-works with inadequate ore importing terminals were given new deeper-water berths. In 1996 Port Talbot's approach channel depth was dredged to 16.7 m to allow access for 150 000 tonne bulk carriers. Spatially separated oil refineries were established on Humberside, and on the Thames a planned port–airport–industrial development at Maplin did not find favour with the government. The Peston and Rees (1970) report was quietly buried.

Vigarié's fourth stage of MIDA development is one in which some of the traditional heavy industries are maintained but in which there are also a larger number of industries based on imported, semifinished materials and products, possibly of a high-technology nature and geared to export. There are already signs of this type of development.

Traditionally, when goods are off-loaded from the ship they become subject to customs duties. Some ports, Hamburg for example, have always claimed to be "free" ports at which goods can be landed and processed before customs duties are payable. Many ports are now creating such "duty-free" areas. They take various forms, of which the simplest is a warehouse operating under customs bond – duties are paid on the wine or tobacco, for example, only when they are taken from the *bonded warehouse*. The free zone might consist of no more than one waterside factory at which goods can be landed, processed and re-exported, all without customs duties being paid. A number of factories might constitute an *export processing zone*, while additional functions such as storage and distribution would produce a *special economic zone*. The extreme case would be a full free port or comprehensive free-trade zone. Such free-port or foreign-trade zones form a hierarchy based on areal extent and range of functions. The object of such free zones is to attract industry and create employment but they are clearly based on the port's break-of-bulk function and an extension of the MIDA concept. In Britain, Liverpool and Southampton have developed free-port zones with product processing, transhipment and distribution functions; and in the 1980s the United States initiated a Foreign Trade Zone (FTZ) programme and a number of ports now have such zones, either for a single trade (e.g. Miami for Latin America) or for general warehousing and industrial purposes (e.g. New York). Customs-free zones of one type or another have become a common feature of ports worldwide.

As a consequence of the developments in sea transport and associated port land use described above, there is increasing differentiation between ports. New criteria for port selection are leading to the emergence of new port hierarchies based on ability to accommodate the largest vessels. As in air transport and distribution in general new hub-and-spoke patterns of activity are emerging.

EXAMPLES OF BULK TRADES

Having considered the transport of bulk cargo, its influence on industrial location and the significance of ports as industrial areas, it is appropriate to bring this together by looking at some of the principal bulk trades in greater detail. The two chosen for further analysis are the coal and grain trades (in the latter case non-grain animal feeds are also discussed). In all these trades, transhipment plays a role in the bulk-transport system but its significance varies considerably – from a UK perspective, transhipment is more important in the coal trade than in the grain trade.

Importantly the transhipment act itself also varies. For example, transhipment may involve the transfer of cargo direct from a large mother ship to smaller feeder vessels or, more typically, it involves transfer to the quayside or storage area for some degree of processing and then for subsequent shipment in a smaller feeder vessel. The degree of storage and processing has important implications for the role of the transhipment port as an industrial area; the more bulk cargo that is transhipped and processed the greater the opportunity for the port area to develop a wider industrial base as related industries decide to locate their activities nearby (Photograph 11.4).

The Coal Trade

World seaborne trade in coal amounts to nearly 400 million tonnes a year, with about 45 per cent of the trade being coking coal which is used in the production of steel and 55 per cent steam coal used primarily for generating electricity in thermal power stations (Organization for Economic Co-operation and Development, 1996). However, this represents only a small proportion of world production, since most coal is not traded internationally but is used to satisfy domestic needs.

The major coal-exporting countries are the USA, Canada, Australia and South Africa and import requirements are greatest in Western Europe and Japan, which between them account for up to 65 per cent of all import tonnage (*International Bulk*

Photograph 11.4   Completed in 1985, Le Havre's 100 ha multipurpose bulk terminal
This can accommodate ships of up to 160 000 tonnes and provides open storage for 400 000 tonnes of coal, facilities for screening and pulverizing coal for local industry and export, and covered storage for grain substitutes for the animal feed industry. Ships and inland waterway craft can be loaded and unloaded at 1500 tonnes/hour (Port of Le Havre)

Journal, 1995a). Clearly this pattern of supply and demand results in long-distance transport by sea. On these deep-sea routes the large bulk carrier plays a key role: vessels of over 80 000 dwt (deadweight tonnes) carry over 50 per cent of coal transported by sea and the general trend in the long-distance coal trades is to use ships in excess of 100 000 dwt. Large ships dominate the world coal trade reflecting the importance of economies of scale in vessel size. As Table 11.4 indicates, the potential economies of scale are significant: almost doubling the size of the ship from 65 000 to 120 000 dwt only increases total costs by 26 per cent. In addition, both the long ocean voyages and the relatively predictable nature of the coal trade promote the use of very large ships. However, demand does vary from year to year and this has implications for the relative importance of

the various exporting areas. For example, US exports dropped to their lowest level for many years at just 56.4 million tonnes in 1994 but demand rebounded strongly in 1995 to 70 million tonnes ensuring that the USA remained the second most important exporter of coal after Australia at 135 million tonnes in 1995 (*International Bulk Journal*, 1995a).

Turning from coal trade at the world level to trade concerning the UK highlights the impact on bulk-freight transport of factors such as national policy and commercial practices. Until the 1970s UK imports of steam coal were insignificant – domestic production was perfectly adequate to satisfy the needs of the Central Electricity Generating Board (CEGB) and since both coal and electricity were nationalized industries there was little incentive to

Table 11.4   Economies of scale in bulk shipping

Ship Size (dwt)	Operating Cost ($'000)	Bunker Costs* ($'000)	Total Cost ($'000)	Cost per dwt ($ p.a.)
40 000	1 315	1 890	3 205	80
65 000	1 540	2 295	3 385	59
120 000	1 780	3 051	4 831	40
170 000	2 120	3 780	5 900	35

*Assuming 270 days at sea per annum at 14 knots.
Source: Stopford (1988), based on Drewry (Shipping Consultants) Ltd (1985).

change their historically close relationship. The CEGB was for many years by far British Coal's most important customer accounting for 77 per cent of purchases (MacKerron, 1988). At the end of the 1980s the CEGB continued to have a binding agreement to take 95 per cent of its coal requirements from British Coal although much of this was at a high price compared with the prevailing price of coal in the international market. Privatization of both the CEGB and British Coal was expected to weaken the relationship between the two nationalized industries and the consumption of coal by the generators has fallen steadily since 1991 largely as a result of the increased use of nuclear power and natural gas. However, at 60 million tonnes in 1995, use of coal at power stations still represents 77 per cent of total coal consumption in the UK.

As a result of contractual agreements and the close relationship between the CEGB and British Coal, purchases of steam coal from abroad remained at low levels throughout the 1980s; even in 1985 following the miners' strike only 4.4 million tonnes were imported. However, from 1990 imports of steam coal started to rise. In 1991 some 9 million tonnes were imported and this increased to just over 11 million tonnes in 1992 (although by 1995 imports had again fallen to 6.3 million tonnes). Most imported steam coal is transported over long distances and much comes under contract from the USA, Colombia and South Africa. Poland is the only truly short sea source although much of the coal imported from, say, the USA arrives in the UK on board a small vessel from a mainland European port as a result of transhipment. For example, in 1986, 3.7

million tonnes of steam coal was imported and an estimated 2 million tonnes of this was transhipped. In the 1990s transhipment volumes have continued at about the same level meaning that, since total imports have risen, the importance of transhipment has to some extent declined.

Much of the transhipped coal moves through two major terminals in the Netherlands: EMO in Rotterdam and OBA in Amsterdam. These terminals are owned by firms that are experienced in transhipment operations to various European destinations including Scandinavia, the Baltic and Germany. They are also large-scale operations taking Cape Size (120 000–140 000 dwt) bulk carriers (EMO can handle coal carriers up to 180 000 dwt), and since they handle very high volumes of cargo, they benefit from scale economies (Dekker, 1995).

However, it has been argued (Browne *et al.*, 1989) that rather than transhipment being seen as a second-best alternative the development of Rotterdam as a European hub for bulk coal movements may provide coal-using industries with a number of significant advantages:

1. *A stock of different grades.* Industrial customers increasingly require various consignments of different grades of coal. These may come from different mining areas. The major terminals, such as those in Rotterdam, can hold stocks of these different grades only a few hundred miles from the customer and in a strategic location, relatively safe from industrial disruption.
2. *A total quality approach from the terminal.* Added value in the forms of screening, blending and

washing is provided for much of the current throughput at the main Rotterdam terminals. These activities require specialist skills and equipment which may only be justified at very high levels of use – so focusing on a hub terminal is a logical strategy.

3. *Reduced storage space required.* Small consignments can be moved from the transhipment point to the destination but these could not be moved economically directly from the source.
4. *Minimizing the overland haul.* Because small vessels are employed for bulk transport after transhipment, it is usually possible to get close to the final destination because there will be a much wider range of ports and terminals able to accept relatively small vessels.

While some or all of these factors may influence decision-makers it is likely that total transport costs will be the most important consideration in comparing transhipment with direct shipment, but the comparison is difficult. Fluctuating costs, particularly freight rates, can radically alter the balance of advantage between transhipment and direct shipping. Lower freight costs achieved by using very large bulk carriers may be largely nullified by extra costs for handling during transhipment.

The hypothetical model shown in Table 11.5 illustrates how in the late 1980s transhipment could be a preferred option for a UK coal importer and shows how changes in handling and transport costs can strongly influence the decision. The model compares rates for coal from Australia and since no small vessels would be used on such a lengthy voyage the options are:

(a) Large bulk carriers transhipping at continental European ports with transfer to final UK destinations on small bulkers. The model considers three typical sizes for large bulk carriers.
(b) Panamax vessels sailing directly to the UK with land or sea transfer to the final destination. The model considers two typical Panamax-size vessels.

Using the costs illustrated, transhipment appears to be the cheaper option. The price ranges per tonne are: (a) for transhipment, $13.75–$20.00; and (b) for direct shipment, $20.00–$23.00. But it is evident that there is some susceptibility to minor fluctuations

Table 11.5 Transport and handling cost model – coal from Australia to UK*

(a) Transhipment

Vessel	Freight Rate: Port of Origin to Transhipment Port	Transhipment Port Handling Cost	Freight Rate: Transhipment Port to UK Power Station	Total Transport Cost per Tonne
110 000 dwt	12.0	3.00	3.00–5.00	18.00–20.00
140 000 dwt	8.15–10.00	3.00	3.00–5.00	14.15–18.00
160 000 dwt	7.75–8.00	3.00	3.00–5.00	13.75–16.00

(b) Direct shipment

Vessel	Freight Rate: Port of Origin to UK Port	Freight Rate: UK Port to Power Station	Total Transport Cost per Tonne
60 000 dwt	20.00	2.00–3.00	22.00–23.00
70 000 dwt	18.00	2.00–3.00	20.00–21.00

*All costs in US$ per tonne of cargo. UK stevedoring costs are assumed to be the same in each case and are therefore omitted from the calculations. The ocean freight rates are based on actual fixtures recorded by Lloyd's Maritime Information Services in 1988.
Source: Browne *et al.* (1989).

since the top of the range for (a) is the same as the bottom of the range for (b).

With this narrow margin there is clearly sensitivity to cost changes in all parts of the model. Continental handling costs rose from $2.50 per tonne in 1984 to $3.00 in 1988 and further rises would make transhipment less competitive. The cost of the small bulker will vary with market fluctuations and there is also a wide difference between rates for geared and gearless vessels. Most significant of all are fluctuations in the charter market for deep-sea bulk carriers. While upward or downward freight rate trends will be approximately followed by the various sizes of vessel, the key to the model as presented here may be the differential between rates for Panamax and large bulk carriers. The narrower the gap, the weaker the case for transhipment from a large vessel. Indeed, fluctuations in rates in this way may be partly responsible for changes in the volume of bulk transhipment from year to year.

Yet it is not only changes in freight rates and ship- or cargo-handling technology that will affect the volume of imported coal. Changes of an institutional type may be just as important: in this case the ownership of one of the main coal buyers, the CEGB. Privatization of the CEGB and the inevitable loosening of the coal-supply agreements between the generating companies and British Coal does indeed seem to have led to an increase in coal imports during the early 1990s.

The future level of steam coal imports will very much depend on how competitive domestically produced coal is with overseas supplies. While the international price has historically been low it is important to note that the market for internationally traded steam coal is quite small (although it has risen from 134 million tonnes in 1985 to 231 million tonnes in 1995). The total world volume of traded steam coal is about four times total UK demand and large-scale buying by the UK electricity industry could cause an increase in price. On the other hand new, low-cost sources including Indonesia, Venezuela, Sumatra, Borneo and China could increase supply. British coal prices could also change significantly as high-cost pits close and low-cost areas increase production following privatization of British Coal.

Within an uncertain picture for the coal trade as a whole, the volume of transhipment is very difficult to forecast. The level of utilization of larger-than-Panamax bulkers for coal is increasing. Until the early 1990s there were no common-user terminals in the UK able to accept a ship of this size. However the picture is changing and PowerGen (one of the privatized successor companies to the CEGB) has enhanced its ability to purchase imported coal by investing in import facilities at the Kingsnorth power station and in a new import terminal at Liverpool. The Liverpool terminal (commissioned in 1993) enables Panamax vessels to be discharged at the rate of 25 000 tonnes per day (*International Bulk Journal*, 1995b). At Rotterdam (Photograph 11.5), floating equipment is often used to handle coal and grain shipments.

The Grain Trade

The grain trade provides a contrast to coal in the size of ships used, the key trading routes and the scope for transhipment. When used in the context of bulk shipping the term "grain" comprises a variety of produce ranging from wheat to soya beans. Wheat and maize dominate seaborne trade in grains, accounting for almost 90 per cent of tonnages shipped (Lloyd's of London, 1990). The major exporting regions are North America, Argentina and Australia and the main trade routes are shown in Table 11.6. World trade in grain ran at about 200 million tonnes a year during the early 1990s. However, trade volumes are more erratic than in the case of coal, since variations in weather conditions and harvests can have a dramatic impact on supply and demand. This volatility and changes in the importance of particular areas have implications for freight rates. For example, in 1996 the high level of grain exports from the USA resulted in increased demand for Panamax-sized vessels while maize exports from South Africa increased the demand for larger ships (Reilly, 1997).

Almost half (48 per cent) of world trade in grain is transported on ships of less than 40 000 dwt and only 6 per cent is moved on those over 80 000 dwt; this is

Photograph 11.5   Floating equipment at Rotterdam allows flexibility of handling
Cargoes can be transferred both to shore for storage and sorting before onward movement (coal in background) and
direct to barges alongside bulk carriers at anchor in stream (grain in foreground) (Interstevedoring, Rotterdam)

Table 11.6   Major trade routes for grain shipments

Route	Volume (billion tonne-miles)
United States to Far East (including 203 btm to Japan)	345
United States to Europe	205
Argentina to Europe	74
United States to Other Americas	64
Canada to Europe	45
Australia to Far East	32
Canada to Far East	32

Source: Lloyd's Maritime Atlas (1990).

a very different pattern from that found in the coal trade and one which clearly has implications for the need to tranship cargo. Although there are economies of scale in the bulk shipment of grain, just as there are for coal shipments, a number of factors limit the use of very large vessels. Among the most important are:

1. *Draught limitations in many of the export loading ports.* For example, the depth of the Mississippi is a critical limiting factor on the optimum ship size for use in trades between the USA and Europe.
2. *The grain trade has been described as opportunistic*, reflecting the vagaries of supply and demand together with its seasonality. This degree of uncertainty makes it difficult to schedule the use of very large vessels. Often it may be better to have the opportunity to use, say, five 30 000 dwt ships rather than one 150 000 dwt vessel. The use of several smaller vessels means grain shippers and buyers can respond in a more flexible way to changing market conditions.
3. *The complex market structure.* Shipments are often made up of consignments from a number of different sellers, which leads to coordination difficulties for very large shipments.

European trade in grain has been much influenced by the agricultural policies of the European Union (EU) and the impact of these policies on the UK has been marked. Since the early 1970s the UK grain trade has experienced substantial changes in both volume and direction resulting from British entry to the EU and the increase in grain production, which has turned the UK from a net grain importer to a net exporter. Between 1970 and 1975 the UK imported up to 9 million tonnes of grain annually, principally from distant countries such as the USA and Canada. But the expansion of UK production led to a dramatic fall in imports and by 1980 they were down to 5 million tonnes with a further fall to 3 million tonnes in 1985 and remaining at broadly this level since then (Department of Transport, 1988; Central Statistical Office, 1996).

UK exports rose to over 2.5 million tonnes by 1980 and continued to increase so that by 1985 they were almost 4 million tonnes and reached 5 million tonnes in 1994. While much of this goes to other EU countries, markets have also been established elsewhere in Europe, North Africa and the Middle East (Department of Transport, 1988; Sewell, 1995). Most of the European cargo is shipped in small vessels from small ports near the production areas.

Larger vessels had been required in earlier years to serve more distant markets economically and lack of grain exporting facilities for larger vessels in the UK had led to transhipment via the Continent. More recently, however, facilities for direct shipment of larger volumes have been available and grain exports in vessels up to 52 000 dwt can be accommodated at Southampton and up to 55 000 dwt at Tilbury Grain Terminal (*International Bulk Journal,* 1995b).

The requirement of some grain buyers for the grain to be bagged has in the past encouraged transhipment. Saudi Arabian buyers of barley for animal feed form a significant part of the non-European export market and throughout the 1980s they purchased bagged grain for ease of distribution locally. This was shipped in bulk to Antwerp and Ghent, which have a good reputation for bagging, then continued break-bulk to Saudi Arabia. This system also enabled small shipments from small UK ports to be grouped on the Continent for sale as larger consignments.

The case for transhipment is more marginal for grain than for coal as very large bulk carriers are not normally used. A large freight-rate differential between vessels able to call in the UK directly and those used in a transhipment operation would be necessary for transhipment to be cheaper. The following example shows that this may only rarely be the case. In 1990 the charter rates per tonne for grain shipments from the US Gulf to Europe varied considerably (Lloyd's List, 1991). The range for two different sizes of vessel were quoted as: (i) for a 50 000 to 60 000 dwt vessel, $11.25 to $16.00; and (ii) for a 70 000 to 85 000 dwt vessel, $11.00 to $14.50. While the largest differential, $5.00, would cover the cost of transhipment and onward carriage from the European continent to the UK, in most cases direct shipment to the UK would have been the cheaper option. In more recent years the differential in rates has generally been lower, providing a further incentive for direct shipment (Photograph 11.6).

Non-Grain Animal Feed

One of the consequences of higher levels of UK grain exports was a shortage of domestically

Photograph 11.6   Le Havre's Quai Hermann du Pasquier grain terminal
This has silo storage for 30 000 tonnes and shed storage for 47 000 tonnes and can be used as an import or export facility for bulk carriers up to 30 000 tonnes. The terminal is equipped for transhipment to and from road vehicles, trains and barges (Port of Le Havre)

produced grain for animal feed. Exchange rates coupled with EU agricultural policy made it attractive for UK compound feed manufacturers to import non-grain substitutes for UK grain. This became a large part of bulk import transhipment during the 1980s (Browne *et al.*, 1989).

Compound feed manufacturers produce several products such as oil cake, cattle feeds, pig feeds and poultry feeds. Each product has perhaps seven or eight main ingredients together with small quantities of additives. The main ingredients can be grains such as barley and maize but increasingly a variety of non-grains is used. This includes soya, sunflower, copra, corn gluten and tapioca. Non-grain animal feeds are imported from distant sources to Europe in approximately the following proportions (Browne *et al.*, 1989): North America, 40 per cent; Far East,

especially Thailand, 30 per cent; South America, especially Brazil and Argentina, 30 per cent. Large vessels are often used, particularly from the Far East where single loads of up to 140 000 tonnes may be exported.

The compound-feed business is intensely competitive consisting of numerous buyers and sellers and little evidence of brand loyalty. The prices of the main raw materials fluctuate wildly but to some extent they are substitutes for one another. This causes manufacturers to buy late and use linear programming techniques to calculate the right mix at lowest prices. Rotterdam has traditionally been the dominant market place for the compound-animal-feed business and most price quotations are based on "cif Rotterdam" (cif = cost, insurance, freight). The size of the market allows buyers and sellers to trade with anonymity and enables last-minute buying because of the large volumes available. It is also a traditional main grain port able to receive the largest vessels.

There is a case for transhipment in the compound-feed industry since each shipload is split and sold in lots of 10 000 tonnes or less to different compound-feed companies and each of these buyers may need only 800 to 2000 tonnes delivered at a time. Each consignment may represent just one of, say, eight ingredients needed to make one of a range of animal-feed products. It would clearly not be practicable to ship such small amounts direct from the distant country of origin. The need to divide and then combine various bulk commodities in this way provides a strong rationale for the use of a central hub such as Rotterdam. Furthermore, compound-feed manufacturers prefer to buy in Europe. A purchase made in South America may have become relatively expensive by the time it reaches Europe because of price fluctuations. This could make the firm's product uncompetitive since 80 per cent of compound-feed manufacturers' total costs are raw materials.

An additional factor that favours the use of a major hub port is concerned with the behaviour of the sellers. Feedstuff shippers in, say, Chicago may prefer to use the major ports and terminals for large consignments of compound feed: they are worried that if only part of the shipload can be sold during the voyage then at a small destination port they will not find the buying infrastructure necessary to deal with the unsold part of the cargo.

As a result of this complex mix of commercial, locational and technical advantages Rotterdam became established as the focal point in Europe for the compound animal-feed business. However, the future for grain and compound-animal-feed transhipment (and by implication the role of Rotterdam) depends to a considerable extent on EU policy. Reform of the Common Agricultural Policy and the EU/USA agreements on subsidized cereal exports in 1994/95 will encourage a reduction in EU grain exports which will in turn reduce export transhipment. As larger vessels can now be handled in the UK, grain export transhipment is likely to fall anyway. In addition, countries currently demanding bagged grain are likely to be able to handle bulk cargo in the future, which in turn will reduce transhipment caused by the use of continental bagging plants.

Furthermore, if grain cannot be exported because of the EU/USA agreements on subsidies, then the EU surplus will have to be dealt with within the EU and it could be used for animal feed. The GATT agreement entered into force in 1995/96 and the Blair House Agreement between the US and the EU requires the EU to achieve a 21 per cent reduction in subsidized exports over six years. One consequence of this will be for a continuing fall in the demand for imported compound animal feed and a reduced role for transhipment. The structural market decline in what are known as "agribulks" has led the largest agribulk handling business in Rotterdam (EBS) to plan for a reduction in handling capacity of around one-third (*International Bulk Journal*, 1996).

Significant investments in UK import facilities may also diminish the attractiveness of transhipment of animal feed via Rotterdam. Import and storage facilities at Bristol allow for the import of over 1 million tonnes of animal feed a year. In Hull, regular shipments of up to 24 000 tonnes of animal feed are received from the Americas and Indian subcontinent and in Newport vessels of up to 35 000 dwt can now be accommodated at the new animal feeds terminal at the Alexandra South Dock (*International Bulk Journal*, 1995b).

CONCLUSIONS

The development of bulk transport by sea has been strongly influenced by technology. Economies of scale have been achieved through the construction of larger ships and this in turn has affected the optimum parcel size, vessel routings and port selection criteria. Port selection is especially relevant because of the strong link between ports and industrial activity. In some cases this activity has been the result of deliberate government policy, as in the case of MIDAs, while in others it merely reflects the commercial and economic advantages of locating activities at the transhipment point. However, technology and vessel design are by no means the only factors at work to influence the patterns of the world bulk trades; government policy, commercial buying practices and physical constraints such as water depth in ports also play a key role.

The transhipment point for bulk cargo may become the focal point for further processing of the bulk commodity. The processing of a cargo at the intermediate transhipment point is of considerable importance. When coal is transhipped it may be screened, washed, blended and graded at the transhipment port, while animal feeds may be tested or inspected during transhipment. Indeed, the scope to add value to the product or cargo at the transhipment port is important to the terminal operators for it enables them to earn revenue, to differentiate their services from those of their competitors and to reduce unit prices by spreading fixed costs over greater terminal throughput.

Although there are important similarities between the bulk shipment and transhipment of grain and coal, there are also important differences. These differences arise in large part from the different pattern of supply and demand and the different type and size of vessel used to service these major world bulk trades. Since coal is shipped over long distances in very large vessels the use of a north European hub at Rotterdam is often the lowest-cost choice. Transhipment by feeder vessel can then be made to smaller ports in the UK and Scandinavia located near the ultimate consuming destination, frequently a power station. A coal-producing country such as the UK has had little need for imported coal, but changes in the ownership of utilities – the privatization of the CEGB – means that the desire to purchase coal on the low-cost open world market may override the traditional arrangements for using almost entirely British coal.

In contrast with the coal trade, grain is shipped in much smaller vessels and transhipment is, as a consequence, far less important. Interestingly in the case of non-grain animal feed, some of the same arguments that lead to the hub concept in coal movement can be applied; again, a logical outcome is increased transhipment. This is firstly because there are physical limitations to the ports which can accommodate these large ships and secondly because there are economic advantages in having a central stockholding point and then distributing smaller parcels of cargo to the buyers. This enables buyers to minimize their inventory without sacrificing to too great an extent the safety or security of buffer stocks held relatively close at hand.

Until recently the individual elements of the transport chain, while functionally related, were operated in a largely disparate way. In the bulk trades, as in maritime transport in general, there is now a realization that the effective operation of through-transport from the producer via the processing industry to the consumer requires a high level of organizational interdependence. It is realistic now, as it has not been before, to view bulk transport as a "system" embracing not only the movement but also the intermediate handling, storage and processing of the commodities involved. It follows from the variety of decision-makers and external influences involved that this system is highly dynamic.

In bulk as in general cargo trades the reduction of inventory and storage costs by just-in-time (JIT) shipments seems set to increase in significance. It seems likely that closer economic integration and the removal of customs barriers in the European Union will stimulate the reorganization of industrial production and distribution and strengthen hub-and-spoke patterns. This is clearly linked with the economies derived from the combined use of the largest possible ocean carriers and efficient mini-bulkers on feeder services. However, as this chapter has demonstrated, within this broad framework, the responses in different trades will vary in detail depending on the nature of the commodities involved, the organization of the processing industries and the geography of the market for their products.

REFERENCES

Amphoux, M. (1949), "Les fonctions portuaires" *Revue de la Porte Océane* (Le Havre), No. 54, 19–22.

Bird, J.H. (1971), *Seaports and seaport terminals* (London: Hutchinson).

Browne, M., Doganis, R. and Bergstrand, S. (1989), *Transhipment of UK trade* (London: British Ports Federation & Department of Transport).

Central Statistical Office (1996), *Annual abstract of statistics 1995* (London: HMSO).

Dekker, J. (1995), "Over the coals", *Port of Rotterdam Magazine* 34 (6), 13–17.

Department of Transport (1988), *Short sea bulk shipping: an analysis of UK performance* (London: Department of Transport).

Drewry (Shipping Consultants) Ltd (1985), *Dry bulk operating costs, past, present and future* (London).

Evans, J.J. (1994), "An analysis of efficiency of bulk shipping markets", *Maritime Policy and Management* 21 (4), 311–29.

Gardiner, R. (ed.) (1992), *The shipping revolution* (London: Conway).

Gay, F.J. (1981), "Urban decision makers and the development of an industrial port: the example of Le Havre", in Hoyle, B.S. and Pinder, D.A. (eds), *Cityport industrialisation and regional development: spatial analysis and planning strategies* (Oxford: Pergamon), 201–22.

Greenhut, M.L. (1956), *Plant location in theory and practice* (Chapel Hill: University of North Carolina).

Hamilton, F.I. (1962), "Models of industrial location", in Chorley, R. and Haggett, P. (eds), *Socio-economic models in geography* (London: Methuen), 362–424.

Heinimann, M. and Cheetham, C. (1986), *Modern river sea traders* (Teignmouth: Cheetham and Heinimann).

Hilling, D. (1966), "Tema – the geography of a new port", *Geography* 52 (2), 111–12.

Hoover, E.M. (1948), *The location of economic activity* (New York: McGraw-Hill).

Hoyle, B.S. and Pinder, D.A. (eds) (1981), *Cityport industrialisation and regional development: spatial analysis and planning strategies* (Oxford: Pergamon).

International Bulk Journal (1995a), "Trade review – seaborne coal", *International Bulk Journal* 15 (3), 5–9.

International Bulk Journal (1995b), "International report – UK", *International Bulk Journal* 15 (3), 21–3.

International Bulk Journal (1996), "OBA sell-off falls through", *International Bulk Journal,* 16 (10), 75.

Lloyd's List (1991), *Weekly freight table* (London: Lloyd's List).

Lloyd's of London (1990), *Lloyd's maritime atlas* (London: Lloyd's).

MacKerron, G. (1988), "The international steam coal market and UK coal", in *Privatising electricity: impact on the UK energy market* (London: Institute for Fiscal Studies).

McLellan, R.G. (1997), "Bigger vessels: how big is too big?", *Maritime Policy and Management* 24 (2), 193–211.

Organization for Economic Co-operation and Development (1996), *Maritime transport* (Paris: OECD).

Peston, M.H. and Rees, R. (1970), *Maritime industrial development areas* (London: National Ports Council).

Pred, A. (1967), *Behaviour and location* (Lund: University of Lund).

Reilly, C. (1997), "Strong recovery in final quarter of 1996", *International Bulk Journal* 17 (1), 56–7.

Rimmer, P.J. (1984), "Japanese seaports: economic development and state intervention", in Hoyle, B.S. and Hilling, D. (eds), *Seaport systems and spatial change* (Chichester: Wiley), 99–133.

Robinson, R. (1981), "Industrialization, new ports and spatial development strategies in less-developed countries: the case of Thailand", in Hoyle, B.S. and Pinder, D.A. (eds), *Cityport industrialisation and regional development: spatial analysis and planning strategies* (Oxford: Pergamon), 305–21.

Sewell, T. (1995), "UK grain – better quality, better exports, less gloom", *International Bulk Journal* 15 (3), 15.

Smith, S.R. (1973), "Ocean borne shipments of petroleum and the impact of straits", *Maritime Studies and Management* 1 (2), 119–30.

Stopford, M. (1988), *Maritime economics* (London: Unwin Hyman).

Stopford, M. (1997), *Maritime economics*, 2nd edn (London: Routledge).

Takel, R.E. (1974), *Industrial port development* (Bristol: Scientechnica).

Takel, R.E. (1981), "The spatial demands of ports and related industry and their relationship with the community", in Hoyle, B.S. and Pinder, D.A. (eds), *Cityport industrialisation and regional development: spatial analysis and planning strategies* (Oxford: Pergamon), 47–68.

Tinsley, D. (1984), *Short-sea bulk traders* (London: Fairplay).

Tuppen, J.N. (1975), "Fos – Europort of the south?", *Geography* 60 (3), 213–17.

Tuppen, J.N. (1981), "The role of Dunkerque in the industrial economy of Nord Pas de Calais", in Hoyle, B.S. and Pinder, D.A. (eds), *Cityport industrialisation and regional development: spatial analysis and planning strategies* (Oxford: Pergamon), 365–79.

Verlaque, C. (1970), *L'industrialisation des ports de la Méditerranée occidentale* (Montpellier: L'Université).

Vigarié, A. (1981), "Maritime industrial development areas: structural evolution and implications for regional development", in Hoyle, B.S. and Pinder, D.A. (eds), *Cityport industrialisation and regional development: spatial analysis and planning strategies* (Oxford: Pergamon), 23–36.

Weber, A. (1909), *Uber den standort der industrien*, transl. Friedrich, C.J. (1929), *Alfred Weber's theory of the location of industries* (Chicago: University of Chicago Press).

Winkelmans, W. (1980), "Transport and location: an inquiry into principal evolutions", in Polak, J.B. and Kamp, J.B. (eds), *Changes in the field of transport studies* (The Hague: Nijhoff), 202–11.

12

INTERMODAL TRANSPORTATION

Brian Slack

In the space of 40 years intermodal transport has spread throughout the world. The marriage of containerization with the through-transport concept has resulted in cargo flows being organized from door to door across several different modes. In this chapter the growth of intermodal transport is treated as a process of spatial diffusion. Some of the evolving characteristics of intermodalism and their impacts are reviewed. The chapter concludes by discussing some of the unresolved challenges that intermodal transport presents to national governments, regional economies and local interests.

INTRODUCTION

Intermodal transport is one of the most dynamic sectors of the transportation industry today.[1] Founded upon a number of technological innovations, intermodalism has spread widely throughout the world during recent decades. Although many of the technologies associated with these innovations have been relatively simple in concept, their impacts have been extensive and profound. The nature of inter-port competition has been changed, the role of shipping lines in the organization and control of trade has been transformed, inland transport flows have been restructured, and the relationships between transport and economic development have been modified and thrown into sharper focus. Intermodalism as a global diffusion process and as an element in the condition of modern transport systems displays significant regional variations. Much of the technology may be standardized, but local market conditions and different regulatory environments give rise to divergences that may ultimately

weaken the global standards that the industry has struggled to establish. This chapter examines the growth and global spread of intermodalism as an innovation, and explores aspects of this phenomenon so as to assess the character of intermodal transport on a global basis at the end of the twentieth century.

It may be useful at the outset to offer some semantic clarifications. The term "intermodal transport" is used widely but is subject to a number of interpretations. Most refer to a flow of goods involving more than one transport mode. This interpretation includes a large proportion of all goods movements: for example, many rail shipments require pick-up and delivery by truck, and the vast majority of ocean flows require inland movement by pipeline, rail, truck or barge. *Multimodal transport* is an appropriate term for these kinds of flows that involve several different modes. In Europe the term *combined transport* is sometimes applied to flows involving several modes, but where the road leg is minimized. Combined transport is being prioritized

---

Modern Transport Geography: second, revised edition. Edited by Brian Hoyle and Richard Knowles.
© 1998 John Wiley & Sons Ltd.

by the European Commission as a means of diverting freight from the roads to rail, inland navigation or coastal shipping.

Intermodal transport, in contrast, has more specific connotations and may be defined as the flow of cargoes from shipper to consignee involving a single cargo unit across at least two different modes of transport under a single through-rate. Historically, shipments have been organized segmentally, where rates were determined and charged by each carrier, and where liability as expressed by the bill of lading was separate to each transport mode. The goal of intermodal transport is to remove the barriers to flows inherent in traditional modal systems, including the technical limits of transferring freight between modes that consider themselves as competitors and the organizational and legal constraints imposed by separate rates and bills of lading so as to provide a seamless system, in which the relative advantages of each mode are combined to produce the most efficient door-to-door service (Hayuth, 1987).

Two basic elements are therefore involved in intermodal transportation. One is the transferability of a unit load, the other the provision of door-to-door service. These two elements have not been developed in a fully integrated manner. In general, it has been easier to improve transferability than to establish the organizational structures necessary to provide single liabilities and through-bills of lading. The former is essentially a technological problem, the latter requires an organizational control that frequently comes up against regulatory restrictions. Transferability has been largely achieved through *containerization*, by means of which cargoes are placed in steel boxes of standard dimensions. The growth and development of containerization has significantly changed the face of transportation systems around the world. The container must be considered, however, as a precursor to the establishment of seamless transportation. A fully developed intermodal system requires structures that can not only transfer freight between modes but also provide an integrated service throughout the entire transport chain. While the two elements are in fact interdependent, they are considered separately in this chapter. They are treated as innovations, and because the growth and development of containerization is most developed it is presented as the first stage in a transport revolution that has spread around the world. The second stage of this revolution is the implementation of seamless transportation chains, a process that is still evolving.

THE FIRST INTERMODAL REVOLUTION AND THE DEVELOPMENT OF CONTAINERIZATION

Historically there have been several attempts to integrate transport modes. Among the earliest was the "piggyback" or trailer-on-flat-car (TOFC), where road trailers are hauled by rail. TOFC was developed as an extensive system by American railroads in the 1950s but its success was limited for several reasons, including regulatory restrictions over the rate structure, a poor reputation for reliability, and low profitability (Muller, 1995). It is significant that the breakthrough with containers took place within the maritime transport industry. For centuries general cargo handling in ports remained essentially unchanged. Gangs of dockers laboured using slings and, later, cranes to lift and stow freight. This was an extremely labour-intensive activity, achieving limited throughputs per shift. The port represented a very significant bottleneck, therefore. Ships spent more than half their time in port, time when no revenues were being generated, but when the fixed depreciation costs and crew salaries were being sustained and when daily port dues were incurred. The slowness of vessel turnarounds meant that shipping lines had to allocate many ships to serve their trade routes.

The Container as an Innovation and as a Spatial Diffusion Process

The concept of placing general cargo in boxes of uniform dimensions had been explored in the 1930s and 1940s but the first major commercial application is credited to Malcolm McLean, a former trucking company executive. He purchased two World War II tankers and on 26 April 1956 shipped 58 containers from Port Newark to Houston on the *Ideal-X*. This is widely regarded as the origin of the modern container revolution. This experiment in coastal shipping proved to be successful and in April 1966 McLean's shipping line, Sea-Land Service, inaugurated the first container service outside American waters with the sailing of a container ship from New York to Rotterdam (*Containerisation International*, 1996).

The action of placing freight in boxes of a standard dimension can be considered as revolutionary. It means that freight can be transferred mechanically, with gantry cranes replacing gangs of dockers, thus achieving significant improvements in the speed of handling. Sea-Land, for example, claims that the loading/unloading of a 40 000 ton container ship demands 750 man-hours, whereas it would have required 24 000 man-hours to handle the same volume of cargo using traditional methods (Chilcote, 1988, 130). The security and safety of cargo is improved also, with less chance of breakage and pilferage. Ship turnaround times are reduced considerably, thereby realizing significant economies for the shipping lines. Vessels now spend much less time in port than before, which means that companies benefit from more revenue-generating voyages per year per vessel.

Containerization has several technical and technological implications. The container itself had to be standardized. In the early days of containerization a number of boxes of different dimensions were employed. The *Ideal-X*, for example, loaded boxes of 35 ft length, the maximum length for a truck in the 1950s, and Matson Line used a 25 ft box on its Hawaiian service. Fortunately, in 1964, just prior to the international debut of the container, the International Standards Organization (ISO) adopted dimensions of 8 ft width, heights of either 8 ft or 8 ft 6 inches and lengths of either 20 or 40 ft. This greatly simplified the development of containerization that followed, and established the TEU (20 ft equivalent unit) as the measure of container activity. Other

technical developments included ship design and handling gear. Although the first container ships were converted tankers, purpose-designed ships were rapidly introduced, which because of their internal configuration are known as cellular vessels. These initial developments, along with special dockside gantry cranes and the container itself, constituted a veritable revolution in maritime transport.

The growth and spread of an innovation is frequently seen as a diffusion process. Geographers have examined a wide range of phenomena that have spread in space and over time (Gould, 1969), and it has been demonstrated that the adoption of the innovation approximates to an S-shaped curve (Figure 12.1a). The rate of early adoption tends to be slow but after a certain period of time the innovation diffuses rapidly through the population and only begins to slow down when a large majority of the population have adopted it.

The year 1956 is widely recognized as the first date of adoption of containerization. Its initial growth was essentially confined to USA domestic trades, including mainland–Puerto Rico and mainland–Hawaii. In 1966, the container entered the North Atlantic trades. By 1970 world container traffic had reached 6 million TEUs, and four years later had climbed to 16 million TEUs. The early 1970s represented the take-off stage for containerization, and its growth thereafter continued explosively (Figure 12.1b). By 1995 world container traffic exceeded 125 million TEUs.

Two processes have been at work here. Firstly, the conversion of cargo from traditional break-bulk traffic has been the major component of growth. Secondly, the growth of world trade, which containerization has facilitated, in turn has swelled the volume of container traffic. It is estimated that by 1995 70 per cent of all maritime general cargo had been containerized, which indicates that future growth of containerization will be derived less from conversions and more from trade expansion.

As a diffusion process, containerization possessed a distinct pattern of global expansion, which Table 12.1 partially demonstrates. An innovation that was essentially American prior to the mid-1960s,

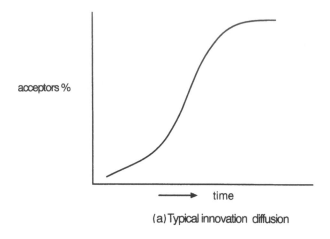

(a) Typical innovation diffusion

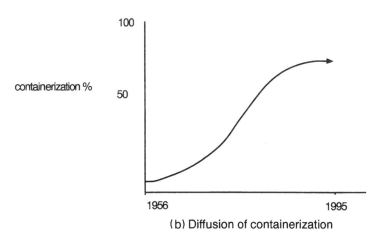

(b) Diffusion of containerization

Figure 12.1   Innovation diffusion

containerization expanded initially across the North Atlantic during the latter part of that decade. The North America–Europe trades became the first international focus of containerization, followed by the establishment of all-container services between Europe and Australia. In the early 1970s containerization spread to include the USA–Japan and Japan–Europe routes. This First World emphasis of containerization, with an east–west orientation of flows, has subsequently been only partially changed. The growth of trade in South Asia as well as the Middle East and Latin America since the 1980s may have established containerization as a global phenomenon, but the importance of the USA, Japan and Europe remains considerable. Containerization has therefore crossed the threshold of being an innovation and can now be considered as a mature transport system. It has spread throughout the world and

Table 12.1 National–container rankings, 1975–95
(in millions of TEUs)

	1975		1982		1987		1995	
1	USA	5.3	USA	8.7	USA	12.8	USA	19.0
2	Japan	1.9	Japan	3.7	Japan	5.9	Hong Kong	11.0
3	UK	1.4	UK	2.7	Taiwan	4.7	Singapore	10.4
4	Netherlands	1.1	Netherlands	2.3	Hong Kong	3.5	Japan	10.1
5	Puerto Rico	0.9	Taiwan	1.9	UK	3.4	Taiwan	7.2
6	Hong Kong	0.8	Germany	1.7	Netherlands	2.9	Netherlands	4.6
7	Italy	0.7	Hong Kong	1.7	Singapore	2.6	UK	4.5
8	Germany	0.7	Australia	1.2	Germany	2.5	Germany	4.3
9	Australia	0.7	Italy	1.2	South Korea	1.9	China	3.9
10	Taiwan	0.5	France	1.2	Belgium	1.5	South Korea	3.2

Source: Containerisation International Yearbooks.

a large majority of all general cargo is now shipped in containers. In 40 years it has become one of the most important elements in international trade and has greatly invigorated the maritime transport industry.

Impacts of Containerization on Ships

The immediate impacts of Malcolm McLean's experiments with hauling containers on ships were relatively minor. The pioneering attempts used vessels that were converted from other trades, and because tankers, with their large holds, could be adapted relatively easily, most of the early container ships were World War II vintage liquid bulk carriers. They were typically 600–650 ft in length and had capacities of less than 1000 TEUs. Containers were stacked in rows of five across the ship, so that early cranes had to have the outreach capacity to lift boxes across the five rows. These vessels comprised the first generation of container ships.

By the late 1960s, with the entry of Japanese and European carriers the first truly cellular ships were ordered, forming a distinct second generation of vessels (Figure 12.2). These were larger than the first-generation converts, typically 700 ft in length and significantly wider, capable of stacking 10 lines of containers on deck. Their capacities extended to 2000 TEUs. This was a period of experimentation,

with some vessels being built to combine break-bulk cargoes with containers – "giving owners the worst of both worlds" (*Containerisation International*, 1996, 43) – or combining roll-on/roll-off with containers, as successfully practised by Atlantic Container Lines (ACL). Other experiments were with speed. During the early 1970s there was a distinct shift towards speed enhancement. From 22 knots in the earliest second-generation container ships, speeds increased dramatically to 27 knots on ships designed for the Europe–Asia trades, and to 33 knots for the Sea-Land vessels designed for the transatlantic service. The romance with speed was abruptly halted by the energy crisis of the mid-1970s. There began a conversion from steam-powered ships to less powerful but more efficient diesel engines.

By the 1980s the emphasis was on size and fuel efficiency, and a new third generation of vessels was introduced. Larger than any predecessors these vessels grew in capacity to up to 4000 TEUs. Some 860 ft in length, they permitted 13 rows of containers to be stacked across the decks. Their dimensions became fixed by the limits of the dimensions of the locks through the Panama Canal, and hence these ships are frequently referred to as *Panamax*. Fuel efficiency was an important design feature of these ships. Indeed, the pendulum swung back from the greyhounds of the second-generation ships as vessels of this generation operate typically at speeds of 22–27 knots.

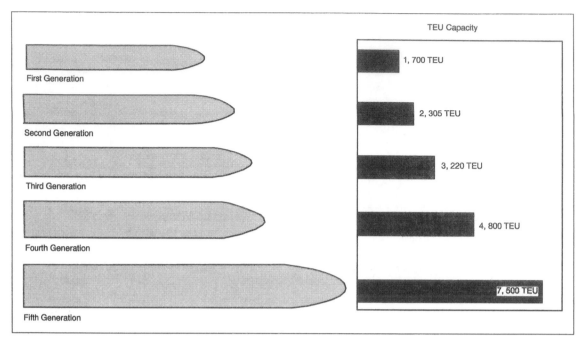

TEU Capacity

First Generation — 1, 700 TEU

Second Generation — 2, 305 TEU

Third Generation — 3, 220 TEU

Fourth Generation — 4, 800 TEU

Fifth Generation — 7, 500 TEU

Figure 12.2   Container ship evolution

In the late 1980s some of the major shipping lines made decisions to breach the limits imposed by the Panama Canal. They placed orders for new ships that because of their dimensions are referred to as *Post-Panamax*. These giants are 900 to 1000 ft in length, stack containers 16 across, and have a capacity of 5000 TEUs. They are commonly referred to as fourth-generation ships. However, just as the major shipping lines began taking delivery of these vessels in the early 1990s, still larger vessels were being ordered. The first of these behemoths, the *Regina Maersk*, was launched in 1996. With a capacity of up to 6700 TEUs, 1100 ft in length, 17 containers across, this vessel operates at a speed of 25 knots (Photograph 12.1). Such giants may ultimately comprise a fifth generation of container ships.

The growth of vessel size and capacity is the dominant feature of the development of containerization. Hybrids and other multimodal alternatives, such as roll-on/roll-off (RORO) and lighter-aboard-ship (LASH), are restricted to niche markets or have fallen by the wayside. The growth in the size of cellular vessels is predicated on the basis of economies of scale. Crew costs remain the same for a 2000 TEU-capacity ship against a 5000 TEU-capacity vessel, thereby helping to reduce differentials in operating costs, and the revenue potential of a larger ship against a smaller vessel is self-evident.

The drive towards larger ships is not, however, without difficulties. Of particular concern for the shipping lines are capital costs. Post-Panamax vessels cost US $100 million per unit. As several ships are required to maintain a regular service between major markets, capital requirements are very considerable. The economies of scale require high load factors. Shipping lines have to fill the slots, and this becomes ever more critical as the size of ships is raised by another notch. For ports, the increasing size of ships is just one additional headache. They are being called upon to provide deeper channels, longer berths, more extensive storage facilities, and handling gear that can service these ever-longer-deeper-wider ships. In the following sections these implications are examined in more detail.

Photograph 12.1   Regina Maersk: one of the latest generation of container ships (Maersk Inc.)

Impacts of Containerization on Shipping

Two major repercussions of containerization are, firstly, the effects on shipping services and routing and, secondly, the effects on the structure and organization of the industry. Pearson and Fossey (1983) suggest that shipping lines develop their service networks as a means of realizing two main objectives. The first is to use their fleet of ships as efficiently as possible. Because container ships represent major capital investments, the goal of the lines is to maximize the number of voyages and minimize port stays. Container services are *liner* services, with regular scheduled arrivals and departures. Service frequency, therefore, becomes a factor in designing the networks. The great majority of container services are based on a weekly cycle, i.e. there is a sailing from each port of call once a week. This constraint determines the number of vessels required for a particular service. Designing an appropriate configuration becomes critical in vessel deployment and hence in the use of capital resources.

The second objective in designing a service schedule is to generate cargo and maintain market share. The selection of a port of call is strongly influenced by cargo availability. Increasing vessel size requires high load factors. Port selection may be based on the particular features of the traffic available, more inbound than outbound for example, that might fit in better with cargo slot capacity. Additional factors that influence port selection include variations in the quality and costs of port services (Willingale, 1984).

Frequently, these two broad objectives are in opposition. Vessel capacity puts demands on traffic generation that frequently cannot be met by one port, and thus calls to other ports have to be made. These additional calls extend the service cycle, however, making it impossible to maintain the desired level of service frequency without adding further vessels. Given the range of factors determining the form and structure of the service networks of individual shipping lines, it is not surprising that no standard container network has developed. Pearson and Fossey (1983) identified 16 different configurations, ranging from simple port-to-port networks to complex overlapping multi-port itineraries. Examples drawn mainly from North America provide a useful indication of global liner shipping networks in terms of their general characteristics and in terms of micro-level features concerning the choice of specific ports of call.

Apart from feeder services, which tend to be short-sea linkages, liner shipping container services are intercontinental in scale. Specifically, they link different maritime ranges. With most of the world's containerized trade flows being concentrated between Europe, the Far East (FE) and North America, a number of important maritime ranges can be recognized: Japan and Korea, East Asia (including Taiwan, Hong Kong and China), West Coast North America (WCNA), East Coast North America (ECNA) and North West Europe. In addition, several other ranges have subsidiary importance, including the US Gulf Coast (USGC), the Mediterranean, Australasia and South Asia. The basic role of services developed by the major shipping lines is to serve two maritime ranges. The majority of services to and from North America are of this kind, usually involving a link from WCNA to Asia, or ECNA to Europe. These services involve single ocean crossings, and hence permit weekly services without a very large commitment of vessels.

Other types of service have been introduced. During the 1980s few developments in containerization gave rise to so much debate as round-the-world (RTW) services. Originally conceived by Evergreen Line and United States Line, RTW was seen as a major break with established container networks. The concept of container ships maintaining regular services around the world was somewhat revolutionary. The financial collapse of USL over the issue in 1985 added fuel to the controversy (Seok-Min, 1996). Evergreen has proved that RTW is an effec-

tive service configuration, permitting a wide market coverage with a relatively small fleet commitment. It operates two services, one east-bound, the other west-bound, and in the process has grown to become one of the largest container lines in the world. Several smaller lines, such as DSR-Senator, have also adopted RTW services.

RTW service demonstrated the advantage of multi-range market coverage. It has a major weakness, however, in that traffic imbalances are endemic. Certain legs generate little traffic, others have cyclical fluctuations, and yet service still has to be provided because of the global itinerary. In order to extend market coverage, while obviating the need to serve low-market areas, many lines have begun to extend their services over several ranges. An example is Maersk (prior to its global alliance with Sea-Land) with a sophisticated network of four overlapping, multi-range services (Figure 12.3a). Although distinct, the services overlap and permit the line to exchange containers between services, and effectively offer a global coverage.

A second type of multi-range model is the pendulum service, where a vessel calls more than once on a high-traffic range in a particular vessel service cycle. Prior to its recent alliance with other trans-Pacific carriers, Nedlloyd operated a pendulum service in the Pacific (Figure 12.3b), which allowed it to call twice in the high-traffic area of the Far East while providing service to North and South America.

It is significant that no major shipping line providing service to North America or Europe concentrates its business at one port only. This indicates that although New York is the major ECNA market, shipping lines find it strategically useful to serve less dense markets as well. Several lines maintain a container service configuration little changed from traditional break-bulk operations. Ships call at several ports up and down a continental range in a regular sequence (Figure 12.4). This type of service enables the line to tap several markets, and thus permits it to serve both major and relatively minor markets. The drawback is that each additional port of call extends the service cycle by several days. This may require

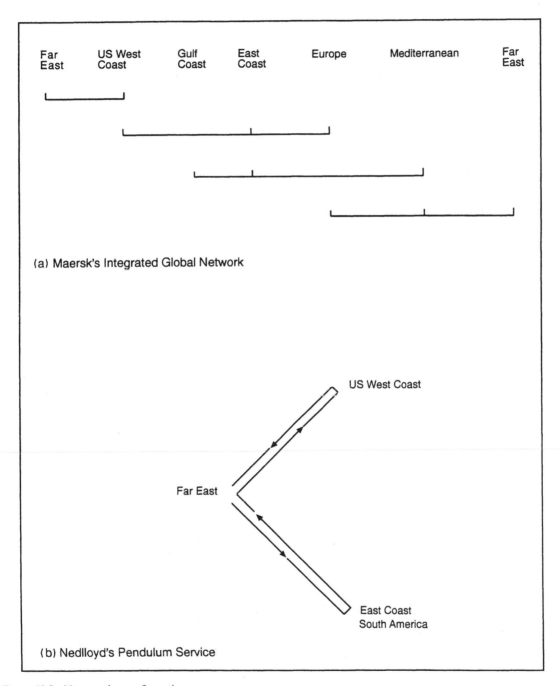

(a) Maersk's Integrated Global Network

(b) Nedlloyd's Pendulum Service

Figure 12.3   New service configurations

additional vessels to be added to maintain an acceptable level of service frequency, which increases the overall cost of the service. It also makes the service less attractive for shippers in the first or second port of call, since their containers are on a ship still in a neighbouring port, while those placed on a competing line at the same time may already be steaming towards their overseas destinations. The result of these disadvantages is that shipping lines operating multi-port itineraries tend to introduce a return leg, usually to the primary market. Thus, POL's more recent services returned to New York after leaving Wilmington (Figure 12.4). Most major carriers are developing more complex networks, involving a number of different services that include some common ports of call. This allows the lines to integrate their operations and permits a very wide geographical market coverage (Figure 12.5).

Strategic Alliances

The capital costs of establishing a containerized liner service have always been very large. Faced with an untested system, some established shipping lines in the early days sought to share the capital costs to form consortia to exploit certain trades. For example, when the decision to containerize the trade between Europe and Australia was made the different lines came together to establish ACT(A); and ACL is a consortium that has had many corporate parents, including Cunard, CGM and Wilhelmsen. While these alliances date from the very beginnings of containerization, it is clear that recent trends in the globalization of markets and in the costs of purchasing fourth- and fifth-generation ships have accelerated the process. The character of these alliances is taking on several different forms,

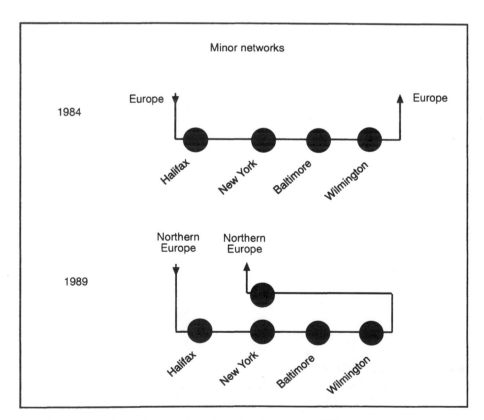

Figure 12.4   Polish Ocean Line's US East Coast service network, 1984 and 1989

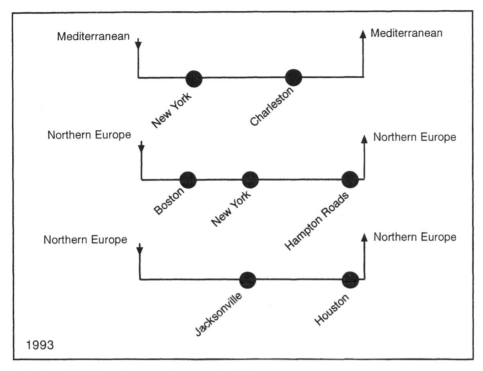

Figure 12.5   Sea-Land's US East Coast service network, 1993

however. At one extreme are the outright mergers, such as Maersk's purchase of EAC in 1994 and the merger in 1996 between P&O and Nedlloyd. More typical are the joint services offered by a number of lines that are forming consortia. Four global groupings have been formed in the mid-1990s: (i) APL, MOL, OOCL and Nedlloyd; (ii) Hapag-Lloyd, P&O and NOL; (iii) Maersk and Sea-Land; and (iv) Hanjin, Cho Yang and DSR-Senator.[2] The lines have vessel sharing agreements (VSA) in which each contributes a certain number of ships required to maintain the desired level of service frequency. Other, less formal, types of alliance are evident, including slot charter arrangements, where a company offers a service on a particular route without committing its own vessels. Instead, it agrees to lease a guaranteed number of container slots per sailing in vessels operated by another line.

Alliances allow lines to establish services at lower cost to themselves. Better vessel utilization, along with the opportunity to employ larger, more economical ships, are the main advantages cited. In addition, service frequencies can be maximized at the lowest cost to the individual carrier, and more extensive port coverage can be realized (Brooks *et al.*, 1993). It is clear that the alliances have very significant geographical implications.

Impacts of Containerization on Ports

Since the primary goal of containerization was to improve cargo-handling rates in ports, it is evident that ports have been affected by the global adoption of this innovation. The scale and intensity of the impacts is far greater than could have been anticipated 40 years ago, however. The box has transformed port operations, led to new siting requirements, and greatly transformed inter-port competition (Heaver, 1995).

While the shipping lines have had to invest billions of dollars to develop a fleet of vessels to accommodate the "box", the commitments of ports have been even greater. They have had to equip themselves with machines to lift and move the containers from ship to shore and around the yards. Particularly costly has been the provision of the berths themselves. Because containerization is a mechanized process, space has to be provided for the mobile equipment to move around. More importantly, because the carrying capacities of the ships greatly exceed those of land transport systems, and because ships can be loaded or unloaded at rates as fast as 150 containers per hour, extensive storage space is required. Compared to the old general cargo berths that might have provided 50 m of berth and 1 ha storage space, modern terminals are 50–100 ha in extent, and berths have to exceed 300 m. The cost of providing such space in crowded (and expensive) urban areas has been a major challenge. Former port sites were often inadequate in area and configuration, and thus have been abandoned. The search for new sites has been the concern of port authorities around the world. In the late 1960s and early 1970s, new docks such as Churchill Dock in Antwerp, Waalhaven in Rotterdam, Seaforth Dock in Liverpool and Port Elizabeth in New York were built. It was an expansion that came on the heels of massive port–industrial development that was already transforming the shape of ports (Hoyle and Pinder, 1981). The growth of containerization and increasing economies of scale have led to even larger demands for terminal space. For some ports, such as Rotterdam with Maasvlatke, Sydney with Botany Bay, Hong Kong with the new airport–port complex, and Vancouver with Deltaport, extensive new sites have been brought on stream. But in many ports limits to expansion, either by urban conflicts such as in Seattle, or environmental constraints such as in Montreal (McCalla, 1994), are providing a brake on a trend towards continued massive growth of port sites. Environmental legislation is likely to be a major constraint on future expansion in many countries of Europe, North America and Australasia, especially relating to the issue of dredging and land reclamation (Vandermeulen, 1996).

Because modern containerization is a capital-intensive activity it is inevitable that many of the effects on port labour have been negative. Traditional methods of cargo handling were labour-intensive and gave rise to significant employment in port cities. The adjustments that port labour has been forced to make because of containerization have been difficult. A sector with a strong tradition of union solidarity, dock labour in many countries has resisted containerization. Restrictive practices have been very common such as the "fifty-mile rule" in New York, whereby longshoremen only could fill or empty containers if the container was within 50 miles of the terminal; or stipulations maintaining unnecessarily large size of gangs as in Australia; or by securing contracts guaranteeing a certain number of hours of work per year regardless of whether the employer needed that number of workers, as in the UK. These labour difficulties have had an impact on the ability of some ports to compete. The growth of Felixstowe and La Spezia as the premier container ports in the UK and Italy, respectively, is due to their freedom from labour difficulties that have beset the former major ports of London and Genoa.

As containerization is spreading into the Third World, the same problems of overmanning, multiple union jurisdictions and reluctance to change are being encountered in the ports. In Brazil and India, acute labour problems are accentuated by strong centralized bureaucracies. Shipping lines see these rigidities as limiting modernization. They are calling for a smaller, more flexible workforce, and a greater freedom to negotiate contracts at the local level, an echo of what has been demanded in the First World ports for the last 40 years.

The relocation of port activities, coupled with the reduction in the demand for port labour, has effectively destroyed docklands and sailortowns (Hilling, 1988). Although containerization may be seen as a positive element in terms of transportation efficiency and trade enhancement, it must not be overlooked that it has had largely negative impacts on traditional labour markets and formerly vibrant urban neighbourhoods.

Impacts of Containerization on Port Traffic and Competition

The conversion of break-bulk trades and the growth of containerization have brought about a transformation of the world port league. Prior to the 1960s, the major general-cargo ports of the world were the leading cities of the developed world – New York, London and Tokyo – as well as a number of seaport gateways that served major industrial hinterlands, such as Rotterdam and Liverpool. The early leaders in containerization were these same ports, which had a large traffic base to build on, although they may not have had adequate facilities to cope with the demands of containerization. As shown in Table 12.2, subsequent changes have been remarkable. Former leaders, such as New York and London, have been eclipsed even in their national standings, and others, such as Rotterdam, have seen their relative global positions weaken. The growth of Hong Kong and Singapore has been remarkable, and along with Pusan, Kaiosiung and Manila reflect the burgeoning export-based growth of the Asian Tigers. Containerization has led to significant changes in port competition worldwide.

When containerization was being introduced, the economies of scale it engendered led some to predict that traffic would be concentrated in a few *load centres* as shipowners would establish a central point on each maritime range through which hinterland traffic would be primarily channelled. Large container ships would then ply between the load centres on each range, supported by localized feeder services. This concept is comparable to what has occurred in air passenger traffic in the USA since deregulation, with flows concentrated at traffic hubs.

The load centre model has been tested for the USA (Hayuth, 1988; Kuby and Reid, 1992). The results in the strictest sense are conflicting, with Hayuth affirming a trend towards traffic dispersal, while Kuby and Reid suggest a tendency towards concentration. While the research results appear to be in conflict, the actual patterns in most of the major maritime facades – ECNA, WCNA, North-West

Table 12.2   Container traffic at the top 20 ranked ports, 1970–94 (in thousands of TEUs)

	1970		1975		1982		1987		1994	
1	New York	930	New York	1730	Rotterdam	2314	Hong Kong	3457	Hong Kong	11050
2	Oakland	340	Rotterdam	1078	New York	2065	Rotterdam	2813	Singapore	10399
3	Rotterdam	300	Kobe	904	Hong Kong	1863	Kaiosiung	2778	Kaiosiung	4899
4	London	160	San Juan	877	Kobe	1623	Singapore	2634	Rotterdam	4539
5	Yokohama	150	Hong Kong	802	Kaiosiung	1479	New York	2089	Pusan	3212
6	Felixstowe	150	Oakland	522	Singapore	1274	Pusan	1949	Kobe	2915
7	Liverpool	140	Seattle	481	Antwerp	1000	Keelung	1939	Hamburg	2725
8	Baltimore	140	Baltimore	421	Seattle	950	Kobe	1877	Long Beach	2573
9			Bremen	409	Keelung	942	Los Angeles	1579	Los Angeles	2518
10			Long Beach	390	Hamburg	930	Long Beach	1460	Yokohama	2317
11			Tokyo	368	Yokohama	925	Hamburg	1451	Antwerp	2208
12			Melbourne	364	San Juan	910	Antwerp	1437	Keelung	2035
13			Yokohama	328	Pusan	883	Yokohama	1348	New York	2033
14			Hamburg	326	Bremen	820	Tokyo	1287	Dubai	1881
15			Antwerp	297	Oakland	804	San Juan	1169	Tokyo	1805
16			Hampton R	292	Long Beach	797	Felixstowe	1053	Felixstowe	1734
17			Sydney	262	Jeddah	775	Bremen	1043	San Juan	1522
18			London	260	Los Angeles	733	Seattle	1026	Bremen	1502
19			Keelung	246	Tokyo	698	Oakland	953	Manila	1501
20			Le Havre	231	Felixstowe	671	Tacoma	697	Oakland	1491

Source: Containerisation International Yearbooks.

Europe and the Mediterranean – are far from being dominated by one load centre. Part of the reason is the diversity of the operational networks of each of the shipping lines. As discussed above, each line has developed its own particular service network, it is rare for all the lines to choose the same port(s) of call, and each line may wish to have several ports of call in order to generate traffic and protect market share. In addition, ports compete with each other and offer particular inducements and incentives to the lines in order to obtain their business. On the WCNA lines have a choice between Seattle, Tacoma and Vancouver for the Pacific North West, and in North-West Europe there is an even bigger choice between Le Havre, Zeebrugge, Antwerp, Rotterdam, Bremen and Hamburg. Small wonder that no port is absolutely dominant there. Only Hong Kong with regard to China (Comtois, 1994) and Singapore with regard to South-East Asia can be said to be load centres in their respective regions; and this is a function of the weakness of competition from other ports rather than the inherent characteristics of containerization.

THE SECOND INTERMODAL REVOLUTION AND THE THROUGH-TRANSPORT CONCEPT

By the early 1990s the first intermodal revolution had reached a state of maturity. While there are still areas of the world where the conversion to containers is still far from complete, particularly in the coastal trades and in Africa, a large majority of general cargo traffic has been containerized. However, as long as the transport chain is made up of a series of separate links, for example with truck–train–ship–train–truck segments, each with their individual ownership, pricing and liability regimes, the organization of shipments remains fragmented (Hayuth, 1987). Regulatory, legal and technical constraints have been among the main obstacles to the establishment of a seamless transportation system.

Regulation

In some jurisdictions, the USA for example, legislation has prevented multimodal ownership, barring any transport firm extending its interests into other modes. In continental Europe, where most of the railways are nationalized, it is very difficult for private share-capital investments to be made. Regulatory restrictions have traditionally extended to freight rates, where intermodal rates were either banned (as in the USA), or were very difficult to establish (as in Europe), and where each mode sought to maximize its own rate advantage to the frequent detriment of the total door-to-door tariff.

From the early 1980s there has been a global assault on these regulatory restrictions. In many respects the USA has led the way. Faced with structural difficulties in its railroad and airline industries, and presented with academic evidence of the inefficiencies of regulation, successive administrations have carried out a substantial liberalization of the USA trucking, airline, rail and shipping industries. The Staggers Act (1980) and the Shipping Act (1984) were among the most important pieces of legislation, removing control over rates and permitting multimodal ownership. The effect of these changes on its northern neighbour forced the Canadian government to begin the deregulation of the transportation industry with its 'Freedom to Move' legislation of 1987.

The winds of deregulatory change have been much slower to spread in Europe. In the vanguard of change has been the UK whose successive Conservative governments (1979–97) have brought about the privatization of the National Bus Company, British Airways, the British Transport Docks Board, and the dismemberment of British Rail, and have thus greatly changed the national transport industry (Bassett, 1993). Elsewhere in Europe, however, the changes are more muted (Whitelegg, 1988). The European Commission has advocated deregulation to a far greater degree than most of the member nations seem ready to accept, as there are strong political and social forces favouring the retention of protection for national industries (Dawson and Renaux, 1989).

Deregulation has become an important force in many other parts of the world. In the former Communist countries market reform is the watchword of economic policy. In Latin America and Mexico the State is retreating from ownership and control of transport infrastructures and carriers. In Australia and New Zealand, too, government regulatory control has been released. The overall pattern is very uneven, however. Few countries have gone as far as New Zealand towards the privatization of transport, but most countries now have some form of deregulation as a policy objective.

Legal and Technical Obstacles

Legal problems relate in particular to the issue of liability. When goods are shipped modally, the issue of liability for loss or damage is fairly clear. Intermodal traffic implies the use of several modes, and how to allocate legal responsibility for shipments is very difficult to assess and regularize. A similar type of problem exists in tracing and documentation. When shippers need to find out exactly where their goods are located, the problem is much simpler if one carrier is involved rather than where there are several. A segmented, multimodal system also confronts the issue of document preparation and dissemination, as well as customs clearance. Shipments may be held up through the slowness of documentation processing (Muller, 1995).

Information technology is addressing many of these problems. Electronic data interchange (EDI) is being implemented by many actors in the intermodal industry, including the carriers, the third parties and the ports. Electronic documentation preparation, filing and transmission is now available for customs clearance, invoices and bills of lading. It is being extended into areas such as claims submissions, tracing, rate requests and fleet management. The establishment of such systems is very expensive, and there are several different systems, which makes integration very difficult. However, the introduction of EDI and other systems, such as automatic equipment identification, helps the planning, management and operation of increasingly complex and extensive networks.

These changes have set the stage for a second intermodal revolution that is characterized by the through-transport concept, in which the organization of trade is considered from door to door, and where there is an attempt to integrate various transport modes into production and consumption systems (Hayuth, 1987; McKenzie *et al.*, 1989). It differs from the first revolution because it involves organizational rather than physical innovations, and because the regulatory and technical changes have come about unevenly in time and space. Unlike the container, for which there was a clear point and date of origin, true intermodality is being established in varying degrees in different parts of the world. The process of innovation, therefore, is not as clearly defined as that involving containerization. We may say that it began in earnest in the early 1980s in North America and has progressed differentially around the world since then. What is interesting is how and where the changes have been implemented, and by whom.

Landward Connections and the Establishment of Door-to-Door Services

It is evident that global door-to-door services imply landward links. The maritime container may have improved the transfer of freight through seaports, but pick-up and delivery to and from ports were largely separate and unintegrated activities. The trucking industry and the railroads were overwhelmingly preoccupied with managing their larger domestic markets in which fierce intermodal competition rather than cooperation was the order of the day. It is not surprising therefore that the most important agents in establishing terrestrial intermodal networks have been the shipping lines.

The deregulation of transportation in the USA in the early 1980s was the catalyst for the intervention of shipping lines into the landward distribution of containers. American President Line (APL) was the earliest innovator. Starting in 1984 it began to lease and ultimately manage blocks of trains from the railroads to haul its maritime containers from West

Coast ports to interior points, particularly to Chicago (McKenzie et al., 1989). The actions of APL were rapidly copied and extended by other trans-Pacific carriers such as Sea-Land, K-Line, Maersk and NYK. The railroads themselves recognized the opportunities for containerized cargoes and began to operate their own block trains to and from Pacific coast ports. With further improvements, such as double stacking (see below), the economies of an intermodal system became increasingly apparent. Several national trucking firms, such as J.B. Hunt and Schneider, joined the railways in strategic alliances to transport their long-haul freight intermodally. CSX, one of the Class 1 railroads, purchased Sea-Land, the world's largest container line. APL began to manage and operate rail freight yards in the Mid-West. Ownership, management and operation of different modes began to be integrated. The growth of intermodal traffic has been a major feature of the USA transport industry since the mid-1980s (Slack, 1990).

The central role played by the shipping lines is important. As the carriers most touched by containerization, they had experience in the management of a unitized transport system, and an interest in exploiting landward connections. They realized that controlling a door-to-door system provided opportunities to increase revenues, and that if costs could be controlled, higher profits would result. Having largely resolved the cost problems in maritime space, it was on land where the new challenges were to be found. They tackled the perceived problems of rail inefficiencies by establishing their own rail services and, because the major obstacles were again to be found in the terminals, some installed their own management and control over intermodal rail yards. In this way they sought to control costs, but at the same time it gave the lines the opportunity to establish their complete control over the transport chain. Tracking, fleet management and the provision of a one-stop customer service gave both clients and the lines important service benefits.

Elsewhere in the world integration has been slower and less complete. In Europe, for example, the existence of national railways has served to limit the opportunities of the shipping lines to integrate a continent-wide service system. Instead, the carriers have been forced to deal with individual railways, as in Holland or Belgium, whose perspectives are guided by national self-interests (Charlier, 1996). There exist in Europe two major international intermodal operations. Intercontainer is a consortium of national railways that is mandated to handle international flows of maritime containers. It depends upon the member railways to provide terminal facilities and equipment. The second major carrier is IURR, a consortium of road freight operators and railways that is preoccupied with intra-European intermodal shipments.

An Evolving Global Intermodal System

A fundamental feature of intermodalism is the emergence of global corporations. The control of such extensive multimodal chains necessitates organizations that have considerable financial resources and that operate internationally. In this regard the shipping lines have been amongst the most ready to exploit intermodalism. However large some carriers may be, their size is proving to be inadequate to offer the intermodal services required. A feature of the contemporary shipping scene is the deepening of strategic alliances among the very largest shipping lines (Bleeke and Ernst, 1993; Brooks et al., 1993). A small number of giant consortia are being established. The fact that these traditional rivals have come together is an indication of the resources required to manage and operate intermodal services that are truly global in scope. The current round of large mergers taking place in the USA railroad industry, such as Burlington Northern (BN) with Atchison Topeka and Santa Fe (ATSF), and Southern Pacific (SP) with Union Pacific (UP), are a further indication of this trend.

Transportation companies are transforming themselves from being modal carriers into intermodal and logistics providers. Traditionally, transport services were provided by a host of small third parties, freight forwarders for example. The emergence of the carrier-based intermodal operators (the so-called fourth parties) is threatening this structure. The mega-carriers argue that quality of service is a paramount factor in transportation today, and when they have to depend upon the variable service provision of a myriad of third parties their core business is imperilled. Service quality, they argue, can be best guaranteed by placing all the links in the intermodal chain under one control. They also achieve cost savings by squeezing out the intermediaries. As a result the mega-carriers are opening their own offices in major inland markets. This trend towards the vertical integration of large intermodal corporations is threatening the lifeblood of the traditional intermediaries which are usually small, locally based firms. A recent study by KPMG highlights the vulnerability of traditional freight forwarders and warehousing firms (KPMG, 1995).

A broader threat from these developments is being felt by ports and port cities. As the shipping lines become ever more immersed in intermodality, ports become just one link among many in intermodal chains. Whereas ports were seen previously by shipping lines as terminals, where cargo was picked up or delivered, they are now one of several possibilities in a network within which non-maritime factors may determine routing choices. A port authority may seek to make its facilities as attractive as possible, but the choices made by shipping lines may be determined by non-port-related considerations (Slack, 1994a).

As the second intermodal revolution progresses it is becoming apparent that, although it is a global process, there exist important regional variations. These divergences are most evident between North America and Western Europe, where the systems are most developed. These differences are contrasted below with developments in Australia and Central and South America.

North America

The impetus towards intermodalism in North America came from the shipping lines engaged in the burgeoning trans-Pacific trades and was focused on West Coast ports. As with the earlier maritime container revolution, the extension of landward intermodal links was facilitated by a relatively simple technological innovation: *double stacking* (DS). By positioning one container on top of another on a rail flat car, twice the number of containers could be hauled with only a small increase in costs (fuel and terminal). Overall cost savings of about 35 per cent over the regular container on flat car (COFC) method mean that the rail haul becomes much more competitive compared to trucking on long hauls (Muller, 1995). From its introduction in 1984 by APL there has been an explosion of DS services operated by shipping lines, the railroads themselves and even ports such as Seattle. Unit DS trains carrying 400 containers are now a common feature on North American railroads (Photograph 12.2).

The growth of this intermodal traffic began with the shipment of maritime containers. Because there was a severe imbalance of trade between the USA and Asian countries, notably Japan, the early innovators of DS such as APL found themselves back-hauling empty boxes to the West Coast ports. They began to offer space in the containers for domestic traffic between interior markets such as Chicago and coastal cities such as Los Angeles. This service proved to be very successful (Slack, 1994b). So great is this traffic that the industry now differentiates between "domestic" containers and the regular maritime boxes. By the 1990s APL was handling more domestic than maritime containers. Because the domestic market became such an important part of their business, the rail intermodal operators now use wider boxes (102 inches) of different lengths to suit particular market niches, such as the 28 ft "pups" for the parcel industry, or the 48 ft and 53 ft containers to compete even more effectively with the trucking industry. Thus what began as a maritime-based industry, with ocean containers whose dimensions were determined by maritime standards, has emerged as a diverse industry in which the domestic container is now almost equally important but cannot be easily handled by ships. Even trucker allies such as J.B. Hunt have converted to the container for their intermodal shipments.

Photograph 12.2   Canadian double-stack train entering the Fraser Gorge (CN)

A distinct intermodal network has been established. The present pattern of DS services numbering over 240 eastbound trains per week has a marked east–west orientation (Figure 12.6). Originating from the West Coast, the network is continent-wide. Although the system in place appears to provide a *land-bridge* between Asia and Europe (whereby containers brought from Asia are transferred to rail at US West Coast ports for delivery to US East Coast ports for shipment to Europe), the actual volume of this traffic is minor. However, two other forms of "bridge" traffic are important: *mini-bridge* and *micro-bridge* (Hayuth, 1988). The former refers to traffic that is destined for a port city, but where in fact delivery is provided by rail from a port on another coast. For example traffic from Japan to New York is routinely delivered by rail from a US West Coast port; similarly European traffic to Houston may be railed from Charleston (South Carolina). In this way the shipping line can offer customers a faster service because it can integrate its ocean and land transport segments to its advantage. *Micro-bridging* is a term applied to the delivery of containers by rail to interior destinations, from Los Angeles to St Louis, for example.

In building this network, the intermodal operators have paid particular attention to the inland terminals. The total number of intermodal facilities has been greatly reduced, from 1107 in 1976 to 199 in 1993 (Slack, 1990). In this way traffic is concentrated at a relatively small number of inland load centres, allowing truck pick-up and delivery over a market range of up to 500 km. The traditional centre of the US rail industry, Chicago, has emerged as the most important hub and now handles more containers (maritime and domestic) than any US port. Because these terminals handle block trains of up to 400 containers at a time, they have to be very long (as much as 2 km), equipped with the kinds of lifting equipment normally found in ports.

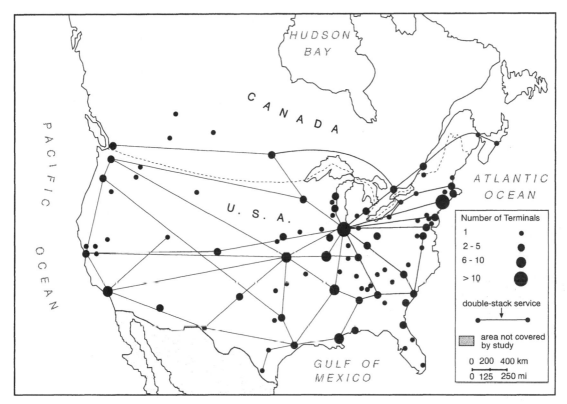

Figure 12.6   Intermodal terminals and double-stack services in North America

The European Union

In the countries of the European Union the container has not played the dominant role as across the Atlantic (Dawson and Renaux, 1989). Intercontainer faced many difficulties in expanding container service, not least being the frequently conflicting national interests of the member countries and high freight rates. Double stacking is not an option the railways can use because of electrification and other overhead restrictions. Other intermodal options have, however, been pursued. Piggyback has received a boost by technological and policy developments in different parts of Europe (European Conference of Ministers of Transport, 1992). The Channel Tunnel forces road freight on to rail for at least the undersea portion of the journey, and there is some expectation that this will provide opportunities for still longer-haul rail shipments between the UK and the rest of Europe. Similarly, Swiss and Austrian policies restricting truck movements across their territories, ostensibly for environmental reasons, is forcing trucks on to the railways for trans-Alpine movements (Charlier and Ridolfi, 1994). Finally, Europe has developed a truck-based unit that can be transferred to rail which is unlike the rigid-box character of the container. The *swap-body* is distinct because its sides are open, and it is wider than the maritime container. These features have made it highly successful, its width permitting two wooden pallets to be loaded side by side.

Distances between markets in the EU are smaller and thus the line-haul economies that favour rail intermodal traffic in North America are not as great. The large market is more diffuse and, reflecting the smaller operating characteristics of European rail-ways, unit trains are significantly shorter. This has meant that terminals need not be as extensive as those in North America. Shorter track lengths are more common, but because containers are not as evident in European facilities, working areas and storage requirements are generally more extensive. European terminals usually conform to a more box-like shape than their more elongated trans-Atlantic counterparts.

In the EU intermodal traffic has still to become an important core business for the railways, which themselves are facing a shrinking share of the trans-port market. In 1993, for example, the rail mode accounted for 15 per cent of the total market (down from 32 per cent in 1970) and intermodal transport accounted for a mere 4 per cent of the rail business. In addition, the development of terminals has been seen largely through national lenses. Each State-owned system has sought to develop terminals in the context of its own national interests, and conse-quently there has not yet been a Europe-wide rationalization. In 1993 there were 254 intermodal terminals in nine member states of the European Union (excluding Greece, Portugal and Eire) (Transport en Logistiek Nederland, 1994). This number is larger than the total for North America and may be taken as an indication of the slower rationalization rate of the European system. Table 12.3 and Figure 12.7 reveal significant differences in the densities of terminals.

Even greater discrepancies between North Amer-ica and Europe are revealed by the fact that many of the 199 US and Canadian terminals are located in the same cities. Forty cities have two or more terminals within their confines, and 15 cities have three or more facilities. Indeed, there are 10 terminals in the Greater New York region, and 14 in metropolitan Chicago (Table 12.4). The result is that if city hubs in North America are considered, irrespective of the number of terminals located therein, there are 98 centres. In Europe, on the other hand, only 21 cities have more than one facility (there are 10 in Rotterdam), and 186 cities have one terminal only. The total number of hub centres in Europe remains high, therefore, at 215.

This is more than double the total for North America, and confirms the fundamental difference in inter-modality between the two areas.

With 41 per cent of the intermodal hubs in North America possessing more than one terminal, a high rate of duplication is suggested, despite the more con-centrated network. This is due mainly to the number of railroads and other operators involved in intermo-dal rail business. Each company has developed its own intermodal network, and because most large cities are served by several railroads, a high degree of duplication has come about. Chicago has so many facilities because it is the main point of contact be-tween all the US railroads, which are essentially regionally based. In Europe, on the other hand, rail-ways have been developed by State monopolies, and there is much less duplication. Only the largest rail hubs, such as Paris, or the largest ports, such as Rot-terdam and Hamburg, have multiple terminals. A fur-ther difference between North America and Europe is the importance of short-sea and inland navigation systems in intermodal transportation (Rissoan, 1994).

Central and South America

Latin America and the Caribbean have traditionally been among the smaller markets in international

Table 12.3 Intermodal terminals in the European Union and North America

	Number of Terminals	Density of Terminals/km²
USA and Canada	199	50 396
European Union*	254	8 145
Belgium	8	3 755
Denmark	14	3 071
France	26	20 923
Germany	119	3 000
Italy	46	6 543
Luxembourg	1	3 000
Netherlands	19	2 210
Spain	14	36 071
United Kingdom	7	34 857

*Excluding Eire, Greece and Portugal.
Source: Transport en Logistiek Nederland (1994).

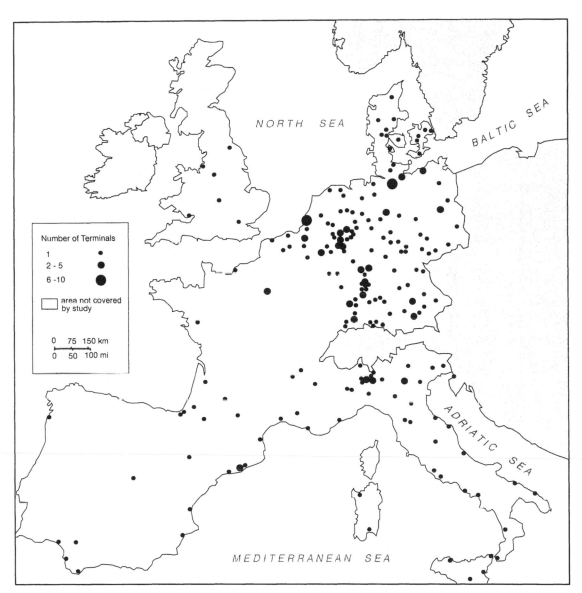

Figure 12.7   Intermodal terminals in Western Europe
Source: Transport en Logistiek Nederland (1994)

Table 12.4   City Distributions of Intermodal Terminals

Number of Terminals per City	1	2	3	4	5	6	7	8	9	10+
Canada and USA	62	26	3	3	1	4	1	0	0	2
EU	186	15	1	2	1	1	0	0	0	1

general cargo trades. With economies largely dependent on the export of bulk commodities, with unstable currencies, with strong government control over ports and shipping lines, and with limited capital available for transport infrastructure, the region has not been attractive for container shipping. State-controlled shipping lines have been given favourable treatment, and the nationalized ports have reputations for congestion. Early developments in containerization were characterized by small vessels, frequently combination cellular/break-bulk ships, operated either by the national carriers such as the Venezuelan carrier CAVN, or by the smaller European lines that had withdrawn from complete participation in the east–west trades to exploit these smaller north–south markets, such as Hamburg Sud. In addition, there was a combined service offered by several Japanese lines (see Table 12.5).

The diffusion of containerization through the region was a very slow process, constrained by many of the factors discussed above. Since 1990, however, it has accelerated, and there are some signs of integration between the modes. Of great significance has been deregulation in the transportation industry. Ports have been privatized in Mexico and Argentina, for example, and restrictions on foreign carriers have been relaxed in Venezuela. A more commercial environment has been imposed by the World Bank, as in the case of Argentina, or by free-trade treaties such as that associating Mexico with the NAFTA.

With these structural changes taking place, and with anticipated regional economic growth, the existing carriers have been increasing their service frequency and adding larger vessels (Table 12.5). In addition, the largest carriers such as Maersk and Sea-Land (now global partners) have entered the market, adding further capacity. Whereas the earlier networks were essentially north–south, the evolving services are being integrated with east–west routes, either through US pivot ports, such as Los Angeles or Miami, or at new intra-regional hubs, such as Kingston (Jamaica) or Colon (Panama).

The increasing interest of the major lines in Central and South America is an indication of the important role that ocean shipping plays in trade development. Certainly, the carriers were attracted by the market potential of the region, especially because of NAFTA and its eventual enlargement, and are positioning themselves to exploit this growth, but they may be seen also as agents of change in their own right, facilitating economic development. The establishment of regular and reliable container services into Central and South America is undoubtedly integrating the region more fully into the global economy. Rates between North America and South America fell by 40 per cent between 1991 and 1993 as new services were put in place.

Because much of the population and many of the markets in the region are coastal, there are few opportunities for the kinds of intermodal exchanges that are occurring in North America and Europe. However, there are some instances where inland services are being provided. For example, a mini-bridge service to Sao Paulo, Brazil, involving rail shipments from the port of Rio de Janeiro is in place. The closer port of Santos is congested and has a poor service record, and thus, despite a costly rail service from Rio, a market niche has been established for shippers requiring a guaranteed and safe delivery. A further example, of a different kind, is the integration of the Mexican rail system into the North American intermodal network. The Mexican railroad has formed several strategic alliances with international shipping lines to serve several Mexican cities from Los Angeles, and there are formal links with BN-ATSF and CN.

Australasia

Because the Australasia–Europe shipping trade route was among the first to be fully unitized, Australia and New Zealand were early adopters of containerization. The pace of subsequent developments, however, has been slower than in North America and Europe. Unique geographical features of the market, particularities of political decision-making, and dock labour problems have been the most important reasons for the slow evolution of intermodality.

Table 12.5 Container shipping services in Central and South America

	1985				1994			
	Joint Services	Individual Services	Mean Frequency (days)	Mean Size (TEUs)	Joint Services	Individual Services	Mean Frequency (days)	Mean Size (TEUs)
K-Line	2	–	1/30	550	3	–	1/30	1000
MOL	2	–	1/30	550	4	3	1/30	1000
Sea-Land	–	–	–	–	2	–	1/10	1000
Maersk	–	–	–	–	1	1	1/14	1000
Hapag-Lloyd	–	3	1/12	1800	2	1	1/21	2200
Nedlloyd	2	–	1/12	1900	3	2	1/14	2000
CCNI	–	6	1/30	400	2	3	1/21	1100
Transroll	–	4	1/30	380	2	1	1/14	1800
CAVN	–	6	1/30	100	–	10	1/30	350

Source: Containerisation International Yearbooks.

Although Australasia represents a relatively small market, containerization did not lead to the establishment of a regional load centre. Instead of establishing one hub linked by feeder services, deep-sea shipping services were provided to many of the smaller markets as well. The pattern of containerization reflects the urban system, with Sydney and Melbourne dominant in Australia, and Auckland in New Zealand; Adelaide, Brisbane, Fremantle (Perth), Wellington, Lyttelton (Christchurch) and Otago (Dunedin) operate as subsidiary centres (see Table 12.6).

The dispersed pattern of containerization is due only in part to the regional market structure,

however. It reflects also the interests of the shipping lines. The economies of containerization on a relatively short ocean service, such as the transatlantic, favour restricting the number of ports of call on each maritime range in order to maximize the number of voyages. The great distance between Europe and Australasia, in contrast, means that extending service beyond gateway ports is a marginal addition in terms of time. For this reason the shipping lines serving Australasia have been willing to add calls to small ports in order to tap into smaller markets.

This process has been facilitated by public policy. Until recently, all ports in Australia and New Zealand were publicly owned. Even small ports sought to establish their right to be players in container traffic by establishing publicly funded container facilities. This has been very much the case in New Zealand, where a limited number of authorized container cranes were dispersed through a number of ports on both North and South Islands, largely because of local political pressures.

From its early start, containerization has been slow to evolve in the region. Dock labour problems have been endemic, resulting in very high terminal costs and low productivity. Improvements have been difficult to implement. In addition, expansion of most of the container terminals has been hampered by site constraints. Land access is generally poor,

Table 12.6 Container traffic at Australian and New Zealand ports, 1975–95 (in thousands of TEUs)

	1975	1983	1987	1995
Melbourne	364	445	536	852
Sydney	262	404	n.a.	669
Auckland	35	146	171	365
Brisbane	50	96	115	249
Fremantle	63	84	113	202
Lyttelton		38	41	127
Burnie		50	74	119
Adelaide	3	11	33	73
Wellington	35	63	71	71
Otago		53	43	3

Source: Containerisation International Yearbooks.

and shallow approach channels limit vessel access in many of the larger ports. Landward distribution of containers has been a particular problem. Not only are most rail yards separated from ports, but the State-controlled railroads themselves expressed little interest in unitized cargoes, and in Australia were restricted to intra-state movements. These issues have served to reinforce the many-ports-of-call model adopted by the lines and to constrain the evolution of intermodalism.

Since the mid-1990s there are signs that the second intermodal revolution is beginning to take hold in Australia and New Zealand. The changes are being driven by both internal and external forces. Of the internal forces, foremost is the growing deregulation of the transport industry. With the privatization of its railway and the commercialization of its ports (including the abolition of restricted trade practices of the dock unions), New Zealand has emerged as one of the most liberal economies in the world. While these changes occurred around 1990, the full force of inter-port competition is only now becoming apparent, with the decline of many of the peripheral ports, such as Otago and Wellington. The railway company, now owned by Wisconsin Central, is becoming much more active in extending intermodal services. In Australia, port reform is still constrained by strong waterfront unions, but changes are evident, with some terminals being run by private firms, Sea-Land in Adelaide for example. A major development in intermodalism was the creation of the National Rail Corporation (NR) in 1991, which began to promote domestic inter-state intermodal services. More recently, NR has established intermodal corridors for overseas containers between Melbourne, Adelaide and Perth, and between Melbourne, Sydney and Brisbane. Double-stack services are operated between Adelaide and Perth.

The external forces arise out of the restructuring of the world's container shipping industry. Many lines that serve Australia and New Zealand are global in scope, and are establishing logistics operations to which the Australasian market is having to adjust. The shipping lines are adding their voices to pressure for reform of the ports industry, and their services to the region are being restructured to complement their global network operations.

The internal and external forces are reshaping containerization in Australia in ways that are still unclear and contentious. Australia and New Zealand used to be served by direct shipping services with the major world markets. This is changing. Maersk, for example, now serves Australia and New Zealand with a feeder service to its Singapore hub. This is seen as a marginalization by some local port authorities and shippers, a loss of direct presence in the markets of Europe and Japan. Others suggest that it enhances competition and will ensure that local products will reach world markets more cheaply by tapping into the mainline networks of the mega-carriers. This debate also is being extended into domestic concerns, in particular to traffic on the Tasman Sea between Australia and New Zealand. Historically, the Tasman trade has excluded foreign vessels. A major domestic carrier, ANL, has withdrawn from the Tasman, leaving the door open for foreign carriers to add this trade to their overseas business. Some ports see this as a threat to their survival, favouring still more concentration of trade at one hub only in the region, and leaving them with a feeder service role.

Improved rail services may have a big impact on inter-port competition as well. Adelaide, Fremantle and Brisbane are putting a great deal of marketing emphasis on the improved NR rail services. Brisbane, in particular, unfettered by the site constraints of Sydney and Melbourne, is closer in sailing time to Asian markets. It hopes to exploit the opportunities afforded by what is essentially a mini-bridge rail service. It must be admitted that there are no signs that this is taking place as yet, but the exploitation of rail services to Brisbane to overcome the urban and environmental difficulties of port expansion in Melbourne and Sydney represents an innovative geographical intermodal possibility.

INTERMODALISM IN THE TWENTY-FIRST CENTURY

An Innovation Facing Maturity

In the space of 40 years intermodalism has changed the character of freight transportation around the world. Containerization is certainly reaching a stage of maturity, having captured 70 per cent of the ocean general freight market. It seems inconceivable that there will be any retreat from the impressive gains that have been made. The land-based extensions that have been developed over the last 15 years, however, have been less spectacular. Modal transport, particularly trucking, is dominant in most markets. The exception is in North America, where gains made by rail-based intermodal systems are important. This success has been brought about by organizations that have exploited technological developments to prove rail intermodal's cost effectiveness for long-haul traffic, and offer a transport service that shippers can rely upon.

The challenges elsewhere are similar: not just the provision of improved transportation infrastructure, but the organizational integration that is at the heart of intermodality. Certainly, there are other alternatives to rail intermodal in some markets, for example inland navigation in Europe, but the eventual success of an appropriate system depends upon the ability to offer through-rates and provide door-to-door service.

Persistence of Regional Differences

Intermodalism is a global system. Whether it involves the unitization of cargoes through containerization, or the establishment of seamless transportation systems, the system and its impacts are being felt around the world. Yet, its character has assumed different forms in different parts of the world. Will these regional differences persist or even grow, or are they but a temporary divergence in a system that is still spreading and evolving? The answer to these questions will depend in part on the extent to which equipment will be standardized. As a technologically based innovation, intermodalism has spawned a range of units, from swap-bodies to the domestic box, as well as different EDI systems. In addition, there are wide variations in regulatory regimes and market conditions in different parts of the world. These forces are tending to produce regional divergences. On the other hand, there are strong centralizing forces, particularly those associated with the increasing dominance of a small number of consortia of mega-carriers who will seek to impose their own systems on the market. It is not clear at present how these conflicting tendencies will be resolved.

Competition Versus Oligopoly

As much as modern intermodalism is a product of deregulation, and is being created out of an industry that is highly competitive, there are significant centralizing forces at work. The costs of new ships, the expense of proprietary electronic management systems, and the need to extend control over the entire transportation chain, strongly favour economies of scale. Among the private carriers, container shipping lines and railroads have always been among the largest corporations. Yet the resources needed to provide intermodal services today exceed the means of even these giants. In the global shipping industry the establishment of global alliances places enormous resources in the hands of a few actors only. The Sea-Land/Maersk consortium, which became operational in 1996, represents a fleet of 175 vessels with a carrying capacity of 500 000 TEUs and controls 75 per cent of the total container capacity between Singapore and Spain. In the US railroad industry the number of western carriers has been reduced from four to two, and there is an imminent takeover of Conrail by CSX (which owns Sea-Land).

Such centralization threatens to give oligarchical control to a few intermodal operators. Already, some ports are being bypassed as the consortia begin to concentrate their traffic at those ports capable of offering the size of terminals required to handle the combined traffic of consortia members. For example, as the new APL terminal in Los Angeles came on stream in 1997, its partners were expected to leave to the neighbouring port of Long Beach. Will the port load centre concept now become a reality?

CONCLUSIONS

Intermodal transportation has become a reality. Shippers, carriers, governments and academics confront a very different world than when the *Ideal-X* sailed on its inaugural voyage. The intermodal alternative is viable in an increasing number of markets and this is reflected in the interests of shippers and many carriers in intermodalism. The old tyranny of modal competition and rivalry has been breached.

If the transportation industry has been alert to the possibilities and opportunities of intermodalism, governments have increasingly left the market-place to determine developments. There are exceptions, such as the interest of the European Commission, but in general governments have still to come to grips with some of the emerging issues brought about by intermodalism. The oligarchical control by a small number of global corporations represents a potential challenge to local and national interests. This is particularly significant in the areas of routing and local competition. The extent to which national interests can be preserved when decisions are made from a global perspective by international corporations has not, in the main, been faced.

Intermodal transport has become part of modern logistics systems, yet its future directions are not entirely clear. Conflicting trends are evident, and one of the challenges that confront academics will be monitoring and interpreting developments. Whatever the changes may be, it seems certain that the importance of intermodalism will not shrink. Geographers have a particularly important role to play in this regard. Intermodalism is transforming societies and the economies at all scales, from the local to the global, and its patterns of development are spatially differentiated. Geographers have a responsibility to provide an understanding of a phenomenon that will undoubtedly help shape the world in the twenty-first century.

NOTES

1. In a field that is changing as rapidly as intermodal transport, trade papers and journals are important sources of information. Most useful are *Containerisation International* and the *Journal of Commerce*.
2. It will be noted that the two merged lines are members of different and competing consortia. At the time of writing it is not clear how this will be resolved.

REFERENCES

Bassett, K. (1993), "British port privatisation and its impact on the port of Bristol", *Journal of Transport Geography* 1, 255–67.

Bleeke, J. and Ernst, D. (eds) (1993), *Collaborating to compete: using strategic alliances and acquisitions in the global marketplace* (New York: Wiley).

Brooks, M.R., Blunden, R.G. and Bidgood, C.I. (1993), "Strategic alliances in the global container transport industry", in Culpan, R. (ed.), *Multinational strategic alliances* (London: International Business Press), 221–50.

Charlier, J. (1996), "The Benelux seaport system", *Tidjschrift voor Economische en Sociale Geografie* 87, 310–21.

Charlier, J. and Ridolfi, G. (1994), "Intermodal transportation in Europe: modes, corridors and routes", *Maritime Policy and Management* 21, 237–50.

Chilcote, P. (1988), "The containerisation story", in Herschman, M.J. (ed.), *Urban ports and harbor management* (New York: Taylor and Francis), 125–46.

Comtois, C. (1994), 'The evolution of containerisation in East Asia", *Maritime Policy and Management* 21, 195–206.

Containerisation International (1996), "40 Years", April (Special Issue).

Dawson, R. and Renaux, G. (1989), *EEC transport policy* (Brussels: Club de Bruxelles).

European Conference of Ministers of Transport (1992), *Improvements in the main intermodal piggyback links* (Paris: ECMT).

Gould, P. (1969), *Spatial diffusion*, Commission on College Geography Resource Paper, No. 4.

Hayuth, Y. (1987), *Intermodality: concept and practice* (Essex: Lloyds of London Press).

Hayuth, Y. (1988), "Rationalisation and deconcentration of the US container port system", *Professional Geographer* 40, 279–88.

Heaver, T. (1995), "The implications of increased competition among ports for port policy and management", *Maritime Policy and Management* 22, 125–33.

Hilling, D. (1988), "Socio-economic change in the maritime quarter: the demise of sailortown", in Hoyle, B.S., Pinder, D.A. and Husain, M.S. (eds), *Revitalizing the waterfront: international dimensions of dockland redevelopment* (London: Belhaven), 20–37.

Hoyle, B.S. and Pinder, D.A. (eds) (1981), *Cityport industrialisation and regional development* (Oxford: Pergamon).

KPMG (1995), *Strategic analysis of intermediary companies in the port of Rotterdam* (Rotterdam: KPMG).

Kuby, M. and Reid, N. (1992), "Technological change and the concentration of US general cargo port system, 1970–88", *Economic Geography* 68, 272–89.

McCalla, R.S. (1994), *Water transport in Canada* (Halifax: Formac).

McKenzie, D.R., North, M.C. and Smith, D.S. (1989), *Intermodal transportation: the whole story* (Omaha: Simmons-Boardman).

Muller, G. (1995), *Intermodal freight transportation* (Westport: Eno Foundation).

Pearson, R. and Fossey, J. (1983), *World deep-sea container shipping* (Aldershot: Gower).

Rissoan, J.P. (1994), "River-sea navigation in Europe", *Journal of Transport Geography* 2, 131–42.

Seok-Min L. (1996), "Round-the-world service: the rise of Evergreen and the fall of US Lines", *Maritime Policy and Management* 23, 119–44.

Slack, B. (1990), "Intermodal transportation in North America and the development of inland load centres", *Professional Geographer* 42, 72–83.

Slack, B. (1994a), "Pawns in the game: ports in a global transport system", *Growth and Change* 24, 597–98.

Slack, B. (1994b), "Domestic containerisation and the load centre concept", *Maritime Policy and Management* 21, 229–36.

Transport en Logistiek Nederland (1994), *Combiplanner voor Gecombineerd Vervoer in Europe* (Rotterdam: Transport en Logistiek Nederland, and Stichting Intermodal Transport).

Vandermeulen, J.H. (1996), "Environmental trends of ports and harbours: implications for planning and management", *Maritime Policy and Management* 23, 55–66.

Whitelegg, J. (1988), *Transport policy in the EEC* (London: Routledge).

Willingale, M.C. (1984), "Ship-operator port-routeing behaviour and the development process", in Hoyle, B.S. and Hilling, D. (eds), *Seaport systems and spatial change* (Chichester, Wiley), 43–59.

13

INTERNATIONAL SURFACE PASSENGER TRANSPORT

Clive Charlton and Richard Gibb

This chapter examines the nature and evolution of international surface passenger transport. A conceptual framework is developed around the two basic concepts associated with interaction: complementarity and transferability. This highlights the structural similarities in international surface passenger transport while at the same time recognizing their great diversity. The constraints and opportunities for the development of this form of transport are then examined using examples from throughout the world but from the European Union in particular. For both economic and political reasons, international surface passenger transport is likely to experience substantial further growth.

INTRODUCTION

The aim of this chapter is to explore the nature, problems and associated solutions of international surface passenger transport (ISPT), which is interpreted here as scheduled public passenger transport, with particular emphasis on rail services. Firstly, the overall character of ISPT and the constraints on its development are examined using a range of examples. This recognizes the structural similarities in ISPT markets, while recognizing their great diversity. Focus then passes to the continental scale, with an evaluation of the attempts by the European Community (EC) to remove the structural constraints on ISPT movements. The slow evolution of the Common Transport Policy (CPT) and policies for the development of Europe-wide transport networks highlights the problems facing the development of ISPT even in a region of growing economic and political unity. The chapter uses as its principal case study what is perhaps the most ambitious contemporary form of ISPT, the development of high-speed rail passenger train services in continental Europe.

To provide a wider context for this main focus on the international rail network in Europe, reference can be made to two basic concepts associated with interaction: complementarity and transferability (Ullman, 1973). In the international case, complementarity represents the demand for travel across frontiers, while transferability is interpreted very broadly as the difficulty or ease of meeting that demand. Both contain conditions that either facilitate and encourage travel, or constrain it.

Complementarity and the Demand for ISPT

The complementarity between States that generates passenger flows is extremely complex. Levels of economic development, economic structure and

Modern Transport Geography: second, revised edition. Edited by Brian Hoyle and Richard Knowles.
© 1998 John Wiley & Sons Ltd.

trade patterns are important. Higher levels of income will sustain a stronger propensity to travel, although increasing wealth tends to divert traffic from surface public transport towards air transport and the private car. This is increasingly apparent in Western Europe and certainly the case across the USA–Canada border, where bus and train are of minor importance. As economies mature, the demand for business and professional travel tends to expand faster than aggregate growth and trade, in association with a shift towards consumer and service-based structures. Trade liberalization and the advance of globalization have generated a substantial exchange of personnel both within and between the many organizations engaged in the process, although, worldwide, air transport caters for the majority of such movements.

International complementarity is also expressed through the enormous growth of tourism, which features a steadily widening range of origins and destinations. However in many international tourism markets, ISPT plays a minor role in comparison with air transport and the private car, despite the importance of coach travel and rail for certain age groups in Western Europe (i.e. 55+ and 18–26), and more generally in Eastern Europe. International migration also stimulates complex patterns of demand for ISPT as social networks involving migrants, their kin and friends spread beyond national boundaries. Many flows can illustrate this point, such as those between Germany and Turkey, between Mexico and the United States, and between a range of African states. Within the EU, the gradual convergence of economies, labour markets, consumer markets and business organizations could be expected to stimulate a steady expansion of international movements.

"Transferability" – the Constraints on ISPT

Transferability can be conceived as a series of constraints on ISPT, which may be modified (usually reduced) to varying degrees. A fundamental factor is the spatial organization of States relative to each other, and especially the locations of principal con-

centrations of population and economic activity. Europe has numerous relatively small but developed and populous political units in close proximity, which generate complex patterns of interaction and surface transport across frontiers, whereas for island States such as Madagascar or New Zealand ISPT is not significant. At the subnational scale, there are a number of examples of international cities which generate fairly intensive short-distance cross-border passenger traffic, including commuter flows, as in the cases of Basel, Lille and Saarbrücken and settlements on the USA–Mexico border such as El Paso/Cuidad Juarez and Laredo/Nuevo Laredo.

National territories are often partly defined and separated by physical barriers, which accentuate the basic spatial constraint of distance. Although major rivers and stretches of sea are readily crossed by ferry services, these are relatively slow, inconvenient and costly, so that water is normally considered to be an additional constraint on ISPT. Where technically feasible, international fixed-link water crossings have been developed. The most notable example is the Channel Tunnel, with the Øresund fixed link under construction between Denmark and Sweden, and the Fehmarn Baelt link between Denmark and Germany in prospect (Munsey, 1997). The international bridge across the Paraná River between Encarnación in Paraguay and Posadas in Argentina, and crossings of the River Uruguay, have eased ISPT in the Plate Basin of South America. Mountain ranges inhibit ISPT both directly and via their influence on political, demographic and economic patterns. Major massifs such as the Andes, Alps and Pyrenees have a profound impact on surface transport; significant improvements are extremely expensive, as in the case of proposed "base tunnels" necessary to upgrade trans-Alpine connections.

Political influences on "transferability" are of central importance in assessing interaction and ISPT. The fractured pattern of ISPT in many parts of the world is a stark testament to the extent of political antipathy between States. Despite strong potential complementarity and physical proximity, travel between the USA and Cuba is normally prohibited; indeed, the island has no ferry services with any of its neighbours. The relative paucity of links between Greece and Turkey, and between Israel and its neighbours, are further examples of how ISPT can be diminished by "political distance". There have been many examples in recent years of substantial changes in the political status of territories and in the relationships between States, with attendant shifts in the patterns of ISPT. This has been especially obvious in Central and Eastern Europe. The elimination of the former "Iron Curtain" has greatly improved the potential for interaction across this former divide (European Conference of Ministers of Transport, 1991). The creation of a series of new independent States such as Latvia, Moldova and Slovenia generates new flows of ISPT in place of domestic movements. However, political breakdown and conflict in the former Yugoslavia has severely disrupted ISPT in and through the Balkan region. Conversely, homogeneity in terms of political control of territory inevitably eliminates ISPT, as in the case of movements in reunified Germany.

Although spatial, physical and economic constraints also apply, political factors have ensured that the majority of Asian States have very weak international surface passenger services, with many "missing links", as between South Asia and South-East Asia (Rhee, 1995). Indeed, as regards railways, post-colonial schisms have curtailed services that once operated (Din, 1990). Even before the Gulf War, rail through-services between Turkey and Iraq had been abandoned. Exceptions are few, but include Thailand–Malaysia and India–Nepal.

The influence of past political and economic patterns is visible in the underdeveloped status of international transport infrastructure in some parts of the Third World. This is true in West Africa, where main transport axes have tended to focus on major ports serving the needs of export-oriented economies, rather than acting as links between adjacent States (Omiunu, 1987). The proposal for a railway linking ECOWAS countries (Economic Community of West African States) from Nigeria round to Senegal and Mauritania is likely to remain a distant prospect for many years.

Many transborder journeys are made more difficult through politically based legal or administrative controls, which can be more than the effects of lengthy border formalities and visa restrictions. A striking example applies at the United States–Mexico frontier, where longer-distance public transport travel still requires a change of vehicle – there are no direct bus or train services from, for example, major Texas cities to Monterrey or Mexico City, despite the large demand for travel. A similar situation holds at the Mexico–Guatemala frontier. Concerns about migration controls and differences in technical standards of transport equipment may underlie what seems an inefficient and inconvenient constraint.

The status of other modes of transport will affect the status of ISPT. Wealthy societies, especially where international travel involves long distances and difficult terrain, will depend to a high degree on air transport. The fast growing international movements in East and South-East Asia are more strongly air-based than their equivalents in Europe, where there is a more balanced mix of modes of international travel.

REMOVING THE BARRIERS: THE EUROPEAN UNION'S COMMON TRANSPORT POLICY

The European Union (EU), and Europe more generally, is the most important market for ISPT in the world. With relatively high disposable incomes, sophisticated trading economies, political diversity and a highly mobile but concentrated population, ISPT has experienced immense growth. In the 1980s, international traffic as a whole increased twice as fast as national traffic in the then European Community (Budd, 1987). However, ISPT is also limited by political frontiers, which still fragment the EU's economy and society to a degree, so that a clear distinction between international and national surface passenger transport can still be discerned. The 15 member States of the EU have developed transport policies and systems tailored principally to suit their national interests, so that the level of ISPT is well below the maximum potential. This chapter now goes on to examine the evolution of the EU's Common Transport Policy (CTP) and proposals for the creation of integrated, supranational transport systems that reflect the aspirations of the European Union. The generation of the Trans-European Networks has become a core dimension of this process.

The founding fathers of the EU recognized the importance of transport to the establishment of an integrated European economy. An important industry in its own right, transport employs over 15 per cent of the Community workforce and accounts for more of the EU's GDP than agriculture. However, it is more critical to the functioning of a truly integrated market than this figure suggests. The free movement of goods and people was a vital foundation of the Treaty of Rome (Ross, 1994), and the broad need to establish a common transport policy was acknowledged in Article 74, although progress was slow until the mid-1980s (Europa, 1996).

The lack of any clear definition of a CTP in the Treaty of Rome itself was first addressed by the European Commission's "Schaus memorandum" of 1961. This document proposed the elimination of all obstacles preventing the development of a free market in transport, in which ISPT would be indistinguishable from national transport movements. This was to be achieved by the removal of national discriminatory policies and rates, by the elimination of policies distorting transport markets and the creation of "healthy competition" in transport services, but with coordination of transport infrastructure investment (Frohnmeyer, 1994). However, these goals were altogether too ambitious for the period. Given the diversity in the structure, regulatory controls and objectives of member States' transport policies, it was unrealistic to assume immediate harmonization. Consequently, the Council of Ministers, with responsibility for ratifying EC legislation, did not reach a consensus on the Schaus memorandum.

Following the accession of the UK, Ireland and Denmark in 1973, there was a subtle shift in emphasis in the approach to a CTP. Most notable was a move away from harmonization as a necessary prerequisite to a common policy. More stress was placed on infrastructure planning and investment as a means of integrating the diverse transport systems of member States. The idea was to promote EC intervention in the planning and financing of an integrated network so that resources could be put to optimum use in terms of the objectives of the Community.

Unfortunately, the 1973 proposals had little more impact than the 1961 memorandum. By the early 1980s, there was little advance towards either a CTP or a common transport market. The most characteristic feature of the stalled progress towards a common policy was the failure to affect the transport policies and markets of EC member States. The persistent divergence of member States' own transport policies were often the product of policies that were sound and justifiable from national perspectives, which had distinct economic, geographical and historical foundations. As pointed out by Bayliss (1979), each State considered its own transport policy to be more suitable than a common policy, which would inevitably involve compromise and additional costs.

In the early 1980s, EC governments recognized that if the Community was to regain its competitive position in the world economy, all restrictions on the free movement of goods and people had to be abandoned. There was also growing understanding of the penalties imposed by an increasingly congested and environmentally damaging road-dominated transport infrastructure. Furthermore, it was recognized that common policies had to replace the divergent actions of individual States. The White Paper that followed the European Council meeting at Fontainebleau in 1984 outlined a programme of legislation deemed necessary to achieve a single integrated European market. This led, through the Single European Act of 1987 – which did not refer to transport policy (Gérardin and Viégas, 1993) – to the major redefinition of the Community's objectives and modes of operation in the Maastricht Treaty, which came into effect in 1993.

The Maastricht Treaty provided a particularly strong stimulus and rationale for the marked progress in the status of European transport policies that has taken place in the 1990s. It was recognized in the provisions of Article 129 that improved transport networks would be necessary if the Treaty's objectives were to be met (alongside energy and telecommunications infrastructure). The freedom of movement and trade required for the achievement of a single market depends on the development of satisfactory communications throughout the Community (Gérardin and Viégas, 1993; Frohnmeyer, 1994; European Conference of Ministers of Transport, 1995). The Treaty also confirms that social and economic cohesion is a central principle for the successful creation and maintenance of the European Union. This requires that peripheral States and regions of the Community are linked to its more central parts by effective transport networks. The dominant thrust of the broad transport objectives enshrined in the Treaty is for an expansion and upgrading of transport connections across national frontiers (CEC, 1992b), with ISPT playing a central role alongside private road, air and freight transport.

Several fundamental concepts with a bearing on ISPT have emerged as central elements of post-Maastricht transport policy. The notion of "interconnectivity" reflects the need to enhance "key links" or to provide "missing links" between existing European transport networks that have evolved under national priorities (Maggi et al., 1992). Much emphasis has also been placed on "interoperability" in the operation of networks (Walrave, 1994; Nijkamp, 1995). Interoperability implies both improved integration between transport modes (such as achieving better interchange facilities between rail and air or bus), and comprehensive technical and organizational harmonization within transport modes, which have tended to develop separately, and often incompatibly to serve national interests. Such harmonization would not only remove constraints on the operation of cross-frontier services, but would also permit a more competitive European market in the supply of international transport services and equipment. This goal was underpinned by European Council Directive 91/440, which provided for the possibility of competing international passenger train operators to have access to the relevant rail infrastructure in the Community (CEC, 1991).

TRANS-EUROPEAN NETWORKS AND ASSOCIATED PAN-EUROPEAN PROPOSALS

Much emphasis has been placed on the development of Trans-European Networks (TENs) as the instruments by which Europe is to establish its single integrated market and economic and social cohesion (CEC, 1990b). Article 129b of the Maastricht Treaty committed the Community to the TENs concept (Dick, 1994), which has been developed and made more precise since 1993. TENs include energy and telecommunications networks, as well as the various modes of passenger and freight transport. In 1994, the Commission set out its vision for a trans-European transport network to be achieved by 2010 (CEC, 1994). The central concern was to identify the networks "of common interest" and particularly those infrastructure projects that should be considered as priorities for early completion. The "Community guidelines for the development of the trans-European transport network" were eventually adopted as a Decision by the Council of Europe and the European Parliament in July 1996 (CEC, 1996a).

The use of the term "trans-European transport network" (singular) here is significant; the Community has confirmed the importance of the "integration of land, sea and air networks", taking account of the comparative advantages of each mode, and encouraging "interoperability" within modes and "intermodality" between them. Several other general principles have been set out as underpinnings for European transport policy into the next century. A key concept is "sustainable mobility of persons and goods", which satisfies the Community's aspirations in terms of "social and safety conditions", competition, environmental protection and economic and social cohesion. The sustainable mobility theme had been adopted in a reassessment of the Common Transport Policy in 1992 (CEC,

1992a), and developed more thoroughly as regards passenger transport in the Commission's Green Paper, "*The Citizens' Network*" (CEC, 1996b). Two rather more cautious ideals also feature in the 1996 trans-European transport network document: that the network should "allow the maximum use of existing capacities" and "be, insofar as possible, economically viable". Finally, the importance of connections with non-EU neighbours is recognized by a requirement that the Community's transport networks should be "capable of connection" to those in European Free Trade Association (EFTA) states, countries of Central and Eastern Europe and the Mediterranean countries.

While it shares the stage with the other modes in this integrated Common Transport Policy, the Community has endorsed its desire to revive the significance of rail transport for both domestic and international transport (*Railway Gazette*, 1996a). A prominent role is confirmed for rail in the trans-European transport network, including conventional passenger services and combined/intermodal freight, but most prominently in the form of a comprehensive trans-European network of high-speed passenger train services. This takes forward earlier proposals, notably that by the Community of European Railways (CER, 1989), which had been developed further by the Commission (CEC, 1990a; Allen, 1991; Charlton, 1994). Their ambitious vision was influenced by the impact of high-speed services to date, but arose also out of concern that the successful national ventures, with their divergent technologies and principles, would not lead to a network that would integrate the community effectively (Frohnmeyer, 1994). The high-speed network comprises purpose-built high-speed lines for operation at 250 km/h or above, specially upgraded (existing) lines for speeds around 200 km/h and also some upgraded routes where special "topographical or town planning constraints" mean that speeds must remain below 200 km/h. The EC's outline plan of 1990 (CEC, 1990a) (Figure 13.1) foresaw around 9000 km of new lines and 15 000 km of upgraded routes. As in earlier versions, the 1996 high-speed rail plan contains some routes that seem distinctly ambitious,

even speculative, such as those into Portugal, southern Italy and Sicily, in Ireland and north of Stockholm, although this would not be expected to be for "maximum" high-speed operations.

In partial recognition of the enormous challenge posed by the full set of proposed trans-European transport networks, a list of 14 transport priority projects has been confirmed (the "Essen 14") (CEC, 1995). It could be reasonably inferred that the EU would be particularly willing to direct European funding to support national and private-sector investments for the links included in this list. Eight of the priority projects feature rail-based ISPT, with five based on high-speed rail. In some cases, a "project" consists of several related links. Those with direct ISPT relevance are shown in Table 13.1.

This list of priority projects appears to combine some realism with an enduring concern to display "balance" between member States. Some of the projects are already committed or are at least very definite prospects (e.g. the high-speed links through Belgium to the Netherlands, between London and the Channel Tunnel, and the Nürnberg–Erfurt route in Germany. Others seem to be on a different scale in terms of Europe-wide significance, as well as likely traffic densities and speeds (e.g. the Cork–Larne axis and parts of the Nordic triangle).

Parallel to the evolution of the EU's own trans-European transport network, there are moves to establish an even more ambitious "pan-European transport policy" incorporating the whole of the continent, including the States of Central and Eastern Europe. The profound political changes in the former Communist bloc are accompanied by both the growth and reorientation of international travel, against a background of an inadequate transport infrastructure. Although a relative modal shift towards the private car and air transport is likely in the international sector, the need to upgrade relevant rail links is also recognized (European Conference of Ministers of Transport, 1991). Progress towards an enhanced continent-wide network, with its emphasis on international surface connections and integration, has been marked by the Prague Declaration of 1991 and the Crete Declaration of 1994, with the

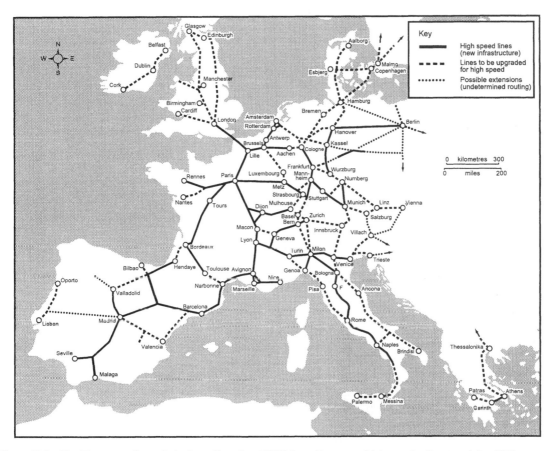

Figure 13.1   The European Commission's outline plan (1990) for a European high-speed rail network for 2010

third pan-European forum taking place in Helsinki in 1997 (CEC, 1996c). A number of organizations have contributed to the process besides the European Community and national governments. These include the European Conference of Ministers of Transport (ECMT), the United Nations Economic Commission for Europe (UN-ECE) (Dente, 1991) and the UIC (Union Internationale des Chemins de fer), the Europe-wide body that focuses on developing and harmonizing technical standards in rail systems. The latter proposes an increase in rail's share in international traffic from 8 per cent to 21 per cent by 2010, albeit dependent on sufficient progress with new rail investments (Walrave, 1994). Among the international routes indicated as of pan-European significance are Berlin–Warsaw–Minsk–Moscow, Trieste–Budapest–

Kiev and, more modestly, Dresden–Prague. In 1997, a "protocol agreement" was signed for the modernization and rehabilitation of the railway lines in the so-called "Crete Corridor 1" Helsinki–Tallinn(ferry)–Riga–Kaunas–Warsaw and Riga–Kaliningrad–Gdansk (UIC, 1997). Generally, the prospective enlargement of the EU by the inclusion of Central and Eastern European States is likely to highlight further the need for investment in appropriate rail infrastructure.

THE DEVELOPMENT OF HIGH-SPEED RAIL PASSENGER SERVICES IN EUROPE

Even a mildly sceptical observer would recognize the immensity of the task if an integrated and

Table 13.1   International high-speed rail elements of the EU's transport network priority projects

Rail Elements	Estimated cost (ecu million)

High-speed rail/combined transport north–south
    Berlin–Leipzig–Erfurt–Nürnberg
    Brenner axis: Verona–Munich
	21 900

High-speed train Paris–Brussels–Cologne–Amsterdam–London
    French/Belgian border–Brussels–Liège–Aachen–Cologne–Frankfurt
    Brussels–Antwerp–Rotterdam–Amsterdam
    Channel Tunnel rail link to London
	15 100

High-speed train south
    Madrid–Barcelona–Perpignan–Montpellier
    Madrid–Vitoria–Dax
	14 200

High-speed train east
    Paris–Metz–Strasbourg–(Karlsruhe), with junctions to
    Saarbrücken–Mannheim and Luxembourg
	4 540

High-speed train/combined transport; France–Italy Lyon–Turin–Milan–Venice–Trieste	12 000
Conventional rail: Ireland Cork–Dublin–Belfast–Larne (for Stranraer)	238
Fixed rail/road link Denmark–Sweden Øresund fixed link and access routes	3 645

"Nordic triangle" rail/road
    Stockholm–Swedish–Norwegian border (towards Oslo)
    Stockholm–Malmo (towards Øresund)
    Malmo–Goteborg–Swedish/Norwegian border (towards Oslo)
    Stockholm–Turku–Helsinki–Finnish/Russian border
	8 780

UK West Coast main line	800

Source: CEC (1995).

comprehensive trans-European high-speed rail network is to be operational by 2010. Despite the very significant progress that has been made over the past decade to establish a more coherent European-wide transport policy, the responsibility for bringing the various projects into being still rests principally with national governments. The progress of high-speed passenger services in Europe has so far been dominated by national priorities and action. This section examines the current and future status of high-speed rail systems in Europe, which has joined Japan at the forefront of world surface passenger transport developments. Japan took the lead role in the development of commercial high-speed rail development with the opening of its *Shinkansen* services in 1964, which have radically altered the relative accessibility of major cities on the network and enhanced the dominance of Tokyo (Murayama, 1994). The opening in 1988 of a *Shinkansen* station at Kakegawa City, initially bypassed by the Tokaido Line between Tokyo and Osaka, has been associated with significant increases in business and tourism activity (Okada, 1994). In the 1990s, the *Shinkansen* system has been enhanced through the introduction of a new series of higher-speed trains, as well as extensions of the network (Semmens, 1997; Taylor, 1997).

The striking progress of European high-speed rail services was achieved initially through a series of autonomous initiatives with national, rather than international, objectives. International rail passenger operations in Europe saw only modest improvements in the earlier phases of high-speed rail development (Savelberg and Vogelaar, 1987), although the number of transfrontier services and projects had advanced significantly by the later 1990s. While the general advance to higher speeds has been an incremental process, a number of benchmarks stand out, which can best be understood by examining both the national contexts in which they have developed and the major international ventures. This is attempted only in outline here; more detailed technical coverage can be found elsewhere, for example in Whitelegg *et al.* (1993) and Haydock (1995).

France

The French TGV (*Train à Grande Vitesse*) is significant both for its role as a high-profile pioneer of high-speed rail in Europe, and because it has evolved as a cornerstone of a wider European high-speed system. Springing from an urgent need to expand capacity in the Paris–Dijon–Lyon corridor, the TGV has been seen both as a regional development strategy and as a prestigious symbol of national technical prowess. Three years after the first TGV services began running between Paris and Lyon in 1981, rail traffic on the LGV (*Ligne à Grande Vitesse*) Sud-Est between the two cities had risen by 45 per cent, much of it diverted from air transport.

The LGV Sud-Est set several fundamental markers in the design and operation of European high-speed rail services. The TGV concept was based on the construction of new railway lines dedicated exclusively to high-speed trains, although these are by no means confined to the new tracks (unlike the Japanese *Shinkansen*). The absence of slower traffic, the use of high-powered electric traction and sophisticated train control systems allow high speeds to be maintained on steeper gradients than normal, thus reducing the line construction costs. Line speeds on the LGV Sud-Est are up to 270 km/h, rising to 300 km/h on the later LGV Atlantique from Paris to Le Mans and Tours. The TGV operates as a high-capacity, high-quality service, with reservations obligatory and supplements payable, between a limited number of access points on the LGV itself (Le Creusot and Mâcon are the only stops on the Paris–Lyon line).

Despite being designed for operation on a specialized infrastructure, TGV trains also run at lower speeds on other electrified lines. This critical flexibility allows a much wider range of destinations to be linked directly into the high-speed network (Figure 13.2). TGV services operate through to points in the south of France such as Nice, Perpignan and Irun (on the Spanish frontier), as well as to locations in the French Alps during the winter sports season.

The early success of the TGV led to a buoyant optimism about its potential in France's transport system and as an instrument of regional development. An ambitious and costly "Master Plan" projected a programme of new LGV projects that would form a comprehensive network of TGV services by the early twenty-first century (*Railway Gazette*, 1990). The LGV Nord-Europe from Paris, through Lille to Calais, was given high priority and opened in 1993. It has played an essential role in forming a high speed connection with the Channel Tunnel, as well as with the Nord Pas de Calais region and the Belgian high-speed line to Brussels, which opened in December 1997. The LGV Sud-Est has been extended via a "Lyon bypass", calling at Lyon Satolas airport (Thompson, 1995), down to Valence in the Rhône corridor. Two shorter, but strategically important, LGV lines have opened around the eastern and southern fringes of Paris (LGVs Jonction Est and Jonction Sud). These extend the scope of the TGV network in several ways: TGV stations serve Paris Charles de Gaulle airport and the Eurodisney theme park east of Paris, and the Jonction lines allow faster through-working of TGV services from northern France to the south. After meeting considerable local resistance on environmental grounds, the LGV Méditerranée is expected to be available for use in 2000. This will extend the high-speed network down the Rhône valley to Marseille and Montpellier, as well as allowing direct TGV services between these two major southern French

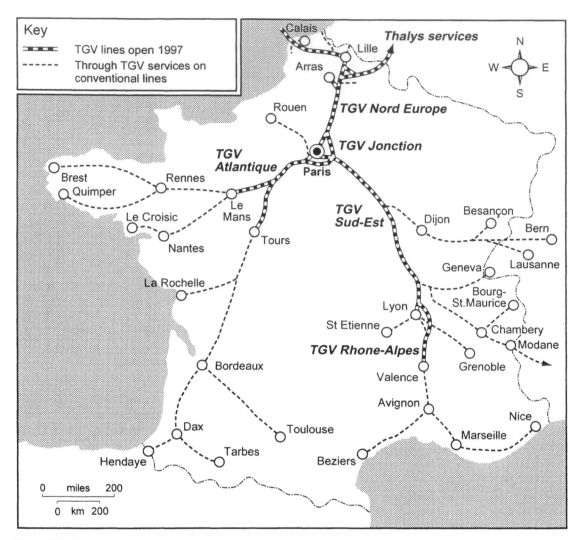

Figure 13.2   The French TGV system, 1997

cities. Beyond this, the next development is likely to be the LGV Est, running through Reims to serve Lorraine and Alsace. Both the LGV Méditerranée and LGV Est would contribute to subsequent higher-speed international services – to Spain (and eventually between Spain and Italy) and to Luxembourg and Germany respectively.

France has also developed further the technologies applied to its TGVs. To meet capacity shortages on its highly successful Paris–Lyon corridor, double-deck trains have been introduced (Haydock, 1995), capable of carrying considerably more passengers at high speeds while remaining within the relatively low French axle-weight limit of 17 tonnes. Once parallel enhancements in track and signalling have been made, capacity on the LGV Sud-Est will rise from 9000 passengers per hour each way to as much as 20 000 per hour. For the future, a "new generation" of TGVs is under development (TGV-NG), which will be capable of even higher speeds, and will also generate less noise and be technically more efficient (Tillier, 1997).

Germany

The German high-speed rail system has its origins in the need for a major reorientation and upgrading of long-distance transport links in the former West Germany. The weakness of north–south rail communications was the prime guiding factor in the choice of routes. The high-speed system has developed on the basis of using a mixture of newly constructed links (*Neubaustrecke)* and existing main lines substantially upgraded to high-speed standards (*Ausbaustrecke*). Passenger services are operated by ICE high-speed trains capable of running at up to 280 km/h. As the high-speed lines were designed to accommodate freight, as well as passenger trains, excessive gradients had to be avoided, which required very expensive engineering of the infrastructure, especially as much of the terrain passed through is hilly. Mitigation of environmental impacts has also added significantly to costs.

Since the opening of the first two key *Neubaustrecke* in 1991 (Mannheim–Stuttgart and Hannover–Würzburg), an extensive network of regular-interval ICE services has developed. German reunification brought dramatic new imperatives to transport planning. Much of the emphasis in more recent high-speed development has reflected the critical need to improve radically the skeletal links between west and east. The Hannover–Berlin *Neubaustrecke* is due to open in 1998, and work has begun on a line from Nürnberg to Erfurt and Leipzig (included in the list of European "priority links") (Jäger, 1996). At the same time as this response to reunification, work is under way on a further strategic high-speed line between Cologne and Frankfurt, which will see journey times fall to one hour. This line is scheduled to begin operating in 2000, and will be exclusively for high-speed passenger services, unlike earlier *Neubaustrecke*. The link will contribute to the international network in north-west Europe; by 2015, it is forecast that 30 per cent of the traffic will be cross-border movements (Jänsch, 1996).

Italy

High-speed train development in Italy is based principally on improving internal inter-city connections, although the Italian approach to high-speed train technology has aroused great interest elsewhere in Europe. Although new line construction for 300 km/h (ETR500) train-sets is an important part of Italian high-speed strategy, notably the Rome–Florence *Direttissima* line (to be followed by high-speed Rome–Naples and Bologna–Milan routes), difficult terrain and modest budgets have made this a very costly option. Until these additional lines are complete, the ETR500 trains operate between Rome and Milan at below their maximum potential speed (Renon, 1997). The alternative solution has been the successful development of tilting-body *Pendolino* trains that can negotiate curves at higher speeds without causing undue passenger discomfort (Giuntini, 1993; Haydock, 1995). The "second-generation" ETR460 tilting trains are capable of speeds up to 250 km/h. *Pendolini* have entered service on a steadily expanding network of routes, including those to a range of points in the Mezzogiorno.

Spain

The rapid completion and subsequent success of the first Spanish high-speed train (*Alta Velocidad Español*), from Madrid to Seville via Córdoba, is a vivid symbol of the country's determination to enter the mainstream of advanced nations in Europe. Although the line has an essentially "internal" objective, Spanish railway aspirations for more efficient connections with European partners were indicated by the decision to build it to the standard 1435 mm gauge, rather than the Spanish 1668 mm gauge. In the early 1990s, there were hopes that the first AVE line would be followed quite rapidly by similar connections through to the French frontier. The process has faltered somewhat, in that the route between Madrid and Barcelona is being upgraded for higher speeds incrementally and initially to the existing Spanish broad gauge. However, agreement has been reached for the construction by 2004 of a standard-gauge AVE line across the Franco-Spanish frontier, which is due to be extended to Barcelona, and will allow through-operations from the French high-speed network. This link is a particular priority for Catalonia as an autonomous Spanish region within the EU (Lopez Pita and Turro Calvet, 1987). Although Spanish high-speed rail strategy is partly determined by the concern for improved international links, the domestic market is also a prominent factor. In 1997, the regional government of Andalucia confirmed a project to extend the pioneer AVE line from Cordoba to Málaga, which would cut the journey time from the latter to Madrid from 4 hours 15 minutes to 2 hours 30 minutes.

EUROPEAN INTERNATIONAL HIGH-SPEED TRAIN SERVICES

While it is clear that national projects with domestic objectives have been very prominent in the evolution of high-speed rail in Europe, there is a widening range of international high-speed services in the late 1990s. Before considering these, it is important to stress some of the constraints on the interoperability required for the completion of a complete trans-European high-speed network. Essentially, independent national rail development has produced a variety of technical and organizational standards and practices that inhibit through-running (Banister *et al.*, 1995). This problem has many dimensions, including differences in power distribution systems for electric trains, train control/signalling systems, technical parameters of high-speed rolling stock and track infrastructure, track gauge (in the case of Spain and Portugal, Finland and the countries of the former Soviet Union), and loading gauge (narrower in Britain) (Puffert, 1993). Separate systems of management, ticketing, marketing and accounting must also be merged or harmonized. In 1996, the European Council issued a Directive confirming its intentions on the interoperability of high-speed trains (CEC, 1996d). Many steps have already been taken to reduce the effects of such divergence; for example, high-speed trains have been developed that

are capable of operating on lines electrified at four different voltages, adjustable wheelsets allow "Talgo" trains to run on the different track gauges of the Spanish and French networks, while considerable technical standardization has been achieved through the work of the UIC and the AEIF (European Association for Interoperability). The internationalization of Europe's railway equipment industry through multinational mergers and rationalization has also reduced divergence (Olivier, 1996).

Despite the strong image of the TGV *within* the French transport system, the French national railway SNCF has also made significant progress in reducing the technical and organizational barriers that have confronted services into its neighbour States. TGV trains operate into Switzerland, serving Geneva, Lausanne, Bern and Brig. To serve the latter two points, a small number of TGV trains have been equipped to operate under the Swiss 15 kV power system, as well as the 25 kV and 1500 V supplies used in France itself. At least as significant, however, was the formation of a Franco-Swiss bilateral route management team for TGV operations into Switzerland (*Railway Gazette*, 1996b).

This organizational model has been adopted for high-speed services connecting Paris and Lyon with Turin and Milan. From 1996, services have been operated via the Fréjus Tunnel using both TGV and Italian tilting ETR460 trains (the latter only as far as Lyon). The joint arrangement in place is seen as a precursor to the long-term goal of a high-speed Franco-Italian route through a new Alpine "base tunnel". Since 1995, TGV trains have also operated a frequent service between Brussels and Paris, again based on a joint operational agreement and the use of multi-current trains. This service has now become part of the international "Thalys" system described below.

There are now also high-speed services into Switzerland from Germany and Italy. German ICE trains operate to Zurich, Bern and Interlaken from a range of points on the ICE network in Germany (Photograph 13.1). In 1996, Italian-built ETR470 *Pendolino* tilting trains began operating joint

Photograph 13.1   A German ICE high-speed train near Stuttgart (C.A. Charlton, R. Gibb)

Italian-Swiss "*Cisalpino*" services through the Alps between Milan and Bern and Zurich, with extension to Stuttgart scheduled for 1997. This marks another advance of the "tilt alternative" approach to faster passenger train services, as well as being a further example of the practical importance of bilateral arrangements in transfrontier high-speed operations (Haydock, 1997).

THE CHANNEL TUNNEL

The opening of the Channel Tunnel in 1994 was clearly a dramatic addition to the nascent European high-speed rail network, especially as the Tunnel's completion coincided with that of the LGV Nord-Europe from the French side of the Channel to Paris, via Lille (Knowles, 1994). The trains constructed for Eurostar services between London and Paris and Brussels, as well as the planning and management of the operation, mark a very significant step forward in international collaboration (Photograph 13.2). The full potential of Eurostar operations will only be realized with the opening of the Channel Tunnel Rail Link (CTRL) from London St Pancras to the Tunnel, although this has suffered a very protracted evolution (Gibb and Knowles, 1994; Haydock, 1995). When eventually completed, high-speed running will be possible throughout, a marked improvement over the performance on the existing lines in Britain. At present, Eurostar trains cannot operate at full power, given the 750 V electrification system on the conventional lines they must share with slower suburban services (Semmens, 1990). Once the CTRL is opened, London–Paris journey times should fall to 2 hours 20 minutes, and London–Brussels to around 2 hours, thus improving further their competitiveness with rival air services.

Photograph 13.2 Eurostar international high-speed passenger train at London's Waterloo international terminal (Eurostar UK Ltd)

Although the core inter-capitals routes will remain the mainstay of Eurostar operations, the range of services using the Tunnel should widen. After some delay, Regional Eurostar services are due to put Birmingham within four hours of Paris, and Manchester five hours. There are also daily Eurostar services from London to Eurodisney, while the trains began to serve a different leisure-based market by operating direct services to the French Alps for winter sports tourists in 1997/8.

THE THALYS NETWORK

The most significant component of the emerging high-speed rail system for north-west Europe is the network of services under development to link Paris and Brussels with Amsterdam and Cologne. This multinational venture operates under the brand name "Thalys", using dedicated high-speed train sets based on the French TGV, but adapted to operate with four different electrical systems as well as the variety of national train control systems. As with the Eurostar trains, this has presented a considerable engineering challenge, as well as costly investment in infrastructure in the form of new high-speed line construction. The first major step forward for the Thalys services was the opening of the new Belgian high-speed line from the French frontier into the suburbs of Brussels in 1997 (Jadot, 1998). This line has accelerated Eurostar services to and from Belgium, and allowed Brussels–Paris journey times to fall to 85 minutes. Even before this, Thalys services had increased rail's share of the latter market from 24 per cent to 40 per cent. Early in the twenty-first century, the network is due to expand with the extension of hourly services onto new and upgraded routes from Brussels to Amsterdam, including a line that will cross the environmentally sensitive "green heart" of the Dutch Randstad in tunnels at an extra cost of £330 million (Hanenbergh, 1996), and from Brussels to Aachen via Liège. An initial Thalys service began operating from Amsterdam to Paris in 1996, using modified French TGV trains; this has attracted a significant traffic flow, even with much of the route confined to conventional tracks. Thalys services have also reduced the Paris–Cologne journey time to 4 hours. Together with the Channel Tunnel, the existing French LGV, the German Cologne–Frankfurt *Neubaustrecke* and new ICE train variants planned for direct Germany–Netherlands and Belgium services, the Thalys operation suggests that aspirations for a trans-European high-speed network by 2010 will be met in the core regions of the EU, if not in its periphery.

FUTURE PROSPECTS: SOME POSSIBLE CHALLENGES AND CONSTRAINTS FACING HIGH-SPEED RAIL IN EUROPE

What in fact are the prospects for high-speed rail in Europe? A simple answer to this question seems more elusive in the late 1990s than it did at the opening of the decade, as the picture has become steadily more complex against an uncertain economic and political background. The various high-speed projects described above must certainly allow some confidence that there will be further progress. The relative advantage of investment in rail should be underscored by a widening understanding that there are environmental and social limits to the continued expansion of private road transport and road construction (although the trans-European networks programme envisages many additional kilometres of motorway). Despite hesitation about its timing and ultimate extent, the "European project" for further economic, social and perhaps political unity still seems broadly on course, with the attendant assumption that more efficient transport is essential. The technical and organizational barriers to better international rail services are no longer as high as in the past. Many high-speed operations, such as the TGV Sud-Est, Spanish AVE and German ICE, have shown an impressive ability to attract new custom. Some high-speed services are proving more successful than might have been predicted a decade ago. These include long-distance trips from Brussels and northern France to the French Riviera, short-distance high-speed AVE services between Madrid and Ciudad Real and Ponferrada, and the 200 km/h AVE services on the conventional broad-gauge "Euromed" route between Barcelona and Valencia. High-speed train connections are widely regarded as highly desirable for regional economic development, and by cities that aspire to "Eurocity" status (Thompson, 1995). Gutiérrez *et al.* (1996) demonstrate that the completion of the EU's plan for the European high-speed network would "bring generalized benefits, in the sense that these will affect the whole of the territory of the European Union, but the greatest increases in accessibility in absolute terms will correspond to the peripheral regions".

Despite its persistent strong profile, it is possible to raise doubts over the realism and validity of Europe's "high-speed" dream. Most daunting are the immense investment costs required. Although the European Community has committed substantial financial resources to the TENs project, the majority of the funding required will need to be raised by national governments or from the private sector. Private investment in transport infrastructure is seen as essential, and in some cases has been forthcoming, as in the case of the Channel Tunnel and CTRL. However, it may be more difficult to attract such input into some of the more adventurous and marginal projects, especially in peripheral regions and in Central and Eastern Europe. Even within the transport sphere, high-speed rail must compete as investment priorities with other modes, and also other rail sectors. There are strong claims for major rail initiatives to improve rail services in Europe's major conurbations, as well as to enhance freight and combined transport flows (such as the Betuwe freight corridor from Rotterdam into Germany). Domestic priorities may override plans for international transport investment, as in Germany, which has strong incentives to continue to improve transport to the east of the reunified country.

Changes in the organization and regulation of European rail systems could have a significant influence in the further evolution of international high-speed services, even if the course this will take is still uncertain. While Britain has chosen the radical path of full privatization, other States have remained more cautious, although most are complying with EU policy in separating the business management of infrastructure from that of train operations. There is also a growing acceptance that private capital will play a more prominent role in future railway investment. However, the principle embodied in EC Directive 91/440, which requires rail infrastructure to be open to competing international passenger train operations, has yet to produce any significant impacts. It is questionable how far a genuine free market is possible within the rail mode: the pioneering international high-speed services such as Eurostar, Thalys and Cisalpino have been based on close collaboration rather than competition.

The viability of international rail passenger services will depend in part on the strength of competition from other modes – air transport, international coach services and not least the private car. The completion of air transport deregulation within Europe is likely to reduce the cost of inter-city air travel, and so hold back a switch to rail which might otherwise be expected as a result of higher rail speeds, although it is clear that the air passenger market is itself very vulnerable to competition over shorter distances (for example, London and Brussels to Paris). The continued expansion of the European motorway and general highway network (Gutiérrez and Urbano, 1996), combined with powerful marketing by the motor industry and rising car ownership, will reinforce the competitive strength of international road transport. There is still a massive latent demand for private car ownership especially in Eastern Europe (Timar, 1991). While an enduring rise in energy prices (which seems eminently likely in the further future) might give rail an advantage for many intra-European journeys, responses can be expected by its competitors.

Also, without infrastructural adjustment and better integration of public transport or profound changes in land-use planning policy, the steady decentralization of population, services and industry will tend to favour the flexibility of road transport, and perhaps also the peri-urban locations of major airports. There are now rather fewer advantages in the location of rail terminals in city centres than in the past. Although there have been some responses to the radical shifts in intra-metropolitan spatial patterns, such as the "parkway" stations in Britain, and TGV stations at Massy in the southern suburbs of Paris and at Paris Charles de Gaulle and Lyon Satolas airports, high-speed rail terminals are still tied closely to locations that were optimal in the nineteenth century.

New high-speed railway construction is likely to encounter increasingly trenchant opposition on environmental grounds, despite its longer-term capacity to reduce energy consumption and road congestion. The first two French TGV lines were built with relatively low perceived environmental impact, but subsequent projects are more problematic. There were strong protests over the construction of the TGV Méditerranée line into Provence, and the Spanish AVE from Madrid to Seville. Mitigation of environmental impacts imposes significant delays and extra costs on high-speed rail projects; this has been especially apparent in Germany, is a major additional expense in the construction of the high-speed line to Amsterdam, and is a factor that has influenced the design of the CTRL.

Further questions focus on the justification for concentrating resources on high-speed inter-city services and involve issues of opportunity cost, and spatial and social equity (Ross, 1994; Vickerman, 1994). Whitelegg (1993) challenges the implications of faster rail services and points out the disproportionate advantages accruing to places and groups in European society that are already well-favoured. Although the TEN programme looks to the cohesion of more peripheral regions, parts of which would experience substantial improvements in accessibility, in practice the main benefits are likely to be concentrated in the European "centre". Here, high-speed rail competes with air transport in terms of service standards and cost, and elevated price levels are necessary for acceptable returns on the great capital investments involved. As direct access from intermediate points is sacrificed to minimize journey times between major cities, less significant centres in the same regions may find themselves with a relatively poorer level of service (European Conference of Ministers of Transport, 1995; Gutiérrez *et al.*, 1996). Accessibility differentials will grow, so that well-connected cities like Lille look forward to buoyant economic development, while Amiens and Mons regret their disadvantage at exclusion from the network.

In practice, this problem is understood and at least partially addressed. The EU's "Citizens' Network" concept reflects a concern to minimize spatial exclusivity in European transport systems. Some regions have relatively widespread access to high-speed services, either direct, or through the operation of feeder routes. The Nord Pas de Calais region in France illustrates this, with TGV through-services to cities such as Dunkerque and Valenciennes, as well as a set of connecting services supported by the regional government.

ALTERNATIVES TO HIGH-SPEED TRAINS

The very high investment costs of new high-speed lines could render them suspect on economic as well as social and environmental grounds. A recent study by the European Commission has cast doubt on the benefits of the Ecu 400 billion TEN transport proposals, suggesting that the additional economic growth that would be generated by the new transport infrastructure would be much less than originally forecast (*The European*, 1997). Perhaps the strongest indication of high-speed ideals not being met is the major reappraisal of the future of the French TGV programme (*Today's Railways*, 1996). The Chirac government that came into power in 1995 effectively scrapped the 1990 Master Plan, out

of concern over the severe financial problems facing SNCF, and the disappointing rate of return calculated for more recent LGVs, including the LGV Nord-Europe. Among factors suggested as explaining the weak actual and predicted performance of much of the TGV network are the country's poor general economic performance, a resistance to pay higher fares for increased speed and the resurgence of competition from a deregulated air transport industry. Although the LGV Est project from Paris to Strasbourg is still retained, its completion could take many years, and other lines in the Master Plan are unlikely to go forward. After years of resistance, SNCF has been persuaded to test tilting trains for use on existing tracks (initially, a modified TGV set), in lieu of new-build LGVs.

This alternative technology, plus an acceptance of "slower" 200–225 km/h maximum speeds, has emerged as the preferred approach elsewhere in Europe, as on the newly privatized railway system in Britain (notably the Virgin West Coast franchise), in Sweden, Portugal, Finland and the Czech Republic. Here, the EU is contributing funds for the upgrading of the Dresden–Prague–Vienna route, which will allow new *Pendolino*-technology train sets to complete the journey from Berlin to the Austrian capital in 6 hours, rather than the present 9.5 hours. In Germany, too, new tilting variants of the ICE high-speed train concept are under development (Kohler, 1997), to complement existing diesel tilting trains for use on secondary inter-city services, including the international route between Munich and Zurich. However, the near-universal enthusiasm for tilting trains as a lower-cost alternative to the "new line" approach (Green, 1997) might need to be tempered by continuing questions over the acceptability of the ride at speed through curves: some passengers report considerable discomfort and nausea, for example on journeys on *Cisalpino* units through the Alps (Ford, 1997).

Passenger train services can be enhanced incrementally through the application of many relatively unspectacular technical and operational developments, including track realignments, signalling improvements and the use of "push–pull" and multiple-unit trains to minimize the time taken to reverse trains. Generally, it is possible that the focus on "maximum" high-speed systems can mask the variety of rail services and potential improvements in rail travel across frontiers. Despite the overall influence of the "frontier effect" on cross-border travel, there are many examples where shorter-range international movements are already substantial, and can be expected to intensify with the further advance of integration in Europe. Relatively modest investments in infrastructure and rolling stock and collaboration in planning and management could enhance the appeal of rail services, through improved frequency, comfort and convenience as well as modest time savings. Improvements in short-range rail services are in prospect across the French-Belgian and Dutch-German frontiers.

Long-distance overnight services are a more traditional form of international rail market that could also have further potential. Although some long-established services have been withdrawn (for example, between Norway and Sweden), and plans for European Night Services through the Channel Tunnel abandoned, certain others have proved fairly successful. Germany plans to introduce night services based on the Spanish "passive tilt" Talgo technology, which is already in use on variable-gauge overnight trains between France and Spain. There could be a variety of markets in the future for such trains, including luxurious "hotel trains" based on premium fares and, in contrast, lower-cost leisure-oriented services. As Europe's tourism market expands and diversifies, there could be a growing role for international rail travel which does not depend on operation at very high speeds, if there is a parallel development of cost-effective and imaginative travel products and packages.

CONCLUSIONS

Despite the various physical, technical, political and economic obstacles to the development of international train services, the market has been expanding to meet a growing demand, even though this has been a somewhat uncoordinated and uneven process. The strength of complementarity across frontiers is growing relative to forces that maintain the effects of distance. ISPT is likely to be a key beneficiary of an era characterized by an increasingly globalized world order. The scale of transfrontier travel is expanding as the *significance* of those frontiers is in many respects diminishing. This is particularly the case in the European Union with its densely populated countries, high levels of disposable income and internationalized economy and labour market, all of which tend to stimulate travel. A similar effect is possible in the longer term in other areas, not least Eastern Europe. ISPT could also gain relative to air transport and the private car if these encounter increasing problems from congestion and higher fuel prices. Nevertheless, there will continue to be serious impediments to the full realization of the potential of international rail travel and ISPT generally, and competing modes will remain formidable competition.

As the European high-speed rail case study shows, the coordination of infrastructure construction and through-services between sovereign States is fraught with difficulties. As may prove to be the case with some of the more ambitious projects in the trans-European transport networks, it is a task not to be underestimated, even in an era of enhanced political and economic cooperation. Equally, the range of experience building up with international transport planning, development and operation in Europe could provide valuable lessons for other parts of the world.

REFERENCES

Allen, G.F. (1991), "EEC high-speed rail plan", *Modern Railways* 48 (511), 188–97.

Banister, D., Capello, R. and Nijkamp, P. (eds) (1995), *European transport and communications networks: policy evolution and change* (Chichester: Wiley).

Bayliss, B.T. (1979), "Transport in the EC", *Journal of Transport Economics and Policy* 13 (1), 28–43.

Budd, S. (1987), *The EEC* (London: Kogan Page).

CEC (1990a), *The European high-speed train network* (Brussels: Commission of the European Communities).

CEC (1990b), *Towards trans-European networks for a Community Action Programme*, COM (90) 585 final (Brussels: Commission of the European Communities).

CEC (1991), "Council Directive of 29 July 1991 on the development of the Community's railways", *Official Journal of the European Communities* OJ L 237 (Brussels: Commission of the European Communities).

CEC (1992a), *The future development of the Common Transport Policy*, COM (92) 424 final (Luxembourg: Commission of the European Communities).

CEC (1992b), "From the Single Act to Maastricht and beyond: the means to our ambitions", *Bulletin of the European Communities*, Supplement 1/92, 13–36 (Brussels: Commission of the European Communities).

CEC (1994), *Community guidelines for the development of a Trans-European Transport Network*, COM (94) 106 final (Brussels: Commission of the European Communities).

CEC (1995), *The Trans-European Transport Network: transforming a patchwork into a network* (Luxembourg: Commission of the European Communities).

CEC (1996a), "Decision No. 1692/96/EC of the European Parliament and of the Council on Community guidelines for the development of the Trans-European Transport Network", *Official Journal of the European Communities* OJ L 228 (Brussels: Commission of the European Communities).

CEC (1996b), *The Citizens' Network*, European Commission Green Paper (Brussels: Commission of the European Communities).

CEC (1996c), "Resolution on the pan-European transport policy", *Official Journal of the European Communities* OJ C 380 (Brussels: Commission of the European Communities).

CEC (1996d), "Council Directive 96/48/EC of 23 July 1996 on the interoperability of the trans-European high-speed rail system", *Official Journal of the European Communities* OJ L 235 (Brussels: Commission of the European Communities).

CER (1989), *Proposals for a European high-speed train network* (Brussels: Community of European Railways).

Charlton, C.A. (1994), "The development of high-speed rail passenger services in Europe", in Gibb, R. (ed.), *The Channel Tunnel: a geographical approach* (Chichester: Wiley), 31–54.

Dente, G. (1991) "The role of the United Nations Economic Commission for Europe in the development of a whole European transport system", in *Prospects for east–west European transport* (Paris: European Conference of Ministers of Transport), 43–63.

Dick, A. (1994), "Trans-European transport networks", *Pan-European transport issues*, Proceedings of Seminar A, 22nd PTRC European Transport Forum, University of Warwick, September 1994, 201–12.

Din, M.A.E. (1990), "The transport importance of the Arabian (Persian) Gulf", *Transport Reviews* 10 (2), 127–48.

Europa (1996), "The European Union's transport policy", Europa World Wide Web site, http://europa.eu.int/en/eupol/trans.html

The European (1997), 9 January.

European Conference of Ministers of Transport (1991), *Prospects for east–west European transport* (Paris: ECMT).

European Conference of Ministers of Transport (1995), *European transport trends and infrastructural needs* (Paris: ECMT).

Ford, R. (1997), "Tilt no longer a novelty in Europe", *Railway Gazette* 153 (4), 249–52.

Frohnmeyer, A. (1994), "Contribution of railways to the Transeuropean Networks", *Pan-European transport issues*, Proceedings of Seminar A, 22nd PTRC European Transport Forum, University of Warwick, September 1994, 65–75.

Gérardin, B. and Viégas, J. (1993), "European transport infrastructure and networks: current policies and trends", in Nijkamp, P. (ed.), *Europe on the move* (Aldershot: Avebury).

Gibb, R. and Knowles, R.D. (1994), "The high-speed rail link: planning and development implications", in Gibb, R. (ed.), *The Channel Tunnel: a geographical approach* (Chichester: Wiley), 177–98.

Giuntini, A. (1993), "High speed trains in Italy: from Fascism to the ETR500", in Whitelegg, J., Húlten, S. and Frank, T., *High speed trains: fast tracks to the future* (Hawes: Leading Edge), 55–65.

Green, C. (1997), "Rail's time has come", *Modern Railways* 54, 784–7.

Gutiérrez, J. and Urbano, P. (1996), "Accessibility in the European Union: the impact of the trans-European road network", *Journal of Transport Geography* 4 (1), 15–25.

Gutiérrez, J., González, R. and Gómez, G. (1996), "The European high-speed train network: predicted effects on accessibility patterns", *Journal of Transport Geography* 4 (4), 227–38.

Hanenbergh, H. (1996), "ICE International drives new line proposals", *Railway Gazette* 152 (7), 430–1.

Haydock, D. (1995) *High speed in Europe* (Sheffield: Platform 5 Publishing).

Haydock, D. (1997), "Cisalpino introduction", *Today's Railways* 16, 18–21.

Jadot, M. (1998), "Entering a new era", *Modern Railways* 55, 104–7.

Jäger, H.R. (1996), "Two lines will add 400 km to Germany's high-speed network", *Railway Gazette* 152 (11), 731–2.

Jänsch, E. (1996), "Evolution of the ICE", *Modern Railways* 53, 513–5.

Knowles, R.D. (1994), "Passenger transport", in Gibb, R. (ed.), *The Channel Tunnel: a geographical approach* (Chichester: Wiley), 55–77.

Kohler (1997), "The ICE pages", Mercurio: the European Railway Server, http://mercurio.iet.unipi.it/ice/ict.html.

Lopez Pita, A. and Turro Calvet, A. (1987), "Faisibilité d'une ligne de chemin de fer à grande vitesse de Barcelone jusqu'à la frontière française", in Proceedings of Seminar A, PTRC Annual Meeting, September 1987, 79–92.

Maggi, R., Masser, I. and Nijkamp, P. (1992), "Missing networks in European transport and communications", *Transport Reviews* 12 (4), 311–21.

Munsey, M. (1997), "DSB: tomorrow's railway", *Today's Railways* 19, 18–20.

Murayama, Y. (1994), "The impact of railways on accessibility in the Japanese urban system", *Journal of Transport Geography* 2 (2), 87–100.

Nijkamp, P. (1995), "From missing networks to interoperable networks: the need for European cooperation in the railway sector", *Transport Policy* 2 (3), 159–67.

Okada, H. (1994), "Features and economic and social effects of the Shinkansen", *Japan Railway and Transport Review* 3, October.

Olivier, M. (1996), "UNIFE tackles the challenge of change", *Railway Gazette* 152 (2), 80–1.

Omiunu, F. (1987), "Towards a transport policy for the ECOWAS sub-region", *Transport Reviews* 7 (4), 327–40.

Puffert, D.J. (1993), "Technical diversity: the integration of the European high-speed train network", in Whitelegg, J., Húlten, S. and Frank, T., *High-speed trains: fast tracks to the future* (Hawes: Leading Edge), 162–71.

Railway Gazette (1990), "3560 km of TGV lines in Master Plan", *Railway Gazette* 146 (7), 503.

Railway Gazette (1996a), "Kinnock charts path to rail's comeback", *Railway Gazette* 152 (2), 74–6.

Railway Gazette (1996b), "Bilateral accords promise dedicated route management", *Railway Gazette* 152 (2), 76.

Renon, R. (1997), "Milano–Bologna will complete Italy's north–south TAV corridor", *Railway Gazette* 153 (10), 687–90.

Rhee, J. (1995), "Development of an Eurasian transportation network: potential and possibilities", *Transportation* 22, 389–412.

Ross, J.F. (1994), "High-speed rail: catalyst for European integration?", *Journal of Common Market Studies* 32 (2), 191–214.

Savelberg, F. and Vogelaar, H. (1987), "Determinants of a high-speed railway", *Transportation* 14, 97–111.

Semmens, P.W.B. (1990), "Government 'no' to high-speed link", *Railway Magazine* 136 (1072).

Semmens, P.W.B. (1997), "Now the bullets fly faster still", *Railway Magazine* 143 (1154), 66–68.

Taylor, C. (1997), "Shinkansen regains speed honours as French cut back: world speed survey, 1997", *Railway Gazette* 153 (10), 669–74.

Thompson, I.B. (1995), "High-speed transport hubs and Eurocity status: the case of Lyon", *Journal of Transport Geography* 3 (1), 29–37.

Tillier, C. (1997), "The TGV pages", Mercurio: the European Railway Server, http://mercurio.iet.unipi.it/tgv/research.html

Timar, A. (1991), "Prospective trends in passenger transport in the East European countries", in *Prospects for east–west European transport* (Paris: European Conference of Ministers of Transport), 227–62.

Today's Railways (1996), "Brake put on TGV", *Today's Railways* 16, 8.

UIC (1997), *Protocol agreement on "Crete Corridor 1" rail links signed at UIC*, UIC Press Release No. 97, 19 June 1997 (Paris: Union Internationale des Chemins de fer).

Ullman, E.L. (1973), *Geography as spatial interaction: studies in regional development, cities and transportation* (Washington, DC: University of Washington Press).

Vickerman, R.W. (1994), "Transport infrastructure and region building in the European Community", *Journal of Common Market Studies* 32 (1), 1–24.

Walrave, M. (1994), "The strategic implications of high-speed rail for Europe", *Pan-European Transport Issues*, Proceedings of Seminar A, 22nd PTRC European Transport Forum, University of Warwick, September 1994, 55–64.

Whitelegg, J. (1993), *Transport for a sustainable future: the case for Europe* (London: Belhaven).

Whitelegg, J., Húlten, S. and Frank, T. (1993), *High-speed trains: fast tracks to the future* (Hawes: Leading Edge).

14

INTERNATIONAL AIR TRANSPORT

Brian Graham

The international air transport industry has been transformed during the past two decades by the combined forces of deregulation (or liberalization), competition and privatization. Against this background, the chapter first explores the geography of demand for air transport and examines its contemporary geopolitics. Secondly, the discussion assesses the response of airlines to the deregulatory environment, concentrating on two particular strategies: hub-and-spoke networks and global alliances. Next, the chapter offers an assessment of the major contemporary air transport markets, followed by a brief examination of the global problems of airport capacity. Finally, the environmental implications of air transport are discussed.

INTRODUCTION

Although the world's air transport networks were largely pioneered prior to World War II, the origins of mass air travel – at least in the developed world – date back no earlier than circa 1960. Since then, aggregate growth rates have been quite dramatic, albeit punctuated by short-term fluctuations caused by external events such as economic recession and the Gulf War of 1991, which severely depressed demand for air travel. Latterly, however, the aviation industry, buoyed by increased profits resulting from the global economic upturn of the mid-1990s, remains bullish about long-term growth trends, despite concerns about fuel supplies and costs, shortages of airport capacity in many key markets, and the negative environmental impacts of air transport. The aggregate growth in demand for air transport has been fuelled by two principal factors – growing disposable incomes in developed countries, accompanied by

radical changes in the geopolitics of the industry, which have resulted in government regulation and control increasingly being replaced by an ethos of deregulation, liberalization, privatization and increased competition.

In the first instance, air transport is a high-cost mode and access to it is notably correlated with personal wealth (Alperovich and Machnes, 1994). Consequently, there is a fair degree of correspondence between gross domestic product (GDP) and revenue passenger-kilometre (mile in United States) (RPK or RPM) flown (Figure 14.1). The RPK/GDP ratio once stood at 2:1 but is now declining. It is estimated that a 3 per cent increase in GDP is now worth only a 4 per cent increase in air traffic, a function of the increasing maturity of the market in many countries. The correlation with wealth ensures that global demand for air transport is spatially skewed, North America, Europe and Asia–Pacific (particularly Australasia and the wealthier countries of the West

Modern Transport Geography: second, revised edition. Edited by Brian Hoyle and Richard Knowles.
© 1998 John Wiley & Sons Ltd.

Pacific Rim) accounting for 90 per cent of total world scheduled, passenger, freight and mail traffic in 1995 (Table 14.1).

Secondly, air transport worldwide was historically subject to stringent government controls and regulation. In 1978, however, the Airlines Deregulation Act swept away Federal government control over domestic air services in the United States, instituting a new global order for the airline industry. These changes are symbolic of the ascendancy throughout the contemporary capitalist world of neo-liberal (or neo-classical or New Right) economic ideologies, committed to ending a previous orthodoxy that envisaged some form of public–private articulation of political economies. The key principles of neo-liberalism include the primacy of the market and profit, and the enhancement of competition, achieved by denationalization and privatization of State-owned companies and, above all, by deregulation – the removal, or restructuring, of the regulatory apparatus applied to business structures and practices. Simultaneously, however, the rapidly escalating interdependence of the world economy means that the economic well-being of individual States is increasingly determined less by national governments than by complex interactions at the global scale (Knox and Agnew, 1994). Economic liberalism has been accompanied by globalization.

It is this dual context of differential access to the mode and deregulation that provides the framework for this chapter's analysis of international air transport. Initially, the basic geographical characteristics of contemporary air transport are established, followed by a discussion of the critical features of deregulatory, competitive aviation environments. Thirdly, the chapter addresses the essentially spatial strategies, which airlines have adopted in coping with the challenge of this radically altered political regime, a discussion extended into brief surveys of the salient characteristics of the world's major contemporary air transport markets. Although one of the principal repercussions of competition has been to help grow demand for air transport, this in turn creates wider issues of precisely how that growth might be sustained. The chapter concludes by examining some of the tensions and conflicts that ensue

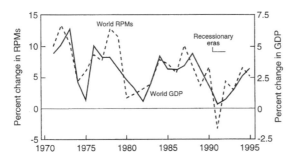

Figure 14.1 World revenue passenger-miles (RPMs) versus economic growth (percentage GDP change)
Source: Boeing (1996, 12)

Table 14.1   Scheduled traffic of commercial air carriers, 1995, preliminary (tonne-kilometres performed by ICAO region of carrier registration)

ICAO Statistical Region of Carrier Registration	Total Tonne-Kilometres Performed (millions)	Percentage of Total Tonne-Kilometres Performed
Europe	77 414	26.54
Africa	5 961	2.04
Middle East	9 953	3.41
Asia–Pacific	77 918	26.73
North America	106 630	36.57
Latin America and Caribbean	13 728	4.71
Total	291 604	100.00

Source: International Civil Aviation Organization (1996, 18).

from the provision of airport capacity and its impact on land-use planning, and the growing concerns over aircraft noise and atmospheric emissions in an age in which environmental issues are becoming an ever-greater public priority.

THE GEOGRAPHY OF AIR TRANSPORT

Given the correlation between GDP and demand for air transport, it not surprising that virtually all the top-ranked countries for scheduled air traffic are located within North America, Europe and Asia–Pacific. The United States alone accounted for 38 per cent of total passenger-kilometres performed on scheduled services in 1995, followed by the United Kingdom and Japan with almost 7 and 6 per cent respectively. Among other factors, the percentage of traffic carried by US airlines reflects the size and domestic nature of the bulk of their market. The largest share of international scheduled traffic – around 30 per cent – is carried by European airlines,

which also account for the most significant single component of the world charter market. The dominant intercontinental traffic axes link Europe with North America and Asia, and Asia with North America. Consequently, at the global scale, the demand for, and provision of, air transport has a pronounced east–west bias, north–south routes into South America, Africa and the South-West Pacific effectively being little more than capillaries within this overall dominant pattern (Figure 14.2).

Not surprisingly, the global distribution of major airline operators correlates directly with the regional traffic patterns shown in Table 14.1 and Figure 14.2. Of the world's top 30 scheduled airline groups in 1996 (ranked by sales), only one – the Brazilian flag-carrier, Varig – is based in a country outside North America, Europe or Asia–Pacific (Table 14.2). No less than seven of the top 15 airlines in this ranking and all top six largest passenger carriers in 1996 were US-domiciled (Table 14.3). European and Asian-Pacific airlines, however, are much more dominant in terms of international passenger traffic, reflecting the political fragmentation of their home regions

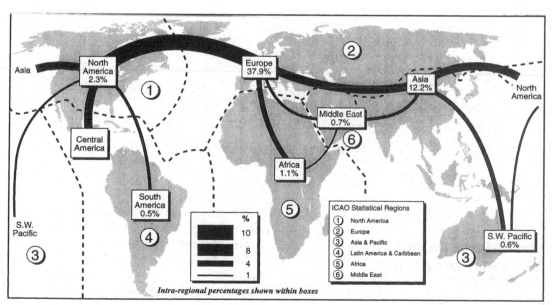

Figure 14.2   Major traffic flows between regions, 1995 (percentage of IATA international scheduled passengers)
Source: International Air Transport Association (1996, 24)

Table 14.2 World's top 30 airline groups by sales, 1996 (in US$ million)

Rank	Airline Group	Country	Sales in 1996
1	American Airlines	USA	17 753
2	United Airlines	USA	16 362
3	Japan Airlines	Japan	13 918
4	Lufthansa	Germany	13 841
5	British Airways	UK	13 247
6	Delta Air Lines	USA	12 465
7	Federal Express	USA	11 520
8	Northwest Airlines	USA	9 880
9	All Nippon Airways	Japan	9 074
10	*Groupe* Air France	France	8 833
11	USAirways	USA	8 142
12	Swissair	Switzerland	6 645
13	Continental Airlines	USA	6 360
14	KLM Royal Dutch Airlines	Netherlands	5 952
15	Qantas	Australia	5 766
16	SAS	Denmark/Norway/Sweden	5 252
17	Singapore Airlines	Singapore	5 115
18	Alitalia	Italy	5 063
19	Korean Air	South Korea	4 341
20	Cathay Pacific	Hong Kong	4 187
21	Iberia Airlines	Spain	3 771
22	Air Canada	Canada	3 578
23	Trans World Airlines	USA	3 554
24	Southwest Airlines	USA	3 406
25	Thai Airways International	Thailand	3 097
26	Varig	Brazil	2 963
27	Japan Air System	Japan	2 832
28	LTU International Airways	Germany	2 674
29	Malaysia Airlines	Malaysia	2 594
30	Ansett Australia	Australia	2 545

Source: *Airline Business* (1997).

and the restricted spatial extent of some domestic markets. Indeed, Singapore Airlines is entirely dependent on international traffic, while the same was also true of Cathay Pacific Airways before Hong Kong reverted to Chinese control in 1997.

THE GEOPOLITICS OF CONTEMPORARY AIR TRANSPORT

Bilateral Agreements

Once it was accepted at the Paris Convention of 1919 that States possess sovereign rights to the air space above their territories, direct government intervention into air transport became inevitable (Doganis, 1991). As airlines developed during the 1920s and 1930s, they were used as investments of State policy to promote trade, mail services, foreign policy and domestic employment, all without much regard to economic implications. Air transport networks developed on the basis of national need, symbolized most presciently by the resultant national or flag-carrier airlines (Graham, 1995). The air relationships between countries were codified in the Chicago Convention of 1944, which recognized the so-called "five freedoms of civil aviation" (to which

Table 14.3 World's largest passenger airlines, 1996 (million passengers)

Rank	Airline	Country	Passengers
1	Delta Air Lines	USA	91.34
2	United Airlines	USA	81.86
3	American Airlines	USA	81.16
4	USAirways	USA	56.64
5	Southwest Airlines	USA	55.49
6	Northwest Airlines	USA	52.70
7	Lufthansa	Germany	41.40
8	All Nippon Airways	Japan	39.72
9	Continental Airlines	USA	38.33
10	British Airways	UK	33.33
11	Japan Airways	Japan	30.19
12	Korean Air	South Korea	23.74
13	Trans World Airlines	USA	23.41
14	Alitalia	Italy	23.14
15	SAS	Denmark/Norway/Sweden	19.83
16	Japan Air System	Japan	18.22
17	America West Airlines	USA	18.18
18	Qantas	Australia	17.49
19	*Groupe* Air France	France	16.40
20	Air France Europe	France	15.50

Source: Airline Business (1997)

four more have since been added) (Figure 14.3; Sealy, 1966; Shearman, 1992). However, the multilateral exchange of these freedoms was rejected, the Chicago Convention agreeing only to the mutual exchange of the first two: the right to overfly a foreign country and the right to make a non-traffic-generating stop, for example, to refuel.

All other freedoms were left to individual bilateral air service agreements, negotiated between pairs of governments. The basic principle of all bilaterals is reciprocity or equivalency, defined as an equal and fair exchange of aviation rights (Debbage, 1994), the agreements covering fares, capacity frequency, number of carriers and routes flown. The key international agreement – because it acted as a model for subsequent bilaterals – was that signed between the United States (US) and United Kingdom (UK) at Bermuda in 1946 (Dobson, 1991). Subsequently liberalized, this now allows multiple designation of carriers on some transatlantic city-pairs and limited fifth-freedom rights, perhaps the

most contested aspect of numerous bilateral negotiations. The original Bermuda accord on the North Atlantic and, even more notably, the 1952 US–Japan bilateral were agreed between unequal partners, a reflection of the political dominance of the United States and the ability of its airlines to operate services following World War II. The US government aggressively sought unreciprocated fifth-freedom rights and these remain highly contentious, especially in Japan where several US carriers, most notably United Airlines and Northwest Airlines, enjoy extensive "beyond" rights, which allow them to use Tokyo Narita as a base for intra-Asian services. Conversely, no foreign airlines are allowed access to the US domestic market because that would constitute eighth-freedom – or cabotage – rights, which are illegal under US law.

Since the imposition of domestic deregulation in 1978, the US government has pursued a global policy – nominally free trade but essentially free trade as compatible with US national interests – to

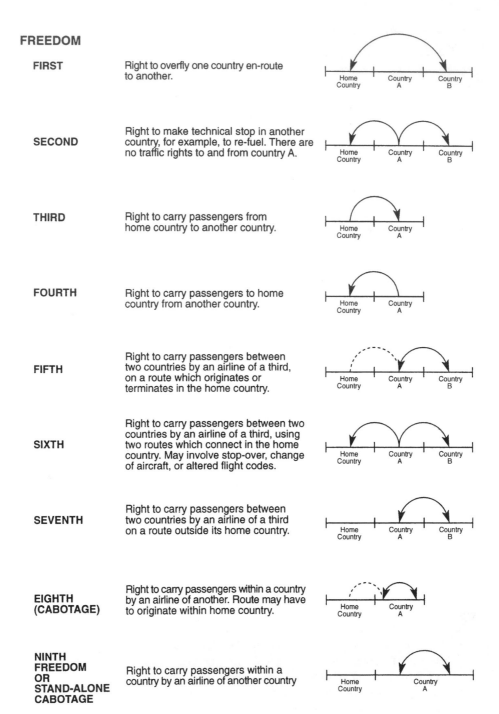

FREEDOM

FIRST — Right to overfly one country en-route to another.

SECOND — Right to make technical stop in another country, for example, to re-fuel. There are no traffic rights to and from country A.

THIRD — Right to carry passengers from home country to another country.

FOURTH — Right to carry passengers to home country from another country.

FIFTH — Right to carry passengers between two countries by an airline of a third, on a route which originates or terminates in the home country.

SIXTH — Right to carry passengers between two countries by an airline of a third, using two routes which connect in the home country. May involve stop-over, change of aircraft, or altered flight codes.

SEVENTH — Right to carry passengers between two countries by an airline of a third on a route outside its home country.

EIGHTH (CABOTAGE) — Right to carry passengers within a country by an airline of another. Route may have to originate within home country.

NINTH FREEDOM OR STAND-ALONE CABOTAGE — Right to carry passengers within a country by an airline of another country

Figure 14.3 Air freedom rights
Source: Association of European Airlines (1997, 21)

liberalize bilaterals. The favoured strategy has been to penetrate both North Atlantic and Pacific markets with "beach-head" agreements. Once these are in place, more recalcitrant governments can be threatened with traffic diversion into renegotiating their own bilaterals, although simultaneously offered the bait of increased access to the world's largest aviation market (Kasper, 1988). Most recently, the US government has sought so-called "open-skies" bilaterals, allowing unrestricted market entry and code-sharing alliances (in which one service is operated under the flight codes of two airlines). A key accord in this respect was that signed with the Netherlands in 1992, this having acted as the model for subsequent open-skies agreements with other European, Asian and, latterly, Central and South American countries. The US–Japan and US–UK bilaterals were for long the most contentious agreements. In early 1998, however, a new US Japan open-skies agreement was negotiated, which effectively redressed the imbalances dating from the 1952 bilateral and granted Japanese carriers parity with their US counterparts. At the time of writing, it is expected also that the US–UK bilateral will finally be renegotiated as an open skies agreement during 1998. The logical outcome of these processes is the replacement of bilateral with multilateral agreements, in which groups of like-minded countries permit any airline virtually unlimited access to any market within their boundaries. Such an agenda, however, is undermined by the continued protection of the US domestic aviation market – the world's largest – from foreign carriers. Indeed, it is probably safe to assume that, whatever the rhetoric, all bilaterals have been, and always will be, negotiated to maximize national interests (Lobbenberg, 1994).

Competition, Deregulation, Liberalization and Privatization

Alongside the constraints of the bilateral system, it was also historically the case that airlines – often publicly owned – had to apply for government licences to operate both domestic and international services, while fare structures were subject to regulatory approval. The basic argument against such structures of airline regulation and public ownership is, by now, well rehearsed. Load factors tended to be low, profitability and service quality poor and fares high. Competition was all but eliminated by what can be regarded as regulatory failure (Kay and Thompson, 1991; Sealy, 1992). Consequent upon US deregulation, air transport – together with other modes – has been progressively freed from price and market entry constraints in many countries. Deregulation refers to a radical process, in which transport modes are exposed to *laissez-faire*, or free-market, forces, achieved through the removal of most regulatory controls over pricing, while permitting carriers to enter and leave markets at will. In everyday use, it is often used incorrectly as a synonym for liberalization, which embraces the idea that the structure of transport industries may necessitate the retention of some form of regulatory protection, if long-term consumer benefits from competition are to be maintained. Hence, liberalization essentially invokes the concept of re-regulation, rather than deregulation.

The academic justification of air transport deregulation depended to a large extent on the theory of the contestable market, one in which an entrant has access to all the production techniques available to incumbents. Thus, entry decisions can be reversed without cost, and there are no barriers to wooing incumbent firms' customers (Baumol, 1982). It was argued that the scheduled airline industry might be contestable because, hypothetically, its low sunk costs (the non-recoverable costs incurred by a firm in entering a market) would ensure that the threat of competition alone should be sufficient to modify the behaviour of incumbents (Alamdari and Black, 1992). Experience has shown, however, that contestability theory is not a good predictor of the air transport market, which, under natural conditions, tends to conform to a non-competitive oligopoly model (Levine, 1987). Sunk costs are also more extensive than formerly predicted, while it has also been shown that actual market entry is essential in order to modify incumbent behaviour. In the United States, for example, airlines adjust pricing strategies to the actual competitive conditions on each route (Oum *et al.*, 1993). In Europe, effective competition occurs only on those few routes served by three carriers; two-airline routes are commonly operated as duopolies (Civil Aviation Authority, 1993, 1995; Commission of the European Communities, 1996).

As it came first, US deregulation has served to demonstrate the policy's benefits but also its many pitfalls. While the empirical evidence is heavily contested, some but not all consumers have gained fare and frequency benefits, although there is some consensus that the former occur only on those routes with head-to-head competition (Civil Aviation Authority, 1993). Morrison and Winston (1995) (who might fairly be described as messianic free-marketeers) estimate that domestic US consumers gained benefits of some US $18.4 billion from deregulation between 1978 and 1993, although Dempsey and Goetz (1992) denounce such claims – calculated on a route-by-route basis – as a "myth" because they do not take into account the point that many passengers are paying more because they have to fly further within hub-and-spoke networks. Moreover, although the initial US legislation in 1978 was followed by a wave of market entry, this merely preceded a marked attenuation of competition (Kahn, 1988). A combination of merger, acquisition, predation and business failure produced a dramatic increase in the size and route networks of some incumbents, most notably American Airlines, United Airlines and Delta Air Lines, which evolved into what are now known as mega-carriers, the emergence of which constitutes what is perhaps the most tangible outcome of US deregulation (Borenstein, 1992; Petzinger, 1995). As Dempsey and Goetz (1992) argue, the US airline industry has become an oligopoly, the eight largest airlines accounting for 95 per cent of the domestic passenger market, while one carrier has more than 60 per cent of traffic at 12 out of 22 hub airports. A second wave of market entry since 1993, mostly by airlines offering low-cost so-called "low/no-frills" services, has not effectively altered this situation.

Concentration, which is expressed in several ways – carrier monopoly, consolidation of air-transport-related employment, market areas – has thus become almost the diagnostic characteristic of deregulation. Consequently, important geographical variations are apparent in the benefits and disbenefits of deregulation. Goetz and Sutton (1997) calculate that, although average fares in the US domestic market have decreased, lower fares are more likely to occur in markets that are not dominated by one or two carriers, particularly if these cities are not unduly peripheral. Fares through the largely unconcentrated international gateway cities have also fallen substantially. Where markets have become more concentrated, however – especially in the core hubs – fares have risen. Moreover, a significant number of semi-peripheral and peripheral cities have suffered reduced air service and higher fares, while some have experienced complete loss of service, despite the provisions under the US Essential Air Services legislation for subsidized local air services to remote communities (Reynolds-Feighan, 1995).

Partly because so much evidence shows airline competition being compromised by the suppliers, many governments have chosen not to follow the US example but opted instead to implement processes of planned gradual liberalization (for details, see Putsay, 1992; Graham, 1995; Hanlon, 1996). Typically – as is also the case in the United States – these policies retain regulatory devices such as competition law and monopoly or anti-trust legislation. Canada, for example, inaugurated a planned gradual liberalization from 1988 onwards (Small, 1993), while European Union (EU) airlines were allowed almost a decade to adjust to the progressive application of three consecutive sets of liberalizing reforms. The so-called Third Package, applied over four years between 1993 and 1997, has effectively completed the transformation of the EU's individual member State networks into a single aviation market.

While there are more general signs – especially in Europe – that the free-market pendulum has swung as far as it is going, the changing regulatory framework for air transport is part and parcel of the global ideological hegemony achieved by the New Right during the 1980s and early 1990s. In addition to the enshrinement of the market and deregulation, this also invoked privatization. Many governments, worldwide, have wholly or partially divested their share-holdings in State airlines and other aviation infrastructure, although some still retain interests in airlines because of their strategic value in wider economic development. In the UK, for example, where privatization was arguably ideologically more important to the New Right than the promotion of competition or the protection of consumer gains, British Airways (BA) was sold off in 1987, while many airports (including the two most important, London Heathrow and London Gatwick) have also been transferred to the private sector. Elsewhere, however, privatization has often been a more pragmatic process, aimed at catering for the financial needs of airlines and airports, while allowing governments to save on investment costs. A dramatic example of the costs potentially involved in subsidizing air transport occurred in 1993–4, when the French, Greek, Irish and Portuguese governments were forced to spend US $7.3 billion on EC-approved subsidies to their ailing flag-carriers, an amount almost twice as large as the entire losses made globally by the airline industry during 1993. Clearly, such payments also distort the competitive process if privately owned airlines, which must make profits on their investments or exit the market, have to compete with subsidized State-controlled carriers. The European Commission (EC) is attempting to apply a "one time/last time" policy, which allows flag-carriers to obtain State aid but only for restructuring within the liberalized environment. One very particular form of privatization has occurred throughout Eastern Europe and the former Soviet Union since 1989, as the airlines of formerly centrally planned States are oriented towards market conditions.

AIRLINE STRATEGIES IN A DEREGULATORY ENVIRONMENT

Although consumers do realize gains from liberalization and deregulation, it also remains the case that incumbent suppliers in any form of capitalist enterprise, including air transport, will seek to develop strategies that constrain or even subvert competition (Button, 1991). In the particular case of the airline industry, these are shaped by the mode's propensity towards oligopoly and concentration, both spatial and structural. In itself, oligopoly is not necessarily a barrier to competition – although the evidence suggests that this is indeed often the case – but there is little doubt that spatial concentration within airline network geographies, allied to structural consolidation manifested through the vertical integration of companies into ever larger alliances, act as serious constraints on the effectiveness of competition. Although there are other aspects of airline operations that compromise competition, two particular repercussions of these processes are emphasized here – the reorganization of networks along hub-and-spoke principles and the construction of airline alliances.

Hub-and-Spoke Networks

This particular strategy to contain competition first emerged in the United States. Although the principal pre-deregulation carriers were geographically concentrated at particular nodes, they essentially operated linear networks, comprising large numbers of point-to-point routes. Since 1978, however, the largest carriers have reoriented these networks around hubs. This term occurs rather loosely in much of the air transport literature, often referring, for example, to any large airport offering multiple connections or even to an airline's principal operating base. In this context, however, it is strictly an integrated air transport interchange through which a single (occasionally two) carrier(s) operate(s) synchronized banks – or waves – of flights. In these, the hub-arrival times of aircraft, originating from cities at the ends of numerous spokes, are coordinated into a short time period. After the minimum interval necessary to redistribute passengers and baggage, an equally large number of aircraft departs to the spoke cities. This pattern is repeated several times during the day (Dennis, 1994a, b; Graham, 1995; Hanlon, 1996).

The hub-and-spoke network is essentially a supplier-driven strategy, which maximizes the on-line (same carrier) connections available to a particular airline at the hub airport. For example, if only six point-to-point services are re-routed through a hub, the number of possible city-pair connections served by the resultant 12-spoke network increases to 36 (Figure 14.4). Furthermore, an exponential increase in possible connecting markets occurs as further spokes are added to the hub (Table 14.4). Dennis (1994b) identifies two forms of hub. The hourglass or directional hub links spokes in one region with those in another, which, broadly speaking, are located in an opposite direction. Conversely, hinterland hubs link long-distance trunk or international routes with short-haul sectors, which feed passengers from the surrounding catchment areas.

For a variety of reasons, hub-and-spoke systems promote concentration and market dominance. Although several airports function as dual hubs (Chicago O'Hare, for example, ranked first in the world for passenger enplanements, functions as a hub for both American and United), most are dominated by a single carrier. In the United States, it is frequently the case that over 70 per cent of enplanements at a hub are handled by the solitary dominant carrier, which, therefore, is effectively operating a quasi-monopoly. The pattern of banks of flights also demands control of airport facilities, both landside and airside. Thus the cumulative effect of this network configuration is to inhibit market entry. Throughout the 1980s it was the case in the United States that a carrier could be challenged effectively at a hub, only if there was a second hub at the other end of the route (Dempsey and Goetz, 1992). In a single-carrier-dominated hub – the "fortress" – no competitor can mount the critical mass of flight frequencies necessary to offer competitive service in a number of city-pair markets. Consequently the hub becomes the first means of market protection, consumers being compensated by the much wider array of connections made possible by this model, albeit often time-consuming and requiring change of aircraft.

Airline Alliances

The reconfiguration of airline networks into geometries of concentration has been accompanied by widespread merger and acquisition and the construction of strategic airline alliances. These latter operate at all sorts of scales from regional services to global agreements between mega-carriers. They are often regarded as being indicative of globalization within the airline industry – the increasing tendency for economic activity to be organized in transnational interconnections. It is, however, all too easy to get carried away with this concept. As is true of service industries generally, only the largest airlines are directly engaged in globalizing strategies, most companies seeing it as a process that they may benefit from indirectly by tapping into the local and national demand created by the behaviour of the largest players (Daniels, 1993). Even the latter remain anchored in domestic markets and

Table 14.4   Growth in the power of a hub

Number of Spokes n	Number of Connection Markets $C = \dfrac{n(n-1)}{2}$	Local Markets Terminating at Hub	Total City-Pair Markets
2	1	2	3
6	15	6	21
10	45	10	55
50	1 225	50	1 275
100	4 950	100	5 050

Source: Dennis (1994b).

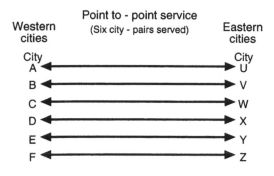

Point to - point service
(Six city - pairs served)

Western cities

Eastern cities

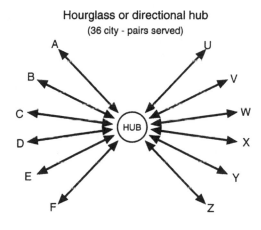

Hourglass or directional hub
(36 city - pairs served)

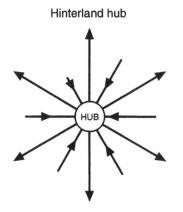

Hinterland hub

Figure 14.4　Hub-and-spoke network systems
Source: based on Kasper (1988) and Dennis (1994b)

circumstances (despite, for example, BA's marketing claim to be a "citizen of the world"). Moreover, globalization invokes concepts of easily crossed, unbounded free space that are not readily separated from the rhetoric of neo-liberalism. That is very much a discourse of the advantaged world, which constitutes air transport's principal market, and when we talk of the globalization of airline activity, BA's "citizens" are largely to be found among the 30 per cent of the world's population who live within the wealthier parts of the northern-hemisphere North America–Europe–Pacific Rim axis.

Nevertheless, the construction of alliances, at whatever scale, again demonstrates the propensity to spatial and structural concentration that is such a salient characteristic of the contemporary air transport industry. If the hub can be best visualized as a means of establishing a quasi-monopoly over a particular airport, then alliances between major carriers aim to extend this control to market area. Thus all alliances are inherently a means of controlling or even subverting competition, at regional, national and global scales. At one level, air transport remains centred on large nationally based carriers, supplemented by an extensive array of local, regional and smaller national companies, heavily dependent on feeding the fortress hubs operated by the major airlines. As the hub-and-spoke concept evolved in the United States and – to a lesser extent – Europe, the industry consolidation produced by horizontal merger and acquisition was accompanied and followed by the vertical integration of the networks of lower-cost regional and commuter airlines into the mega-carriers' operations. Thus all the largest US carriers have their regional affiliates – American Eagle, Continental Express, Delta Connection, Northwest Airlink, United Express – to provide hub-feed (Davies and Quastler, 1995). These carriers initially depended largely on turbo-prop aircraft but, more recently, their operations have been transformed by the introduction of 50-seater (or less) regional jets, which can fly much longer, thin routes. A similar process has occurred in Europe, where the rapidly accelerating integration of regional airline activities into the operations of the major carriers has emerged as one of the most visible repercussions of liberalization. No European regional airline of any substance is now entirely independent. Some, such as Lufthansa CityLine, KLM Cityhopper and KLMuk (the former Air UK), are fully owned subsidiaries of major carriers, while a number of regionals now operate as franchisees. Originally pioneered by BA (as BA Express) this strategy – in which the regional carrier remains independent but offers the fully branded product of the major airline – has also been adapted by Lufthansa (Team Lufthansa), Air France (Air France Express), Iberia (Iberia Express) and Alitalia (Alitalia Express).

If regional airlines provide hub-feed connections and thus contribute to hub control and regional market dominance, then transnational alliances attempt to extend this strategy to global markets. To be successful, an alliance must have a firm geographical base in an area of high demand for air transport. An effective global alliance, however, must also incorporate strong partners in each of North America, Europe and the Pacific Rim, together with feeder partners in the capillary regions such as South America and Africa. Clearly, this limits the number of potential global alliances to little more than a handful of airline groups (Table 14.5). Oum *et al.* (1993) identify two models for global airline alliances. The first involves the expensive strategy of a mega-carrier creating an alliance by taking equity shares in several junior partners operating in other countries and continents. Although BA attempted to construct a global alliance on this basis, buying into the Australian carrier, Qantas, and USAir (now USAirways), it found it very difficult to develop and sustain the strategy. In 1997, BA severed its linkages with USAirways and sold off its shareholding, opting instead – through the proposed alliance with American – to pursue the now-ubiquitous second model. This is an alliance of more or less equal partners in several continents, each supplemented by its regional feeder airlines. The best example is the Star Alliance, which incorporates Lufthansa, Scandinavian Airline System (SAS), United, Thai International, Air Canada and Varig, together with a number of associated and subsidiary carriers. (At the time of writing, there were persistent rumours that the Star Alliance would be extended to include Cathay Pacific and/or the Singapore Airlines–Ansett Australia–Air New Zealand grouping.) These carriers offer extensive code-sharing, shared passenger lounges, through-ticketing and joint "Frequent Flyer Programmes". The proposed deal between BA and American (which was still seeking regulatory approval in mid-1997) would create an alliance of similar size because its principal members would include: Qantas (Australia), Canadian Airlines International, Aerolineas Argentinas, Avianca (Colombia), TAM (Brazil), Finnair, and possibly the Iberia/Aviaco group in Spain. While the Star Alliance remains heavily dominant in Central and Northern Europe, a BA–American–Iberia alliance would have an estimated 60 per cent of the most important intercontinental market, the North Atlantic, and also be the most powerful force in Latin America.

THE MAJOR CONTEMPORARY AIR TRANSPORT MARKETS

The evolution of the hub-and-spoke strategy, and the emergence of complex networks of alliances at a variety of scales ranging from the regional to the global, emphasize that, because liberalization has been accompanied by concentration, the most powerful airline companies have been able to capture the new deregulatory regimes to their own advantage. For example, it is fair to say that all alliances, at whatever scale, are anti-competitive. There are, however, considerable geographical variations in these general processes and this section of the chapter briefly addresses their implications for the major international air transport markets.

North America

Although virtually all the principal US carriers have adopted networks based on hub-and-spoke principles, the geographical constraints of this network system have caused them considerable difficulties. Whether directional or hinterland in function (or

Table 14.5 Major strategic airline alliances, 1996–7

Alliance and Major Carriers	Revenue 1996 (US$ million)	Fleet	Passengers 1996 (million)
Star Alliance	46 166	1 450	185.3
United			
Lufthansa			
SAS			
Air Canada			
Thai International			
Varig			
American/BA*	45 370	1 368	171.6
American			
BA			
Qantas			
Iberia/Aviaco			
Canadian International			
Aerolineas Argentinas			
Avianca			
TAM			
Continental Group†	24 143	865	111.6
Continental			
Air France			
Air France Europe			
Alitalia			
America West			
Delta Group	23 519	982	120.1
Delta/Delta Connection			
Swissair			
Sabena			
Austrian			
Northwest/KLM‡	17 672	661	75.9
Northwest/Northwest Airlink			
KLM			
Martinair Holland			
Air UK, now KLMuk, KLM Cityhopper, KLMexel			
Eurowings			
Kenya Airways			
SIA Group	9 663	241	30.3
Singapore Airlines			
Ansett Australia			
Air New Zealand			

*The American/BA alliance had not received regulatory approval from the European Commission in early 1998. Finnair and BA agreed an extensive alliance in early 1998.
†Virgin Atlantic has an alliance with Continental only.
‡Since these data were compiled, KLM has bought 30% of the Norwegian carrier, Braathens SAFE, and concluded a comprehensive alliance with Alitalia. In January 1998, Northwest and Continental agreed a far-reaching deal which, ultimately, may lead to a coalescence of their respective global alliances.
Source: Airline Business (1997, 31).

indeed both), any hub has to fulfil certain characteristics. Firstly, it must be located centrally with regard to the markets served. In the United States, the major north–south traffic flows link Los Angeles–San Francisco–Seattle, Minneapolis/St Paul–St Louis–Atlanta–Miami, and New York–Atlanta–Miami. The dominant east–west flows connect California with Chicago, New York City, Washington DC and Florida across central hubs such as Denver and Dallas/Fort Worth (Williams, 1993; Figure 14.5). Secondly, as the attainment of market dominance is a primary reason for establishing hubs, airlines are seeking a near-monopoly over passenger market share at those airports. Finally, a successful hub also requires the locational attributes of centrality and intermediacy; the former refers to its ability to generate direct services to local markets – the hinterland role – while intermediacy describes its geographical "in-betweenness" or suitability for generating connecting traffic, in other words its directional function (Fleming and Hayuth, 1994).

As Figure 14.5 demonstrates, these combined requirements serve to constrain possible hub locations. The earliest hub-and-spoke networks were based on large-city connecting airports such as Chicago O'Hare and Atlanta Hartsfield. However, the distances involved in the continental United States, combined with the airlines' desire to achieve regional domination while, simultaneously, developing services throughout the country, meant that almost all were forced to develop multiple hubs, supported in turn by secondary or mini-hubs to command feeder traffic. These were commonly medium-sized cities, such as Charlotte, Pittsburgh, Cincinnati, Raleigh–Durham and Nashville, selected as much for their locations in relation to the principal passenger flows rather than as sources of originating traffic (Ivy, 1993). Thus Delta, for example, operates a multidirectional hub at its main base, Atlanta, together with three east–west hubs at Cincinnati, Salt Lake City and Dallas/Fort Worth. Secondary nuclei at Boston, Orlando, Los Angeles and Portland effectively act as local hubs in the four "corners" of the contiguous 48 states, while New York, Portland and Atlanta function as the principal intercontinental gateways. The primary and secondary hubs are also fed by Delta Connection regional carriers (Figure 14.6). Owing to the concentration of hubs in the

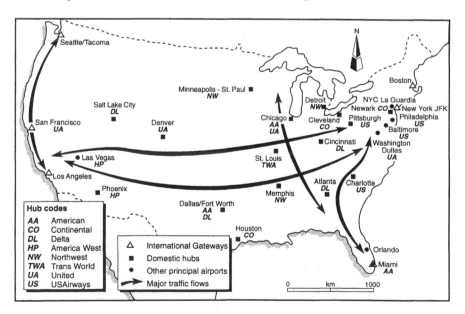

Figure 14.5   Distribution of principal US hubs and traffic flows, 1997
Source: partly based on Williams (1993)

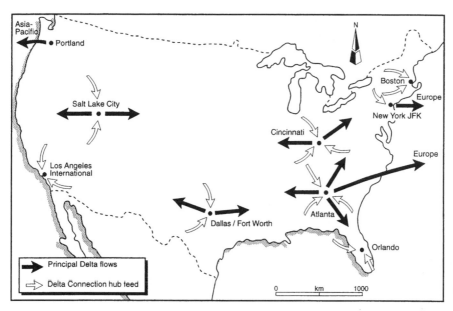

Figure 14.6 Delta airlines hub-and-spoke system

same geographical regions and the insufficiency of originating traffic suffered by some cities, all the major airlines have experienced difficulties with the system. However, although some hubs including Nashville and Raleigh–Durham – have been downsized or even shut down completely, this does not detract from the effectiveness of the strategy for the major carriers, which now enjoy quasi-monopolies at their respective hubs.

Nevertheless, there is another model for US airline networks. Southwest Airlines, based in Dallas and now the eighth-ranked US carrier in terms of sales, pioneered the concept of low-cost, low or "no frills" services, operated over short-haul routes within an essentially linear point-to-point network. Although this has now evolved certain almost random hubbing characteristics, most notably at Phoenix, the model of an airline driven by stringent control over operating costs and basic cabin service has spawned a string of hopeful imitators, particularly since 1993. Indeed, mega-carriers United and Delta both operate their own low-cost, "no-frills" units – Shuttle by United and Delta Express – to compete head-on with Southwest. However, the entire "no frills" start-up market in the United States was seriously damaged by the sharp decline in public confidence that followed the crash of a Valu-Jet DC-9 in Florida in 1996 and the subsequent grounding – for safety violations – of what was then the fastest-growing US airline (Schiavo, 1997). Despite the evident success of Southwest, however, and while there will always be niche markets for start-up airlines around the edges of the major carriers' hub-and-spoke networks, the cumulative outcome of US deregulation has been concentration.

Moreover, the emergence of the mega-carriers and their fortress hubs has created a powerful domestic base on which these airlines have been able to build international operations. The biggest domestic US airlines, Southwest apart, have become global operators, largely secure in the now relatively uncontested geometry of their core domestic hub-and-spoke networks. The negotiation of more liberal bilaterals has also allowed the mega-carriers to increase the number of international gateways to the United States, leading to the "fragmentation" effects apparent, for example, on the North Atlantic routes, where the number of city-pairs has proliferated, the routes being flown largely by smaller twin-engined jets (Dennis, 1994c; Graham 1995). This trend, however, has not altered the patterns of concentration. Rather, the strategy allows the airlines to offer higher frequency in some of the busier markets and also to connect their hubs to what are effectively spoke cities in Europe and elsewhere, thereby enhancing the viability of the US domestic hubs. In turn, the most important international carriers outside the United States are serving more US cities as extensions of their own hub-based networks.

Europe

Although the liberalization of the European industry was a much more gradual process than that which occurred in the United States, many of the same – apparently inexorable – processes of spatial concentration can be observed. By the early 1980s, European airlines were incurring operating costs substantially in excess of those in the United States. Scheduled fares were higher, there was little competition, while capacities, fares and frequencies were controlled through a plethora of intergovernmental bilateral agreements. The policy of gradual liberalization realized through the successive implementation, of the "Three Packages" between 1988 and 1997, was designed to modify this situation, part and parcel of the reconfiguration of national air transport networks into the infrastructure of a more competitive and flexible Single European Market (Table 14.6). The First and Second Packages were largely

concerned with liberalization of bilateral agreements, and served to demonstrate that consumer gains – price competition, increased frequencies, more city- and airport-pairs – could be realized only when there was effective competition, largely created by providing opportunities for market entry. The Third Package transformed national airlines into Community carriers. Effective 1 April 1997, all EU airlines have had open access to virtually all routes within the Community, including cabotage – the ninth-freedom right to operate domestic services in a State other than that in which the airline is registered (Figure 14.3).

While the liberalization process has led to unquestioned consumer gains such as lower economy fares on the densest routes, the evidence seems to suggest that these are realized only when an airport- or (possibly) city-pairing is served by at least three carriers engaged in head-to-head competition (Civil Aviation Authority, 1995). Two airlines will tend to operate as a duopoly, although the Association of European Airlines (1997) contends that the three-carrier argument is less applicable to domestic routes, formerly served by only one airline. In these cases, the advent of a second airline should provide real competition. In 1996, of 520 airport-pairings within the EU, only 31 (6 per cent) – admittedly including some of the most important – were served by more than two airlines (including, however, the densest routes). Almost two-thirds of airport pairings (64 per cent) were operated as monopolies, although these include a large number of low-density

Table 14.6 The three European Commission air transport liberalization packages

1	Implemented from 1.1.88	Allowed multiple designation, fifth-freedom rights, automatic approval of discount fares;
2	Implemented from 1.11.90	Double disapproval rule applied to full fares in Second Package
3	Implemented from 1.1.93 final implementation 1.4.97	Permits • Free pricing on all fares • Full access to all routes including cabotage • Abandonment of distinction between charter and scheduled carriers • Protection for routes designated as public service obligations • EC retention of right to intervene against excessive fares, predatory pricing and seat dumping

Source: Graham (1995, 142).

routes unlikely to support competition (Table 14.7). Thus, consumer benefits related to fares are largely confined to the densest airport- and city-pairs. Otherwise fares have risen to an extent adjudged sufficiently excessive for the EC to threaten regulatory intervention (Commission of the European Communities, 1996).

As in the United States, liberalization has been accompanied by a wave of market entry (Cranfield University/CEC, 1997). As we have seen, however, European air transport remains dominated by the largest carriers. Many of the secondary airlines, such as British Midland Airways, Braathens SAFE, KLMuk and Lauda Air, are affiliates of the major carriers, while the same is also true of all the most important regionals. There are a few scheduled low-cost operators, the three most significant being Ireland's Ryanair, Brussels-based Virgin Express and Luton-based easyJet, but nothing that remotely emulates Southwest. One reason for this, of course, is the existence of a substantial leisure-oriented "charter" sector, which caters very efficiently with holiday traffic. The Third Package abolished the distinction between scheduled and charter airlines, the latter now effectively offering low-cost, low-frequency scheduled services to a wide variety of tourism destinations.

The cumulative effect of European liberalization has been to allow the major European carriers to restructure their formerly national networks effectively into trans-European feed systems to their hubs, all located in the EU's most prosperous "vital axis" (Dunford and Perrons, 1994) (Figure 14.7). If there is effective airline competition in Europe it is between these hubs, the most important of which are London, Amsterdam, Frankfurt and Paris. As we have seen, however, the intracontinental alliances, which enable these hubs to function, are also part of wider global agreements, demonstrating once again the apparent inevitability of concentration in the contemporary air transport industry (Graham, 1997). The balance of power always appears to lie with the most powerful airlines, which have captured the deregulatory environment to their own advantage. In Europe, as in the United States, the balance of advantage also lies with the most prosperous regions in which, inevitably, the most important airports are located.

Asia–Pacific

The Asia–Pacific region has been the world's fastest-growing air transport market, although the rate of increase has slowed substantially as some of its most dynamic economies – located in the West Pacific Rim – suffered a sharp financial downturn at the end of 1997. Air transport is of particular importance in this macro-region because of the dominance of its cities in economic development, the rapidly developing importance of tourism and the fragmented geography of the region (Debbage, 1994). While there has been significant liberalization in many countries, most Asian States have as yet stopped short of relinquishing outright control of flag-carriers to the private sector. As Bowen and Leinbach (1995) maintain, this reflects the importance of the air transport

Table 14.7 Effects of the Third Package on competition: Internal Community routes (airport to airport)

Routes	Jan. 1992		Jan. 1993		Jan. 1994		Jan. 1995		Jan. 1996	
	No.	%	No.	%	No.	%	No.	%	No.	%
Total	510	–	488	–	482	–	522	–	518	–
monopoly	283	56	296	61	318	66	342	66	329	64
2 carriers	208	40	182	37	150	31	154	29	158	30
>2 carriers	19	4	10	2	14	3	26	5	31	6

Source: Commission of the European Communities (1996).

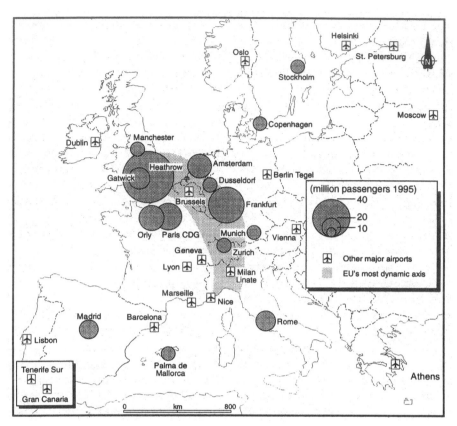

Figure 14.7   The distribution of Europe's principal airports
(millions of passengers handled, 1995)
Source: Airports Council International (1997)

industry and the desire of governments to pursue selective, pragmatic and deliberate development policies. O'Connor (1995) argues that the key to understanding the region's air transport infrastructure lies in the same concepts of centrality and intermediacy that have also been seen as diagnostic features of US hubs. Three South-East Asian airports in particular – Singapore, Bangkok and Hong Kong – fulfil these joint roles and they have emerged as the dominant nodes. Traditionally, intermediacy was most relevant to east–west traffic (for example, the location of Singapore on the Europe–Australia routes) but the increasing importance of a north–south axis, linking Australia to the West Pacific Rim, particularly favours Hong Kong. Further east and north, Seoul, Osaka and, above all, Tokyo are the

dominant airports. The density of traffic generated in the largely urban markets of the West Pacific Rim is reflected in Table 14.8, which shows that no less than 15 of the world's leading 25 international city-pairs for passenger air traffic in 1995 are located within – or else linked to – the region (Figure 14.8). In addition, Japanese domestic routes are among the densest in the world, Tokyo–Sapporo and Tokyo–Fukuoka accounting for almost 8 million and 6 million passengers per annum respectively. There is also enormous potential for further growth, particularly in China, which is the world's fastest-growing air transport market.

As Figure 14.8 demonstrates, the most important international routes link the major cities of the West Pacific Rim to each other and to the dominant east–

Table 14.8 Most important West Pacific Rim international city-pairs for scheduled passenger traffic
(12 months ending 31 March 1995) (million passengers)

	City-Pair	Passengers	World Ranking
1	Hong Kong–Taipei	4 100	1
2	Kuala Lumpur–Singapore	2 315	5
3	Honolulu–Tokyo	2 294	6
4	Seoul–Tokyo	2 189	8
5	Bangkok–Hong Kong	1 903	9
6	Hong Kong–Tokyo	1 877	10
7	Jakarta–Singapore	1 632	11
8	Taipei–Tokyo	1 584	12
9	Bangkok–Singapore	1 465	13
10	Hong Kong–Singapore	1 418	14
11	Hong Kong–Manila	1 120	18
12	Singapore–Tokyo	1 104	19
13	Los Angeles–Tokyo	1 047	20
14	Hong Kong–Seoul	1 006	22
15	London–Tokyo	997	24

Source: International Civil Aviation Organization (1996, 22).

west axis of global aviation. This is perhaps one of the most convincing manifestations of globalization, the idea of world cities that serve as the gatekeepers of the world service economy (Daniels, 1993). Cities such as London, New York, Chicago, Tokyo, Singapore and Hong Kong constitute a set of commercial and financial nodes, joined by a series of linkages including transport flows. Inevitably, they have become the interconnection points for global airline networks.

Asia–Pacific also provides a very clear example of the relationship between air transport and tourism. Initially, the airlines and hotel companies concentrated on the key gateway cities but, more recently, a considerable array of secondary destinations such as Penang (Malaysia), Phuket (Thailand) and Bali (Indonesia) have been substantially developed. It has been argued that air transport liberalization is one of the most significant factors promoting tourism growth (World Tourism Organization, 1994). In Australia, for example, it is claimed that airline deregulation has been accompanied by strong tourism growth, especially in more isolated cities such as Perth (Western Australia) and Cairns (Queensland). This is, however, an unduly limited explanation,

reflecting the often-blinkered way in which proponents of air transport deregulation tend to exaggerate its causal effects. Tourism demand and increased propensity to travel by air are related above all else to levels of disposable income. What actually seems to be happening is that the rapid increase in tourism demand in Asia–Pacific has been a function of increased wealth within the region (particularly in Japan) and the expanding demand for long-haul holidays from affluent consumers in Europe and North America. Although the highly competitive nature of the Asian–Pacific airline industry is encouraging tourism in a macro-region in which over 80 per cent of all tourists arrive by air, the mode in itself – whatever the regulatory regime – cannot create tourism demand, that ultimately being a function of very much more complex articulations of economic development. It is expected that the Asian financial crisis, which began towards the end of 1997, will substantially reduce tourism traffic by air.

Rest of the World

If the east–west, largely northern-hemisphere, axis that links Asia–Pacific, North America and Europe

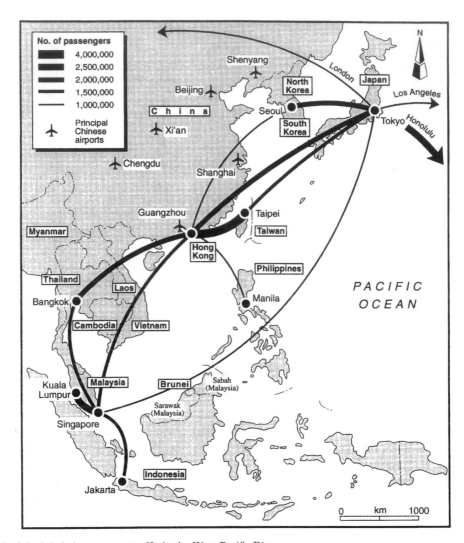

Figure 14.8   Scheduled air passenger traffic in the West Pacific Rim
Data for densest city-pairs, 1995
Source: International Civil Aviation Organization (1996, 22)

contributes the dominant characteristic of international air transport, the remainder of the world – despite the size of its population – is of relatively minor importance. Australia and New Zealand, of course, are firmly integrated within the rapidly developing north–south axis that links them to the West Pacific Rim, but the Middle East, Africa and South America play no more than peripheral roles in global air transport patterns.

The Middle East has a high potential for traffic growth but has a relatively small population base, which constrains demand, no matter how wealthy some of its States are. Political tensions between Israel and its neighbours also reduce the potential for intra-regional traffic (Feiler and Goodovitch, 1994). The Persian Gulf airports used to be important stopovers on the routes between Europe and Asia but the development of longer-range aircraft now allows these services to be flown non-stop. Thus, the region has become something of a spoke, and even a little isolated from the principal international air transport flows.

Despite a geography of distance and fragmentation that is ideally suited to air transport, Africa accounts for less than 3 per cent of world international scheduled air traffic. Intercontinental traffic is largely north–south, much of it generated by inbound tourism from Europe. International and domestic services within the continent – the Republic of South Africa excepted – are poorly developed in absolute and frequency terms. Many airlines remain in State ownership while very few are integrated into global alliances. The principal reason for these trends, of course, is poverty and dependence, reflecting again the central point that propensity to travel by air is conditional on wealth.

Finally, Central and South America, together with the Caribbean, account for around 6.5 per cent of world international scheduled passenger traffic. South America shares with Africa an air transport network largely shaped by the dictates of economic and political colonialism. International traffic is dominated by routes to the United States and often by the US mega-carriers (particularly American), which have adopted almost imperialistic attitudes to South America. European services are channelled through Madrid and, to a lesser extent, Lisbon, the former colonial capitals. Many South American governments have opted recently for abrupt deregulation on the US model and it remains to be seen how the region's airlines can cope with this new environment. Although some are growing rapidly, it does seem, however, that an alliance with a US mega-carrier will be a necessary condition for survival in the crucial North American market.

AIRPORTS

Not surprisingly, given the global pre-eminence of US carriers and the size and spatial extent of the US domestic market, the principal US airports dominate the world rankings for passenger traffic. Of the top 30 airports worldwide in 1995, ranked by total passengers handled, no less than 17 were located within the 48 contiguous states, compared to seven in Asia–Pacific (including Honolulu) and six in Europe (Table 14.9). On this measure, Chicago O'Hare, at 67.3 million passengers, is by far the world's busiest airport, followed by Atlanta Hartsfield (57.7 million) and Dallas/Fort Worth (56.5 million). However, with the exception of New York JFK, all the top 10 airports for international traffic are located in Europe or Asia, London Heathrow being by far the most important airport worldwide in this respect. Given that Gatwick is also included in this ranking, London emerges as the dominant international node in the global air transport network. Memphis, Tennessee, home hub of the world's largest cargo carrier, Federal Express, leads the air freight rankings.

Airport congestion – both airside (runways and aprons) and landside (terminals and parking) – and mounting public hostility to the provision of additional capacity are among the most serious problems facing the liberalized air transport industry. Many airport operators have been fully or, more commonly, partially privatized, but that strategy in itself, while leading to increased profits, is essentially irrelevant to the capacity issue – for a convincing summary of airport operations, see Doganis (1992). Most major European airports, and a significant number in the United States and Asia–Pacific, are capacity-constrained, which effectively means that airline access is rationed. Yet, not least because of environmental objections, very few new airports or even runways are currently being built or even planned in Europe. The reconstructed airports at Oslo Gardermoen (which will succeed Fornebu) and Milan Malpensa (which will replace Linate as Northern Italy's principal airport) will both be completed in 1998, followed by Manchester's second runway. In the United States, the controversial Denver International, which finally opened to traffic in 1995 following serious delays and escalating costs (largely incurred by the failure of a high-technology baggage system), remains the only important recent airport (Dempsey *et al.*, 1997; Goetz and Szyliowicz, 1997). The most substantial airport developments

Table 14.9 Top 30 Airports (1995) by Terminal Passengers Handled (millions)

Rank	Airport	Total Terminal Passengers Handled
1	Chicago O'Hare Int'l	67.3
2	Atlanta Hartsfield	57.7
3	Dallas/Fort Worth Int'l	56.5
4	London Heathrow	54.5
5	Los Angeles Int'l	53.9
6	Tokyo Haneda	45.8
7	Frankfurt Rhein/Main	38.2
8	San Francisco Int'l	36.3
9	Miami Int'l	33.2
10	Denver Int'l	31.0
11	Seoul Kimpo Int'l	30.9
12	New York JFK	30.4
13	Paris Charles de Gaulle	28.4
14	Detroit Metro Wayne County	28.2
15	Hong Kong Kai Tak	28.0
16	Las Vegas McCarran Int'l	28.0
17	Phoenix Sky Harbor Int'l	27.9
18	Minneapolis/St Paul Int'l	26.8
19	Paris Orly	26.6
20	Newark Int'l	26.6
21	Lambert–St Louis Int'l	25.7
22	Amsterdam Schiphol	25.3
23	Houston Intercontinental	24.7
24	Boston Logan Int'l	24.4
25	Tokyo Narita	24.2
26	Honolulu Int'l	23.7
27	Singapore Changi	23.2
28	Bangkok Int'l	23.1
29	Seattle/Tacoma Int'l	22.8
30	London Gatwick	22.5

Source: Airports Council International (1997).

are taking place in Asia including Kansai International, sited on an artificial island in Osaka Bay and opened in 1994, Macau and Chek Lap Kok in Hong Kong, while other new airports are being constructed at Seoul and Kuala Lumpur. China is also radically enhancing and extending its airport capacity. As O'Connor (1996) demonstrates, however, this additional capacity will not address the intractable problem created by the concentration of West Pacific Rim air traffic in the Tokyo–Singapore corridor (Figure 14.8).

The general shortage of airport capacity is a fundamental impediment to the development of a more competitive airline industry. Indeed, it is likely to become the major constraint, functioning as a barrier to market entry and favouring incumbency through the priority given to historic rights in the allocation of scarce runway landing and take-off slots. Moreover, liberalization increases demand for airport capacity because frequency of flights is a major marketing tool in business markets. Thus it is not sufficient merely to begin competitive service in a market; entrants have to match the frequencies offered by incumbents. Hubbing also demands airport dominance to ensure the availability of capacity sufficient to handle the waves of flights. Consequently, major policy tensions exist between the implementation of more competitive airline industries offering tariff, frequency and service benefits to consumers, and widespread political and public opposition to the construction of new airport capacity. Runways are particularly controversial but even additional terminals arouse bitter protest because of their propensity to increase aircraft movements. By early 1998, the Public Planning Enquiry assessing the case for an additional Terminal Five at London Heathrow had sat longer than any other similar body in UK planning history.

It is estimated that world passenger air traffic will continue to rise by around 5 per cent per annum until 2010, essentially a doubling of 1993's 1171 million scheduled air passengers. As there are no plans to have doubled existing world airport capacity in the same period – indeed, in Europe, capacity is being restricted with, for example, more and more airports tightening restrictions on night flights – how might at least some of this growth be accommodated? A number of strategies can be applied to reduce demand at congested airports, especially at peak times. It has been suggested that proximate airports – for example, Amsterdam Schiphol/Charleroi (Brussels South)/Brussels National (supplemented perhaps by off-shore runways), or Frankfurt/ Dusseldorf Rhein-Ruhr and Moenchengladbach Dusseldorf Express/Cologne-Bonn – could be marketed as effectively single destinations. The airports in each group would be linked by high-speed trains (HSTs), while again there is some potential, especially in Europe, for modal shift, HSTs being more efficient people-carriers than aircraft over city-pairs of less than 500 km. Another set of options includes measures to spread peak traffic demand through price discrimination, in particular by allowing airlines to trade slots and imposing traffic distribution rules (TDRs) that restrict the activities of other airport users. Finally, considerable scope exists to increase capacity through technological and operational improvements. None of these options, however, are likely to be sufficient if projected air transport growth rates are to be maintained.

AIR TRANSPORT AND THE ENVIRONMENT

Clearly, therefore, and despite the undoubted economic benefits that can accrue from an efficient air transportation system (Caves, 1994), an unresolved and rapidly escalating tension exists between projected air transport growth rates and the provision of sufficient infrastructural capacity. The foregoing discussion has been couched in terms of how these two sets of factors might be reconciled. None the less, another option does exist. Should they be reconciled at all or is it in the wider public interest that increasing demand for air transport be restrained in other ways? The general issues raised by transport and environmental sustainability are addressed in Chapter 15, so it is sufficient here to emphasize three of the more particular ways – congestion, noise and atmospheric emissions – in which air transport negatively impacts on environment, and to examine briefly how these might relate to the argument that the mode's growth rate might have to be constrained through some form of re-regulation.

Air transport creates congestion in several ways. Despite improved Air Traffic Control procedures, airport capacity constraints mean that aircraft routinely circulate in holding patterns until landing slots are available. Not only does this practice consume fuel, but it also increases noise and emissions levels. Airports create road traffic congestion and consume large areas of land as parking space for these vehicles, a factor that contributes significantly to the severance effects imposed on land use and its planning by the sheer physical size of the facilities. Aware that alleviation of these environmental considerations is crucial to the political approval of future infrastructural development, airport operators (particularly in Europe but also in Asia–Pacific) are taking increasingly radical steps – including the effective rationing of parking through pricing and space restriction strategies – which aim at forcing airport users and employees to switch to public transport. Many European airports are now fully integrated into conventional light and heavy and even high-speed rail networks (see Chapter 2). For example,

Manchester's strategic plan sets a public transport target figure of 25 per cent for all journeys to the airport by 2005 (compared to the present 15 per cent), while Heathrow's plan seeks an even more ambitious 50 per cent. Population density and magnitude within an airport catchment, together with the latter's geographical extent, constitute the primary determinants constraining the potential for public-transport modal shift. In North America, where airports generally have much poorer public-transport links than their European counterparts, the new Denver International, for example (handling in excess of 30 million passengers a year), is served only by road access, a reflection of the dispersed, low-density and car-oriented nature of the metropolitan area that it serves.

The air transport industry has also made considerable efforts to address noise pollution. Commercial jet transports currently in service are divided into Stage II and III types, classifications that relate to Chapters 2 and 3 of Annexe 16 to the Chicago Convention. Chapter 2 aircraft will have to be phased out of service by 2002 unless they are hush-kitted to Stage III standards or re-engined. However, that will not remove the problem of aircraft noise. Stage III aircraft are not quiet; rather they are less noisy than their predecessors, and many modern types, including, for example, a fully loaded B747–400, only marginally comply with Stage III requirements. Faced with mounting public opposition to noise, and the failure of the air transport industry to agree new standards beyond Chapter 3 of the Convention, it is likely that individual airport operators will, for example, increasingly impose their own restrictions on night flights and impose fines for noise violations. Airlines, however, aware that they will habitually infringe noise limits, can simply include that penalty in ticket price.

Finally, air transport contributes to the damage wrought by hydrocarbon emissions on the atmosphere (Somerville, 1993). Although much less culpable than road traffic, particularly in respect to carbon dioxide (CO_2) emissions, modern high-bypass-ratio aircraft turbo-fans operate at high temperatures, which increases emissions of nitrogen ox-

ides (NO_x). The effect of this pollution on the upper atmosphere is as yet unknown, but NO_x are believed to deplete ozone by converting it to oxygen, while contributing to petrochemical smog and acid rain and increasing susceptibility to bronchial infections (Whitelegg, 1993).

CONCLUSIONS

Although the negative environmental impacts of air transport are markedly less than those attributable to road vehicles, nevertheless they contribute to an increasing awareness – especially in Europe – that unconstrained growth of mobility in general cannot be sustained along a whole series of environmental alignments. As we have seen, the demand for air transport has risen rapidly since the 1960s, particularly in North America, Europe and parts of Asia–Pacific. The driving force has been increased personal disposable income, combined with air transport's unchallenged capacity to reduce the friction of distance. But it is also apparent that regulatory change – most notably the implementation of liberalization – has also helped grow demand through increased competition. However, the strategies adopted by the airlines to contain that competition and adapt the liberalized environment to their own ends have in turn exacerbated the issue of insufficient air transport infrastructure.

As the Millennium approaches, bringing with it the inevitability of diminishing hydrocarbon reserves but also ever more sophisticated evidence of the environmental damage being caused by transport systems organized around personal mobility and profit, serious issues of sustainability surround air transport. It is almost certainly the case that individual governments and other agencies such as the EC will eventually have to legislate to cap demand for air transport. In effect, this is already beginning to happen in Europe with the emphasis placed on HSTs in the Trans-European Transport Network being constructed to help integrate the Single European Market. Again, Amsterdam Schiphol has a legally binding upper limit of 44 million passengers per annum, a figure that it will reach before 2015. It may well be that these examples symbolize the growing realization that, in the final essence, an air transport industry, controlled by free-market principles, is a sustainable proposition only if it is accepted that the interests of that industry constitute the fundamental priority to be pursued at the expense of all else.

ACKNOWLEDGEMENTS

I am very grateful to Kenneth Sealy, not only for his comments on an earlier draft of this chapter, but also for writing *The geography of air transport*, which – more years ago than I now care to remember – acted as a major stimulus to my interest in air transportation.

REFERENCES

Airline Business (1997), "Airline Business 100", September, 4–35.
Airports Council International (1997), *Annual airport traffic statistics, 1995* (Geneva: ACI).
Alamdari, F.E. and Black, I.G. (1992), "Passengers' choice of airline under competition: the use of the logit model", *Transport Reviews* 12, 153–70.
Alperovich, G. and Machnes, Y. (1994), "The role of wealth in the demand for international air travel", *Journal of Transport Economics and Policy* 28, 163–73.
Association of European Airlines (1997), *Yearbook 1997* (Brussels: AEA).
Baumol, W.J. (1982), "Contestable markets: an uprising in the theory of industrial structure", *American Economic Review* 72, 1–15.
Boeing (1996), *Boeing Market Outlook* (Seattle: Boeing).
Borenstein, S. (1992), "The evolution of US airline competition", *Journal of Economic Perspectives* 6, 45–73.
Bowen, J.T. and Leinbach, T.R. (1995), "The state and liberalization: the airline industry in the East Asian NICs", *Annals of the Association of American Geographers* 85, 468–93.
Button, K.J. (ed.) (1991), *Airline deregulation: international experiences* (London: Fulton).
Caves, R.E. (1994), "Aviation and society – redrawing the balance", *Transportation Planning and Technology* 18, 3–19 and 21–36.
Civil Aviation Authority (1993), *Airline competition in the Single European Market*, CAP 623 (London: CAA).
Civil Aviation Authority (1995), *The Single European Aviation Market: progress so far*, CAP 654 (London: CAA).

Commission of the European Communities (1996), *Impact of the Third Package of air transport liberalization measures* (Brussels: CEC).
Cranfield University/CEC (1997), *The Single Market Review: impact on services: air transport* (Luxembourg: CEC, and London: Kogan Page).
Daniels, P.W. (1993), *Service industries in the world economy* (Oxford: Blackwell).
Davies, R.E.G. and Quastler, I.E. (1995), *Commuter airlines of the United States* (Washington, DC: Smithsonian Institution Press).
Debbage, K.G. (1994), "The international airline industry: globalization, regulation and strategic alliances", *Journal of Transport Geography* 2, 190–203.
Dempsey, P.S. and Goetz, A.R. (1992), *Airline deregulation and laissez-faire mythology* (Westport, Conn.: Quorum).
Dempsey, P.S., Goetz, A.R. and Szyliowicz, J.S. (1997), *Denver International Airport: lessons learned* (New York: McGraw-Hill).
Dennis, N. (1994a), "Airline hub operations in Europe", *Journal of Transport Geography* 2, 219–33.
Dennis, N. (1994b), "Scheduling strategies for airline hub operations", *Journal of Air Transport Management* 1, 131–44.
Dennis, N. (1994c), "The North Atlantic air travel market", *EIU Travel and Tourism Analyst* 2, 4–23.
Dobson, A.P. (1991), *Peaceful air warfare: the USA, Britain and the politics of international aviation* (Oxford: Clarendon).
Doganis, R. (1991), *Flying off course: the economics of international airlines*, 2nd edn (London: HarperCollins).
Doganis, R. (1992), *The airport business* (London: Routledge).
Dunford, M. and Perrons, D. (1994), "Regional inequality, regimes of accumulation and economic development in contemporary Europe", *Transactions of the Institute of British Geographers* NS 19, 163–82.
Feiler, G. and Goodovitch, T. (1994), "Decline and growth, privatization and protectionism in the Middle East airline industry", *Journal of Transport Geography* 2, 55–64.
Fleming, D.K. and Hayuth, Y. (1994), "Spatial characteristics of transportation hubs: centrality and intermediacy", *Journal of Transport Geography* 2, 3–18.
Goetz, A.R. and Sutton, C.J. (1997), "The geography of deregulation in the U.S. airline industry", *Annals of the Association of American Geographers* 87, 238–63.
Goetz, A.R. and Szyliowicz, J.S. (1997), "Revisiting transportation planning and decision making theory: the case of Denver International Airport", *Transportation Research A* 31A, 263–80.
Graham, B. (1995), *Geography and air transport* (Chichester: Wiley).
Graham, B. (1997), "Air transport liberalization in the European Union: an assessment", *Regional Studies* 31, 807–12.
Hanlon, J.P. (1996), *Global airlines: competition in a transnational industry* (Oxford: Butterworth-Heinemann).
International Air Transport Association (1996), *World air transport statistics, No. 40*, WATS 6/96 (Geneva: IATA).

International Civil Aviation Organization (1996), *Civil aviation statistics of the world, 1995* (Montreal: ICAO).

Ivy, R.L. (1993), "Variations in hub service in the US domestic air transportation network", *Journal of Transport Geography* 1, 211–18.

Kahn, A.E. (1988), "Surprises of airline deregulation", *American Economic Review* 78, 316–22.

Kasper, D.M. (1988), *Deregulation and globalization: liberalizing international trade in air services* (Cambridge, MA: Ballinger).

Kay, J. and Thompson, D. (1991), "Regulatory reform in transport in the United Kingdom: principles and application", in Bannister, D. and Button, K. (eds), *Transport in a free market economy* (Basingstoke: Macmillan), 19–42.

Knox, P. and Agnew, J. (1994), *The geography of the world-economy*, 2nd edn (London: Edward Arnold).

Levine, M.E. (1987), "Airline competition in deregulated markets: theory, firm strategy and public policy", *Yale Journal on Regulation* 4, 393–494.

Lobbenberg, A. (1994), "Government relations on the North Atlantic: a case study of five Europe–USA relationships", *Journal of Air Transport Management* 1, 47–62.

Morrison, S.A. and Winston, C. (1995), *Evolution of the airline industry* (Washington, DC: Brookings Institution).

O'Connor, K. (1995), "Airport development in Southeast Asia", *Journal of Transport Geography* 3, 269–79.

O'Connor, K. (1996), "Airport development: a Pacific–Asian perspective", *Built Environment* 22, 212–22.

Oum, T.H., Taylor, A.J. and Zhang, A. (1993), "Strategic airline policy in the globalizing airline networks", *Transportation Journal* 32, 14–30.

Petzinger, T. (1995), *Hard landing* (New York: Times Books).

Putsay, M.W. (1992), "Towards a global airline industry: prospects and impediments", *Logistics and Transportation Review* 28, 103–28.

Reynolds-Feighan, A.J. (1995), "European and American approaches to air transport liberalisation: some implications for small communities", *Transportation Research A* 29A, 467–83.

Schiavo, M. (1997), *Flying blind, flying safe* (New York: Avon Books).

Sealy, K.R. (1966), *The geography of air transport*, 2nd edn (London: Hutchinson).

Sealy, K.R. (1992), "International air transport", in Hoyle, B.S. and Knowles, R.D. (eds), *Modern transport geography* (London: Belhaven), 233–56.

Shearman, P. (1992), *Air transport: strategic issues in planning and development* (London: Pitman).

Small, N.O. (1993), "A victim of geography, not policy? Canada's airline industry since deregulation", *Journal of Transport Geography* 1, 182–94.

Somerville, H. (1993), "The airline industry's perspective", in Banister, D. and Button, K. (eds), *Transport, the environment and sustainable development* (London: Spon), 161–74.

Whitelegg, J. (1993), *Transport for a sustainable future: the case for Europe* (London: Belhaven).

Williams, G. (1993), *The airline industry and the impact of deregulation* (Aldershot: Ashgate).

World Tourism Organization (1994), *Aviation and tourism policies: balancing the benefits* (London: Routledge).

15

SUSTAINABILITY OF TRANSPORT

William R. Black

The non-sustainability of the current dominant transport modes has been recognized for about a decade. The nature of this sustainability problem is identified here along with the major factors that create the problem. The latter include the finite nature of petroleum (the principal fuel used for transport today), the environmental degradation attributable to the transport sector and its impact on local and global environmental problems, the high rates of accidents and fatalities for highways, the high levels of congestion in the transport sector, and the tendency for transport to stimulate sprawl. An examination of past and current transport modes in terms of sustainability leads us to conclude that historical transport modes were more sustainable, but this conclusion is more apparent than real. The problem is not with any single mode, but rather with the excessive number of vehicles necessary to satisfy the demand for transport. This is illustrated using the case of ship-building during the seventeenth and eighteenth centuries. Moves towards sustainability range from town parking schemes to international agreements that would limit the amount of carbon emitted into the atmosphere. It should be apparent that the former will accomplish very little in the absence of the latter. The chapter concludes with the suggestion that sustainable transport must be measurable so that we can assess progress towards attaining it. Such a measurement system is proposed and illustrated for a selected set of 14 countries.

INTRODUCTION

Several of the chapters in this book have made reference to whether certain transport modes or vehicles are sustainable. As transport notions go, this is a relatively new idea. Although several definitions exist, one that follows very closely the initial definition of sustainable development as given in the Brundtland Report (World Commission on Environment and Development, 1987) has been offered by Black (1996). It defines sustainable transport as "satisfying current transport and mobility needs without compromising the ability of future generations to meet these needs" (Black, 1996, 151). Such a definition is analogous to the European use of the term "sustainable mobility". There is a certain vagueness to even this definition since there is no limit placed on "future generations" and nothing is sustainable forever.

Greene and Wegener (1997) offer a different definition attributed to Daly (1991). The latter actually defines sustainable development, but the definition is transferable to sustainable transport. Within this context transport is sustainable if it satisfies three

Modern Transport Geography: second, revised edition. Edited by Brian Hoyle and Richard Knowles.
© 1998 John Wiley & Sons Ltd.

conditions: (i) its rates of use of renewable resources do not exceed their rates of regeneration; (ii) its rates of use of non-renewable resources do not exceed the rate at which sustainable renewable substitutes are developed; and (iii) its rates of pollution emission do not exceed the assimilative capacity of the environment. Gordon (1995) does not believe sustainable transport is able to be precisely defined or achieved, but rather should be something we try to move towards. We will return to this later in the chapter.

These definitions or perspectives do not change the basic point, which is that the future of transport is fraught with problems and will probably have to be offered in a somewhat different form than it is currently offered.

PRINCIPAL BARRIERS TO SUSTAINABILITY

Let us examine in detail the factors that are limiting the sustainability of transport. These include uncertainties regarding the future availability of petroleum, the impact of vehicular traffic on the local environment as well as its impact on global atmospheric problems, the high level of accidents for current transport modes, traffic congestion, and the perspective that the provision of transport leads to urban sprawl. The significance of these factors varies geographically. Most are exemplified by our major urban areas, but rural and less-developed areas also have some of these barriers and even there the number of components is increasing.

The Future of Petroleum

There is a cartoon from several years ago that shows a banker or financier rejecting the motor vehicle ideas of a man named Henry (presumably Ford) with the statement that such a vehicle would require the construction of thousands of miles of surfaced highways, and therefore it was not a feasible undertaking. Given the automobile, one could construct a similar cartoon that had a banker rejecting the idea of a petrol- or gasoline-powered motor vehicle over a water-based steam engine. The former would require the construction of thousands of stations where one could acquire this highly volatile and combustible fuel. In comparison, the water for a steam engine was completely safe, free and ubiquitous. Why would anyone buy a petroleum-based fuel?

Ironically, the automobile became the dominant personal transport vehicle in the developed world, the highways were built and gasoline or petrol did become the major fuel. Even today it is not clear what happened to the steam-powered automobile in the first two decades of the twentieth century. Some believe that the early manufacturers were poor entrepreneurs. Others believe the vehicle was not as good as its gasoline-powered competitor. The latter is a belief without foundation if one examines the steam-powered automobiles of the Stanley Brothers or Abner Doble in America, or of Leon Serpollet in France (Jamison, 1970). These vehicles could travel at high speeds and in the case of Doble's vehicle could go more than 1000 miles on 25 gallons of water. Nevertheless, the gasoline-powered automobile became the personal transport mode for the rest of the century.

The consumption of petroleum for transport has increased consistently during the century, slowing only when the economy slowed. Current world consumption of petroleum for all uses is in the neighbourhood of 65 million barrels a day. If the world continues consuming petroleum at these levels without an increase in the rate of annual consumption, the world's known petroleum reserves will be gone by 2032. If the rate of growth in consumption increases at 2.3 per cent per annum, which is the current growth rate, then known petroleum reserves will be gone by 2021 (Black, 1996). Although some researchers note that we are continually finding new petroleum reserves, they also question if any large fields remain. MacKenzie (1995) argues that if actual reserves are 2.6 times greater than current proven reserves, and the rate of annual growth in consumption is the previously noted 2.3 per cent, then we will run out of petroleum in 2050.

An economist trained in the classical tradition will argue that we will never run out of petroleum. In other words, as supplies dwindle, the price of petroleum-based fuels will begin to rise to the point where consumption ceases, except for the uses that have no alternative. A fuel price of US $20 a gallon may extend the life of petroleum, but from an urban transport perspective, the fuel has ceased to exist. So whether this fuel source is consumed entirely or priced out of the market in the next five decades makes little difference. It is not a sustainable fuel since future generations will not be able to use it.

Environmental Degradation Attributable to Transport

A second barrier to sustainability is the environmental degradation of our current transport modes and practices. Table 15.1 identifies the impacts of transport on humans, animal life, vegetation, soils, geomorphology, waters, climate and the atmosphere. The list could be refined and in the process significantly extended. Society and policy today tend to ignore several of these impact areas and focus on the environmental impacts on climate and the atmosphere that can affect humans. This practice will be followed here as well, but the reader should be aware of the other areas that are negatively affected by transport even though they may not impact the sustainability of transport as it has been defined here.

Urban air quality has received more attention than any other area of environmental impacts related to the transport sector. The identification of the major air pollutants in the United States and the establishment of emission standards for these were significant accomplishments for the 1970s. These pollutants and the proportion of these attributable to the transport sector in the US are: oxides of nitrogen NO_x) (41 per cent), sulphur oxides (5 per cent), hydrocarbons (38 per cent), particulate matter (23 per cent), carbon monoxide (67 per cent) and carbon dioxide (30 per cent) (Gordon, 1991). Similar source levels exist for most developed countries of the world. The oxides of nitrogen and the hydrocarbons

combine in the presence of sunlight to form urban ozone. Ozone and its components, as well as particulate matter, can have significant impacts on the human respiratory system. Such impacts would include ailments ranging from breathing difficulties from any one of these to lung cancer from carcinogenic hydrocarbons or particulate matter. Carbon monoxide can lead to death from asphyxiation in the extreme case, but it can also contribute to heart disease in some cases. Overall the emissions and ailments attributable to the transport sector are attributable to the use of petroleum.

A second impact area related to emissions would be the impact of these on the global atmospheric problems of acid deposition (acid rain), stratospheric ozone depletion and global climate change. The problem of acid deposition is one that impacts primarily fresh-water marine life and plant life. Emissions from one region are atmospherically transported by winds to another region where they are deposited on plants, soils, or water bodies in wet or dry forms of sulphuric and nitric acids. Depending on local buffering ability of soils (due primarily to parent material, natural acidity or soil thickness) trees can die or marine populations can be impacted by the loss of food sources (e.g. insects) or contamination attributable to aluminium leached from the soils by acidic water that passes through these and into ponds and lakes. In North America the problem exists in the northeastern part of the US and the southeastern part of Canada, where the pollutants come from sulphur oxides emitted by Midwest power-generating facilities. Similar problems exist in Scandinavia with emissions from Great Britain, and in the Korean peninsula with emissions from China. Recall that the transport sector emits only about 5 per cent of the sulphur oxides in the USA so the transport sector is not the primary culprit. Nevertheless, there are areas where acid deposition is primarily nitric acid (e.g. Pasadena, California) and this is generally attributed to the automobile.

Stratospheric ozone depletion is attributable primarily to man-made chlorofluorocarbons (CFCs) used to make lightweight packaging (e.g. for fast

Table 15.1   Transport impacts contributing to non-sustainability

Impact Area	Mode	Impact
Vegetation	Highways	Loss of species during right-of-way clearance
	Highway–motor carrier	Damage due to chemical spills
	Aircraft	*Salvinia* introduction to water bodies in Africa
Soils	All land modes	Erosion during construction
	Highway	Changes in soil quality due to poor drainage
	Highway	Contamination due to chemical spills
	Highway	Contamination–chemical use for snow removal
	Railroad	Contamination–use of creosol to preserve wood
	Railroad	Contamination due to PCB use in brake systems
	Pipelines	Contamination due to breaks in oil pipelines
Geomorphology	All land modes	Construction changes in landforms
	Aviation	Loss of wetlands due to airport construction
	Water	Loss of wetlands due to dredging and dumping
	Highway	Off-road vehicle damage in dune areas
Animal	Highway–railroads	Fatalities due to animals in right-of-way
	Highway–railroads	Barriers to movement due to fencing
	Canals	Introduction of predator species
	Pipelines	Barriers to movement when at grade
	Highway	Loss of habitat or interference in same
Water	Highway	Run-off (rubber, petrol, asbestos, phenols, etc.)
	Highway–streets	Flooding due to network density increases
	Water–ocean ships	Garbage dumped from vessels
	Water–ocean tankers	Major petroleum spills
Atmosphere	Highway modes	General air pollution
	Motor vehicles	Ozone layer loss–CFC use in air conditioning
	Aviation	Ozone layer loss–exhaust from supersonic transport
	Major land modes	Global warming due to CO_2 from fossil-fuel use
	Major land modes	Global warming due to methane escapes
	Water–ocean tankers	Global warming–methane escape from tankers
	Highway–railroad	Hazardous material release during accidents
	Highway modes	Possible role in sulphur-based acid deposition
Humans	Motor vehicles	Excessive fatalities and injuries
	Motor vehicles	Medical problems attributable to air pollutants
	Motorized land modes	Various ailments attributable to noise pollution

food), as a propellant (e.g. in spray cans of paint, deodorant and so forth), as a cleaning solution (for computer circuitry), or as a coolant (in air conditioners or refrigeration). CFCs' link to the transport sector is through motor vehicle air conditioning systems. These systems tend to leak CFCs as the vehicle ages. Recharging of air conditioning units was once practised in a very careless manner resulting in the escape of this compound to the environment. Re-claiming of the vehicle through crushing also did little to capture these compounds. The compounds would then enter the atmosphere and be transported to the polar areas of the planet. A geographically unique set of environmental conditions would result in the freeing of the compound's chlorine, which would then attack ozone in the vicinity, resulting in its destruction and the formation of what have been called "holes" in the ozone layer of the planet.

These holes have resulted in an increase in ultraviolet radiation reaching the surface and this may lead to various eye ailments (e.g. retinal damage, cataracts or blindness) and skin diseases (benign and malignant skin cancers), as well as negatively impacting land and marine plant and animal life.

The third major area of transport-related climate and atmospheric impacts is global warming. This planet is surrounded by a layer of gases that is transparent to incoming solar radiation allowing this to reach and heat the surface. The heat so generated would escape the planet if it were not for the same layer of gases, which absorbs or reflects this heat back to the surface. It is this layer of gases, sometimes called the "greenhouse gases", that results in this planet being warm enough for human life. This warming of the planet is called the "greenhouse effect". The effect and carbon dioxide's role in its existence have been known since the late 1800s. More recently it has been argued that increasing the amount of carbon dioxide will result in a "forcing" of the greenhouse effect, which will result in a further warming of the planet. The scientific community is unanimous in its belief in the existence of the greenhouse effect and carbon's role in it. The only questions argued are whether the warming has already begun and how great the warming will be.

As the single largest source of human-generated carbon emissions, the transport sector is in large part responsible for the problem of global warming. At the same time the transport sector could be significantly impacted by the same global warming (Black, 1990). The Intergovernmental Panel on Climate Change (1996) has recently estimated an increase in temperatures for the year 2100 of 1.5–3.5°C. This amount of warming could result in partial melting of the polar ice-caps and mid-latitude glaciers, which along with thermal expansion would result in a sea-level rise of 0.3 to approximately 1.0 m by 2100 according to the IPCC. While coastal flooding of urban transit, railroads and highways could result during storm surges, and port facilities might require significant amounts of reconstruction for the same reason, it is expected that the major impacts will result from shifts in the distribution of agricultural production.

We have no reason to believe that dry areas will become drier or wet areas would be wetter. However, if storm activity increases (due to increases in evaporation) and ocean currents change due to a warming planet, then there is reason to believe that anything could happen in terms of the location of climate changes. Therefore it is possible that areas of agricultural production will change and we have no idea if the "new" areas will be adequately served by transport.

Accidents and Fatalities of Highway Travel

In the last decade the USA has improved its highway safety record by dropping under 50 000 annual fatalities. The country's highways were until that point wiping out the population of a small metropolitan area each year. Outside the USA the picture is not much brighter. Downey (1995) has given global estimates of 250 000 fatalities annually and another 10 million persons injured. Forecasts of one million fatalities worldwide by 2020 would not be unbelievable, though they would be unreasonable. These numbers should be unacceptable to us, but all too often we simply shake our heads and turn to page two of the morning paper.

If we had no other barriers to sustainability, would not this single one be enough to prevent our transport system from being sustainable? I believe it would. If sustainability is enabling future generations to satisfy their transport needs, is not the elimination of part of that generation inconsistent with the objective? All indications are that this barrier will grow in importance.

Congestion

The excessive number and use of automobiles in larger urban areas have led to high levels of traffic congestion. The standard response to congestion in the past was the construction of additional highways in the form of major arterials or bypasses. Even the Interstate Highway system of the United States was built, in part, so that commercial vehicles could bypass the congested highways of urban areas in that country. This system provided some relief to the traffic congestion of urban areas, but the relief was short-lived since the system tended to dump traffic at the edge of the city where existing roads and streets could not cope with the volumes. An extension of the Interstate Highways into urban areas followed and this also provided some temporary relief to the congestion problem.

There seems to be some recognition now that the construction of additional highways stimulates more travel and that any reduction in congestion due to the project will quickly be absorbed by this traffic, leading to similar or worse levels of traffic congestion. This statement applies to areas of high congestion and rapid growth. One can still get relief from traffic congestion outside of urban areas through highway construction, but these are not the areas where the major problems exist today.

Urban Sprawl and Excessive Land Use

The suburbanization of major urban areas has been facilitated by the construction of transport facilities into these areas. Highways are often blamed for this outward movement, but streetcars and inter-urban railroads were probably responsible for some of this trend before the automobile. While it is true that transportation made suburbanization possible, it did not have to play a causal role in urban sprawl. The latter is a leapfrog type of development that leaves large pockets of undeveloped land between itself and the urban core, increasing the costs of serving these areas with municipal services, transport lines and utilities. It is not apparent that sprawl needs to be a barrier to sustainable transport.

The excessive use of land for highway transport in urban areas is also viewed as non-sustainable, since it will essentially prevent the use of the land for more productive activities. This use of land has increased over the past half-century, but we have also seen major abandonments of railroad property in these same urban areas and it is possible that the overall "transport" use has not changed that much.

These are the major barriers preventing the world from having a sustainable transport system. They seem to be overwhelming and difficult, if not impossible, to resolve.

A BRIEF HISTORY OF NON-SUSTAINABLE TRANSPORT

Many of the barriers to sustainability seem to be a product of modern times and the automobile, and some believe that if we were to go back to a simpler time the problems would disappear. This is true. If we did not use petroleum, its reserves and emissions would not be a problem. If vehicles moved slower, there would certainly be fewer fatalities. But congestion and sprawl would probably continue to be problems, if not barriers to sustainability. It is likely that another series of barriers to sustainability would be created.

History would suggest that, rather than the transport vehicle itself, it is the excessive use of the vehicle that creates the problem. As an example, most would probably consider the horse and buggy as a sustainable transport mode, and it is in its non-intensive rural context. But we have also seen photographs of the congestion created by these vehicles in New York and London in the 1880s. That was only part of the problem. It has been estimated that "in New York City alone at the turn of the century, horses deposited on the streets every day an estimated 2.5 million pounds of manure and 60 000 gallons of urine, accounting for about two-thirds of the filth that littered the city's streets" (Flink, 1988, 136). In an urban context with high utilization even this mode of transport becomes non-sustainable.

We may view the wind-driven wooden ships of the fifteenth through to the mid-nineteenth century as an early sustainable transport mode. In terms of their use of wind energy, a renewable energy source, they were sustainable. However, these ships placed excessive demands on the lumber resources of the countries that operated these fleets: Great Britain, France, Spain and Holland. The demands were excessive enough to lead to the deforestation of most of these countries, a deforestation from which they have never really recovered. This occurred at a time when lumber was *the natural resource* used for heating, cooking and shelter. By the early 1700s Great Britain was securing the lumber for main or "great" masts for its naval and merchant vessels from the American colonies and other parts of Europe. Table 15.2 reflects the origin of the main masts imported by Great Britain in 1775, and indicates the impact that the war with the American colonies would have on lumber supplies for shipbuilding.

Of course lumber was used for all parts of merchant and naval ships of this era. On average, building a merchant ship required 97 average oak trees, and a typical naval vessel would involve the use of approximately 1400 of these trees. It is easy to see how Great Britain would have a lumber crisis by the beginning of the 1800s. In the case of Great Britain, less than 2 per cent of the 15 300 vessels registered in 1790 were navy ships, the remaining 98 per cent were merchant ships. However, since the naval vessels were considerably larger (they weighed in the neighbourhood of 13 times more than a merchant ship), the lumber demanded by the Navy was 21 per cent (391 450 tons) of the total, with the merchant ships using the remainder (1 460 823) (Albion, 1965). From this perspective the iron-clad ships of the late 1800s were a necessity.

Table 15.2 Origins and volume of imports of "great masts" into Great Britain for ship-building, 1775

Nova Scotia	87
New England	239
New York	73
Pennsylvania	295
Virginia–Maryland	28
Carolina	2
Total, America	724
Russia	561
"East Country"	106
Denmark–Norway	31
Sweden	0
Total, Baltic	698
Total, America and Baltic	1422

Source: Albion (1965).

The empires of Greece and Rome had managed to deforest most of the Mediterranean Basin with similar excessive uses of lumber for the construction of their naval fleets (Hughes, 1975). Wood was also used for various other purposes at that time as well.

To reiterate, the problem is not necessarily with the mode or vehicle, it is the use of excessive numbers of these that creates the problem. Even the motor vehicle is sustainable, but not when the world fleet in use reaches a thousand million vehicles.

THE SUSTAINABILITY OF CONTEMPORARY AND FUTURE TRANSPORT MODES

While the transport modes of the past are not as sustainable as we might have believed, what can be said of the sustainability of current transport modes and vehicles? Unfortunately, there is very little that one can say about the sustainability of the vehicles that make up our contemporary transport system. The primary reason for this is that the significant modes, those that handle large numbers of passengers or large tonnages of freight (automobiles, buses, rail, aircraft, or motor carriers), all consume fuels derived from petroleum. We sometimes confuse this point by talking about miles per gallon, or seat miles per gallon, as though energy efficiency has some meaning in terms of sustainability. Recall that the sustainability of transport with regard to petroleum is that the fuel is finite and its practical end is foreseeable, and that emissions from petroleum-based fuels are damaging the local and global atmospheric environments. Increasing fuel efficiency has the potential of increasing the life of the fuel by insignificant amounts. Given the additional problem of emissions, one might argue that decreasing the fuel consumed per unit of travel will lessen atmospheric pollution. This is true in the short run, but the reality is that the same amount of vehicular emissions will get into the atmosphere in seven years as opposed to five years. In addition, growth of transport in the developing world may counter the impact of reductions in the developed world. If we are looking at pollutants that remain in the atmosphere for more than 100 years, then vehicle fuel efficiency has little impact on its sustainability.

The less significant modes in terms of traffic carried are also insignificant in terms of sustainability. These modes usually include the so-called non-motorized modes, of which bicycles are the most universal example. Considered by many to be the leading sustainable transport vehicle since it uses human energy and (its user) emits minor amounts of carbon dioxide, it has some problems. Its utility tends to be seasonal in temperate climates, its range is limited, and its safety record for injuries and fatalities is one of the highest on a passenger-mile basis (Black *et al.*, 1995). This last point should raise some question about its sustainability.

We could look at some other modes, but the point is that, although some of these appear to be attractive, they would not be capable of moving the freight and passengers in the numbers that the current modes carry. Since there is a desire for movement and transport, one could say it is an economic imperative, then the current dominant modes must be the modes of the future, and we must make them more sustainable. This implies a different fuel source, less or no harmful emissions, and improvements in vehicle safety. Congestion and sprawl will continue to be problems of any future transport systems, but they are perhaps manageable by regulatory or policy actions.

SOLUTIONS TO THE SUSTAINABLE TRANSPORT PROBLEM?

Proposed solutions to the transport sustainability problem may be thought of as lying along a continuum that ranges from minor traffic ordinances in small towns to global agreements involving most nations of the world. Between these extremes we have metropolitan area programmes for urban public transit or congestion pricing in certain corridors, State programmes mandating a portion of the new car market share must use alternative fuels (e.g.

California's programme), national regulations or standards (e.g. laws requiring the use of seat belts), or CAFE (corporate average fuel economy) standards that require the fuel consumption of an average vehicle manufactured by a firm to be 27.5 miles per gallon. Beyond the national level we may very well have multinational agreements on a regional level, such as the European Union's goal of reducing carbon emissions by the year 2000 to 1990 levels. This would be followed by global agreements to eliminate the production and use of certain chemicals that are detrimental to the environment. Examples exist for all of these cases and several of these are discussed elsewhere. Beyond these policy types of actions there are also proposals for new (neo-classical) types of urban design that decrease the need for travel, or the substitution of walking or biking for automobiles, or high-speed rail to replace freeways. Examples of each of these also exist, but all have shortcomings ranging from limited utility and impracticability to excessive costs that have made them experiments to watch rather than solutions to try. Of concern here are the previously noted policy solutions that seem to have general utility and the extent to which these programmes at various scales are successful.

In terms of a resolution to the transport sustainability problem, it seems apparent that any action below the national level at this point in time will have little effect on the total problem. This is not to say that a subnational area could not enact traffic regulations that would significantly reduce highway accidents and fatalities within its border. It could and this would reduce the global totals for accidents and fatalities, but probably not significantly. Similarly, California can enact statute after statute to improve its air quality, but unless the US (or a significant number of states) enacts similar laws or regulations, it is doubtful that the California action will have much of an impact beyond its borders.

Some might argue that even a single nation can have little impact on the global sustainability of transport. If the country is a major contributor to the non-sustainability of some component of transport, it can have a global impact. An example is available in the US action to remove lead from gasoline sold in that country. Medical evidence on the impacts of lead on children's development led the US Environmental Protection Agency (EPA) to reduce significantly the standard for lead content in gasoline beginning in 1974. Emissions dropped immediately and further tightening of the standard reduced emissions between 1982 and 1991 by 89 per cent. Lead was completely removed from gasoline in the USA in 1992, in part because of the medical evidence previously cited. Lead in gasoline also interfered with the use of catalytic converters on newer automobiles. Since these actions were taken, global lead levels have been decreasing, which is a reflection in part of the significant role the USA played in such emissions.

Multinational agreements that set targets for their signatories have a mixed record of success, but the potential benefits are so great that these nations must continue to try to meet the provisions of the agreements. The aforementioned European Union's attempt to reduce year-2000 carbon emissions to 1990 levels will probably not be achieved, with the possible exceptions of Great Britain, France and Germany. Nevertheless, the exercise did raise the public's awareness and stimulated reductions that might not have occurred otherwise.

With regard to the five major barriers to transport sustainability mentioned earlier in this chapter, it does seem that some steps can be taken to remove them, but these actions will for the most part take time and significant monetary resources. Let us briefly examine each of the barriers in turn: diminishing reserves of petroleum, environmental (primarily atmospheric) degradation, excessive highway accidents, traffic congestion and urban sprawl.

Diminishing Reserves of Petroleum – Alternatives

Faced with the loss of any natural resource, countries will differ in terms of the way in which they respond. One approach is what could be called the technological approach, e.g. to develop an alternative or substitute. A second approach is a policy response to the problem, which would seek to control consumption of the resource through regulation, taxation, or rationing. A third approach is what could be called a behavioural approach wherein the citizenry is expected to cut back voluntarily on consumption or to conserve. In general, Americans tend to believe a "technological fix" is possible for most problems. Policy approaches are far more typical of European countries and they have generally been very successful in this area. In the short run, nearly every country will take the policy approach to a crisis. The OPEC embargoes of the 1970–1980 period resulted in national pleas for conservation and rationing schemes in the USA, but at the same time major ethanol production and hybrid vehicle schemes were initiated.

There seems to be a growing recognition that the petroleum problem will not be solved by policy actions. These can extend the life of that fossil fuel, but given the rate at which consumption is growing globally, a few more years will be of little help. Of course, if we allow the market to determine price, then an implicit rationing will result and this will extend the life of the fuel. Fuel at excessive prices will not power our future transport systems, but it will stimulate the development of alternatives. It is at this point that policy solutions lead into technological solutions, or in some cases confuse technological solutions.

Gordon (1991) evaluates several alternative fuels that are currently under consideration as the "new" transport fuel or fuels of the future. It seems reasonable to set aside petroleum-based fuels since these would also become scarce. This takes away reformulated gasoline and oxygenated additives for gasoline fuels (MTBE and ETBE). Liquefied petroleum gas (LPG), also called propane, would be dropped from most lists if it is of petroleum origin. LPG can also be produced from natural gas. This fossil fuel, while not as environmentally damaging as petroleum, does contribute to many of the same environmental problems and probably should not be considered as a major alternative fuel. These latter comments also apply to compressed natural gas (CNG), or methanol, if it is produced from fossil fuels. We have essentially raided the technologist's cupboard and found it mostly empty.

We are left with ethanol, hydrogen, fuel cells, solar power and electric vehicles. Ethanol is often held up as the solution to our future transport fuel problems. Here we have a renewable fuel produced from plant biomass, e.g. corn or sugar cane. This fuel is frequently added to gasoline to make gasohol in the USA; it is 90 per cent gasoline and 10 per cent ethanol. Ethanol is not as environmentally benign as some believe, but this is not its primary problem. Two major interrelated problems argue against ethanol as a long-term solution to global fuel needs. Firstly, this fuel would require the dedication of massive amounts of acreage for the plant stock that would be used to produce ethanol, and even this dedication of land might not be sufficient. A recent study in the USA estimated that if all corn, barley, oats and sorghum grown in that country were dedicated to ethanol production, i.e. none would be used for human consumption, then that country would only be able to fuel its transport system for a little more than two weeks (16.6 days) with ethanol (Pearson, 1996). Secondly, with global populations expected to reach 10 000 million by 2100, it is probable that most arable land will be devoted to food production for human consumption. So ethanol as well will probably drop from the scene.

We are left with electric vehicles, solar energy, fuel cells, and hydrogen. Electric vehicles offer some potential if we could produce the electricity from something other than fossil fuels. Such vehicles could be used to meet most urban transport needs, but technological problems exist for this fuel in long-distance transport. These problems are diminishing each day, but we will undoubtedly face the urge to continue using coal to produce electric power and this will not solve our current transport fuel problems as it mortgages our environmental future.

It is technically feasible to produce hydrogen from water, as many former high-school chemistry students will recall. This act in itself requires an energy source. Solar energy could be used as the power source for hydrogen production. The hydrogen could be used to power vehicles directly or in a fuel cell. The by-products of burning hydrogen are oxygen and water vapour and it is reasonable to assume that the latter could be captured in some way and used to produce additional hydrogen by the vehicle, making the fuel environmentally benign. Of course estimates of the cost of this fuel suggest it would be double or triple the price of gasoline. However, if the price of gasoline included its external environmental costs (Black *et al.*, 1996), then hydrogen would be competitive. There will undoubtedly be opposition to moving towards such a fuel by existing petrochemical industries.

The Global Environment – Choices?

If we examine the major pollutants harming the atmosphere of the planet or the air of our cities, we must view the finite nature of petroleum as a blessing. Choices between the various alternative fuels must be made with care. Several alternative fuels discussed above were rejected because of their environmental impacts. This may appear rash, but we are at a cross-roads where we have the possibility of solving long-term fuel supply and environmental quality problems at the same time. Why would we opt to solve only one of these if a fuel choice existed that would solve both? There may be many ways in which hydrogen can power our transport systems and these should all be examined, but there appears to be no reasonable alternative to this fuel if we are to solve the dual fuel-supply/air-quality problems that confront the planet.

Highway Injuries and Fatalities

Highway accidents are attributable to environmental factors (snow, ice, rain), design factors in roads and vehicles, and human error. We have the capability of reducing vehicle accidents with technological innovations that would in part take the human error out of the accident equation. This would involve making automobiles "smarter" with more computerized components. This solution is expensive, but it is generally expected to be common in vehicles of the future.

Policy solutions would involve legislation mandating the use of seat belts in all vehicles, as well as controls on speed. It is not evident that high speeds result in more accidents on exceptionally good highways for the simple reason that these facilities are made for vehicles that travel at high speed. Nevertheless, there is a tendency for vehicles to travel at higher speeds on poorer roads if an area increases speeds on its better highways.

There are also behavioural changes that would help with this problem, e.g. deciding not to travel during poorer weather conditions, trip chaining to minimize the number of trips, defensive driving, and so forth. These are the hardest changes to make, however.

Congestion

Assume for the moment that the motor vehicle problem has been solved in terms of minimizing air pollution and a new renewable resource base has been identified to fuel a new generation of vehicles. Assume further that we have accidents under control. The next problem will be highway congestion or in some cases just space in which to keep a car. We have come up with solutions to the highway congestion problem through technology (highway construction), policy (toll roads and similar policy provisions), but the former is no longer viewed as a solution and the latter works only in certain corridors where the geography or route structure is cooperative. Parking space will most likely be available outside of urban areas and transit vehicles will move drivers from central to peripheral sites. This is already common in the most congested areas.

It seems the most effective solution to transport congestion in urban areas is a change in personal and business behaviour, or at least more flexibility. Staggering of work hours keeps congestion under control in many metropolitan areas. Deliveries during the night would also lessen daytime congestion. Stronger funding of urban transit, which would permit a higher level of service (lower headways) as well as more comfortable and attractive vehicles, is also necessary. We may see an increase in the level of interest in car pooling or van pooling, but this appears unattractive based on recent trends. Trends throughout the developed and developing world suggest a continual increase in the market for private automobiles. Neighbourhood electric vehicles could already serve most of our urban transport needs, but this too will require some modifications in the behaviour and attitudes of drivers.

Urban Sprawl

Urban sprawl is a land-use or land-control issue. If an area does not want sprawl then it need only put in place a local zoning ordinance, building permits, taxes and restrictions and enforce these. One should hardly view urban expansion, no matter how much it sprawls, as caused by transport when regulatory controls exist that can prevent it. If the sprawl already exists then it may be necessary to tax services or control growth to contiguous areas based on the cost of providing urban services.

SOCIAL AND ECONOMIC IMPACTS OF SOLUTIONS

It should be evident that the transport sustainability that is possible will not be free. It carries a significant cost for those countries that attempt to achieve it. This is amply illustrated by examining the price of electric vehicles today. These are so expensive that governments or electric utility operators are willing to subsidize their purchase. Similarly, none of the current alternative fuels have a price that is lower than gasoline, which is 97.9 cents per US gallon (approximately 0.833 of a British gallon) or 25 cents per litre in the American Midwest at the time of writing (March 1998). Shifts to an alternative fuel will increase the costs of travel and transport. Reductions in motor vehicle accidents and their severity can be achieved through various intelligent vehicle accessories, but these will also increase the price of motor vehicles. Increasing the price of transport through fees or tolls is the policy option that appears the most attractive today for handling congestion, but this would create an inequitable situation since the lowest-paid workers have jobs that require that they travel at times when the tolls would be highest. Assuming this problem could be handled with fee waivers for the lowest income levels, it would still be a burden on others who are not quite as poor. Even the control of urban sprawl would generate costs since this would deny the rich and the poor low-cost land on the urban periphery. As we look at nearly all of these "solutions" we can see costs for the citizenry that exceed current costs and we want to ask: "Can we afford to implement these solutions?" But that is not the question we should be asking. That question is: "Can we afford *not* to implement them?" We have all too often taken the lowest-cost solution in the past and that is why the options available now seem to cost so much more.

If we take these actions and the cost of transport increases, this will have ramifications on other needs of individuals and families. There will simply be less money available for shelter, food and nutrition, clothing and social activities. Perhaps in other cases it will take away the little discretionary income that remains after all other needs are met. Life will become harder for individuals and families with lower incomes. Those with middle-range incomes will be inconvenienced but they will survive. High-income individuals or families will hardly notice the change. Those advocating the use of prices to control travel demand have not really taken the next step and begun to look at the impact this will have on society. Perhaps we should do that first, because if we increase the price of travel and then set in place mechanisms to lessen or remove the impact of these price increases on lower-income drivers, we might also eliminate the impact that price increases would otherwise have on travel demand. Increasing the price only on those who can afford to pay it will not eliminate congestion.

Higher transport prices will also have to be paid by private-sector businesses and industries. The difference is that we would expect all members of a single industry to be impacted the same way and this would result in no real change in trade or market areas. Although increases in transport costs will increase the costs of operations for the firm, these increases are often passed along to consumers, so the end-result of retail and industrial transport price increases is higher prices for consumer goods for the individuals and families noted previously.

KNOWING WHERE WE STAND

It was suggested at the outset of this chapter that sustainable transportation may not be definable. Gordon (1995) has suggested that it may be a goal towards which we should strive, rather than try to define it precisely. Even fuzzy goals have underlying objectives that enable us to evaluate whether we have accomplished the goals, so it seems that we should try to set out some measures of the various components of transport sustainability so that we will at least know where we stand and if we are moving in the right direction.

It has been suggested in this chapter that a transport system based on petroleum is non-sustainable since that fuel is non-renewable and has a limited economic life. The fuel also negatively impacts local air quality and pollutes the global atmospheric environment. The major transport systems and modes today are also non-sustainable at present because of the high level of accidents and fatalities, and vehicle congestion. Urban sprawl is facilitated by transport lines, but its major causal factor is an inability to control land use.

Measuring those factors that contribute to non-sustainability in transport is usually not possible, but we can identify other indices that may assist us in monitoring conditions that reflect non-sustainability. Since most policies in this area are national, we would want to have national-level indices to compare one country with another. One of the easiest indices would be a measure of the number of highway accidents involving personal injuries. We might standardize this value by dividing by population to get an index of highway accidents involving personal injuries per person in the country. The higher this value, the less sustainable the transport sector of the country. If we wanted higher values to reflect higher levels of sustainable transport, we could simply take the reciprocal of the index (1/index). While most would find this index acceptable as one dimension of sustainable transport, others would argue that some countries record and report accidents more conscientiously than others. Nevertheless, we will hold this index as one dimension of our transport sustainability index.

Automobile dependence is also something to avoid in terms of sustainability. An index of some value here would be the number of people per motor vehicle in the country. As this number rises, there are fewer motor vehicles than would be expected given the population of the country. This index would also reflect fuel consumption in that the fewer people per car, the more vehicles available, and therefore the more vehicles in use and fuel consumed.

Local and global atmospheric impacts also come from the excessive use of motor vehicles. The index above could also be used to reflect petroleum-based fuel consumption or atmospheric pollution. Although it would not recognize a country's move towards alternative fuels, such moves are minor with the exception of the use of compressed natural gas in New Zealand or ethanol in Brazil. For the most part as the index increases (more people per vehicle) this translates into lower levels of atmospheric pollution. So we will include this index as a surrogate for such pollution. Viewing this measure as a motor vehicle pollution index, then, as its value increases, pollution should decrease and sustainability should increase.

Congestion is another dimension of non-sustainable transport. It is defined in several ways in the literature (see *inter alia*, Shrank *et al.*, 1993; National Research Council, 1994), but most of these approaches require considerable data. We will measure congestion as a ratio of motor vehicles to miles of highway. Division of the former by the latter would yield motor vehicles per mile of highway. It recognizes the size of the network involved and, as the index increases, congestion is increasing and therefore transport is non-sustainable.

Although not discussed implicitly here, a sustainable transport network is one that has alternative modes available. To get some indication of the availability of alternative modes, it is possible to propose an index of miles of rail track divided by a country's area. This becomes a track density measure and, the greater its value, the more sustainable the country's transport system would be since alternative modes would be available.

With some minor mathematical adjustments we can take the five values above and convert them to indices with a mean of 100. The five values can then be summed and divided by five to yield an index of transport sustainability. This final index also has a mean of 100, with values below the mean indicating less sustainable transport and values above the mean implying more sustainable transport. One could obviously question whether an equal weight should be applied to the five components of sustainable transport, or whether the persons per vehicle index should have been used to reflect both automobile dependence and pollution tendencies. However, the approach enables the reader to see exactly why a given country has the transport sustainability index value obtained. Differential weighting often obscures this. The index has been applied to 14 countries and the resulting values of the indices are displayed in Table 15.3. What the table shows us is that, under the assumptions made here, the least sustainable transport is found in Canada and the United States. Japan and France are tending in the same direction. More sustainable transport situations exist in Brazil and Germany. In the former, the low number of accidents per capita pushes Brazil into the sustainability area, while the presence of a dense rail alternative places Germany in that field. Some incorporation of Brazil's use of ethanol in the measures used here would push it further in the direction of a sustainable transport situation.

Table 15.3 reveals where each country stands and implicitly what it has to take care of if it is to improve its overall position. In the case of the USA with its automobile culture, just about anything could be done to improve the situation as all indices are among the lowest in the table. The UK situation

Table 15.3   Sustainability indices for 14 selected countries

Country	Petroleum Dependence	Environmental Impacts	Accidents and Injuries	Alternative Modes	Congestion	Transport Sustainability
Brazil	243.90	243.90	10.09	6.56	161.28	133.15
Canada	39.02	39.02	166.42	12.58	8.70	53.15
Costa Rica	234.15	234.15	191.64	32.70	170.96	172.72
France	46.34	46.34	75.41	110.25	95.14	74.70
Germany	46.34	46.34	52.71	436.41	166.64	149.69
Italy	43.90	43.90	80.07	93.08	264.70	105.12
Japan	48.78	48.78	41.84	94.39	139.05	74.57
Malaysia	170.73	170.73	59.31	11.81	79.15	98.35
Saudi Arabia	151.22	151.22	126.49	1.09	47.90	95.59
South Africa	180.49	180.49	103.03	30.73	77.84	114.51
Sweden	56.10	56.10	122.53	42.22	71.32	69.65
Switzerland	48.78	48.78	65.75	214.37	124.95	100.53
United Kingdom	60.98	60.98	52.43	272.89	152.02	119.86
United States	29.27	29.27	24.94	40.69	88.52	42.54

is much better than the USA in terms of alternative (rail) mode availability and congestion, and slightly better in terms of automobile dependence, air pollution and accidents. As crude as these measures may be, they do reveal some very basic truths about the sustainability of transport among the selected countries of the world examined here. In addition, it enables us to identify where improvements need to be made.

changes in human behaviour and attitudes. There may be the substitution of communication for some travel, but improvements in communications over the last 100 years have actually generated more travel. Finally, there will be increases in taxation; these will be necessary to maintain the systems as well as to inhibit overuse of them. By 2100 the world will be different, but our transport systems will be sustainable.

CONCLUSIONS

In this chapter we touched on the non-sustainable nature of our current transport systems and networks. Resource depletion and environmental damage will force society to confront this sustainability problem within the lifetime of most who will read this chapter. That confrontation will address the problem with a mixture of changes in technology, policy instruments and changes in human behaviour. The systems can be made sustainable, but this will necessitate the use of a new fuel that results in fewer emissions that are detrimental to the environment. Future generations will probably have less freedom than the current generation in terms of the use of private vehicles and this will necessitate

REFERENCES

Albion, R.G. (1965), *Forests and sea power: the timber problem of the Royal Navy 1652–1862* (Hamden, CT: Archon Books).

Black, W.R. (1990), "Global warming: impacts on the transportation infrastructure", *TR (Transportation Research) News* 150 (2–8), 34.

Black, W.R. (1996), "Sustainable transportation: a US perspective", *Journal of Transport Geography* 4, 151–9.

Black, W.R., Munn, D.L., Black, R.J. and Xie, B.J. (1995), *Modal choices: approaches to comparing the cost of alternate transportation modes* (Bloomington, IN: Transportation Research Center, Indiana University).

Daley, E.E. (1991), *Steady state economics* (Washington, DC: Island Press).

Downey, M.L. (1995), "Transportation trends", paper presented at the *Symposium on Challenges and Opportunities for Global Transportation in the 21st century*, Volpe Transportation Systems Center, Cambridge, MA.

Flink, J.J. (1988), *The automobile age* (Cambridge, MA: MIT Press).

Gordon, D. (1991), *Steering a new course: transportation, energy and the environment* (Washington, DC: Island Press).

Gordon, D. (1995), "Sustainable transportation: what do we mean and how do we get there?", in Sperling, D. and Shaheen, S.A. (eds), *Transportation and energy: strategies for a sustainable transportation system* (Washington, DC: American Council for an Energy Efficient Economy).

Greene, D.L. and Wegener, M. (1997), "Sustainable transport", *Journal of Transport Geography* 5, 177–90.

Hughes, J.D. (1975), *Ecology in ancient civilizations* (Albuquerque: University of New Mexico Press).

Intergovernmental Panel on Climate Change (1996), *Climate change 1995* (Cambridge: Cambridge University Press).

Jamison, A. (1970), *The steam-powered automobile* (Bloomington, IN: Indiana University Press).

MacKenzie, J.J. (1995), "Alternative fuels to reduce petroleum consumption, global gases, and urban air pollution", paper presented at the *Symposium on Challenges and Opportunities for Global Transportation in the 21st century*, Volpe Transportation Systems Center, Cambridge, MA.

National Research Council (1994), *Curbing gridlock: peak period fees to relieve traffic congestion*, Vols 1 and 2, Special Report 242. Transportation Research Board and Commission on Behavioral and Social Sciences and Education (Washington, DC: National Academy Press).

Pearson, B. (1996), "An estimation of potential production of agri-based ethanol", Department of Geography, Indiana University, Bloomington, Indiana (unpublished).

Shrank, D., Turner, S. and Lomax, T. (1993), *Estimates of urban roadway congestion, 1990*, Report 1131–5 (College Station: Texas Transportation Institute).

World Commission on Environment and Development (1987), *Our common future* (Oxford: Oxford University Press).

LIST OF FIGURES

LIST OF PHOTOGRAPHS

LIST OF TABLES

NOTES ON CONTRIBUTORS

William R. Black received his doctorate from the University of Iowa and has been a member of the geography faculty at Indiana University since 1969. Doctoral research on rail network expansion led to positions as Director of Rail Planning for Indiana, member of the Activation Task Force that created the Consolidated Rail Corporation (better known as Conrail) and Director of the Indiana Department of Transportation. Professor Black served two terms as Chairman of the Transportation Specialty Group of the Association of American Geographers and was the 1995 recipient of that group's Ullman Award. He is active in the Transportation Research Board of the National Research Council and chairs its Committee on Social and Economic Factors in Transportation. Since 1995 he has been the North American Associate Editor of the *Journal of Transport Geography*. Currently he is Co-Chair of a National Science Foundation–European Science Foundation committee involved in designing a transatlantic research programme on social change and sustainable transport. He has directed 20 research projects and is the author of three books and more than 100 research papers and reports.
Department of Geography, 120 Student Building, Indiana University, Bloomington, IN 47405-6101, USA

Michael Browne is the Exel Logistics Professor of Transport at the University of Westminster where he specializes in international logistics. He teaches freight transport and logistics on the University's Master's programme in Transport Planning and Management and is responsible for directing research and consultancy activities in logistics. He has worked on studies for the European Commission, the UK Departments of Transport and Trade, and commercial organizations. He has acted as a Specialist Adviser to the House of Commons Select Committee on Transport.
Transport Studies Group, University of Westminster, 35 Marylebone Road, London, NW1 5LS, UK

Clive Charlton is a Senior Lecturer in the Department of Geographical Sciences at the University of Plymouth. His research interests include railway operations and policy, rural tourism and recreation, and environmental issues in Iberia. He helped set up the Devon and Cornwall Rail Partnership, based at the University of Plymouth, which promotes and researches the use of rural railways for recreation and tourism.
Department of Geographical Sciences, University of Plymouth, Plymouth, Devon, PL4 8AA, UK

John Farrington is a Senior Lecturer in the Department of Geography, University of Aberdeen. Dr Farrington specializes in transport geography with particular reference to policy and environmental impact. Recent research includes work on environmental assessments of transport projects, and on car dependence in rural Scotland for the Scottish Office.
Department of Geography, University of Aberdeen, Elphinstone Road, Old Aberdeen, AB24 3UF, UK

Richard Gibb is a Reader in Geography in the Department of Geographical Sciences at the University of Plymouth. His principal research interests focus on regional economic integration and cooperation, with particular emphasis on southern Africa and the European Union. He has published widely on these themes, as well as on various aspects of transport, including rail privatization and the Channel Tunnel.
Department of Geographical Sciences, University of Plymouth, Plymouth, Devon, PL4 8AA, UK

Genevieve Giuliano is Professor and Acting Dean in the School of Urban Planning and Development of the University of Southern California. She received her Ph.D. in Social Sciences from the University of California, Irvine. Professor Giuliano is a faculty fellow of the Lincoln Institute of Land Policy and a member of the Editorial Boards of *Urban Studies, Transportation Research* and the *Journal of Transport Statistics*. Her research interests include relationships between land use and transportation, transportation policy evaluation, and impacts of information technology on transportation and travel behaviour.
School of Urban Planning and Development, University of Southern California, Los Angeles, CA 90089-0042, USA

Brian Graham is Professor of Human Geography in the School of Environmental Studies, University of Ulster. He has published extensively on many aspects of transport and cultural geography. His publications include *Geography and air transport* (Wiley, 1995), together with an edited collection, *In search of Ireland: a cultural geography* (Routledge, 1997). Recent papers have addressed such diverse topics as the liberalization of the EU's air transport industry, loyalism in Ulster, the nature of European heritage, and the contested meanings of the pilgrimage routes to Santiago de Compostela. His most recent edited book is *Modern Europe: place, culture and identity* (Arnold, 1998).
School of Environmental Studies, University of Ulster, Coleraine, Co. Londonderry, Northern Ireland, BT52 1SA, UK

Derek Hall is Head of the Department of Leisure and Tourism Management at The Scottish Agricultural College. His research interests include tourism and transport development processes in restructuring societies and peripheral regions. His recent publications include *Transport and economic development in the new Central and Eastern Europe* (editor, Belhaven, 1993), *Albania and the Albanians* (Pinter, 1994), *Tourism: a gender analysis* (co-editor with Vivian Kinnaird, Wiley, 1994), and *Reconstructing the Balkans* (co-editor with Darrick Danta, Wiley, 1995). Dr Hall has served as Secretary (1990–93) and Chairman (1993–96) of the Transport Geography Study Group of the Institute of British Geographers.
Department of Leisure and Tourism Management, The Scottish Agricultural College, Auchincruive, Ayr, KA6 5HW, UK

David Hilling retired in summer 1996 after nearly 40 years in university teaching, most recently as Senior Lecturer in Geography at Royal Holloway College, University of London, where he is now an Honorary Research Fellow. He is Fellow of the Chartered Institute of Transport, and of the Permanent International Association of Navigation Congresses; and is a Vice-Chairman of the Inland Shipping Group (Inland Waterways Association). His teaching and research interests are in maritime transport and associated problems of port development. He is the author of *Barge*

carrier systems (Benn, 1978) and *Transport and developing countries* (Routledge, 1996); author with A.B. Mountjoy of *Africa: geography and development* (Hutchinson, 1988); and editor with B.S. Hoyle of *Seaports and development in Tropical Africa* (Macmillan, 1970) and *Seaport systems and spatial change* (Wiley, 1984).
4 Torrington Road, Berkhamsted, Hertfordshire, HP4 3DD, UK

Brian Hoyle is a Reader in Geography in the Department of Geography, University of Southampton. His research interests include ports and port-cities; waterfront revitalization; and transport/development relationships, particularly in Africa and Canada. He has authored or edited 15 books and many papers in these fields. Recent publications include *European port cities in transition* (edited with David Pinder, Belhaven, 1992); *Cityports, coastal zones and regional change* (edited, Wiley, 1996); and *Insularity and development* (edited with Emilio Biagini, Cassell, 1998). Dr Hoyle served as Secretary (1987–90) and Chairman (1990–93) of the Transport Geography Study Group of the Institute of British Geographers. He is a Fellow of the Chartered Institute of Transport, an elected Member of the Council of the Royal Geographical Society with the Institute of British Geographers, and a Member of the Belgian Royal Academy of Overseas Sciences of which he was the 1995 recipient of the Suykens Prize for port studies.
Department of Geography, University of Southampton, Southampton, Hampshire, SO17 1BJ, UK

Colin Hunter is a Lecturer in the Department of Geography, University of Aberdeen. Dr Hunter teaches and researches in the broad field of environmental management, specializing in environmental sustainability issues with particular interests in tourism, urban development and fresh water resources. Recent co-authored books include *Sustainable cities* (Jessica Kingsley/Regional Studies Association, 1994) and *Tourism and the environment: a sustainable relationship?* (Routledge, 1995).
Department of Geography, University of Aberdeen, Elphinstone Road, Old Aberdeen, AB24 3UF, UK

Richard Knowles is a Reader in the Department of Geography, University of Salford. Dr Knowles is Editor of the international *Journal of Transport Geography* (published by Elsevier Science Ltd) and a former Secretary (1984–87) and Chairman (1987–90) of the Transport Geography Study Group of the Institute of British Geographers. He has been a member of the Greater Manchester Passenger Transport Authority since 1988. He has written widely on transport issues. His research interests include examining the effects of bus deregulation and rail privatization and the impacts of the new Manchester Metrolink transit system and of new fixed links such as the Channel Tunnel.
Department of Geography, University of Salford, Salford, Lancashire, M5 4WT, UK

Thomas R. Leinbach is currently serving as Director of the Geography and Regional Science Program, United States National Science Foundation, on leave of absence from the University of Kentucky, Lexington, where he is Professor of Geography and Editor of the journal *Growth and Change: a Journal of Urban and Regional Policy*. Professor Leinbach's interests focus on transportation, industrialization and population issues in the developing world but especially South-East Asia. He is the author of over 60 refereed publications on these themes. He has also recently co-authored *Southeast Asian transport issues in development* (Oxford University Press, 1989) and co-edited *Collapsing space and time: geographic aspects of communication and information* (Routledge, 1991).

Department of Geography, University of Kentucky, Lexington, KY 40506, USA; and
Geography and Regional Science Program, Room 995, National Science Foundation, 4201 Wilson Blvd, Arlington, VA 22230, USA

Stephen Nutley is a Lecturer in Geography in the School of Environmental Studies, University of Ulster, Northern Ireland (UK). He has degrees from the Universities of Durham and Aberdeen, and has previously worked at the University of Wales and the former Liverpool Polytechnic. His main interests are transport geography and rural geography, with research focusing on social change in rural areas, mobility, accessibility, transport and planning. His publications include *Transport policy appraisal and personal accessibility in rural Wales* (GeoBooks, 1983) and *Unconventional and community transport in the United Kingdom* (Gordon and Breach, 1990).

School of Environmental Studies, University of Ulster, Coleraine, Co. Londonderry, Northern Ireland, BT52 1SA, UK

Stephen Page is Associate Professor in Tourism Management and Director, Centre for Tourism Research, Massey University at Albany, Auckland, New Zealand. He is the author of *Transport for tourism* (Routledge, 1994). His research on transport and tourism has examined the tourism implications of developing the Channel Tunnel and he has published various transport reports for the journal *Travel and Tourism Analyst*. He is also the author of five other books on tourism and the Associate Editor of the journal *Tourism Management*.

Centre for Tourism Research, Massey University at Albany, Private Bag 102904, NSMC, Auckland, New Zealand

Brian Slack is Professor of Geography at Concordia University, Montreal, Canada. He has a long-standing interest in the geography of ports and maritime transport. During the past 10 years his research has extended into intermodal transportation, which has led to academic publications in the *Professional Geographer* and in *Maritime Policy and Management*, and to reports for Transport Canada including an intermodal monitor.

Department of Geography, Concordia University, 1455 De Maisonneuve Blvd Ouest, Montreal, Québec, H3G 1M8, Canada

José Smith is a Lecturer in the Department of Geography, University of Salford. She has undertaken research projects on transport and development in Kenya, Uganda and Zimbabwe. She is a former Secretary (1993–96) and Chair (1996–99) of the Transport Geography Research Group of the Royal Geographical Society with the Institute of British Geographers.

Department of Geography, University of Salford, Salford, Lancashire, M5 4WT, UK

Andrew Spencer was a Lecturer in Geography at the National University of Singapore and subsequently taught at the University of Westminster as a member of the Transport Studies Group. Currently he is a freelance lecturer and researcher/consultant. He has published several articles on transport planning and policy issues, particularly in relation to East Asia and other developing areas.

78 Limbury Road, Luton, Bedfordshire, LU3 2PL, UK

Brian Turton is a Senior Lecturer in the Department of Environmental Social Sciences in the University of Keele. Dr Turton is the joint author (with Rodney Tolley) of *Transport systems, policy and planning* (Longman, 1995) and has recently completed contributions on transport geography to the third edition of *The changing geography of the United Kingdom* and to *Applied Geography*, edited by Michael Pacione (1998). On the basis of numerous visits to Zimbabwe in recent years he has published research on colonial road transport in the former Rhodesia, on aspects of tourist development and on problems of rail and air transport.

Department of Environmental Social Sciences, University of Keele, Keele, Staffordshire, ST5 5BG, UK

William Walton is a Lecturer in the Department of Land Economy, University of Aberdeen. Mr Walton teaches and researches in the areas of town planning and environmental policy with particular reference to road policy. Recent publications include "Policy changes in the Government's road building policy" in the *Town Planning Review* and "The potential scope for the application of tradable pollution permits to reducing car ownership in the UK: some preliminary thoughts" in *Transport Policy*.

Department of Land Economy, University of Aberdeen, Elphinstone Road, Old Aberdeen, AB24 3UF, UK

INDEX

Learning Resources
Centre